Companies Act 1989

AUSTRALIA
The Law Book Company Ltd.
Sydney : Melbourne : Brisbane : Perth

CANADA
The Carswell Company Ltd.
Toronto : Calgary : Vancouver : Ottawa

INDIA
N. M. Tripathi Private Ltd.
Bombay
and
Eastern Law House Private Ltd.
Calcutta
M.P.P. House
Bangalore

ISRAEL
Steimatzky's Agency Ltd.
Jerusalem : Tel Aviv : Haifa

PAKISTAN
Pakistan Law House
Karachi

Companies Act 1989

with annotations by

Geoffrey Morse
LL.B., Barrister, Herbert Smith Professor of Company Law, Nottingham University

with

Michael Bridge, LL.M. (London), Barrister, Hind Professor of Commercial Law, Nottingham University

David Milman, LL.B., Ph.D., Herbert Smith Professor of Company and Commercial Law, University of Manchester

Richard Morris, B.A., M.Sc., F.C.A., Professor of Accounting, University of Liverpool

Christopher Ryan, LL.M., Barrister and Solicitor (N.Z.), Senior Lecturer in Law, London University

LONDON
SWEET & MAXWELL
1990

Published in 1990 by
Sweet & Maxwell Limited of,
South Quay Plaza,
183 Marsh Wall, London,
and printed in Great Britain
by The Eastern Press Limited
of London and Reading

British Library Cataloguing in Publication Data

Great Britain
    [Companies Act 1989]. Companies Act 1989. — (Current law statutes annotated reprints).
    1. Great Britain. Companies. Law. Great Britain. Companies Act 1989.
    I. [Companies Act 1989].   II. Title.   III. Morse, Geoffrey.   IV. Series.
    344.106'66

    ISBN 0–421–41960–1

All rights reserved.
No part of this publication may be
reproduced or transmitted in any form
or by any means, electronic, mechanical, photocopying,
recording or otherwise, or stored in any retrieval
system of any nature, without the written permission
of the copyright holder, application for which
shall be made to the publisher

© Sweet & Maxwell 1990

CONTENTS

Companies Act 1989

References are to page numbers

Table of Cases		vii
Table of Statutes		ix
Part I:	Company Accounts	40–11
Part II:	Eligibility for Appointment as Company Auditor	40–63
Part III:	Investigations and Powers to Obtain Information	40–85
Part IV:	Registration of Company Charges	40–111
Part V:	Other Amendments of Company Law	40–136
Part VI:	Mergers and Related Matters	40–200
Part VII:	Financial Markets and Insolvency	40–213
Part VIII:	Amendments of the Financial Services Act 1986	40–245
Part IX:	Transfer of Securities	40–260
Part X:	Miscellaneous and General Provisions	40–261
Schedules		40–266
Index		[1]

TABLE OF CASES

References are to section and Schedule number

Annagel Glory Compania Naviera S.A. *v.* Golodetz; Middle East Marketing
  Corp.; Anngel Glory, The, 1988 PCC 37; [1988] 1 Lloyd's Rep. 45 .... s.93
Associated Provincial Picture Houses Ltd. *v.* Wednesbury Corpn. [1948] 1 K.B.
  223; [1948] L.J.R. 190; 177 L.T. 641; 63 T.L.R. 623; 112 J.P. 55, 92 S.J.
  26; [1947] 2 All E.R. 682; 45 L.G.R. 635, C.A., affirming [1947] L.J.R.
  678 .... s.117
Automobile Association (Canterbury) Inc. *v.* Australasian Secured Deposits Ltd.
  [1973] 1 N.Z.L.R. 417 .... s.93

Baillee *v.* Oriental Telephone and Electronic Co. Ltd. [1915] Ch. 503 .... s.108
Barrett & Co. *v.* Livesey (1981) 131 N.L.J. 1213 .... s.93
Bradley *v.* Eagle Star Insurance Co. Ltd. s.141
Brady *v.* Brady [1988] 2 W.L.R. 1308; (1988) 132 S.J. 820; [1988] 2 All E.R. 617;
  (1988) 4 BCC 390; 1988 PCC 316; [1988] 2 FTLR 181; [1988] BCLC 579;
  H.L.; reversing [1988] BCLC 20; 1977 PCC 434; (1987) 3 BCC 535; [1987]
  2 FTLR 414; (1987) 137 New L.J. 898, C.A. s.132
Brightlife, *Re* [1987] Ch. 200; [1987] 2 W.L.R. 197; (1987) 131 S.J. 132; [1986] 3
  All E.R. 673; 1986 PCC 435; (1987) 84 L.S. Gaz. 653 .... s.93, s.100
British Eagle International Airlines Ltd. *v.* Compagnie Nationale Air France
  [1975] 1 W.L.R. 758; 119 S.J. 368; [1975] 2 All E.R. 390; [1975] 2 Lloyd's
  Rep. 43, H.L.; reversing in part [1974] 1 Lloyd's Rep. 429, C.A.; affirming
  [1973] 1 Lloyd's Rep. 414 .... s.154
Brunton *v.* Electrical Engineering Corp. [1892] 1 Ch. 434 .... s.93

Cane *v.* Jones [1980] 1 W.L.R. 1451; (1979) 124 S.J. 542; [1981] 1 All E.R. 533 ..... s.113
Colman *v.* Eastern Counties Ry Co. (1846) 10 Beav. 1 .... s.108
Commissioner of the Police for the Metropolis *v.* Caldwell [1982] A.C. 341;
  [1981] 2 W.L.R. 509; [1981] 125 S.J. 239; [1981] 1 All E.R. 961; (1981) 73
  Cr.App.R. 13; [1981] Crim.L.R. 392, H.L.; affirming *sub nom.* R. *v.*
  Caldwell (1980) 71 Cr.App.R. 237; [1980] Crim.L.R. 572, C.A. s.151
Company, *Re, ex p.* Glossop [1988] BCLC 570 .... Sch. 19

Earle *v.* Hemsworth Rural District Council (1928) 44 T.L.R. 758 .... s.103

Halt Garage (1964) *Re* [1982] 3 All E.R. 1016 .... s.108
Harris Simons Construction Ltd., *Re* [1989] 1 W.L.R. 368 .... s.97
Hoare *v.* British Columbia Development Association (1912) 107 L.T. 602 .... s.93
Holmes (Eric) (Property), *Re* [1965] Ch. 1052; [1965] 2 W.L.R. 1260; 109 S.J.
  251; [1965] 2 All E.R. 333 .... s.97
Houldsworth *v.* City of Glasgow Bank (1880) 7 R (H.L.) 53 .... s.131

Independent Automatic Sales Ltd. *v.* Knowles and Foster [1962] 1 W.L.R. 974;
  106 S.J. 720; [1962] 3 All E.R. 27 .... s.95
International Sales and Agencies Ltd. *v.* Marcus [1982] 3 All E.R. 551; [1982] 2
  C.M.L.R. 46 .... s.108

Lloyd Cheyham and Co. Ltd. *v.* Littlejohn and Co., 1986 PCC 389; [1987] BCLC
  303 .... s.19
London and Cheshire Insurance Co. *v.* Laplagrene Property Co. [1971] Ch. 499;
  [1971] 2 W.L.R. 257; (1970) 114 S.J. 912; [1971] 1 All E.R. 766; 22 P. &
  C.R. 108 .... s.93
Lonrho *v.* Bond (No. 2) (1989) 5 BCC 776 .... s.135

TABLE OF CASES

McGuinness v. Bremner [1988] BCLC 673 .... Sch. 19
Mechanisations (Eaglescliffe) Ltd., Re [1966] Ch. 20; [1965] 2 W.L.R. 702; 109 S.J. 230; [1984] 3 All E.R. 840 .... s.97
Mercantile Bank of India v. Chartered Bank of India [1937] 1 All E.R. 231 .... s.95
Monolithic Building Co. Ltd., Re [1915] 1 Ch. 643 .... s.95, s.99
Montague's Settlements, Re; Duke of Manchester v. National Westminster Bank [1987] Ch. 264; [1987] 2 W.L.R. 1192; (1987) 131 S.J. 411; (1987) 84 L.S.Gaz. 1057 .... s.108

National Provincial and Union Bank of England v. Charnley [1924] 1 K.B. 431 .... s.97
Nelson v. Anglo American Mortgage Agency [1897] 1 Ch. 130 .... s.101
N.V. Slavenburg's Bank v. Intercontinental Natural Resources [1980] 1 W.L.R. 1076; (1980) 124 S.J. 374; [1980] 1 All E.R. 955 .... s.94
Nye (C.L.), Re [1971] Ch. 442; [1970] 3 W.L.R. 158; 114 S.J. 413; [1970] 3 All E.R. 1061, C.A.; reversing [1969] 2 W.L.R. 1380; 113 S.J. 466; [1969] 2 All E.R. 587 .... s.97

Permanent Houses (Holdings) Ltd., Re [1988] BCLC 563 .... s.100
Plaut v. Steiner (1989) 5 BCC 352 .... s.132

R. v. Caldwell, see Commissioner of the Police for the Metropolis v. Caldwell.
—— v. Cunningham [1957] 2 Q.B.D. 396; [1957] 3 W.L.R. 76; 121 J.P. 451; 101 S.J. 503; [1957] 2 All E.R. 412; 41 Cr.App.R. 155, C.C.A.; reversing [1957] Crim.L.R. 32 .... s.151
—— v. Registrar of Companies, ex p. Central Bank of India [1986] Q.B. 1114; [1986] 2 W.L.R. 177; (1985) 129 S.J. 755; [1986] 1 All E.R. 105; 1986 PCC 235, C.A.; reversing R. v. Registrar of Companies, ex p. Central Bank of India [1986] Q.B. 1114 .... s.94, s.95

Smith v. Croft (No. 3) [1988] Ch. 114; [1987] 3 W.L.R. 405; (1987) 131 S.J. 1038; [1987] 3 All E.R. 909; [1987] BCLC 355; [1987] 1 FTLR 319; 1986 PCC 209; (1987) 84 L.S.Gaz. 2449 .... s.108
Standard Rotary Machine Co. Ltd., Re (1906) 95 L.T. 829 .... s.103
Stoneleigh Finance v. Phillips [1965] 2 Q.B. 537; [1965] 2 W.L.R. 508; 109 S.J. 68; [1965] 1 All E.R. 513, C.A.; reversing (1964) 108 S.J. 319 .... s.93
Sun Tai Cheung Credits v. Att.-Gen. of Hong Kong [1987] 1 W.L.R. 948; (1987) 131 S.J. 938; [1987] 3 BCC 357; (1987) 84 L.S.Gaz. 1965, P.C. s.95

Trade Development Bank v. Warriner and Mason (Scotland) Ltd., 1980 S.C. 74 .... s.103

Wallis and Simmonds (Builders) Ltd., Re [1974] 1 W.L.R. 391; (1973) 118 S.J. 203; [1974] 1 All E.R. 561; (1973) 28 P. & C.R. 37; [1974] 1 Lloyd's Rep. 272 .... s.93
Weller (Sam) & Sons Ltd., Re (1989) 5 BCC 810 .... Sch. 19
Welsh Irish Ferries Ltd., Re [1986] Ch. 471; [1985] 3 W.L.R. 610; 1985 PCC 303; (1985) 129 S.J. 683; [1985] 2 Lloyd's Rep. 372 .... s.93
Wilson v. Kelland [1910] 2 Ch. 306 .... s.103
Windward Enterprises Ltd., Re [1983] BCLC 293 .... Sch. 19
Wright v. Horton (1887) 12 App.Cas. 371 .... s.101
Wrightson v. MacArthur & Hutchinson Ltd. [1921] 2 K.B. 807 .... s.93

Yolland, Husson and Birkett Ltd., Re [1908] 1 Ch. 152 .... s.97
Yorkshire Woolcombers Association Ltd., Re [1903] 2 Ch. 284 .... s.93

TABLE OF STATUTES

Indicates those sections affected by the provisions of the Companies Act 1989

1844	Joint Stock Companies Act ... s.126	1964	Trading Stamps Act (c.71) s.17, s.34
1889	Judicial Factors (Scotland) Act s.39	1967	General Rate Act (c.9)—
	s.11A s.182		s.32A(6) .... Sch. 18(6)
1907	Limited Partnerships Act (7 Edw. 7, c.24)—		Companies Act (c.81)—
			s.13(1) s.25, s.31, s.34
	s.4(2) .... Sch. 19(16)	1968	Civil Evidence Act (c.64)—
1925	Law of Property Act (15 & 16 Geo. 5, c.20)—		s.5 .... s.126
			Transport Act (c.73)—
	s.74 .... s.130		Pt. V .... Sch. 18(7)
	s.198 .... s.142	1969	Post Office Act (c.48)—
	Criminal Justice Act (15 & 16 Geo. 5, c.86)—		s.86 .... Sch. 18(8)
		1970	Conveyancing and Feudal Reform (Scotland) Act (c.35)—
	s.33 .... s.44, s.91		
1934	Law Reform (Miscellaneous Provisions) Act (24 & 25 Geo. 5, c.41)—		s.27(2) s.99
			(7) s.99
		1971	Coal Industry Act (c.16)—
	s.1(2)(c) s.141		s.8 .... Sch. 10(27)
1945	Criminal Justice Act (Northern Ireland)—	1972	Land Charges Act (c.61)—
			s.37 .... s.142, Sch. 16(1)
	s.18 .... s.91		(8) .... Sch. 16(1)
1946	Coal Industry Nationalisation Act (9 & 10 Geo. 6, c.59)—		Industry Act (c.63)—
			s.10(9) .... Sch. 18(9)
			European Communities Act (c.68)—
	Sched. 2A, para. 5 .... Sch. 18(1)		s.9(1) s.108
1947	Electricity Act (10 & 11 Geo. 6, c.54)—	1973	Coal Industry Act (c.8)—
			s.12(1) .... Sch. 18(10)
	s.67 .... Sch. 18(2)		Fair Trading Act (c.41) s.153
1954	Landlord and Tenant Act (2 & 3 Eliz. 2, c.56)—		Pt. I s.152
			Pt. IV s.151
	s.42 .... Sch. 18(3)		Pt. V s.151, s.152
1960	Charities Act (8 & 9 Eliz. 2, c.58)—		Pt. VI s.151
			Pt. VII s.152
	s.30 .... s.111		Pt. VIII s.152
	(1)* s.111		s.7(1)(c) .... Sch. 14(8)
	(2)* s.111		s.46 .... Sch. 20(1), Sch. 24
	s.30A s.111		s.49 .... Sch. 14(8)
	(1) s.112		s.50 .... Sch. 14(8)
	(2) s.112		s.51 .... Sch. 14(8)
	s.30B s.111		ss.57–61 .... s.152
	(1) s.108, s.112		s.58(1) s.152
	(2) s.112		s.60 .... Sch. 20(2)
	(3) s.112		s.63(1) .... Sch. 20(3)
	(4) s.112		s.64 .... s.147, s.152
	s.30C s.111, s.112		s.65 .... s.149, s.150
	s.46 .... s.111		(2)–(4) s.149, s.150
1962	Transport Act (10 & 11 Eliz. 2, c.46)—		s.66 .... Sch. 20(4)
			s.66A s.150
	s.92(1) .... Sch. 18(4)		s.67(2)(a) .... Sch. 20(5)
1963	Betting, Gaming and Lotteries Act (c.2)—		s.68(4) .... Sch. 20(6)
			s.71 .... Sch. 20(7), Sch. 24
	Sched. 2, para. 24 .... Sch. 10(25)		s.74(1) .... Sch. 20(8), Sch. 24
1964	Harbours Act (c.40)—		s.75(4) .... Sch. 20(9)
	s.42(2) .... Sch. 10(26)		s.76(2) .... Sch. 20(11)
	(6) .... Sch. 10(26), Sch. 24		s.83(3A) .... Sch. 20(12)
	(9) .... Sch. 10(26)		s.85(5) .... Sch. 20(13), Sch. 24
	s.57(1) .... Sch. 18(5)		(6) .... Sch. 20(13), Sch. 24

TABLE OF STATUTES

1973 Fair Trading Act—cont.
    s.85(7) .... Sch. 20(13)
    (7A) .... Sch. 20(13)
    s.88 .... Sch. 20(14), Sch. 24
    s.89 .... Sch. 20(15), Sch. 24
    s.90 .... Sch. 20(16)
    s.73(1)(b) s.149
    s.75 .... s.147, s.152
    (4A)–(4M) s.149
    (4K) s.146
    s.75A s.146
    (1) s.152
    s.75B s.146
    s.75C s.146
    s.75D s.146
    s.75E s.146
    s.75F s.146
    s.75G s.147, s.148
    s.75H s.147
    s.75J s.147
    s.75K s.147
    s.76 .... s.147
    (b) s.146
    s.77(1) s.149, s.150
    (4)–(6) s.149, s.150
    s.85(6)–(8) .... Sch. 14(4)
    s.88 .... s.148
    s.90 .... s.149
    s.93 .... s.149
    s.93A s.148
    s.93B s.151
    s.129(1) s.151
    s.132(1) .... Sch. 20(17)
    Sched. 3,
    para. 16 .... Sch. 20(18)
    Sched. 9 .. ... Sch. 20(20), Sch. 24
    Sched. 8 .... Sch. 20(19)
    para. 9A s.147
    paras. 12–12C s.147
    Northern Ireland Constitution Act (c.36) s.88
    s.3 .... s.213
    (1)(a) s.213
    Sched. 3 .... s.213

1974 Northern Ireland Act (c.28)—
    Sched. 1,
    para. 1 .... s.214
    Trade Union and Labour Relations Act (c.52)—
    s.11(3) s.124
    (9) s.124
    Sched. 2,
    paras. 6–15 .... s.124
    paras. 16–21 .... s.124

1975 Criminal Procedure (Scotland) Act (c.21)—
    s.74 .... s.44, s.91
    s.331 .... s.43
    Industry Act (c.68)—
    s.37(1) .... Sch. 18(11)
    Scottish Development Agency Act (c.69)—
    s.25(1) .... Sch. 18(12)
    Welsh Development Agency Act (c.70)—
    s.27(1) .... Sch. 18(13)

1975 Policyholders Protection Act (c.75)—
    Sched. 3,
    para. 4 .... s.210
    para. 5(3) s.210
    para. 6 .... s.210
    para. 8 .... s.210
1976 Damages (Scotland) Act (c.13) s.141
    Fatal Accidents Act (c.30) s.141
    Industrial Common Ownership Act (c.78)—
    s.2(5) .... Sch. 18(15)
    Restrictive Trade Practices Act (c.34) .... Sch. 18(14)
    s.8(2) .... Sch. 14(9)
    s.16(3) .... Sch. 14(9)
    s.24 .... Sch. 14(9)
    Sched. 2 .... Sch. 14(9)
1977 Aircraft and Shipbuilding Industries Act (c.3)—
    s.17(1)(c) .... Sch. 10(28)
    (9) .... Sch. 10(28)
    (10) .... Sch. 10(28)
    s.56(1) .... Sch. 18(16)
    Nuclear Industries (Finance) Act (c.7)—
    s.3 .... Sch. 18(17)
    Coal Industry Act (c.39)—
    s.14(1) .... Sch. 18(18)
    Insurance Brokers (Registration) Act (c.46) s.87
1978 Shipbuilding (Redundancy Payments) Act (c.11)—
    s.1(4) .... Sch. 18(19)
    Interpretation Act (c.30) s.53, s.144
    s.7 .... s.49
    s.17(2)(a) s.144
    s.23(3) s.144
1979 Capital Gains Tax Act (c.14)—
    s.149(7) .... Sch. 18(20)
    Crown Agents Act (c.43)—
    s.22 .... Sch. 10(29)
    s.31(1) .... Sch. 18(21)
1980 Competition Act (c.21) s.151, s.153,
                            Sch. 14(10)
    s.3(8) .... Sch. 20(21)
    s.4 .... s.148
    (4) .... Sch. 20(22)
    s.9 .... s.148
    (4) .... Sch. 20(23)
    s.11(3)(f) .... Sch. 18(22)
    s.12 .... Sch. 18(22)
    s.29(1)(a) .... Sch. 20(24)
    British Aerospace Act (c.26)—
    s.14(1) .... Sch. 18(23)
    Magistrates' Courts Act (c.43)—
    s.127(1) s.43
    Sched. 3 .... s.44, s.91
    Limitation Act (c.58)—
    s.11 .... s.141
    s.14 .... s.141

x

Table of Statutes

1980 Local Government, Planning
and Land Act (c.65)—
    s.100(1) .... Sch. 18(24)
    s.170(1)(d) .... Sch. 18(24)
    (2) .... Sch. 18(24)
Solicitors (Scotland) Act Sch. 19(16)
1981 British Telecommunications
Act (c.38)—
    s.85 .... Sch. 18(25)
    s.75 .... Sch. 10(30)
Transport Act (c.56)—
    s.4(2) .... Sch. 18(26)
    s.11(4) .... Sch. 10(31)
1982 Iron and Steel Act (c.25)—
    s.24(5) .... Sch. 10(32)
    Sched. 4 .... s.120
Civil Jurisdiction and Judgments Act (c.27)—
    Sched. 5,
    para. 10 .... s.200
Stock Transfer Act (c.42)—
    Sched. 1 .... s.173, Sch. 22(10)
Insurance Companies Act
(c.50) s.82, s.196
    Pt. II s.13
    s.44 .... s.65, s.68, s.75, s.81, s.87
    (2) s.77
    (4) s.77
    (6) s.77
    s.44A s.77
    s.47A(1) s.77
    s.71(2A) s.77
    (6) s.77
1983 Value Added Tax Act
(c.55)—
    s.29 .... Sch. 18(27)
1984 London Regional Transport
Act (c.32)—
    s.68 .... Sch. 18(29)
Telecommunications Act
(c.21) s.151, s.153
    s.13(9) .... Sch. 20(25)
    s.73(1) .... Sch. 18(28)
Inheritance Tax Act (c.51)—
    s.13(5) .... Sch. 18(30)
    s.103(2) .... Sch. 18(30)
    s.234 .... Sch. 18(30)
Ordnance Factories and Military Services Act
(c.59)—
    s.14 .... Sch. 18(31)
Police and Criminal Evidence
Act (c.60)—
    s.69(2) s.126
1985 Companies Act (c.6) s.196
    Pt. VII s.1, s.53, s.103
    Pt. XIV s.56, s.58, s.60, s.69,
        s.71, s.82, s.87
    Pt. XV s.135
    Pt. IV s.105
    Pt. XI s.24
    Pt. XXIII s.105
    s.3A s.110
    s.4 .... s.110, s.111
    s.5 .... s.110
    s.6(1)(a)(b) s.111
    (3) s.111

1985 Companies Act—cont.
    s.8A s.128
    s.10 .... s.136
    s.13(1) s.127
    s.23 .... s.129, Sch. 18(32)
    s.35 . ... s.108, s.109, s.110, s.111,
        s.112, s.142
    (3) s.109, s.111
    s.35* s.108
    s.35A ... s.108, s.109, s.110, s.111,
        s.112, s.142
    (2) s.109
    s.35B ... s.108, s.109, s.110, s.111
    s.36 .... s.130
    s.36(1)* s.130
    (4)* s.130
    s.36A s.130
    s.36B .... s.130, Sch. 17
    s.36C s.130
    s.38(1)(2) .... Sch. 17(1)
    s.38A .... Sch. 17
    s.39(1)–(3) .... Sch. 17(2)
    s.40 .... Sch. 17(3)
    s.41 .... Sch. 17(4)
    s.43(3) .... s.23, Sch. 10(1)
    s.46 .... s.23
    (2)–(6) .... Sch. 10(1)
    s.80(1) s.115
    (4) s.115
    (5) s.115
    (6) s.115
    s.80A s.115, s.116
    s.95(2) s.114
    (5) s.114
    (6) s.114
    s.111A s.131
    s.116 .... s.131
    s.120A s.134
    s.131 .... Sch. 2(10)
    (1) .... Sch. 19(1)
    (2) .... Sch. 3(10)(29)
    s.132 .... Sch. 2(10)
    s.144(3) s.137
    (4) s.137
    s.152 .... s.132
    s.153 .... Sch. 18(33)
    (1) s.132
    (2) s.132
    (4)(b) s.132
    s.155(4) s.114
    (5) s.114
    s.157(4)(a) s.114
    s.159(3) s.133
    s.159A s.133
    s.160(3) .... s.133, Sch. 24
    (4) s.133
    s.162(2) s.133
    s.164 .... s.114
    (2) s.114
    (3) s.114
    (4) s.114
    (5) s.114
    (6) s.114
    (7) s.114
    s.165 .... s.114
    (2) s.114

1985 Companies Act—*cont.*		1985 Companies Act—*cont.*	
s.167(2)	s.114	s.227(1)*	s.4, s.22
s.169(5)	s.143, Sch. 24	(2)*	s.3
s.173	s.103	(3)*	s.4
(2)	s.114	(4)*	s.3
s.174(2)	s.114	s.228	s.1, s.3, s.5, Sch. 3(9)
(4)	s.114	(1)*	s.4
s.175(6)	s.143, Sch. 24	(2)*	s.4
s.186	Sch. 17(5)	(4)*	s.4
s.188	Sch. 17(6)	(5)*	s.4
s.191(1)	s.143, Sch. 24	(6)*	s.4
(2)	s.143	(7)*	s.5
(3)	s.143, Sch. 24	s.229	s.1, s.5, Sch. 3(1)
s.198(2)	s.134	(3)	s.6
s.199(2)	s.134	(c)	Sch. 7, Pt. II(6)
(2)	s.134	(4)	s.6, s.11, Sch. 2(18), Sch. 7, Pt. II(1)
s.201	Sch. 24		
s.201(1)*	s.134	s.229(1)*	s.5
s.202(1)	s.134, Sch. 24	(3)*	s.5
(3)	s.134	(a)*	s.5
(4)	s.134	(d)*	s.5
s.206(8)	s.134	(5)*	s.5
(8)	s.134	s.230	s.1, s.5, s.22
s.208	s.134	s.230(1)*	s.5
(5)	s.134	(2)*	s.5
s.209	s.134	(4)*	s.5
(1)(j)	s.134, Sch. 24	(5)*	s.5
(5)(a)(i)	Sch. 10(2)	(6)*	s.5
s.210(5)	s.135	s.231	s.1, s.6
s.211(9)	Sch. 10(3)	s.231(1)*	s.6
s.212	s.134	(d)*	s.6
s.215(4)	Sch. 10(3)	(4)*	s.6
s.216(1)	s.135	s.232	s.1, s.6
(2)	s.135	s.232*	s.6, Sch. 4
s.219(1)	s.143	s.233	s.1, s.6, s.7, Sch. 6(7)
(2)	s.143	(1)	s.5
s.221	s.1, s.2, s.14	(4)	s.14
s.221(2)–(4)*	s.2	s.233*	s.6, Sch. 4
s.222	s.1, s.2	s.234	s.1, s.8, s.22
s.222(4)*	s.2	(1)(b)	s.18
s.223	s.1, s.2, s.3, s.22, Sch. 10(13)	s.234*	s.6, Sch. 4
		s.234A	s.1, s.8
s.223(1)*	s.2	s.235	s.1, s.9, s.10, Sch. 6(8)(10)
(2)*	s.2		
(3)*	s.2	(1)	s.16
s.224	s.1. s.3, s.22, Sch. 10(13)	s.235(1)*	s.8
s.224(2)	s.1	(2)*	s.8
s.224(1)*	s.3	(3)–(5)*	s.8
(2)*	s.3	(7)*	s.8
(3)*	s.3	s.236	s.1, s.9, Sch. 6(8)
(4)*	s.3	s.236(1)*	s.9
(5)*	s.3	(2)*	s.9
s.225	s.1, s.3, s.11, Sch. 10(13)	s.237	s.1, s.9
s.225(1)*	s.3	(2)	s.10, s.15
(4)*	s.3	(3)	s.10
(6)(c)*	s.3	s.237(1)*	s.9
(7)*	s.3	(2)*	s.9
(8)*	s.3	(3)*	s.118
s.226	s.1, s.3, s.4, s.22	(4)*	s.9
(2)	s.1, s.19, s.22	(5)*	s.9
(4)	s.18	(6)*	s.9
(5)	s.18	s.238	s.1, s.10, s.12, s.14, s.119, s.122, s.123
s.227	s.1, s.3, s.5, s.22		
s.227(2)	s.1	(1)	s.12, s.15, s.16
(3)	s.1, s.19, s.22	(5)	s.16
(5)	s.18	s.238(1)*	s.7
(6)	s.18	(2)*	s.7

Table of Statutes

1985 Companies Act—*cont.*
s.239 .... s.1, s.10, s.14
s.240 ... s.1, s.10, s.15, Sch. 6(10)
   (3)(*b*) s.17
   (5) s.17
s.240* s.10
s.241 .... s.1, s.11, s.16
   (1)* s.11, s.17
   (3)* s.11
s.242 .... s.1, s.4, s.11, s.13, s.16,
        s.17, Sch. 7, Pt. II(6)
s.242(1)* s.11
   (2)* s.11
   (3)* s.11
   (4)* s.11
   (5)* s.11
   (6)* s.11
s.242A s.1, s.4, s.11
s.243 .... s.1, s.11
   (1)* s.11
   (2)* s.11
   (3)* s.11
   (4)* s.11
   (5)* s.11
s.244 .... s.1, s.11, s.22
   (1)* s.11
   (2)* s.11
s.245 .... s.1, s.12
   (1)* s.13
   (2)* s.13
s.245A s.1, s.12
   B s.1, s.12
   C s.1, s.12
s.246 .... s.1, s.9, s.10, s.13, s.14,
        Sch. 6
   (1)* s.10
   (2)* s.10
s.247 ... s.1, s.9, s.10, s.13, Sch. 6
   (2)* s.13
   (3)* s.13
s.248 ... s.1, s.9, s.10, s.13, Sch. 6
   (2)* s.13
   (3)* s.13
   (4)* s.13
   (5)* s.13
s.249 ... s.1, s.9, s.10, s.13, Sch. 6
   (2)–(6)* s.13
s.250 .... s.1, s.9, s.14, s.119,
        Sch. 6(9)
   (2)* s.13
s.251 .... s.1, s.10, s.12, s.15
s.252 .... s.1, s.16, s.116, s.119
s.252* s.14
   (1)* s.14, s.118
   (2)* s.14
   (3)* s.14
   (4)* s.14
   (5)* s.14
   (6)* s.14
   (7)* s.118
s.253 .... s.1, s.16, s.116
   (2) s.119
s.253* s.14
s.253(1)–(3)* s.14
s.254 .... s.1, s.17

1985 Companies Act—*cont.*
s.254* s.10
   (2)* s.10
   (3)* s.10
   (4)* s.10
s.255 .... s.1, s.9, s.18, s.22
s.255* s.10
   (1)* s.10
   (3)* s.10
   (4)* s.10
   (5)* s.10
s.255A s.1, s.9, s.18, s.22
   (3) s.22
   (4) s.22
s.255B s.1, s.9, s.18
   C s.1, s.9, s.18
   D s.1, s.9, s.18
s.256 .... s.1, s.19, s.22
s.256* s.20
s.257 .... s.1, s.20
   (3)* s.18
s.258 .... s.1, s.5, s.20, s.21, s.22,
        Sch. 9
   (2) .... Sch. 3(15)
   (4) .... s.22, Sch. 3(15)
s.258(1)(*a*)* s.18
   (2)* s.18
   (4)* s.18
s.259 .... s.1, s.22
   (1)–(3) s.22
   (4) s.22
   (5) s.22
s.259(3)* s.18
   (4)* s.18
s.260 .... s.1, s.22
   (1)* s.18
   (2)* s.18
s.261 .... s.1, s.22
   (1) s.22
   (2) s.22
s.261(1)* .... s.18, Sch. 8
   (3)* s.18
   (4)* s.18
   (6)* s.18
s.262 .... s.1, s.22
   (1) s.22
   (2) s.22
   (3) s.22
s.262A s.1, s.22
s.263 .... s.4
s.264 .... s.4
   (2) .... Sch. 10(1)
   (3) .... Sch. 10(1)
s.265 .... s.4
s.266 .... s.4
s.267 .... s.4
s.268 .... s.4
s.269 .... s.4
s.270(3) s.16
   (4) s.4, s.9, s.16
s.271 .... s.9
   (3) .... Sch. 10(4)
   (4) s.16
s.272 .... s.4
   (3) .... Sch. 10(5)
   (5) .... Sch. 10(6)

Table of Statutes

1985 Companies Act—*cont.*
s.273 .... s.4, s.9
   (7) .... Sch. 10(6)
s.274 .... s.4
s.275 .... s.4
s.276 .... s.4
   (b) .... Sch. 10(7)
s.279 .... Sch. 10(8)
s.287 .... s.136
   (3)* s.136
s.288(3) .... s.143, Sch. 24
s.289 .... Sch. 19(2)
   (4) .... Sch. 10(9)
s.290 .... Sch. 19(3)
s.293 .... Sch. 18(34)
s.305 .... Sch. 19(4)
s.310(2) s.137
   (3) s.137
s.314 .... Sch. 4(10)
s.315 .... Sch. 4(10)
s.318(7) .... s.143, Sch. 24
s.319(1) s.114
   (5) s.114
s.320(2) s.16
s.321(4) .... Sch. 19(8)
s.322A s.108, s.109, s.111
s.330 .... Sch. 7, Pt. IV(2)
s.332(1)(b) s.138
s.334 .... s.138
s.335 .... s.138
s.337(3)(a) s.114
s.338(4) .... s.138, Sch. 10(10)
   (6) s.138
s.339(4) .... Sch. 10(10)
s.342(2) .... Sch. 10(11)
s.343(1)(a) .... Sch. 10(10)
   (4) .... Sch. 10(11)
s.344(2) .... Sch. 10(10)
s.346 .... Sch. 4(13)
   (2)–(4) ... s.109, s.111, s.112
s.350(1) .... Sch. 17(7)
s.351(1)(a) .... Sch. 19(14)
s.356(1) .... s.143, Sch. 24
   (2) .... s.143, Sch. 24
   (3) s.143
   (4) .... s.143, Sch. 24
s.363 .... s.139
s.364 .... s.139
s.364A s.139
s.365 .... s.139
s.366 .... s.115
   (1) s.115
   (4) s.115
s.366A s.115, s.116
s.368(8) .... Sch. 19(9)
s.369(4) s.115, s.116
s.378(3) s.115, s.116
s.379A ... s.16, s.115, s.116, s.117, s.119
   (2) s.116
   (3) s.115
   (4) s.115
s.380 .... s.116
s.381A s.113, s.114
s.381A(1) s.114
   B s.113
   C s.113

1985 Companies Act—*cont.*
s.382 .... s.113
   (5) s.113
s.382A s.113
s.383 .... s.113
   (1) .... s.143, Sch. 24
   (2) .... s.143, Sch. 24
   (3) .... s.143, Sch. 24
s.384 ...... s.14, s.24, s.53, s.118, s.119
   (4) s.118
s.384(1)–(3)* s.118
   (5)* s.118
ss.384–394A s.9
s.385 .... s.118, s.119
   (2) s.119
s.385(1)–(3)* s.118
s.385A s.118, s.119
   (2) s.119
s.386 ... s.116, s.118, s.119, s.122
   (1)–(3)* s.118
s.387 .... s.118, s.119, s.121
   (2)* s.118
s.388 .... s.118, s.119
   (1)* s.118
   (2)* s.118
s.388A s.14, s.118, s.119
s.389 ... s.31, s.50, s.118, Sch. 24
   (1)(a) s.31, s.50
s.389* s.212
s.389A s.118, s.120
s.390 .... s.120, s.122
   (1) s.118
   (2) s.118
s.390* s.118
   (2)* s.118
   (3)* s.118
   (5)* s.118
   (6)* s.118
   (7)* s.118
s.390A s.118, s.121
   B s.118, s.121
s.391 .... s.118, s.122
   (1)–(7)* s.118
s.391A s.118, s.122
s.392 .... s.118, s.122
s.392(1)(a)* s.118
   (b)* s.118
   (2)* s.118
s.392A s.118, s.122
s.393 .... s.116, s.118, s.119
s.393* s.118
s.394 .... s.118, s.122, s.123
s.394* s.118, s.124
s.394A s.118, s.123
s.395 .... s.93
   (2) .... s.104, Sch. 15
   (3) .... Sch. 15
   (4) s.94, s.101, s.104
s.395* s.95
ss.395–408 .... s.92
s.396 ... s.93, s.104, s.105, Sch. 15
   (1)(d) s.104
   (4) s.104
   (6) s.104, s.105
s.396* s.93

xiv

1985 Companies Act—*cont.*
   s.397 .... s.94, s.105
      (3)–(5) .... Sch. 15
   s.397* s.100
   s.398 .... s.95
      (1) s.100
      (2) .... Sch. 15
      (4) .... s.96, Sch. 15
      (5) .... s.96, Sch. 15
   s.399 .... s.95, s.104, Sch. 15
      (2) s.97, s.98, s.99, s.104
   s.399* s.95
   ss.399–406 .... s.105
   s.400 .... s.95, s.104, Sch. 15
   s.400* s.95
   s.401 .... s.96, Sch. 15
      (2)(*b*)* s.94
      (4) s.98
   s.402 ..... s.95, s.96, s.97, Sch. 15
   s.403 .... s.98, s.104, Sch. 15
      (1)* s.98
   s.404 .... s.99, Sch. 15
   s.404* s.97
   s.405 .... s.99, Sch. 15
   s.405* s.100
   s.406 .... s.95, s.99, Sch. 15
      (1) s.104
   s.406* s.101
   s.407 .... s.99, Sch. 15
   s.407* s.101
   s.408 .... s.100, Sch. 15
   s.408* s.101
   ss.408–410 .... s.105
   s.409 ... s.92, s.100, s.105, Sch. 15
   s.410 .... s.100, s.104, s.105,
                           Sch. 15
   ss.410–423 .... s.92
   s.411 .... s.101, s.105, Sch. 15
   s.412 .... s.101, s.105, Sch. 15
   s.413 ..... s.93, s.100, s.102, s.104
      (2) s.95
      (3) s.98
      (4) s.98
      (6) s.98
   s.414 .... s.103, s.104, Sch. 15
   s.415 ..... s.94, s.95, s.100, s.103,
                           Sch. 15
      (1) s.104
      (2) s.104
      (3) s.97, s.104
   s.416 .... s.103, s.142, Sch. 15
   s.417 .... s.98, s.103, Sch. 15
   s.418 ... s.93, s.100, s.104, Sch. 15
   s.419 .... s.93, s.104, Sch. 15
      (2) s.95
      (5) s.95
   s.420 .... s.104, s.105
   s.424 .... s.92
   s.427A s.114
   s.431 .... s.59, s.61, s.69, s.70
      (2)(*a*)(*b*) s.62
   s.432 .... s.61, s.69
      (1) s.57
      (2A) s.55
   s.433 .... s.69
   s.434 .... s.69
      (1) s.56

1985 Companies Act—*cont.*
   s.434(2) s.56
      (3) s.56
      (6) s.56
   ss.434–446 .... s.68
   s.435* .... s.212, Sch. 24
   s.436(1) s.56
   s.437 .... s.58, s.61
      (1)(*a*) s.58
      (1A) s.57
      (1B) s.57
      (3) s.55
   s.438 .... s.58, s.70
   s.439(1) s.59
      (4) s.59
      (5) s.59
   s.440 .... s.60
   s.440* .... s.212, Sch. 24
   s.441 .... s.61
   s.442(3) s.59, s.62
      (3A) s.62
      (3B) s.62
      (3C) s.62
   ss.442–445 .... s.70
   s.443 .... s.69
      (4) .... Sch. 24
   s.444 .... s.58, s.62, s.68
   s.445 .... s.135
   s.446 .... s.69, s.70, Sch. 24
   s.447 ... s.55, s.58, s.65, s.68, s.75,
                          s.81, s.87
      (1) .... Sch. 24
      (1)–(6) s.63
      (9) s.63
   s.448 .... s.58, s.64, s.65
      (5) s.64
      (7) s.64
   s.449 .... s.64, s.68, s.88
      (1) .... s.65, Sch. 24
      (1A) s.65
      (1B) s.65
      (2) s.65
      (3) s.65
   s.450(1) s.66
      (4) s.66
      (5) s.66
   s.451 .... s.67
   s.451A s.64, s.68
      (5) s.68
   s.452(1) .... s.69, s.70, Sch. 24
      (1A) s.69
      (1B) s.69
   s.453(1A) s.70
      (1B) s.70
   s.454(2)(3) .... Sch. 19(10)
   s.456(3) .... Sch. 19(10)
   s.459 .... s.108
      (1) .... Sch. 19(11)
   s.460(1) .... Sch. 19(11), Sch. 24
   s.462(2) .... Sch. 17(8)
   s.463(1) s.140
   s.464(1)(*b*) s.140
      (1A) s.140
      (3) s.140
      (5) .... s.140, Sch. 24
      (6) s.140

TABLE OF STATUTES

1985 Companies Act—*cont.*
   s.466(2) .... Sch. 17(9), Sch. 24
      (4)–(6) .... s.140, Sch. 24
   s.651(1) .... s.141, Sch. 24
      (4)–(7) s.141
   s.684(1) .... Sch. 19(12)
   s.686 .... Sch. 19(5)
   s.691 ... s.104, Sch. 15, Sch. 19(6)
   s.696 .... Sch. 19(13)
      (4) .... Sch. 15
   s.699(3) .... Sch. 10(12)
   s.700 .... Sch. 10(13)
   ss.700–703 .... s.23
   s.701 .... Sch. 10(13)
   s.702 .... Sch. 10(13)
   s.703 .... Sch. 10(13)
   s.703A .... s.105, Sch. 15
   s.703B .... s.105, Sch. 15
   s.703C .... s.105, Sch. 15
   s.703D .... s.105, Sch. 15
   s.703E .... s.105, Sch. 15
   s.703F .... s.105, Sch. 15
   s.703G .... s.105, Sch. 15
   s.703H .... s.105, Sch. 15
   s.703I .... s.105, Sch. 15
   s.703J .... s.105, Sch. 15
   s.703K .... s.105, Sch. 15
   s.703L .... s.105, Sch. 15
   s.703M .... s.105, Sch. 15
   s.703N .... s.105, Sch. 15
   s.704(5) s.127
   s.705 .... Sch. 19(14)
   s.706 .... s.125
      (1) s.127
   s.707 .... s.125
      (1) s.127
   s.707A s.126
      (1) s.127
   s.708(1) s.127
      (*a*) s.127
      (*b*) .... Sch. 24
      (4) s.127
   s.709 .... s.126
      (1) s.127
      (3) s.127
   s.709* s.126
   s.710 .... s.126
   s.710* s.126
   s.710A s.126, s.127
   s.711(1)(*k*) .... Sch. 10(14)
   s.711A s.142
   s.712* s.126, s.127, s.212,
                          Sch. 24
   s.713(1) s.127
   s.715* s.126, s.127, s.212,
                          Sch. 24
   s.715A s.124, s.127
   s.716 .... Sch. 19(15), Sch. 24
   s.717 .... Sch. 19(16), Sch. 24
   s.718(3) s.106, s.109, s.130
      (6) s.130
   s.719 .... Sch. 18(36)
   s.723A s.143
   s.727 .... s.137
   s.730 .... Sch. 19(17)
   s.732 ... s.63, s.64, s.65, s.66, s.67

1985 Companies Act—*cont.*
   s.733 ... s.63, s.64, s.65, s.66, s.67,
                   s.90, s.123, Sch. 24
   s.734 ... s.63, s.64, s.65, s.66, s.67,
                     s.120, s.123
      (5) .... Sch. 19(18)
      (6) .... Sch. 19(18)
   s.734A .... Sch. 19(19), Sch. 24
   s.735(1) .... Sch. 22(15)
   s.735A(2) s.127
   s.735B s.127
   s.736 ..... s.21, s.53, s.144, s.149,
                           Sch. 18
   s.736A s.21, s.144, s.149
   s.736B s.21, s.144
   s.742 .... Sch. 10(15)
      (1) s.23
      (2) s.23
   s.742* s.22
   s.743 .... s.132, Sch. 18(37)
   s.744 .... Sch. 10(16)
   s.744* .... s.22, Sch. 21
   s.744A .... s.22, Sch. 19(20)
   s.745(1) s.213
   s.746 .... Sch. 24
   Sched. 1 .... Sch. 19(7)
    para. 2 .... Sch. 10(17)
   Sched. 2 ..... s.129, Sch. 3(6)(20),
                Sch. 10(18), Sch. 24
    Pt. II s.23
   Sched. 3,
    Pt. II .... Sch. 10(19)
   Sched. 4 .... s.4, s.5, s.13, s.18,
                 Sch. 1, Sch. 2, Sch. 6
    Pt. I s.18, s.22
    para. 3(5) s.14
    para. 4(3) s.14
    para. 11 .... Sch. 1(5)
    para. 12 .... Sch. 10(20)
    paras. 17–19 .... Sch. 7,
                          Pt. II(3)
    para. 21 ... Sch. 2(18), Sch. 7,
                           Pt. II(3)
    para. 29 .... s.22
    para. 34(3)–(3B) ... Sch. 1(6)
    para. 35* s.22
    para. 36A ..... s.13, Sch. 1(7)
    para. 47 .... Sch. 1(8)
    para. 51(2) .... Sch. 1(9)
    para. 56 .... s.13
    para. 58(3) .... Sch. 1(10)
    para. 59 ... Sch. 1(11), Sch. 2,
                 Sch. 7, Pt. II(2)
    para. 59A .... Sch. 1(11)
    para. 60* .... Sch. 3
    para. 65* .... Sch. 3
    paras. 68–70* .... Sch. 3
    para. 75* .... Sch. 3
    para. 77* s.22
    para. 79* s.22
    para. 81* s.22
    para. 83 .... s.22
    para. 84 .... s.22
    para. 88 .... s.22
    para. 89 .... s.22
    para. 90* s.22
    para. 91* s.22

1985 Companies Act—*cont.*
Sched. 4—*cont.*
Pt. I—*cont.*
para. 92(1)* s.22
para. 93 .... s.22
para. 94(1)–(3) s.22
para. 95* s.22
paras. 10–15* s.22
paras. 17–19 .... Sch. 2(18)
Sched. 4A s.1, s.5, s.13, s.18,
Sch. 1(10), Sch. 2
para. 1 .... Sch. 7, Pt. II(2)
para. 17 .... Sch. 7, Pt. II(4)
para. 19 .... Sch. 3(21)
para. 20 .... s.22
paras. 20–22 ... Sch. 7, Pt. II(4)
Sched. 5 . ... s.1, s.6, s.18, Sch. 3,
Sch. 10(18)
Pt. I* s.6
Pt. V .... s.6, Sch. 6
Pt. V* .... Sch. 4
Pt. VI* .... Sch. 4, Sch. 6
paras. 1–6* .... Sch. 3
para. 7 ...... Sch. 7, Pt. III(1)
paras. 7–21* .... Sch. 3
para. 9 ...... Sch. 7, Pt. III(1)
para. 13* .... Sch. 3
para. 16* .... Sch. 3
para. 17* .... Sch. 3
para. 19* .... Sch. 3
para. 23 .... Sch. 7, Pt. III(1)
para. 25 .... Sch. 7, Pt. III(1)
para. 26 .... Sch. 7, Pt. III(1)
para. 28 .... Sch. 7, Pt. III(1)
Sched. 6 .... s.1, s.6, s.18,
Sch. 1(10), Sch. 7, Pt. IV
Pt. I .... Sch. 4
Pt. I* s.6
Pt. II .... Sch. 4
Pt. II* s.6
Pt. III .... Sch. 4
Sched. 7 .... s.18
para. 1 .... Sch. 5(2)
paras. 2–2B .... Sch. 5(3)
para. 5A s.137
Sched. 8 .... s.13, Sch. 6
para. 8 .... s.9
Sched. 9 ..... s.18, Sch. 7, Sch. 24
Pt. I s.18
para. 17 .... Sch. 8(2)
Pt. II .... s.18, Sch. 7, Pt. II
Pt. III .... s.18, Sch. 7
Pt. IV ... ... s.18, Sch. 7, Pt. IV
para. 6 .... s.18
para. 8 .... s.18
para. 10(1)(*c*) .... Sch. 7(1)
para. 13 .... s.18, Sch. 7(2)
para. 17 .... Sch. 7(3)
paras. 18A–18C .... Sch. 7(4)
para. 19 .... Sch. 7(5)
para. 20 .... Sch. 7(6)
paras. 21–26 .... Sch. 7(7)
para. 27 .... s.18, Sch. 7(8)
para. 28 .... s.18, Sch. 7(9)
para. 28A ..... s.9, Sch. 7(10)
paras. 29–31 .... Sch. 7(11)
para. 32 .. ... s.22, Sch. 7(12)

1985 Companies Act—*cont.*
Sched. 9—*cont.*
Pt. IV—*cont.*
para. 33 .... s.22
para. 34 .... s.22
para. 36 .. .... s.22, Sch. 7(13)
Sched. 10 .... s.18, Sch. 8
Sched. 10* .... Sch. 8
Sched. 10A ... s.1, s.20, s.21, s.22,
Sch. 9
Sched. 11 .. .... s.127, Sch. 10(21),
Sch. 24
Sched. 13,
para. 25 .... s.143, Sch. 24
para. 26 .... s.143
Sched. 14 .... s.139
Sched. 15 .... Sch. 24
paras. 3, 5 .... s.139
Sched. 15A s.113, s.114
Sched. 15A* s.23, s.114,
Sch. 10(22)
Sched. 15B s.23, s.114,
Sch. 10(22)
Sched. 21,
para. 6 .... s.108
Sched. 22 .... s.21, s.106, s.108,
s.109, s.123, s.130, s.142,
s.143, Sch. 10(23),
Sch. 19(21), Sch. 24
Sched. 24... s.23, s.63, s.64, s.119,
s.120, s.122, s.123, s.139,
Sch. 10(24), Sch. 16(2),
Sch. 24
Sched. 25 .... Sch. 18(38)
Company Securities (Insider
Dealing) Act (c.8) .. s.82, s.196
s.1 .... s.76
s.2 .... s.76
s.4 .... s.76
s.5 .... s.76
s.8(2) s.209
Oil and Pipelines Act
(c.62)—
Sched. 3,
para. 9 .... Sch. 10(33)
Insolvency Act (c.65)—
Sched. 6 .... Sch. 24
Bankruptcy (Scotland) Act
(c.66) s.159, s.161, s.180,
s.182, s.189, s.190,
Sch. 22
s.32(8) s.164, s.175
s.34 .... s.165, Sch. 22(8)
s.36 .... s.165, Sch. 22(8)
s.42 .... s.164
s.73(1) .... s.163, Sch. 22(6)
Transport Act (c.67)—
s.137(1) .... Sch. 18(39)
Housing Act (c.68)—
s.622 .... Sch. 18(40)
Housing Associations Act
(c.69)—
s.101 .... Sch. 18(41)
1986 Atomic Energy Authority
Act (c.3)—
s.9 .... Sch. 18(42)

Table of Statutes

1986 Airports Act (c.31) s.151
    s.82 .... Sch. 18(43)
  Patents, Designs and Marks
    Act (c.39)—
  Sched. 2,
    para. 1 .... Sch. 10(34)
  Gas Act (c.44)—
    s.48(1) .... Sch. 18(44)
    s.61(1) .... Sch. 18(44)
  Insolvency Act (c.45) ... s.87, s.111,
        s.127, s.159, s.180, s.189
    Pt. II s.3, s.182
    Pt. IV s.182
    Pt. V s.182
    Pt. IX s.182
    s.9(3) .... Sch. 16(3)
    s.10(1)(*b*)... s.175, Sch. 22(11)(12)
      (*c*) s.161
    s.11(2) .... s.175, Sch. 22(11)
      (3) .... s.161, Sch. 22(5)
      (*c*) .... s.175, Sch. 22(11)
      (*d*) .... Sch. 22(12)
    s.15(1) .... s.175, Sch. 22(11)
      (2) .... s.175, Sch. 22(11)
    s.39 .... s.100
    s.40 .... s.163
    s.43 .... s.175
    s.45(4) s.100
      (5) .... Sch. 16(3), Sch. 24
    s.46 .... s.100
    s.53 .... s.100
      (2) .... Sch. 24
      (3) .... Sch. 17(10)
    s.54 .... s.100
      (3) .... Sch. 16(3), Sch. 24
    s.61 .... s.175
    s.62 .... s.100
      (5) .... Sch. 16(3), Sch. 24
    s.86 .... s.158
    s.98 .... s.163
    s.107 .... s.154
    s.123 .... s.95
    s.124(4) s.60
    s.124A s.60
    s.126 .... s.161
    s.127 .... s.164, s.175,
              Sch. 22(7)(11)
    s.128 .... s.161
    s.129 .... s.158, s.163
    s.130 .... s.161, Sch. 22(5)
      (3) .... Sch. 22(12)
    s.143(2) s.160
    s.175 .... s.163
    s.178 .... s.164, Sch. 22(7)
    s.185 .... s.161
    s.186 .... s.164, Sch. 22(7)
    s.218(5) s.78
    s.235 .... s.160
    s.238 .... s.165, Sch. 22(8)
    ss.238–241 .... s.95
    s.239 ..... s.159, s.165, Sch. 22(8)
    s.242 .... s.165, Sch. 22(8)
    s.243 .... s.165, Sch. 22(8)
    s.245 .... s.95, s.97, s.99
    s.247 .... s.163
      (2) s.140

1986 Insolvency Act—*cont.*
    s.249 .... s.95
    s.251 .... s.100, s.190, Sch. 22(14)
    s.278 .... s.158, s.163
    s.284 .... s.164, s.175,
              Sch. 22(7)(11)
    s.285 .... s.161, Sch. 22(5)
      (3) .... Sch. 22(12)
    s.304 .... s.161
    s.315 .... s.164, Sch. 22(7)
    s.322 .... s.159
    s.323 ..... s.159, s.163, Sch. 22(6)
    s.324 .... s.161
    s.328(3) s.154
    s.339 .... s.165, Sch. 22(8)
    s.340 .... s.165, Sch. 22(8)
    s.345 .... s.164, Sch. 22(7)
    s.382 .... s.159
    s.411 .... s.2
    s.423 .... s.165, Sch. 22(8)
    s.426 .... s.183
      (4) s.183
      (11) s.183
    s.431 .... s.208
    s.441(2) s.213
    Sched. 5 .... s.159
    Sched. 10 .... Sch. 24
    Sched. 13,
      Pt. I .... Sch. 24
    Sched. 14 .... s.111
  Company Directors Disqual-
    ification Act (c.46) s.127
    s.3(3)(*b*) .... Sch. 10(35)
    s.8 .... s.79
    s.11 .... s.208
    s.13 .... s.208
    s.21(2) .... Sch. 24
      (4) s.208
    s.22(5) s.211
    s.22A s.211
    Sched. 1 .... s.211
      para. 4 .... s.139, Sch. 16(4)
      para. 5 .... Sch. 10(35)
  Building Societies Act (c.53) ... s.87
    s.53 .... s.80, s.88
    s.54 .... s.88
    s.104(2) s.211
    s.110 .... s.211
    s.119 .... Sch. 18(45)
    Sched. 15 .... s.211, Sch. 24
    Sched. 18 .... Sch. 24
  Financial Services Act (c.60) .. s.13,
       s.14, s.82, s.87, s.129,
       s.153, s.155, s.170, s.176,
       s.190, s.207, Sch. 22(15)
    Pt. IV s.131
    Pt. V s.131
    s.4 .... s.76
    s.12 .... s.156, s.169, s.204
    s.13 .... Sch. 23(1), Sch. 24
    s.28 .... s.192, s.196
    s.33 .... s.192, s.196
    s.37 .... s.155
      (7)(i) s.169
      (8) s.169

Table of Statutes

1986 Financial Services Act—*cont.*
   s.39 .... s.155
     (4) s.156
     (8) s.169
   s.40(2) s.156
   s.47 .... s.76
   s.47A s.192
   s.47B s.192
   s.48 .... s.194, Sch. 23(2)
   s.49 .... s.194, Sch. 23(3)
   s.50 .... s.194
     (4) .... Sch. 23(4)
   s.52 .... Sch. 23(5)
   s.54 .... s.65, s.87
   s.55 .... s.194, Sch. 23(6), Sch. 24
   s.56 .... s.194
     (7) .... Sch. 23(7)
     (7A) .... Sch. 23(7)
   s.59 .... s.192, s.196
   s.60 .... s.192, s.196
   s.61 .... s.169
     (1) s.192, s.196
   s.62 .... s.192, s.193
   s.62A s.193
   s.63A s.194, s.195
     B s.194
     C s.195
   s.86 .... Sch. 23(8)
   s.94 ... s.60, s.65, s.68, s.76, s.81, s.87
     (7) s.72
     (7A) s.72
     (8A) s.72
     (8B) s.72
     (10) s.72
   s.95(3) .... Sch. 23(9)
   s.105 .... s.55, s.60, s.76
     (7) .... s.7, Sch. 24
     (9) s.73
     (11) s.73
   s.106 .... s.65, s.76, s.81, s.87
     (2A) s.73
   s.107 .... Sch. 23(10)
     A .... Sch. 23(11)
   s.114 .... s.168, s.206, Sch. 23(12)
     (5) s.193
   s.115 .... Sch. 23(13)
     (2) s.204
     (3)–(5) s.168
   s.117(4) .... Sch. 10(36)
     (5) .... Sch. 10(36)
   s.119 .... s.169, Sch. 23(14)
     (5) .... Sch. 24
   s.121 .... s.169, Sch. 23(15)
   s.122 .... Sch. 23(16)
   s.123(5) .... Sch. 20(26)
   s.124 .... Sch. 23(17)
   s.128A s.196
     B s.196
     C s.196
   s.130 .... s.76
   s.133 .... s.76
   s.150(6) s.197
   s.154(5) s.197
   s.159 .... s.198
     (1) .... s.198, Sch. 24
     (3) s.198

1986 Financial Services Act—*cont.*
   s.160 .... s.198
     (1) .... s.198, Sch. 24
     (6) s.198
   s.160A s.198
   s.161 .... s.198
   s.162(3) s.201
   s.170(2)–(4) s.199
   s.171 .... s.198
     (2) s.76
     (3) s.76
   s.177 ... s.55, s.60, s.65, s.68, s.76, s.81, s.87
     (2A) s.74
     (5A) s.74
     (8) s.74
     (10) s.74
     (11) s.74
   s.179 .... s.88
     (3) .... s.75, Sch. 24
   s.180 .... s.88
     (1) s.75
     (1A) s.75
     (3) s.75
     (6) .... s.75, Sch. 24
     (9) s.75
   s.188 .... s.200
   s.192 .... s.201
   s.195 .... s.202
   s.196(3) .... Sch. 24
   s.198(1) .... Sch. 24
   s.199(1)(2) s.76
     (3)(*b*) s.76
     (5)(*b*) s.76
     (7) s.76
     (8) s.76
     (9) .... s.76, Sch. 24
   s.204 .... s.169
   s.205 .... Sch. 23(18)
     A .... Sch. 23(18)
   s.206(1) .... Sch. 23(19)
   s.207(1) s.205
   Sched. 1,
     para. 30 .... Sch. 10(36)
   Sched. 2 .... s.196
     para. 3 .... s.203
     para. 3A s.204
     para. 4 .... s.192, s.194, Sch. 23(20)
   Sched. 3 .... s.196
     para. 3 .... s.203
     para. 3A s.204
     para. 4 .... s.192, Sch. 23(21)
   Sched. 4 .... s.155, s.156, s.159
     para. 6 .... s.205
   Sched. 5,
     para. 2 .... s.171
   Sched. 7,
     para. 2 .... Sch. 23(22)
     para. 2A s.204
   Sched. 8 .... Sch. 23(23)
   Sched. 9 .... Sch. 23(24)
   Sched. 10,
     para. 4 .... Sch. 23(25)
   Sched. 11 .... s.204, Sch. 23(26)–(43), Sch. 24
     para. 18 .... s.65

Table of Statutes

1986 Financial Services Act—*cont.*
    Sched. 11—*cont.*
        para. 22A s.193
        para. 28 .... s.193, s.206
    Sched. 16,
        para. 22 .... Sch. 19(15)(16), Sch. 24

.1987 Debtors (Scotland) Act (c.18) s.161
    Banking Act (c.22) . s.13, s.18, s.22, s.82, s.87, s.196, Sch. 7
        s.46(2) .... s.119, Sch. 10(37)
            (4) s.119
        s.84(1) .... s.81, s.171, Sch. 24
        s.90(1) .... Sch. 24
        s.105A .... Sch. 10(37)
        Sched. 6 .... Sch. 24
    Criminal Justice Act (c.38)—
        s.2 .... s.60
    Criminal Justice (Scotland) Act (c.41)—
        s.52 .... s.60
        s.55(*a*) .... Sch. 24

1988 Income and Corporation Taxes Act (c.1)—
        s.141(7) .... Sch. 18(46)
        s.180 .... Sch. 10(38)
        s.186 .... s.132
        s.565(6) .... s.139, Sch. 10(38), Sch. 24
    Dartford-Thurrock Crossing Act (c.20)—
        s.33(2) .... Sch. 10(39)
    Criminal Justice Act (c.33)—
        s.145(*a*) .... Sch. 24
    British Steel Act (c.35)—
        s.15(1) .... Sch. 18(47)
    Court of Session Act (c.36)—
        s.45 ... s.29, s.35, s.36, s.40, s.166, s.167, s.201
    Copyright, Designs and Patents Act (c.48)—
    Sched. 7,
        para. 31 .... Sch. 24

1989 Water Act (c.15)—
    s.29 .... s.152
    s.30 .... s.152
1989 Finance Act (c.26) s.132
1989 Law of Property (Miscellaneous Amendments) Act ... s.130
1989 Companies Act (c.40)—
    Pt. II s.75, s.80, s.81, s.87
    Pt. III s.75, s.80, s.81, s.87
    Pt. VII s.75, s.80, s.81, s.87
    s.1 .... s.1
    s.2 .... s.1, s.2
    s.3 .... s.1, s.3
    s.3A s.108
    s.4 .... s.1, s.4, s.19, s.108
    s.5 .... s.1, s.5, s.19
    s.6 .... s.1, s.6
    s.7 .... s.1, s.7
    s.8 .... s.1, s.8
    s.9 .... s.1, s.9
    s.10 ... s.1, s.10, s.17, s.119, s.123

1989 Companies Act—*cont.*
    s.11 .... s.1, s.4, s.11, s.16
    s.12 .... s.1, s.10, s.12
    s.13 .... s.1, s.9, s.13, Sch. 6
    s.14 ...... s.1, s.9, s.14, s.46, s.119
    s.15 .... s.1, s.10, s.15
    s.16 .... s.1, s.16, s.116, s.119
    s.17 .... s.1, s.17
    s.18 .... s.1, s.9, s.18
    s.19 .... s.1, s.19
        (5) s.191
    s.20 .... s.1, s.20
    s.21 .... s.1, s.21, s.144, Sch. 9
    s.22 .... s.1, s.22
    s.23 .... s.23
    s.24 .... s.24
        (1) s.54
        (2) s.54
    ss.24–53 .... s.118
    s.25 ... s.25, s.31, s.34, Sch. 13(10)
    s.26 .... s.26
    s.27 .... s.27
    s.28 .... s.28
    s.29 .... s.29
    s.30 .... s.30, Sch. 11
        (2) s.54
        (3) s.54
        (4) s.54
        (5) s.54
    s.31 .... s.31, s.54
    s.32 .... s.32, Sch. 12
        (1) s.54
        (2) s.54
        (3) s.54
        (4) s.54
    s.33 .... s.25, s.31, s.33
        (3) s.46
        (4) s.31
    s.34 .... s.25, s.31, s.34
    s.35 .... s.35, s.41, s.48
    s.36 .... s.36, s.48
    s.37 .... s.37
    s.38 .... s.38, s.46
    s.39 .... s.39
    s.40 .... s.40, s.46
    s.41 .... s.41
    s.42 .... s.42
    s.43 .... s.43
    s.44 .... s.44
    s.45 .... s.45
    s.46 ... s.40, s.46, s.47, s.54, s.75, s.87, Sch. 13
    s.47 .... s.46, s.47, Sch. 14
    s.48 .... s.48
    s.49 .... s.49
    s.50 .... s.50
    s.51 .... s.51
    s.52 .... s.52, s.54
    s.53 .... s.53
        (1) s.54
        (2) s.54
    s.54 .... s.54
    s.55 .... s.55
    s.56 .... s.56
    s.57 .... s.57
    s.58 .... s.58
    s.59 .... s.59

Table of Statutes

1989 Companies Act—*cont.*
s.60 .... s.60
s.61 .... s.61
s.62 .... s.62
s.63 .... s.63
s.64 .... s.64, s.76
s.65 .... s.65
s.66 .... s.66
s.67 .... s.67
s.68 .... s.68
s.69 .... s.69
s.70 .... s.70
s.71 .... s.71
s.72 .... s.72
s.73 .... s.72, s.73
s.74 .... s.72, s.74
s.75 .... s.75
s.76 .... s.76
s.77 .... s.76, s.77
s.78 .... s.78
s.79 .... s.79
s.80 .... s.80
s.81 .... s.81
s.82 .... s.75, s.82, s.87
ss.82–91 .... s.213
s.83 ... s.60, s.79, s.82, s.83, s.84,
       s.85, s.86, s.88
s.84 ... s.65, s.68, s.75, s.81, s.84,
       s.87, s.88
s.85 .... s.85, s.89, s.90, s.91
s.86 .... s.86, s.88, s.89, s.90, s.91
s.87 .... s.86, s.87, s.88
s.88 .... s.88
s.89 .... s.88, s.89
s.90 .... s.90
s.91 .... s.91
s.92 .... s.92
s.93 .... s.93
s.94 .... s.94
s.95 .... s.95
s.96 .... s.96
s.97 .... s.97
s.98 .... s.98
s.99 .... s.99
s.100 .... s.100
s.101 .... s.101
s.102 .... s.102
s.103 .... s.103
s.104 .... s.104
s.105 .... s.105
s.106 .... s.106
s.107 .... s.107
s.108 ... s.108, s.109, s.111, s.139,
       s.142
s.109 .... s.108, s.109, s.139
s.110 ... s.108, s.110, s.111, s.112
s.111 .... s.108, s.111, s.112
  (2) s.112
s.112 ... s.108, s.111, s.112, s.116
  (3) s.108
s.113 .... s.109, s.113
s.114 .... s.113, s.114
s.115 .... s.115, s.116
s.116 .... s.16, s.113, s.115, s.116,
       s.117
s.117 .... s.115, s.116, s.117

1989 Companies Act—*cont.*
s.118 .... s.118
s.119 ..... s.14, s.116, s.118, s.119
ss.119–123 .... s.9
s.120 ... s.113, s.116, s.118, s.120,
       s.122
s.121 .... s.118, s.121
s.122 .... s.116, s.118, s.122
s.123 .... s.118, s.122, s.123
  (7) .... Sch. 17
s.124 .... s.118, s.124
s.125 .... s.125, s.127
s.126 .... s.126, s.127
s.127 .... s.124, s.127
  (3) s.126
s.128 .... s.128
s.129 .... s.129
s.130 .... s.130
s.131 .... s.131
s.132 .... s.132
s.133 .... s.133
s.134 .... s.134
s.135 .... s.135
s.136 .... s.136
s.137 .... s.137
s.138 .... s.138
s.139 .... s.139
s.140 .... s.140
s.141 .... s.141, s.215
s.142 .... s.103, s.142
s.143 .... s.143
s.144 .... s.21, s.144, Sch. 18
s.145 .... s.145
s.146 .... s.146
s.147 .... s.147, s.151, s.215
s.148 .... s.148, s.215
s.149 .... s.149, s.215
s.150 .... s.150, s.215
s.151 .... s.151
s.152 .... s.152
s.153 .... s.153, s.215
s.154 .... s.154, s.213
s.155 ... s.154, s.155, s.213, s.191
  (2) s.191
ss.155–172 .... s.154
s.156 .... s.155, s.156, s.213,
       Sch. 21
  (2)(*c*) s.170
  (3) s.157
s.157 .... s.157, s.213, Sch. 21
s.158 .... s.158, s.167, s.174,
       Sch. 21
s.159 .... s.159, s.167, Sch. 21
ss.159–165 .... s.158
s.160 .... s.160, s.167, s.213,
       Sch. 21
s.161 .... s.161, s.167, Sch. 21
s.162 ... s.159, s.162, s.167, s.213,
       Sch. 21
s.163 .... s.163, s.167, s.175,
       Sch. 21
  (4) s.159
  (6) s.175
s.164 .... s.164, s.167, s.175,
       Sch. 21
  (3) s.175
  (4) s.159, s.175
  (6) s.175

1989 Companies Act—*cont.*
　s.165 .... s.165, s.167
　　(1) s.159
　　(2) s.159
　　(3) s.159
　　(4) s.159
　s.166 .... s.166, s.168, s.213,
　　　　　　　　　　　　　Sch. 21
　　(2)(*a*) s.167
　s.167 .... s.167, s.213, Sch. 21
　s.168 .... s.168, s.213
　s.169 .... s.169, s.213
　s.170 ... s.154, s.156, s.170, s.176,
　　　　　　　　s.181, s.213, Sch. 21
　s.171 ... s.154, s.171, s.176, s.181,
　　　　　　　　　　　　　　　s.213
　s.172 ... s.154, s.172, s.181, s.213
　s.173 .... s.173, s.191
　　(1) s.176
　　(1)(*c*) s.174
　　(2) s.176
　　(5) s.176
　ss.173–176 .... s.154
　s.174 .... s.174, s.176, Sch. 21
　s.175 .... s.174, s.175, s.176
　s.176 .... s.176, s.181
　s.177 .... s.164, s.177, s.181
　ss.177–181 .... s.154
　s.178 .... s.178, s.179, s.181
　s.179 .... s.179, s.181
　s.180 .... s.180, s.181
　s.181 .... s.181
　s.182 .... s.182, Sch. 22
　s.183 .... s.183
　s.184 .... s.184, s.213
　s.185 .... s.185, s.186, s.213
　s.186 .... s.186, s.213
　s.187 ... s.175, s.187, s.191, s.213
　s.188 .... s.188, s.191, s.213,
　　　　　　　　　　　　　Sch. 21
　　(2) s.158
　s.189 .... s.189, s.191, s.213
　s.190 .... s.190, s.213
　　(1) s.173, s.191
　　(3) s.164, s.191
　　(4) s.191
　　(6) s.191
　　(7)(*a*) s.191
　　(7)(*b*) s.191
　s.191 .... s.191, s.213
　s.192 ... s.192, s.194, s.195, s.206,
　　　　　　　　　　　　　Sch. 23
　s.193 .... s.193
　s.194 .... s.194, s.206, Sch. 23
　s.195 .... s.195, s.206, Sch. 23
　s.196 .... s.196
　s.197 .... s.197
　s.198 .... s.197, s.198, s.199
　s.199 .... s.197, s.199
　s.200 .... s.200
　s.201 .... s.201
　s.202 .... s.197, s.202, s.215
　s.203 .... s.203

1989 Companies Act—*cont.*
　s.204 .... s.204
　s.205 .... s.205
　s.206 .... s.206, Sch. 23
　s.207 .... s.207
　s.208 .... s.208
　s.209 .... s.209
　s.210 .... s.210
　s.211 .... s.211
　s.212 .... s.212, s.215
　s.213 .... s.213
　s.214 .... s.213, s.214
　s.215 .... s.213, s.215
　s.216 .... s.213, s.216
　Sched. 1 .... s.4, Sch. 1
　　para. 7 .... s.13
　Sched. 2 ... ... s.1, s.5, s.13, Sch. 2
　Sched. 3 .... s.6, Sch. 3
　Sched. 4 .... s.1, s.6, Sch. 4
　Sched. 5 .... s.8, Sch. 5
　Sched. 6 .... s.9, s.13, Sch. 6
　Sched. 7 .... s.18, Sch. 7
　　Pt. I s.9
　Sched. 8 .... s.18, Sch. 8
　Sched. 9 .... s.1, s.21, Sch. 9
　Sched. 10 .... s.23, Sch. 10
　Sched. 11 ..... s.39, s.54, Sch. 11
　　Pt. I s.30
　　Pt. II s.30, s.48
　　para.16 .... s.48
　Scheds. 11–14 .... s.118
　Sched. 12 ...... s.39, s.54, Sch. 12
　Sched. 12,
　　Pt. I s.32
　Sched. 12,
　　Pt. II s.32
　Sched. 12,
　　para. 2(1) s.54
　Sched. 13 ...... s.46, s.201, Sch. 13
　Sched. 14 ...... s.46, s.47, Sch. 14
　Sched. 14,
　　Pt. I s.46
　　para. 1(1) s.54
　　para. 1(3) s.47
　　para. 6 .... s.47
　　paras. 1–7 .... s.47
　Sched. 15 .... s.105, Sch. 15
　Sched. 16 .... s.107, Sch. 16
　Sched. 17 .... s.130, Sch. 17
　Sched. 18 .... s.144, Sch. 18
　Sched. 19 .... s.145, Sch. 19
　　para. 20 .... s.22
　Sched. 20 ... s.153, s.215, Sch. 20
　Sched. 21 ..... s.156, s.159, s.169,
　　　　　　　　　　s.188, s.213, Sch. 21
　　Pt. III s.170
　　para. 4 .... s.155
　　para. 5 .... s.184
　　para. 12 .... s.184
　Sched. 22 .... s.182, Sch. 22
　Sched. 24 .... s.22, s.118, s.212,
　　　　　　　　　　　　s.215, Sch. 24

1989 c. 40

COMPANIES ACT 1989*

(1989 c. 40)

Arrangement of Sections

Part I

Company Accounts

Introduction

SECT.
1. Introduction.

Provisions applying to companies generally

2. Accounting records.
3. A company's financial year and accounting reference periods.
4. Individual company accounts.
5. Group accounts.
6. Additional disclosure required in notes to accounts.
7. Approval and signing of accounts.
8. Directors' report.
9. Auditors' report.
10. Publication of accounts and reports.
11. Laying and delivering of accounts and reports.
12. Remedies for failure to comply with accounting requirements.

Exemptions and special provisions

13. Small and medium-sized companies and groups.
14. Dormant companies.
15. Public listed companies: provision of summary financial statement.
16. Private companies: election to dispense with laying of accounts and reports before general meeting.
17. Unlimited companies: exemption from requirement to deliver accounts and reports.
18. Banking and insurance companies and groups: special provisions.

Supplementary provisions

19. Accounting standards.
20. Power to alter accounting requirements.
21. Parent and subsidiary undertakings.
22. Other interpretation provisions.

Consequential amendments

23. Consequential amendments.

Part II

Eligibility for Appointment as Company Auditor

Introduction

24. Introduction.

Eligibility for appointment

25. Eligibility for appointment.
26. Effect of appointment of partnership.

---

* Annotations by Geoffrey Morse, LL.B., Barrister, Herbert Smith Professor of Company Law, Nottingham University; with Michael Bridge, LL.M. (London), Barrister, Hind Professor of Commercial Law, Nottingham University; David Milman, LL.B., Ph.D., Herbert Smith Professor of Company and Commercial Law, University of Manchester; Richard Morris, B.A., M.Sc., F.C.A., Professor of Accounting, University of Liverpool; Christopher Ryan, LL.M., Barrister and Solicitor (NZ), Senior Lecturer in Law, City University.

SECT.
27. Ineligibility on ground of lack of independence.
28. Effect of ineligibility.
29. Power of Secretary of State to require second audit.

Recognition of supervisory bodies and professional qualifications

30. Supervisory bodies.
31. Meaning of "appropriate qualification".
32. Qualifying bodies and recognised professional qualifications.
33. Approval of overseas qualifications.
34. Eligibility of individuals retaining only 1967 Act authorisation.

Duties of recognised bodies

35. The register of auditors.
36. Information about firms to be available to public.
37. Matters to be notified to the Secretary of State.
38. Power to call for information.
39. Compliance orders.
40. Directions to comply with international obligations.

Offences

41. False and misleading statements.
42. Offences by bodies corporate, partnerships and unincorporated associations.
43. Time limits for prosecution of offences.
44. Jurisdiction and procedure in respect of offences.

Supplementary provisions

45. Fees.
46. Delegation of functions of Secretary of State.
47. Restrictive practices.
48. Exemption from liability for damages.
49. Service of notices.
50. Power to make consequential amendments.
51. Power to make provision in consequence of changes affecting accountancy bodies.
52. Meaning of "associate".
53. Minor definitions.
54. Index of defined expressions.

PART III

INVESTIGATIONS AND POWERS TO OBTAIN INFORMATION

Amendments of the Companies Act 1985

55. Investigations by inspectors not leading to published report.
56. Production of documents and evidence to inspectors.
57. Duty of inspectors to report.
58. Power to bring civil proceedings on the company's behalf.
59. Expenses of investigating a company's affairs.
60. Power of Secretary of State to present winding-up petition.
61. Inspectors' reports as evidence.
62. Investigation of company ownership.
63. Secretary of State's power to require production of documents.
64. Entry and search of premises.
65. Provision for security of information obtained.
66. Punishment for destroying, mutilating, &c. company documents.
67. Punishment for furnishing false information.
68. Disclosure of information by Secretary of State or inspector.
69. Protection of banking information.
70. Investigation of oversea companies.
71. Investigation of unregistered companies.

Amendments of the Financial Services Act 1986

SECT.
72. Investigations into collective investment schemes.
73. Investigations into affairs of persons carrying on investment business.
74. Investigations into insider dealing.
75. Restrictions on disclosure of information.
76. Entry and search of premises.

Amendments of other enactments

77. Amendments of the Insurance Companies Act 1982.
78. Amendment of the Insolvency Act 1986.
79. Amendment of the Company Directors Disqualification Act 1986.
80. Amendment of the Building Societies Act 1986.
81. Amendments of the Banking Act 1987.

Powers exercisable to assist overseas regulatory authorities

82. Request for assistance by overseas regulatory authority.
83. Power to require information, documents or other assistance.
84. Exercise of powers by officer, &c.
85. Penalty for failure to comply with requirement, &c.
86. Restrictions on disclosure of information.
87. Exceptions from restrictions on disclosure.
88. Exercise of powers in relation to Northern Ireland.
89. Prosecutions.
90. Offences by bodies corporate, partnerships and unincorporated associations.
91. Jurisdiction and procedure in respect of offences.

PART IV

REGISTRATION OF COMPANY CHARGES

Introduction

92. Introduction.

Registration in the companies charges register

93. Charges requiring registration.
94. The companies charges register.
95. Delivery of particulars for registration.
96. Delivery of further particulars.
97. Effect of omissions and errors in registered particulars.
98. Memorandum of charge ceasing to affect company's property.
99. Further provisions with respect to voidness of charges.
100. Additional information to be registered.

Copies of instruments and register to be kept by company

101. Copies of instruments and register to be kept by company.

Supplementary provisions

102. Power to make further provision by regulations.
103. Other supplementary provisions.
104. Interpretation, &c.
105. Charges on property of oversea company.
106. Application of provisions to unregistered companies.
107. Consequential amendments.

PART V

OTHER AMENDMENTS OF COMPANY LAW

A company's capacity and related matters

108. A company's capacity and the power of the directors to bind it.
109. Invalidity of certain transactions involving directors.

SECT.
110. Statement of company's objects.
111. Charitable companies.
112. Charitable companies (Scotland).

De-regulation of private companies

113. Written resolutions of private companies.
114. Written resolutions: supplementary provisions.
115. Election by private company to dispense with certain requirements.
116. Elective resolution of private company.
117. Power to make further provision by regulations.

Appointment and removal of auditors and related matters

118. Introduction.
119. Appointment of auditors.
120. Rights of auditors.
121. Remuneration of auditors.
122. Removal, resignation, &c. of auditors.
123. Statement by person ceasing to hold office as auditor.
124. Auditors of trade unions and employers' associations.

Company records and related matters

125. Delivery of documents to the registrar.
126. Keeping and inspection of company records.
127. Supplementary provisions as to company records and related matters.

Miscellaneous

128. Form and articles for partnership company.
129. Membership of holding company.
130. Company contracts and execution of documents by companies.
131. Members' rights to damages, &c.
132. Financial assistance for purposes of employees' share scheme.
133. Issue of redeemable shares.
134. Disclosure of interests in shares.
135. Orders imposing restrictions on shares.
136. A company's registered office.
137. Effecting of insurance for officers and auditors of company.
138. Increase of limits on certain exemptions.
139. Annual returns.
140. Floating charges (Scotland).
141. Application to declare dissolution of company void.
142. Abolition of doctrine of deemed notice.
143. Rights of inspection and related matters.
144. "Subsidiary", "holding company" and "wholly-owned subsidiary".
145. Minor amendments.

PART VI

MERGERS AND RELATED MATTERS

146. Restriction on references where prior notice given.
147. Undertakings as alternative to merger reference.
148. Enforcement of undertakings.
149. Temporary restrictions on share dealings.
150. Obtaining control by stages.
151. False or misleading information.
152. Fees.
153. Other amendments about mergers and related matters.

Part VII

Financial Markets and Insolvency

Introduction

SECT.
154. Introduction.

Recognised investment exchanges and clearing houses

155. Market contracts.
156. Additional requirements for recognition: default rules, &c.
157. Changes in default rules.
158. Modifications of the law of insolvency.
159. Proceedings of exchange or clearing house take precedence over insolvency procedures.
160. Duty to give assistance for purposes of default proceedings.
161. Supplementary provisions as to default proceedings.
162. Duty to report on completion of default proceedings.
163. Net sum payable on completion of default proceedings.
164. Disclaimer of property, rescission of contracts, &c.
165. Adjustment of prior transactions.
166. Powers of Secretary of State to give directions.
167. Application to determine whether default proceedings to be taken.
168. Delegation of functions to designated agency.
169. Supplementary provisions.

Other exchanges and clearing houses

170. Certain overseas exchanges and clearing houses.
171. Certain money market institutions.
172. Settlement arrangements provided by the Bank of England.

Market charges

173. Market charges.
174. Modifications of the law of insolvency.
175. Administration orders, &c.
176. Power to make provision about certain other charges.

Market property

177. Application of margin not affected by certain other interests.
178. Priority of floating market charge over subsequent charges.
179. Priority of market charge over unpaid vendor's lien.
180. Proceedings against market property by unsecured creditors.
181. Power to apply provisions to other cases.

Supplementary provisions

182. Powers of court in relation to certain proceedings begun before commencement.
183. Insolvency proceedings in other jurisdictions.
184. Indemnity for certain acts, &c.
185. Power to make further provision by regulations.
186. Supplementary provisions as to regulations.
187. Construction of references to parties to market contracts.
188. Meaning of "default rules" and related expressions.
189. Meaning of "relevant office-holder".
190. Minor definitions.
191. Index of defined expressions.

Part VIII

Amendments of the Financial Services Act 1986

192. Statements of principle.
193. Restriction of right to bring action for contravention of rules, regulations, &c.

SECT.
194. Application of designated rules and regulations to members of self-regulating organisations.
195. Codes of practice.
196. Relations with other regulatory authorities.
197. Construction of references to incurring civil liability.
198. Offers of unlisted securities.
199. Offers of securities by private companies and old public companies.
200. Jurisdiction of High Court and Court of Session.
201. Directions to secure compliance with international obligations.
202. Offers of short-dated debentures.
203. Standard of protection for investors.
204. Costs of compliance.
205. Requirements for recognition of investment exchange.
206. Consequential amendments and delegation of functions on commencement.

PART IX

TRANSFER OF SECURITIES

207. Transfer of securities.

PART X

MISCELLANEOUS AND GENERAL PROVISIONS

Miscellaneous

208. Summary proceedings in Scotland for offences in connection with disqualification of directors.
209. Prosecutions in connection with insider dealing.
210. Restriction of duty to supply statements of premium income.
211. Building societies: miscellaneous amendments.

General

212. Repeals.
213. Provisions extending to Northern Ireland.
214. Making of corresponding provision for Northern Ireland.
215. Commencement and transitional provisions.
216. Short title.

SCHEDULES:
    Schedule 1—Form and content of company accounts.
    Schedule 2—Form and content of group accounts.
    Schedule 3—Disclosure of information: related undertakings.
        Part I—Companies not required to prepare group accounts.
        Part II—Companies required to prepare group accounts.
    Schedule 4—Disclosure of information: emoluments and other benefits of directors and others.
    Schedule 5—Matters to be included in directors' report.
    Schedule 6—Exemptions for small and medium-sized companies.
        Part I—Small companies.
        Part II—Medium-sized companies.
        Part III—Supplementary provisions.
    Schedule 7—Special provisions for banking and insurance companies and groups.
        Part I—Form and content of accounts.
        Part II—Accounts of banking or insurance group.
        Part III—Additional disclosure: related undertakings.
        Part IV—Additional disclosure: emoluments and other benefits of directors and others.
    Schedule 8—Directors' report where accounts prepared in accordance with special provisions for banking or insurance companies or groups.
    Schedule 9—Parent and subsidiary undertakings: supplementary provisions.
    Schedule 10—Amendments consequential on Part I.
        Part I—Amendments of the Companies Act 1985.
        Part II—Amendments of other enactments.

Schedule 11—Recognition of supervisory body.
   Part I—Grant and revocation of recognition.
   Part II—Requirements for recognition.
Schedule 12—Recognition of professional qualification.
   Part I—Grant and revocation of recognition.
   Part II—Requirements for recognition.
Schedule 13—Supplementary provisions with respect to delegation order.
Schedule 14—Supervisory and qualifying bodies: restrictive practices.
   Part I—Prevention of restrictive practices.
   Part II—Consequential exemptions from competition law.
Schedule 15—Charges on property of oversea companies.
Schedule 16—Amendments consequential on Part IV.
Schedule 17—Company contracts, seals, &c.: further provisions.
Schedule 18—"Subsidiary" and related expressions: consequential amendments and savings.
Schedule 19—Minor amendments of the Companies Act 1985.
Schedule 20—Amendments about mergers and related matters.
Schedule 21—Additional requirements for recognition.
   Part I—UK investment exchanges.
   Part II—UK clearing houses.
   Part III—Overseas investment exchanges and clearing houses.
Schedule 22—Financial markets and insolvency: provisions applying to pre-commencement cases.
Schedule 23—Consequential amendments of the Financial Services Act 1986.
   Part I—General amendments.
   Part II—Amendments relating to friendly societies.
Schedule 24—Repeals.

An Act to amend the law relating to company accounts; to make new provision with respect to the persons eligible for appointment as company auditors; to amend the Companies Act 1985 and certain other enactments with respect to investigations and powers to obtain information and to confer new powers exercisable to assist overseas regulatory authorities; to make new provision with respect to the registration of company charges and otherwise to amend the law relating to companies; to amend the Fair Trading Act 1973; to enable provision to be made for the payment of fees in connection with the exercise by the Secretary of State, the Director General of Fair Trading and the Monopolies and Mergers Commission of their functions under Part V of that Act; to make provision for safeguarding the operation of certain financial markets; to amend the Financial Services Act 1986; to enable provision to be made for the recording and transfer of title to securities without a written instrument; to amend the Company Directors Disqualification Act 1986, the Company Securities (Insider Dealing) Act 1985, the Policyholders Protection Act 1975 and the law relating to building societies; and for connected purposes. [November 16, 1989]

PARLIAMENTARY DEBATES
   Hansard, H.L. Vol. 502, cols. 1363; Vol. 503, cols. 6, 876, 890, 961, 995; Vol. 504, cols. 73, 508, 615, 1145, 1260; Vol. 505, cols. 461, 1016, 1195; Vol. 506, cols. 131, 943, 988, 1377; Vol. 512, cols. 548, 673, 1088. H.C. Vol. 152, col. 291; Vol. 158, cols. 879, 951, 1068, 1126, 1181.
   The Bill was considered in Standing Committee D from May 16 to June 29, 1989.

INTRODUCTION AND GENERAL NOTE
   Pt. I of the Act implements the seventh EC directive on company law (83/349/EEC O.J. Vol. 26, L193) which relates to group accounts. All groups above a certain size will be required to produce consolidated accounts on a defined basis. These will include new

provisions on the effect of acquisitions on the position of a group. This Part also allows listed companies to provide their members with summary financial statements as an alternative to the full accounts. A new definition of subsidiary undertakings is introduced to control the phenomenon of off-balance sheet financing.

Pt. II implements the eighth EC directive on company law (84/253/EEC, O.J. Vol. 27, L126) which concerns the qualifications of auditors. This required statutory force to be given to rules which were previously set and governed by the professional bodies. The directive requires maximum standards for qualification and regulation of those qualified to audit company accounts but allows professional bodies to be designated as approving authorities. The Act does not specify who the designated bodies for approving auditors are to be, but lays down the criteria under which the Secretary of State can recognise professional bodies. As a consequence, any existing professional body of accountants and auditors is able to apply to the Secretary of State to become a "recognised supervisory body" to supervise the operation of the rules contained in the Act. The Secretary of State will, however, have powers to set up by statutory instrument a body corporate to oversee the profession. Professional bodies will also be able to apply to become "a recognised qualifying body", whose qualification will become "a recognised professional qualification". In addition, audit firms will be permitted to become incorporated provided a majority of voting rights is held by (and a majority of the directors comprise) individuals or firms which are qualified to act as auditors.

Pt. III amends and extends provisions relating to investigations under the Insurance Companies Act 1982, the Companies Act 1985, the Insolvency Act 1986 and the Financial Services Act 1986 and confers a new investigations power to assist overseas regulatory authorities. The aim of all these provisions is to preserve fair and efficient markets and to enhance the scope and flexibility of the powers in order to speed up investigations and make them more effective. The new provisions will in general terms operate in three main ways, namely by adjusting or extending the circumstances in which inspectors may be appointed and in which such appointments may be directed or terminated; by simplifying or enhancing powers to obtain and disclose information; and by enabling investigations to take place in this country on behalf of overseas regulators in a spirit of reciprocity. As financial markets and trade become increasingly international and as European commitments multiply, the need has grown for the Department of Trade and Industry to be sufficiently equipped to liaise and join with its opposite numbers in other countries in order to provide and enforce regulations in relation to banking, insurance, financial services and the securities industry. The current investigative policy of the Department is set out in its booklet *Investigations: How they work*, and the current law is contained largely in Pt. XIV, ss.431–453 of the Companies Act 1985 and ss.177 and 199 of the Financial Services Act 1986, both as amended by Pt. III of this Act.

Pt. IV concerns the registration of company charges. This will simplify the registration procedure for company charges, especially for registration of charges by oversea companies. It inserts a new Pt. XII into the Companies Act 1985. There are substantive changes to the law, *e.g.* in the case of late delivery of the particulars of the charge to the registrar.

The aims of Pt. IV were explained by Lord Young as follows:

"Part IV of the Bill concerns the registration of company charges. The main aim is to reduce the burden on companies who register charges at Companies House. The present system is cumbersome and inflexible. We propose to reduce the amount of documentation that companies must supply to Companies House and to make it easier for companies to update information already on the register.

A second objective is to reduce the task of dealing with charges at Companies House, with a consequent reduction in costs. Staff currently employed on this work will be redeployed elsewhere to cope with the growing workload of the registrar.

Thirdly, we are taking the opportunity to make some essential changes to the system of registration of charges by overseas companies. Court decisions have revealed serious defects which must be put right." (*Hansard*, H.L. Vol. 503, col. 11 (January 16, 1989)).

The reforms introduced here are best viewed as interim measures. The publication of the Diamond Report *A Review of Security Interests in Property* on January 27, 1989, as the 1989 Act was undergoing its Parliamentary passage, may herald a more radical revision of the system, if its proposals are accepted by the Government. The Diamond Report opts for the solution favoured by the Crowther Committee in 1971 (Cm. 4596), *i.e.* comprehensive registration of all security interests. However, as the deadline for the submission of comments on Pts. I and II of the Diamond Report was September 1, 1989, it was always unlikely that the radical proposals contained in that report would find a home in this particular Companies Bill. For a full discussion of the implications of this report see *Lawson* [1989] J.B.L. 287.

The provisions now to be found in Pt. IV of the 1989 Act have had a chequered history in terms of their evolution. The original version was amended considerably in the debates in both the Lords and the Commons. This version was (for reasons that have never been fully explained) then abandoned by the Government which introduced a completely new set of provisions right at the end of the Parliamentary passage of the Bill. This has resulted in a much more complex framework, which will become even more sophisticated once the secondary legislation, upon which this Part of the Act so much depends, appears.

The basic legislative technique adopted in the 1989 Act of substituting new provisions into Pts. XII and XXIII of the 1985 consolidation Act is once again adopted here so as to maintain the cosmetic integrity of that legislation. However, the match is not perfect in that completely new sections have been introduced and room has had to be found for them by transferring other provisions to different Parts of the Act. Furthermore, certain sections in the original Pt. XII have not been retained in its updated version, *e.g.* s.402 (endorsement of certificate of registration on debentures). This provision had been recommended for repeal some 25 years ago by the Jenkins Committee (Cm. 1749, para. 303). At last, this recommendation, which met with the approval of the Diamond Committee (para. 28.4.2) has been taken up by the 1989 Act.

It should be noted that the new system of registration applies (with suitable modifications where appropriate) to both England and Wales on the one hand and to Scotland on the other. People in Scotland need not view this in terms of a loss of national identity, for several useful ideas from the former Scottish system have been adopted by the new unified framework.

When analysing the background to Pt. IV of the 1989 Act, the new legislation may conveniently be broken down into four main areas:

(1) *The public system of charge registration (ss.93–100)*: This system was created by the Companies Act 1900 on the recommendation of the Davey Committee on Company Law Amendment in 1895 (C.7779). It operates by the establishment of a charges register at the Companies Registry at Cardiff which is open to public inspection. The aim of the system is to provide an accurate source of information for persons interested in the creditworthiness of companies—see *Re Jackson & Bassford Ltd.* [1906] 2 Ch. 467 at 476 *per* Buckley J. This register contains details of registrable charges created over company assets. Failure to submit particulars of charge within the specified 21-day deadline may result in invalidation of the charge. It has been apparent for a number of years that this system was not achieving its desired aim. The reasons for this are as follows:

(a) Not all charges are registrable, and more importantly, not all security transactions result in a registrable charge being created. Thus a charge over a company's holdings of shares in another company is not included in the list of registrable charges in s.396, nor is the interest created by a properly drafted title retention clause (*Clough Mill* v. *Martin* [1985] 1 W.L.R. 111), nor an artificial trust device (*Carreras Rothmans* v. *Freeman Mathews Treasure Ltd.* [1985] Ch. 207, nor a block discounting agreement (*Lloyds and Scottish Finance* v. *Cyril Lord Carpets* (1979) 129 New L.J. 366. The decision of Mervyn Davies J. in *Re Sugar Properties (Derisley Wood) Ltd.* [1988] B.C.L.C. 146 to the effect that charges created over a company's share in a racehorse were not registrable again indicates a lacuna in the registration net. On the other hand, other security transactions which commercial practitioners had for years treated as non-registrable might suddenly become registrable as the result of a surprise judgment of the courts—see, for example, *Re Welsh Irish Ferries Ltd.* [1986] Ch. 471.

(b) Once details of charge have been registered, the chargee is fully protected, even if the recorded particulars do not reveal the full extent of his security. This curious result is produced as a result of the conclusive nature of the registrar's certificate— see the Companies Act 1985, s.401(2)(b) as originally enacted. This certificate is immune from challenge in ordinary civil proceedings (*R.* v. *Registrar of Companies, ex p. Central Bank of India* [1986] Q.B. 1114).

(c) The doctrine of constructive notice, which applied to the recorded details required to be registered at Cardiff, was increasingly out of step with the needs of commercial practice.

(d) Procedures for late registration of charges and amendment of the register were in urgent need of revision. In addition the administrative burdens imposed on the registrar arising from his obligation to check the furnished particulars against the instrument of charge needed to be reduced.

(e) The English registration system had no satisfactory mechanisms to deal with the registration of negative pledge and automatic crystallisation clauses, now commonly contained in debentures creating floating charges.

(2) *The domestic registration system (s.101)*: It is sometimes overlooked that there is also a requirement to register details of all charges created over a company's assets at the registered office of the company concerned and to retain copies of instruments of charge. This requirement, which was first imposed in 1862, is not, however, supported by the sanction of invalidity in the event of non-compliance. There was one major problem with this domestic system of charge registration and that concerned the public's inspection rights.

(3) *Registration of charges created by oversea companies (s.105 and Sched. 15)*: This registration system, which can be traced back to the Companies Act 1928, s.43, was introduced on the recommendation of the Greene Committee (1926) (Cmd. 2657). It has grown in importance with the expansion of international trade and the internationalisation of corporate finance. The rule formerly found in the Companies Act 1985, s.409 was presumably designed to ensure that an oversea company recorded details of charge alongside the other information kept on that company at Cardiff. The scope of this provision was widened considerably by Lloyd J. in *N.V. Slavenburg's Bank* v. *Intercontinental Natural Resources* [1980] 1 W.L.R. 1076 where it was held that the registration requirement extended to any foreign company with an established place of business in this country, even if it had not been registered as an oversea company under Pt. XXIII of the Act. For discussion of this case see *Milman* (1981) 125 S.J. 294. One result of this ruling was the establishment of the so-called "Slavenburg Register" at Companies House. S.105 and Sched. 15 do away with this register, and seek to put the law on a more orderly basis.

Pt. V contains a large number of unrelated amendments to the Companies Act 1985. These include: the abolition of constitutional restrictions on the capacity of the company and the authority of its directors to bind it; the introduction of written and elective resolutions for private companies; a re-casting of the 1985 sections on the appointment and removal of auditors; new enabling provisions for the registrar to adapt to modern technology; the abolition of the need for a corporate seal; amendments to the share disclosure rules; changes to the law on a change of address of a company's registered office; directors' indemnity policies; annual returns; abolition of the constructive notice doctrine in relation to matters held on the company's file; and a new definition of holding and subsidiary companies for all purposes (except group accounting in Pt. I).

Pt. VI concerns merger references and related matters under the Fair Trading Act. The major changes are the introduction of a pre-notification system to avoid the problems of an announced merger being referred to the Monopolies and Mergers Commission; provisions for undertakings to be given to allow the merger to proceed without a reference; and restrictions on the acquisitions of shares once a merger is referred to the M.M.C.

Pt. VII deals with the relationship between the insolvency laws and the financial markets. It will allow netting to take place prior to the insolvency process taking effect.

Pt. VIII is concerned with amendments to the Financial Services Act 1986. Many changes are technical, but there are major changes to the way in which the Securities and Investment Board (S.I.B.), will publish its own rulebook and will authorise Self-regulatory organisations (S.R.Os.), in accordance with their rulebooks. The Secretary of State's functions under Pt. VIII will be delegated to the S.I.B. as with the parent act. One other major change will be to disallow actions for damages for breach of an S.R.O. or S.I.B. rule for all but private investors.

Pt. IX of the Act enables the Secretary of State to introduce a system of "paperless shares" or "dematerialisation"—*i.e.* a procedure by which the title to and transfer of shares may be recorded without formal documentation. This would be a radical departure from established principles of Company Law in the U.K. (see C.A. 1985, ss.183, 185 and 186), though to some extent it does continue a trend towards computerisation started by the Stock Exchange (Completion of Bargains) Act 1976. The idea was mooted in the 1985 White Paper "Financial Services in the U.K." (Cm. 9432), para. 7.21. Pt. IX was a late addition to the Bill introduced in Standing Committee D in the House of Commons, though it is clear that reform in this area was on the agenda from as early as November 1988, when the D.T.I. issued a Consultative Document on the subject.

To some extent this change has been forced on the authorities who are keen to maintain London's position as an international centre for securities dealings; this new system will enable the TAURUS scheme as proposed by the International Stock Exchange to proceed. It is also hoped that the new system will speed up share transfers and reduce transactions costs. For a full rehearsal of the alleged advantages of the new system: see Francis Maude's comments in Standing Committee D (*supra*, col. 679).

The finer details of this new regime are to be mapped out in regulations made by the Secretary of State in pursuance of his power under s.207. The terms of s.207 are vague, apparently because the Government itself does not know how the TAURUS scheme will eventually turn out. Persons wishing to gain a better idea of what these regulations might contain should examine the November 1988 Consultative Paper, the later D.T.I. Press Release 89/432 and the discussions in Standing Committee D in the House of Commons (*supra*). The Government would appear committed to the "principle of transparency", which permits public access to details of shareholdings, and is opposed to the idea of compelling shareholders to give up their certificates in place of a computer entry. The Government will also have to take into account the fear held by many public companies that the new system will make it more difficult to identify new shareholders and thereby frustrate the service of s.212 notices.

Pt. X contains a number of miscellaneous amendments to the Company Directors Disqualification Act 1986, the Company Securities (Insider Dealing) Act 1986, the Policyholders Protection Act 1975 and the Building Societies Act 1986. It also contains the usual repeals, transitional and commencement provisions.

Scheds. 1–10 relate to the changes in accounting procedures in Pt. I. Scheds. 11–14 supplement Pt. II on the qualification of auditors. Scheds. 15 and 16 are consequent on Pt. IV (company charges). Scheds. 17 and 18 are consequent on the reforms relating to the corporate seal and holding company definitions. Sched. 19 contains further separate amendments to the Companies Act 1985 by way of additions to those in Pt. V of the Act. Sched. 20 is consequential on Pt. VI (mergers) and Scheds. 21 and 22 on Pt. VII (insolvency and the financial markets). Sched. 23 contains consequential amendments of the Financial Services Act 1986 following Pt. VII and Sched. 24 is the repeals Schedule.

ABBREVIATIONS

1985 Act	: Companies Act 1985.
C.A. 1985	: Companies Act 1985.
Diamond Report	: A Review of Security Interests in Property.
D.T.I.	: Department of Trade and Industry.
E.E.I.G.	: European Economic Interest Grouping.
F.S.A. 1986	: Financial Services Act 1986.
I.A. 1986	: Insolvency Act 1986.
M.M.C.	: Monopolies and Mergers Commission.
O.F.T.	: Office of Fair Trading.
Principal Act	: Companies Act 1985.
RCH	: recognised clearing house.
RIE	: recognised investment exchange.
RPB	: recognised professional bodies.
S.I.B.	: Securities and Investments Board.
SORPS	: Statements of Recommended Practice.
S.R.O.	: Self-regulatory Organisation.
SSAP	: Statement of Standard Accounting Practice.

PART I

COMPANY ACCOUNTS

Introduction

Introduction

1. The provisions of this Part amend Part VII of the Companies Act 1985 (accounts and audit) by—
  (a) inserting new provisions in place of sections 221 to 262 of that Act, and
  (b) amending or replacing Schedules 4 to 10 to that Act and inserting new Schedules.

GENERAL NOTE

This section establishes the scope of the provisions dealing with company accounts. These are contained in ss.1–23 of the new Act and in Scheds. 1–10.

Essentially, ss.1–22 of the new Act replace ss.221–262 of the 1985 Act as follows:

Companies Act 1989

Sections of the 1989 Act	Replacement sections in the 1985 Act	Topic
2	221	Accounting records
	222	
3	223	A company's financial year and accounting reference periods
	224	
	225	
4	226	Individual company accounts
5	227	Group accounts
	228	
	229	
	230	
6	231	Additional disclosure required in notes to accounts
	232	
7	233	Approval and signing of accounts
8	234	Directors' report
	234A	
9	235	Auditors' report
	236	
	237	
10	238	Publication of accounts and reports
	239	
	240	
11	241	Laying and delivery of accounts and reports
	242	
	242A	
	243	
	244	
12	245	Remedies for failure to comply with accounting requirements
	245A	
	245B	
	245C	
13	246	Small and medium sized companies and groups
	247	
	248	
	249	
14	250	Dormant companies
15	251	Public listed companies: provision of summary financial statement
16	252	Private companies: election to dispense with laying of accounts and reports before general meeting
	253	
17	254	Unlimited companies: exemption from requirement to deliver accounts and reports
18	255	Banking and insurance groups: special provisions
	255A	
	255B	
	255C	
	255D	
19	256	Accounting standards
20	257	Power of the Secretary of State to alter accounting requirements
21	258	Definitions of parent and subsidiary undertakings
22	259	Meaning of "undertaking"
	260	Meaning of "participating interests"
	261	Notes to the accounts
	262	Minor definitions
	262A	Index of defined expressions

The main changes are as follows:
 (1) The European Community's Seventh Company Law Directive (83/349/EEC) is

implemented by the revised ss.227–230 of the 1985 Act, as inserted by s.5 of the new Act. Under the new provisions, consolidated accounts are the only form of group accounts permitted (s.227(2)). However, there are exceptions for intermediate holding companies (new s.228) and small or medium sized groups (new ss.248–249, as inserted by s.13 of the 1989 Act). New definitions of parent and subsidiary undertakings have also been introduced by new s.258 and Sched. 10A, as inserted respectively by s.21 of and Sched. 9 to the 1989 Act, and the circumstances in which the accounts of a subsidiary may be excluded from consolidation have also been extended (new s.229). The procedures for effecting consolidation, including acquisition and merger accounting, the treatment of joint ventures, and accounting for associated undertakings are detailed in a new Sched. 4A, inserted by Sched. 2 to the new Act. This Schedule also introduces various new disclosure requirements concerning such matters as new acquisitions, the cumulative amount of goodwill written off, and details of disposals of subsidiaries.

(2) The requirements relating to the approval of accounts by the board of directors have been altered. Under s.233, as inserted by s.7 of the new Act, only one director need sign a company's individual balance sheet instead of the present two. Likewise, the directors' report will similarly have to be approved and signed under new s.234A, as inserted by s.8 of the 1989 Act.

(3) Under s.251, as inserted by s.15 of the 1989 Act, listed companies will, under certain conditions, be able to send summary financial statements to shareholders who do not wish to receive full statutory accounts.

(4) Under ss.226(2) and 227(3), as inserted respectively by ss.4 and 5 of the 1989 Act, it will be possible to use the true and fair view override without first having to demonstrate that a true and fair view cannot be given by compliance with the Act supplemented by further disclosure.

(5) Under ss.252–253, as inserted by s.16 of the 1989 Act, members of a private company are able to elect to dispense with the laying of accounts and reports before the company in general meeting.

(6) Under s.224(2), as inserted by s.3 of the 1989 Act, new companies will have nine (instead of the previous six) months in which to notify the Registrar of their accounting reference dates.

(7) Under ss.255, 255A, 255B, 255C and 255D, as inserted by s.18 of the 1989 Act, a number of changes have been made to the provisions relating to banking and insurance companies. The main innovation relates to the ability to prepare "special category" group accounts. Whereas in the past any parent company which has had a banking or insurance subsidiary has been able to prepare "special category" group accounts, this facility will now only be available where the parent is itself a banking or insurance company or where the activities of the group are predominantly in these areas.

(8) Under s.256, as inserted by s.19 of the 1989 Act, new provisions have been introduced with regard to accounting standards and bodies concerned with issuing them.

(9) Under para. 8(3) of Sched. 6 to the 1985 Act (as amended by Sched. 4 to the new Act), directors' compensation for loss of office will henceforward include the value of benefits receivable other than in direct cash terms.

(10) The provisions of the former Pt. VI of Sched. 5 to the 1985 Act have been repealed, and it is no longer necessary to disclose the emoluments of higher paid employees other than directors.

Provisions applying to companies generally

Accounting records

2. The following sections are inserted in Part VII of the Companies Act 1985 at the beginning of Chapter I (provisions applying to companies generally)—

"Accounting records

Duty to keep accounting records

221.—(1) Every company shall keep accounting records which are sufficient to show and explain the company's transactions and are such as to—

(a) disclose with reasonable accuracy, at any time, the financial position of the company at that time, and
(b) enable the directors to ensure that any balance sheet and profit and loss account prepared under this Part complies with the requirements of this Act.

(2) The accounting records shall in particular contain—
   (a) entries from day to day of all sums of money received and expended by the company, and the matters in respect of which the receipt and expenditure takes place, and
   (b) a record of the assets and liabilities of the company.

(3) If the company's business involves dealing in goods, the accounting records shall contain—
   (a) statements of stock held by the company at the end of each financial year of the company,
   (b) all statements of stocktakings from which any such statement of stock as is mentioned in paragraph (a) has been or is to be prepared, and
   (c) except in the case of goods sold by way of ordinary retail trade, statements of all goods sold and purchased, showing the goods and the buyers and sellers in sufficient detail to enable all these to be identified.

(4) A parent company which has a subsidiary undertaking in relation to which the above requirements do not apply shall take reasonable steps to secure that the undertaking keeps such accounting records as to enable the directors of the parent company to ensure that any balance sheet and profit and loss account prepared under this Part complies with the requirements of this Act.

(5) If a company fails to comply with any provision of this section, every officer of the company who is in default is guilty of an offence unless he shows that he acted honestly and that in the circumstances in which the company's business was carried on the default was excusable.

(6) A person guilty of an offence under this section is liable to imprisonment or a fine, or both.

Where and for how long records to be kept

222.—(1) A company's accounting records shall be kept at its registered office or such other place as the directors think fit, and shall at all times be open to inspection by the company's officers.

(2) If accounting records are kept at a place outside Great Britain, accounts and returns with respect to the business dealt with in the accounting records so kept shall be sent to, and kept at, a place in Great Britain, and shall at all times be open to such inspection.

(3) The accounts and returns to be sent to Great Britain shall be such as to—
   (a) disclose with reasonable accuracy the financial position of the business in question at intervals of not more than six months, and
   (b) enable the directors to ensure that the company's balance sheet and profit and loss account comply with the requirements of this Act.

(4) If a company fails to comply with any provision of subsections (1) to (3), every officer of the company who is in default is guilty of an offence, and liable to imprisonment or a fine or both, unless he shows that he acted honestly and that in the circumstances in which the company's business was carried on the default was excusable.

(5) Accounting records which a company is required by section 221 to keep shall be preserved by it—

(a) in the case of a private company, for three years from the date on which they are made, and

(b) in the case of a public company, for six years from the date on which they are made.

This is subject to any provision contained in rules made under section 411 of the Insolvency Act 1986 (company insolvency rules).

(6) An officer of a company is guilty of an offence, and liable to imprisonment or a fine or both, if he fails to take all reasonable steps for securing compliance by the company with subsection (5) or intentionally causes any default by the company under that subsection.".

DEFINITIONS AND CROSS REFERENCES
"accounting records": the use of computers and other non-documentary methods for keeping company records is dealt with in ss.722–723, C.A. 1985. For the directors' duty to account properly see Technical Release TR 573 of the Consultative Committee of Accountancy Bodies (March 1985).
"officer": s.744, C.A. 1985.
"parent company": s.258, C.A. 1985 as inserted by s.21, 1989 Act; and Sched. 10(A), C.A. 1985 as inserted by Sched. 9, 1989 Act.
"private company": s.1(3), C.A. 1985.
"public company": s.1(3), C.A. 1985.
"the requirements of this Act": under ss.226 and 227, C.A. 1985, as inserted by ss.4–5, annual accounts must comply as to form and content with the requirements of Scheds. 4–10 of the Principal Act and in particular give a true and fair view of the company's and/or groups financial position and of its profit and loss.

GENERAL NOTE
This section inserts new ss.221 and 222 into the 1985 Act. These re-enact, without substantive change, existing provisions dealing with the requirement to keep proper accounting records and the length of time over which they should be retained.
The derivations are as follows: s.221(1)–(3) from s.221(2)–(4) of the 1985 Act; s.221(4) was inserted during the passage of the Bill to ensure that a parent company takes reasonable steps to ensure that proper accounting records are kept by a subsidiary undertaking to which the provisions of the new s.221(1)–(3) do not apply; s.221(5)–(6) derives from the previous s.223(1) and (3) respectively. S.222(1)–(3) derives from s.222(1)–(3) of the original 1985 Act; s.222(4) from the former s.223(1); s.222(5) from what was s.222(4); and s.222(6) from the former s.223(2).

A company's financial year and accounting reference periods

3. The following sections are inserted in Part VII of the Companies Act 1985—

"A company's financial year and accounting reference periods

A company's financial year
223.—(1) A company's "financial year" is determined as follows.

(2) Its first financial year begins with the first day of its first accounting reference period and ends with the last day of that period or such other date, not more than seven days before or after the end of that period, as the directors may determine.

(3) Subsequent financial years begin with the day immediately following the end of the company's previous financial year and end with the last day of its next accounting reference period or such other date, not more than seven days before or after the end of that period, as the directors may determine.

(4) In relation to an undertaking which is not a company, references in this Act to its financial year are to any period in respect of which a profit and loss account of the undertaking is required to be made up

(by its constitution or by the law under which it is established), whether that period is a year or not.

(5) The directors of a parent company shall secure that, except where in their opinion there are good reasons against it, the financial year of each of its subsidiary undertakings coincides with the company's own financial year.

Accounting reference periods and accounting reference date

224.—(1) A company's accounting reference periods are determined according to its accounting reference date.

(2) A company may, at any time before the end of the period of nine months beginning with the date of its incorporation, by notice in the prescribed form given to the registrar specify its accounting reference date, that is, the date on which its accounting reference period ends in each calendar year.

(3) Failing such notice, a company's accounting reference date is—
  (a) in the case of a company incorporated before the commencement of section 3 of the Companies Act 1989, 31st March;
  (b) in the case of a company incorporated after the commencement of that section, the last day of the month in which the anniversary of its incorporation falls.

(4) A company's first accounting reference period is the period of more than six months, but not more than 18 months, beginning with the date of its incorporation and ending with its accounting reference date.

(5) Its subsequent accounting reference periods are successive periods of twelve months beginning immediately after the end of the previous accounting reference period and ending with its accounting reference date.

(6) This section has effect subject to the provisions of section 225 relating to the alteration of accounting reference dates and the consequences of such alteration.

Alteration of accounting reference date

225.—(1) A company may by notice in the prescribed form given to the registrar specify a new accounting reference date having effect in relation to the company's current accounting reference period and subsequent periods.

(2) A company may by notice in the prescribed form given to the registrar specify a new accounting reference date having effect in relation to the company's previous accounting reference period and subsequent periods if—
  (a) the company is a subsidiary undertaking or parent undertaking of another company and the new accounting reference date coincides with the accounting reference date of that other company, or
  (b) an administration order under Part II of the Insolvency Act 1986 is in force.

A company's "previous accounting reference period" means that immediately preceding its current accounting reference period.

(3) The notice shall state whether the current or previous accounting reference period—
  (a) is to be shortened, so as to come to an end on the first occasion on which the new accounting reference date falls or fell after the beginning of the period, or
  (b) is to be extended, so as to come to an end on the second occasion on which that date falls or fell after the beginning of the period.

(4) A notice under subsection (1) stating that the current accounting reference period is to be extended is ineffective, except as mentioned below, if given less than five years after the end of an earlier accounting reference period of the company which was extended by virtue of this section.

This subsection does not apply—
  (a) to a notice given by a company which is a subsidiary undertaking or parent undertaking of another company and the new accounting reference date coincides with that of the other company, or
  (b) where an administration order is in force under Part II of the Insolvency Act 1986,
or where the Secretary of State directs that it should not apply, which he may do with respect to a notice which has been given or which may be given.

(5) A notice under subsection (2)(a) may not be given if the period allowed for laying and delivering account and reports in relation to the previous accounting reference period has already expired.

(6) An accounting reference period may not in any case, unless an administration order is in force under Part II of the Insolvency Act 1986, be extended so as to exceed 18 months and a notice under this section is ineffective if the current or previous accounting reference period as extended in accordance with the notice would exceed that limit.".

DEFINITIONS AND CROSS REFERENCES
"accounting reference period": revised s.224, C.A. 1985, as inserted by s.3, 1989 Act; s.742(1), C.A. 1985, as amended by Sched. 10, para. 15, 1989 Act.
"financial year": s.233, C.A. 1985 as inserted by s.3, 1989 Act; s.742(1), C.A. 1985, as amended by Sched. 10, para. 15, 1989 Act.
"parent company": see DEFINITIONS to s.2.
"subsidiary company": s.258, C.A. 1985, as inserted by s.21, 1989 Act; ss.36, 736A and 736B, C.A. 1985, as inserted by s.144, 1989 Act; Sched. 10A, C.A. 1985, as inserted by Sched. 9, 1989 Act; SSAP. 14, para. 7.
"oversea companies": s.744, C.A. 1985; s.701, C.A. 1985, as inserted by Sched. 10, para. 13, 1989 Act.

GENERAL NOTE
This section inserts new ss.223–5 into the 1985 Act which re-enact, with some amendments, provisions determining a company's financial year and accounting reference period covered in the former ss.224–7. The wording has been improved, and the main change is an extension to the period allowed for the initial election of an accounting reference period from six to nine months.

New s.223
This new section indicates that a company's financial year is determined by its accounting reference period, a matter which is dealt with in the new s.224. Some flexibility is afforded by subss. (2) and (3) to enable directors to align the reporting period with the end of a trading week. Subss. (5) requires directors to align the financial years of parent companies and subsidiary undertakings. Subs. (4) allows for the situation where an undertaking, (e.g. a joint venture) is not a separate company.

Subss. (2) and (3) are substantially derived from the previous s.227(2); and subs. (5) from the previous s.227(4).

New s.224
This indicates that a company's accounting reference periods are determined by its accounting reference date, notice of which must be given in prescribed form to the Registrar of Companies within nine months of a company's incorporation. Failing this, the reference date is deemed to be March 31 for companies incorporated prior to the implementation of the 1989 Act; and for those incorporated thereafter, the end of the month 12 months

following its incorporation. The reference date must be such that a company's first accounting reference period, ending on the reference date, will be at least six months, but no greater than 18 months, in length; thereafter the accounting reference period will normally be 12 months, unless altered under the terms of the revised s.225.

Derivations are as follows: Subs. (1) from the previous s.224(1); subs. (2) from the previous s.224(2)–(3) (except that six months is changed to nine); subs. (3)(a) from the former s.224(3) (but (b) is new); subs. (4)–(5) from the previous s.224(4); subs. (6) from the previous s.224(5).

New s.225

This gives limited rights to shorten or extend an existing financial year, and accounting periods of parent companies and subsidiary companies can be aligned under the provisions of subs. (2)(a).

Subs. (4) is aimed at preventing companies from changing their accounting reference dates frequently—unless there are special circumstances and permission is given by the Secretary of State, changes will not be allowed within five years of a previous change.

Subs. (6) limits an extension of the current or previous accounting reference period to a maximum of 18 months.

Derivations are as follows: s.225(1) from the previous s.225(1); s.225(2) from the previous s.225(6)(c) and s.225(8) (as inserted); s.225(3) from the previous s.225(4); s.225(4) from the previous s.225(6)–(8); s.225(5) from the previous s.225(3)(b); and s.225(6) from the previous s.225(5) and s.225(8) (as inserted).

Individual company accounts

4.—(1) The following section is inserted in Part VII of the Companies Act 1985—

"Annual accounts

Duty to prepare individual company accounts

226.—(1) The directors of every company shall prepare for each financial year of the company—
 (a) a balance sheet as at the last day of the year, and
 (b) a profit and loss account.

Those accounts are referred to in this Part as the company's 'individual accounts'.

(2) The balance sheet shall give a true and fair view of the state of affairs of the company as at the end of the financial year; and the profit and loss account shall give a true and fair view of the profit or loss of the company for the financial year.

(3) A company's individual accounts shall comply with the provisions of Schedule 4 as to the form and content of the balance sheet and profit and loss account and additional information to be provided by way of notes to the accounts.

(4) Where compliance with the provisions of that Schedule, and the other provisions of this Act as to the matters to be included in a company's individual accounts or in notes to those accounts, would not be sufficient to give a true and fair view, the necessary additional information shall be given in the accounts or in a note to them.

(5) If in special circumstances compliance with any of those provisions is inconsistent with the requirement to give a true and fair view, the directors shall depart from that provision to the extent necessary to give a true and fair view.

Particulars of any such departure, the reasons for it and its effect shall be given in a note to the accounts".

(2) Schedule 4 to the Companies Act 1985 (form and content of company accounts) is amended in accordance with Schedule 1 to this Act.

DEFINITIONS AND CROSS REFERENCES
 "annual accounts": s.262(1), C.A. 1985, as inserted by s.22, 1989 Act; s.742(1), C.A. 1985, as amended by Sched. 10, para. 15, 1989 Act.

"financial year": see DEFINITIONS to s.3.
"profit and loss account": "balance sheet": For details of prescribed format and contents, see Scheds. 4–10, C.A. 1985, as amended by Scheds. 1–7, 1989 Act; For use in determining amounts available for distribution, see s.270 *et seq.*, Sched. 11, C.A. 1985; For undertakings not trading for profit, see s.261(2), C.A. 1985, as inserted by s.22, 1989 Act.
"true and fair view": Scheds. 4–10, C.A. 1985 as amended by Scheds. 1–7, 1989 Act (*esp* Sched. 4, paras. 10–15); Stock Exchange's 'Admission of Services to Listing' para. 20, p.516; EC's Fourth Council Directive on the annual accounts of companies (78/660/EEC), art. 2.

GENERAL NOTE
Subss. (1) and (3) of the new s.226 require company directors to prepare an individual profit and loss account and balance sheet for a financial year, which, with regard to form and content, and including the notes thereto, must be in accordance with the provisions of Sched. 4 to the principal Act, as amended by Sched. 1 in the new legislation. However, under subs. (2) of the inserted section, there is an overriding requirement that the financial statements should give a true and fair view of the state of affairs on the company at the end of its financial year and of its profit and loss for that period, and if necessary the directors must disclose additional information and/or depart from the prescribed form and content of the accounts and notes thereto contained in Sched. 4 (as amended), indicating that they have done so and the reasons therefore in a note (subss. (3) and (4)).

In addition to preparing a balance sheet and profit and loss account, companies with an annual turnover or gross income of more than £25,000 are required by Statement of Standard Accounting Practice No. 10, "Statements of Source and Application of Funds", to produce a flow of funds statement. (See also International Accounting Standard No. 7, "Statement of Changes in Financial Position".)

See s.272 of the 1985 Act for the requirement (where relevant) that a public company should prepare full interim accounts to help determine the maximum amount that can be distributed by a company under ss.263–9 and 274–6 of the principal Act.

See s.273 of the 1985 Act for the requirement (where relevant) that a public company in its first accounting reference period should prepare full initial accounts (s.270(4) of the 1985 Act) to help determine the maximum amount that can be distributed by a company under ss.263–9 and 274–6 of the principal Act.

See ss.242 and 242A of the 1985 Act, as inserted by s.11 of this Act, for the penalties for laying accounts before the company in general meeting and for filing the accounts with the Registrar of Companies which do not comply with the requirements of the Act.

Derivations are as follows: s.226(1) in part from the previous ss.227(1) and 227(3); s.226(2) from the former s.228(2); s.226(3) from the previous s.228(1); s.226(4) from the previous s.228(4); and s.226(5) from the former ss.228(5) and 228(6).

Group accounts

5.—(1) The following section is inserted in Part VII of the Companies Act 1985—

"Duty to prepare group accounts
227.—(1) If at the end of a financial year a company is a parent company the directors shall, as well as preparing individual accounts for the year, prepare group accounts.
(2) Group accounts shall be consolidated accounts comprising—
  (a) a consolidated balance sheet dealing with the state of affairs of the parent company and its subsidiary undertakings, and
  (b) a consolidated profit and loss account dealing with the profit or loss of the parent company and its subsidiary undertakings.
(3) The accounts shall give a true and fair view of the state of affairs as at the end of the financial year, and the profit or loss for the financial year, of the undertakings included in the consolidation as a whole, so far as concerns members of the company.
(4) A company's group accounts shall comply with the provisions of Schedule 4A as to the form and content of the consolidated balance sheet and consolidated profit and loss account and additional information to be provided by way of notes to the accounts.
(5) Where compliance with the provisions of that Schedule, and the other provisions of this Act, as to the matters to be included in a

company's group accounts or in notes to those accounts, would not be sufficient to give a true and fair view, the necessary additional information shall be given in the accounts or in a note to them.

(6) If in special circumstances compliance with any of those provisions is inconsistent with the requirement to give a true and fair view, the directors shall depart from that provision to the extent necessary to give a true and fair view.

Particulars of any such departure, the reasons for it and its effect shall be given in a note to the accounts.".

(2) Schedule 2 to this Act (form and content of group accounts) is inserted after Schedule 4 to the Companies Act 1985, as Schedule 4A.

(3) The following sections are inserted in Part VII of the Companies Act 1985—

"Exemption for parent companies included in accounts of larger group

228.—(1) A company is exempt from the requirement to prepare group accounts if it is itself a subsidiary undertaking and its immediate parent undertaking is established under the law of a member State of the European Economic Community, in the following cases—

(a) where the company is a wholly-owned subsidiary of that parent undertaking;

(b) where that parent undertaking holds more than 50 per cent. of the shares in the company and notice requesting the preparation of group accounts has not been served on the company by shareholders holding in aggregate—

(i) more than half of the remaining shares in the company, or

(ii) 5 per cent. of the total shares in the company.

Such notice must be served not later than six months after the end of the financial year before that to which it relates.

(2) Exemption is conditional upon compliance with all of the following conditions—

(a) that the company is included in consolidated accounts for a larger group drawn up to the same date, or to an earlier date in the same financial year, by a parent undertaking established under the law of a member State of the European Economic Community;

(b) that those accounts are drawn up and audited, and that parent undertaking's annual report is drawn up, according to that law, in accordance with the provisions of the Seventh Directive (83/349/EEC);

(c) that the company discloses in its individual accounts that it is exempt from the obligation to prepare and deliver group accounts;

(d) that the company states in its individual accounts the name of the parent undertaking which draws up the group accounts referred to above and—

(i) if it is incorporated outside Great Britain, the country in which it is incorporated,

(ii) if it is incorporated in Great Britain, whether it is registered in England and Wales or in Scotland, and

(iii) if it is unincorporated, the address of its principal place of business;

(e) that the company delivers to the registrar, within the period allowed for delivering its individual accounts, copies of those group accounts and of the parent undertaking's annual report, together with the auditors' report on them; and

(f) that if any document comprised in accounts and reports delivered in accordance with paragraph (e) is in a language other than English, there is annexed to the copy of that document delivered a translation of it into English, certified in the prescribed manner to be a correct translation.

(3) The exemption does not apply to a company any of whose securities are listed on a stock exchange in any member State of the European Economic Community.

(4) Shares held by directors of a company for the purpose of complying with any share qualification requirement shall be disregarded in determining for the purposes of subsection (1)(a) whether the company is a wholly-owned subsidiary.

(5) For the purposes of subsection (1)(b) shares held by a wholly-owned subsidiary of the parent undertaking, or held on behalf of the parent undertaking or a wholly- owned subsidiary, shall be attributed to the parent undertaking.

(6) In subsection (3) "securities" includes—
(a) shares and stock,
(b) debentures, including debenture stock, loan stock, bonds, certificates of deposit and other instruments creating or acknowledging indebtedness,
(c) warrants or other instruments entitling the holder to subscribe for securities falling within paragraph (a) or (b), and
(d) certificates or other instruments which confer—
  (i) property rights in respect of a security falling within paragraph (a), (b) or (c).
  (ii) any right to acquire, dispose of, underwrite or convert a security, being a right to which the holder would be entitled if he held any such security to which the certificate or other instrument relates, or
  (iii) a contractual right (other than an option) to acquire any such security otherwise than by subscription.

Subsidiary undertakings included in the consolidation

229.—(1) Subject to the exceptions authorised or required by this section, all the subsidiary undertakings of the parent company shall be included in the consolidation.

(2) A subsidiary undertaking may be excluded from consolidation if its inclusion is not material for the purpose of giving a true and fair view; but two or more undertakings may be excluded only if they are not material taken together.

(3) In addition, a subsidiary undertaking may be excluded from consolidation where—
(a) severe long-term restrictions substantially hinder the exercise of the rights of the parent company over the assets or management of that undertaking, or
(b) the information necessary for the preparation of group accounts cannot be obtained without disproportionate expense or undue delay, or
(c) the interest of the parent company is held exclusively with a view to subsequent resale and the undertaking has not previously been included in consolidated group accounts prepared by the parent company.

The reference in paragraph (a) to the rights of the parent company and the reference in paragraph (c) to the interest of the parent company are, respectively, to rights and interests held by or attributed to the company for the purposes of section 258 (definition of "parent undertaking") in the absence of which it would not be the parent company.

(4) Where the activities of one or more subsidiary undertakings are so different from those of other undertakings to be included in the consolidation that their inclusion would be incompatible with the obligation to give a true and fair view, those undertakings shall be excluded from consolidation.

This subsection does not apply merely because some of the undertakings are industrial, some commercial and some provide services, or because they carry on industrial or commercial activities involving different products or provide different services.

(5) Where all the subsidiary undertakings of a parent company fall within the above exclusions, no group accounts are required."

(4) The following section is inserted in Part VII of the Companies Act 1985—

"**Treatment of individual profit and loss account where group accounts prepared**

230.—(1) The following provisions apply with respect to the individual profit and loss account of a parent company where—
  (a) the company is required to prepare and does prepare group accounts in accordance with this Act, and
  (b) the notes to the company's individual balance sheet show the company's profit or loss for the financial year determined in accordance with this Act.

(2) The profit and loss account need not contain the information specified in paragraphs 52 to 57 of Schedule 4 (information supplementing the profit and loss account).

(3) The profit and loss account must be approved in accordance with section 233(1) (approval by board of directors) but may be omitted from the company's annual accounts for the purposes of the other provisions below in this Chapter.

(4) The exemption conferred by this section is conditional upon its being disclosed in the company's annual accounts that the exemption applies.".

DEFINITIONS AND CROSS REFERENCES
"[annual] accounts": see DEFINITIONS to s.4.
"auditors' report": ss.235, 236, C.A. 1985, as inserted by s.9, 1989 Act; see also Auditing Standard, 'The Audit Report' of the Auditing Practices Committee.
"delivery of accounts to the Registrar": ss.242–4, C.A. 1985, as inserted by s.11, 1989 Act.
"financial year": see DEFINITIONS to s.3.
"group accounts": s.227(2), C.A. 1985, as inserted by s.5, 1989 Act; Sched. 4A, C.A. 1985, as inserted by Sched. 2, 1989 Act. See also Statements of Standard Accounting Practice nos. 1, 14, 22 and 23.
"individual accounts": s.262(1), C.A. 1985, as inserted by s.22, 1989 Act. For format and contents, see Scheds. 4–10, C.A. 1985, as amended by Scheds. 1–7, 1989 Act; For use in determining amounts available for distribution, see s.270 *et seq.* and Sched. 11, C.A. 1985; For undertakings not trading for profit, see s.261(2), C.A. 1985, as inserted by s.22, 1989 Act.
"notes to the accounts": s.261, C.A. 1985, as inserted by s.22, 1989 Act; Sched. 4A, C.A. 1985, as inserted by Sched. 2, 1989 Act; Sched. 4, C.A. 1985 as amended by Sched. 1, 1989 Act, Scheds. 5, 6, C.A. 1985, as amended by Scheds. 3, 4 1989 Act.
"parent company": see DEFINITIONS to s.2.
"parent undertaking": s.258, C.A. 1985, as inserted by s.21, 1989 Act; Sched. 10A, C.A. 1985, as inserted by Sched. 9, 1989 Act.
"securities": s.228(6), C.A. 1985, as inserted by s.5, 1989 Act.
"subsidiary undertaking": see DEFINITIONS to s.3 ("subsidiary company").
"true and fair view": see DEFINITIONS to s.4.

GENERAL NOTE
S.5, together with Sched. 2, inserts new ss.227–230 into the 1985 Act, recasting existing provisions on group accounts in line with the requirements of the European Commission's

Seventh Directive on the harmonisation of company laws (83/349/EEC: see Palmer, vol. IV, K.66–K.118). The new s.227 deals with the obligation to prepare group accounts and their form (further dealt with in Sched. 4A to the 1985 Act, inserted by Sched. 2 to this Act). The new s.228 makes exemptions from the provisions of the new s.227; and the new s.229 requires that subsidiary undertakings should be included in consolidated accounts, subject to exceptions set out in that section. The new s.230 makes concessions in respect of individual profit and loss accounts where group accounts are prepared.

New s.227
This is derived as follows: subs. (1) from the former s.229(1); subs. (2) from the previous s.229(5), but expanded; subs. (3) from the previous s.230(2); subs. (4) replaces the requirement of the previous s.230(1) that group accounts should, so far as possible, comply with the old Sched. 4 to the 1985 Act; subs. (5) from the previous s.230(4); and subs. (6) from the former s.230(5) and (6).

New s.228
This implements the provisions of Articles 7–9 of the Seventh Directive. Essentially, sub-groups need not prepare group accounts if the immediate parent undertaking of the sub-group prepares group accounts under the law of an EC member state and the subsidiary undertaking is wholly owned by the sub-group parent, or it holds more than 50 per cent. of the shares and there is no request by a specified minority of shareholders for such sub-group accounts to be prepared.

New s.229
This is derived as follows: subs. (1) from the former s.229(5); subs. (2) is new but partly implements the provisions of the previous s.229(3)(a); subs. (3) is new, but as well as dealing with Art. 5 of the Seventh Directive covers the provisions of the previous s.229(3); subs. (4) elaborates the provisions of the previous s.229(3)(d), but clarifies the extent to which the "true and fair view" derogation can be used to justify exclusion from consolidation; subs. (5) derives from the former s.229(3).

New s.230
This essentially, re-enacts the provisions of the previous s.228(7)—*i.e.* where a parent undertaking prepares a consolidated profit and loss account, it need not publish a separate individual profit and loss account as long as it discloses how much of the consolidated profit or loss has been dealt with in the company's individual accounts and that it is taking advantage of this exemption.

Reference should also be made to the various Statements of Standard Accounting Practice that deal with group accounts: SSAP. 14 "Group Accounts" (which incidentally identifies four circumstances when a subsidiary must be excluded from consolidation); SSAP. 1 "Accounting for Associated Companies"; SSAP. 23 "Accounting for Acquisitions and Mergers"; and SSAP. 22 "Accounting for Goodwill" (see Palmer, Vol. III, section F). For Stock Exchange requirements, see para. 20, p.5.16 of the Stock Exchange's "Admission of Securities to Listing".

Additional disclosure required in notes to accounts

6.—(1) The following section is inserted in Part VII of the Companies Act 1985—

"Disclosure required in notes to accounts: related undertakings

231.—(1) The information specified in Schedule 5 shall be given in notes to a company's annual accounts.

(2) Where the company is not required to prepare group accounts, the information specified in Part I of that Schedule shall be given; and where the company is required to prepare group accounts, the information specified in Part II of that Schedule shall be given.

(3) The information required by Schedule 5 need not be disclosed with respect to an undertaking which—
   (a) is established under the law of a country outside the United Kingdom, or
   (b) carries on business outside the United Kingdom,

if in the opinion of the directors of the company the disclosure would be seriously prejudicial to the business of that undertaking, or to the business of the company or any of its subsidiary undertakings, and the Secretary of State agrees that the information need not be disclosed.

This subsection does not apply in relation to the information required under paragraph 5(2), 6 or 20 of that Schedule.

(4) Where advantage is taken of subsection (3), that fact shall be stated in a note to the company's annual accounts.

(5) If the directors of the company are of the opinion that the number of undertakings in respect of which the company is required to disclose information under any provision of Schedule 5 to this Act is such that compliance with that provision would result in information of excessive length being given, the information need only be given in respect of—
  (a) the undertakings whose results or financial position, in the opinion of the directors, principally affected the figures shown in the company's annual accounts, and
  (b) undertakings excluded from consolidation under section 229(3) or (4).

This subsection does not apply in relation to the information required under paragraph 10 or 29 of that Schedule.

(6) If advantage is taken of subsection (5)—
  (a) there shall be included in the notes to the company's annual accounts a statement that the information is given only with respect to such undertakings as are mentioned in that subsection, and
  (b) the full information (both that which is disclosed in the notes to the accounts and that which is not) shall be annexed to the company's next annual return.

For this purpose the "next annual return" means that next delivered to the registrar after the accounts in question have been approved under section 233.

(7) If a company fails to comply with subsection (6)(b), the company and every officer of it who is in default is liable to a fine and, for continued contravention, to a daily default fine.".

(2) Schedule 3 to this Act (disclosure of information: related undertakings) is substituted for Schedule 5 to the Companies Act 1985.

(3) The following section is inserted in Part VII of the Companies Act 1985—

"**Disclosure required in notes to accounts: emoluments and other benefits of directors and others**

232.—(1) The information specified in Schedule 6 shall be given in notes to a company's annual accounts.

(2) In that Schedule—
  Part I relates to the emoluments of directors (including emoluments waived), pensions of directors and past directors, compensation for loss of office to directors and past directors and sums paid to third parties in respect of directors' services,
  Part II relates to loans, quasi-loans and other dealings in favour of directors and connected persons, and
  Part III relates to transactions, arrangements and agreements made by the company or a subsidiary undertaking for officers of the company other than directors.

(3) It is the duty of any director of a company, and any person who is or has at any time in the preceding five years been an officer of the

company, to give notice to the company of such matters relating to himself as may be necessary for the purposes of Part I of Schedule 6.

(4) A person who makes default in complying with subsection (3) commits an offence and is liable to a fine.".

(4) Schedule 6 to the Companies Act 1985 is amended in accordance with Schedule 4 to this Act.

DEFINITIONS AND CROSS REFERENCES
"annual accounts": see DEFINITIONS to s.4.
"annual return": ss.363–365, C.A. 1985, as inserted by s.139, 1989 Act.
"compensation for loss of office": Sched. 6, para. 8, C.A. 1985, as inserted by Sched. 4, 1989 Act.
"credit transactions": C.A. 1985; s.331(7); Sched. 6, paras. 15–30, C.A. 1985, as amended by Sched. 4, paras. 4–7, 1989 Act.
"director": s.741, C.A. 1985.
"group accounts": see DEFINITIONS to s.5.
"officer": s.744, C.A. 1985.
"quasi-loan": s.331(2), C.A. 1985.
"subsidiary undertakings": see DEFINITIONS to s.3 ("subsidiary companies").

GENERAL NOTE
S.6, together with Sched. 3 and 4, inserts new ss.231–2 into the 1985 Act, re-enacting with amendments existing provisions. The new s.231 requires the information specified in Sched. 5 to the 1985 Act (which deals with information about undertakings that are related to the reporting company) to be disclosed, subject to various exceptions. The new s.232 requires the disclosure of information on the emoluments of directors and other benefits in favour of directors and others.

Sched. 3 substantially recasts Sched. 5 to the 1985 Act and extends it to reflect disclosure requirements relating to a group as specified in the EC's Seventh Directive.

Sched. 4 amends Sched. 6 to the 1985 Act, first by introducing provisions equivalent to Pt. V of Sched. 5 to the 1985 Act (Chairman's and Directors' Emoluments, Pensions and Compensation for Loss of Office); and second, by making further minor amendments. (The most significant change is probably the repeal of Pt. VI of the old Sched. 5, which required disclosure of particulars relating to the number of employees remunerated at higher rates).

New s.231
This is derived as follows: subs. (1) from the first sentence of the previous s.231(1); subs. (2) is new, indicating that Pt. I of the revised Sched. 5 is appropriate where a company is not required to prepare group accounts, but where group accounts are required, reference must be made to Pt. II; subs. (3) recasts Sched. 5, Pt. I, para. 3; subs. (4) is new and was inserted during the passage of the Bill through Parliament; subs. (5) recasts Sched. 5, Pt. I, para. 4; subs. (6) recasts Sched. 5, Pt. I, para. 5; subs. (7) re-enacts the last sentence of the previous s.231(4).

New s.232
This replaces the former ss.231(2)(d), 232, 233 and 234. In subs. (2), Pt. I of the revised Sched. 6 to the 1985 Act is identified as relating to the emoluments of directors (including emoluments waived), pensions of directors and past directors, and compensation for loss of office to directors and past directors: it is derived from the former Sched. 5, Pt. V, paras. 22–34; Pt. II of the revised Sched. 6 to the 1985 Act is identified as relating to loans, quasi-loans and other dealings in favour of directors and connected persons: it derives from the previous Sched. 6, Pt. I, paras. 1–16; Pt. III of the revised Sched. 6 to the 1985 Act relates to transactions, arrangements and agreements made by the company or a subsidiary undertaking for officers of the company other than directors: it derives from the previous Sched. 6, Pt. II, paras. 15–17.

Approval and signing of accounts

7. The following section is inserted in Part VII of the Companies Act 1985—

"*Approval and signing of accounts*

Approval and signing of accounts

233.—(1) A company's annual accounts shall be approved by the board of directors and signed on behalf of the board by a director of the company.

(2) The signature shall be on the company's balance sheet.

(3) Every copy of the balance sheet which is laid before the company in general meeting, or which is otherwise circulated, published or issued, shall state the name of the person who signed the balance sheet on behalf of the board.

(4) The copy of the company's balance sheet which is delivered to the registrar shall be signed on behalf of the board by a director of the company.

(5) If annual accounts are approved which do not comply with the requirements of this Act, every director of the company who is party to their approval and who knows that they do not comply or is reckless as to whether they comply is guilty of an offence and liable to a fine.

For this purpose every director of the company at the time the accounts are approved shall be taken to be a party to their approval unless he shows that he took all reasonable steps to prevent their being approved.

(6) If a copy of the balance sheet—
- (a) is laid before the company, or otherwise circulated, published or issued, without the balance sheet having been signed as required by this section or without the required statement of the signatory's name being included, or
- (b) is delivered to the registrar without being signed as required by this section,

the company and every officer of it who is in default is guilty of an offence and liable to a fine.".

DEFINITIONS AND CROSS REFERENCES
"annual accounts": see DEFINITIONS to s.4.
"balance sheet": see DEFINITIONS to s.4.
"delivering the accounts to the Registrar": ss.242–244, C.A. 1985, as inserted by s.11, 1989 Act.
"director": s.741, C.A. 1985.
"dormant companies' accounts": s.250, C.A. 1985, as inserted by s.14, 1989 Act.
"filing abbreviated (formerly 'modified') accounts": ss.246–249, C.A. 1985, as inserted by s.13, 1989 Act; Sched. 8, C.A. 1985, as inserted by Sched. 6, 1989 Act.
"interim accounts": ss.270(4)(a) and 272, C.A. 1985.
"laying the accounts before the company": ss.241–244, C.A. 1985, as inserted by s.11, 1989 Act.
"officer": s.744, C.A. 1985.
"publication of accounts": ss.238–240, C.A. 1985, as inserted by s.10, 1989 Act.

GENERAL NOTE
This section inserts a new s.233 into the 1985 Act, replacing and clarifying the existing provisions for the approval and signing of accounts. The principal change is that the accounts can be signed on behalf of the board by a single director rather than by two directors, which has been the requirement hitherto.

The derivation of the new s.233 is as follows: subss. (1) and (2) are drawn from the former s.238(1), as modified to take account of the changes referred to above; subs. (3) is a new requirement that the name of the person signing the balance sheet shall be stated on any copy of it (although this is accepted practice, in fact, only one copy actually being signed); subs. (5) replaces s.238(2).

Directors' report

8.—(1) The following sections are inserted in Part VII of the Companies Act 1985—

"Directors' report

Duty to prepare directors' report

234.—(1) The directors of a company shall for each financial year prepare a report—
  (a) containing a fair review of the development of the business of the company and its subsidiary undertakings during the financial year and of their position at the end of it, and
  (b) stating the amount (if any) which they recommend should be paid as dividend and the amount (if any) which they propose to carry to reserves.

(2) The report shall state the names of the persons who, at any time during the financial year, were directors of the company, and the principal activities of the company and its subsidiary undertakings in the course of the year and any significant change in those activities in the year.

(3) The report shall also comply with Schedule 7 as regards the disclosure of the matters mentioned there.

(4) In Schedule 7—
  Part I relates to matters of a general nature, including changes in asset values, directors' shareholdings and other interests and contributions for political and charitable purposes,
  Part II relates to the acquisition by a company of its own shares or a charge on them,
  Part III relates to the employment, training and advancement of disabled persons,
  Part IV relates to the health, safety and welfare at work of the company's employees, and
  Part V relates to the involvement of employees in the affairs, policy and performance of the company.

(5) In the case of any failure to comply with the provisions of this Part as to the preparation of a directors' report and the contents of the report, every person who was a director of the company immediately before the end of the period for laying and delivering accounts and reports for the financial year in question is guilty of an offence and liable to a fine.

(6) In proceedings against a person for an offence under this section it is a defence for him to prove that he took all reasonable steps for securing compliance with the requirements in question.

Approval and signing of directors' report

234A.—(1) The directors' report shall be approved by the board of directors and signed on behalf of the board by a director or the secretary of the company.

(2) Every copy of the directors' report which is laid before the company in general meeting, or which is otherwise circulated, published or issued, shall state the name of the person who signed it on behalf of the board.

(3) The copy of the directors' report which is delivered to the registrar shall be signed on behalf of the board by a director or the secretary of the company.

(4) If a copy of the directors' report—
  (a) is laid before the company, or otherwise circulated, published or issued, without the report having been signed as required by this section or without the required statement of the signatory's name being included, or

(b) is delivered to the registrar without being signed as required by this section,

the company and every officer of it who is in default is guilty of an offence and liable to a fine.".

(2) Schedule 7 to the Companies Act 1985 (matters to be included in directors' report) is amended in accordance with Schedule 5 to this Act.

DEFINITIONS AND CROSS REFERENCES
"director": s.741, C.A. 1985.
"dividend": ss.263–281, C.A. 1985; Companies (Tables A–F) Regulations 1985, paras. 102–108.
"financial year": see DEFINITIONS to s.3.
"political and charitable purposes": Sched. 7, para. 5, C.A. 1985.
"secretary": s.283, C.A. 1985.
"subsidiary undertakings": see DEFINITIONS to s.3 ("subsidiary companies").

GENERAL NOTE
This section inserts new ss.234 and 234A into the 1985 Act, replacing previous provisions dealing with the directors' report. The new s.234 requires the directors' report to comply with Sched. 7 to the 1985 Act, as revised by s.234A. S.234A introduces a requirement that the directors' report should be formally approved by the board and be signed on its behalf by a director or secretary.

The derivations of the new s.234 are as follows: subs. (1) from the previous s.235(1); subs. (2) from the former s.235(2); subss. (3)–(4) from s.235(3)–(5); subss. (5)–(6) from s.235(7).

Auditors' report

9. The following sections are inserted in Part VII of the Companies Act 1985—

"Auditors' report

Auditors' report

235.—(1) A company's auditors shall make a report to the company's members on all annual accounts of the company of which copies are to be laid before the company in general meeting during their tenure of office.

(2) The auditors' report shall state whether in the auditors' opinion the annual accounts have been properly prepared in accordance with this Act, and in particular whether a true and fair view is given—
  (a) in the case of an individual balance sheet, of the state of affairs of the company as at the end of the financial year,
  (b) in the case of an individual profit and loss account, of the profit or loss of the company for the financial year,
  (c) in the case of group accounts, of the state of affairs as at the end of the financial year, and the profit or loss for the financial year, of the undertakings included in the consolidation as a whole, so far as concerns members of the company.

(3) The auditors shall consider whether the information given in the directors' report for the financial year for which the annual accounts are prepared is consistent with those accounts; and if they are of opinion that it is not they shall state that fact in their report.

Signature of auditors' report

236.—(1) The auditors' report shall state the names of the auditors and be signed by them.

(2) Every copy of the auditors' report which is laid before the company in general meeting, or which is otherwise circulated, published or issued, shall state the names of the auditors.

(3) The copy of the auditors' report which is delivered to the registrar shall state the names of the auditors and be signed by them.

(4) If a copy of the auditors' report—
  (a) is laid before the company, or otherwise circulated, published or issued, without the required statement of the auditors' names, or
  (b) is delivered to the registrar without the required statement of the auditors' names or without being signed as required by this section,
the company and every officer of it who is in default is guilty of an offence and liable to a fine.

(5) References in this section to signature by the auditors are, where the office of auditor is held by a body corporate or partnership, to signature in the name of the body corporate or partnership by a person authorised to sign on its behalf.

Duties of auditors

237.—(1) A company's auditors shall, in preparing their report, carry out such investigations as will enable them to form an opinion as to—
  (a) whether proper accounting records have been kept by the company and proper returns adequate for their audit have been received from branches not visited by them, and
  (b) whether the company's individual accounts are in agreement with the accounting records and returns.

(2) If the auditors are of opinion that proper accounting records have not been kept, or that proper returns adequate for their audit have not been received from branches not visited by them, or if the company's individual accounts are not in agreement with the accounting records and returns, the auditors shall state that fact in their report.

(3) If the auditors fail to obtain all the information and explanations which, to the best of their knowledge and belief, are necessary for the purposes of their audit, they shall state that fact in their report.

(4) If the requirements of Schedule 6 (disclosure of information: emoluments and other benefits of directors and others) are not complied with in the annual accounts, the auditors shall include in their report, so far as they are reasonably able to do so, a statement giving the required particulars.".

DEFINITIONS AND CROSS REFERENCES
  "accounting records": see DEFINITIONS to s.2.
  "annual accounts": see DEFINITIONS to s.4.
  "auditing firm (*i.e.* partnership)": s.53(1), 1989 Act.
  "auditors' report": see DEFINITIONS to s.5.
  "delivery of accounts to the Registrar": see DEFINITIONS to s.5.
  "directors' report": ss.234, 234A, C.A. 1985, as inserted by s.8, 1989 Act; Sched. 7, C.A. 1985, as amended by Sched. 5, 1989 Act.
  "financial year": see DEFINITIONS to s.3.
  "group accounts": see DEFINITIONS to s.5.
  "individual accounts (*i.e.* profit and loss account and balance sheet)": see DEFINITIONS to s.5.
  "laying the accounts before the company": see DEFINITIONS to s.7.
  "parent company": see DEFINITIONS to s.2.
  "parent undertaking": s.258, C.A. 1985; as inserted by s.21, 1989 Act; Sched. 10A, C.A. 1985, as inserted by Sched. 9, 1989 Act.
  "publication of accounts": see DEFINITIONS to s.7.
  "subsidiary undertaking": see DEFINITIONS to s.3 ("subsidiary companies").
  "true and fair view": see DEFINITIONS to s.4.

GENERAL NOTE
  This section inserts new ss.235–7 into the 1985 Act. They recast existing provisions relating to the auditors' report and the rights of auditors to information. The main change is in the new s.236, which for the first time formally requires the report to be signed.

New s.235

This requires that the auditors shall report to the company's shareholders on the annual accounts. The report should include their opinion on whether the annual accounts have been properly prepared in accordance with the Companies Act and in particular whether a true and fair view is given. They are also required to ensure that information given in the directors' report is consistent with the annual accounts. Corresponding sections in the 1985 Act are: subs. (1), the former s.236(1); subs. (2), the previous s.236(2), greatly simplified; subs. (3), the previous s.237(6).

New s.236

This requires that the auditors' report should state the names of the auditors and be signed by them. Subs. (4) indicates that the penalty for default is a fine.

New s.237

This deals with the duties of auditors, indicating that they are required to undertake investigations to enable them to form an opinion as to whether (a) proper accounting records have been kept and adequate branch returns have been made available; and (b) the accounts are in agreement with such records and returns. If proper accounting records have not been kept, or they and the explanations offered are inadequate for their purposes, and/or the accounts do not agree with the records and returns, such matters must be stated in the auditors' report. The auditors are also required to give particulars of directors' remuneration; and of the group's transactions with the directors or officers and of any loan, guarantees, etc., made to them, if such details are not otherwise disclosed in the notes to the accounts. The derivations are as follows: subs. (1) from the previous s.237(1); subs. (2) from the former s.237(2); subs. (3) from the previous s.237(4); subs. (4) from the previous s.237(5).

Provisions relating to the appointment, remuneration, resignation or removal, qualifications, rights, etc., of auditors are covered in ss.384–394A of the 1985 Act, as inserted by ss.119–123 of this Act.

Most auditors will, by virtue of their qualifications (see s.31) additionally have to ensure that the company's (and, where relevant, the group's) financial statements, etc., have been prepared in accordance with the Statements of Standard Accounting Practice laid down by the Accounting Standards Committee. The latter body also issues persuasive Statements of Recommended Practice (SORPs). Listed companies also have to ensure their financial statements comply with the requirements of the Stock Exchange's "Admission of Securities to Listing" (para. 21(a), p.5.17).

Where modified accounts are filed with the Registrar of Companies (see ss.246–9 of the 1985 Act, as inserted by s.13 of this Act), a special auditors' report has to accompany such financial statements, which will reproduce within it the full auditors' report (Sched. 8, para. 8, in the 1985 Act, as inserted by Sched. 6 to this Act).

A company which is "dormant" under the provisions of s.250 of the 1985 Act, as inserted by s.14 of this Act, may exempt itself from the obligation to appoint auditors, in which case an auditors' report need not accompany the accounts.

Where full individual and/or group accounts are published by a company, they must be accompanied by the auditors' report. However, where unofficial abridged accounts are published, they must not be accompanied by the full auditors' report, though they must refer to such a report and indicate whether it contains any qualifications.

Requirements for the auditors' report for banking and insurance companies' accounts (see ss.255–255D, as inserted by s.18 of this Act) are detailed in Sched. 9, para. 28A, as inserted by Sched. 7, Pt. I, para. 10 to this Act.

See s.271 of the 1985 Act for the requirement that where an auditors' report is qualified, the auditors must prepare a statement in writing indicating whether in their opinion the matter which is the subject of qualification is material in determining whether a distribution can legally be made.

See s.273 of the 1985 Act for the auditors' report on any initial accounts (s.270(4)) prepared by a public company.

Publication of accounts and reports

10. The following sections are inserted in Part VII of the Companies Act 1985—

"Publication of accounts and reports

Persons entitled to receive copies of accounts and reports

238.—(1) A copy of the company's annual accounts, together with a copy of the directors' report for that financial year and of the auditors' report on those accounts, shall be sent to—
  (a) every member of the company,
  (b) every holder of the company's debentures, and
  (c) every person who is entitled to receive notice of general meetings,
not less than 21 days before the date of the meeting at which copies of those documents are to be laid in accordance with section 241.

(2) Copies need not be sent—
  (a) to a person who is not entitled to receive notices of general meetings and of whose address the company is unaware, or
  (b) to more than one of the joint holders of shares or debentures none of whom is entitled to receive such notices, or,
  (c) in the case of joint holders of shares or debentures some of whom are, and some not, entitled to receive such notices, to those who are not so entitled.

(3) In the case of a company not having a share capital, copies need not be sent to anyone who is not entitled to receive notices of general meetings of the company.

(4) If copies are sent less than 21 days before the date of the meeting, they shall, notwithstanding that fact, be deemed to have been duly sent if it is so agreed by all the members entitled to attend and vote at the meeting.

(5) If default is made in complying with this section, the company and every officer of it who is in default is guilty of an offence and liable to a fine.

(6) Where copies are sent out under this section over a period of days, references elsewhere in this Act to the day on which copies are sent out shall be construed as references to the last day of that period.

Right to demand copies of accounts and reports

239.—(1) Any member of a company and any holder of a company's debentures is entitled to be furnished, on demand and without charge, with a copy of the company's last annual accounts and directors' report and a copy of the auditors' report on those accounts.

(2) The entitlement under this section is to a single copy of those documents, but that is in addition to any copy to which a person may be entitled under section 238.

(3) If a demand under this section is not complied with within seven days, the company and every officer of it who is in default is guilty of an offence and liable to a fine and, for continued contravention, to a daily default fine.

(4) If in proceedings for such an offence the issue arises whether a person had already been furnished with a copy of the relevant document under this section, it is for the defendant to prove that he had.

Requirements in connection with publication of accounts

240.—(1) If a company publishes any of its statutory accounts, they must be accompanied by the relevant auditors' report under section 235.

(2) A company which is required to prepare group accounts for a financial year shall not publish its statutory individual accounts for

that year without also publishing with them its statutory group accounts.

(3) If a company publishes non-statutory accounts, it shall publish with them a statement indicating—
  (a) that they are not the company's statutory accounts,
  (b) whether statutory accounts dealing with any financial year with which the non-statutory accounts purport to deal have been delivered to the registrar,
  (c) whether the company's auditors have made a report under section 235 on the statutory accounts for any such financial year, and
  (d) whether any report so made was qualified or contained a statement under section 237(2) or (3) (accounting records or returns inadequate, accounts not agreeing with records and returns or failure to obtain necessary information and explanations);

and it shall not publish with the non-statutory accounts any auditors' report under section 235.

(4) For the purposes of this section a company shall be regarded as publishing a document if it publishes, issues or circulates it or otherwise makes it available for public inspection in a manner calculated to invite members of the public generally, or any class of members of the public, to read it.

(5) References in this section to a company's statutory accounts are to its individual or group accounts for a financial year as required to be delivered to the registrar under section 242; and references to the publication by a company of "non-statutory accounts" are to the publication of—
  (a) any balance sheet or profit and loss account relating to, or purporting to deal with, a financial year of the company, or
  (b) an account in any form purporting to be a balance sheet or profit and loss account for the group consisting of the company and its subsidiary undertakings relating to, or purporting to deal with, a financial year of the company,

otherwise than as part of the company's statutory accounts.

(6) A company which contravenes any provision of this section, and any officer of it who is in default, is guilty of an offence and liable to a fine.".

DEFINITIONS AND CROSS REFERENCES
"accounting records and returns": ss.221–2, C.A. 1985, as inserted by s.2, 1989 Act.
"annual accounts": see DEFINITIONS to s.4.
"auditors' report": see DEFINITIONS to s.5.
"debentures": s.744, C.A. 1985.
"delivering of the accounts to the Registrar": see DEFINITIONS to s.7.
"directors' report": see DEFINITIONS to s.9.
"financial year": see DEFINITIONS to s.3.
"meetings": ss.366–383, C.A. 1985.
"member of a company": s.22, C.A. 1985.
"non-statutory accounts": s.240(5), C.A. 1989, as inserted by s.10, 1989 Act.
"officer": s.744, C.A. 1985.
"persons entitled to notice of a general meeting": s.370, C.A. 1985.
"publication of accounts": see DEFINITIONS to s.7.
"share capital": ss.117–124, C.A. 1985.
"special auditors' report for abbreviated accounts": Sched. 8, para. 8, C.A. 1985, as inserted by Sched. 6, 1989 Act.
"statutory group accounts": s.5; Sched. 2.
"statutory individual company accounts": s.227(2), C.A. 1985, as inserted by s.5, 1989 Act; Sched. 4(A), C.A. 1985, as inserted by Sched. 2, 1989 Act; SSAPs 1, 14, 22, 23.
"subsidiary undertaking": see DEFINITIONS to s.3 ("subsidiary company").

GENERAL NOTE
This section inserts new ss.238–240 into the 1985 Act, recasting and extending existing requirements relating to the circulation and publication of a company's accounts and the directors' and auditors' reports.

New s.238
This is derived from the previous s.240, with subs. (1) from the former s.240(1); subs. (2) from the former s.240(3); subs. (3) from the former s.240(2) (albeit in a somewhat simplified form); subs. (4) from the former s.240(4); and subs. (5) from the former s.240(5).

New s.238(6)
This is new and was inserted during committee in parliament. Briefly, the revised section requires that copies of a company's accounts and reports will be sent to all persons entitled to receive notice of a general meeting at least 21 days prior to its being held. However, if the accounts and reports are sent within a period less than 21 days before the meeting, they can nevertheless be deemed to have been sent out at the proper time interval if all members entitled to attend and vote at the meeting so agree. Failure to comply with these requirements renders the company and every defaulting officer liable to a fine.

New s.239
This deals with the right of members of a company or holders of its debentures to demand copies of its accounts and reports. As previously, they are entitled to such copies free on demand, and failure to comply with a request for such copies within seven days renders officers in default liable to a fine. The new subs. (1) is derived from the former s.246(1) (although the specific reference to the directors' and auditors' reports here is new); subs. (2) is new; subs. (3) is from the former s.246(2); and subs. (4) is new.

New s.240
This specifies requirements in connection with the publication of accounts previously covered in the former ss.254 and 255 of the 1985 Act. It distinguishes between a company's "statutory" and "non-statutory" accounts, the former being defined in subs. (5) as the full individual or group accounts properly filed with the Registrar of Companies. However, statutory accounts also include abbreviated (formerly "modified") individual or group accounts where properly filed under the new ss.246–249, as inserted by s.12. The new s.240(1) makes it clear that the statutory accounts must be accompanied by the relevant auditors' report.

New s.240(3). This deals with the publication of "non-statutory" accounts (referred to in the previous legislation as "abridged accounts", a term possibly misleading in view of the concessions enabling small and medium sized companies quite properly to file abbreviated (formerly "modified") accounts). Where "non-statutory" accounts are published, a statement must accompany them indicating (a) that they are not the statutory accounts; (b) whether statutory accounts for the year in question have been delivered to the registrar; and (c) whether the auditors have made a report on the statutory accounts, and if so whether or not it was qualified.
The non-statutory accounts must not be published with the auditors' report relating to the statutory accounts.

New s.240(2). This requires a company which is obliged to prepare group accounts not to publish its individual accounts without also publishing its group accounts. (This is a change in the emphasis from the provisions of the former s.255(3) from which subs. (2) is derived.)

New s.240(6) This indicates that contravention of the provisions of the revised section renders the company and defaulting officers liable to a fine.
Non-statutory accounts include "Preliminary Announcements" made by companies whose shares are listed on The Stock Exchange, London, and which comply with the "Admission of Securities to Listing" regulations (see paras. 8 and 24–25, pp.5.11 and 5.28–5.31). Other summarised financial statements qualifying as non-statutory accounts would appear to be the simplified accounts often circulated by large companies to their employees and shareholders. (The latter are now covered by s.251 of the 1985 Act, as inserted by s.15 of this Act.)
The new subs. (1) is derived from the former s.254(2)(4); subs. (2) from the former s.254(3); subs. (3) from the former s.255(3)(4) (as modified and with (d) now referring to a

qualified rather than an unqualified auditors' report); subs. (4) is new; subs. (5) is in part derived from the former s.255(1); and subs. (6) from the former s.255(5).

Laying and delivering of accounts and reports

11. The following sections are inserted in Part VII of the Companies Act 1985—

"Laying and delivering of accounts and reports

Accounts and reports to be laid before company in general meeting

241.—(1) The directors of a company shall in respect of each financial year lay before the company in general meeting copies of the company's annual accounts, the directors' report and the auditors' report on those accounts.

(2) If the requirements of subsection (1) are not complied with before the end of the period allowed for laying and delivering accounts and reports, every person who immediately before the end of that period was a director of the company is guilty of an offence and liable to a fine and, for continued contravention, to a daily default fine.

(3) It is a defence for a person charged with such an offence to prove that he took all reasonable steps for securing that those requirements would be complied with before the end of that period.

(4) It is not a defence to prove that the documents in question were not in fact prepared as required by this Part.

Accounts and reports to be delivered to the registrar

242.—(1) The directors of a company shall in respect of each financial year deliver to the registrar a copy of the company's annual accounts together with a copy of the directors' report for that year and a copy of the auditors' report on those accounts.

If any document comprised in those accounts or reports is in a language other than English, the directors shall annex to the copy of that document delivered a translation of it into English, certified in the prescribed manner to be a correct translation.

(2) If the requirements of subsection (1) are not complied with before the end of the period allowed for laying and delivering accounts and reports, every person who immediately before the end of that period was a director of the company is guilty of an offence and liable to a fine and, for continued contravention, to a daily default fine.

(3) Further, if the directors of the company fail to make good the default within 14 days after the service of a notice on them requiring compliance, the court may on the application of any member or creditor of the company or of the registrar, make an order directing the directors (or any of them) to make good the default within such time as may be specified in the order.

The court's order may provide that all costs of and incidental to the application shall be borne by the directors.

(4) It is a defence for a person charged with an offence under this section to prove that he took all reasonable steps for securing that the requirements of subsection (1) would be complied with before the end of the period allowed for laying and delivering accounts and reports.

(5) It is not a defence in any proceedings under this section to prove that the documents in question were not in fact prepared as required by this Part.

Civil penalty for failure to deliver accounts

242A.—(1) Where the requirements of section 242(1) are not complied with before the end of the period allowed for laying and delivering accounts and reports, the company is liable to a civil penalty.

This is in addition to any liability of the directors under section 242.

(2) The amount of the penalty is determined by reference to the length of the period between the end of the period allowed for laying and delivering accounts and reports and the day on which the requirements are complied with, and whether the company is a public or private company, as follows:—

Length of period	Public company	Private company
Not more than 3 months.	£ 500	£ 100
More than 3 months but not more than 6 months.	£1,000	£ 250
More than 6 months but not more than 12 months.	£2,000	£ 500
More than 12 months.	£5,000	£1,000

(3) The penalty may be recovered by the registrar and shall be paid by him into the Consolidated Fund.

(4) It is not a defence in proceedings under this section to prove that the documents in question were not in fact prepared as required by this Part.

Accounts of subsidiary undertakings to be appended in certain cases

243.—(1) The following provisions apply where at the end of the financial year a parent company has as a subsidiary undertaking—

(a) a body corporate incorporated outside Great Britain which does not have an established place of business in Great Britain, or

(b) an unincorporated undertaking,

which is excluded from consolidation in accordance with section 229(4) (undertaking with activities different from the undertakings included in the consolidation).

(2) There shall be appended to the copy of the company's annual accounts delivered to the registrar in accordance with section 242 a copy of the undertaking's latest individual accounts and, if it is a parent undertaking, its latest group accounts.

If the accounts appended are required by law to be audited, a copy of the auditors' report shall also be appended.

(3) The accounts must be for a period ending not more than twelve months before the end of the financial year for which the parent company's accounts are made up.

(4) If any document required to be appended is in a language other than English, the directors shall annex to the copy of that document delivered a translation of it into English, certified in the prescribed manner to be a correct translation.

(5) The above requirements are subject to the following qualifications—

(a) an undertaking is not required to prepare for the purposes of this section accounts which would not otherwise be prepared, and if no accounts satisfying the above requirements are prepared none need be appended;

(b) a document need not be appended if it would not otherwise be required to be published, or made available for public inspection, anywhere in the world, but in that case the reason for not appending it shall be stated in a note to the company's accounts;

(c) where an undertaking and all its subsidiary undertakings are excluded from consolidation in accordance with section 229(4), the accounts of such of the subsidiary undertakings of that undertaking as are included in its consolidated group accounts need not be appended.

(6) Subsections (2) to (4) of section 242 (penalties, &c. in case of default) apply in relation to the requirements of this section as they apply in relation to the requirements of subsection (1) of that section.

Period allowed for laying and delivering accounts and reports

244.—(1) The period allowed for laying and delivering accounts and reports is—
  (a) for a private company, 10 months after the end of the relevant accounting reference period, and
  (b) for a public company, 7 months after the end of that period.
This is subject to the following provisions of this section.

(2) If the relevant accounting reference period is the company's first and is a period of more than 12 months, the period allowed is—
  (a) 10 months or 7 months, as the case may be, from the first anniversary of the incorporation of the company, or
  (b) 3 months from the end of the accounting reference period,
whichever last expires.

(3) Where a company carries on business, or has interests, outside the United Kingdom, the Channel Islands and the Isle of Man, the directors may, in respect of any financial year, give to the registrar before the end of the period allowed by subsection (1) or (2) a notice in the prescribed form—
  (a) stating that the company so carries on business or has such interests, and
  (b) claiming a 3 month extension of the period allowed for laying and delivering accounts and reports;
and upon such a notice being given the period is extended accordingly.

(4) If the relevant accounting period is treated as shortened by virtue of a notice given by the company under section 225 (alteration of accounting reference date), the period allowed for laying and delivering accounts is that applicable in accordance with the above provisions or 3 months from the date of the notice under that section, whichever last expires.

(5) If for any special reason the Secretary of State thinks fit he may, on an application made before the expiry of the period otherwise allowed, by notice in writing to a company extend that period by such further period as may be specified in the notice.

(6) In this section "the relevant accounting reference period" means the accounting reference period by reference to which the financial year for the accounts in question was determined.".

DEFINITIONS AND CROSS REFERENCES
  "accounting reference period": see DEFINITIONS to s.3.
  "annual accounts": see DEFINITIONS to s.4.
  "auditors' report": see DEFINITIONS to s.5.
  "date of incorporation": s.13(3), C.A. 1985.
  "directors": s.741, C.A. 1985.
  "directors' report": see DEFINITIONS to s.9.
  "financial year": see DEFINITIONS to s.3.
  "group accounts": see DEFINITIONS to s.5.
  "individual accounts": see DEFINITIONS to s.5.
  "meetings": ss.366–383, C.A. 1985.
  "members": s.22, C.A. 1985.
  "parent undertaking": see DEFINITIONS to s.5.
  "private company": s.1(3), C.A. 1985.

"public company": s.1(3), C.A. 1985.
"subsidiary undertaking": see DEFINITIONS to s.3 ("subsidiary company").

GENERAL NOTE
This section inserts new ss.241–244 into the 1985 Act. These sections for the most part re-enact without change of substance the previous provisions dealing with the laying and delivery of a company's accounts and reports, although the structure of the sections has been altered. The main innovation is in the new s.243, which implements a requirement of the EC's Seventh Council Directive for the accounts of certain subsidiaries excluded from a consolidation to be attached to the group accounts of reporting companies.

New s.241
This specifies that in respect of each financial year a company's directors must lay before the company in general meeting copies of its accounts and the directors' and auditors' reports. Failure to do so within the specified time renders the directors liable to fines. The derivation of the new section is from the former ss.241(1) and 243(1)(2)(5), although specific reference to the directors' and auditors' reports is an innovation.

New s.242
This requires directors to deliver copies of the accounts and the directors' and auditors' reports to the Registrar of Companies within the specified period. Where documents are in a foreign language they must be accompanied by a certified English translation. Failure to comply with the provisions of the sections renders both the directors and the company liable to a fine. The company may also be directed by the Courts to make good its failure to file its accounts, etc. The derivation of the new section is as follows: subs. (1) from the former s.241(3) (although formal reference to the directors' and auditors' reports is now made); subs. (2) from the previous s.243(1); subs. (3) from s.244(1) (2); subs. (4) from s.243(2); subs. (5) from s.243(5).

New s.242A
S.242A was inserted in committee and indicates that in addition to any fines imposed on directors under s.242, the company may also be subject to a penalty. The size of the latter depends on whether the company is public or private, and it escalates according to the length of the delay. The derivation is from the previous s.243(3)(4), but with increased penalties.

New s.243
This deals with the situation where a parent company has an unconsolidated subsidiary which is either registered and operates outside Great Britain or is an unincorporated business. (In either case, the subsidiary will not be liable to file its individual accounts with the Registrar.) When this is the situation, copies of the subsidiary's latest accounts (including, where appropriate, its group accounts) have to be filed, together with the auditors' report. Where necessary a certified English translation must be included. Exemptions from these requirements (*i.e.* where such a business does not prepare or publish its accounts elsewhere, or where its activities are so different from those of the rest of the group that consolidation would be inappropriate) are given in subs. (5).

New s.244
This specifies the periods allowed for laying and delivering a company's accounts and the directors' and auditors' reports. As previously, the period normally allowed is ten months after the reference period for a private company and seven months for a public company, although if either has interests outside the U.K. the directors can give notice to the Registrar and claim a further three months' extension. Certain modifications are allowed where companies are in their first accounting reference period or where they shorten their accounting reference periods; moreover, the Secretary of State has powers to extend the period for laying and delivering accounts for any company by giving it notice in writing.

The modified rules for a company in its first reference period are that, where such a reference period is greater than 12 months in length, the accounts must nevertheless be laid and delivered within 22 months of its date of incorporation if it is a private company, or 19 months if it is a public company, but both subject to a three months' extension if it has overseas interests. However, this is subject to the proviso that there should always be a minimum allowed period of three months between the end of the reference period and the last date for laying and delivering accounts. Where a company's reference period is shortened under the new s.225 (inserted by s.3 of this Act), the period allowed for laying and delivering the accounts is that which expires later of (a) the period normally allowed; and (b) three months from the date of the notice of the change in the accounting reference period given under s.225.

Listed companies are required by the Stock Exchange's "Admission of Securities to Listing" (para. 20, p.5.16) to issue an annual report and accounts within six months of the end of the financial period to which they relate.

This section is derived as follows: subs. (1) from the previous s.242(1)(2); subs. (2) from the former s.242(4) (but clarified); subs. (3) from the former s.242(3); subs. (4) from the previous s.242(5); subs. (5) from the former s.242(6); and subs. (6) from the previous s.242(1).

Remedies for failure to comply with accounting requirements

12. The following sections are inserted in Part VII of the Companies Act 1985—

"Revision of defective accounts and reports

Voluntary revision of annual accounts or directors' report

245.—(1) If it appears to the directors of a company that any annual accounts of the company, or any directors' report, did not comply with the requirements of this Act, they may prepare revised accounts or a revised report.

(2) Where copies of the previous accounts or report have been laid before the company in general meeting or delivered to the registrar, the revisions shall be confined to—
  (a) the correction of those respects in which the previous accounts or report did not comply with the requirements of this Act, and
  (b) the making of any necessary consequential alterations.

(3) The Secretary of State may make provision by regulations as to the application of the provisions of this Act in relation to revised annual accounts or a revised directors' report.

(4) The regulations may, in particular—
  (a) make different provision according to whether the previous accounts or report are replaced or are supplemented by a document indicating the corrections to be made;
  (b) make provision with respect to the functions of the company's auditors in relation to the revised accounts or report;
  (c) require the directors to take such steps as may be specified in the regulations where the previous accounts or report have been—
      (i) sent out to members and others under section 238(1),
      (ii) laid before the company in general meeting, or
      (iii) delivered to the registrar,
    or where a summary financial statement based on the previous accounts or report has been sent to members under section 251;
  (d) apply the provisions of this Act (including those creating criminal offences) subject to such additions, exceptions and modifications as are specified in the regulations.

(5) Regulations under this section shall be made by statutory instrument which shall be subject to annulment in pursuance of a resolution of either House of Parliament.

Secretary of State's notice in respect of annual accounts

245A.—(1) Where copies of a company's annual accounts have been sent out under section 238, or a copy of a company's annual accounts has been laid before the company in general meeting or delivered to the registrar, and it appears to the Secretary of State that there is, or may be, a question whether the accounts comply with the requirements of this Act, he may give notice to the directors of the company indicating the respects in which it appears to him that such a question arises, or may arise.

(2) The notice shall specify a period of not less than one month for the directors to give him an explanation of the accounts or prepare revised accounts.

(3) If at the end of the specified period, or such longer period as he may allow, it appears to the Secretary of State that no satisfactory explanation of the accounts has been given and that the accounts have not been revised so as to comply with the requirements of this Act, he may if he thinks fit apply to the court.

(4) The provisions of this section apply equally to revised annual accounts, in which case the references to revised accounts shall be read as references to further revised accounts.

Application to court in respect of defective accounts

245B.—(1) An application may be made to the court—
  (a) by the Secretary of State, after having complied with section 245A, or
  (b) by a person authorised by the Secretary of State for the purposes of this section,

for a declaration or declarator that the annual accounts of a company do not comply with the requirements of this Act and for an order requiring the directors of the company to prepare revised accounts.

(2) Notice of the application, together with a general statement of the matters at issue in the proceedings, shall be given by the applicant to the registrar for registration.

(3) If the court orders the preparation of revised accounts, it may give directions with respect to—
  (a) the auditing of the accounts,
  (b) the revision of any directors' report or summary financial statement, and
  (c) the taking of steps by the directors to bring the making of the order to the notice of persons likely to rely on the previous accounts,

and such other matters as the court thinks fit.

(4) If the court finds that the accounts did not comply with the requirements of this Act it may order that all or part of—
  (a) the costs (or in Scotland expenses) of and incidental to the application, and
  (b) any reasonable expenses incurred by the company in connection with or in consequence of the preparation of revised accounts,

shall be borne by such of the directors as were party to the approval of the defective accounts.

For this purpose every director of the company at the time the accounts were approved shall be taken to have been a party to their approval unless he shows that he took all reasonable steps to prevent their being approved.

(5) Where the court makes an order under subsection (4) it shall have regard to whether the directors party to the approval of the defective accounts knew or ought to have known that the accounts did not comply with the requirements of this Act, and it may exclude one or more directors from the order or order the payment of different amounts by different directors.

(6) On the conclusion of proceedings on an application under this section, the applicant shall give to the registrar for registration an office copy of the court order or, as the case may be, notice that the application has failed or been withdrawn.

(7) The provisions of this section apply equally to revised annual accounts, in which case the references to revised accounts shall be read as references to further revised accounts.

Other persons authorised to apply to court

245C.—(1) The Secretary of State may authorise for the purposes of section 245B any person appearing to him.
  (a) to have an interest in, and to have satisfactory procedures directed to securing, compliance by companies with the accounting requirements of this Act,
  (b) to have satisfactory procedures for receiving and investigating complaints about the annual accounts of companies, and
  (c) otherwise to be a fit and proper person to be authorised.

(2) A person may be authorised generally or in respect of particular classes of case, and different persons may be authorised in respect of different classes of case.

(3) The Secretary of State may refuse to authorise a person if he considers that his authorisation is unnecessary having regard to the fact that there are one or more other persons who have been or are likely to be authorised.

(4) Authorisation shall be by order made by statutory instrument which shall be subject to annulment in pursuance of a resolution of either House of Parliament.

(5) Where authorisation is revoked, the revoking order may make such provision as the Secretary of State thinks fit with respect to pending proceedings.

(6) Neither a person authorised under this section, nor any officer, servant or member of the governing body of such a person, shall be liable in damages for anything done or purporting to be done for the purposes of or in connection with—
  (a) the taking of steps to discover whether there are grounds for an application to the court,
  (b) the determination whether or not to make such an application, or
  (c) the publication of its reasons for any such decision,
unless the act or omission is shown to have been in bad faith.".

DEFINITIONS AND CROSS REFERENCES
"accounts delivered to the Registrar": ss.242–244, C.A. 1985, as inserted by s.11, 1989 Act.
"accounts laid before the company in general meeting": ss.241–244, C.A. 1985, as inserted by s.11, 1989 Act.
"annual accounts": see DEFINITIONS to s.4.
"company's auditors": ss.384–388A, C.A. 1985, as inserted by s.119, 1989 Act.
"directors": s.741, C.A. 1985.
"directors' report": see DEFINITIONS to s.9.
"summary financial statement": s.251, C.A. 1985, as inserted by s.15, 1989 Act.

GENERAL NOTE
This section was inserted into the Bill during its progress through Parliament, and it implements recommendations of the Dearing Report to the Consultative Committee of Accountancy Bodies, "The Making of Accounting Standards" (September 1988). These relate to a new statutory power for the Secretary of State or authorised bodies to apply to the Courts for an order requiring the revision of accounts that do not give a true and fair view (s. 10.3(b) of the Report). Such authority could be delegated to a Review Panel or a similar body, such as the Stock Exchange (s. 15.12 of the Report).
S.12 inserts new ss.245, 245A, 245B and 245C into the 1985 Act.

New s.245

This is concerned with the revision of annual accounts and/or a directors' report which do not comply with the provisions of the Companies Acts. This may be done voluntarily by the directors, but where the financial statements have been laid before the company in general meeting or delivered to the Registrar, the revisions should just deal with the corrections and the consequential effects. However, the Secretary of State will be able to make regulations by statutory instrument concerning such revisions in respect of the extent of replacing or supplementing the original documents, the function of the auditors in relation to the amendments, remedial steps with regard to publication of the revised information, and the general application of the provisions of the Companies Acts.

New s.245A

This gives the Secretary of State power to give notice to the directors of a company indicating respects in which he believes the financial statements laid before the company or delivered to the Registrar may not comply with the Acts' requirements. The notice must specify a period of up to one month, in which time the directors must either explain satisfactorily the accounts or prepare revised financial statements, failing which the Secretary of State may apply to the Courts under new s.245B. The same actions can be applied against revised accounts.

New s.245B

This gives the Secretary of State or his nominee (see new s.245C) authority to apply to the Courts for a declaration that the accounts are in breach of the Acts and for an order requiring directors to prepare revised financial statements. The latter order may give directions with respect to the audit, the revision of the directors' report or summary financial statements, steps to be taken by directors to bring the making of the order to the notice of those likely to rely on the defective accounts, and any other pertinent matters. The Courts may also order that some or all of the directors approving defective accounts should be liable to pay all or part of the costs of the action. Such proceedings can also be applied against revised accounts.

New s.245C

This empowers the Secretary of State to delegate by statutory instrument his powers under new s.245B to a fit and proper person, either generally or for particular classes of case. Such a person, however, is given some protection under subs. (6) from actions for damages.

Exemptions and special provisions

Small and medium-sized companies and groups

13.—(1) The following sections are inserted in Part VII of the Companies Act 1985, as the beginning of a Chapter II—

"CHAPTER II

EXEMPTIONS, EXCEPTIONS AND SPECIAL PROVISIONS

Small and medium-sized companies and groups

Exemptions for small and medium-sized companies

246.—(1) A company which qualifies as a small or medium-sized company in relation to a financial year—
    (a) is exempt from the requirements of paragraph 36A of Schedule 4 (disclosure with respect to compliance with accounting standards), and
    (b) is entitled to the exemptions provided by Schedule 8 with respect to the delivery to the registrar under section 242 of individual accounts and other documents for that financial year.

(2) In that Schedule—
   Part I relates to small companies,
   Part II relates to medium-sized companies, and
   Part III contains supplementary provisions.

(3) A company is not entitled to the exemptions mentioned in subsection (1) if it is, or was at any time within the financial year to which the accounts relate—
   (a) a public company,
   (b) a banking or insurance company, or
   (c) an authorised person under the Financial Services Act 1986,
or if it is or was at any time during that year a member of an ineligible group.

(4) A group is ineligible if any of its members is—
   (a) a public company or a body corporate which (not being a company) has power under its constitution to offer its shares or debentures to the public and may lawfully exercise that power,
   (b) an authorised institution under the Banking Act 1987,
   (c) an insurance company to which Part II of the Insurance Companies Act 1982 applies, or
   (d) an authorised person under the Financial Services Act 1986.

(5) A parent company shall not be treated as qualifying as a small company in relation to a financial year unless the group headed by it qualifies as a small group, and shall not be treated as qualifying as a medium-sized company in relation to a financial year unless that group qualifies as a medium-sized group (see section 249).

Qualification of company as small or medium-sized

247.—(1) A company qualifies as small or medium-sized in relation to a financial year if the qualifying conditions are met—
   (a) in the case of the company's first financial year, in that year, and
   (b) in the case of any subsequent financial year, in that year and the preceding year.

(2) A company shall be treated as qualifying as small or medium-sized in relation to a financial year—
   (a) if it so qualified in relation to the previous financial year under subsection (1); or
   (b) if it was treated as so qualifying in relation to the previous year by virtue of paragraph (a) and the qualifying conditions are met in the year in question.

(3) The qualifying conditions are met by a company in a year in which it satisfies two or more of the following requirements—

Small company

1.	Turnover	Not more than £2 million
2.	Balance sheet total	Not more than £975,000
3.	Number of employees	Not more than 50

Medium-sized company

1.	Turnover	Not more than £8 million
2.	Balance sheet total	Not more than £3.9 million
3.	Number of employees	Not more than 250.

(4) For a period which is a company's financial year but not in fact a year the maximum figures for turnover shall be proportionately adjusted.

(5) The balance sheet total means—
   (a) where in the company's accounts Format 1 of the balance

sheet formats set out in Part I of Schedule 4 is adopted, the aggregate of the amounts shown in the balance sheet under the headings corresponding to items A to D in that Format, and

(b) where Format 2 is adopted, the aggregate of the amounts shown under the general heading "Assets".

(6) The number of employees means the average number of persons employed by the company in the year (determined on a weekly basis). That number shall be determined by applying the method of calculation prescribed by paragraph 56(2) and (3) of Schedule 4 for determining the corresponding number required to be stated in a note to the company's accounts.".

(2) Schedule 6 to this Act is substituted for Schedule 8 to the Companies Act 1985.

(3) The following sections are inserted in Part VII of the Companies Act 1985—

"Exemption for small and medium-sized groups

248.—(1) A parent company need not prepare group accounts for a financial year in relation to which the group headed by that company qualifies as a small or medium-sized group and is not an ineligible group.

(2) A group is ineligible if any of its members is—
  (a) a public company or a body corporate which (not being a company) has power under its constitution to offer its shares or debentures to the public and may lawfully exercise that power,
  (b) an authorised institution under the Banking Act 1987,
  (c) an insurance company to which Part II of the Insurance Companies Act 1982 applies, or
  (d) an authorised person under the Financial Services Act 1986.

(3) If the directors of a company propose to take advantage of the exemption conferred by this section, it is the auditors' duty to provide them with a report stating whether in their opinion the company is entitled to the exemption.

(4) The exemption does not apply unless—
  (a) the auditors' report states that in their opinion the company is so entitled, and
  (b) that report is attached to the individual accounts of the company.

Qualification of group as small or medium-sized

249.—(1) A group qualifies as small or medium-sized in relation to a financial year if the qualifying conditions are met—
  (a) in the case of the parent company's first financial year, in that year, and
  (b) in the case of any subsequent financial year, in that year and the preceding year.

(2) A group shall be treated as qualifying as small or medium-sized in relation to a financial year—
  (a) if it so qualified in relation to the previous financial year under subsection (1); or
  (b) if it was treated as so qualifying in relation to the previous year by virtue of paragraph (a) and the qualifying conditions are met in the year in question.

(3) The qualifying conditions are met by a group in a year in which it satisfies two or more of the following requirements—

Small group

1. Aggregate turnover — Not more than £2 million net (or £2.4 million gross)
2. Aggregate balance sheet total — Not more than £1 million net (or £1.2 million gross)
3. Aggregate number of employees — Not more than 50

Medium-sized group

1. Aggregate turnover — Not more than £8 million net (or £9.6 million gross)
2. Aggregate balance sheet total — Not more than £3.9 million net (or £4.7 million gross)
3. Aggregate number of employees — Not more than 250.

(4) The aggregate figures shall be ascertained by aggregating the relevant figures determined in accordance with section 247 for each member of the group.

In relation to the aggregate figures for turnover and balance sheet total, "net" means with the set-offs and other adjustments required by Schedule 4A in the case of group accounts and "gross" means without those set-offs and other adjustments; and a company may satisfy the relevant requirement on the basis of either the net or the gross figure.

(5) The figures for each subsidiary undertaking shall be those included in its accounts for the relevant financial year, that is—

(a) if its financial year ends with that of the parent company, that financial year, and

(b) if not, its financial year ending last before the end of the financial year of the parent company.

(6) If those figures cannot be obtained without disproportionate expense or undue delay, the latest available figures shall be taken.".

DEFINITIONS AND CROSS REFERENCES

"accounting standards": s.256, C.A. 1985, as inserted by s.19, 1989 Act.
"accounts delivered to the Registrar": see DEFINITIONS to s.12.
"[annual] accounts": see DEFINITIONS to s.5.
"auditors' report": see DEFINITIONS to s.5.
"banking company": s.744, C.A. 1985, as inserted by Sched. 10, para. 16, 1989 Act; for "banking group" see s.255A(3), C.A. 1985, as inserted by s.18, 1989 Act.
"debentures": s.744, C.A. 1985.
"financial year": see DEFINITIONS to s.3.
"group": s.262(1), C.A. 1985, as inserted by s.22, 1989 Act, SSAP. 14, para. 9.
"group accounts": see DEFINITIONS to s.5.
"individual accounts": see DEFINITIONS to s.5.
"insurance company", "insurance group", s.255A(4), 1985 Act, as inserted by s.18, 1989 Act.
"parent company": see DEFINITIONS to s.2.
"public company": s.1(3), C.A. 1985.
"shares": s.259(2), C.A. 1985, as inserted by s.22, 1989 Act; s.744, C.A. 1985.
"subsidiary undertaking": see DEFINITIONS to s.3 ("subsidiary company").
"turnover": s.262(1), C.A. 1985, as inserted by s.22, 1989 Act.

GENERAL NOTE

S.13 inserts new ss.246–249 into the 1985 Act which, together with para. 36A of the revised Sched. 4 (inserted by para. 7 of Sched. 1 to the new Act) and the revised Sched. 8 (inserted by Sched. 6 to the new Act), contain exemptions from accounting provisions for small and medium-sized companies and groups. New s. 246 and 247 re-enact, with minor amendments, existing provisions on the delivery of abbreviated (formerly "modified") individual accounts by small and medium-sized companies. New ss.248 and 249 contain a new exemption for the parent undertakings of small and medium-sized groups from the obligation to prepare group accounts.

New s.246
Under subs. (1), small and medium-sized companies (defined in the new s.247) are exempt from the requirement introduced into the revised Sched. 4 that the notes should specifically state that the financial statements comply with accounting standards. (This modification to Sched. 4 was made on the recommendation of the Dearing Committee's Report, "The Making of Accounting Standards", submitted to the Consultative Committee of Accountancy Bodies in September 1988: s.10.3(a).) Small or medium-sized companies or groups (which must not include public companies, banks, insurance companies, or authorised persons under the Financial Services Act 1986) are also entitled to prepare abbreviated (formerly "modified") accounts as prescribed in the revised Sched. 8 for delivery to the Registrar. However, for this purpose a parent undertaking does not qualify as small or medium-sized unless the group it heads is so classified. Subs. (3) is similar to the previous s.247(2); subs. (4) to the former s.247(3); and subs. (5) to the previous s.250(2).

New s.247
Under this section a company qualifies as small or medium-sized where it meets the qualifying criteria
(1) in its first financial year; or
(2) subsequently in the current and previous years; or
(3) it was so qualified in the previous financial year.
The qualifying criteria are that it should meet at least two of three conditions concerning annualised turnover, balance sheet totals and the average weekly number of employees as follows:

	Small-sized	*Medium-sized*
(1) annualised turnover	≤ £2 m	≤ £8 m
(2) balance sheet total	≤ £975,000	≤ £3.9m
(3) average weekly number of employees	≤ 50	≤ 250

Guidance on how to calculate balance sheet totals, the average weekly number of employees, and annualised turnover is given in subss. (4)–(6).
The derivations are as follows: subs. (1) from the previous s.248(2); subs. (3) from the former s.248(1)(2), as amended by S.I. 1986, No. 1865; subs. (4) from the previous s.248(5); subs. (5) from the former s.248(3); and subs. (6) from the previous s.248(4). Subs. (2) clarifies the provisions of the former s.249(2)–(6).

New s.248
Under this section, a parent company of a group which qualifies as a small or medium-sized group (defined in the new s.249) need not prepare group accounts. However, to take advantage of this, the company's auditors must provide the directors with a report stating that in their opinion the company is entitled to the exemptions, and this must be attached to the company's individual accounts. A group is not eligible for the exemption if any of its members are public companies, banks, insurance companies or authorised persons under the Financial Services Act 1986.

New s.249
Under this section, a group qualifies as small or medium-sized where it meets the qualifying criteria:
(1) in its first financial year; or
(2) subsequently in the current and previous years; or
(3) it was qualified in the previous financial year.
The qualifying criteria are that it should meet at least two of three conditions concerning annualised turnover, balance sheet totals and the average weekly number of employees as follows:

	Small-sized		*Medium-sized*	
	Net	*Gross*	*Net*	*Gross*
(1) annualised turnover	≤ £2m	≤ £2.4m	≤ £8m	≤ £9.6m
(2) balance sheet total	≤ £1m	≤ £2.1m	≤ £3.9m	≤ £4.7m
(3) average weekly number of employees		≤ 50		≤ 250

40–45

Guidance on how to calculate the aggregate balance sheet totals, the average weekly number of employees and annualised turnover is given in subss. (4)–(6). In particular, "net" means after set-offs required by Sched. 4A (inserted by Sched. 2 of the new Act); "gross" means before those set-offs.

Subs. (2)
This inserts, by Schedule 6 to the new Act, a new Sched. 8 into the 1985 Act. This deals with "Exemptions for small and medium-sized companies."

Dormant companies

14. The following section is inserted in Part VII of the Companies Act 1985—

"*Dormant companies*

Resolution not to appoint auditors
250.—(1) A company may by special resolution make itself exempt from the provisions of this Part relating to the audit of accounts in the following cases—
   (a) if the company has been dormant from the time of its formation, by a special resolution passed before the first general meeting of the company at which annual accounts are laid;
   (b) if the company has been dormant since the end of the previous financial year and—
      (i) is entitled in respect of its individual accounts for that year to the exemptions conferred by section 246 on a small company, or would be so entitled but for being a member of an ineligible group, and
      (ii) is not required to prepare group accounts for that year, by a special resolution passed at a general meeting of the company at which the annual accounts for that year are laid.
(2) A company may not pass such a resolution if it is—
   (a) a public company,
   (b) a banking or insurance company, or
   (c) an authorised person under the Financial Services Act 1986.
(3) A company is "dormant" during a period in which no significant accounting transaction occurs, that is, no transaction which is required by section 221 to be entered in the company's accounting records; and a company ceases to be dormant on the occurrence of such a transaction.
For this purpose there shall be disregarded any transaction arising from the taking of shares in the company by a subscriber to the memorandum in pursuance of an undertaking of his in the memorandum.
(4) Where a company is, at the end of a financial year, exempt by virtue of this section from the provisions of this Part relating to the audit of accounts—
   (a) sections 238 and 239 (right to receive or demand copies of accounts and reports) have effect with the omission of references to the auditors' report;
   (b) no copies of an auditors' report need be laid before the company in general meeting;
   (c) no copy of an auditors' report need be delivered to the registrar, and if none is delivered, the copy of the balance sheet so delivered shall contain a statement by the directors, in a position immediately above the signature required by section

233(4), that the company was dormant throughout the financial year; and

(d) the company shall be treated as entitled in respect of its individual accounts for that year to the exemptions conferred by section 246 on a small company notwithstanding that it is a member of an ineligible group.

(5) Where a company which is exempt by virtue of this section from the provisions of this Part relating to the audit of accounts—
  (a) ceases to be dormant, or
  (b) would no longer qualify (for any other reason) to make itself exempt by passing a resolution under this section,
it shall thereupon cease to be so exempt.".

DEFINITIONS AND CROSS REFERENCES
"abbreviated (formerly 'modified') accounts": s.13; Sched. 6.
"accounting records": see DEFINITIONS to s.2.
"accounting transactions": s.221, C.A. 1985, as inserted by s.2, 1989 Act.
"accounts laid before the company in general meeting": see DEFINITIONS to s.12.
"annual accounts": see DEFINITIONS to s.3.
"appointment of auditors": ss.384–388A, C.A. 1985, as inserted by s.119, 1989 Act.
"auditors' report": see DEFINITIONS to s.5.
"delivery of accounts to the Registrar": see DEFINITIONS to s.5.
"directors": s.741, C.A. 1985.
"directors' statement of qualification as a small company": Sched. 8, para. 7, C.A. 1985, as inserted by Sched. 6, 1989 Act.
"dormant": s.250, C.A. 1985, as inserted by s.14, 1989 Act.
"financial year": see DEFINITIONS to s.3.
"meetings": ss.366–383, C.A. 1985.
"signing of the balance sheet": s.233, C.A. 1985, as inserted by s.17, 1989 Act.
"small company": ss.247, 249, C.A. 1989, as inserted by s.17, 1989 Act.
"special resolution": s.378, C.A. 1985.
"special auditors' report with abbreviated (formerly 'modified') accounts": see DEFINITIONS to s.10.

GENERAL NOTE
This section inserts new s.250 into the 1985 Act which re-enacts, with minor amendments, the provisions relating to dormant companies contained in the former ss.252–253.

New s.250
This indicates that under certain circumstances a company may effectively make itself a dormant company, thus avoiding the need to appoint auditors under s.384 (see s.388A, as inserted by s.119 of this Act). This, in turn, under the new s.250(4), enables the company to dispense with the auditors' report when laying financial statements before the company and filing them with the Registrar of Companies. To qualify as dormant, no significant accounting transaction (other than the issue price for its shares from the subscribers to the memorandum of association) must occur in the period in question. The company may then pass a special resolution exempting itself from the obligation under s.384 (as inserted by s.119 of this Act) to appoint auditors. Such a special resolution may be passed by a company (other than a public or special category company or an authorised person under the 1986 Financial Services Act) at an extraordinary general meeting held before the first general meeting at which the accounts are to be laid before the company, so long as it has been dormant since its formation. In other circumstances, such a special resolution may be passed at a general meeting at which the accounts for a particular financial year are to be laid before the company, but only where the following conditions are met: (a) the company is not required to prepare group accounts; (b) the directors must be entitled to file small company accounts under s.246, or would be so entitled but for being a member of an ineligible group; (c) the company must have been dormant since the end of the previous financial year.

In order to take advantage of the dormant company provisions, steps will also have to be taken to change its articles where they require it to appoint an auditor (as, indeed, would generally be the case for any company adopting Table A prior to the new form which under S.I. 1985 No.85 (The Companies (Tables A to F) Regulations 1985 of May 22, 1985) took effect from July 1, 1985.)

Where a company qualifies as dormant and is exempted from the obligation to appoint auditors, an auditors' report need not be included with the accounts laid before the company or be delivered to the Registrar. However, in such circumstances a statement that the company was dormant throughout the financial year must appear immediately above the directors' signatures on the balance sheet.

It will be necessary for a company to prepare a profit and loss account in the year in which it becomes dormant, since paras. 3(5) and 4(3) of Sched. 4 to the principal Act require the previous year's figures to be disclosed even where there are no current year's figures.

The derivation of the new s.250 is as follows: subs. (1) from the former s.252(1), (a) from the previous s.252(3), (b) from the former s.252(2); subs. (2) from the previous s.252(4); subs. (3) from the previous s.252(5); subs. (4) from the former s.253(1)–(3); and subs. (5) from the previous s.252(6).

Public listed companies: provision of summary financial statement

15. The following section is inserted in Part VII of the Companies Act 1985—

"Listed public companies

Provision of summary financial statement to shareholders

251.—(1) A public company whose shares, or any class of whose shares, are listed need not, in such cases as may be specified by regulations made by the Secretary of State, and provided any conditions so specified are complied with, send copies of the documents referred to in section 238(1) to members of the company, but may instead send them a summary financial statement.

In this subsection "listed" means admitted to the Official List of The International Stock Exchange of the United Kingdom and the Republic of Ireland Limited.

(2) Copies of the documents referred to in section 238(1) shall, however, be sent to any member of the company who wishes to receive them; and the Secretary of State may by regulations make provision as to the manner in which it is to be ascertained whether a member of the company wishes to receive them.

(3) The summary financial statement shall be derived from the company's annual accounts and the directors' report and shall be in such form and contain such information as may be specified by regulations made by the Secretary of State.

(4) Every summary financial statement shall—
  (a) state that it is only a summary of information in the company's annual accounts and the directors' report;
  (b) contain a statement by the company's auditors of their opinion as to whether the summary financial statement is consistent with those accounts and that report and complies with the requirements of this section and regulations made under it;
  (c) state whether the auditors' report on the annual accounts was unqualified or qualified, and if it was qualified set out the report in full together with any further material needed to understand the qualification;
  (d) state whether the auditors' report on the annual accounts contained a statement under—
    (i) section 237(2) (accounting records or returns inadequate or accounts not agreeing with records and returns), or
    (ii) section 237(3) (failure to obtain necessary information and explanations),
and if so, set out the statement in full.

(5) Regulations under this section shall be made by statutory instrument which shall be subject to annulment in pursuance of a resolution of either House of Parliament.

(6) If default is made in complying with this section or regulations made under it, the company and every officer of it who is in default is guilty of an offence and liable to a fine.

(7) Section 240 (requirements in connection with publication of accounts) does not apply in relation to the provision to members of a company of a summary financial statement in accordance with this section.".

DEFINITIONS AND CROSS REFERENCES
"accounting records and returns": see DEFINITIONS to s.10.
"annual accounts,": see DEFINITIONS to s.11.
"auditors' report": see DEFINITIONS to s.5.
"directors' report": see DEFINITIONS to s.9.
"listed company": s.251(1), C.A. 1985, as inserted by s.15, 1989 Act.
"member": s.22, C.A. 1985.
"publication of accounts": see DEFINITIONS to s.7.
"public company": s.1(3), C.A. 1985.
"qualification in an auditors' report": s.262(1), C.A. 1985, as inserted by s.22, 1989 Act.
"shares": see DEFINITIONS to s.13.

GENERAL NOTE
This section inserts a new s.251 into the 1985 Act which allows listed companies to provide summarised (rather than full) financial statements to members when conditions to be specified in regulations by the Secretary of State are fulfilled.

New s.251
Subs. (3) indicates the summary financial statements will be derived from the company's annual accounts and directors' report.
Subs. (4) specifies that such summarised financial statements must include statements (a) indicating they are only summarised financial information; (b) by the auditors as to whether the information given is consistent with the full accounts and the directors' report; (c) whether the full auditors' report was qualified, and if so include that full report; (d) whether the auditors' report contained a statement concerning the accounting records and/or the adequacy of the information and explanations received, and if so include such statements in full.
Subs. (2) indicates that members are entitled to receive the full accounts and the directors' report, notwithstanding their receipt of summarised financial information.
Subs. (6) indicates that the company and every officer in default over the provisions of the new s.251 is liable to a fine; and subs. (7) states that the provisions of the revised s.240 (inserted by s.10 and which deals with the publication of "statutory" and "non-statutory" (*i.e.* previously "abridged") financial statements) do not apply.

Private companies: election to dispense with laying of accounts and reports before general meeting

16. The following sections are inserted in Part VII of the Companies Act 1985—

"*Private companies*

Election to dispense with laying of accounts and reports before general meeting

252.—(1) A private company may elect (by elective resolution in accordance with section 379A) to dispense with the laying of accounts and reports before the company in general meeting.

(2) An election has effect in relation to the accounts and reports in respect of the financial year in which the election is made and subsequent financial years.

(3) Whilst an election is in force, the references in the following provisions of this Act to the laying of accounts before the company in

general meeting shall be read as references to the sending of copies of the accounts to members and others under section 238(1)—
- (a) section 235(1) (accounts on which auditors are to report),
- (b) section 270(3) and (4) (accounts by reference to which distributions are justified), and
- (c) section 320(2) (accounts relevant for determining company's net assets for purposes of ascertaining whether approval required for certain transactions);

and the requirement in section 271(4) that the auditors' statement under that provision be laid before the company in general meeting shall be read as a requirement that it be sent to members and others along with the copies of the accounts sent to them under section 238(1).

(4) If an election under this section ceases to have effect, section 241 applies in relation to the accounts and reports in respect of the financial year in which the election ceases to have effect and subsequent financial years.

Right of shareholder to require laying of accounts

253.—(1) Where an election under section 252 is in force, the copies of the accounts and reports sent out in accordance with section 238(1)—
- (a) shall be sent not less than 28 days before the end of the period allowed for laying and delivering accounts and reports, and
- (b) shall be accompanied, in the case of a member of the company, by a notice informing him of his right to require the laying of the accounts and reports before a general meeting;

and section 238(5) (penalty for default) applies in relation to the above requirements as to the requirements contained in that section.

(2) Before the end of the period of 28 days beginning with the day on which the accounts and reports are sent out in accordance with section 238(1), any member or auditor of the company may by notice in writing deposited at the registered office of the company require that a general meeting be held for the purpose of laying the accounts and reports before the company.

(3) If the directors do not within 21 days from the date of the deposit of such a notice proceed duly to convene a meeting, the person who deposited the notice may do so himself.

(4) A meeting so convened shall not be held more than three months from that date and shall be convened in the same manner, as nearly as possible, as that in which meetings are to be convened by directors.

(5) Where the directors do not duly convene a meeting, any reasonable expenses incurred by reason of that failure by the person who deposited the notice shall be made good to him by the company, and shall be recouped by the company out of any fees, or other remuneration in respect of their services, due or to become due to such of the directors as were in default.

(6) The directors shall be deemed not to have duly convened a meeting if they convene a meeting for a date more than 28 days after the date of the notice convening it.".

DEFINITIONS AND CROSS REFERENCES
"annual accounts": see DEFINITIONS to s.4.
"auditor": s.24(2), 1989 Act.
"auditors' report": see DEFINITIONS to s.8.
"auditors' report on the validity of proposed distributions": s.271(4), C.A. 1985.
"directors": s.741, C.A. 1985.
"distribution based on accounts": s.270 *et seq.*, C.A. 1985.

"financial year": see DEFINITIONS to s.3.
"laying of accounts before the company in general meeting": see DEFINITIONS to s.7.
"meetings": ss.366–383, C.A. 1985.
"members": s.22, C.A. 1985.
"private companies": s.1(3), C.A. 1985

GENERAL NOTE
This section inserts two new sections (ss.252 and 253) into the 1985 Act. The first permits private companies by unanimous election to dispense with the requirement to lay accounts. The second empowers a member or the auditor of the company to require that a general meeting be held so that the accounts may be laid.

New s.252
This empowers a private company by elective resolution in accordance with s.379A of the 1985 Act (as inserted by s.116 of the current legislation) to dispense with the laying of the annual accounts and the directors' and auditors' reports before the company in general meeting. Such a resolution relates to the financial statements for the year in which it is made and the election carries over to subsequent financial years. While the election is in force, references in the 1985 Act to the laying of the accounts in ss.235(1), 270(3) and (4) and 320(2), together with the reference in s.271(4) to the reading of the auditors' report, are to be interpreted as referring to the circulation of such statements to the members under s.238(1).

New s.253
This indicates that where an election under s.252 is in force, copies of the accounts and directors' and auditors' reports shall be sent to members at least 28 days before the period allowed for laying and delivering accounts (as given in the revised ss.241–242, inserted by s.11), together with a notice of their rights to require the laying of accounts, etc., before a general meeting. Failure to do so renders the company and its officers liable to fines. An objecting member or auditor must then inform the company within 28 days of the accounts being circulated, and the directors must then convene a general meeting within 21 days, failing which the objecting party may do so himself. Such a meeting must be held within three months. Where an objecting party has to convene a meeting, he may recover reasonable expenses from the company.

Unlimited companies: exemption from requirement to deliver accounts and reports

17. The following section is inserted in Part VII of the Companies Act 1985—

"Unlimited companies

Exemption from requirements to deliver accounts and reports
254.—(1) The directors of an unlimited company are not required to deliver accounts and reports to the registrar in respect of a financial year if the following conditions are met.

(2) The conditions are that at no time during the relevant accounting reference period—
  (a) has the company been, to its knowledge, a subsidiary undertaking of an undertaking which was then limited, or
  (b) have there been, to its knowledge, exercisable by or on behalf of two or more undertakings which were then limited, rights which if exercisable by one of them would have made the company a subsidiary undertaking of it, or
  (c) has the company been a parent company of an undertaking which was then limited.

The references above to an undertaking being limited at a particular time are to an undertaking (under whatever law established) the liability of whose members is at that time limited.

(3) The exemption conferred by this section does not apply if at any time during the relevant accounting period the company carried on business as the promoter of a trading stamp scheme within the Trading Stamps Act 1964.

(4) Where a company is exempt by virtue of this section from the obligation to deliver accounts, section 240 (requirements in connection with publication of accounts) has effect with the following modifications—
  (a) in subsection (3)(b) for the words from 'whether statutory accounts' to 'have been delivered to the registrar' substitute 'that the company is exempt from the requirement to deliver statutory accounts', and
  (b) in subsection (5) for 'as required to be delivered to the registrar under section 242' substitute 'as prepared in accordance with this Part and approved by the board of directors'.".

DEFINITIONS AND CROSS REFERENCES
"accounting reference period": s.244(6), C.A. 1985, as inserted by s.11, 1989 Act.
"[annual] accounts": see DEFINITIONS to s.5.
"delivery of statutory accounts to the Registrar": see DEFINITIONS to s.5.
"directors": s.741, C.A. 1985.
"financial year": see DEFINITIONS to s.3.
"members": s.22, C.A. 1985.
"parent company": see DEFINITIONS to s.2.
"subsidiary undertaking": see DEFINITIONS to s.3 ("subsidiary company").
"unlimited company": s.1(2)(c), C.A. 1985.
"undertaking": s.259(1), C.A. 1985, as inserted by s.22, 1989 Act.

GENERAL NOTE
This section inserts a new s.254 into the 1985 Act which re-enacts, with minor modifications, existing exemptions for certain unlimited companies from the requirement to deliver their annual accounts and reports to the Registrar of Companies. Such exemptions are lost if any connected company has limited liability or the company itself is a promoter of a trading stamp scheme.

The derivation of the new s.254 is as follows: subss. (1)–(3) from the former s.241(4). Subs. (4) deals with modifications to the new s.240 (inserted by s.10 and which is concerned with the publication of "statutory" and "non-statutory" (*i.e.* previously "abridged") accounts).

Banking and insurance companies and groups: special provisions

18.—(1) The following sections are inserted in Part VII of the Companies Act 1985—

"*Banking and insurance companies and groups*

Special provisions for banking and insurance companies

255.—(1) A banking or insurance company may prepare its individual accounts in accordance with Part I of Schedule 9 rather than Schedule 4.

(2) Accounts so prepared shall contain a statement that they are prepared in accordance with the special provisions of this Part relating to banking companies or insurance companies, as the case may be.

(3) In relation to the preparation of individual accounts in accordance with the special provisions of this Part relating to banking or insurance companies, the references to the provisions of Schedule 4 in section 226(4) and (5) (relationship between specific requirements and duty to give true and fair view) shall be read as references to the provisions of Part I of Schedule 9.

(4) The Secretary of State may, on the application or with the consent of the directors of a company which prepares individual accounts in accordance with the special provisions of this Part relating to banking or insurance companies, modify in relation to the company any of the requirements of this Part for the purpose of adapting them to the circumstances of the company.

This does not affect the duty to give a true and fair view.

Special provisions for banking and insurance groups

255A.—(1) The parent company of a banking or insurance group may prepare group accounts in accordance with the provisions of this Part as modified by Part II of Schedule 9.

(2) Accounts so prepared shall contain a statement that they are prepared in accordance with the special provisions of this Part relating to banking groups or insurance groups, as the case may be.

(3) References in this Part to a banking group are to a group where—
  (a) the parent company is a banking company, or
  (b) at least one of the undertakings in the group is an authorised institution under the Banking Act 1987 and the predominant activities of the group are such as to make it inappropriate to prepare group accounts in accordance with the formats in Part I of Schedule 4.

(4) References in this Part to an insurance group are to a group where—
  (a) the parent company is an insurance company, or
  (b) the predominant activity of the group is insurance business and activities which are a direct extension of or ancillary to insurance business.

(5) In relation to the preparation of group accounts in accordance with the special provisions of this Part relating to banking or insurance groups, the references to the provisions of Schedule 4A in section 227(5) and (6) (relationship between specific requirements and duty to give true and fair view) shall be read as references to those provisions as modified by Part II of Schedule 9.

(6) The Secretary of State may, on the application or with the consent of the directors of a company which prepares group accounts in accordance with the special provisions of this Part relating to banking or insurance groups, modify in relation to the company any of the requirements of this Part for the purpose of adapting them to the circumstances of the company.

Modification of disclosure requirements in relation to banking company or group

255B.—(1) In relation to a company which prepares accounts in accordance with the special provisions of this Part relating to banking companies or groups, the provisions of Schedule 5 (additional disclosure: related undertakings) have effect subject to Part III of Schedule 9.

(2) In relation to a banking company, or the parent company of a banking company, the provisions of Schedule 6 (disclosure: emoluments and other benefits of directors and others) have effect subject to Part IV of Schedule 9.

Directors' report where accounts prepared in accordance with special provisions

255C.—(1) The following provisions apply in relation to the directors' report of a company for a financial year in respect of which it prepares accounts in accordance with the special provisions of this Part relating to banking or insurance companies or groups.

(2) The information required to be given by paragraph 6, 8 or 13 of Part I of Schedule 9 (which is allowed to be given in a statement or report annexed to the accounts), may be given in the directors' report instead.

Information so given shall be treated for the purposes of audit as forming part of the accounts.

(3) The reference in section 234(1)(b) to the amount proposed to be carried to reserves shall be construed as a reference to the amount proposed to be carried to reserves within the meaning of Part I of Schedule 9.

(4) If the company takes advantage, in relation to its individual or group accounts, of the exemptions conferred by paragraph 27 or 28 of Part I of Schedule 9, paragraph 1 of Schedule 7 (disclosure of asset values) does not apply.

(5) The directors' report shall, in addition to complying with Schedule 7, also comply with Schedule 10 (which specifies additional matters to be disclosed).".

(2) The following section is inserted in Part VII of the Companies Act 1985—

"Power to apply provisions to banking partnerships

255D.—(1) The Secretary of State may by regulations apply to banking partnerships, subject to such exceptions, adaptations and modifications as he considers appropriate, the provisions of this Part applying to banking companies.

(2) A "banking partnership" means a partnership which is an authorised institution under the Banking Act 1987.

(3) Regulations under this section shall be made by statutory instrument.

(4) No regulations under this section shall be made unless a draft of the instrument containing the regulations has been laid before Parliament and approved by a resolution of each House.".

(3) Schedule 9 to the Companies Act 1985 (form and content of special category accounts) is amended in accordance with Schedule 7 to this Act.

(4) In that Schedule—

> Part I contains amendments relating to the form and content of accounts of banking and insurance companies and groups,
>
> Part II contains provisions with respect to the group accounts of banking and insurance groups,
>
> Part III contains provisions adapting the requirements of Schedule 5 to the Companies Act 1985 (additional disclosure: related undertakings), and
>
> Part IV contains provisions relating to the requirements of Schedule 6 to that Act (additional disclosure: emoluments and other benefits of directors and others).

(5) Schedule 8 to this Act (directors' report where accounts prepared in accordance with special provisions for banking and insurance companies and groups) is substituted for Schedule 10 to the Companies Act 1985.

DEFINITIONS AND CROSS REFERENCES
"banking group": s.255A, C.A. 1985, as inserted by s.18, 1989 Act.
"directors": s.741, C.A. 1985.
"directors' emoluments": Sched. 6, Pt. I, para. 1(4), C.A. 1985, as inserted by Sched. 4, para. 3, 1989 Act.
"directors' report": s.8.
"financial year": see DEFINITIONS to s.3.
"group accounts": see DEFINITIONS to s.5.
"individual company accounts": see DEFINITIONS to s.5.
"insurance group": see DEFINITIONS to s.13.
"parent company": see DEFINITIONS to s.2.

"reserves": Sched. 9, para. 32, C.A. 1985.
"true and fair view": see DEFINITIONS to s.4.
"undertakings": s.259(1), C.A. 1985, as inserted by s.22, 1989 Act.

GENERAL NOTE
This section inserts new ss.255, 255A, 255B, 255C and 255D into the 1985 Act. These new sections contain provisions relating to banking and insurance companies and groups.

New s.255
This substantially re-enacts the "special category" requirements of the former ss.257 and 258, while the new s.255A effectively re-enacts the provisions relating to "special category" group accounts of the former s.259. The new s.255 indicates that a banking or insurance company *may* prepare its accounts in accordance with the provisions of Sched. 9 to the 1985 Act (as amended by Sched. 7 of the new legislation). Where it does so, the accounts should contain a statement indicating that they are so prepared, and they should still give a true and fair view. Moreover, the Secretary of State may, on application, or with the consent of the directors, adapt the requirements to the circumstances of the company.
The derivations are as follows: subs. (1) from the previous s.258(2); subs. (2) from the former s.257(3); subs. (3) from the previous s.258(1)–(2); subs. (4) from the former s.258(4) and s.258(1)(a).

New s.255A
This introduces parallel provisions to s.255 but dealing with groups of companies. For this purpose, banking and insurance groups are defined respectively as existing where either the parent company or one of the undertakings in the group is in the relevant industry and this is the predominant activity of the group.
The derivations are as follows: subs. (1) from the former s.259(3); subs. (2) from the previous s.257(3); subs. (5) from the former s.258(1)(2) and s.259(3); subs. (6) from the former s.259(4).

New s.255B
This deals with the modification of disclosure requirements relating to banking or insurance companies or groups in respect of Scheds. 5 and 6 to the principal Act. These deal with additional disclosures in notes about related undertakings and directors' emoluments. The derivations are: subs. (1) from the previous s.260(1); subs. (2) from the former s.260(2).

New s.255C
This deals with the directors' report for companies which are taking advantage of the special provisions relating to banking and insurance companies. Subs. (2) relates to items which may be disclosed in the directors' report rather than the accounts; subs. (3) to amounts proposed to be carried to reserves; and subss. (4) and (5) to specific items which must be disclosed in the directors' report. The derivations are: subs. (1) from the former s.261(1); subs. (2) from the previous s.261(3) and (4); and subs. (5) from the former s.261(6).

New s.255D
This empowers the Secretary of State to apply the above provisions to banking partnerships, the latter being defined in subs. (2).
S.18(3)–(4) deals with the amendments to Sched. 9 to the 1985 Act, concerning the special accounting requirements for banking and insurance concerns. These are detailed in Sched. 7 to the new Act. S.18(5) substitutes a new Sched. 10 to the 1985 Act, dealing with the contents of the directors' report for banking and insurance concerns. The details are in Sched. 8 to the new Act.

Supplementary provisions

Accounting standards

19. The following section is inserted in Part VII of the Companies Act 1985, as the beginning of a Chapter III—

"CHAPTER III

SUPPLEMENTARY PROVISIONS

Accounting standards

Accounting standards

256.—(1) In this Part "accounting standards" means statements of standard accounting practice issued by such body or bodies as may be prescribed by regulations.

(2) References in this Part to accounting standards applicable to a company's annual accounts are to such standards as are, in accordance with their terms, relevant to the company's circumstances and to the accounts.

(3) The Secretary of State may make grants to or for the purposes of bodies concerned with—
  (a) issuing accounting standards,
  (b) overseeing and directing the issuing of such standards, or
  (c) investigating departures from such standards or from the accounting requirements of this Act and taking steps to secure compliance with them.

(4) Regulations under this section may contain such transitional and other supplementary and incidental provisions as appear to the Secretary of State to be appropriate.

DEFINITIONS AND CROSS REFERENCES
"accounting standards": see DEFINITIONS to s.13.
"annual accounts": see DEFINITIONS to s.4.

GENERAL NOTE
This section, inserting a new s.256 into the 1985 Act, was inserted into the Companies Bill during its progress through Parliament, and it is a direct response to the publication of a report ("The Making of Accounting Standards") in September 1988 by a committee chaired by Sir Ron Dearing. Briefly, the latter proposes that a broadly-based Financial Reporting Council should be created to guide the work of the standard setting body, the Accounting Standards Board, which will determine its pronouncements on the basis of a two thirds majority. The standards themselves would not be incorporated into law, but directors would be required to state in notes to the accounts whether the financial statements are drawn up in accordance with applicable standards; and a new statutory power should exist enabling the Secretary of State to apply to the Courts for an order requiring revision of a company's accounts that do not give a true and fair view. The Accounting Standards Board would also publish guidance on so-called "emerging issues", and a Review Panel would examine contentious departures from accounting standards by large companies.

New s.256
This indicates that "accounting standards" will be such standards issued by bodies prescribed by statutory regulations and which are relevant in the circumstances to a company's accounts. The Secretary of State is specifically empowered to delegate authority concerning the issuing of standards, the overseeing of the promulgation of such standards, the investigation of departures from such standards, and taking steps to ensure compliance.

The status of accounting standards in helping to clarify the meaning of the phrase "a true and fair view" (see the revised ss.226(2) and 227(3), respectively inserted by ss.4 and 5 of this Act) has been examined in the case of *Lloyd Cheyham and Co. Ltd.*, v. *Littlejohn and Co.* [1986] P.C.C. 389. In that case Woolf J. considered the evidential role of accounting standards and held that "while they are not conclusive . . . and they are not . . . rigid rules, they are very strong evidence as to what is the proper standard which should be adopted . . ."

Power to alter accounting requirements

20. The following section is inserted in Part VII of the Companies Act 1985—

"Power to alter accounting requirements

Power of Secretary of State to alter accounting requirements

257.—(1) The Secretary of State may by regulations made by statutory instrument modify the provisions of this Part.

(2) Regulations which—
   (a) add to the classes of documents required to be prepared, laid before the company in general meeting or delivered to the registrar,
   (b) restrict the classes of company which have the benefit of any exemption, exception or special provision,
   (c) require additional matter to be included in a document of any class, or
   (d) otherwise render the requirements of this Part more onerous,

shall not be made unless a draft of the instrument containing the regulations has been laid before Parliament and approved by a resolution of each House.

(3) Otherwise, a statutory instrument containing regulations under this section shall be subject to annulment in pursuance of a resolution of either House of Parliament.

(4) Regulations under this section may—
   (a) make different provision for different cases or classes of case,
   (b) repeal and re-enact provisions with modifications of form or arrangement, whether or not they are modified in substance,
   (c) make consequential amendments or repeals in other provisions of this Act, or in other enactments, and
   (d) contain such transitional and other incidental and supplementary provisions as the Secretary of State thinks fit.

(5) Any modification by regulations under this section of section 258 or Schedule 10A (parent and subsidiary undertakings) does not apply for the purposes of enactments outside the Companies Acts unless the regulations so provide.".

DEFINITIONS AND CROSS REFERENCES
"delivery of accounts to the Registrar": see DEFINITIONS to s.5.
"laying accounts before the company in general meeting": see DEFINITIONS to s.7.
"parent undertaking": see DEFINITIONS to s.5.
"subsidiary undertaking": see DEFINITIONS to s.5.

GENERAL NOTE
This section inserts a new s.257 into the 1985 Act which outlines the powers of the Secretary of State to make alterations by statutory instrument to the regulations concerning the contents of annual accounts laid before a company in general meeting or filed with the Registrar of Companies.

The new section represents a simplification of the former s.256, and the derivation of the new subss. (1) and (2) is substantially from the former s.256(1)–(6). Subss. (3)–(5) are new.

Parent and subsidiary undertakings

21.—(1) The following section is inserted in Part VII of the Companies Act 1985—

"Parent and subsidiary undertakings

Parent and subsidiary undertakings

258.—(1) The expressions "parent undertaking" and "subsidiary undertaking" in this Part shall be construed as follows; and a "parent company" means a parent undertaking which is a company.

(2) An undertaking is a parent undertaking in relation to another undertaking, a subsidiary undertaking, if—

(a) it holds a majority of the voting rights in the undertaking, or
(b) it is a member of the undertaking and has the right to appoint or remove a majority of its board of directors, or
(c) it has the right to exercise a dominant influence over the undertaking—
  (i) by virtue of provisions contained in the undertaking's memorandum or articles, or
  (ii) by virtue of a control contract, or
(d) it is a member of the undertaking and controls alone, pursuant to an agreement with other shareholders or members, a majority of the voting rights in the undertaking.

(3) For the purposes of subsection (2) an undertaking shall be treated as a member of another undertaking—
(a) if any of its subsidiary undertakings is a member of that undertaking, or
(b) if any shares in that other undertaking are held by a person acting on behalf of the undertaking or any of its subsidiary undertakings.

(4) An undertaking is also a parent undertaking in relation to another undertaking, a subsidiary undertaking, if it has a participating interest in the undertaking and—
(a) it actually exercises a dominant influence over it, or
(b) it and the subsidiary undertaking are managed on a unified basis.

(5) A parent undertaking shall be treated as the parent undertaking of undertakings in relation to which any of its subsidiary undertakings are, or are to be treated as, parent undertakings; and references to its subsidiary undertakings shall be construed accordingly.

(6) Schedule 10A contains provisions explaining expressions used in this section and otherwise supplementing this section.".

(2) Schedule 9 to this Act (parent and subsidiary undertakings: supplementary provisions) is inserted after Schedule 10 to the Companies Act 1985, as Schedule 10A.

DEFINITIONS AND CROSS REFERENCES
"articles of association": ss.7–9, 744, C.A. 1985.
"control contract": Sched. 10A, C.A. 1989, as inserted by Sched. 9, 1989 Act.
"directors": s.741, C.A. 1985.
"dominant influence": Sched. 10A, C.A. 1985, as inserted by Sched. 9, 1989 Act.
"members": s.22, C.A. 1985.
"parent company": see DEFINITIONS to s.2.
"parent undertaking": see DEFINITIONS to s.5.
"participating interest": s.260, C.A. 1985, as inserted by s.22, 1989 Act.
"subsidiary undertaking": ss.21, 144; see DEFINITIONS to s.5.
"voting rights": Sched. 10A, C.A. 1985, as inserted by Sched. 9, 1989 Act.

GENERAL NOTE
This section inserts a new s.258 into the 1985 Act which, together with Sched. 10A (as inserted by Sched. 9 to the new Act), defines parent and subsidiary undertakings. The primary use of these terms is for the determination of the undertakings to be taken into group accounts, and the new provisions bring British legislation into line with the EC's Seventh Council Directive, arts. 1–3.

A parent undertaking is essentially defined in relation to a subsidiary if (a) it holds a majority of the voting rights; (b) it is a member of the subsidiary and has power to appoint and remove a majority of its directors; or (c) it can exert a dominant influence over the subsidiary (e.g. by virtue of a contract) or the companies are managed on a unified basis. The new Sched. 10A gives guidance on the interpretation of the section on matters including voting rights, powers to appoint and remove a majority of directors, and rights to exercise a dominant influence.

Definitions of "holding company", "subsidiary" and "wholly owned subsidiary" are given in a new s.736 to the principal Act, as inserted by s.144 of the new legislation, which replaces the former section that dealt with these matters. S.144 also inserts s.736A, which explains the meaning of the terms used; while s.736B empowers the Secretary of State to alter the definitions.

The new legislation defines a group in broader terms than previously, and entities which have in the past been managed on a central and unified basis will now be formally recognised in law. This will affect units such as Unilever and Royal Dutch Shell, which already voluntarily publish fully consolidated joint venture accounts as well as the strictly legal financial statements of their British participant companies as required by previous Companies Acts.

It should be noted that the proposed Statement of Standard Accounting Practice 42, "Accounting for Special Purpose Transactions", identifies circumstances where it may be appropriate for the accounts of a company which does not fulfil the Companies Act definition of a subsidiary to be consolidated with that of another company to ensure that the latter's financial statements reflect a true and fair view.

Other interpretation provisions

22. The following sections are inserted in Part VII of the Companies Act 1985—

"Other interpretation provisions

Meaning of "undertaking" and related expressions

259.—(1) In this Part "undertaking" means—
(a) a body corporate or partnership, or
(b) an unincorporated association carrying on a trade or business, with or without a view to profit.

(2) In this Part references to shares—
(a) in relation to an undertaking with a share capital, are to allotted shares;
(b) in relation to an undertaking with capital but no share capital, are to rights to share in the capital of the undertaking; and
(c) in relation to an undertaking without capital, are to interests—
(i) conferring any right to share in the profits or liability to contribute to the losses of the undertaking, or
(ii) giving rise to an obligation to contribute to the debts or expenses of the undertaking in the event of a winding up.

(3) Other expressions appropriate to companies shall be construed, in relation to an undertaking which is not a company, as references to the corresponding persons, officers, documents or organs, as the case may be, appropriate to undertakings of that description.

This is subject to provision in any specific context providing for the translation of such expressions.

(4) References in this Part to "fellow subsidiary undertakings" are to undertakings which are subsidiary undertakings of the same parent undertaking but are not parent undertakings or subsidiary undertakings of each other.

(5) In this Part "group undertaking", in relation to an undertaking, means an undertaking which is—
(a) a parent undertaking or subsidiary undertaking of that undertaking, or
(b) a subsidiary undertaking of any parent undertaking of that undertaking.

Participating interests

260.—(1) In this Part a "participating interest" means an interest held by an undertaking in the shares of another undertaking which it holds on a long-term basis for the purpose of securing a contribution to its activities by the exercise of control or influence arising from or related to that interest.

(2) A holding of 20 per cent. or more of the shares of an undertaking shall be presumed to be a participating interest unless the contrary is shown.

(3) The reference in subsection (1) to an interest in shares includes—
  (a) an interest which is convertible into an interest in shares, and
  (b) an option to acquire shares or any such interest;
and an interest or option falls within paragraph (a) or (b) notwithstanding that the shares to which it relates are, until the conversion or the exercise of the option, unissued.

(4) For the purposes of this section an interest held on behalf of an undertaking shall be treated as held by it.

(5) For the purposes of this section as it applies in relation to the expression "participating interest" in section 258(4) (definition of "subsidiary undertaking")—
  (a) there shall be attributed to an undertaking any interests held by any of its subsidiary undertakings, and
  (b) the references in subsection (1) to the purpose and activities of an undertaking include the purposes and activities of any of its subsidiary undertakings and of the group as a whole.

(6) In the balance sheet and profit and loss formats set out in Part I of Schedule 4, "participating interest" does not include an interest in a group undertaking.

(7) For the purposes of this section as it applies in relation to the expression "participating interest"—
  (a) in those formats as they apply in relation to group accounts, and
  (b) in paragraph 20 of Schedule 4A (group accounts: undertakings to be accounted for as associated undertakings),
the references in subsections (1) to (4) to the interest held by, and the purposes and activities of, the undertaking concerned shall be construed as references to the interest held by, and the purposes and activities of, the group (within the meaning of paragraph 1 of that Schedule).

Notes to the accounts

261.—(1) Information required by this Part to be given in notes to a company's annual accounts may be contained in the accounts or in a separate document annexed to the accounts.

(2) References in this Part to a company's annual accounts, or to a balance sheet or profit and loss account, include notes to the accounts giving information which is required by any provision of this Act, and required or allowed by any such provision to be given in a note to company accounts.

Minor definitions

262.—(1) In this Part—
  "annual accounts" means—
    (a) the individual accounts required by section 226, and
    (b) any group accounts required by section 227,
    (but see also section 230 (treatment of individual profit and loss account where group accounts prepared));
  "annual report", in relation to a company, means the directors' report required by section 234;

"balance sheet date" means the date as at which the balance sheet was made up;

"capitalisation", in relation to work or costs, means treating that work or those costs as a fixed asset;

"credit institution" means an undertaking carrying on a deposit-taking business within the meaning of the Banking Act 1987;

"fixed assets" means assets of a company which are intended for use on a continuing basis in the company's activities, and "current assets" means assets not intended for such use;

"group" means a parent undertaking and its subsidiary undertakings;

"included in the consolidation", in relation to group accounts, or "included in consolidated group accounts", means that the undertaking is included in the accounts by the method of full (and not proportional) consolidation, and references to an undertaking excluded from consolidation shall be construed accordingly;

"purchase price", in relation to an asset of a company or any raw materials or consumables used in the production of such an asset, includes any consideration (whether in cash or otherwise) given by the company in respect of that asset or those materials or consumables, as the case may be;

"qualified", in relation to an auditors' report, means that the report does not state the auditors' unqualified opinion that the accounts have been properly prepared in accordance with this Act or, in the case of an undertaking not required to prepare accounts in accordance with this Act, under any corresponding legislation under which it is required to prepare accounts;

"true and fair view" refers—

(a) in the case of individual accounts, to the requirement of section 226(2), and

(b) in the case of group accounts, to the requirement of section 227(3);

"turnover", in relation to a company, means the amounts derived from the provision of goods and services falling within the company's ordinary activities, after deduction of—

(i) trade discounts,

(ii) value added tax, and

(iii) any other taxes based on the amounts so derived.

(2) In the case of an undertaking not trading for profit, any reference in this Part to a profit and loss account is to an income and expenditure account; and references to profit and loss and, in relation to group accounts, to a consolidated profit and loss account shall be construed accordingly.

(3) References in this Part to "realised profits" and "realised losses", in relation to a company's accounts, are to such profits or losses of the company as fall to be treated as realised in accordance with principles generally accepted, at the time when the accounts are prepared, with respect to the determination for accounting purposes of realised profits or losses.

This is without prejudice to—

(a) the construction of any other expression (where appropriate) by reference to accepted accounting principles or practice, or

(b) any specific provision for the treatment of profits or losses of any description as realised.

Index of defined expressions

262A. The following Table shows the provisions of this Part defining or otherwise explaining expressions used in this Part (other than expressions used only in the same section or paragraph)—

accounting reference date and accounting reference period	section 224
accounting standards and applicable accounting standards	section 256
annual accounts	
(generally)	section 262(1)
(includes notes to the accounts)	section 261(2)
annual report	section 262(1)
associated undertaking (in Schedule 4A)	paragraph 20 of that Schedule
balance sheet (includes notes)	section 261(2)
balance sheet date	section 262(1)
banking group	section 255A(3)
capitalisation (in relation to work or costs)	section 262(1)
credit institution	section 262(1)
current assets	section 262(1)
fellow subsidiary undertaking	section 259(4)
financial year	section 223
fixed assets	section 262(1)
group	section 262(1)
group undertaking	section 259(5)
historical cost accounting rules (in Schedule 4)	paragraph 29 of that Schedule
included in the consolidation and related expressions	section 262(1)
individual accounts	section 262(1)
insurance group	section 255A(4)
land of freehold tenure and land of leasehold tenure (in relation to Scotland)	
—in Schedule 4	paragraph 93 of that Schedule
—in Schedule 9	paragraph 36 of that Schedule
lease, long lease and short lease	
—in Schedule 4	paragraph 83 of that Schedule
—in Schedule 9	paragraph 34 of that Schedule
listed investment	
—in Schedule 4	paragraph 84 of that Schedule
—in Schedule 9	paragraph 33 of that Schedule
notes to the accounts	section 261(1)
parent undertaking (and parent company)	section 258 and Schedule 10A
participating interest	section 260
pension costs (in Schedule 4)	paragraphs 94(2) and (3) of that Schedule
period allowed for laying and delivering accounts and reports	section 244
profit and loss account	
(includes notes)	section 261(2)
(in relation to a company not trading for profit)	section 262(2)
provision	
—in Schedule 4	paragraphs 88 and 89 of that Schedule
—in Schedule 9	paragraph 32 of that Schedule
purchase price	section 262(1)
qualified	section 262(1)
realised losses and realised profits	section 262(3)
reserve (in Schedule 9)	paragraph 32 of that Schedule
shares	section 259(2)
social security costs (in Schedule 4)	paragraph 94(1) and (3) of that Schedule

special provisions for banking and
    insurance companies and groups   sections 255 and 255A
subsidiary undertaking   section 258 and Schedule 10A
true and fair view   section 262(1)
turnover   section 262(1)
undertaking and related expressions   section 259(1) to (3)".

GENERAL NOTE

This section inserts new ss.259–262 into the 1985 Act containing interpretations and definitions for the purposes of Pt. VII of the Act.

New s.259

This indicates the broad nature of the word "undertaking," which covers partnership and other commercial unincorporated associations as well as companies (subs. (1)); the meaning of the word "shares" in relation to different types of business entity (subs. (2)); how expressions appropriate to companies should be interpreted in relation to non-corporate entities (subs. (3)); the meaning of "fellow subsidiary undertakings" (subs. (4)); and the meaning of "group undertaking" (subs. (5)).

The Seventh Council Directive of the European Community specifically refers to undertakings rather than companies, and this is reflected in its definition of group relationships where the conditions are appropriate for the preparation of consolidated accounts (Arts. 1–3).

New s.260

This defines the meaning of a "participating interest", which corresponds to that of a "related company" as given in the former para. 92(1) of Sched. 4, to the 1985 Act (subs. (1)). Subs. (2) indicates that a holding of 20% will give rise to the presumption of there being a "participating interest" unless the contrary is shown. Subss. (3)–(7) offer further clarifications in relation to a "participating interest."

New s.261

This indicates that information to be disclosed in notes may be included in the accounts themselves or in notes annexed thereto. This corresponds to the former para. 35 of Sched. 4 to the 1985 Act.

New s.262

This contains a number of definitions, many of which are derived from previous legislation—

    "annual accounts": *cf.* "accounts" in the original s.742 in the 1985 Act.
    "balance sheet date": in the original s.742 in the 1985 Act.
    "capitalisation": para. 79 in the original Sched. 4 to the 1985 Act.
    "fixed assets": para. 77 in the original Sched. 4 to the 1985 Act.
    "group": para. 81 in the original Sched. 4 to the 1985 Act.
    "income and expenditure account": the former s.227(1) of the 1985 Act.
    "purchase price": para. 90 in the original Sched. 4 to the 1985 Act.
    "realised profits and losses": para. 91 in the original Sched. 4 to the 1985 Act.
    "true and fair view": Scheds. 4–10 to the 1985 Act generally, but especially Sched. 4, paras. 10–15.
    "turnover": para. 95 in the original Sched. 4 to the 1985 Act.

The definition of "qualified" in an auditors' report should be read in conjunction with the Auditing Standard, "The Audit Report", of the Auditing Practices Committee.

New s.262A

This gives a table of expressions, indicating the sections in which definitions or explanations of them can be found. The following expressions given in the original s.744 of the 1985 Act have been repealed under Sched. 24 of the new legislation: "annual return"; "authorised institution"; "authorised minimum"; "expert"; "floating charge"; "joint stock company"; and "undistributable reserves".

A full index of defined expressions in the 1985 Act is given in s.744A, as inserted by para. 20 of Sched. 19 to this Act.

Consequential amendments

Consequential amendments

23. The enactments specified in Schedule 10 have effect with the amendments specified there, which are consequential on the amendments made by the preceding provisions of this Part.

GENERAL NOTE

This section, together with Sched. 10, makes consequential amendments to Pt. VII of th 1985 Act. Para. 1 of the Schedule alters s.46 with regard to the meaning of an "unqualified auditors' report, as referred to in s.43(3); para. 13 substitutes new ss.700–703 dealing with the preparation and delivery of accounts and reports by oversea companies; para. 15 substitutes new subss. (1)–(2) in s.742, which deals with the generality of the definitions used for "annual accounts," "accounting reference date," "balance sheet date," "current assets," "financial year," "fixed assets," "profit and loss account," "realised profits" and "realised losses"; para. 18(7) inserts a second part to the former Sched. 2, dealing with "beneficial interests"; para. 19 modifies Sched. 3 to the 1985 Act, which deals with auditors' and accountants' reports in prospectuses; para. 22 modifies Sched. 15A (renumbered 15B), dealing with provisions applicable to mergers and divisions of public companies; and para. 24(3) amends Sched. 24 dealing with "punishment of offences."

PART II

ELIGIBILITY FOR APPOINTMENT AS COMPANY AUDITOR

Introduction

Introduction

24.—(1) The main purposes of this Part are to secure that only persons who are properly supervised and appropriately qualified are appointed company auditors, and that audits by persons so appointed are carried out properly and with integrity and with a proper degree of independence.

(2) A "company auditor" means a person appointed as auditor under Chapter V of Part XI of the Companies Act 1985; and the expressions "company audit" and "company audit work" shall be construed accordingly.

DEFINITIONS

"company auditor": s.24(2), 1989 Act.
"company audit": s.24(2), 1989 Act.
"company audit work": s.24(2), 1989 Act.

Subs. (1)

This sets out the purpose of this Part of the Act: (1) that only persons who are properly supervised and appropriately qualified can be appointed as company auditors; and (2) that audits are carried out properly with integrity and with a proper degree of independence.

Subs. (2)

This defines the terms "company auditor", "company audit" and "company audit work" in terms of the provisions of s.384 of the 1985 Act.

Eligibility for appointment

Eligibility for appointment

25.—(1) A person is eligible for appointment as a company auditor only if he—
 (a) is a member of a recognised supervisory body, and
 (b) is eligible for the appointment under the rules of that body.

(2) An individual or a firm may be appointed a company auditor.

(3) In the cases to which section 34 applies (individuals retaining only 1967 Act authorisation) a person's eligibility for appointment as a company auditor is restricted as mentioned in that section.

DEFINITIONS
"company auditor": s.24(2), 1989 Act.
"recognised supervisory body": ss.31, 32, 1989 Act.

GENERAL NOTE
This section restricts eligibility for appointment as a statutory company auditor to members of a recognised supervisory body. The section allows individuals and firms to be appointed. The eligibility of persons with overseas qualifications is dealt with in s.33; and the eligibility of individuals authorised under s.13(1) of the Companies Act 1967 in s.34.

Effect of appointment of partnership

26.—(1) The following provisions apply to the appointment as company auditor of a partnership constituted under the law of England and Wales or Northern Ireland, or under the law of any other country or territory in which a partnership is not a legal person.

(2) The appointment is (unless a contrary intention appears) an appointment of the partnership as such and not of the partners.

(3) Where the partnership ceases, the appointment shall be treated as extending to—
  (a) any partnership which succeeds to the practice of that partnership and is eligible for the appointment, and
  (b) any person who succeeds to that practice having previously carried it on in partnership and is eligible for the appointment.

(4) For this purpose a partnership shall be regarded as succeeding to the practice of another partnership only if the members of the successor partnership are substantially the same as those of the former partnership; and a partnership or other person shall be regarded as succeeding to the practice of a partnership only if it or he succeeds to the whole or substantially the whole of the business of the former partnership.

(5) Where the partnership ceases and no person succeeds to the appointment under subsection (3), the appointment may with the consent of the company be treated as extending to a partnership or other person eligible for the appointment who succeeds to the business of the former partnership or to such part of it as is agreed by the company shall be treated as comprising the appointment.

DEFINITIONS
"company auditor": ss.24(2).
"eligible for appointment": ss.25, 27, 1989 Act.

GENERAL NOTE
This section, which was inserted during the progress of the Bill through Parliament, deals with the effect of appointing a partnership as the company's auditors, where such a firm is constituted under the law of any country where it is not a separate legal person. (Effectively this means England and Wales and Northern Ireland within the U.K.).

Subs. (2)
This indicates that the appointment will normally be interpreted as relating to the partnership rather than to an individual partner.

Subss. (3) and (4)
These indicate that where the membership of a partnership changes, a succeeding practice will be eligible for appointment, so long as the members or the business are substantially the same as before.

Subs. (5)
This deals with other circumstances where part of a practice is taken over by another partnership or person eligible for appointment.

Ineligibility on ground of lack of independence

27.—(1) A person is ineligible for appointment as company auditor of a company if he is—
 (a) an officer or employee of the company, or
 (b) a partner or employee of such a person, or a partnership of which such a person is a partner,

or if he is ineligible by virtue of paragraph (a) or (b) for appointment as company auditor of any associated undertaking of the company.

For this purpose an auditor of a company shall not be regarded as an officer or employee of the company.

(2) A person is also ineligible for appointment as company auditor of a company if there exists between him or any associate of his and the company or any associated undertaking a connection of any such description as may be specified by regulations made by the Secretary of State.

The regulations may make different provisions for different cases.

(3) In this section "associated undertaking", in relation to a company, means—
 (a) a parent undertaking or subsidiary undertaking of the company, or
 (b) a subsidiary undertaking of any parent undertaking of the company.

(4) Regulations under this section shall be made by statutory instrument which shall be subject to annulment in pursuance of a resolution of either House of Parliament.

DEFINITIONS
 "associated undertaking of the company": s.27(3), 1989 Act.
 "company auditor": ss.24(2), 1989 Act.
 "officer of the company": s.744, C.A. 1985.
 "parent undertaking": see DEFINITIONS to s.2.
 "subsidiary undertaking": see DEFINITIONS to s.5.

GENERAL NOTE
This section defines the circumstances in which a person is ineligible for appointment as a statutory auditor on grounds of lack of independence—*i.e.* if he is an officer or employee of the company or a parent or subsidiary undertaking, or a partner or employee of such a person. A person may also be ineligible if there is a connection between him or any associate of his and the group of companies, the nature of such a connection being specified in regulations made by the Secretary of State.

Effect of ineligibility

28.—(1) No person shall act as a company auditor if he is ineligible for appointment to the office.

(2) If during his term of office a company auditor becomes ineligible for appointment to the office, he shall thereupon vacate office and shall forthwith give notice in writing to the company concerned that he has vacated it by reason of ineligibility.

(3) A person who acts as company auditor in contravention of subsection (1), or fails to give notice of vacating his office as required by subsection (2), is guilty of an offence and liable—
 (a) on conviction on indictment, to a fine, and
 (b) on summary conviction, to a fine not exceeding the statutory maximum.

(4) In the case of continued contravention he is liable on a second or subsequent summary conviction (instead of the fine mentioned in subsection (3)(b)) to a fine not exceeding one-tenth of the statutory maximum in respect of each day on which the contravention is continued.

(5) In proceedings against a person for an offence under this section it is a defence for him to show that he did not know and had no reason to believe that he was, or had become, ineligible for appointment.

DEFINITIONS
"company auditor": ss.24(2), 1989 Act.
"eligibility": ss.25, 27, 1989 Act.

GENERAL NOTE
This section makes acting as a statutory auditor when ineligible an offence, and the guilty party is liable on conviction to a fine and on summary conviction to a fine not exceeding the statutory maximum. In the case of continued contravention, the person will be liable on a second or subsequent summary conviction to a fine of up to one tenth of the statutory maximum for each day on which the offence is continued. However, it is a defence to show that there was no knowledge and no reason to believe that the person concerned was ineligible.

In this context, a person may either be ineligible *or become* ineligible. In the latter case, he should vacate office and give notice in writing to the company that he has resigned because of ineligibility.

Power of Secretary of State to require second audit

29.—(1) Where a person appointed company auditor was, for any part of the period during which the audit was conducted, ineligible for appointment to that office, the Secretary of State may direct the company concerned to retain a person eligible for appointment as auditor of the company—
(a) to audit the relevant accounts again, or
(b) to review the first audit and to report (giving his reasons) whether a second audit is needed;
and the company shall comply with such a direction within 21 days of its being given.

(2) If a second audit is recommended the company shall forthwith take such steps as are necessary to comply with the recommendation.

(3) Where a direction is given under this section, the Secretary of State shall send a copy of the direction to the registrar of companies; and the company shall within 21 days of receiving any report under subsection (1)(b) send a copy of it to the registrar of companies.

The provisions of the Companies Act 1985 relating to the delivery of documents to the registrar apply for the purposes of this subsection.

(4) Any statutory or other provisions applying in relation to the first audit shall apply, so far as practicable, in relation to a second audit under this section.

(5) If a company fails to comply with the requirements of this section, it is guilty of an offence and liable on summary conviction to a fine not exceeding the statutory maximum; and in the case of continued contravention it is liable on a second or subsequent summary conviction (instead of the fine mentioned above) to a fine not exceeding one-tenth of the statutory maximum in respect of each day on which the contravention is continued.

(6) A direction under this section is, on the application of the Secretary of State, enforceable by injunction or, in Scotland, by an order under section 45 of the Court of Session Act 1988.

(7) If a person accepts an appointment, or continues to act, as company auditor at a time when he knows he is ineligible, the company concerned may recover from him any costs incurred by it in complying with the requirements of this section.

DEFINITIONS
"company audit": s.24(2), 1989 Act.
"company auditor": s.24(2), 1989 Act.
"provisions relating to the delivery of documents to the registrar": s.29(3), 1989 Act.

GENERAL NOTE
Where a company audit has been carried out by an ineligible person, the Secretary of State may direct that an eligible person be appointed, either to undertake a second audit or to review the first audit and report whether a second audit is needed. When such a direction is given, a copy will be sent to the Registrar of Companies, and the company must comply within 21 days. On receiving any report on the possible need for a second audit, the company must forward a copy to the Registrar within 21 days. Failure to comply with the provisions of the section is an offence, liable on summary conviction to a fine not exceeding the statutory maximum; and in the case of continued contravention, on a second or subsequent summary conviction to a fine of one tenth of the statutory maximum for each day on which the offence takes place.

The company is entitled to recover costs incurred complying with this section if the ineligible person knew he was ineligible.

Recognition of supervisory bodies and professional qualifications

Supervisory bodies

30.—(1) In this Part a "supervisory body" means a body established in the United Kingdom (whether a body corporate or an unincorporated association) which maintains and enforces rules as to—

(a) the eligibility of persons to seek appointment as company auditors, and

(b) the conduct of company audit work,

which are binding on persons seeking appointment or acting as company auditors either because they are members of that body or because they are otherwise subject to its control.

(2) In this Part references to the members of a supervisory body are to the persons who, whether or not members of the body, are subject to its rules in seeking appointment or acting as company auditors.

(3) In this Part references to the rules of a supervisory body are to the rules (whether or not laid down by the body itself) which the body has power to enforce and which are relevant for the purposes of this Part.

This includes rules relating to the admission and expulsion of members of the body, so far as relevant for the purposes of this Part.

(4) In this Part references to guidance issued by a supervisory body are to guidance issued or any recommendation made by it to all or any class of its members or persons seeking to become members which would, if it were a rule, fall within subsection (3).

(5) The provisions of Parts I and II of Schedule 11 have effect with respect to the recognition of supervisory bodies for the purposes of this Part.

DEFINITIONS
"company auditor": s.24(2), 1989 Act.
"company audit work": s.24(2), 1989 Act.
"guidance issued by a supervisory body": s.30(4), 1989 Act.
"members of a supervisory body": s.30(2), 1989 Act.
"rules of a supervisory body": s.30(3), 1989 Act.
"supervisory body": s.30(1), 1989 Act.

GENERAL NOTE
This section and the following sections should be read in conjunction with Sched. 11, "Recognition of a Supervisory Body."

Examples of recognised supervisory bodies are likely to be the Institute of Chartered Accountants in England and Wales; the Institute of Chartered Accountants of Scotland; the Institute of Chartered Accountants in Ireland; and the Chartered Association of Certified Accountants. Guidance would then refer to the pronouncements of the Auditing Practices Committee.

Meaning of "appropriate qualification"

31.—(1) A person holds an appropriate qualification for the purposes of this Part if—
(a) he was, by virtue of membership of a body recognised for the purposes of section 389(1)(a) of the Companies Act 1985, qualified for appointment as auditor of a company under that section immediately before 1st January 1990 and immediately before the commencement of section 25 above,
(b) he holds a recognised professional qualification obtained in the United Kingdom, or
(c) he holds an approved overseas qualification and satisfies any additional educational requirements applicable in accordance with section 33(4).

(2) A person who, immediately before 1st January 1990 and immediately before the commencement of section 25 above, was qualified for appointment as auditor of a company under section 389 of the Companies Act 1985 otherwise than by virtue of membership of a body recognised for the purposes of section 389(1)(a)—
(a) shall be treated as holding an appropriate qualification for twelve months from the day on which section 25 comes into force, and
(b) shall continue to be so treated if within that period he notifies the Secretary of State that he wishes to retain the benefit of his qualification.

The notice shall be in writing and shall contain such information as the Secretary of State may require.

(3) If a person fails to give such notice within the time allowed he may apply to the Secretary of State, giving such information as would have been required in connection with a notice, and the Secretary of State may, if he is satisfied—
(a) that there was good reason why the applicant did not give notice in time, and
(b) that the applicant genuinely intends to practise as an auditor in Great Britain,

direct that he shall be treated as holding an appropriate qualification for the purposes of this Part.

(4) A person who—
(a) began before 1st January 1990 a course of study or practical training leading to a professional qualification in accountancy offered by a body established in the United Kingdom, and
(b) obtained that qualification on or after that date and before 1st January 1996,

shall be treated as holding an appropriate qualification if the qualification is approved by the Secretary of State for the purposes of this subsection.

(5) Approval shall not be given unless the Secretary of State is satisfied that the body concerned has or, as the case may be, had at the relevant time adequate arrangements to ensure that the qualification is, or was, awarded only to persons educated and trained to a standard equivalent to that required in the case of a recognised professional qualification.

(6) A person shall not be regarded as holding an appropriate qualification for the purposes of this Part except in the above cases.

DEFINITIONS

"overseas qualification": s.33, 1989 Act.
"qualified for appointment as an auditor otherwise than by membership of a recognised body": s.34, 1989 Act.
"qualifying body": s.32, 1989 Act.

GENERAL NOTE

This section defines the circumstances in which a person may be regarded as holding an appropriate qualification. These are where (1) he was a member on December 31, 1989 of a body recognised for the purpose of s.389(1) of the 1985 Act as being qualified to be a company auditor (*i.e.* a member of one of the three Institutes of Chartered Accountants or the Chartered Association of Certified Accountants) and was a member when s.25 comes into force; (2) he holds a recognised professional qualification obtained in the U.K.; or (3) he holds an approved overseas qualification (see s.33).

Anyone otherwise qualified to be a company auditor before s.25 comes into force, (*e.g.* being authorised under s.13(1) of the 1967 Companies Act: see s.34) will be treated as holding an appropriate qualification. This will be extended if he indicates to the Secretary of State in writing that he wishes to retain that benefit.

Subss. (4) and (5)

These contain transitional provisions that deal with the position of someone who is not a member of one of the recognised supervisory bodies when s.25 comes into force, but who commenced studying and/or training for a professional qualification of such a body before January 1, 1990 and who qualified before January 1, 1996.

Qualifying bodies and recognised professional qualifications

32.—(1) In this Part a "qualifying body" means a body established in the United Kingdom (whether a body corporate or an unincorporated association) which offers a professional qualification in accountancy.

(2) In this Part references to the rules of a qualifying body are to the rules (whether or not laid down by the body itself) which the body has power to enforce and which are relevant for the purposes of this Part.

This includes rules relating to—

(a) admission to or expulsion from a course of study leading to a qualification,

(b) the award or deprivation of a qualification, or

(c) the approval of a person for the purposes of giving practical training or the withdrawal of such approval,

so far as relevant for the purposes of this Part.

(3) In this Part references to guidance issued by any such body are to any guidance which the body issues, or any recommendation it makes to all or any class of persons holding or seeking to hold a qualification, or approved or seeking to be approved by the body for the purpose of giving practical training, which would, if it were a rule, fall within subsection (2).

(4) The provisions of Parts I and II of Schedule 12 have effect with respect to the recognition for the purposes of this Part of a professional qualification offered by a qualifying body.

DEFINITIONS AND CROSS REFERENCES
"guidance": s.32(3), 1989 Act.
"qualifying body": s.32(1), 1989 Act.
"rules": s.32(2), 1989 Act.

GENERAL NOTE

This section defines a "qualifying body" (subs. (1)), its "rules" (including those relating to admission to and expulsion from a training contract, the award or revocation of a qualification, and the approval of a training partner) (subs. (2)), and the "guidance" it offers. This section and the following sections should be read in conjunction with Sched. 12, "Recognition of Professional Qualification".

Examples of qualifying bodies are likely to be the Institute of Chartered Accountants in England and Wales; the Institute of Chartered Accountants of Scotland; the Institute of Chartered Accountants in Ireland; and the Chartered Association of Certified Accountants.

Approval of overseas qualifications

33.—(1) The Secretary of State may declare that persons who—
  (a) are qualified to audit accounts under the law of a specified country or territory outside the United Kingdom, or
  (b) hold a specified professional qualification in accountancy recognised under the law of a country or territory outside the United Kingdom,
shall be regarded for the purposes of this Part as holding an approved overseas qualification.

(2) A qualification shall not be so approved by the Secretary of State unless he is satisfied that it affords an assurance of professional competence equivalent to that afforded by a recognised professional qualification.

(3) In exercising the power conferred by subsection (1) the Secretary of State may have regard to the extent to which persons—
  (a) eligible under this Part for appointment as a company auditor, or
  (b) holding a professional qualification recognised under this Part,
are recognised by the law of the country or territory in question as qualified to audit accounts there.

(4) The Secretary of State may direct that a person holding an approved overseas qualification shall not be treated as holding an appropriate qualification for the purposes of this Part unless he holds such additional educational qualifications as the Secretary of State may specify for the purpose of ensuring that such persons have an adequate knowledge of the law and practice in the United Kingdom relevant to the audit of accounts.

(5) Different directions may be given in relation to different qualifications.

(6) The Secretary of State may if he thinks fit, having regard to the considerations mentioned in subsections (2) and (3), withdraw his approval of an overseas qualification in relation to persons becoming qualified as mentioned in subsection (1)(a), or obtaining such a qualification as is mentioned in subsection (1)(b), after such date as he may specify.

DEFINITIONS AND CROSS REFERENCES
  "company auditor": s.24(2), 1989 Act.
  "recognised professional qualification": ss.31–32, 1989 Act.

GENERAL NOTE
  This section defines the circumstances in which the Secretary of State must be satisfied that the person is equivalently competent to someone with a U.K. recognised professional qualification. In reaching his conclusions, he may take into account reciprocal arrangements for persons professionally qualified in the U.K. to audit overseas; and he may require additional qualifications to ensure an adequate knowledge of law and practice in the U.K. relevant to the audit of accounts. He may also withdraw recognition of an overseas qualification after a specified date if he is no longer satisfied that there is equivalent competence or there are inadequate reciprocal arrangements.

Eligibility of individuals retaining only 1967 Act authorisation

34.—(1) A person whose only appropriate qualification is that he retains an authorisation granted by the Board of Trade or the Secretary of State under section 13(1) of the Companies Act 1967 is eligible only for appointment as auditor of an unquoted company.

(2) A company is "unquoted" if, at the time of the person's appointment, no shares or debentures of the company, or of a parent undertaking of which it is a subsidiary undertaking, have been quoted on a stock exchange (in Great Britain or elsewhere) or offered (whether in Great Britain or elsewhere) to the public for subscription or purchase.

(3) This section does not authorise the appointment of such a person as auditor of a company that carries on business as the promoter of a trading stamp scheme within the meaning of the Trading Stamps Act 1964.

(4) References to a person eligible for appointment as company auditor under section 25 in enactments relating to eligibility for appointment as auditor of a body other than a company do not include a person to whom this section applies.

DEFINITIONS AND CROSS REFERENCES
"company auditor": s.24(2), 1989 Act.
"debentures": s.744, C.A. 1985.
"parent undertaking": see DEFINITIONS to s.5.
"shares": see DEFINITIONS to s.13.
"subsidiary undertaking": see DEFINITIONS to s.5.
"unquoted company": s.34(2), 1989 Act.

GENERAL NOTE
This section provides that a person whose only appropriate qualification is one previously granted under s.13(1) of the Companies Act 1967 is only eligible for appointment as an auditor of an "unquoted" company: *i.e.* when he was appointed, no shares or debentures of the company or of its parent or subsidiary undertakings, were quoted on a stock exchange or were offered to the public for subscription or purchase. Such a person is also ineligible to audit a company which is a promoter of a trading stamp scheme, or of any other body where reference to s.25 is made.

Duties of recognised bodies

The register of auditors

35.—(1) The Secretary of State shall make regulations requiring the keeping of a register of—
  (a) the individuals and firms eligible for appointment as company auditor, and
  (b) the individuals holding an appropriate qualification who are responsible for company audit work on behalf of such firms.
(2) The regulations shall provide that each person's entry in the register shall give—
  (a) his name and address, and
  (b) in the case of a person eligible as mentioned in subsection (1)(a), the name of the relevant supervisory body,
together with such other information as may be specified by the regulations.
(3) The regulations may impose such obligations as the Secretary of State thinks fit—
  (a) on recognised supervisory bodies,
  (b) on persons eligible for appointment as company auditor, and
  (c) on any person with whom arrangements are made by one or more recognised supervisory bodies with respect to the keeping of the register.
(4) The regulations may include provision—
  (a) requiring the register to be open to inspection at such times and places as may be specified in the regulations or determined in accordance with them,
  (b) enabling a person to require a certified copy of an entry in the register, and
  (c) authorising the charging of fees for inspection, or the provision of copies, of such reasonable amount as may be specified in the regulations or determined in accordance with them;
and may contain such other supplementary and incidental provisions as the Secretary of State thinks fit.
(5) Regulations under this section shall be made by statutory instrument which shall be subject to annulment in pursuance of a resolution of either House of Parliament.

(6) The obligations imposed by regulations under this section on such persons as are mentioned in subsection (3)(a) or (c) are enforceable on the application of the Secretary of State by injunction or, in Scotland, by an order under section 45 of the Court of Session Act 1988.

DEFINITIONS AND CROSS REFERENCES
"appropriate qualification": ss.31–34, 1989 Act.
"company auditor": s.24(2), 1989 Act.
"company audit work": ss.9, 24(2), 1989 Act.
"eligible for appointment as company auditor": ss.25 , 27, 1989 Act.
"recognised supervisory body": s.30, 1989 Act.

GENERAL NOTE
Under the provisions of this section the Secretary of State will make regulations through a statutory instrument requiring that a register be kept of all individuals and firms eligible for appointment as company auditors and of the qualified persons responsible for company audit work on their behalves. The register will give their names and addresses and indicate the relevant supervisory body. The regulations may require further information to be disclosed on the register, and the Secretary of State can impose further obligations on the recognised supervisory bodies, on persons eligible to be company auditors, and on anyone charged by one or more supervisory bodies to keep the register. The regulations may also include provisions concerning the availability of the register for public inspection, for copies of entries being made available, and for appropriate fees to be charged for such services.

Information about firms to be available to public

36.—(1) The Secretary of State shall make regulations requiring recognised supervisory bodies to keep and make available to the public the following information with respect to the firms eligible under their rules for appointment as a company auditor—
  (a) in relation to a body corporate, the name and address of each person who is a director of the body or holds any shares in it,
  (b) in relation to a partnership, the name and address of each partner,
and such other information as may be specified in the regulations.
(2) The regulations may impose such obligations as the Secretary of State thinks fit—
  (a) on recognised supervisory bodies,
  (b) on persons eligible for appointment as company auditor, and
  (c) on any person with whom arrangements are made by one or more recognised supervisory bodies with respect to the keeping of the information.
(3) The regulations may include provision—
  (a) requiring that the information be open to inspection at such times and places as may be specified in the regulations or determined in accordance with them,
  (b) enabling a person to require a certified copy of the information or any part of it, and
  (c) authorising the charging of fees for inspection, or the provision of copies, of such reasonable amount as may be specified in the regulations or determined in accordance with them;
and may contain such other supplementary and incidental provisions as the Secretary of State thinks fit.
(4) The regulations may make different provision in relation to different descriptions of information and may contain such other supplementary and incidental provisions as the Secretary of State thinks fit.
(5) Regulations under this section shall be made by statutory instrument which shall be subject to annulment in pursuance of a resolution of either House of Parliament.
(6) The obligations imposed by regulations under this section on such persons as are mentioned in subsection (2)(a) or (c) are enforceable on

the application of the Secretary of State by injunction or, in Scotland, by an order under section 45 of the Court of Session Act 1988.

DEFINITIONS AND CROSS REFERENCES
"company auditor": s.24(2), 1989 Act.
"director": s.53(1).
"eligible for appointment as a company auditor": ss.25, 27, 1989 Act.
"recognised supervisory body": s.30, 1989 Act.

GENERAL NOTE
Under the provisions of this section, the Secretary of State will make regulations through a statutory instrument requiring a recognised supervisory body to make available to the public information about firms which are eligible under its rules to act as statutory auditors. The information to be disclosed will be the names and addresses of all directors and shareholders, if the firm is a company; or of all the partners if it is a partnership. The regulations may require further information to be disclosed, and the Secretary of State can impose further obligations on the recognised supervisory bodies, on persons eligible to be company auditors, and on anyone charged by one or more supervisory bodies to keep such information. The regulations may also include provisions concerning the availability of the information for public inspection, for copies of information being made available, and for appropriate fees to be charged for such services. However, the regulations may make different provisions for different types of information.

Matters to be notified to the Secretary of State

37.—(1) The Secretary of State may require a recognised supervisory or qualifying body—
 (a) to notify him forthwith of the occurrence of such events as he may specify in writing and to give him such information in respect of those events as is so specified;
 (b) to give him, at such times or in respect of such periods as he may specify in writing, such information as is so specified.

(2) The notices and information required to be given shall be such as the Secretary of State may reasonably require for the exercise of his functions under this Part.

(3) The Secretary of State may require information given under this section to be given in a specified form or verified in a specified manner.

(4) Any notice or information required to be given under this section shall be given in writing unless the Secretary of State specifies or approves some other manner.

DEFINITIONS AND CROSS REFERENCES
"qualifying body": s.32, 1989 Act.
"recognised supervisory body": s.30, 1989 Act.

GENERAL NOTE
This section enables the Secretary of State to require a recognised supervisory or qualifying body to notify him of the occurrence of such events as he may specify in writing and to give him information in respect of those events for particular periods. Such information should generally be submitted in writing and may be required to be in a specified form or to have been verified in a particular way.

Power to call for information

38.—(1) The Secretary of State may by notice in writing require a recognised supervisory or qualifying body to give him such information as he may reasonably require for the exercise of his functions under this Part.

(2) The Secretary of State may require that any information which he requires under this section shall be given within such reasonable time and verified in such manner as he may specify.

DEFINITIONS AND CROSS REFERENCES
"qualifying body": s.32, 1989 Act.
"recognised supervisory body": s.30, 1989 Act.

GENERAL NOTE
This section enables the Secretary of State by notice in writing to require a recognised supervisory body or qualifying body to give him such information as he may reasonably require. It may be required within a reasonable time and may have to be verified in a particular way.

Compliance orders

39.—(1) If at any time it appears to the Secretary of State—
(a) in the case of a recognised supervisory body, that any requirement of Schedule 11 is not satisfied,
(b) in the case of a recognised professional qualification, that any requirement of Schedule 12 is not satisfied, or
(c) that a recognised supervisory or qualifying body has failed to comply with an obligation to which it is subject by virtue of this Part,

he may, instead of revoking the relevant recognition order, make an application to the court under this section.

(2) If on such application the court decides that the subsection or requirement in question is not satisfied or, as the case may be, that the body has failed to comply with the obligation in question it may order the supervisory or qualifying body in question to take such steps as the court directs for securing that the subsection or requirement is satisfied or that the obligation is complied with.

(3) The jurisdiction conferred by this section is exercisable by the High Court and the Court of Session.

DEFINITIONS AND CROSS REFERENCES
"recognised professional qualification": s.32, 1989 Act.
"recognised qualifying body": s.32, 1989 Act.
"recognised supervisory body": s.30, 1989 Act.

GENERAL NOTE
This section enables the Secretary of State, as an alternative to revoking a recognition order in relation to a recognised supervisory body, a qualifying body, or a recognised professional qualification, to apply to the court for an order directing the recognised body to take the necessary steps to meet particular requirements or obligations.

Directions to comply with international obligations

40.—(1) If it appears to the Secretary of State—
(a) that any action proposed to be taken by a recognised supervisory or qualifying body, or a body established by order under section 46, would be incompatible with Community obligations or any other international obligations of the United Kingdom, or
(b) that any action which that body has power to take is required for the purpose of implementing any such obligations,

he may direct the body not to take or, as the case may be, to take the action in question.

(2) A direction may include such supplementary or incidental requirements as the Secretary of State thinks necessary or expedient.

(3) A direction under this section is enforceable on the application of the Secretary of State by injunction or, in Scotland, by an order under section 45 of the Court of Session Act 1988.

DEFINITIONS
"recognised qualifying body": s.32, 1989 Act.
"recognised supervisory body": s.30, 1989 Act.

GENERAL NOTE
This section enables the Secretary of State to require appropriate steps to be taken by the body concerned if it appears that any action proposed to be taken by a recognised body or a body established under s.46 would be incompatible with European Community or other international obligations, or that any action which the body has power to take is necessary to meet such obligations.

Offences

False and misleading statements

41.—(1) A person commits an offence if—
(a) for the purposes of or in connection with any application under this Part, or
(b) in purported compliance with any requirement imposed on him by or under this Part,
he furnishes information which he knows to be false or misleading in a material particular or recklessly furnishes information which is false or misleading in a material particular.

(2) It is an offence for a person whose name does not appear on the register of auditors kept under regulations under section 35 to describe himself as a registered auditor or so to hold himself out as to indicate, or be reasonably understood to indicate, that he is a registered auditor.

(3) It is an offence for a body which is not a recognised supervisory or qualifying body to describe itself as so recognised or so to describe itself or hold itself out as to indicate, or be reasonably understood to indicate, that it is so recognised.

(4) A person guilty of an offence under subsection (1) is liable—
(a) on conviction on indictment, to imprisonment for a term not exceeding two years or to a fine or both;
(b) on summary conviction, to imprisonment for a term not exceeding six months or to a fine not exceeding the statutory maximum or both.

(5) A person guilty of an offence under subsection (2) or (3) is liable on summary conviction to imprisonment for a term not exceeding six months or to a fine not exceeding level 5 on the standard scale or both.

Where a contravention of subsection (2) or (3) involves a public display of the offending description, the maximum fine that may be imposed is (in place of that mentioned above) an amount equal to level 5 on the standard scale multiplied by the number of days for which the display has continued.

(6) It is a defence for a person charged with an offence under subsection (2) or (3) to show that he took all reasonable precautions and exercised all due diligence to avoid the commission of the offence.

DEFINITIONS AND CROSS REFERENCES
"recognised qualifying body": s.32, 1989 Act.
"recognised supervisory body": s.30, 1989 Act.
"register of auditors": s.35, 1989 Act.

GENERAL NOTE
This section deals with offences in relation to Pt. II of the Act. Thus a person who supplies false or misleading information is guilty of an offence (subs. (1)) and is liable either on conviction or indictment to a term of imprisonment of up to two years and/or to a fine; or on summary conviction to a term of imprisonment of up to six months and/or to a fine not exceeding the statutory maximum (subs. (3)). It is also an offence for a person whose name is not on the register of auditors to hold himself out as a registered auditor (subs. (2)); or likewise for a body which is not a recognised supervisory or qualifying body to hold itself out as such. Offences under subss. (2) and (3) render a person liable on summary conviction

to a term of imprisonment of up to six months and/or a fine not exceeding level 5 on the standard scale. However, where a false description is given in public, the maximum fine instead is an amount equal to level 5 on the standard scale, multiplied by the number of days over which the public display occurred.

Offences by bodies corporate, partnerships and unincorporated associations

42.—(1) Where an offence under this Part committed by a body corporate is proved to have been committed with the consent or connivance of, or to be attributable to any neglect on the part of, a director, manager, secretary or other similar officer of the body, or a person purporting to act in any such capacity, he as well as the body corporate is guilty of the offence and liable to be proceeded against and punished accordingly.

(2) Where the affairs of a body corporate are managed by its members, subsection (1) applies in relation to the acts and defaults of a member in connection with his functions of management as to a director of a body corporate.

(3) Where an offence under this Part committed by a partnership is proved to have been committed with the consent or connivance of, or to be attributable to any neglect on the part of, a partner, he as well as the partnership is guilty of the offence and liable to be proceeded against and punished accordingly.

(4) Where an offence under this Part committed by an unincorporated association (other than a partnership) is proved to have been committed with the consent or connivance of, or to be attributable to any neglect on the part of, any officer of the association or any member of its governing body, he as well as the association is guilty of the offence and liable to be proceeded against and punished accordingly.

DEFINITIONS AND CROSS REFERENCES
  "body corporate": s.740, C.A. 1985.
  "director": s.53(1).
  "member (of a company)": s.22, C.A. 1985.
  "member (of a supervisory body)": s.30(2), 1989 Act.
  "officer"; s.744, C.A. 1985.
  "secretary": s.283, C.A. 1985.

GENERAL NOTE
This section extends liability for offences to directors, secretaries, managers, other officers and (even in certain circumstances) members of corporate bodies if they have contributed to their commission (subss. (1) and (2)). Liability is also extended to partners and officers, etc., of unincorporated associations.

Time limits for prosecution of offences

43.—(1) An information relating to an offence under this Part which is triable by a magistrates' court in England and Wales may be so tried on an information laid at any time within twelve months after the date on which evidence sufficient in the opinion of the Director of Public Prosecutions or the Secretary of State to justify the proceedings comes to his knowledge.

(2) Proceedings in Scotland for an offence under this Part may be commenced at any time within twelve months after the date on which evidence sufficient in the Lord Advocate's opinion to justify the proceedings came to his knowledge or, where such evidence was reported to him by the Secretary of State, within twelve months after the date on which it came to the knowledge of the latter.

For the purposes of this subsection proceedings shall be deemed to be commenced on the date on which a warrant to apprehend or to cite the accused is granted, if the warrant is executed without undue delay.

(3) Subsection (1) does not authorise the trial of an information laid, and subsection (2) does not authorise the commencement of proceedings, more than three years after the commission of the offence.

(4) For the purposes of this section a certificate of the Director of Public Prosecutions, the Lord Advocate or the Secretary of State as to the date on which such evidence as is referred to above came to his knowledge is conclusive evidence.

(5) Nothing in this section affects proceedings within the time limits prescribed by section 127(1) of the Magistrates' Courts Act 1980 or section 331 of the Criminal Procedure (Scotland) Act 1975 (the usual time limits for criminal proceedings).

GENERAL NOTE
This section indicates the time limits for prosecution for offences under Pt. II of the Act. Essentially proceedings must commence within 12 months of evidence relating to the offence coming to the notice of the prosecuting party, but action cannot be initiated more than three years after the offence took place. These provisions do not affect the usual time limits for criminal proceedings.

Jurisdiction and procedure in respect of offences

44.—(1) Summary proceedings for an offence under this Part may, without prejudice to any jurisdiction exercisable apart from this section, be taken against a body corporate or unincorporated association at any place at which it has a place of business and against an individual at any place where he is for the time being.

(2) Proceedings for an offence alleged to have been committed under this Part by an unincorporated association shall be brought in the name of the association (and not in that of any of its members), and for the purposes of any such proceedings any rules of court relating to the service of documents apply as in relation to a body corporate.

(3) Section 33 of the Criminal Justice Act 1925 and Schedule 3 to the Magistrates' Courts Act 1980 (procedure on charge of offence against a corporation) apply in a case in which an unincorporated association is charged in England and Wales with an offence under this Part as they apply in the case of a corporation.

(4) In relation to proceedings on indictment in Scotland for an offence alleged to have been committed under this Part by an unincorporated association, section 74 of the Criminal Procedure (Scotland) Act 1975 (proceedings on indictment against bodies corporate) applies as if the association were a body corporate.

(5) A fine imposed on an unincorporated association on its conviction of such an offence shall be paid out of the funds of the association.

DEFINITIONS
"body corporate": s.740, C.A. 1985.

GENERAL NOTE
This section deals with the jurisdiction of the courts and the procedures to be adopted. The main point is that proceedings against an unincorporated association are effectively to be undertaken as against corporate bodies, *i.e.* in their names and at any places where they carry on business. Likewise, any fines are payable from an unincorporated association's funds.

Supplementary provisions

Fees

45.—(1) An applicant for a recognition order under this Part shall pay such fee in respect of his application as may be prescribed; and no application shall be regarded as duly made unless this subsection is complied with.

(2) Every recognised supervisory or qualifying body shall pay such periodical fees to the Secretary of State as may be prescribed.

(3) In this section "prescribed" means prescribed by regulations made by the Secretary of State, which may make different provision for different cases or classes of case.

(4) Regulations under this section shall be made by statutory instrument which shall be subject to annulment in pursuance of a resolution of either House of Parliament.

(5) Fees received by the Secretary of State by virtue of this Part shall be paid into the Consolidated Fund.

DEFINTIONS AND CROSS REFERENCES
"recognised qualifying body": s.32, 1989 Act.
"recognised supervisory body": s.30, 1989 Act.

GENERAL NOTE
This section provides for the payment of fees by applicants for recognition and of periodical fees by recognised supervisory and qualifying bodies. Regulations governing the payment of fees will be set by statutory instrument, and the fees will be paid into the consolidated fund.

Delegation of functions of Secretary of State

46.—(1) The Secretary of State may by order (a "delegation order") establish a body corporate to exercise his functions under this Part.

(2) A delegation order has the effect of transferring to the body established by it, subject to such exceptions and reservations as may be specified in the order, all the functions of the Secretary of State under this Part except—
   (a) such functions under Part I of Schedule 14 (prevention of restrictive practices) as are excepted by regulations under section 47, and
   (b) his functions in relation to the body itself;
and the order may also confer on the body such other functions supplementary or incidental to those transferred as appear to the Secretary of State to be appropriate.

(3) Any transfer of the functions under the following provisions shall be subject to the reservation that they remain exercisable concurrently by the Secretary of State—
   (a) section 38 (power to call for information), and
   (b) section 40 (directions to comply with international obligations);
and any transfer of the function of refusing to approve an overseas qualification, or withdrawing such approval, on the grounds referred to in section 33(3) (lack of reciprocity) shall be subject to the reservation that the function is exercisable only with the consent of the Secretary of State.

(4) A delegation order may be amended or, if it appears to the Secretary of State that it is no longer in the public interest that the order should remain in force, revoked by a further order under this section.

(5) Where functions are transferred or resumed, the Secretary of State may by order confer or, as the case may be, take away such other functions supplementary or incidental to those transferred or resumed as appear to him to be appropriate.

(6) The provisions of Schedule 13 have effect with respect to the status, constitution and proceedings of a body established by a delegation order, the exercise by it of certain functions transferred to it and other supplementary matters.

(7) An order under this section shall be made by statutory instrument.

(8) An order which has the effect of transferring or resuming any functions shall not be made unless a draft of it has been laid before and approved by resolution of each House of Parliament; and any other description of order shall be subject to annulment in pursuance of a resolution of either House of Parliament.

DEFINITIONS AND CROSS REFERENCES
"body corporate" s.740, C.A. 1985.
"delegation order": s.46, 1989 Act.
"directions to comply with international obligations": s.40, 1989 Act.
"lack of reciprocity with regard to recognising professional qualifications": s.33(3), 1989 Act.
"overseas professional qualifications": s.33, 1989 Act.
"power to call for relevant information from recognised supervisory and qualifying bodies": s.38, 1989 Act.
"prevention of restrictive practices": s.47; Sched. 14, 1989 Act.

GENERAL NOTE
This section enables the Secretary of State, by order made by statutory instrument, to set up a body corporate to exercise his functions under Pt. II of the Act, concerning the Eligibility for Appointment as a Company Auditor. The order can delegate some or all of the Secretary of State's powers, except those preventing restrictive practices (s.14 and Sched. 14) and his relations with such a delegated body; and if this is done, the Secretary of State will still be able concurrently to exercise his power to call for relevant information from a recognised supervisory or qualifying body (s.38) and to give directions so that such bodies should comply with European Community and other international obligations (s.40). Moreover, the delegated body will only be able to refuse or withdraw approval of an overseas qualification on the grounds of lack of reciprocity (s.33(3)) with the consent of the Secretary of State.

Subss. (4) and (5) provide that a delegation order can be revoked in whole or in part or be varied by a further order made by statutory statement. Sched. 13, "Supplementary provisions with respect to delegation order", has effect with regard to the delegation of the Secretary of State's powers, and its provisions deal with the status, constitution and proceedings of the delegated body, the exercise by it of functions transferred to it, and other supplementary matters.

Restrictive practices

47.—(1) The provisions of Schedule 14 have effect with respect to certain matters relating to restrictive practices and competition law.

(2) The Secretary of State may make provision by regulations as to the discharge of the functions under paragraphs 1 to 7 of that Schedule when a delegation order is in force.

(3) The regulations may—
(a) except any function from the effect of the delegation order,
(b) modify any of the provisions mentioned in subsection (2), and
(c) impose such duties on the body established by the delegation order, the Secretary of State and Director General of Fair Trading as appear to the Secretary of State to be appropriate.

(4) The regulations shall contain such provision as appears to the Secretary of State to be necessary or expedient for reserving to him the decision—
(a) to refuse recognition on the ground mentioned in paragraph 1(3) of that Schedule, or
(b) to exercise the powers conferred by paragraph 6 of that Schedule.

(5) For that purpose the regulations may—
(a) prohibit the body from granting a recognition order without the leave of the Secretary of State, and
(b) empower the Secretary of State to direct the body to exercise its powers in such manner as may be specified in the direction.

(6) Regulations under this section shall be made by statutory instrument which shall be subject to annulment in pursuance of a resolution of either House of Parliament.

DEFINITIONS AND CROSS REFERENCES
"delegation order": s.46(1), 1989 Act.
"recognition of a professional qualification": ss.31–33, 1989 Act.
"recognition of a supervisory body": s.30, Sched. 11, 1989 Act.

GENERAL NOTE
This section, together with Sched. 14, provides a special competition regime for recognised supervisory and qualifying bodies. The Secretary of State is placed under a duty not to recognise a body unless he is satisfied that its rules and guidance do not restrict, distort or prevent competition to a greater extent than is reasonably justifiable having regard to the purposes of Pt. II of the Act. He may also take action if he subsequently regards any rules or practices as unjustifiably restricting, distorting or preventing competition. He may only exercise his powers after he has considered any report from the Director General of Fair Trading, who is also charged with keeping the rules and guidance in question under review. Certain consequential exemptions are made to competition law.

Subs. (2)
Under this subsection, where a delegation order is in force (see s.46) the Secretary of State can by regulations established by statutory instrument make provision for the discharge of functions under Sched. 14, paras. 1–7.

Subs. (3)
Under this subsection, the regulations may exempt any function from the delegation order, modify the provisions of Sched. 14, paras. 1–7 and impose other appropriate duties on the delegated body.

Subs. (4)
By this subsection, the regulations may also reserve powers to the Secretary of State where competition appears to be significantly impeded both to refuse recognition of a supervisory or qualifying body; and to revoke recognition or to direct the body to remedy the position or alter its rules.

Subs. (5)
In order to ensure that such authority is not overridden, this subsection indicates that the regulations may prohibit the delegated body from issuing a recognition order without the consent of the Secretary of State and empower him to direct the body to use its powers in a particular way.

Exemption from liability for damages

48.—(1) Neither a recognised supervisory body, nor any of its officers or employees or members of its governing body, shall be liable in damages for anything done or omitted in the discharge or purported discharge of functions to which this subsection applies, unless the act or omission is shown to have been in bad faith.

(2) Subsection (1) applies to the functions of the body so far as relating to, or to matters arising out of—
  (a) such rules, practices, powers and arrangements of the body to which the requirements of Part II of Schedule 11 apply, or
  (b) the obligations with which paragraph 16 of that Schedule requires the body to comply,
  (c) any guidance issued by the body, or
  (d) the obligations to which the body is subject by virtue of this Part.

(3) Neither a body established by a delegation order, nor any of its members, officers or employees, shall be liable in damages for anything done or omitted in the discharge or purported discharge of the functions exercisable by virtue of an order under section 46, unless the act or omission is shown to have been in bad faith.

DEFINITIONS AND CROSS REFERENCES
"guidance (of a supervisory body)": s.30(4), 1989 Act.
"members of its governing body": s.30(2), 1989 Act.

"officers": see s.744, C.A. 1985.
"recognised supervisory body": s.30, 1989 Act.

GENERAL NOTE
This section (which was inserted into the Bill during its progress through Parliament) deals with the exemption of recognised supervisory bodies and delegated bodies, and their officers, employees and governing members, from liability for damages unless it is shown that their acts or omissions were made in bad faith. With regard to supervisory bodies, this relates to the rules, practices, powers and arrangements of the body concerned with the granting of professional qualifications and the means of assuring that members are fit and proper persons to be auditors, as well as dealing with such matters as professional integrity and independence; technical standards; procedures for maintaining competence; monitoring and enforcing compliance with rules; procedures relating to the admission, discipline and expulsion of members; the investigation of complaints; meeting claims arising out of audit work; the keeping of a register of auditors open to public scrutiny (see ss.35–36); and the promotion and maintenance of standards. The exemptions from liability to damages also extends to any guidance offered by the supervisory body and the obligations to which it is subject under Pt. II of the Act.

Service of notices

49.—(1) This section has effect in relation to any notice, direction or other document required or authorised by or under this Part to be given to or served on any person other than the Secretary of State.

(2) Any such document may be given to or served on the person in question—
  (a) by delivering it to him,
  (b) by leaving it at his proper address, or
  (c) by sending it by post to him at that address.

(3) Any such document may—
  (a) in the case of a body corporate, be given to or served on the secretary or clerk of that body;
  (b) in the case of a partnership, be given to or served on any partner;
  (c) in the case of an unincorporated association other than a partnership, be given to or served on any member of the governing body of the association.

(4) For the purposes of this section and section 7 of the Interpretation Act 1978 (service of documents by post) in its application to this section, the proper address of any person is his last known address (whether of his residence or of a place where he carries on business or is employed) and also—
  (a) in the case of a person who is eligible under the rules of a recognised supervisory body for appointment as company auditor and who does not have a place of business in the United Kingdom, the address of that body;
  (b) in the case of a body corporate, its secretary or its clerk, the address of its registered or principal office in the United Kingdom;
  (c) in the case of an unincorporated association (other than a partnership) or a member of its governing body, its principal office in the United Kingdom.

DEFINITIONS AND CROSS REFERENCES
"address": s.49(4), 1989 Act.
"body corporate": s.740, C.A. 1985.
"secretary": s.283, C.A. 1985.

GENERAL NOTE
This section sets out the manner in which a notice, direction or other document can be given or served on any person other than the Secretary of State. Service may be by delivery or by leaving or posting the document to the proper address (defined in subs. (4)). In the

case of a body corporate it should be served on the secretary, while for a partnership or an unincorporated association respectively on a partner or a member of the governing body.

Power to make consequential amendments

50.—(1) The Secretary of State may by regulations make such amendments of enactments as appear to him to be necessary or expedient in consequence of the provisions of this Part having effect in place of section 389 of the Companies Act 1985.

(2) That power extends to making such amendments as appear to the Secretary of State necessary or expedient of—
  (a) enactments referring by name to the bodies of accountants recognised for the purposes of section 389(1)(a) of the Companies Act 1985, and
  (b) enactments making with respect to other statutory auditors provision as to the matters dealt with in relation to company auditors by section 389 of the Companies Act 1985.

(3) The provision which may be made with respect to other statutory auditors includes provision as to—
  (a) eligibility for the appointment,
  (b) the effect of appointing a partnership which is not a legal person and the manner of exercise of the auditor's rights in such a case, and
  (c) ineligibility on the ground of lack of independence or any other ground.

(4) The regulations may contain such supplementary, incidental and transitional provision as appears to the Secretary of State to be necessary or expedient.

(5) The Secretary of State shall not make regulations under this section with respect to any statutory auditors without the consent of—
  (a) the Minister responsible for their appointment or responsible for the body or person by, or in relation to whom, they are appointed, or
  (b) if there is no such Minister, the person by whom they are appointed.

(6) In this section a "statutory auditor" means a person appointed auditor in pursuance of any enactment authorising or requiring the appointment of an auditor or auditors.

(7) Regulations under this section shall be made by statutory instrument which shall be subject to annulment in pursuance of a resolution of either House of Parliament.

GENERAL NOTE

The Bill presented to Parliament included a Schedule detailing the extensive consequential amendments to other enactments which contain provisions for appointing auditors who would be qualified to audit company accounts. In committee the Schedule was dropped, and s.50(1) now empowers the Secretary of State to make regulations to secure the necessary equivalence. Subss. (2)–(7) indicate his obligations in this respect and the limits to his powers.

Power to make provision in consequence of changes affecting accountancy bodies

51.—(1) The Secretary of State may by regulations make such amendments of enactments as appear to him to be necessary or expedient in consequence of any change of name, merger or transfer of engagements affecting—
  (a) a recognised supervisory or qualifying body under this Part, or
  (b) a body of accountants referred to in, or approved, authorised or otherwise recognised for the purposes of, any other enactment.

(2) Regulations under this section shall be made by statutory instrument which shall be subject to annulment in pursuance of a resolution of either House of Parliament.

DEFINITIONS AND CROSS REFERENCES
"recognised qualifying body": s.32, 1989 Act.
"recognised supervisory body": s.30, 1989 Act.

GENERAL NOTE
This section was inserted in committee and empowers the Secretary of State to make amendments by statutory instrument required because of changes in the names of recognised supervisory or qualifying bodies or because of mergers between bodies.

Meaning of "associate"

52.—(1) In this Part "associate," in relation to a person, shall be construed as follows.
(2) In relation to an individual "associate" means—
   (a) that individual's spouse or minor child or step-child,
   (b) any body corporate of which that individual is a director, and
   (c) any employee or partner of that individual.
(3) In relation to a body corporate "associate" means—
   (a) any body corporate of which that body is a director,
   (b) any body corporate in the same group as that body, and
   (c) any employee or partner of that body or of any body corporate in the same group.
(4) In relation to a Scottish firm, or a partnership constituted under the law of any other country or territory in which a partnership is a legal person, "associate" means—
   (a) any body corporate of which the firm is a director,
   (b) any employee of or partner in the firm, and
   (c) any person who is an associate of a partner in the firm.
(5) In relation to a partnership constituted under the law of England and Wales or Northern Ireland, or the law of any other country or territory in which a partnership is not a legal person, "associate" means any person who is an associate of any of the partners.

DEFINITIONS AND CROSS REFERENCES
"body corporate": s.740, C.A. 1985.
"firm": s.53(1), 1989 Act.

GENERAL NOTE
This section defines the meaning of the word "associate" in relation to an individual (subs. (1)), a body corporate (subs. (2)), a partnership where that is a separate legal person (*e.g.* in Scotland) (subs. (3)) and a partnership where that is *not* a separate legal person (*e.g.* in England and Wales or in Northern Ireland) (subs. (5)).

Minor definitions

53.—(1) In this Part—
"address" means—
   (a) in relation to an individual, his usual residential or business address, and
   (b) in relation to a firm, its registered or principal office in Great Britain;
"company" means any company or other body to which section 384 of the Companies Act 1985 (duty to appoint auditors) applies;
"director", in relation to a body corporate, includes any person occupying in relation to it the position of a director (by whatever name called) and any person in accordance with whose directions or instructions (not being advice given in a

professional capacity) the directors of the body are accustomed to act;

"enactment" includes an enactment contained in subordinate legislation within the meaning of the Interpretation Act 1978;

"firm" means a body corporate or a partnership;

"group", in relation to a body corporate, means the body corporate, any other body corporate which is its holding company or subsidiary and any other body corporate which is a subsidiary of that holding company; and

"holding company" and "subsidiary" have the meaning given by section 736 of the Companies Act 1985;

"parent undertaking" and "subsidiary undertaking" have the same meaning as in Part VII of the Companies Act 1985.

(2) For the purposes of this Part a body shall be regarded as "established in the United Kingdom" if and only if—

(a) it is incorporated or formed under the law of the United Kingdom or a part of the United Kingdom, or

(b) its central management and control is exercised in the United Kingdom;

and any reference to a qualification "obtained in the United Kingdom" is to a qualification obtained from such a body.

GENERAL NOTE

This section defines the meaning of the following: "address," "company," "director," "enactment", "firm," "group," "holding company," "subsidiary," "parent undertaking," "subsidiary undertaking," "established in the United Kingdom," and (with regard to a professional qualification) "obtained in the United Kingdom."

Index of defined expressions

54. The following Table shows provisions defining or otherwise explaining expressions used in this Part (other than provisions defining or explaining an expression used only in the same section)—

address	section 53(1)
appropriate qualification	section 31
associate	section 52
company	section 53(1)
company auditor, company audit and company audit work	section 24(2)
delegation order	section 46
director (of a body corporate)	section 53(1)
Director (in Schedule 14)	paragraph 1(1) of that Schedule
enactment	section 53(1)
established in the United Kingdom	section 53(2)
firm	section 53(1)
group (in relation to a body corporate)	section 53(1)
guidance	
-of a qualifying body	section 32(3)
-of a supervisory body	section 30(4)
holding company	section 53(1)
member (of a supervisory body)	section 30(2)
obtained in the United Kingdom	section 53(2)
parent undertaking	section 53(1)
purposes of this Part	section 24(1)
qualifying body	section 32(1)
recognised	

-in relation to a professional qualification	section 32(4) and Schedule 12
-in relation to a qualifying body	paragraph 2(1) of Schedule 12
-in relation to a supervisory body	section 30(5) and Schedule 11
rules	
-of a qualifying body	section 32(2)
-of a supervisory body	section 30(3)
subsidiary and subsidiary undertaking	section 53(1)
supervisory body	section 30(1)

GENERAL NOTE

This section provides an index of provisions defining or otherwise explaining expressions used in Pt. II of the Act concerning the Eligibility for Appointment as Company Auditor.

PART III

INVESTIGATIONS AND POWERS TO OBTAIN INFORMATION

Amendments of the Companies Act 1985

Investigations by inspectors not leading to published report

55. In section 432 of the Companies Act 1985 (appointment of inspectors by Secretary of State), after subsection (2) (investigation of circumstances suggesting misconduct) insert—

"(2A) Inspectors may be appointed under subsection (2) on terms that any report they may make is not for publication; and in such a case, the provisions of section 437(3) (availability and publication of inspectors' reports) do not apply.".

GENERAL NOTE

This section inserts a new subsection into s.432 of the Companies Act 1985 (Other company investigations either at the instigation of the court or at the discretion of the Secretary of State) which provides that inspectors may be appointed on terms that any report they make will not be for publication and in such cases the existing usual rules governing the availability and publication of inspectors' reports do not apply. In such instances, the fact that an investigation is taking place will not be announced, as is the case currently in relation to investigations under s.447 of the Companies Act 1985 and ss.105 and 177 of the Financial Services Act 1986. The aim of the provision is to speed up the investigation, the purpose of which is to decide whether an offence has been committed or whether there are grounds for regulatory action. It is not intended to be used where the public interest requires a published report.

Production of documents and evidence to inspectors

56.—(1) Section 434 of the Companies Act 1985 (production of documents and evidence to inspectors) is amended as follows.

(2) In subsection (1) (duty of officers to assist inspectors), for "books and documents" substitute "documents".

(3) For subsection (2) (power to require production of documents, attendance or other assistance) substitute—

"(2) If the inspectors consider that an officer or agent of the company or other body corporate, or any other person, is or may be in possession of information relating to a matter which they believe to be relevant to the investigation, they may require him—

(a) to produce to them any documents in his custody or power relating to that matter,
(b) to attend before them, and
(c) otherwise to give them all assistance in connection with the investigation which he is reasonably able to give;

and it is that person's duty to comply with the requirement.".

(4) For subsection (3) (power to examine on oath) substitute—

"(3) An inspector may for the purposes of the investigation examine any person on oath, and may administer an oath accordingly.

(5) After subsection (5) insert—

"(6) In this section "documents" includes information recorded in any form; and, in relation to information recorded otherwise than in legible form, the power to require its production includes power to require the production of a copy of the information in legible form.".

(6) In section 436 of the Companies Act 1985 (obstruction of inspectors treated as contempt of court), for subsections (1) and (2) substitute—

"(1) If any person—
(a) fails to comply with section 434(1)(a) or (c),
(b) refuses to comply with a requirement under section 434(1)(b) or (2), or
(c) refuses to answer any question put to him by the inspectors for the purposes of the investigation,

the inspectors may certify that fact in writing to the court.".

GENERAL NOTE

This section amends and extends the provisions of ss.434 and 436 of the Companies Act 1985. In the past, the power of inspectors to question people generally was limited to those persons who are or who had been officers or agents of the company being investigated. This section extends this power of interrogation to include "any person" and correspondingly makes that person liable also for contempt proceedings, should he or she deliberately or recklessly answer falsely or refuse to cooperate.

This section is also the first of many instances where the previously used term "books and papers" has been replaced wherever it appears in Pt. XIV of the Companies Act 1985 by the more widely defined term "documents," which includes information recorded in any form, together with a power to require a copy to be produced in a legible form.

Duty of inspectors to report

57. In section 437 of the Companies Act 1985 (inspectors' reports), after subsection (1A) insert—

"(1B) If it appears to the Secretary of State that matters have come to light in the course of the inspectors' investigation which suggest that a criminal offence has been committed, and those matters have been referred to the appropriate prosecuting authority, he may direct the inspectors to take no further steps in the investigation or to take only such further steps as are specified in the direction.

(1C) Where an investigation is the subject of a direction under subsection (1B), the inspectors shall make a final report to the Secretary of State only where—
(a) they were appointed under section 432(1) (appointment in pursuance of an order of the court), or
(b) the Secretary of State directs them to do so.".

GENERAL NOTE

This section inserts new subsections into s.437 of the Companies Act 1985 to enable the Secretary of State to order an investigation by inspectors appointed under that Act to be stopped or to be proceeded with only as directed by him, where it appears that evidence of a criminal offence has been uncovered and which has been referred to the relevant prosecuting authority. In such instances the inspectors shall not make a final report unless directed to do so by the Secretary of State or if appointed by the court. It is a matter of D.T.I. practice that the relevant prosecuting authorities are consulted in appropriate cases.

Note this provision does not give the Secretary of State carte blanche to stop or curtail an investigation for any reason. Matters must have come to light suggesting a criminal offence and these matters referred to the appropriate prosecuting authority. If the latter did not decide to prosecute, then it would still be open to the Secretary of State, in light of new facts and if it was in the public interest, to appoint inspectors to carry out a new investigation. Indeed, he could reappoint the same persons as inspectors so that they could carry on where they left off.

Power to bring civil proceedings on the company's behalf

58. In section 438 of the Companies Act 1985 (power to bring civil proceedings on the company's behalf), for the opening words of subsection (1) down to "it appears to the Secretary of State" substitute "If from any report made or information obtained under this Part it appears to the Secretary of State".

GENERAL NOTE

This section extends s.438 of the Companies Act 1985 so that the Secretary of State may bring civil proceedings on behalf of the investigated company on the basis of any report made or information received under Pt. XIV of the Companies Act 1985 and not simply, as previously was the case, on information obtained under ss.447 and 448 or reports under s.437. Now action may be taken on information obtained under s.444 (power to investigate share ownership without the appointment of inspectors) and s.437(1)(a), which enable information to be given or obtained from inspectors without a formal report.

Expenses of investigating a company's affairs

59.—(1) Section 439 of the Companies Act 1985 (expenses of investigating a company's affairs) is amended as follows.

(2) For subsection (1) substitute—

"(1) The expenses of an investigation under any of the powers conferred by this Part shall be defrayed in the first instance by the Secretary of State, but he may recover those expenses from the persons liable in accordance with this section.

There shall be treated as expenses of the investigation, in particular, such reasonable sums as the Secretary of State may determine in respect of general staff costs and overheads.".

(3) In subsection (4) for "the inspectors' report" substitute "an inspectors' report".

(4) For subsection (5) substitute—

"(5) Where inspectors were appointed—
  (a) under section 431, or
  (b) on an application under section 442(3),
the applicant or applicants for the investigation is or are liable to such extent (if any) as the Secretary of State may direct.".

GENERAL NOTE

This section amends s.439 of the Companies Act 1985 so as to extend the circumstances in which the costs and expenses of an investigation under that section can be recovered. While these monies usually will be defrayed initially by the Secretary of State, he is empowered to recover them from the persons liable, in accordance with s.439 (*e.g.* from the applicants under s.431, or any party successfully prosecuted).

Note "expenses" are such reasonable sums as he may determine in respect of general staff costs and overheads. "Staff costs" are the investigators' salaries. While outside investigators' fees were recoverable, now the costs of official salaries (*i.e.* internal D.T.I. investigative staff salaries) are also recoverable.

Power of Secretary of State to present winding-up petition

60.—(1) Section 440 of the Companies Act 1985 (power of Secretary of State to present winding-up petition) is repealed; but the following amendments have the effect of re-enacting that provision, with modifications.

(2) In section 124(4) of the Insolvency Act 1986 (application by Secretary of State for company to be wound up by the court), for paragraph (b) substitute—

"(b) in a case falling within section 124A below.".

(3) After that section insert—

"Petition for winding up on grounds of public interest

124A.—(1) Where it appears to the Secretary of State from—

(a) any report made or information obtained under Part XIV of the Companies Act 1985 (company investigations, &c.),

(b) any report made under section 94 or 177 of the Financial Services Act 1986 or any information obtained under section 105 of that Act,

(c) any information obtained under section 2 of the Criminal Justice Act 1987 or section 52 of the Criminal Justice (Scotland) Act 1987 (fraud investigations), or

(d) any information obtained under section 83 of the Companies Act 1989 (powers exercisable for purpose of assisting overseas regulatory authorities),

that it is expedient in the public interest that a company should be wound up, he may present a petition for it to be wound up if the court thinks it just and equitable for it to be so.

(2) This section does not apply if the company is already being wound up by the court.".

GENERAL NOTE

This section repeals s.440 of the Companies Act 1985, which gave the Secretary of State power to present a winding up petition to the court and amends the Insolvency Act 1986. The provisions of s.440 are re-enacted in that latter Act, entitling him, after receiving information from various types of investigation, to petition that it is expedient and in the public interest that the company investigated be wound up if the court thinks it just and equitable to do so.

Inspectors' reports as evidence

61. In section 441 of the Companies Act 1985 (inspectors' reports to be evidence), in subsection (1) for "sections 431 or 432" substitute "this Part".

GENERAL NOTE

This section extends s.441 of the Companies Act 1985 so that all reports made by inspectors under s.437 of that Act and not just those made under ss.431 and 432, are admissible in any legal proceedings as evidence of the opinion of the inspectors in relation to any matter contained in a report.

Investigation of company ownership

62. In section 442 of the Companies Act 1985 (power to investigate company ownership), for subsection (3) (investigation on application by members of company) substitute—

"(3) If an application for investigation under this section with respect to particular shares or debentures of a company is made to the Secretary of State by members of the company, and the number of applicants or the amount of shares held by them is not less than that required for an application for the appointment of inspectors under section 431(2)(a) or (b), then, subject to the following provisions, the Secretary of State shall appoint inspectors to conduct the investigation applied for.

(3A) The Secretary of State shall not appoint inspectors if he is satisfied that the application is vexatious; and where inspectors are appointed their terms of appointment shall exclude any matter in so far as the Secretary of State is satisfied that it is unreasonable for it to be investigated.

(3B) The Secretary of State may, before appointing inspectors, require the applicant or applicants to give security, to an amount not exceeding £5,000, or such other sum as he may by order specify, for payment of the costs of the investigation.

An order under this subsection shall be made by statutory instrument which shall be subject to annulment in pursuance of a resolution of either House of Parliament.

(3C) If on an application under subsection (3) it appears to the Secretary of State that the powers conferred by section 444 are sufficient for the purposes of investigating the matters which inspectors would be appointed to investigate, he may instead conduct the investigation under that section."

GENERAL NOTE

This section remodels s.442(3) of the Companies Act 1985 so that the Secretary of State's obligation to appoint inspectors under s.442, if an application is made by the requisite number of people, is removed in certain circumstances, namely, if the application is vexatious or it is unreasonable for the matter to be investigated (which grounds are not new), but also he may now decline to appoint inspectors if it appears to him that the powers in s.444 are sufficient to deal with the matter.

In addition, if he does decide to appoint inspectors he may require those persons seeking the investigation to give security of up to £5,000. He may also increase the maximum figure as security by a statutory instrument subject only to annulment by a resolution of either House of Parliament.

Secretary of State's power to require production of documents

63.—(1) Section 447 of the Companies Act 1985 (power of Secretary of State to require production of documents) is amended as follows.

(2) Omit subsection (1) (bodies in relation to which powers exercisable), and—
  (a) in subsections (2) and (3) for "any such body" substitute "a company",
  (b) in subsections (4) and (5) for "any body" and "a body" substitute "a company", and
  (c) in subsections (5) and (6) for "the body" substitute "the company".

(3) For "books or papers", wherever occurring, substitute "documents".

(4) In subsection (3) (power to authorise officer to require production of documents) after "an officer of his" insert "or any other competent person", after "the officer" in the first place where it occurs insert "or other person" and for "the officer" in the second place where it occurs substitute "he (the officer or other person)".

(5) In subsection (4) (power to require production of documents in possession of third party) after "an officer of his" and after "the officer" (twice) insert "or other person".

(6) In subsection (6), for the second sentence substitute—
  "Sections 732 (restriction on prosecutions), 733 (liability of individuals for corporate default) and 734 (criminal proceedings against unincorporated bodies) apply to this offence.".

(7) After subsection (8) insert—
  "(9) In this section "documents" includes information recorded in any form; and, in relation to information recorded otherwise than in legible form, the power to require its production includes power to require the production of a copy of it in legible form.".

(8) In Schedule 24 to the Companies Act 1985 (punishment of offences), in the entry relating to section 447(6), for "books and papers" substitute "documents".

GENERAL NOTE

This section amends s.447 of the Companies Act 1985, which empowers the Secretary of State to require the production of documents so as to allow him to authorise any competent person (including persons who are not his officers) to exercise on his behalf certain powers conferred by that section.

Entry and search of premises

64.—(1) For section 448 of the Companies Act 1985 (entry and search of premises) substitute—

"**Entry and search of premises**

448.—(1) A justice of the peace may issue a warrant under this section if satisfied on information on oath given by or on behalf of the Secretary of State, or by a person appointed or authorised to exercise powers under this Part, that there are reasonable grounds for believing that there are on any premises documents whose production has been required under this Part and which have not been produced in compliance with the requirement.

(2) A justice of the peace may also issue a warrant under this section if satisfied on information on oath given by or on behalf of the Secretary of State, or by a person appointed or authorised to exercise powers under this Part—

(a) that there are reasonable grounds for believing that an offence has been committed for which the penalty on conviction on indictment is imprisonment for a term of not less than two years and that there are on any premises documents relating to whether the offence has been committed,

(b) that the Secretary of State, or the person so appointed or authorised, has power to require the production of the documents under this Part, and

(c) that there are reasonable grounds for believing that if production was so required the documents would not be produced but would be removed from the premises, hidden, tampered with or destroyed.

(3) A warrant under this section shall authorise a constable, together with any other person named in it and any other constables—

(a) to enter the premises specified in the information, using such force as is reasonably necessary for the purpose;

(b) to search the premises and take possession of any documents appearing to be such documents as are mentioned in subsection (1) or (2), as the case may be, or to take, in relation to any such documents, any other steps which may appear to be necessary for preserving them or preventing interference with them;

(c) to take copies of any such documents; and

(d) to require any person named in the warrant to provide an explanation of them or to state where they may be found.

(4) If in the case of a warrant under subsection (2) the justice of the peace is satisfied on information on oath that there are reasonable grounds for believing that there are also on the premises other documents relevant to the investigation, the warrant shall also authorise the actions mentioned in subsection (3) to be taken in relation to such documents.

(5) A warrant under this section shall continue in force until the end of the period of one month beginning with the day on which it is issued.

(6) Any documents of which possession is taken under this section may be retained—
  (a) for a period of three months; or
  (b) if within that period proceedings to which the documents are relevant are commenced against any person for any criminal offence, until the conclusion of those proceedings.

(7) Any person who intentionally obstructs the exercise of any rights conferred by a warrant issued under this section or fails without reasonable excuse to comply with any requirement imposed in accordance with subsection (3)(d) is guilty of an offence and liable to a fine.

Sections 732 (restriction on prosecutions), 733 (liability of individuals for corporate default) and 734 (criminal proceedings against unincorporated bodies) apply to this offence.

(8) For the purposes of sections 449 and 451A (provision for security of information) documents obtained under this section shall be treated as if they had been obtained under the provision of this Part under which their production was or, as the case may be, could have been required.

(9) In the application of this section to Scotland for the references to a justice of the peace substitute references to a justice of the peace or a sheriff, and for the references to information on oath substitute references to evidence on oath.

(10) In this section 'document' includes information recorded in any form.".

(2) In Schedule 24 to the Companies Act 1985 (punishment of offences), in the entry relating to section 448(5)—
  (a) in the first column for "448(5)" substitute "448(7)", and
  (b) for the entry in the second column substitute—
   "Obstructing the exercise of any rights conferred by a warrant or failing to comply with a requirement imposed under subsection (3)(d).".

GENERAL NOTE

This section amends and extends the power to enter and search premises available to inspectors under s.448 of the Companies Act 1985. It enables any person exercising investigation powers under Pt. XIV of that Act to apply for an entry and search warrant in respect of documents which have not been produced in compliance with a requirement imposed under those powers. The section also introduces in subs. (2) a provision enabling such warrants to be granted in relation to documents which have not been requested where there are reasonable grounds for believing that a serious offence has been committed and that the relevant documents may be tampered with or destroyed. Documents seized may be copied and persons named in the warrant asked to explain them. Each warrant is valid for one month and seized documents may be retained for up to three months or longer if criminal proceedings are commenced within that time. It is an offence to obstruct a search or fail to explain seized documents.

Provision for security of information obtained

65.—(1) Section 449 of the Companies Act 1985 (provision for security of information obtained) is amended as follows.

(2) In subsection (1) (purposes for which disclosure permitted)—
  (a) in the opening words for "body" (twice) substitute "company";
  (b) for paragraph (c) substitute—
   "(c) for the purposes of enabling or assisting any inspector

appointed under this Part, or under section 94 or 177 of the Financial Services Act 1986, to discharge his functions;";
  (c) after that paragraph insert —
    "(cc) for the purpose of enabling or assisting any person authorised to exercise powers under section 44 of the Insurance Companies Act 1982, section 447 of this Act, section 106 of the Financial Services Act 1986 or section 84 of the Companies Act 1989 to discharge his functions;";
  (d) in paragraph (d) for "or the Financial Services Act 1986" substitute, ", the Financial Services Act 1986 or Part II, III or VII of the Companies Act 1989,";
  (e) omit paragraph (e);
  (f) in paragraph (h) for "(n) or (1p)" substitute "or (n)";
  (g) after that paragraph insert—
    "(hh) for the purpose of enabling or assisting a body established by order under section 46 of the Companies Act 1989 to discharge its functions under Part II of that Act, or of enabling or assisting a recognised supervisory or qualifying body within the meaning of that Part to discharge its functions as such;";
  (h) after paragraph (l) insert—
    "(ll) with a view to the institution of, or otherwise for the purposes of, any disciplinary proceedings relating to the discharge by a public servant of his duties;";
  (i) for paragraph (m) substitute—
    "(m) for the purpose of enabling or assisting an overseas regulatory authority to exercise its regulatory functions.".
(3) For subsection (1A) substitute—
  "(1A) In subsection (1)—
    (a) in paragraph (ll) "public servant" means an officer or servant of the Crown or of any public or other authority for the time being designated for the purposes of that paragraph by the Secretary of State by order made by statutory instrument; and
    (b) in paragraph (m) "overseas regulatory authority" and "regulatory functions" have the same meaning as in section 82 of the Companies Act 1989.".
(4) In subsection (1B) (disclosure to designated public authorities) for "designated for the purposes of this section" substitute "designated for the purposes of this subsection".
(5) In subsection (2), for the second sentence substitute—
  "Sections 732 (restriction on prosecutions), 733 (liability of individuals for corporate default) and 734 (criminal proceedings against unincorporated bodies) apply to this offence.".
(6) For subsection (3) substitute—
  "(3) For the purposes of this section each of the following is a competent authority—
    (a) the Secretary of State,
    (b) an inspector appointed under this Part or under section 94 or 177 of the Financial Services Act 1986,
    (c) any person authorised to exercise powers under section 44 of the Insurance Companies Act 1982, section 447 of this Act, section 106 of the Financial Services Act 1986 or section 84 of the Companies Act 1989,
    (d) the Department of Economic Development in Northern Ireland,
    (e) the Treasury,
    (f) the Bank of England,
    (g) the Lord Advocate,

(h) the Director of Public Prosecutions, and the Director of Public Prosecutions for Northern Ireland,
(i) any designated agency or transferee body within the meaning of the Financial Services Act 1986, and any body administering a scheme under section 54 of or paragraph 18 of Schedule 11 to that Act (schemes for compensation of investors),
(j) the Chief Registrar of friendly societies and the Registrar of Friendly Societies for Northern Ireland,
(k) the Industrial Assurance Commissioner and the Industrial Assurance Commissioner for Northern Ireland,
(l) any constable,
(m) any procurator fiscal.

(3A) Any information which may by virtue of this section be disclosed to a competent authority may be disclosed to any officer or servant of the authority.".

(7) In subsection (4) (orders) for "subsection (1B)" substitute "subsection (1A)(a) or (1B).".

GENERAL NOTE

This section amends s.449 of the Companies Act 1985, which provides for the security of information obtained, to extend the purposes for which and the persons to whom information obtained under ss.447 and 448 of that Act may be disclosed. It prohibits the unauthorised disclosure of information obtained under investigation powers to any person other than a competent authority as defined in s.449 as extended by this new section. A competent authority now includes any officer or servant of the authority. In particular this section permits disclosure for the purposes of any disciplinary proceedings against public servants for misconduct, breach of instructions or even gross negligence for example in relation to price-sensitive information.

Punishment for destroying, mutilating, &c. company documents

66.—(1) Section 450 of the Companies Act 1985 (punishment for destroying, mutilating, &c. company documents) is amended as follows.

(2) In subsection (1) for the opening words down to "insurance company" substitute "An officer of a company, or of an insurance company," for "body's" substitute "company's" and for "the body" substitute "the company".

(3) For subsection (4) substitute—

"(4) Sections 732 (restriction on prosecutions), 733 (liability of individuals for corporate default) and 734 (criminal proceedings against unincorporated bodies) apply to an offence under this section.".

(4) After that subsection insert—

"(5) In this section "document" includes information recorded in any form.".

GENERAL NOTE

This section makes minor amendments to s.450 of the Companies Act 1985, which provides punishments for the destruction or mutilation of company documents to conceal its state of affairs or frustrate an investigation.

Punishment for furnishing false information

67. In section 451 of the Companies Act 1985 (punishment for furnishing false information), for the second sentence substitute—

"Sections 732 (restriction on prosecutions), 733 (liability of individuals for corporate default) and 734 (criminal proceedings against unincorporated bodies) apply to this offence.".

GENERAL NOTE

This section makes a minor amendment to s.451 of the Companies Act 1985 which provides punishment for giving false information in an investigation.

Disclosure of information by Secretary of State or inspector

68. For section 451A of the Companies Act 1985 (disclosure of information by the Secretary of State) substitute—

> **"Disclosure of information by Secretary of State or inspector**
>
> 451A.—(1) This section applies to information obtained under sections 434 to 446.
>
> (2) The Secretary of State may, if he thinks fit—
>
>   (a) disclose any information to which this section applies to any person to whom, or for any purpose for which, disclosure is permitted under section 449, or
>
>   (b) authorise or require an inspector appointed under this Part to disclose such information to any such person or for any such purpose.
>
> (3) Information to which this section applies may also be disclosed by an inspector appointed under this Part to—
>
>   (a) another inspector appointed under this Part or an inspector appointed under section 94 or 177 of the Financial Services Act 1986, or
>
>   (b) a person authorised to exercise powers under section 44 of the Insurance Companies Act 1982, section 447 of this Act, section 106 of the Financial Services Act 1986 or section 84 of the Companies Act 1989.
>
> (4) Any information which may by virtue of subsection (3) be disclosed to any person may be disclosed to any officer or servant of that person.
>
> (5) The Secretary of State may, if he thinks fit, disclose any information obtained under section 444 to—
>
>   (a) the company whose ownership was the subject of the investigation,
>
>   (b) any member of the company,
>
>   (c) any person whose conduct was investigated in the course of the investigation,
>
>   (d) the auditors of the company, or
>
>   (e) any person whose financial interests appear to the Secretary of State to be affected by matters covered by the investigation.".

GENERAL NOTE

This section amends and extends s.451A of the Companies Act 1985 (disclosure of information by the Secretary of State) so as to permit inspectors appointed under Pt. XIV of that Act also to disclose information obtained under ss.443 to 446 of that Act. Information may be disclosed by the Secretary of State or an inspector to assist any other inspector or person authorised acting under Pt. XIV of the 1985 Act or under relevant provisions of the Companies Act 1989 or the Financial Services Act 1986.

Under the 1989 Act, disclosure is permitted to assist the new supervisory bodies for company auditors (see Pt. II) or in relation to disciplinary proceedings against public servants or to assist an overseas regulatory authority (see Pt. III). In relation to the power to obtain information concerning persons interested in shares, the Secretary of State now may disclose information obtained to certain persons (s.451A(5)) at his discretion.

Protection of banking information

69.—(1) Section 452 of the Companies Act 1985 (privileged information) is amended as follows.

(2) In subsection (1), omit paragraph (b) (disclosure by bankers of information relating to their customers).

(3) After that subsection insert—

"(1A) Nothing in section 434, 443 or 446 requires a person (except as mentioned in subsection (1B) below) to disclose information or produce documents in respect of which he owes an obligation of confidence by virtue of carrying on the business of banking unless—
(a) the person to whom the obligation of confidence is owed is the company or other body corporate under investigation,
(b) the person to whom the obligation of confidence is owed consents to the disclosure or production, or
(c) the making of the requirement is authorised by the Secretary of State.

(1B) Subsection (1A) does not apply where the person owing the obligation of confidence is the company or other body corporate under investigation under section 431, 432 or 433.".

(4) In subsection (3) after "officer of his" insert "or other person".

GENERAL NOTE

This section amends s.452 of the Companies Act 1985 (privileged information) in so far as it relates to the disclosure of banking information for the purposes of investigations under the Companies Act 1985. Banker's information remains confidential and privileged except in so far as it relates to the company under investigation, or the person or client to whom the banker's obligation of confidence is owed has consented to disclosure, or the Secretary of State has made or authorised the request to a bank for the information.

Investigation of oversea companies

70. In section 453 of the Companies Act 1985 (investigation of oversea companies), for subsection (1) substitute—

"(1) The provisions of this Part apply to bodies corporate incorporated outside Great Britain which are carrying on business in Great Britain, or have at any time carried on business there, as they apply to companies under this Act; but subject to the following exceptions, adaptations and modifications.

(1A) The following provisions do not apply to such bodies—
(a) section 431 (investigation on application of company or its members),
(b) section 438 (power to bring civil proceedings on the company's behalf),
(c) sections 442 to 445 (investigation of company ownership and power to obtain information as to those interested in shares, &c.), and
(d) section 446 (investigation of share dealings).

(1B) The other provisions of this Part apply to such bodies subject to such adaptations and modifications as may be specified by regulations made by the Secretary of State.".

GENERAL NOTE

This section re-enacts with modification the provisions of s.453(1) of the Companies Act 1985, which relates to the investigation of overseas companies which operate or which have operated in Great Britain but were incorporated outside Great Britain. This new subsection states that ss.431, 438 and 442–446 do not operate in relation to such companies.

Investigation of unregistered companies

71. In Schedule 22 to the Companies Act 1985 (provisions applying to unregistered companies), for the entry relating to Part XIV substitute—

"Part XIV (except section 446)	Investigation of companies and their affairs; requisition of documents.	—".

GENERAL NOTE
   This section makes a minor amendment to Sched. 22 of the Companies Act 1985 relating to Pt. XIV.

Amendments of the Financial Services Act 1986

Investigations into collective investment schemes

72.—(1) Section 94 of the Financial Services Act 1986 (investigations into collective investment schemes) is amended as follows.

(2) For subsection (7) (privilege on grounds of banker's duty of confidentiality) substitute—

"(7) Nothing in this section requires a person (except as mentioned in subsection (7A) below) to disclose any information or produce any document in respect of which he owes an obligation of confidence by virtue of carrying on the business of banking unless—
  (a) the person to whom the obligation of confidence is owed consents to the disclosure or production, or
  (b) the making of the requirement was authorised by the Secretary of State.

(7A) Subsection (7) does not apply where the person owing the obligation of confidence or the person to whom it is owed is—
  (a) the manager, operator or trustee of the scheme under investigation, or
  (b) a manager, operator or trustee whose own affairs are under investigation.".

(3) After subsection (8) (duty of inspectors to report) insert—

"(8A) If it appears to the Secretary of State that matters have come to light in the course of the inspectors' investigation which suggest that a criminal offence has been committed, and those matters have been referred to the appropriate prosecuting authority, he may direct the inspectors to take no further steps in the investigation or to take only such further steps as are specified in the direction.

(8B) Where an investigation is the subject of a direction under subsection (8A), the inspectors shall make a final report to the Secretary of State only where the Secretary of State directs them to do so.".

(4) After subsection (9) add—

"(10) A person who is convicted on a prosecution instituted as a result of an investigation under this section may in the same proceedings be ordered to pay the expenses of the investigation to such extent as may be specified in the order.

There shall be treated as expenses of the investigation, in particular, such reasonable sums as the Secretary of State may determine in respect of general staff costs and overheads.".

GENERAL NOTE
   This section amends s.94 of the Financial Services Act 1986 (investigations into collective investment schemes), to make the investigative provisions under the latter identical to those under the Companies Act 1985 in many respects. For example, the banker's privilege of non-disclosure applies unless waived by the client or unless the request for information has been made by or endorsed by the Secretary of State. Likewise, his power to halt an investigation now applies to this type of investigation (*i.e.* where evidence of a criminal offence is uncovered and passed to the relevant prosecuting authority). It also enables the costs and expenses of an investigation to be recovered from the convicted person in cases

where it results in a successful prosecution. *Cf.* ss.73 and 74 below, which make corresponding amendments in relation to investigations of the affairs of persons carrying on investment business and into insider dealing.

Investigations into affairs of persons carrying on investment business

73.—(1) Section 105 of the Financial Services Act 1986 (investigation into affairs of person carrying on investment business) is amended as follows.

(2) Omit subsection (7) (privilege on grounds of banker's duty of confidentiality).

(3) In subsection (9) (interpretation), in the definition of "documents", for "references to its production include references to producing" substitute "the power to require its production includes power to require the production of".

(4) After subsection (10) add—

"(11) A person who is convicted on a prosecution instituted as a result of an investigation under this section may in the same proceedings be ordered to pay the expenses of the investigation to such extent as may be specified in the order.

There shall be treated as expenses of the investigation, in particular, such reasonable sums as the Secretary of State may determine in respect of general staff costs and overheads.".

(5) In section 106 of the Financial Services Act 1986 (exercise of investigation powers by officer, &c.), after subsection (2) insert—

"(2A) A person shall not by virtue of an authority under this section be required to disclose any information or produce any documents in respect of which he owes an obligation of confidence by virtue of carrying on the business of banking unless—
   (a) he is the person under investigation or a related company,
   (b) the person to whom the obligation of confidence is owed is the person under investigation or a related company,
   (c) the person to whom the obligation of confidence is owed consents to the disclosure or production, or
   (d) the imposing on him of a requirement with respect to such information or documents has been specifically authorised by the Secretary of State.

In this subsection "documents", "person under investigation" and "related company" have the same meaning as in section 105.".

GENERAL NOTE
See the note to s.72.

Investigations into insider dealing

74.—(1) Section 177 of the Financial Services Act 1986 (investigations into insider dealing) is amended as follows.

(2) After subsection (2) (power to limit period or scope of investigation) insert—

"(2A) At any time during the investigation the Secretary of State may vary the appointment by limiting or extending the period during which the inspector is to continue his investigation or by confining the investigation to particular matters.".

(3) After subsection (5) (duty of inspectors to report) insert—

"(5A) If the Secretary of State thinks fit, he may direct the inspector to take no further steps in the investigation or to take only such further steps as are specified in the direction; and where an investigation is the subject of such a direction, the inspectors shall make a final report to the Secretary of State only where the Secretary of State directs them to do so.".

(4) For subsection (8) (privilege on grounds of banker's duty of confidentiality) substitute—

"(8) A person shall not under this section be required to disclose any information or produce any document in respect of which he owes an obligation of confidence by virtue of carrying on the business of banking unless—
  (a) the person to whom the obligation of confidence is owed consents to the disclosure or production, or
  (b) the making of the requirement was authorised by the Secretary of State.".

(5) In subsection (10) (definition of "documents") for "references to its production include references to producing" substitute "the power to require its production includes power to require the production of."

(6) After subsection (10) add—

"(11) A person who is convicted on a prosecution instituted as a result of an investigation under this section may in the same proceedings be ordered to pay the expenses of the investigation to such extent as may be specified in the order.

There shall be treated as expenses of the investigation, in particular, such reasonable sums as the Secretary of State may determine in respect of general staff costs and overheads.".

GENERAL NOTE
See the note to s.72.
This section also enables the Secretary of State to vary the appointment of an investigator during an investigation into insider dealing and to terminate or curtail the investigation, in which case a final report will be made to the Secretary of State only if he requests it.

Restrictions on disclosure of information

75.—(1) In section 179(3) of the Financial Services Act 1986 (persons who are "primary recipients" for purposes of provisions restricting disclosure of information)—
  (a) omit the word "and" preceding paragraph (i);
  (b) in that paragraph, after "any such person" insert "as is mentioned in paragraphs (a) to (h) above";
  (c) after that paragraph insert—
    "(j) any constable or other person named in a warrant issued under this Act.".

(2) Section 180 of the Financial Services Act 1986 (exceptions from restrictions on disclosure) is amended as follows.

(3) In subsection (1) (purposes for which disclosure permitted)—
  (a) in paragraph (c), after "insolvency" insert "or by Part II, III or VII of the Companies Act 1989";
  (b) for paragraph (e) substitute—
    "(e) for the purpose—
      (i) of enabling or assisting a designated agency to discharge its functions under this Act or Part VII of the Companies Act 1989,
      (ii) of enabling or assisting a transferee body or the competent authority to discharge its functions under this Act, or
      (iii) of enabling or assisting the body administering a scheme under section 54 above to discharge its functions under the scheme;";
  (c) after paragraph (h) insert—
    "(hh) for the purpose of enabling or assisting a body established by order under section 46 of the Companies Act 1989 to discharge its functions under Part II of that Act, or of enabling or

assisting a recognised supervisory or qualifying body within the meaning of that Part to discharge its functions as such;";
  (d) after paragraph (o) insert—
    "(oo) with a view to the institution of, or otherwise for the purposes of, any disciplinary proceedings relating to the discharge by a public servant of his duties;";
  (e) in paragraph (p), after "under" insert "section 44 of the Insurance Companies Act 1982, section 447 of the Companies Act 1985", and after "above" insert "or section 84 of the Companies Act 1989";
  (f) after paragraph (q) insert—
    "(qq) for the purpose of enabling or assisting an overseas regulatory authority to exercise its regulatory functions;".
  (4) After that subsection insert—
    "(1A) In subsection (1)—
    (a) in paragraph (oo) "public servant" means an officer or servant of the Crown or of any public or other authority for the time being designated for the purposes of that paragraph by order of the Secretary of State; and
    (b) in paragraph (qq) "overseas regulatory authority" and "regulatory functions" have the same meaning as in section 82 of the Companies Act 1989.".
  (5) In subsection (3) (disclosure to designated public authorities) for "designated for the purposes of this section" substitute "designated for the purposes of this subsection".
  (6) Omit subsection (6) (disclosure to certain overseas authorities).
  (7) In subsection (9) (orders) for "subsection (3) or (8)" substitute "subsection (1A)(a), (3) or (8)."

GENERAL NOTE
  This section amends ss.179(3) and 180 of the Financial Services Act 1986, concerning the restrictions on disclosure of information obtained in an investigation under that Act and the exceptions thereto. Primary recipients of information are duty bound to disclose it only to the listed competent authorities, which now include a designated agency, transferee body, competent authority or body administering a compensation scheme under that Act or the new Companies Act 1989 to enable them to discharge their functions or to take disciplinary proceedings relating to the discharge by a public servant of his duties.

Entry and search of premises

76.—(1) Section 199 of the Financial Services Act 1986 (powers of entry) is amended as follows.
  (2) For subsections (1) and (2) substitute—
    "(1) A justice of the peace may issue a warrant under this section if satisfied on information on oath given by or on behalf of the Secretary of State that there are reasonable grounds for believing that an offence has been committed—
    (a) under section 4, 47, 57, 130, 133 or 171(2) or (3) above, or
    (b) section 1, 2, 4 or 5 of the Company Securities (Insider Dealing) Act 1985,
    and that there are on any premises documents relevant to the question whether that offence has been committed.
    (2) A justice of the peace may also issue a warrant under this section if satisfied on information on oath given by or on behalf of the Secretary of State, or by a person appointed or authorised to exercise powers under section 94, 106 or 177 above, that there are reasonable grounds for believing that there are on any premises documents whose production has been required under section 94, 105 or 177 above and which have not been produced in compliance with the requirement.".
  (3) In subsection (3)(b) for "subsection (1)(a) or (b)" substitute "subsection (1)".

(4) In subsection (5) (period for which documents may be retained), for paragraph (b) substitute—
"(b) if within that period proceedings to which the documents are relevant are commenced against any person for any criminal offence, until the conclusion of those proceedings.".

(5) In subsection (6) (offences) after "Any person who" insert "intentionally".

(6) In subsection (7) for "subsection (1)(a) above" substitute "subsection (1) above".

(7) For subsection (8) substitute—
"(8) In the application of this section to Scotland for the references to a justice of the peace substitute references to a justice of the peace or a sheriff, and for the references to information on oath substitute references to evidence on oath.".

(8) In subsection (9) (definition of "documents"), omit the words from "and, in relation" to the end.

GENERAL NOTE
This section amends s.199 of the Financial Services Act 1986 (powers of entry and search of premises) and extends it so far as it relates to search and entry warrants in respect of documents which have been requested but not produced in the course of an investigation under that Act.

Cf. s.64, which makes corresponding changes in relation to investigations under the Companies Act 1985, and s.77 which does likewise in relation to insurance company investigations.

Amendments of other enactments

Amendments of the Insurance Companies Act 1982

77.—(1) Part II of the Insurance Companies Act 1982 is amended as follows.

(2) In section 44 (power to obtain information and require production of documents), for "books or papers" (wherever occurring) substitute "documents", and for subsection (6) substitute—
"(6) In this section "document" includes information recorded in any form; and, in relation to information recorded otherwise than in legible form, the power to require its production includes power to require the production of a copy of the information in legible form.".

(3) After that section insert—

"**Entry and search of premises**
44A.—(1) A justice of the peace may issue a warrant under this section if satisfied on information on oath given by or on behalf of the Secretary of State, or by a person authorised to exercise powers under section 44 above, that there are reasonable grounds for believing that there are on any premises documents whose production has been required under section 44(2) to (4) above and which have not been produced in compliance with the requirement.

(2) A justice of the peace may also issue a warrant under this section if satisfied on information on oath given by or on behalf of the Secretary of State, or by a person authorised to exercise powers under section 44 above—
   (a) that there are reasonable grounds for believing that an offence has been committed for which the penalty on conviction on indictment is imprisonment for a term of not less than two years and that there are on any premises documents relating to whether the offence has been committed,
   (b) that the Secretary of State or, as the case may be, the

authorised person has power to require the production of the documents under section 44(2) to (4) above, and

(c) that there are reasonable grounds for believing that if production was so required the documents would not be produced but would be removed from the premises, hidden, tampered with or destroyed.

(3) A warrant under this section shall authorise a constable, together with any other person named in it and any other constables—

(a) to enter the premises specified in the information, using such force as is reasonably necessary for the purpose;

(b) to search the premises and take possession of any documents appearing to be such documents as are mentioned in subsection (1) or (2), as the case may be, or to take, in relation to any such documents, any other steps which may appear to be necessary for preserving them or preventing interference with them;

(c) to take copies of any such documents; and

(d) to require any person named in the warrant to provide an explanation of them or to state where they may be found.

(4) If in the case of a warrant under subsection (2) the justice of the peace is satisfied on information on oath that there are reasonable grounds for believing that there are also on the premises other documents relevant to the investigation, the warrant shall also authorise the actions mentioned in subsection (3) to be taken in relation to such documents.

(5) A warrant under this section shall continue in force until the end of the period of one month beginning with the day on which it is issued.

(6) Any documents of which possession is taken under this section may be retained—

(a) for a period of three months; or

(b) if within that period proceedings to which the documents are relevant are commenced against any person for any criminal offence, until the conclusion of those proceedings.

(7) In the application of this section to Scotland for the references to a justice of the peace substitute references to a justice of the peace or a sheriff, and for the references to information on oath substitute references to evidence on oath.

(8) In this section "document" includes information recorded in any form.".

(4) In section 47A(1) (restriction on disclosure of information), after "section 44(2) to (4)" insert "or 44A".

(5) In section 71 (offences and penalties), after subsection (2) insert—

"(2A) A person who intentionally obstructs the exercise of any rights conferred by a warrant issued under section 44A above or fails without reasonable excuse to comply with any requirement imposed in accordance with subsection (3)(d) of that section is guilty of an offence and liable—

(a) on conviction on indictment, to a fine, and

(b) on summary conviction, to a fine not exceeding the statutory maximum.".

(6) In section 71(6) (defence to failure to comply with requirement to produce books or papers) for "books or papers" substitute "documents".

GENERAL NOTE

This section amends Pt. II of the Insurance Companies Act 1982. It enables warrants to be granted for the entry and search of premises and makes related provisions. It also substitutes the word "document" for "books and papers" wherever the latter appears in s.44

of that Act and defines "document" so as to correspond with the definition provided by this Act for investigation purposes in Pt. XIV of the Companies Act 1985 and the relevant parts of the Financial Services Act 1986.

Amendment of the Insolvency Act 1986

78. In section 218(5) of the Insolvency Act 1986 (investigation by Secretary of State on report by liquidator), for paragraph (a) substitute—

"(a) shall thereupon investigate the matter reported to him and such other matters relating to the affairs of the company as appear to him to require investigation, and".

GENERAL NOTE

This section amends s.218(5) of the Insolvency Act 1986 in that the investigative powers of the Secretary of State on receipt of a report from liquidators under that Act are extended to include such affairs of the Company as appear, at his discretion, to require investigation.

Amendment of the Company Directors Disqualification Act 1986

79. In section 8 of the Company Directors Disqualification Act 1986 (disqualification after investigation of company), after "section 52 of the Criminal Justice (Scotland) Act 1987" insert "or section 83 of the Companies Act 1989".

GENERAL NOTE

This section amends s.8 of the Company Director Disqualification Act 1986 to enable the Secretary of State to apply to the court for an order disqualifying a director or other person from acting as a company director in future, following the outcome of gathering information under the new investigative powers operative to assist overseas regulatory authorities instituted by ss.82–91 of this Act.

Amendment of the Building Societies Act 1986

80. In section 53 of the Building Societies Act 1986 (confidentiality of information obtained by the Building Societies Commission), in subsection (7)(b) (functions of Secretary of State for purposes of which disclosure may be made) after sub-paragraph (ii) insert—

", or
(iii) Part II, III or VII of the Companies Act 1989;".

GENERAL NOTE

This section amends s.53 of the Building Societies Act 1986 to permit the Building Societies Commission to disclose confidential information to the Secretary of State for purposes of his investigatory functions under this Act.

Amendments of the Banking Act 1987

81.—(1) In section 84(1) of the Banking Act 1987 (disclosure of information obtained under that Act), the Table showing the authorities to which, and functions for the purposes of which, disclosure may be made is amended as follows.

(2) In the entry relating to the Secretary of State, in column 2, for "or the Financial Services Act 1986" substitute ", the Financial Services Act 1986 or Part II, III or VII of the Companies Act 1989".

(3) For the entry relating to inspectors appointed by the Secretary of State substitute—

| "An inspector appointed under Part XIV of the Companies Act 1985 or section 94 or 177 of the Financial Services Act 1986. | Functions under that Part or that section.". |

(4) For the entry beginning "A person authorised by the Secretary of State" substitute—

"A person authorised to exercise powers under section 44 of the Insurance Companies Act 1982, section 447 of the Companies Act 1985, section 106 of the Financial Services Act 1986 or section 84 of the Companies Act 1989. | Functions under that section.".

(5) For the entry relating to a designated agency or transferee body or the competent authority (within the meaning of the Financial Services Act 1986) substitute—

"A designated agency (within the meaning of the Financial Services Act 1986). | Functions under the Financial Services Act 1986 or Part VII of the Companies Act 1989.

A transferee body or the competent authority (within the meaning of the Financial Services Act 1986). | Functions under the Financial Services Act 1986.".

GENERAL NOTE

This section amends s.84(1) of the Banking Act 1987 to permit disclosure of information to the Secretary of State for purposes of his investigatory functions under this Act.

Powers exercisable to assist overseas regulatory authorities

Request for assistance by overseas regulatory authority

82.—(1) The powers conferred by section 83 are exercisable by the Secretary of State for the purpose of assisting an overseas regulatory authority which has requested his assistance in connection with inquiries being carried out by it or on its behalf.

(2) An "overseas regulatory authority" means an authority which in a country or territory outside the United Kingdom exercises—
(a) any function corresponding to—
    (i) a function under the Financial Services Act 1986 of a designated agency, transferee body or competent authority (within the meaning of that Act),
    (ii) a function of the Secretary of State under the Insurance Companies Act 1982, the Companies Act 1985 or the Financial Services Act 1986, or
    (iii) a function of the Bank of England under the Banking Act 1987, or
(b) any function in connection with the investigation of, or the enforcement of rules (whether or not having the force of law) relating to, conduct of the kind prohibited by the Company Securities (Insider Dealing) Act 1985, or
(c) any function prescribed for the purposes of this subsection by order of the Secretary of State, being a function which in the opinion of the Secretary of State relates to companies or financial services.

An order under paragraph (c) shall be made by statutory instrument which shall be subject to annulment in pursuance of a resolution of either House of Parliament.

(3) The Secretary of State shall not exercise the powers conferred by section 83 unless he is satisfied that the assistance requested by the overseas regulatory authority is for the purposes of its regulatory functions.

An authority's "regulatory functions" means any functions falling within subsection (2) and any other functions relating to companies or financial services.

(4) In deciding whether to exercise those powers the Secretary of State may take into account, in particular—
  (a) whether corresponding assistance would be given in that country or territory to an authority exercising regulatory functions in the United Kingdom;
  (b) whether the inquiries relate to the possible breach of a law, or other requirement, which has no close parallel in the United Kingdom or involves the assertion of a jurisdiction not recognised by the United Kingdom;
  (c) the seriousness of the matter to which the inquiries relate, the importance to the inquiries of the information sought in the United Kingdom and whether the assistance could be obtained by other means;
  (d) whether it is otherwise appropriate in the public interest to give the assistance sought.

(5) Before deciding whether to exercise those powers in a case where the overseas regulatory authority is a banking supervisor, the Secretary of State shall consult the Bank of England.

A "banking supervisor" means an overseas regulatory authority with respect to which the Bank of England has notified the Secretary of State, for the purposes of this subsection, that it exercises functions corresponding to those of the Bank under the Banking Act 1987.

(6) The Secretary of State may decline to exercise those powers unless the overseas regulatory authority undertakes to make such contribution towards the costs of their exercise as the Secretary of State considers appropriate.

(7) References in this section to financial services include, in particular, investment business, insurance and banking.

GENERAL NOTE

The major innovation of Pt. III of this Act is the creation of a new power of investigation in order to assist overseas regulatory authorities, *i.e.* power to investigate companies and persons in Great Britain on behalf of the equivalent regulatory bodies abroad to the Securities and Investments Board (S.I.B.), the Bank of England, the Stock Exchange, the Securities Association, etc. The new provisions enable the Secretary of State to obtain the information necessary to enable reciprocity with overseas regulators. The powers given to him are similar in scope to the domestic investigatory powers under Pt. XIV of the Companies Act 1985. He must, however, be satisfied that the requested assistance is bona fide and for the purposes of the overseas authority's regulatory functions. In the Secretary of State's view a request will only be acceded to if a bilateral memorandum exists limiting disclosures and use by the requesting authority.

The section specifies criteria which he may take into account in deciding whether to exercise the powers and requires him to consult the Bank of England before taking such a decision in certain cases. He is given power by statutory instrument to add to the list of overseas regulators able to call on him for assistance.

Power to require information documents or other assistance

83.—(1) The following powers may be exercised in accordance with section 82, if the Secretary of State considers there is good reason for their exercise.

(2) The Secretary of State may require any person—
  (a) to attend before him at a specified time and place and answer

questions or otherwise furnish information with respect to any matter relevant to the inquiries,
  (b) to produce at a specified time and place any specified documents which appear to the Secretary of State to relate to any matter relevant to the inquiries, and
  (c) otherwise to give him such assistance in connection with the inquiries as he is reasonably able to give.

(3) The Secretary of State may examine a person on oath and may administer an oath accordingly.

(4) Where documents are produced the Secretary of State may take copies or extracts from them.

(5) A person shall not under this section be required to disclose information or produce a document which he would be entitled to refuse to disclose or produce on grounds of legal professional privilege in proceedings in the High Court or on grounds of confidentiality as between client and professional legal adviser in proceedings in the Court of Session, except that a lawyer may be required to furnish the name and address of his client.

(6) A statement by a person in compliance with a requirement imposed under this section may be used in evidence against him.

(7) Where a person claims a lien on a document, its production under this section is without prejudice to his lien.

(8) In this section "documents" includes information recorded in any form; and, in relation to information recorded otherwise than in legible form, the power to require its production includes power to require the production of a copy of it in legible form.

GENERAL NOTE

This section empowers the Secretary of State to require any person to give information to him on oath, to produce documents or give other assistance in relation to his inquiries, and makes related provisions.

Exercise of powers by officer, &c.

84.—(1) The Secretary of State may authorise an officer of his or any other competent person to exercise on his behalf all or any of the powers conferred by section 83.

(2) No such authority shall be granted except for the purpose of investigating—
  (a) the affairs, or any aspects of the affairs, of a person specified in the authority, or
  (b) a subject-matter so specified,
being a person who, or subject-matter which, is the subject of the inquiries being carried out by or on behalf of the overseas regulatory authority.

(3) No person shall be bound to comply with a requirement imposed by a person exercising powers by virtue of an authority granted under this section unless he has, if required, produced evidence of his authority.

(4) A person shall not by virtue of an authority under this section be required to disclose any information or produce any documents in respect of which he owes an obligation of confidence by virtue of carrying on the business of banking unless—
  (a) the imposing on him of a requirement with respect to such information or documents has been specifically authorised by the Secretary of State, or
  (b) the person to whom the obligation of confidence is owed consents to the disclosure or production.

In this subsection "documents" has the same meaning as in section 83.

(5) Where the Secretary of State authorises a person other than one of his officers to exercise any powers by virtue of this section, that person

shall make a report to the Secretary of State in such manner as he may require on the exercise of those powers and the results of exercising them.

GENERAL NOTE
This section enables the Secretary of State to authorise one of his officers or any competent person to exercise on his behalf the investigative powers conferred by s.83, but he may only make such an authorisation for specific purposes defined by reference to the persons subject to the enquiry or the subject matter of the enquiry being conducted by an overseas regulator.

The section requires an investigator, other than a D.T.I. officer, to make a report to the Secretary of State, and it specifies the circumstances in which banking information may be required.

Penalty for failure to comply with requirement, &c.

85.—(1) A person who without reasonable excuse fails to comply with a requirement imposed on him under section 83 commits an offence and is liable on summary conviction to imprisonment for a term not exceeding six months or to a fine not exceeding level 5 on the standard scale, or both.

(2) A person who in purported compliance with any such requirement furnishes information which he knows to be false or misleading in a material particular, or recklessly furnishes information which is false or misleading in a material particular, commits an offence and is liable—
   (a) on conviction on indictment, to imprisonment for a term not exceeding two years or to a fine, or both;
   (b) on summary conviction, to imprisonment for a term not exceeding six months or to a fine not exceeding the statutory maximum, or both.

GENERAL NOTE
This section provides criminal penalties for persons who unreasonably refuse to comply with requirements imposed under s.83, or who in purported compliance furnish false or misleading information. As to the effect and scope of the words "knowingly" and "recklessly," see the General Note to s.151.

Restrictions on disclosure of information

86.—(1) This section applies to information relating to the business or other affairs of a person which—
   (a) is supplied by an overseas regulatory authority in connection with a request for assistance, or
   (b) is obtained by virtue of the powers conferred by section 83, whether or not any requirement to supply it is made under that section.

(2) Except as permitted by section 87 below, such information shall not be disclosed for any purpose—
   (a) by the primary recipient, or
   (b) by any person obtaining the information directly or indirectly from him,
without the consent of the person from whom the primary recipient obtained the information and, if different, the person to whom it relates.

(3) The "primary recipient" means, as the case may be—
   (a) the Secretary of State,
   (b) any person authorised under section 84 to exercise powers on his behalf, and
   (c) any officer or servant of any such person.

(4) Information shall not be treated as information to which this section applies if it has been made available to the public by virtue of being disclosed in any circumstances in which, or for any purpose for which, disclosure is not precluded by this section.

(5) A person who contravenes this section commits an offence and is liable—
- (a) on conviction on indictment, to imprisonment for a term not exceeding two years or to a fine, or both;
- (b) on summary conviction, to imprisonment for a term not exceeding three months or to a fine not exceeding the statutory maximum, or both.

GENERAL NOTE

This section imposes restrictions on the disclosure of information supplied by an overseas regulator in connection with a request for assistance or obtained by virtue of the investigatory powers under s.83. Neither the Secretary of State nor persons acting on his behalf nor their officers or agents nor persons obtaining information directly or indirectly from them shall disclose it, except for the purposes stated in the Act, unless they have the consent of the person from whom it came and, if different, the person to whom it relates.

Exceptions from restrictions on disclosure

87.—(1) Information to which section 86 applies may be disclosed—
- (a) to any person with a view to the institution of, or otherwise for the purposes of, relevant proceedings,
- (b) for the purpose of enabling or assisting a relevant authority to discharge any relevant function (including functions in relation to proceedings),
- (c) to the Treasury, if the disclosure is made in the interests o investors or in the public interest,
- (d) if the information is or has been available to the public fron other sources,
- (e) in a summary or collection of information framed in such a way as not to enable the identity of any person to whom the information relates to be ascertained, or
- (f) in pursuance of any Community obligation.

(2) The relevant proceedings referred to in subsection (1)(a) are—
- (a) any criminal proceedings,
- (b) civil proceedings arising under or by virtue of the Financial Services Act 1986 and proceedings before the Financial Services Tribunal, and
- (c) disciplinary proceedings relating to—
    - (i) the exercise by a solicitor, auditor, accountant, valuer or actuary of his professional duties, or
    - (ii) the discharge by a public servant of his duties.

(3) In subsection (2)(c)(ii) "public servant" means an officer or servant of the Crown or of any public or other authority for the time being designated for the purposes of that provision by order of the Secretary of State.

(4) The relevant authorities referred to in subsection (1)(b), and the relevant functions in relation to each such authority, are as follows—

Authority	Functions
The Secretary of State.	Functions under the enactments relating to companies, insurance companies or insolvency, or under the Financial Services Act 1986 or Part II, this Part or Part VII of this Act.

An inspector appointed under Part XIV of the Companies Act 1985 or section 94 or 177 of the Financial Services Act 1986.	Functions under that Part or that section.
A person authorised to exercise powers under section 44 of the Insurance Companies Act 1982, section 447 of the Companies Act 1985, section 106 of the Financial Services Act 1986 or section 84 of this Act.	Functions under that section.
An overseas regulatory authority.	Its regulatory functions (within the meaning of section 82 of this Act).
The Department of Economic Development in Northern Ireland or a person appointed or authorised by that Department.	Functions conferred on it or him by the enactments relating to companies or insolvency.
A designated agency within the meaning of the Financial Services Act 1986.	Functions under that Act or Part VII of this Act.
A transferee body or the competent authority within the meaning of the Financial Services Act 1986.	Functions under that Act.
The body administering a scheme under section 54 of the Financial Services Act 1986.	Functions under the scheme.
A recognised self-regulating organisation, recognised professional body, recognised investment exchange, recognised clearing house or recognised self-regulating organisation for friendly societies (within the meaning of the Financial Services Act 1986).	Functions in its capacity as an organisation, body, exchange or clearing house recognised under that Act.
The Chief Registrar of friendly societies, the Registrar of Friendly Societies for Northern Ireland and the Assistant Registrar of Friendly Societies for Scotland.	Functions under the Financial Services Act 1986 or the enactments relating to friendly societies or building societies.
The Bank of England.	Functions under the Banking Act 1987 and any other functions.
The Deposit Protection Board.	Functions under the Banking Act 1987.
A body established by order under section 46 of this Act.	Functions under Part II of this Act.
A recognised supervisory or qualifying body within the meaning of Part II of this Act.	Functions as such a body.
The Industrial Assurance Commissioner and the Industrial Assurance Commissioner for Northern Ireland.	Functions under the enactments relating to industrial assurance.

The Insurance Brokers Registration Council.	Functions under the Insurance Brokers (Registration) Act 1977.
The Official Receiver or, in Northern Ireland, the Official Assignee for company liquidations or for bankruptcy.	Functions under the enactments relating to insolvency.
A recognised professional body (within the meaning of section 391 of the Insolvency Act 1986).	Functions in its capacity as such a body under the Insolvency Act 1986.
The Building Societies Commission.	Functions under the Building Societies Act 1986.
The Director General of Fair Trading.	Functions under the Financial Services Act 1986.

(5) The Secretary of State may by order amend the Table in subsection (4) so as to—
(a) add any public or other authority to the Table and specify the relevant functions of that authority,
(b) remove any authority from the Table, or
(c) add functions to, or remove functions from, those which are relevant functions in relation to an authority specified in the Table;
and the order may impose conditions subject to which, or otherwise restrict the circumstances in which, disclosure is permitted.

(6) An order under this section shall be made by statutory instrument which shall be subject to annulment in pursuance of a resolution of either House of Parliament.

GENERAL NOTE
This section sets out the exceptions from the disclosure restrictions contained in s.86.

Exercise of powers in relation to Northern Ireland

88.—(1) The following provisions apply where it appears to the Secretary of State that a request for assistance by an overseas regulatory authority may involve the powers conferred by section 83 being exercised in Northern Ireland in relation to matters which are transferred matters within the meaning of the Northern Ireland Constitution Act 1973.

(2) The Secretary of State shall before deciding whether to accede to the request consult the Department of Economic Development in Northern Ireland, and if he decides to accede to the request and it appears to him—
(a) that the powers should be exercised in Northern Ireland, and
(b) that the purposes for which they should be so exercised relate wholly or primarily to transferred matters,
he shall by instrument in writing authorise the Department to exercise in Northern Ireland his powers under section 83.

(3) The following provisions have effect in relation to the exercise of powers by virtue of such an authority with the substitution for references to the Secretary of State of references to the Department of Economic Development in Northern Ireland—
(a) section 84 (exercise of powers by officer, &c.),
(b) section 449 of the Companies Act 1985, section 53 or 54 of the Building Societies Act 1986, sections 179 and 180 of the Financial Services Act 1986, section 84 of the Banking Act 1987 and sections 86 and 87 above (restrictions on disclosure of information), and
(c) section 89 (authority for institution of criminal proceedings);

and references to the Secretary of State in other enactments which proceed by reference to those provisions shall be construed accordingly as being or including references to the Department.

(4) The Secretary of State may after consultation with the Department of Economic Development in Northern Ireland revoke an authority given to the Department under this section.

(5) In that case nothing in the provisions referred to in subsection (3)(b) shall apply so as to prevent the Department from giving the Secretary of State any information obtained by virtue of the authority; and (without prejudice to their application in relation to disclosure by the Department) those provisions shall apply to the disclosure of such information by the Secretary of State as if it had been obtained by him in the first place.

(6) Nothing in this section affects the exercise by the Secretary of State of any powers in Northern Ireland—
  (a) in a case where at the time of acceding to the request it did not appear to him that the circumstances were such as to require him to authorise the Department of Economic Development in Northern Ireland to exercise those powers, or
  (b) after the revocation by him of any such authority;
and no objection shall be taken to anything done by or in relation to the Secretary of State or the Department on the ground that it should have been done by or in relation to the other.

GENERAL NOTE
  This section, permitting the Secretary of State to exercise the powers conferred by s.83 in Northern Ireland, is necessary because of the Northern Ireland Constitution. Traditionally, and constitutionally, it has been the practice for the Northern Ireland authority to carry out most of the executive functions of government, including in particular most company law functions.
  Under the developed powers of the Constitution Act 1973, provisions may be enacted by an Order in Council, which procedure is followed in this section and the 1989 Act generally for provisions affecting company law and insolvency law.

Prosecutions

89. Proceedings for an offence under section 85 or 86 shall not be instituted—
  (a) in England and Wales, except by or with the consent of the Secretary of State or the Director of Public Prosecutions;
  (b) in Northern Ireland, except by or with the consent of the Secretary of State or the Director of Public Prosecutions for Northern Ireland.

Offences by bodies corporate, partnerships and unincorporated associations

90.—(1) Where an offence under section 85 or 86 committed by a body corporate is proved to have been committed with the consent or connivance of, or to be attributable to any neglect on the part of, a director, manager, secretary or other similar officer of the body, or a person purporting to act in any such capacity, he as well as the body corporate is guilty of the offence and liable to be proceeded against and punished accordingly.

(2) Where the affairs of a body corporate are managed by its members, subsection (1) applies in relation to the acts and defaults of a member in connection with his functions of management as to a director of a body corporate.

(3) Where an offence under section 85 or 86 committed by a partnership is proved to have been committed with the consent or connivance of, or to be attributable to any neglect on the part of, a partner, he as well as

the partnership is guilty of the offence and liable to be proceeded against and punished accordingly.

(4) Where an offence under section 85 or 86 committed by an unincorporated association (other than a partnership) is proved to have been committed with the consent or connivance of, or to be attributable to any neglect on the part of, any officer of the association or any member of its governing body, he as well as the association is guilty of the offence and liable to be proceeded against and punished accordingly.

GENERAL NOTE
This provision is similar to that contained in s.733 of the Companies Act 1985. It permits the veil of incorporation to be lifted to allow prosecution of individuals, as well as the company, where ss.85 and 86 have been contravened.

Jurisdiction and procedure in respect of offences

91.—(1) Summary proceedings for an offence under section 85 may, without prejudice to any jurisdiction exercisable apart from this section, be taken against a body corporate or unincorporated association at any place at which it has a place of business and against an individual at any place where he is for the time being.

(2) Proceedings for an offence alleged to have been committed under section 85 or 86 by an unincorporated association shall be brought in the name of the association (and not in that of any of its members), and for the purposes of any such proceedings any rules of court relating to the service of documents apply as in relation to a body corporate.

(3) Section 33 of the Criminal Justice Act 1925 and Schedule 3 to the Magistrates' Courts Act 1980 (procedure on charge of offence against a corporation) apply in a case in which an unincorporated association is charged in England and Wales with an offence under section 85 or 86 as they apply in the case of a corporation.

(4) In relation to proceedings on indictment in Scotland for an offence alleged to have been committed under section 85 or 86 by an unincorporated association, section 74 of the Criminal Procedure (Scotland) Act 1975 (proceedings on indictment against bodies corporate) applies as if the association were a body corporate.

(5) Section 18 of the Criminal Justice Act (Northern Ireland) 1945 and Schedule 4 to the Magistrates' Courts (Northern Ireland) Order 1981 (procedure on charge of offence against a corporation) apply in a case in which an unincorporated association is charged in Northern Ireland with an offence under section 85 or 86 as they apply in the case of a corporation.

(6) A fine imposed on an unincorporated association on its conviction of such an offence shall be paid out of the funds of the association.

PART IV

REGISTRATION OF COMPANY CHARGES

Introduction

Introduction

92. The provisions of this Part amend the provisions of the Companies Act 1985 relating to the registration of company charges—
  (a) by inserting in Part XII of that Act (in place of sections 395 to 408 and 410 to 423) new provisions with respect to companies registered in Great Britain, and

(b) by inserting as Chapter III of Part XXIII of that Act (in place of sections 409 and 424) new provisions with respect to oversea companies.

GENERAL NOTE
This section simply outlines the techniques of statutory substitution and transferral to be adopted by this Part of the Act. A full explanation is provided in the Introductory Note to Pt. IV above.

Registration in the companies charges register

Charges requiring registration

93. The following sections are inserted in Part XII of the Companies Act 1985—

"*Registration in the company charges register*

Introductory provisions

395.—(1) The purpose of this Part is to secure the registration of charges on a company's property.
 (2) In this Part—
  "charge" means any form of security interest (fixed or floating) over property, other than an interest arising by operation of law; and
  "property", in the context of what is the subject of a charge, includes future property.
 (3) It is immaterial for the purposes of this Part where the property subject to a charge is situated.
 (4) References in this Part to "the registrar" are—
  (a) in relation to a company registered in England and Wales, to the registrar of companies for England and Wales, and
  (b) in relation to a company registered in Scotland, to the registrar of companies for Scotland;
and references to registration, in relation to a charge, are to registration in the register kept by him under this Part.

Charges requiring registration

396.—(1) The charges requiring registration under this Part are—
 (a) a charge on land or any interest in land, other than—
  (i) in England and Wales, a charge for rent or any other periodical sum issuing out of the land,
  (ii) in Scotland, a charge for any rent, ground annual or other periodical sum payable in respect of the land;
 (b) a charge on goods or any interest in goods, other than a charge under which the chargee is entitled to possession either of the goods or of a document of title to them;
 (c) a charge on intangible movable property (in Scotland, incorporeal moveable property) of any of the following descriptions—
  (i) goodwill,
  (ii) intellectual property,
  (iii) book debts (whether book debts of the company or assigned to the company),
  (iv) uncalled share capital of the company or calls made but not paid;
 (d) a charge for securing an issue of debentures; or

Companies Act 1989

(e) a floating charge on the whole or part of the company's property.

(2) The descriptions of charge mentioned in subsection (1) shall be construed as follows—

(a) a charge on a debenture forming part of an issue or series shall not be treated as falling within paragraph (a) or (b) by reason of the fact that the debenture is secured by a charge on land or goods (or on an interest in land or goods);

(b) in paragraph (b) "goods" means any tangible movable property (in Scotland, corporeal moveable property) other than money;

(c) a charge is not excluded from paragraph (b) because the chargee is entitled to take possession in case of default or on the occurrence of some other event;

(d) in paragraph (c)(ii) "intellectual property" means—
   (i) any patent, trade mark, service mark, registered design, copyright or design right, or
   (ii) any licence under or in respect of any such right;

(e) a debenture which is part of an issue or series shall not be treated as a book debt for the purposes of paragraph (c)(iii);

(f) the deposit by way of security of a negotiable instrument given to secure the payment of book debts shall not be treated for the purposes of paragraph (c)(iii) as a charge on book debts;

(g) a shipowner's lien on subfreights shall not be treated as a charge on book debts for the purposes of paragraph (c)(iii) or as a floating charge for the purposes of paragraph (e).

(3) Whether a charge is one requiring registration under this Part shall be determined—

(a) in the case of a charge created by a company, as at the date the charge is created, and

(b) in the case of a charge over property acquired by a company, as at the date of the acquisition.

(4) The Secretary of State may by regulations amend subsections (1) and (2) so as to add any description of charge to, or remove any description of charge from, the charges requiring registration under this Part.

(5) Regulations under this section shall be made by statutory instrument which shall be subject to annulment in pursuance of a resolution of either House of Parliament.

(6) In the following provisions of this Part references to a charge are, unless the context otherwise requires, to a charge requiring registration under this Part.

Where a charge not otherwise requiring registration relates to property by virtue of which it requires to be registered and to other property, the references are to the charge so far as it relates to property of the former description.".

GENERAL NOTE

This section substitutes fresh ss.395 and 396 into the Companies Act 1985. There are changes of both form and substance to note here.

New s.395

This is in fact a completely new explanatory provision.

Subss. (1)–(2)

These subsections define terms frequently used in Pt. IV. The definition of "charge" is not particularly helpful; it is not clear, for example, whether it covers a charge to secure a non-monetary obligation. Under the former system, it seems that such a charge was not registrable—see *Stoneleigh Finance* v. *Phillips* [1965] 2 Q.B. 537. Diamond supported the view that such charges should be registrable and there were voices in Parliament in favour of such a change—(*Hansard*, H.L. Vol. 504, col. 139–40, February 14, 1989). It will be left to the courts to determine whether a title retention clause creates a "security interest". Charges by operation of law are excluded. This merely confirms the common law—*Brunton v. Electrical Engineering Corp.* [1892] 1 Ch. 434 (solicitor's lien); *London and Cheshire Insurance Co. v. Laplagrene Property Co.* [1971] Ch. 499 (unpaid vendor's lien). The Government amended the Bill to make this clear—see *Hansard*, H.L. Vol. 504, col. 125, February 14, 1989. See also s.396(6) for further guidance on the meaning of "charge" for the purposes of the following provisions.

Subss. (3) and (4)
There is of course a separate Companies Registry in Scotland but the new provisions apply equally to both jurisdictions, a departure from the previous system where there were separate registration rules for Scotland.

New s.396
This represents a modified list of registrable charges and is based on s.396 of the 1985 Act. It has a simplified and more coherent structure than its predecessor. The idea of the list has not been abandoned; it was criticised by Manson in (1900) 16 L.Q.R. 414 at 417 when it was first introduced but it did receive the support of the Jenkins Committee in 1962 (Cm. 1749, para. 301). The Diamond Report in its prescription for interim reform also recommended its retention. Not all charges are registrable; a specific charge over shares still escapes the net, as do many other common security transactions (see Diamond paras. 23.4.4 and 23.6.9 here). For criticism of the former lacuna see the Jenkins Report, Cm. 1749, para. 301, and the Cork report, Cm. 8558, para. 1520. It was surprising that the Diamond Report (para. 23.8.13) favoured the status quo but his view did meet with the approval of the Government (*Hansard*, H.L. Vol. 504, col. 121–3, February 14, 1989 and the discussion in the House of Commons, Standing Committee D, cols. 402–4, June 20, 1989).

Subs. (1)
(a) *Land or any interest in land:* This category, which had been introduced as a result of the recommendations of the Loreburn Committee in 1906 (Cd. 3052, para. 37), was formerly contained in s.396(1)(d). Note the exclusion for rent charges—see superseded C.A. 1985, s.396(1)(d) here for a similar exclusion. The mode of creation of the charge is irrelevant— *Re Wallis and Simmonds (Builders) Ltd.* [1974] 1 W.L.R. 391. Note the limitation imposed by subs. (2)(a).

(b) *Goods or any interest in goods:* There is no real change in the substance of the law here, although ships and aircraft are no longer treated as a discrete category. Pledges were not registrable under the previous law, even though this was not made clear in the statute—*Wrightson v. MacArthur & Hutchinsons Ltd.* [1921] 2 K.B. 807 and *Barrett & Co. v. Livesey* (1981) 131 N.L.J. 1213. Note also subs. (2)(b) and (c).

(c) *Intangible movable property:* This covers a wide range of corporate assets. It has been extended to cover registered designs and design rights—see subs. (2)(d). Note the term "book debts" has been extended to cover book debts of another company assigned to a factoring company. The decision of Hoffmann J. in *Re Brightlife* [1987] Ch. 200 to the effect that a company's credit in its bank account could not be regarded as a book debt owed to it was supported by the Diamond Committee (para. 23.4.12) and has remained undisturbed by this legislation. Charges over book debts first became registrable as a result of the recommendations of the Loreburn Committee in 1906 (Cd. 3052, para. 38). The recommendation of the Diamond Committee (para. 23.9.25) that the more up to date term "receivables" should be substituted has not been accepted and the Government still refuses to define the term "book debts"—(*Hansard*, H.L. Vol. 504, col. 115–7, February 14, 1989). Charges over unpaid and uncalled capital are now also subsumed in this category. Note also subs. (2)(e)–(g).

(d) *A charge for securing an issue of debenture:* For years it was unclear whether this meant an issue of single debentures or just a large-scale issue. There is some tenuous Commonwealth authority to support the latter interpretation—*Automobile Association (Canterbury) Inc. v. Australasian Secured Deposits Ltd.* [1973] 1 N.Z.L.R. 417. The Diamond Committee (para. 23.9.11) supported this narrower interpretation and it would appear from s.419 that it is now the position in English law. Scotland had felt able to do without this discrete category but Diamond supported its retention.

(e) *A floating charge:* This makes it clear that a floating charge is registrable, irrespective of its scope. This was not clear from the wording in the former s.396(1)(f), though there was authority at common law to support this conclusion—*Re Yorkshire Woolcombers Association*

Ltd. [1903] 2 Ch. 284 at 294 *per* Romer L.J. and *Hoare* v. *British Columbia Development Association* (1912) 107 L.T. 602.

Subs. (2)
This subsection seeks to clarify points arising out of the list in subs. (1). An important change in the law deserves to be mentioned here. As a result of decisions such as *Re Welsh Irish Ferries Ltd.* [1986] Ch. 471 and *Annangel Glory Compania Naviera S.A.* v. *Golodetz* 1988 P.C.C. 37, shipowner's liens on subfreights were registrable, either on the grounds that they constituted charges over book debts or alternatively because they amounted to a floating charge. For criticisms of this view, see Milman (1985) 6 Co. Law 224. These decisions have both been reversed by s.396(2)(g).

Subs. (3)
This was a last minute addition to the Bill to help to identify whether a particular transaction fell within the registration net.

Subss. (4) and (5)
These subsections introduce welcome flexibility into the list of registrable charges. Further changes to the registrable categories can be made without the need for amending legislation—note here ss.413 and 418. The negative resolution procedure for statutory instruments is standard practice.

Subs. (6)
This attempts to offer clarification but would never win a prize in a plain English competition. In essence it deals with the case of hybrid security, part of which falls within the registration net and the remainder of which does not. The provisions in the Act relate only to the former element. See also s.395(2) on "property."

The companies charges register

94. The following section is inserted in Part XII of the Companies Act 1985—

"The companies charges register
397.—(1) The registrar shall keep for each company a register, in such form as he thinks fit, of charges on property of the company.

(2) The register shall consist of a file containing with respect to each charge the particulars and other information delivered to the registrar under the provisions of this Part.

(3) Any person may require the registrar to provide a certificate stating the date on which any specified particulars of, or other information relating to, a charge were delivered to him.

(4) The certificate shall be signed by the registrar or authenticated by his official seal.

(5) The certificate shall be conclusive evidence that the specified particulars or other information were delivered to the registrar no later than the date stated in the certificate; and it shall be presumed unless the contrary is proved that they were not delivered earlier than that date.".

GENERAL NOTE
This section inserts completely new substituted s.397 in the Companies Act 1985.

New s.397
Subs. (1)
Note the discretion enjoyed by the registrar (see s.395(4)) as to the form of the charges register.

Subs. (2)
This provides guidance as to the contents of the register. An illustrative list contained in early versions of the Bill has been omitted. See also s.415 for more guidance.

Subs. (3)
This system of demanding what is in effect a receipt is new. It replaces the old certificate of registration, which was supplied as a matter of course. This new document is available to any person on application to the registrar.

Subss. (4) and (5)
Under the original version of the Bill the receipt was no longer to enjoy the conclusive nature which the erstwhile certificate of registration possessed under the C.A. 1985—see the former s.401(2)(b) and *R.* v. *Registrar of Companies* ex p. *Central Bank of India* [1986] Q.B. 1114. This radical change in the law had its critics amongst the Opposition parties— (*Hansard*, H.L. Vol. 504, cols. 126–32, February 14, 1989). Therefore the Government thought again and came up with the compromise solution that is expressed in subs. (5). For a discussion of this, see *Hansard*, H.L. Vol. 505, col. 1209–16, April 6, 1989. Thus, we now have a degree of rebuttable conclusiveness with regard to date of registration, but not in connection with the other aspects of the security transaction, (*e.g.* amount of loan or extent of the security). Possession of a receipt that is conclusive as to date is evidentially important when one considers that a charge is immune from invalidation if particulars have been submitted for registration within the 21 days, even if the registrar fails to file those particulars—*per* Lloyd J. in *N.V. Slavenburg's Bank* v. *Intercontinental Natural Resources* [1980] 1 W.L.R. 1076.

Delivery of particulars for registration

95. The following sections are inserted in Part XII of the Companies Act 1985—

"**Company's duty to deliver particulars of charge for registration**
398.—(1) It is the duty of a company which creates a charge or acquires property subject to a charge—
(a) to deliver the prescribed particulars of the charge, in the prescribed form, to the registrar for registration, and
(b) to do so within 21 days after the date of the charge's creation or, as the case may be, the date of the acquisition;
but particulars of a charge may be delivered for registration by any person interested in the charge.

(2) Where the particulars are delivered for registration by a person other than the company concerned, that person is entitled to recover from the company the amount of any fees paid by him to the registrar in connection with the registration.

(3) If a company fails to comply with subsection (1), then, unless particulars of the charge have been delivered for registration by another person, the company and every officer of it who is in default is liable to a fine.

(4) Where prescribed particulars in the prescribed form are delivered to the registrar for registration, he shall file the particulars in the register and shall note, in such form as he thinks fit, the date on which they were delivered to him.

(5) The registrar shall send to the company and any person appearing from the particulars to be the chargee, and if the particulars were delivered by another person interested in the charge to that person, a copy of the particulars filed by him and of the note made by him as to the date on which they were delivered.

Effect of failure to deliver particulars for registration
399.—(1) Where a charge is created by a company and no prescribed particulars in the prescribed form are delivered for registration within the period of 21 days after the date of the charge's creation, the charge is void against—
(a) an administrator or liquidator of the company, and
(b) any person who for value acquires an interest in or right over property subject to the charge,

where the relevant event occurs after the creation of the charge, whether before or after the end of the 21 day period.

This is subject to section 400 (late delivery of particulars).

(2) In this Part "the relevant event" means—
   (a) in relation to the voidness of a charge as against an administrator or liquidator, the beginning of the insolvency proceedings, and
   (b) in relation to the voidness of a charge as against a person acquiring an interest in or right over property subject to a charge, the acquisition of that interest or right;

and references to "a relevant event" shall be construed accordingly.

(3) Where a relevant event occurs on the same day as the charge is created, it shall be presumed to have occurred after the charge is created unless the contrary is proved.

Late delivery of particulars

400.—(1) Where prescribed particulars of a charge created by a company, in the prescribed form, are delivered for registration more than 21 days after the date of the charge's creation, section 399(1) does not apply in relation to relevant events occurring after the particulars are delivered.

(2) However, where in such a case—
   (a) the company is at the date of delivery of the particulars unable to pay its debts, or subsequently becomes unable to pay its debts in consequence of the transaction under which the charge is created, and
   (b) insolvency proceedings begin before the end of the relevant period beginning with the date of delivery of the particulars,

the charge is void as against the administrator or liquidator.

(3) For this purpose—
   (a) the company is "unable to pay its debts" in the circumstances specified in section 123 of the Insolvency Act 1986; and
   (b) the "relevant period" is—
      (i) two years in the case of a floating charge created in favour of a person connected with the company (within the meaning of section 249 of that Act),
      (ii) one year in the case of a floating charge created in favour of a person not so connected, and
      (iii) six months in any other case.

(4) Where a relevant event occurs on the same day as the particulars are delivered, it shall be presumed to have occurred before the particulars are delivered unless the contrary is proved.".

GENERAL NOTE

This section introduces three substituted sections into the Companies Act 1985. Again we have late changes in the original clause in the Bill. For an explanation, see *Hansard*, H.C. Vol. 158, col. 1157, October 26, 1989.

New s.398

This again is a new provision, though it is partly based on the old ss.395 and 400.

Subs. (1)

This subsection, in effect, preserves the status quo with regard to the imposition of a duty to register on the company (see the old s.399) and the 21 day deadline. The D.T.I. received submissions to the effect that this period should be changed but in the end it concluded that 21 days was about right. Diamond agreed with this view (see para. 25.1.5). For "the creation of the charge" see s.419(2).

There is now no duty to send the instrument of charge to the registrar for checking against the furnished particulars. This will result in a considerable saving of staff time at the registry, which often takes several days to conduct the necessary inquiries—see the discussion in the House of Commons Standing Committee D, cols. 397–400, June 20, 1989. Both the Jenkins Committee (Cm. 1749, para. 300(g)) and the Diamond Committee favoured lifting this obligation from the shoulders of the Companies Registry, and the 1973 Bill, if enacted, would have achieved this. Diamond also rejected the suggestion that the instrument of charge should be registered (para. 22.1.9). It would appear that the Secretary of State may revert to the former position by exercising his power under s.413(2).

For the prescribed particulars see s.415. Note that this provision also covers property acquired by the company that is subject to a charge.

Subs. (2)
An indemnity is available where registration is effected by some party other than the company. Currently no fees are payable to register a charge but clearly fees are envisaged under the new system.

Subs. (3)
Criminal sanctions are visited upon the company in the event of failure to register. The key deterrent, however, is the resulting invalidity of the charge—see s.399.

Subs. (4)
The registrar must register particulars provided they are in the prescribed form. There is no duty to register improperly prepared particulars—*Sun Tai Cheung Credits* v. *Att.-Gen. of Hong Kong* [1987] 1 W.L.R. 948. Note that the registrar no longer has to check the particulars of a charge submitted to him against any instrument of charge.

Subs. (5)
This wider distribution pattern is new and seeks to ensure that the company and the person who appears to be the chargee know what the register contains and is vital in view of the revised s.402. There was a minor amendment of this provision in the Lords by which the word "chargee" was replaced by "the person appearing from the particulars to be the chargee"—(*Hansard*, H.L. Vol. 504, col. 137, February 14, 1989).

New s.399
Subs. (1)
The sanction of invalidity is retained in the event of failure to register in time, subject to late registration under the new s.400. However, there appears to be a subtle change in the nature of that invalidity, for under the old law the security automatically became invalid once the 21 days for registration had elapsed; under the new system it becomes potentially invalid at that date but invalidity is only consummated once a relevant event occurs. Invalidity may be exploited by administrators and bona fide purchasers (but not creditors in general). Under the former law, an unregistered charge was not void as against a bona fide purchaser. However, an unregistered security that had been realised by the chargee is still (subject to s.406) unaffected by the fact of non-registration—*Mercantile Bank of India* v. *Chartered Bank of India* [1937] 1 All E.R. 231. The company itself cannot assert the invalidity of the charge—*Re Monolithic Building Co. Ltd.* [1915] 1 Ch. 643, *Independent Automatic Sales Ltd.* v. *Knowles and Foster* [1962] 1 W.L.R. 974.

Although the duty to register in s.398 applies both to charges created by the company and to property acquired by the company which is subject to a charge, it would appear from the wording of subs. (1) that the sanction of invalidity will only operate in the former case. This in fact preserves the position at common law—*Capital Finance Co.*v. *Stokes* [1969] 1 Ch. 261 at 278 *per* Harman L.J.

Subss. (2) and (3)
These subsections provide guidance on "relevant event" in subs. (1). See also s.419(5).

New s.400
This provision had no counterpart in the 1985 legislation. Under the previous system in the wake of *R.* v. *Registrar of Companies* ex p. *Central Bank of India* [1986] 2 Q.B. 1114, the only way in which particulars could be registered after the elapse of the 21 day period was through a court order. The provision noted below reverts to a position of administrative convenience, subject to suitable safeguards. Diamond proposed such a change (see para.

25.3.3). This provision initially had three additional subsections, but they were abandoned by the Government in the House of Lords at Committee stage (*Hansard*, H.L. Vol. 504, cols. 138–9, February 14, 1989).

Subs. (1)
Late delivery of particulars is now possible, with the result that s.399 avoidance will not operate.

Subss. (2) and (3)
These limit the effect of the aforementioned concession by rendering nugatory late registration where the company is insolvent and it goes into liquidation or administration within a specified period. There are shades here of s.238–241 and 245 of the Insolvency Act 1986 and the time limits adopted therein. For the beginning of insolvency proceedings see s.419(5).

Subs. (4)
For "relevant event", see s.399(2).

Delivery of further particulars

96. The following section is inserted in Part XII of the Companies Act 1985—

> "**Delivery of further particulars**
>
> 401.—(1) Further particulars of a charge, supplementing or varying the registered particulars, may be delivered to the registrar for registration at any time.
>
> (2) Further particulars must be in the prescribed form signed by or on behalf of both the company and the chargee.
>
> (3) Where further particulars are delivered to the registrar for registration and appear to him to be duly signed, he shall file the particulars in the register and shall note, in such form as he thinks fit, the date on which they were delivered to him.
>
> (4) The registrar shall send to the company and any person appearing from the particulars to be the chargee, and if the particulars were delivered by another person interested in the charge to that other person, a copy of the further particulars filed by him and of the note made by him as to the date on which they were delivered.".

GENERAL NOTE
This inserts a new s.410 into the Companies Act 1985 that had no precedent in the former statutory regime. There was no need to update the register because the chargee was fully protected by his initial registration once the certificate of registration had been obtained. Things are now different in view of the new s.402.

New s.401
Subss. (1) and (2)
The register may be amended or updated by submission of particulars in the prescribed form.

Subss. (3) and (4)
Mutatis mutandis these provisions mirror ss.(4) and (5) of the revised s.398. The wording of subs. (3) was amended at House of Lords Report stage to clarify the rôle of the registrar (*Hansard*, H.L. Vol. 505, cols. 1221–2, April 6, 1989).

Effect of omissions and errors in registered particulars

97. The following section is inserted in Part XII of the Companies Act 1985—

> "**Effect of omissions and errors in registered particulars**
>
> 402.—(1) Where the registered particulars of a charge created by a company are not complete and accurate, the charge is void, as

mentioned below, to the extent that rights are not disclosed by the registered particulars which would be disclosed if they were complete and accurate.

(2) The charge is void to that extent, unless the court on the application of the chargee orders otherwise, as against—
  (a) an administrator or liquidator of the company, and
  (b) any person who for value acquires an interest in or right over property subject to the charge,
where the relevant event occurs at a time when the particulars are incomplete or inaccurate in a relevant respect.

(3) Where a relevant event occurs on the same day as particulars or further particulars are delivered, it shall be presumed to have occurred before those particulars are delivered unless the contrary is proved.

(4) The court may order that the charge is effective as against an administrator or liquidator of the company if it is satisfied—
  (a) that the omission or error is not likely to have misled materially to his prejudice any unsecured creditor of the company, or
  (b) that no person became an unsecured creditor of the company at a time when the registered particulars of the charge were incomplete or inaccurate in a relevant respect.

(5) The court may order that the charge is effective as against a person acquiring an interest in or right over property subject to the charge if it is satisfied that he did not rely, in connection with the acquisition, on registered particulars which were incomplete or inaccurate in a relevant respect.

(6) For the purposes of this section an omission or inaccuracy with respect to the name of the chargee shall not be regarded as a failure to disclose the rights of the chargee.".

GENERAL NOTE

This inserts new s.402 into the C.A. 1985. It is largely new, though it does contain elements from the old s.404 which dealt with late registration by court order. Under the old law, once the chargee had received his certificate of registration he was in the clear, even if the recorded particulars of charge did not accurately reflect the true extent of his security rights. In this context see *Re Yolland, Husson and Birkett Ltd.* [1908] 1 Ch. 152; *National Provincial and Union Bank of England* v. *Charnley* [1924] 1 K.B. 431; *Re Holmes (Eric) (Property)* [1965] Ch. 1052; *Re Mechanisations (Eaglescliffe) Ltd.* [1966] Ch. 20 and *Re Nye (C.L.)* [1971] Ch. 442. The revised system will not allow the chargee to adopt such a "laid back" approach and constitutes a major move towards restoring public confidence in the integrity of the register of charges. See the discussion in the House of Commons Standing Committee D, cols. 398–9, June 20, 1989.

New s.402
Subss. (1), (2) and (3)

A chargee will be deprived of the benefit of his security to the extent that it is not reflected by the recorded particulars. This notion of partial invalidity of security is also used in s.245 of the Insolvency Act 1986. For "registered particulars" see s.415(3). "Relevant event" is defined in s.399(2).

Subss. (4) and (5)

The court has the power to waive the invalidating effect of subs. (2) where no harm has been done to unsecured creditors or where no unsecured creditor is likely to have been misled. For an interpretation of "likely" in subs. (4)(a) that might be adopted in this context, see Hoffmann J. in *Re Harris Simons Construction Ltd.* [1989] 1 W.L.R. 368. The scope of subs. (4)(b) is wide and could limit the extent of this power of waiver. Those secured creditors or bona fide purchasers who did not rely on the registered particulars cannot take advantage of subs. (2)(b).

Subs. (6)

This seeks to explain subs. (1). Misstating the name of the chargee is of no consequence.

Memorandum of charge ceasing to affect company's property

98. The following section is inserted in Part XII of the Companies Act 1985—

"**Memorandum of charge ceasing to affect company's property**

403.—(1) Where a charge of which particulars have been delivered ceases to affect the company's property, a memorandum to that effect may be delivered to the registrar for registration.

(2) The memorandum must be in the prescribed form signed by or on behalf of both the company and the chargee.

(3) Where a memorandum is delivered to the registrar for registration and appears to him to be duly signed, he shall file it in the register, and shall note, in such form as he thinks fit, the date on which it was delivered to him.

(4) The registrar shall send to the company and any person appearing from the memorandum to be the chargee, and if the memorandum was delivered by another person interested in the charge to that person, a copy of the memorandum filed by him and of the note made by him as to the date on which it was delivered.

(5) If a duly signed memorandum is delivered in a case where the charge in fact continues to affect the company's property, the charge is void as against—

(a) an administrator or liquidator of the company, and
(b) any person who for value acquires an interest in or right over property subject to the charge,

where the relevant event occurs after the delivery of the memorandum.

(6) Where a relevant event occurs on the same day as the memorandum is delivered, it shall be presumed to have occurred before the memorandum is delivered unless the contrary is proved.".

GENERAL NOTE

This inserts new s.403 into the C.A. 1985. This provision may be supplemented by regulations made under s.413 (see ss.(3), (4) and (6) of that section). Reference should also be made to s.417.

New s.403
Subss. (1) and (2)
There is nothing new in subs. (1) here, though there is no explicit mention of the statutory declaration that was formerly required. Presumably this may be required by the forthcoming secondary regulations. Note the lack of obligation in subs. (1). The fact that both parties must sign this memorandum is a new idea imported from the Scottish system.

Subs. (3)
There is an interesting change to note here; under the old law (see C.A. 1985, s.403(1) as originally enacted) the registrar had a discretion whether to file a memorandum of satisfaction or release, now he is *obliged* to do this. As in the case of s.401(4), the wording here was amended at House of Lords Report stage to clarify the duties of the registrar (*Hansard*, H.L. Vol. 505, col. 1225, April 6, 1989).

Subs. (4)
This provision has been extended so as to extend the entitlement to the chargee.

Subss. (5) and (6)
Once again these provisions are novel and deal with improperly procured memoranda. For "relevant event", see s.399(2).

Further provisions with respect to voidness of charges

99. The following sections are inserted in Part XII of the Companies Act 1985—

"Further provisions with respect to voidness of charges

Exclusion of voidness as against unregistered charges

404.—(1) A charge is not void by virtue of this Part as against a subsequent charge unless some or all of the relevant particulars of that charge are duly delivered for registration.

(a) within 21 days after the date of its creation, or
(b) before complete and accurate relevant particulars of the earlier charge are duly delivered for registration.

(2) Where relevant particulars of the subsequent charge so delivered are incomplete or inaccurate, the earlier charge is void as against that charge only to the extent that rights are disclosed by registered particulars of the subsequent charge duly delivered for registration before the corresponding relevant particulars of the earlier charge.

(3) The relevant particulars of a charge for the purposes of this section are those prescribed particulars relating to rights inconsistent with those conferred by or in relation to the other charge.

Restrictions on voidness by virtue of this Part

405.—(1) A charge is not void by virtue of this Part as against a person acquiring an interest in or right over property where the acquisition is expressly subject to the charge.

(2) Nor is a charge void by virtue of this Part in relation to any property by reason of a relevant event occurring after the company which created the charge has disposed of the whole of its interest in that property.

Effect of exercise of power of sale

406.—(1) A chargee exercising a power of sale may dispose of property to a purchaser freed from any interest or right arising from the charge having become void to any extent by virtue of this Part—

(a) against an administrator or liquidator of the company, or
(b) against a person acquiring a security interest over property subject to the charge;

and a purchaser is not concerned to see or inquire whether the charge has become so void.

(2) The proceeds of the sale shall be held by the chargee in trust to be applied—

First, in discharge of any sum effectively secured by prior incumbrances to which the sale is not made subject;

Second, in payment of all costs, charges and expenses properly incurred by him in connection with the sale, or any previous attempted sale, of the property;

Third, in discharge of any sum effectively secured by the charge and incumbrances ranking *pari passu* with the charge;

Fourth, in discharge of any sum effectively secured by incumbrances ranking after the charge;

and any residue is payable to the company or to a person authorised to give a receipt for the proceeds of the sale of the property.

(3) For the purposes of subsection (2)—

(a) prior incumbrances include any incumbrance to the extent that the charge is void as against it by virtue of this Part; and
(b) no sum is effectively secured by a charge to the extent that it is void as against an administrator or liquidator of the company.

(4) In this section—

(a) references to things done by a chargee include things done by a receiver appointed by him, whether or not the receiver acts as his agent;

(b) "power of sale" includes any power to dispose of, or grant an interest out of, property for the purpose of enforcing a charge (but in relation to Scotland does not include the power to grant a lease), and references to "sale" shall be construed accordingly; and

(c) "purchaser" means a person who in good faith and for valuable consideration acquires an interest in property.

(5) The provisions of this section as to the order of application of the proceeds of sale have effect subject to any other statutory provision (in Scotland, any other statutory provision or rule of law) applicable in any case.

(6) Where a chargee exercising a power of sale purports to dispose of property freed from any such interest or right as is mentioned in subsection (1) to a person other than a purchaser, the above provisions apply, with any necessary modifications, in relation to a disposition to a purchaser by that person or any successor in title of his.

(7) In Scotland, subsections (2) and (7) of section 27 of the Conveyancing and Feudal Reform (Scotland) Act 1970 apply to a chargee unable to obtain a discharge for any payment which he is required to make under subsection (2) above as they apply to a creditor in the circumstances mentioned in those subsections.

Effect of voidness on obligation secured

407.—(1) Where a charge becomes void to any extent by virtue of this Part, the whole of the sum secured by the charge is payable forthwith on demand; and this applies notwithstanding that the sum secured by the charge is also the subject of other security.

(2) Where the charge is to secure the repayment of money, the references in subsection (1) to the sum secured include any interest payable.".

GENERAL NOTE

This completely new clause was introduced at the eleventh hour of the Parliamentary passage of the Companies Bill—(*Hansard,* H.C. Vol. 158, col. 1160, October 26, 1989). It creates *four* new sections for the 1985 Act, *i.e.* ss.404–7.

New s.404
Subss. (1) and (3)

These describe the effect of invalidation of security as against a later unregistered charge in the event of failure to register full prescribed particulars, as defined by subs. (3). It would appear that timing will be the key factor governing priority.

Subs. (2)

A security may clearly be partially invalid. This is not a novel concept—see Insolvency Act 1986, s.245.

New s.405
Subs. (1)

An unregistered charge is not void against a person taking an interest in the security with actual notice of the existence of the charge and on the understanding that he takes subject to the charge. Although the logic behind this rule is unimpeachable, it does represent a departure from the underlying philosophy of the previous law—see *Re Monolithic Building Co. Ltd.* [1915] 1 Ch. 643.

Subs. (2)

This also restricts the invalidating effect of non-registration. It prevents a charge being invalidated retrospectively, and will prevent genuine executed commercial transactions from having to be unravelled. For "relevant event" see s.399(2).

New s.406
Subss. (1) and (4)
This authorises the holder of an unregistered charge (or his receiver—subs. (4)(a)) to realise his security with some degree of confidence. Again it confirms the existing position that invalidity can only be raised if the security still subsists.

Subss. (2) and (3)
This is the sting in the tail as far as subs. (1) is concerned; freedom to enforce the security does not mean a complete licence to walk away with the proceeds of realisation. A statutory distribution order is imposed.

Subs. (5)
This attempts to preserve existing priority rules which take preference over the order in subs. (2).

Subs. (6)
This extends the scope of subs. (2) to later sales where an attempt has been made by the chargee to avoid his obligations under subs. (2), *e.g.* by giving away property. In such a case the donee becomes subject to the above provisions. For "purchaser" see subs. (4)(c).

Subs. (7)
This makes special provision for Scotland.

New s.407
Subss. (1) and (2)
Invalidity of the security accelerates the duty to repay the debt. This is a reflection of a well-established principle in this area of law but there may be an unintentional change in the law deferring the obligation to repay because the security does not become immediately invalid on the expiry of the 21 day period, but only after the relevant event occurs.

Additional information to be registered

100. The following sections are inserted in Part XII of the Companies Act 1985—

"*Additional information to be registered*

Particulars of taking up of issue of debentures

408.—(1) Where particulars of a charge for securing an issue of debentures have been delivered for registration, it is the duty of the company—
  (a) to deliver to the registrar for registration particulars in the prescribed form of the date on which any debentures of the issue are taken up, and of the amount taken up, and
  (b) to do so before the end of the period of 21 days after the date on which they are taken up.

(2) Where particulars in the prescribed form are delivered to the registrar for registration under this section, he shall file them in the register.

(3) If a company fails to comply with subsection (1), the company and every officer of it who is in default is liable to a fine.

Notice of appointment of receiver or manager, &c.

409.—(1) If a person obtains an order for the appointment of a receiver or manager of a company's property, or appoints such a receiver or manager under powers contained in an instrument, he shall within seven days of the order or of the appointment under those powers, give notice of that fact in the prescribed form to the registrar for registration.

(2) Where a person appointed receiver or manager of a company's property under powers contained in an instrument ceases to act as

such receiver or manager, he shall, on so ceasing, give notice of that fact in the prescribed form to the registrar for registration.

(3) Where a notice under this section in the prescribed form is delivered to the registrar for registration, he shall file it in the register.

(4) If a person makes default in complying with the requirements of subsection (1) or (2), he is liable to a fine.

(5) This section does not apply in relation to companies registered in Scotland (for which corresponding provision is made by sections 53, 54 and 62 of the Insolvency Act 1986).

Notice of crystallisation of floating charge, &c.

410.—(1) The Secretary of State may by regulations require notice in the prescribed form to be given to the registrar of—
  (a) the occurrence of such events as may be prescribed affecting the nature of the security under a floating charge of which particulars have been delivered for registration, and
  (b) the taking of such action in exercise of powers conferred by a fixed or floating charge of which particulars have been delivered for registration, or conferred in relation to such a charge by an order of the court, as may be prescribed.

(2) The regulations may make provision as to—
  (a) the persons by whom notice is required to be, or may be, given, and the period within which notice is required to be given;
  (b) the filing in the register of the particulars contained in the notice and the noting of the date on which the notice was given; and
  (c) the consequences of failure to give notice.

(3) As regards the consequences of failure to give notice of an event causing a floating charge to crystallise, the regulations may include provision to the effect that the crystallisation—
  (a) shall be treated as ineffective until the prescribed particulars are delivered, and
  (b) if the prescribed particulars are delivered after the expiry of the prescribed period, shall continue to be ineffective against such persons as may be prescribed,
subject to the exercise of such powers as may be conferred by the regulations on the court.

(4) The regulations may provide that if there is a failure to comply with such of the requirements of the regulations as may be prescribed, such persons as may be prescribed are liable to a fine.

(5) Regulations under this section shall be made by statutory instrument which shall be subject to annulment in pursuance of a resolution of either House of Parliament.

(6) Regulations under this section shall not apply in relation to a floating charge created under the law of Scotland by a company registered in Scotland.".

GENERAL NOTE

Three new sections for the 1985 Act are contained in this provision.

New s.408

This provision, which deals with the registration of particulars of charge relating to a series of debentures, is derived from s.397 of the Companies Act 1985, though it is framed in much simpler terms, leaving the details to be fleshed out by regulation.

Subss. (1) and (3)

As with s.398(1), the primary duty with regard to registration is imposed on the company, this duty being enforced by criminal sanctions. Note the modified 21 day time limit in subs. (1)(b)—this is new.

Subs. (2)
Once again the registrar is only obliged to file particulars if delivered to him in the prescribed form. See s.415.

New s.409
This amounts to a reformulation of the original s.405 of the 1985 Act and will make little difference in practice. Diamond (para. 28.4.5) wanted this provision extended to cover the case where a chargee takes possession, but the legislature has not seen fit to implement this recommendation.

Subss. (1) and (3)
The seven day time limit is familiar. The notice form is prescribed by subs. (3) and regulations thereunder. Note also the notification obligations laid down by ss.39 and 46 of the Insolvency Act 1986.

Subss. (2) and (3)
Immediate notice, again in prescribed form, is required on leaving office. For administrative receivers see also Insolvency Act 1986, s.45(4).

Subs. (4)
There is no civil sanction to worry about.

Subs. (5)
Special provision is made for receiverships of Scottish companies.

News s.410
This is an entirely novel provision designed to cope with one of the practical difficulties thrown up by the widespread adoption of automatic crystallisation clauses in debentures creating floating charges. Such clauses, after years of uncertainty and in spite of criticism from the Cork Committee (Cm. 8558, para. 1579), have now received the seal of judicial approval in English law—*Re Brightlife Ltd.* [1987] 2 W.L.R. 197 and *Re Permanent Houses (Holdings) Ltd.* [1988] BCLC 563. For another legislative provision designed to combat the abuse of automatic crystallisation, see Insolvency Act 1986, s.251.

Subss. (1) and (2)
The Secretary of State may require registration of *inter alia* the occurrence of events leading to automatic crystallisation of a floating charge. For regulations under this provision see ss.413 and 418. The current intentions of the Government as to the possibility of such regulations being made in the immediate future are unclear. At the House of Lords Report Stage the Government was able to reassure the Opposition Lords about the intended operation of this new provision (*Hansard,* H.L. Vol. 505, cols. 1225–7, April 6, 1989).

Subs. (3)
The aforementioned regulations may, in the event of failure to register, render nugatory a floating charge that has crystallised by the above method. The court may be given a reserve rôle.

Subs. (4)
Criminal sanctions may also be provided for.

Subs. (5)
This negative resolution procedure for the creation of secondary legislation is well established.

Subs. (6)
These provisions do not apply to Scottish floating charges created by Scottish companies, where the characteristics of a floating charge and the circumstances under which it may attach are governed by statute.

Copies of instruments and register to be kept by company

Copies of instruments and register to be kept by company

101. The following sections are inserted in Part XII of the Companies Act 1985—

"*Copies of instruments and register to be kept by company*

Duties to keep copies of instruments and register

411.—(1) Every company shall keep at its registered office a copy of every instrument creating or evidencing a charge over the company's property.

In the case of a series of uniform debentures, a copy of one debenture of the series is sufficient.

(2) Every company shall also keep at its registered office a register of all such charges, containing entries for each charge giving a short description of the property charged, the amount of the charge and (except in the case of securities to bearer) the names of the persons entitled to it.

(3) This section applies to any charge, whether or not particulars are required to be delivered to the registrar for registration.

(4) If a company fails to comply with any requirement of this section, the company and every officer of it who is in default is liable to a fine.

Inspection of copies and register

412.—(1) The copies and the register referred to in section 411 shall be open to the inspection of any creditor or member of the company without fee; and to the inspection of any other person on payment of such fee as may be prescribed.

(2) Any person may request the company to provide him with a copy of—
  (a) any instrument creating or evidencing a charge over the company's property, or
  (b) any entry in the register of charges kept by the company, on payment of such fee as may be prescribed.

This subsection applies to any charge, whether or not particulars are required to be delivered to the registrar for registration.

(3) The company shall send the copy to him not later than ten days after the day on which the request is received or, if later, on which payment is received.

(4) If inspection of the copies or register is refused, or a copy requested is not sent within the time specified above—
  (a) the company and every officer of it who is in default is liable to a fine, and
  (b) the court may by order compel an immediate inspection of the copies or register or, as the case may be, direct that the copy be sent immediately.".

GENERAL NOTE

This provision deals with the domestic registration of charges at the company's registered office, a system that was first set in place in 1862. It repeats the pattern found above in that it re-enacts in amended form ss.406–408 of the 1985 legislation, which are now ss.411 and 412.

New s.411

This new provision combines the original ss.406 and 407 of the Companies Act 1985.

Subss. (1)–(3)
The company must keep, at its registered office, copies of *all* instruments of charge plus a register of basic details of all charges, even if such charges are not registrable at the Companies Registry. For registrar see s.395(4).

Subs. (4)
This is a weak sanction. There is no question of the security being invalidated, as the House of Lords confirmed in *Wright* v. *Horton* (1887) 12 App.Cas. 371.

New s.412
This is based on the original s.408 of the 1985 Act but extends the right of the public to inspect and take copies.

Subss. (1)–(3)
This group of provisions regulates inspection rights. Under the old law, although the register of charges was open to inspection by anyone, the crucial right to inspect the copies of instruments of charge was only extended to current members and creditors. The new provision plugs an important loophole by allowing any person to inspect the copies of instruments of charge. The original version of the Bill contained specific details of inspection hours and fees for exercising inspection rights or taking copies, but this detail was removed at House of Lords Report stage on the grounds that such minutiae were best left to be prescribed by statutory instrument (*Hansard*, H.L. Vol. 505, col. 1227, April 6, 1989).

Note the right to demand copies and the 10 day deadline imposed by subs. (3). This is a new departure in the statute, even though at common law the right to inspect probably encompassed the taking of copies—see *Nelson* v. *Anglo American Land Mortgage Agency* [1897] 1 Ch. 130. On this point note the Diamond Report (para. 22.1.8).

Subs. (4)
Enforcement is achieved through criminal sanctions and court orders.

Supplementary provisions

Power to make further provision by regulations

102. The following section is inserted in Part XII of the Companies Act 1985—

"Supplementary provisions

Power to make further provision by regulations

413.—(1) The Secretary of State may by regulations make further provision as to the application of the provisions of this Part in relation to charges of any description specified in the regulations.

Nothing in the following provisions shall be construed as restricting the generality of that power.

(2) The regulations may require that where the charge is contained in or evidenced or varied by a written instrument there shall be delivered to the registrar for registration, instead of particulars or further particulars of the charge, the instrument itself or a certified copy of it together with such particulars as may be prescribed.

(3) The regulations may provide that a memorandum of a charge ceasing to affect property of the company shall not be accepted by the registrar unless supported by such evidence as may be prescribed, and that a memorandum not so supported shall be treated as not having been delivered.

(4) The regulations may also provide that where the instrument creating the charge is delivered to the registrar in support of such a memorandum, the registrar may mark the instrument as cancelled before returning it and shall send copies of the instrument cancelled to such persons as may be prescribed.

(5) The regulations may exclude or modify, in such circumstances and to such extent as may be prescribed, the operation of the provisions of this Part relating to the voidness of a charge.

(6) The regulations may require, in connection with the delivery of particulars, further particulars or a memorandum of the charge's ceasing to affect property of the company, the delivery of such supplementary information as may be prescribed, and may—
  (a) apply in relation to such supplementary information any provisions of this Part relating to particulars, further particulars or such a memorandum, and
  (b) provide that the particulars, further particulars or memorandum shall be treated as not having been delivered until the required supplementary information is delivered.

(7) Regulations under this section shall be made by statutory instrument which shall be subject to annulment in pursuance of a resolution of either House of Parliament.".

GENERAL NOTE
This, again, was a very late addition to the Bill and, being introduced under the guillotine, we have no guidance on the thinking behind it.

New s.413
Subs. (1)
Once again we see the use of delegated legislation to supplement the provisions of a Companies Act.

Subss. (2)–(6)
These subsections give us some idea what these regulations might provide for. It is clear from subs. (1) that we are not here presented with an exhaustive list. The possibility that these regulations might require an instrument of charge to be submitted to the Registrar instead of prescribed particulars is odd to say the least, as this legislation was supposed to be moving away from that requirement and the burden which it imposed on the Registrar. Subs. (5) confers considerable latitude on the Secretary of State to amend primary legislation—a so-called "Henry VIII clause".

Subs. (7)
The use of the negative resolution procedure is now standard practice.

Other supplementary provisions

103. The following sections are inserted in Part XII of the Companies Act 1985—

"Date of creation of charge
414.—(1) References in this Part to the date of creation of a charge by a company shall be construed as follows.

(2) A charge created under the law of England and Wales shall be taken to be created—
  (a) in the case of a charge created by an instrument in writing, when the instrument is executed by the company or, if its execution by the company is conditional, upon the conditions being fulfilled, and
  (b) in any other case, when an enforceable agreement is entered into by the company conferring a security interest intended to take effect forthwith or upon the company acquiring an interest in property subject to the charge.

(3) A charge created under the law of Scotland shall be taken to be created—
  (a) in the case of a floating charge, when the instrument creating the floating charge is executed by the company, and

(b) in any other case, when the right of the person entitled to the benefit of the charge is constituted as a real right.

(4) Where a charge is created in the United Kingdom but comprises property outside the United Kingdom, any further proceedings necessary to make the charge valid or effectual under the law of the country where the property is situated shall be disregarded in ascertaining the date on which the charge is to be taken to be created.

Prescribed particulars and related expressions

415.—(1) References in this Part to the prescribed particulars of a charge are to such particulars of, or relating to, the charge as may be prescribed.

(2) The prescribed particulars may, without prejudice to the generality of subsection (1), include—
  (a) whether the company has undertaken not to create other charges ranking in priority to or *pari passu* with the charge, and
  (b) whether the charge is a market charge within the meaning of Part VII of the Companies Act 1989 or a charge to which the provisions of that Part apply as they apply to a market charge.

(3) References in this Part to the registered particulars of a charge at any time are to such particulars and further particulars of the charge as have at that time been duly delivered for registration.

(4) References in this Part to the registered particulars of a charge being complete and accurate at any time are to their including all the prescribed particulars which would be required to be delivered if the charge were then newly created.

Notice of matters disclosed on register

416.—(1) A person taking a charge over a company's property shall be taken to have notice of any matter requiring registration and disclosed on the register at the time the charge is created.

(2) Otherwise, a person shall not be taken to have notice of any matter by reason of its being disclosed on the register or by reason of his having failed to search the register in the course of making such inquiries as ought reasonably to be made.

(3) The above provisions have effect subject to any other statutory provision as to whether a person is to be taken to have notice of any matter disclosed on the register.

Power of court to dispense with signature

417.—(1) Where it is proposed to deliver further particulars of a charge, or to deliver a memorandum of a charge ceasing to affect the company's property, and—
  (a) the chargee refuses to sign or authorise a person to sign on his behalf, or cannot be found, or
  (b) the company refuses to authorise a person to sign on its behalf,
the court may on the application of the company or the chargee, or of any other person having a sufficient interest in the matter, authorise the delivery of the particulars or memorandum without that signature.

(2) The order may be made on such terms as appear to the court to be appropriate.

(3) Where particulars or a memorandum are delivered to the registrar for registration in reliance on an order under this section, they must be accompanied by an office copy of the order.

In such a case the references in sections 401 and 403 to the particulars or memorandum being duly signed are to their being otherwise duly signed.

(4) The registrar shall file the office copy of the court order along with the particulars or memorandum.".

GENERAL NOTE
This clause inserts four new provisions into the Companies Act 1985.

New s.414
Subss. (1) and (2)
These define the date of creation of a charge for the purposes of English law. The key date is that of execution of the debenture (not date of issue), unless that date is postponed (*e.g.* by an escrow).

Subs. (3)
This is a parallel provision for Scotland.

Subs. (4)
The fact that a charge created in this country requires further steps to be performed before it is valid abroad does not lead to a deferral in its date of creation.

New s.415
Subss. (1)–(4)
This is a fairly bland and uninformative interpretation provision. Hidden away in subs. (2), however, is a clear hint that negative pledge clauses may have to be registered. For discussion of this issue see the undertaking given by the Government in House of Commons Standing Committee D, cols. 407–8, June 20, 1989.
For "market charges" see Companies Act 1989, s.173.

New s.416
Subss. (1) and (2)
These represent yet another (and hopefully the final) attempt in this Bill to deal with the vexed question of constructive notice. For earlier discussion see *Hansard*, H.L. Vol. 505, cols. 1216–21, April 6, 1989). The current position at common law, as reflected by a stream of authority running from *Re Standard Rotary Machine Co. Ltd.* (1906) 95 L.T. 829, *Wilson* v. *Kelland* [1910] 2 Ch. 306, *Earle* v. *Hemsworth Rural District Council* (1928) 44 T.L.R. 758 to the Scottish case of *Trade Development Bank* v. *Warriner and Mason (Scotland) Ltd.* 1980 S.C. 74 is that registration of the charge at the Companies Registry constitutes notice to the world of the existence (but not the contents) of the charge. At one time it appeared that this doctrine was to be swept away by the 1989 Act and indeed s.142 does just that for most areas of company law. However, this apparently is not to be the case for registration of charges. We now have in subs. (1) a reformulated doctrine which ascribes notice to later chargees of the registered particulars in so far as they are required to be registered.
Gratuitous registration of supplementary information will have no effect. The position on notice is more relaxed for later non-chargees (subs. (2)). For date of creation of the charge see s.414.

Subs. (3)
This is a saving provision which may well be relevant to the land charges area of company charges.

New s.417
Subss. (1) and (2)
These are useful provisions which have been relocated from earlier versions of the Bill. The idea appears to have been derived from Scotland.

Subss. (3) and (4)
These deal with the mechanics of registration, but note the mandatory tone of subs. (4).

Interpretation, &c.

104. The following sections are inserted in Part XII of the Companies Act 1985—

"**Regulations**
418. Regulations under any provision of this Part, or prescribing anything for the purposes of any such provision—
   (a) may make different provision for different cases, and

(b) may contain such supplementary, incidental and transitional provisions as appear to the Secretary of State to be appropriate.

Minor definitions

419.—(1) In this Part—

"chargee" means the person for the time being entitled to exercise the security rights conferred by the charge;

"issue of debentures" means a group of debentures, or an amount of debenture stock, secured by the same charge; and

"series of debentures" means a group of debentures each containing or giving by reference to another instrument a charge to the benefit of which the holders of debentures of the series are entitled *pari passu*.

(2) References in this Part to the creation of a charge include the variation of a charge which is not registrable so as to include property by virtue of which it becomes registrable.

The provisions of section 414 (construction of references to date of creation of charge) apply in such a case with any necessary modifications.

(3) References in this Part to the date of acquisition of property by a company are—

(a) in England and Wales, to the date on which the acquisition is completed, and

(b) in Scotland, to the date on which the transaction is settled.

(4) In the application of this Part to a floating charge created under the law of Scotland, references to crystallisation shall be construed as references to the attachment of the charge.

(5) References in this Part to the beginning of insolvency proceedings are to—

(a) the presentation of a petition on which an administration order or winding-up order is made, or

(b) the passing of a resolution for voluntary winding up.

Index of defined expressions

420. The following Table shows the provisions of this Part defining or otherwise explaining expressions used in this Part (other than expressions used only in the same section)—

"charge	sections 395(2) and 396(6)
charge requiring registration	section 396
chargee	section 419(1)
complete and accurate (in relation to registered particulars)	section 415(4)
creation of charge	section 419(2)
crystallisation (in relation to Scottish floating charge)	section 419(4)
date of acquisition (of property by a company)	section 419(3)
date of creation of charge	section 414
further particulars	section 401
insolvency proceedings, beginning of	section 419(5)
issue of debentures	section 419(1)
memorandum of charge ceasing to affect company's property	section 403
prescribed particulars	section 415(1) and (2)
property	section 395(2)
registered particulars	section 415(3)

registrar and registration in relation to a charge	section 395(4)
relevant event	section 399(2)
series of debentures	section 419(1).".

GENERAL NOTE
This section inserts three new sections into the Companies Act 1985.

New s.418
This underlines the extensive powers of the Secretary of State when it comes to making regulations in this area. Note here regulations under ss.396(4) and 406(1). It is difficult to see why this provision is needed in view of the wide scope of s.413.

New s.419
Subss. (1) and (2)
This is a useful definition section, which, *inter alia,* makes suitable amendments for Scottish law. The definition of beginning of insolvency proceedings is relevant to ss.399 and 400. The significance of the phrase "issue of debentures" is apparent when one considers s.396(1)(d).

New s.420
This form of tabular assistance to interpretation is fairly novel, though used extensively throughout this Act. It may prove useful in practice.

Charges on property of oversea company

105. The provisions set out in Schedule 15 are inserted in Part XXIII of the Companies Act 1985 (oversea companies), as a Chapter III (registration of charges).

GENERAL NOTE
This provision paves the way for Sched. 15, which seeks to clarify the law on the registration of charges over the assets of oversea companies (see the Introductory Note). It also makes a structural change in the 1985 Act by transferring the relevant provisions from Pt. IV to a more appropriate location in Pt. XXIII. For discussion, see House of Commons Standing Committee D, cols. 408–10, June 20, 1989.

New s.703A
Subss. (1) and (3)
These define the extent of ss.703A–N and have the effect of overturning the *Slavenburg* ruling [1980] 1 W.L.R. 1076 by providing that the duty to register details of charge should only apply to *registered oversea companies* and not merely to foreign companies which do business in this country. Diamond favoured this solution—see para. 27.11 of his Report.

Subs. (2)
This simply defines terms.

Subs. (4)
See s.703E.

New s.703B
Subs. (1)
This tells us what has to be registered. See the list in s.396.

Subs. (2)
This states *when* registration is required.

Subs. (3)
This is purely explanatory and mirrors s.396(6).

New s.703C
Subss. (1) and (2)
These are the counterparts of s.397.

Subs. (3)
The provisions in s.397 with regard to the giving of receipts are made applicable to the oversea companies charges register.

New s.703D
Subs. (1)
This deals with the registration of existing charges created by companies wishing to register as oversea companies under s.691.

Subs. (2)
The obligation to register arises after the elapse of 21 days but only if it is the case that the property has remained in Great Britain for longer than that period.

Subs. (3)
This provision would appear to be in the nature of a back-up to subs. (2) by imposing a secondary four month registration deadline for cases where charged property finds its way into Great Britain. The method of expressing the timing sequence here leaves much to be desired. For an explanation of its raison d'être, see House of Commons Standing Committee D, col. 409, June 20, 1989.

Subs. (4)
Anyone can register particulars of charge.

Subs. (5)
The sanction for non-registration is a fine. But note s.703F for a more Draconian consequence of non-registration.

Subs. (6)
This is a late amendment and involves relocation of an existing provision in the Bill.

New s.703E
Subs. (1)
This provides a link with registration of the oversea company under s.691.

Subss. (2) and (3)
Problems caused by the multiple registration system for oversea companies and their charges are addressed by these provisions.

Subs. (4)
The position of companies which cease to fall within the scope of s.691 is dealt with by this subsection, but there is to be no retrospective advantage to be gained here.

New s.703F
Subss. (1)–(3)
Ss.399–406, plus ss.409–410 are hereby extended to this area, subject to minor modifications. Note the special four month time limit for cases governed by s.703D(3).

New s.703G
This again merely extends provisions governing general charge registration to this specialised area of the subject.

New s.703H
Subss. (1) and (2)
Again, this provides a link with the basic rules on charge registration subject to the special four month time limit for cases falling under s.703D(3).

New s.703I
Subss. (1)–(3)
Ss.408–410 are thus made applicable.

New s.703J
Subss. (1)–(3)
This extends ss.411 and 412 to registered oversea companies. This domestic register must be kept at the oversea company's principal place of business in Great Britain. By definition it will not have a registered office here.

New s.703K
Subss. (1) and (2)
Once again, the Secretary of State is given wide power to amend this area of law.

New s.703L
Subs. (1)
This is a definition section that lays down guidance for determining the location of vehicles belonging to oversea companies.

Subs. (2)
Problems posed by charges over future assets are tackled here.

New s.703M
This is the final provision coupling the provisions on general charge registration to this particular area.

New s.703N
This is the counterpart to s.420.

Application of provisions to unregistered companies

106. In Schedule 22 to the Companies Act 1985 (provisions applying to unregistered companies), at the appropriate place insert—
"Part XII   Registration of company   Subject to section 718(3).".
             charges; copies of
             instruments and register to
             be kept by company.

GENERAL NOTE
This makes the provisions relating to registration of company charges applicable to unregistered companies (see C.A. 1985, s.718 and Sched. 22). If the E.E.I.G. becomes popular these provisions may grow in importance. For background information see House of Commons Standing Committee D, cols. 411–2, June 20, 1989.

Consequential amendments

107. The enactments specified in Schedule 16 have effect with the amendments specified there, which are consequential on the amendments made by the preceding provisions of this Part.

GENERAL NOTE
This section, which must be read in the light of Sched.16, effects a number of amendments to existing companies legislation consequent upon the enactment of the provisions of Pt. IV. For the most part these changes are largely cosmetic. Note the new tabulation of criminal sanctions for breach of registration obligations.

Part V

Other amendments of Company Law

A company's capacity and related matters

A company's capacity and the power of the directors to bind it

108.—(1) In Chapter III of Part I of the Companies Act 1985 (a company's capacity; formalities of carrying on business), for section 35 substitute—

"**A company's capacity not limited by its memorandum**

35.—(1) The validity of an act done by a company shall not be called into question on the ground of lack of capacity by reason of anything in the company's memorandum.

(2) A member of a company may bring proceedings to restrain the doing of an act which but for subsection (1) would be beyond the company's capacity; but no such proceedings shall lie in respect of an act to be done in fulfilment of a legal obligation arising from a previous act of the company.

(3) It remains the duty of the directors to observe any limitations on their powers flowing from the company's memorandum; and action by the directors which but for subsection (1) would be beyond the company's capacity may only be ratified by the company by special resolution.

A resolution ratifying such action shall not affect any liability incurred by the directors or any other person; relief from any such liability must be agreed to separately by special resolution.

(4) The operation of this section is restricted by section 30B(1) of the Charities Act 1960 and section 112(3) of the Companies Act 1989 in relation to companies which are charities; and section 322A below (invalidity of certain transactions to which directors or their associates are parties) has effect notwithstanding this section.

Power of directors to bind the company

35A.—(1) In favour of a person dealing with a company in good faith, the power of the board of directors to bind the company, or authorise others to do so, shall be deemed to be free of any limitation under the company's constitution.

(2) For this purpose—
  (a) a person "deals with" a company if he is a party to any transaction or other act to which the company is a party;
  (b) a person shall not be regarded as acting in bad faith by reason only of his knowing that an act is beyond the powers of the directors under the company's constitution; and
  (c) a person shall be presumed to have acted in good faith unless the contrary is proved.

(3) The references above to limitations on the directors' powers under the company's constitution include limitations deriving—
  (a) from a resolution of the company in general meeting or a meeting of any class of shareholders, or
  (b) from any agreement between the members of the company or of any class of shareholders.

(4) Subsection (1) does not affect any right of a member of the company to bring proceedings to restrain the doing of an act which is beyond the powers of the directors; but no such proceedings shall lie

in respect of an act to be done in fulfilment of a legal obligation arising from a previous act of the company.

(5) Nor does that subsection affect any liability incurred by the directors, or any other person, by reason of the directors' exceeding their powers.

(6) The operation of this section is restricted by section 30B(1) of the Charities Act 1960 and section 112(3) of the Companies Act 1989 in relation to companies which are charities; and section 322A below (invalidity of certain transactions to which directors or their associates are parties) has effect notwithstanding this section.

No duty to enquire as to capacity of company or authority of directors
35B. A party to a transaction with a company is not bound to enquire as to whether it is permitted by the company's memorandum or as to any limitation on the powers of the board of directors to bind the company or authorise others to do so.".

(2) In Schedule 21 to the Companies Act 1985 (effect of registration of companies not formed under that Act), in paragraph 6 (general application of provisions of Act), after sub-paragraph (5) insert—

"(6) Where by virtue of sub-paragraph (4) or (5) a company does not have power to alter a provision, it does not have power to ratify acts of the directors in contravention of the provision.".

(3) In Schedule 22 to the Companies Act 1985 (provisions applying to unregistered companies), in the entries relating to Part I, in the first column for "section 35" substitute "sections 35 to 35B".

GENERAL NOTE

This section substitutes new ss.35, 35A and 35B into the Companies Act 1985, replacing the existing s.35 (*i.e.* the consolidated s.9(1) of the European Communities Act 1985). There is also a consequential amendment to Sched. 22 to the 1985 Act applying to unregistered companies. This, and the following four sections, are the result of a D.T.I. consultative document following a report in 1985 by Dr. Prentice of Oxford University, "Reform of the Ultra Vires Rule". Their intention is to perfect the imperfect abolition of constitutional restrictions on the capacity of the company and the authority of its directors with regard to third parties under the former s.35, whilst preserving the internal function of those restrictions as a measure of shareholder protection. In legislating in this area the U.K. is bound by Art. 9, para. 1 of the first EC directive on company law (1968). This reads as follows:

"Acts done by the organs of the company shall be binding upon it, even if those acts are not within the objects of the company, unless such acts exceed the powers that the law confers or allows to be conferred on those organs."

In attempting to implement this directive, U.K. law suffers from the problem that it has no concept in commercial transactions of an organ of the company. U.K. law depends upon the law of agency to establish a valid corporate transaction; see the note to new s.35A(1) below.

The scheme of the new legislation is that corporate capacity is dealt with in new s.35 and the authority of the directors to act outside that capacity in new ss.35A and 35B. These new sections should be read as being subject to C.A. 1985, new s.322A (introduced by s.109) if the third party is a director or connected person, and to ss.111 and 112 of this Act if the company concerned is a charitable company. Measures to simplify the content and alteration of the objects clause are contained in new ss.3A and 4 of the 1985 Act, introduced by s.110 of this Act.

New s.35
Subs. (1)

This effectively abolishes the doctrine of *ultra vires* in so far as most companies are concerned. The company will have full capacity as regards third parties. For the effect of such limits in the memorandum on the authority of its directors see new s.35A below. This new subsection will only apply if it is an "act done by a company" which presupposes in commercial transactions that an agent doing the act either has authority to bind the company or the company ratifies his act. The word "act" clearly includes gifts as well as contractual transactions. The wording will apply either in favour of or against the company concerned.

Unlike the former s.35 or the new s.35A, it does not depend upon the knowledge of the third party. The use of the word "memorandum" rather than simply the objects clause was a late alteration, so that it could obviate any infringement of the other clauses in that document, *e.g.* the capital clause. The reality is that it will apply to the objects clause.

Subs. (2)

This is intended to preserve an individual shareholder's right to seek an injunction to prevent a proposed act which is contrary to the memorandum. This is a personal right of any shareholder (see, *e.g. Colman* v. *Eastern Counties Ry Co.* (1846) 10 Beav. 1). This right will be lost, however, if the company is already under a legal obligation arising from a previous act of the company. This raises the question as to an act previous to what? The logical answer is an act previous to the act sought to be restrained and if that first act (*e.g.* the making of an executory contract) is valid under new s.35A, no injunction will lie to prevent, *e.g.* the execution of that contract. In practice it is difficult to envisage circumstanced in which a shareholder will be able to bring such an action. Since the right to an injunction is a personal one, no question of a derivative action arises, but, because ratification is now possible, (see subs.(3)) it may well be lost *de facto* on such ratification. The alternative of a petition under C.A. 1985, s.459 for unfairly prejudicial conduct on the failure of legitimate expectation ground may be more rewarding for a minority shareholder in such circumstances.

Subs. (3)

This preserves the fiduciary liability of directors who act outside the memorandum of the company. Any such action must be brought by the company itself or by a derivative action. The latter was, in fact, limited recently in *Smith* v. *Croft (No. 3)* [1988] Ch. 114. However, the act itself may now be ratified by a special resolution of the company, although a separate special resolution will be needed to relieve the directors of personal liability to the company. It may be, therefore, that a derivative action will lie if ratification or relief is attempted by anything less on the principle established in *Baillie* v. *Oriental Telephone and Electronic Co. Ltd.* [1915] 1 Ch. 503.

The power to ratify an act contrary to the objects clause by special resolution is included because that clause itself can now be so altered at any time under C.A. 1985, new s.4, (see s.110). It is strange, however, that it was included in new s.35 as opposed to new s.35A (where it lay until the final stages of the Bill). Ratification of the act, as opposed to relief for the directors, will only be needed if the third party cannot rely on new s.35A—the company has capacity in all circumstances under new s.35(1).

Subs. (4)

This provides for the restrictions both for directors as third parties and charitable companies in England and Scotland. See the notes to ss.109, 111 and 112 (below).

New s.35A

Abolishing restrictions on corporate capacity under new s.35 will not protect third parties. Under the law of agency, any restrictions imposed by the company's constitution will affect the agent's authority to bind the company and so negative the value of new s.35. Accordingly, new s.35A is intended to remove all such consitutional limitations on the authority of the directors in favour of third parties, whilst again preserving the internal rights of the shareholders if the directors do so act. The continental theory of the directors as the organs of the company who, if registered, bind the company automatically and who do not if not so registered, and upon which the first directive was based, does not apply in the U.K.

Subs. (1)

This is negative only in that it removes, for the benefit of most third parties, the fetters to the board's authority to act or to delegate their authority to act which flow from the company's constitution. The agent must still have authority to act under the general law of agency, *i.e.* actual, implied or apparent authority. This concept is alien to the organic theory set out below. One consequence of this subsection will be that the board's powers of holding out giving another agent apparent authority will be virtually limitless. Lord Wedderburn, in debate, styled this new authority as 'ghost' authority. Even if this subsection does not apply, the act may be ratified by the company under new s.35(3). The precise effect of new subs. (1) is defined in new subss. (2) and (3).

Subs. (2)

This relates to two concepts required for subs. (1) to operate. First, that subsection only operates in favour of a person *dealing* with a company. Para. (a) makes it clear that both transactions and other acts are covered. It is not clear what the precise difference between these two concepts are, but it is clear that gratuitous acts will be covered by this wording, one of the difficulties in the former s.35 (see *Re Halt Garage (1964)* [1982] 3 All E.R. 1016). In other new sections the distinction, if any, may be relevant; see, *e.g.* new s.35B.

The second requirement for subs. (1) to apply is that the person dealing with the company be acting in good faith. Paras. (b) and (c) of subs. (2) provide two important presumptions in this respect. Para. (b) reverses the views expressed on the former s.35 that knowledge of the defect alone would defeat the section (see *International Sales and Agencies Ltd.* v. *Marcus* [1982] 3 All E.R. 551). Something else will be required to establish bad faith, *i.e.* understanding, which may be subjectively or objectively assessed. It is possible, if the former is adopted, that a third party could be so protected under new s.35A yet retain his liability as a constructive trustee as propounded in *Re Montagu's S.T.* [1987] Ch. 264. The second presumption is that good faith is to be presumed unless the contrary is proved. This was found in the former s.35. Note also new s.35B as to the lack of any duty of a third party to investigate the possibility of any such defect.

Subs. (3)

This widens the definition as to which limitations on the directors' powers are to be excluded by subs. (1). There is no comprehensive definition of a company's constitution for this purpose but it includes ordinary resolutions and contractual restrictions. It is an open question whether a restriction as to the composition of the board (*e.g.* as to quorum) in the articles, or otherwise in the constitution, will be a limitation freed by subs. (1). It may or may not be regarded as a limitation on the powers of the board.

Subs. (4)

This is intended to prevent the removal of restrictions in subs. (1) affecting the rights of shareholders to restrain an act contrary to such restrictions. This right will be lost if the company is already bound to carry out that act. See the note on new s.35(2).

Subs. (5)

This preserves the liability of the directors to the company if they act outside their constitutional limits. Any such action must be brought by the company or by way of a derivative action. See the note to new s.35(3).

Subs. (6)

This provides for the restrictions both for directors as third parties and charitable companies in England and Scotland. See the notes to ss.108, 111 and 112 (below).

New s.35B

This section re-enacts the removal of any duty on a third party to enquire as to whether the transaction is contrary to the company's constitution. This section should be read with new s.35A(2). It applies, however, only to transactions and not to acts. *Quaere* whether that will produce any practical difficulties in relation to gratuitous acts?

Invalidity of certain transactions involving directors

109.—(1) In Part X of the Companies Act 1985 (enforcement of fair dealing by directors), after section 322 insert—

"**Invalidity of certain transactions involving directors, etc.**

322A.—(1) This section applies where a company enters into a transaction to which the parties include—
  (a) a director of the company or of its holding company, or
  (b) a person connected with such a director or a company with whom such a director is associated,
and the board of directors, in connection with the transaction, exceed any limitation on their powers under the company's constitution.

(2) The transaction is voidable at the instance of the company.

(3) Whether or not it is avoided, any such party to the transaction as is mentioned in subsection (1)(a) or (b), and any director of the company who authorised the transaction, is liable—
  (a) to account to the company for any gain which he has made directly or indirectly by the transaction, and

(b) to indemnify the company for any loss or damage resulting from the transaction.

(4) Nothing in the above provisions shall be construed as excluding the operation of any other enactment or rule of law by virtue of which the transaction may be called in question or any liability to the company may arise.

(5) The transaction ceases to be voidable if—
    (a) restitution of any money or other asset which was the subject-matter of the transaction is no longer possible, or
    (b) the company is indemnified for any loss or damage resulting from the transaction, or
    (c) rights acquired bona fide for value and without actual notice of the directors' exceeding their powers by a person who is not party to the transaction would be affected by the avoidance, or
    (d) the transaction is ratified by the company in general meeting, by ordinary or special resolution or otherwise as the case may require.

(6) A person other than a director of the company is not liable under subsection (3) if he shows that at the time the transaction was entered into he did not know that the directors were exceeding their powers.

(7) This section does not affect the operation of section 35A in relation to any party to the transaction not within subsection (1)(a) or (b).

But where a transaction is voidable by virtue of this section and valid by virtue of that section in favour of such a person, the court may, on the application of that person or of the company, make such order affirming, severing or setting aside the transaction, on such terms, as appear to the court to be just.

(8) In this section "transaction" includes any act; and the reference in subsection (1) to limitations under the company's constitution includes limitations deriving—
    (a) from a resolution of the company in general meeting or a meeting of any class of shareholders, or
    (b) from any agreement between the members of the company or of any class of shareholders.".

(2) In Schedule 22 to the Companies Act 1985 (provisions applying to unregistered companies), in the entries relating to Part X, insert—

"section 322A   Invalidity of certain   Subject to section
                       transactions involving   718(3).".
                       directors, etc.

GENERAL NOTE

This section introduces a new s.322A into the Companies Act 1985 and applies that section to unregistered companies so far as the Secretary of State may decide by regulations. The new section modifies the operation of C.A. 1985, new ss.35, 35A and 35B (s.108 above) where the third party is a director or connected person.

New s.322A

When a board of directors has exceeded its powers under the company's constitution in a transaction where the third party is a director of that company or its holding company, or is a person connected with such a director or with an associated company of a director (see C.A. 1985, s.346(2)(4)) then the transaction is voidable at the company's option (subss. (1) and (2)). This reverses the presumption of validity in new s.35A (s.108). As originally drafted, this section rendered all such transactions void unless ratified by the company. This was changed to the concept of voidability on the basis that third party rights would be prejudiced. For "limits" under the constitution see subs. (8) and the note to new s.35A(2).

Note that a transaction includes any act (subs. (8)); *cf.* new s.35B. Subs. (4) makes it clear that this does not affect any other defect in the transaction. It does not appear to apply to shadow directors.

The transaction is voidable and not void. Subs. (5) provides that the company will lose its right to avoid the transaction if: (a) restitution is not possible; (b) the company is indemnified against any loss; (c) it would affect rights acquired by a bona fide purchaser without actual notice of the defect (to protect *inter alia* the Land Registry); (d) if the transaction is ratified by the company (whether by an ordinary resolution, special resolution (if s.35(3) operates) or the articles have been infringed, or otherwise, *e.g.* by a written resolution under s.113 of this Act; see below). There is nothing in the section to prevent the director concerned voting on such a resolution. Since the transaction is voidable it does not need to be ratified in this way, it could be ratified by the company adopting the transaction. The company may presumably also lose the right to avoid the contract under the general law, *e.g.* due to the operation of *laches*.

Whether or not the transaction itself is ratified, the director or connected person, or any director who authorised the transaction, is liable to account for any gain arising and to indemnify the company against any loss. A non-director will not, however, be so liable if he can show that he had no knowledge of the defect at the time of the transaction (subss. (2) and (6)). "Know" will presumably mean "actual knowledge."

By virtue of subs. (7) this new section will not affect the operation of new s.35A in relation to a third party who is neither a director nor a connected person within subs. (1). Thus it is possible that if a director and an independent person are involved as third parties, the transaction will be both voidable against the director under this section and valid as against the other party under new s.35A. In such a case either the independent party or the company may apply to the court who may affirm, sever or set aside the transaction on "just" terms.

Statement of company's objects

110. In Chapter I of Part I of the Companies Act 1985 (company formation), after section 3 (forms of memorandum) insert—

"**Statement of company's objects: general commercial company**

3A. Where the company's memorandum states that the object of the company is to carry on business as a general commercial company—

(a) the object of the company is to carry on any trade or business whatsoever, and

(b) the company has power to do all such things as are incidental or conducive to the carrying on of any trade or business by it.".

(2) In the same Chapter, for section 4 (resolution to alter objects) substitute—

"**Resolution to alter objects**

4.—(1) A company may by special resolution alter its memorandum with respect to the statement of the company's objects.

(2) If an application is made under the following section, an alteration does not have effect except in so far as it is confirmed by the court.".

GENERAL NOTE

This section introduces a new s.3A and substitutes a new s.4 into the Companies Act 1985. The effect is to allow the use of short objects clauses giving wide powers (new s.3A) and to allow a general right to alter the objects clauses (new s.4). These changes are part of the reform of the law on objects clauses contained in new C.A. 1985, ss.35, 35A and 35B (s.101 above). Since such clauses are now, for most practical purposes, purely internal restrictions, it was agreed to simplify them and to allow for changes to be made. Other possibilities, such as the abolition of the objects clause, or making one optional, were not adopted. The basic law on the objects clause itself therefore remains the same.

New s.3A

Companies may now adopt a single object, *i.e.* to carry on business as a general commercial company. By virtue of this new section the company does not have unlimited powers but may carry on any business or trade and do all such things as are incidental or conducive to any such trade or business. It is not clear, however, whether a company may adopt this objects clause with exceptions and still take the benefit of the section subject to those exceptions. Such a clause may, on the other hand, be extended by the shareholders.

New s.4

Companies may now alter their objects clause by special resolution. The present restrictions on the purposes for which such a change may be made are abolished. However, such a right remains subject to a dissentient minority petition under the existing C.A. 1985, s.5 and if such an application is made, any change will only have effect as and when confirmed by the court under that section.

Charitable companies

111.—(1) In the Charities Act 1960, for section 30 (charitable companies) substitute—

"**Charitable companies: winding up**

30. Where a charity may be wound up by the High Court under the Insolvency Act 1986, a petition for it to be wound up under that Act by any court in England or Wales having jurisdiction may be presented by the Attorney General, as well as by any person authorised by that Act.

Charitable companies: alteration of objects clause

30A.—(1) Where a charity is a company or other body corporate having power to alter the instruments establishing or regulating it as a body corporate, no exercise of that power which has the effect of the body ceasing to be a charity shall be valid so as to affect the application of—
   (a) any property acquired under any disposition or agreement previously made otherwise than for full consideration in money or money's worth, or any property representing property so acquired,
   (b) any property representing income which has accrued before the alteration is made, or
   (c) the income from any such property as aforesaid.

(2) Where a charity is a company, any alteration by it of the objects clause in its memorandum of association is ineffective without the prior written consent of the Commissioners; and it shall deliver a copy of that consent to the registrar of companies under section 6(1)(a) or (b) of the Companies Act 1985 along with the printed copy of the memorandum as altered.

(3) Section 6(3) of that Act (offences) applies in relation to a default in complying with subsection (2) as regards the delivery of a copy of the Commissioners' consent.

Charitable companies: invalidity of certain transactions

30B.—(1) Sections 35 and 35A of the Companies Act 1985 (capacity of company not limited by its memorandum; power of directors to bind company) do not apply to the acts of a company which is a charity except in favour of a person who—
   (a) gives full consideration in money or money's worth in relation to the act in question, and
   (b) does not know that the act is not permitted by the company's memorandum or, as the case may be, is beyond the powers of the directors,
or who does not know at the time the act is done that the company is a charity.

(2) However, where such a company purports to transfer or grant an interest in property, the fact that the act was not permitted by the

company's memorandum or, as the case may be, that the directors in connection with the act exceeded any limitation on their powers under the company's constitution, does not affect the title of a person who subsequently acquires the property or any interest in it for full consideration without actual notice of any such circumstances affecting the validity of the company's act.

(3) In any proceedings arising out of subsection (1) the burden of proving—
   (a) that a person knew that an act was not permitted by the company's memorandum or was beyond the powers of the directors, or
   (b) that a person knew that the company was a charity,
lies on the person making that allegation.

(4) Where a company is a charity, the ratification of an act under section 35(3) of the Companies Act 1985, or the ratification of a transaction to which section 322A of that Act applies (invalidity of certain transactions to which directors or their associates are parties), is ineffective without the prior written consent of the Commissioners.

Charitable companies: status to appear on correspondence, etc.

30C.—(1) Where a company is a charity and its name does not include the word "charity" or the word "charitable", the fact that the company is a charity shall be stated in English in legible characters—
   (a) in all business letters of the company,
   (b) in all its notices and other official publications,
   (c) in all bills of exchange, promissory notes, endorsements, cheques and orders for money or goods purporting to be signed by or on behalf of the company,
   (d) in all conveyances purporting to be executed by the company, and
   (e) in all its bills of parcels, invoices, receipts and letters of credit.

(2) In subsection (1)(d) "conveyance" means any instrument creating, transferring, varying or extinguishing an interest in land.

(3) Section 349(2) to (4) of the Companies Act 1985 (offences in connection with failure to include required particulars in business letters, &c.) apply in relation to a contravention of subsection (1) above.".

(2) In section 46 of the Charities Act 1960 (definitions), at the appropriate place insert—

"'company' means a company formed and registered under the Companies Act 1985, or to which the provisions of that Act apply as they apply to such a company;".

GENERAL NOTE

This section substitutes a new s.30, introduces new ss.30A, 30B and 30C and amends s.46 of the Charities Act 1960. It does not apply to Scotland (see s.112 below). The main purpose of the section is to adopt the new regime for corporate transactions in new ss.35 and 35A (s.108) and for objects clauses (s.110) to charitable companies. Charitable companies cannot be given freedom of alteration of such clauses, nor is it proper to allow all third parties to deal with such companies without reference to the objects clause. The solution is to control any such alterations and to protect only innocent third parties who deal with charitable companies for full consideration, or who are unaware that it is a charitable company, and subsequent transferees for full consideration without notice of the defect. To assist in this process, charitable companies will have to disclose their charitable status. New s.30 of the 1960 Act is, however, outside this scheme and is simply an update of the existing section on the winding up of such companies. A similar process is involved in the amendment to s.46 of the Charities Act 1960 which now includes a definition of a company for the purpose of that Act. The major developments occur in new ss.30A (alteration of objects), 30B (third party rights) and 30C (disclosure of charitable status).

New s.30 Charities Act 1960

This section re-enacts the former s.30(1) of the Charities Act 1960. Former s.30(2) is re-enacted as new s.30(A)(1). The only change from the original wording is that the Insolvency Act 1986 replaces a reference to the Companies Act 1948. This was effected in any event by Sched. 14 to the Insolvency Act 1986.

New s.30A Charities Act 1960

This section, by subs. (2), restricts the general rights of the alteration of the objects clause given to other companies by C.A. 1985, new s.4 (s.110). It also, in subs. (1), re-enacts the former s.30(2) of the Charities Act 1960, as to the effect of any alteration by any company or body corporate by virtue of which it ceases to be a charity.

The new restriction, in subs. (2), is that any change of its objects by a charitable company under C.A. 1985, new s.4, will be ineffective unless the company has the prior written consent of the Charity Commissioners. Such consent must be sent to the registrar under C.A. 1985, s.6, following such a change. Failure to do so will be an offence under C.A. 1985, s.6(3).

New s.30B Charities Act 1960

This section disapplies C.A. 1985, new ss.35 and 35A (s.108 above) as to persons dealing with a charitable company in so far as they obviate any restrictions on corporate transactions flowing from the capacity of the company (both as to its own capacity and its capacity to authorise agents to act on its behalf). Such restrictions will still apply to render any such transactions or acts void except in favour of:

(a) a person who gives full consideration in money or money's worth and has no knowledge of the lack of capacity or authority;

(b) a person who does not know at that time that the company is a charity (see s.30C below); or

(c) a person who acquires title subsequent to any invalid transfer or grant of an interest in property by a charitable company for full consideration without actual notice of the original invalidity (subss. (1) and (2)).

In cases (a) or (b) the burden of proof as to the knowledge of the third party is on the person seeking to make that allegation (subs. (3)).

If the charitable company seeks to ratify such an act under new C.A. 1985, s.35(3) by a special resolution, that will be ineffective without the consent of the Charity Commissioners. A similar rule applies to any ratification under C.A. 1985, new s.322A, where the third party is a director. That section applies in full to charitable companies, so that the transaction will be voidable only if the third party is a director, but void under common law in other cases where new ss.35 and 35A are disapplied by this section. It is doubtful whether this is the intended result.

New s.30C Charities Act 1960

This section is intended to clarify the situation in relation to the exception for third parties who deal with a company unaware that it is a charitable company contained in s.30B(1). It only applies if the company's name does not include the word charity or the word charitable. In such cases it requires disclosure of its charitable status on the documents set out in subs. (1). A conveyance in subs. (1)(d) is defined in subs. (2).

Charitable companies (Scotland)

112.—(1) In the following provisions (which extend to Scotland only)—

(a) "company" means a company formed and registered under the Companies Act 1985, or to which the provisions of that Act apply as they apply to such a company; and

(b) "charity" means a body established for charitable purposes only (that expression having the same meaning as in the Income Tax Acts).

(2) Where a charity is a company or other body corporate having power to alter the instruments establishing or regulating it as a body corporate, no exercise of that power which has the effect of the body ceasing to be a charity shall be valid so as to affect the application of—

(a) any property acquired by virtue of any transfer, contract or obligation previously effected otherwise than for full consideration in money or money's worth, or any property representing property so acquired,

(b) any property representing income which has accrued before the alteration is made, or

(c) the income from any such property as aforesaid.

(3) Sections 35 and 35A of the Companies Act 1985 (capacity of company not limited by its memorandum; power of directors to bind company) do not apply to the acts of a company which is a charity except in favour of a person who—

(a) gives full consideration in money or money's worth in relation to the act in question, and

(b) does not know that the act is not permitted by the company's memorandum or, as the case may be, is beyond the powers of the directors,

or who does not know at the time the act is done that the company is a charity.

(4) However, where such a company purports to transfer or grant an interest in property, the fact that the act was not permitted by the company's memorandum or, as the case may be, that the directors in connection with the act exceeded any limitation on their powers under the company's constitution, does not affect the title of a person who subsequently acquires the property or any interest in it for full consideration without actual notice of any such circumstances affecting the validity of the company's act.

(5) In any proceedings arising out of subsection (3) the burden of proving—

(a) that a person knew that an act was not permitted by the company's memorandum or was beyond the powers of the directors, or

(b) that a person knew that the company was a charity,

lies on the person making that allegation.

(6) Where a company is a charity and its name does not include the word "charity" or the word "charitable", the fact that the company is a charity shall be stated in English in legible characters—

(a) in all business letters of the company,

(b) in all its notices and other official publications,

(c) in all bills of exchange, promissory notes, endorsements, cheques and orders for money or goods purporting to be signed by or on behalf of the company,

(d) in all conveyances purporting to be executed by the company, and

(e) in all its bills of parcels, invoices, receipts and letters of credit.

(7) In subsection (6)(d) "conveyance" means any document for the creation, transfer, variation or extinction of an interest in land.

(8) Section 349(2) to (4) of the Companies Act 1985 (offences in connection with failure to include required particulars in business letters, &c.) apply in relation to a contravention of subsection (6) above.

GENERAL NOTE

This section applies only to Scotland. It mirrors the amendments to the new regime for corporate transactions (C.A. 1985, new ss.35 and 35A (s.108 above)) and objects clauses (s.110 above) made by s.111 to charitable companies in England and Wales. See the General Note to s.111 for the reasoning involved.

Subs. (1)

This defines the concept of charity and company for the purposes of this section. It includes all companies subject to the C.A. 1985.

Subs. (2)
This is identical to new s.30A(1) of the Charities Act 1960 introduced by s.111—see the note to that section. There is no equivalent to s.30A(2) of the 1960 Act, however, since the Charity Commission has no authority in Scotland.

Subss. (3)–(5)
These are identical to new s.30B(1)–(3) of the Charities Act 1960, introduced by s.111. Again there is no equivalent of s.30B(4) since that involves the Charity Commissioners.

Subss. (6) and (7)
These are equivalent to new s.30C of the Charities Act 1960, introduced by s.111.

Subs. (8)
This is equivalent to s.111(2).

De-regulation of private companies

Written resolutions of private companies

113.—(1) Chapter IV of Part XI of the Companies Act 1985 (meetings and resolutions) is amended as follows.

(2) After section 381 insert—

"Written resolutions of private companies

Written resolutions of private companies

381A.—(1) Anything which in the case of a private company may be done—
 (a) by resolution of the company in general meeting, or
 (b) by resolution of a meeting of any class of members of the company,
may be done, without a meeting and without any previous notice being required, by resolution in writing signed by or on behalf of all the members of the company who at the date of the resolution would be entitled to attend and vote at such meeting.

(2) The signatures need not be on a single document provided each is on a document which accurately states the terms of the resolution.

(3) The date of the resolution means when the resolution is signed by or on behalf of the last member to sign.

(4) A resolution agreed to in accordance with this section has effect as if passed—
 (a) by the company in general meeting, or
 (b) by a meeting of the relevant class of members of the company,
as the case may be; and any reference in any enactment to a meeting at which a resolution is passed or to members voting in favour of a resolution shall be construed accordingly.

(5) Any reference in any enactment to the date of passing of a resolution is, in relation to a resolution agreed to in accordance with this section, a reference to the date of the resolution, unless section 381B(4) applies in which case it shall be construed as a reference to the date from which the resolution has effect.

(6) A resolution may be agreed to in accordance with this section which would otherwise be required to be passed as a special, extraordinary or elective resolution; and any reference in any enactment to a special, extraordinary or elective resolution includes such a resolution.

(7) This section has effect subject to the exceptions specified in Part I of Schedule 15A; and in relation to certain descriptions of resolution

under this section the procedural requirements of this Act have effect with the adaptations specified in Part II of that Schedule.

Rights of auditors in relation to written resolution

381B.—(1) A copy of any written resolution proposed to be agreed to in accordance with section 381A shall be sent to the company's auditors.

(2) If the resolution concerns the auditors as auditors, they may within seven days from the day on which they receive the copy give notice to the company stating their opinion that the resolution should be considered by the company in general meeting or, as the case may be, by a meeting of the relevant class of members of the company.

(3) A written resolution shall not have effect unless—
  (a) the auditors notify the company that in their opinion the resolution—
    (i) does not concern them as auditors, or
    (ii) does so concern them but need not be considered by the company in general meeting or, as the case may be, by a meeting of the relevant class of members of the company, or
  (b) the period for giving a notice under subsection (2) expires without any notice having been given in accordance with that subsection.

(4) A written resolution previously agreed to in accordance with section 381A shall not have effect until that notification is given or, as the case may be, that period expires.

Written resolutions: supplementary provisions

381C.—(1) Sections 381A and 381B have effect notwithstanding any provision of the company's memorandum or articles.

(2) Nothing in those sections affects any enactment or rule of law as to—
  (a) things done otherwise than by passing a resolution, or
  (b) cases in which a resolution is treated as having been passed, or a person is precluded from alleging that a resolution has not been duly passed.".

(3) After section 382 insert—

"Recording of written resolutions

382A.—(1) Where a written resolution is agreed to in accordance with section 381A which has effect as if agreed by the company in general meeting, the company shall cause a record of the resolution (and of the signatures) to be entered in a book in the same way as minutes of proceedings of a general meeting of the company.

(2) Any such record, if purporting to be signed by a director of the company or by the company secretary, is evidence of the proceedings in agreeing to the resolution; and where a record is made in accordance with this section, then, until the contrary is proved, the requirements of this Act with respect to those proceedings shall be deemed to be complied with.

(3) Section 382(5) (penalties) applies in relation to a failure to comply with subsection (1) above as it applies in relation to a failure to comply with subsection (1) of that section; and section 383 (inspection of minute books) applies in relation to a record made in accordance with this section as it applies in relation to the minutes of a general meeting.".

GENERAL NOTE

This section introduces four new sections into the Companies Act 1985, new ss.381A, 381B, 381C and 382A. It is qualified and adapted by s.114, which introduces a new Sched.

15A into the 1985 Act. The general theme is to provide a procedure whereby private companies have the right to substitute the unanimous written agreement of their shareholders for resolutions of a general or class meeting. Nothing in the company's constitution will be able to alter this right, but the existing law on "informal resolutions" is not affected. Note that regulation 53 of Table A provides a similar procedure for general meetings only—it is not clear whether this has been preserved by new s.381C(2)(b).

New s.381A
This new section creates the basic power for private companies to adopt written resolutions. There are no notice requirements since it is essential that all eligible shareholders sign for the resolution to be effective—a single omission will render the resolution inoperative. Creditors could insist on receiving copies by contractual agreement. Signature may be made by proxy and will be valid if the proxy was in existence at the date of the signature. There are no provisions as to the withdrawal of a signature prior to the signature of the last to sign—the Government view is that once a signature has been made it is irrevocable on general grounds.

Subs. (2)
There is no requirement either for all the signatures to be on a single document or for the wording on each signed document to be identical. Several letters may therefore be sent for signature.

Subss. (3) and (5)
The final signature fixes the date of the resolution. Under subs. (5) this is also the date of the passing of the resolution for general purposes, unless one of the relevant periods or events set out in new s.381B expires or occurs later than the date of the resolution. Such later date is referred to as the date when the resolution has effect, which then becomes the date of the passing of the resolution.

Subss. (4) and (6)
These subsections provide the legal authority of written resolutions under this section. For elective resolutions, see s.109 below.

Subs. (7)
The limits of this procedure and its adaptation to specific resolutions are set out in new Sched.15A to the Companies Act 1985. See the note to s.107 below.

New s.381B
This new section requires that a copy of every proposed written resolution be sent to the company's auditors. The wording in subs. (1), if strictly construed, precludes such a copy being sent if the resolution has already been agreed to (*i.e.* signed) by all concerned. It follows that there could be a technical difficulty if the copy was sent to the auditors after the final signature.

On receipt of the copy, the auditors may adopt any of the following, with the appropriate consequences:
 (a) do nothing for seven days from receipt (*quaere* how will the company know when that is?) In that case the resolution, if already agreed to, will become effective from that date—see note on new s.381A(3)(b);
 (b) within that seven-day period, notify the company that the resolution does not concern them as auditors. On such receipt by the company, the resolution, if already agreed to, will become effective from that date—see note on new s.381A(3)(b);
 (c) within that seven-day period, notify the company that although it concerns them as auditors, it need not be considered by a formal meeting. On such receipt by the company the consequences are as in (b) above;
 (d) within that seven-day period the auditors considering that the matter concerns them as auditors, notify the company that it should be considered by a meeting. In that event the resolution, even if agreed to, has no effect. Under substituted C.A. 1985, s.390(2) (s.120 of this Act) the auditors have the right to attend and speak at the meeting if it is convened.

New s.381C
It is clear that nothing in the company's memorandum or articles can restrict the availability of this written resolution procedure. It is less clear whether a simpler alternative

form of written resolution procedure in the articles (*e.g.* Table A, reg. 53) will continue to be available. Subs. (2) preserves the existing case-law on informal resolutions having effect—see *e.g. Cane* v. *Jones* [1980] 1 W.L.R. 1451; *Palmer* para. 54–12.

New s.382A
This section concerns the procedural aspects of recording written resolutions passed under new s.381A. The evidential and other provisions are similar to those in C.A. 1985, s.382, for resolutions passed by meetings in the ordinary way.

Subs. (1)
It is not thought that the actual signature need be recorded. A written resolution which takes effect as a special resolution must also be registered in the normal way.

Written resolutions: supplementary provisions

114.—(1) In the Companies Act 1985 the following Schedule is inserted after Schedule 15—

"SCHEDULE 15A

WRITTEN RESOLUTIONS OF PRIVATE COMPANIES

PART I

EXCEPTIONS

1. Section 381A does not apply to—
    (a) a resolution under section 303 removing a director before the expiration of his period of office, or
    (b) a resolution under section 391 removing an auditor before the expiration of his term of office.

PART II

ADAPTATION OF PROCEDURAL REQUIREMENTS

Introductory

2.—(1) In this Part of this Schedule (which adapts certain requirements of this Act in relation to proceedings under section 381A)—
    (a) a "written resolution" means a resolution agreed to, or proposed to be agreed to, in accordance with that section, and
    (b) a "relevant member" means a member by whom, or on whose behalf, the resolution is required to be signed in accordance with that section.
(2) A written resolution is not effective if any of the requirements of this Part of this Schedule is not complied with.

Section 95 (disapplication of pre-emption rights)

3.—(1) The following adaptations have effect in relation to a written resolution under section 95(2) (disapplication of pre-emption rights), or renewing a resolution under that provision.
(2) So much of section 95(5) as requires the circulation of a written statement by the directors with a notice of meeting does not apply, but such a statement must be supplied to each relevant member at or before the time at which the resolution is supplied to him for signature.
(3) Section 95(6) (offences) applies in relation to the inclusion in any such statement of matter which is misleading, false or deceptive in a material particular.

Section 155 (financial assistance for purchase of company's own shares or those of holding company)

4. In relation to a written resolution giving approval under section 155(4) or (5) (financial assistance for purchase of company's own shares or those of holding company), section 157(4)(a) (documents to be available at meeting) does not apply, but the documents referred to in that provision must be supplied to each relevant member at or before the time at which the resolution is supplied to him for signature.

Sections 164, 165 and 167 (authority for off-market purchase or contingent purchase contract of company's own shares)

5.—(1) The following adaptations have effect in relation to a written resolution—
  (a) conferring authority to make an off-market purchase of the company's own shares under section 164(2),
  (b) conferring authority to vary a contract for an off-market purchase of the company's own shares under section 164(7), or
  (c) varying, revoking or renewing any such authority under section 164(3).

(2) Section 164(5) (resolution ineffective if passed by exercise of voting rights by member holding shares to which the resolution relates) does not apply; but for the purposes of section 381A(1) a member holding shares to which the resolution relates shall not be regarded as a member who would be entitled to attend and vote.

(3) Section 164(6) (documents to be available at company's registered office and at meeting) does not apply, but the documents referred to in that provision and, where that provision applies by virtue of section 164(7), the further documents referred to in that provision must be supplied to each relevant member at or before the time at which the resolution is supplied to him for signature.

(4) The above adaptations also have effect in relation to a written resolution in relation to which the provisions of section 164(3) to (7) apply by virtue of—
  (a) section 165(2) (authority for contingent purchase contract), or
  (b) section 167(2) (approval of release of rights under contract approved under section 164 or 165).

Section 173 (approval for payment out of capital)

6.—(1) The following adaptations have effect in relation to a written resolution giving approval under section 173(2) (redemption or purchase of company's own shares out of capital).

(2) Section 174(2) (resolution ineffective if passed by exercise of voting rights by member holding shares to which the resolution relates) does not apply; but for the purposes of section 381A(1) a member holding shares to which the resolution relates shall not be regarded as a member who would be entitled to attend and vote.

(3) Section 174(4) (documents to be available at meeting) does not apply, but the documents referred to in that provision must be supplied to each relevant member at or before the time at which the resolution is supplied to him for signature.

Section 319 (approval of director's service contract)

7. In relation to a written resolution approving any such term as is mentioned in section 319(1) (director's contract of employment for more than five years), section 319(5) (documents to be available at company's registered office and at meeting) does not apply, but the documents referred to in that provision must be supplied to each relevant member at or before the time at which the resolution is supplied to him for signature.

Section 337 (funding of director's expenditure in performing his duties)

8. In relation to a written resolution giving approval under section 337(3)(a) (funding a director's expenditure in performing his duties), the requirement of that provision that certain matters be disclosed at the meeting at which the resolution is passed does not apply, but those matters must be disclosed to each relevant member at or before the time at which the resolution is supplied to him for signature.".

(2) The Schedule inserted after Schedule 15 to the Companies Act 1985 by the Companies (Mergers and Divisions) Regulations 1987 is renumbered "15B"; and accordingly, in section 427A of that Act (also inserted by those regulations), in subsections (1) and (8) for "15A" substitute "15B".

GENERAL NOTE
This section introduces a new Sched. 15A into the C.A. 1985. The existing Sched. 15A (Mergers and Divisions) is to be renumbered Sched. 15B to that Act: (subs. (2)). S.427A of the C.A. 1985 is also amended accordingly.
The new Schedule provides two exceptions to the written resolution procedure laid down by s.113 and adapts the procedure of five specific types of resolution required by the C.A. 1985 to accommodate their being passed by the written resolution procedure.

New Sched. 15A—Pt. I
Resolutions to remove a director or auditor before their term of office expires are excluded from the written resolution procedure. In both cases the subject of the resolution has a right to address the meeting and so could not be easily accommodated into the new procedure.

New Sched. 15A—Pt. II
Pt. II adapts five procedural requirements for the proper forming of a resolution to achieve a specific purpose under the C.A. 1985 so as to allow for those resolutions to be passed by the written resolution procedure. Note (para. 2(2)) that the written resolution will be ineffective if the adapted procedure is not complied with.
Para. 3—disapplication of pre-emption rights: The written statement required to be sent out with the notice of the meeting is instead to be supplied to each member at or before the time the resolution is supplied for signature. A relevant member is defined in para. 2(1)(b) as any member who will need to sign the resolution for it to become effective. The definition of "written resolution" in para. 2(1)(a) allows for a draft resolution. *Quaere* if the written statement is sent out with draft one of the resolution which is not agreed to but omitted from draft two which is signed and agreed to by all concerned?
Para. 4—private company exemption from financial assistance prohibition: The requisite documents must be sent to each relevant member prior to his signature instead of being available at the meeting.
Para. 5—off market purchases and contingent purchase contracts by a company for its own shares: There are two adaptations of the procedure whereby a company may authorise an off-market purchase of its own shares, vary such a contract, vary, revoke or renew such authority, authorise a contingent purchase contract or approve the release of rights under either acquisition procedure. The first disapplies the ban on the vendor shareholder voting on such a resolution but at the same time does not require his signature for the resolution to be effective. The vendor may sign, but it is not necessary. The second relates to the necessary documents which would normally be available both at the company's registered office and at the meeting. Such documents must be supplied to the members before signature.
Para. 6—approval of redemption or purchase of shares out of capital: The two adaptations to this procedure are identical in form to those noted in para. 5, *i.e.* to the vendor's position and the relevant documents.
Para. 7—approval of director's service contract: The standard adaptation of the documents to be provided at a meeting is included here—see the note to para. 2.
Para. 8—finding of director's expenditure: The usual disclosure at the meeting is adapted to disclosure to the members before signature in the standard form—see the note to para. 2.

Election by private company to dispense with certain requirements

115.—(1) In Part IV of the Companies Act 1985 (allotment of shares and debentures), in section 80(1) (authority of company required for certain allotments) after "this section" insert "or section 80A"; and after that section insert—

"**Election by private company as to duration of authority**
80A.—(1) A private company may elect (by elective resolution in accordance with section 379A) that the provisions of this section shall

apply, instead of the provisions of section 80(4) and (5), in relation to the giving or renewal, after the election, of an authority under that section.

(2) The authority must state the maximum amount of relevant securities that may be allotted under it and may be given—
   (a) for an indefinite period, or
   (b) for a fixed period, in which case it must state the date on which it will expire.

(3) In either case an authority (including an authority contained in the articles) may be revoked or varied by the company in general meeting.

(4) An authority given for a fixed period may be renewed or further renewed by the company in general meeting.

(5) A resolution renewing an authority—
   (a) must state, or re-state, the amount of relevant securities which may be allotted under the authority or, as the case may be, the amount remaining to be allotted under it, and
   (b) must state whether the authority is renewed for an indefinite period or for a fixed period, in which case it must state the date on which the renewed authority will expire.

(6) The references in this section to the maximum amount of relevant securities that may be allotted shall be construed in accordance with section 80(6).

(7) If an election under this section ceases to have effect, an authority then in force which was given for an indefinite period or for a fixed period of more than five years—
   (a) if given five years or more before the election ceases to have effect, shall expire forthwith, and
   (b) otherwise, shall have effect as if it had been given for a fixed period of five years.".

(2) In Chapter IV of Part XI of the Companies Act 1985 (meetings and resolutions), after section 366 (annual general meeting) insert—

"Election by private company to dispense with annual general meetings

366A.—(1) A private company may elect (by elective resolution in accordance with section 379A) to dispense with the holding of annual general meetings.

(2) An election has effect for the year in which it is made and subsequent years, but does not affect any liability already incurred by reason of default in holding an annual general meeting.

(3) In any year in which an annual general meeting would be required to be held but for the election, and in which no such meeting has been held, any member of the company may, by notice to the company not later than three months before the end of the year, require the holding of an annual general meeting in that year.

(4) If such a notice is given, the provisions of section 366(1) and (4) apply with respect to the calling of the meeting and the consequences of default.

(5) If the election ceases to have effect, the company is not obliged under section 366 to hold an annual general meeting in that year if, when the election ceases to have effect, less than three months of the year remains.

This does not affect any obligation of the company to hold an annual general meeting in that year in pursuance of a notice given under subsection (3).".

(3) In the same Chapter, in sections 369(4) and 378(3) (majority required to sanction short notice of meeting) insert—

"A private company may elect (by elective resolution in accordance with section 379A) that the above provisions shall have effect in relation to the company as if for the references to 95 per cent. there were substituted references to such lesser percentage, but not less than 90 per cent., as may be specified in the resolution or subsequently determined by the company in general meeting.".

GENERAL NOTE

This section, together with ss.116 and 117, introduces a new elective regime for private companies. This will allow private companies to dispense with certain internal requirements of the Companies Act 1985 by means of an elective resolution. Elective resolutions are defined in s.116 where the five areas of election are also set out. S.117 allows for subsequent additions by regulation.

S.115 provides for three of the new elective areas by introducing new ss.80A and 366A into the C.A. 1985 and inserting additional words into ss.369(4) and 378(3) of that Act.

New s.80A

A private company may pass an elective resolution (see s.116) that new s.80A shall apply instead of s.80(4) and (5) in relation to the restrictions on the authority given to the directors to allot unissued shares. Currently, any such authority cannot be given or renewed for more than five years. If the new s.80A applies, the company will be able to give such authority, either for an indefinite period or a fixed period of any length. In the latter case, the authority may be renewed for a fixed or indefinite period by the company. The only restrictions are that any such authority must state the maximum amount of shares which may be allotted under it and, if it is for a fixed period, the date on which it is to expire.

In any event, this authority can be revoked or varied at any time by an ordinary resolution, If the election itself is revoked (see new s.379A(3) and (4)), then the authority given under new s.80A will be construed as one for five years only. If it has already been in existence for more than that time, it will cease immediately.

New s.366A

A private company may, by elective resolution, dispense with the holding of an annual general meeting. Such an election cannot, however, be made retrospectively. Any member may still require a meeting by giving notice to that effect to the copany at least three months before the end of the year in question. The notice and default provisions of s.366 of the C.A. 1985 will then apply. (For related elections on accounts and auditors see the note on s.116).

If the election is revoked (see new s.379A(3) and (4)) an annual general meeting need not be held in that year if there are less than three months of the year left, unless a notice requiring one has already been given.

Amendments to ss.369(4) and 378(3)

Under these amendments a private company may, by elective resolution, (see s.116) reduce the usual percentage of members required to sanction short notice being given of any meeting (s.369) or of a special resolution (s.378) from 95 per cent. to 90 per cent.

Elective resolution of private company

116.—(1) Chapter IV of Part XI of the Companies Act 1985 (meetings and resolutions) is amended as follows.

(2) After section 379 insert—

"Elective resolution of private company

379A.—(1) An election by a private company for the purposes of—

    (a) section 80A (election as to duration of authority to allot shares),

    (b) section 252 (election to dispense with laying of accounts and reports before general meeting),

    (c) section 366A (election to dispense with holding of annual general meeting),

40–154

(d) section 369(4) or 378(3) (election as to majority required to authorise short notice of meeting), or

(e) section 386 (election to dispense with appointment of auditors annually),

shall be made by resolution of the company in general meeting in accordance with this section.

Such a resolution is referred to in this Act as an "elective resolution".

(2) An elective resolution is not effective unless—
  (a) at least 21 days' notice in writing is given of the meeting, stating that an elective resolution is to be proposed and stating the terms of the resolution, and
  (b) the resolution is agreed to at the meeting, in person or by proxy, by all the members entitled to attend and vote at the meeting.

(3) The company may revoke an elective resolution by passing an ordinary resolution to that effect.

(4) An elective resolution shall cease to have effect if the company is re-registered as a public company.

(5) An elective resolution may be passed or revoked in accordance with this section, and the provisions referred to in subsection (1) have effect, notwithstanding any contrary provision in the company's articles of association.".

(3) In section 380 (registration of resolutions), in subsection (4) (resolutions to which the section applies), after paragraph (b) insert—

"(bb) an elective resolution or a resolution revoking such a resolution;".

GENERAL NOTE

This section, by inserting new s.379A into the Companies Act 1985, provides the central plank in the elective resolution regime for private companies. It defines both an elective resolution and its uses. It should be read in conjunction with ss.16, 115, 117, 119, 120 and 122 of this Act, which amplify the uses of an elective resolution.

Subs. (3)

Note that an elective resolution or a resolution revoking an elective resolution must be registered as if it were a special resolution under s.380 of the C.A. 1985.

New s.379A

An elective resolution (as defined in s.379A(2)) may be made by a private company for any one of five purposes:

(1) to apply C.A. 1985, new s.80A in relation to the authority for directors to allot unissued shares—see the note on C.A. 1989, s.115;

(2) to dispense with the laying of accounts and reports before a general meeting under C.A. 1985, s.252, substituted by C.A. 1989, s.16. For the rights of shareholders to require a meeting for the accounts, etc., to be laid, see substituted C.A. 1985, s.253 (C.A. 1989, s.16). See generally the note on C.A. 1989, s.16 above;

(3) to apply C.A. 1985, new s.366A to dispense with the requirement to hold an annual general meeting—see the note on C.A. 1989, s.115 above;

(4) to reduce the percentage for sanctioning short notice of meetings or special resolutions under the amended ss.369(4) and 378(3) of the C.A. 1985—see the note on C.A. 1989, s.115 above;

(5) to dispense with the annual appointment of auditors under C.A. 1985, s.386, substituted by C.A. 1989, s.119. For members' rights see substituted C.A. 1985, s.393 (C.A. 1989, s.122).

An elective resolution requires 21 days notice and unanimous agreement of all those entitled to attend and vote. The written resolution procedure under C.A. 1989, s.113 may be used. It can, however, be revoked at any time by an ordinary resolution and is automatically revoked if the company becomes a public company. Nothing in the company's memorandum or articles is to have any effect on this elective regime.

Power to make further provision by regulations

117.—(1) The Secretary of State may by regulations make provision enabling private companies to elect, by elective resolution in accordance with section 379A of the Companies Act 1985, to dispense with compliance with such requirements of that Act as may be specified in the regulations, being requirements which appear to the Secretary of State to relate primarily to the internal administration and procedure of companies.

(2) The regulations may add to, amend or repeal provisions of that Act; and may provide for any such provision to have effect, where an election is made, subject to such adaptations and modifications as appear to the Secretary of State to be appropriate.

(3) The regulations may make different provision for different cases and may contain such supplementary, incidental and transitional provisions as appear to the Secretary of State to be appropriate.

(4) Regulations under this section shall be made by statutory instrument.

(5) No regulations under this section shall be made unless a draft of the instrument containing the regulations has been laid before Parliament and approved by a resolution of each House.

GENERAL NOTE

This section allows the Secretary of State to alter the contents of the elective resolution regime (see the note on s.116 above) by regulations requiring the affirmative resolution procedure. It thus allows the five existing areas of election to be added to, amended or restricted, but only if it appears to the Secretary of State to be a matter relating primarily to the internal administration and procedure of private companies. However, any challenge to the Secretary of State's powers would have to show unreasonableness of a nature as defined in *Associated Provincial Picture Houses Ltd.* v. *Wednesbury Corpn.* [1948] 1 K.B. 223.

Appointment and removal of auditors and related matters

Introduction

118.—(1) The following sections amend the provisions of the Companies Act 1985 relating to auditors by inserting new provisions in Chapter V of Part XI of that Act.

(2) The new provisions, together with the amendment made by section 124, replace the present provisions of that Chapter except section 389 (qualification for appointment as auditor) which is replaced by provisions in Part II of this Act.

GENERAL NOTE

Ss.118–124 were inserted into the Bill during its progress through Parliament, and they replace the previous section comprising Chapter V of Pt. XI of the 1985 Act (dealing with Auditors), with the exception of s.389 (the qualification for appointment as auditor), which is repealed under Sched. 24 and replaced by the provisions of Pt. II of the new Act (ss.24–53 and Scheds. 11–14).

The new Chapter V appears as follows:

Inserted by 1989 Act		New sections of 1985 Act	Former sections of 1985 Act
s.119	Duty to appoint auditors	384	384(1) plus new material
	Appointment of auditors at a general meeting at which the accounts are laid	385	384(1)–(3)
	Appointment of auditors by a private company which is not obliged to lay accounts	385A	new, but partly based on former s.384(2)–(3)

	Election by a private company to dispense with the annual appointment of the auditor	386	new
	Appointment of an auditor by the Secretary of State in default of appointment by a company	387	384(5)
	Filling of casual vacancies	388	384(4), 388(1)–(2)
	Dormant company's exemption from the obligation to appoint auditors	388A	subss. (1)–(3), (5), are based on the former s.252(1)(7); subs. (4) is new.
[ss.24–53 and Scheds. 11–14 of the 1989 Act]	Qualification for appointment as auditor	389	
s.120	Rights of auditors to obtain information	389A	237(3), 393, 392(1)(a), 392(2), 392(1)(b), 392(2).
	Rights of auditors to attend company meetings	390(1) 390(2)	387(1) new, but partly based on former s.387(2)
s.121	Remuneration of auditors	390A	385(1)–(3) plus new material
	Remuneration of auditors or their associates for non-audit work	390B	new
s.122	Removal of auditors	391	386(1)–(3) plus new material based on former s.387(2)
	Rights of auditors	391A	388(1)(d)(a), 2(a)(b), (3)–(5)
	Resignation of auditors	392	390(1)(2)(3)(a)(7)
	Rights of resigning auditors	392A	391(1)–(7)
	Termination of appointment of auditors not appointed annually	393	new
s.123	Statement by a person ceasing to hold office as an auditor	394	390(2), (3)(a), (5), (6) modified
	Offences of failing to comply with new s.394	394A	390(7) plus new material
s.124	Duties of trade unions and employers' associations with regard to auditors	—	394

Appointment of auditors

119.—(1) The following sections are inserted in Chapter V of Part XI of the Companies Act 1985 (auditors)—

"Appointment of auditors

Duty to appoint auditors

384.—(1) Every company shall appoint an auditor or auditors in accordance with this Chapter.

This is subject to section 388A (dormant company exempt from obligation to appoint auditors).

(2) Auditors shall be appointed in accordance with section 385 (appointment at general meeting at which accounts are laid), except in the case of a private company which has elected to dispense with

the laying of accounts in which case the appointment shall be made in accordance with section 385A.

(3) References in this Chapter to the end of the time for appointing auditors are to the end of the time within which an appointment must be made under section 385(2) or 385A(2), according to whichever of those sections applies.

(4) Sections 385 and 385A have effect subject to section 386 under which a private company may elect to dispense with the obligation to appoint auditors annually.

Appointment at general meeting at which accounts laid

385.—(1) This section applies to every public company and to a private company which has not elected to dispense with the laying of accounts.

(2) The company shall, at each general meeting at which accounts are laid, appoint an auditor or auditors to hold office from the conclusion of that meeting until the conclusion of the next general meeting at which accounts are laid.

(3) The first auditors of the company may be appointed by the directors at any time before the first general meeting of the company at which accounts are laid; and auditors so appointed shall hold office until the conclusion of that meeting.

(4) If the directors fail to exercise their powers under subsection (3), the powers may be exercised by the company in general meeting.

Appointment by private company which is not obliged to lay accounts

385A.—(1) This section applies to a private company which has elected in accordance with section 252 to dispense with the laying of accounts before the company in general meeting.

(2) Auditors shall be appointed by the company in general meeting before the end of the period of 28 days beginning with the day on which copies of the company's annual accounts for the previous financial year are sent to members under section 238 or, if notice is given under section 253(2) requiring the laying of the accounts before the company in general meeting, the conclusion of that meeting.

Auditors so appointed shall hold office from the end of that period or, as the case may be, the conclusion of that meeting until the end of the time for appointing auditors for the next financial year.

(3) The first auditors of the company may be appointed by the directors at any time before—
 (a) the end of the period of 28 days beginning with the day on which copies of the company's first annual accounts are sent to members under section 238, or
 (b) if notice is given under section 253(2) requiring the laying of the accounts before the company in general meeting, the beginning of that meeting;

and auditors so appointed shall hold office until the end of that period or, as the case may be, the conclusion of that meeting.

(4) If the directors fail to exercise their powers under subsection (3), the powers may be exercised by the company in general meeting.

(5) Auditors holding office when the election is made shall, unless the company in general meeting determines otherwise, continue to hold office until the end of the time for appointing auditors for the next financial year; and auditors holding office when an election ceases to have effect shall continue to hold office until the conclusion of the next general meeting of the company at which accounts are laid.

Election by private company to dispense with annual appointment

386.—(1) A private company may elect (by elective resolution in accordance with section 379A) to dispense with the obligation to appoint auditors annually.

(2) When such an election is in force the company's auditors shall be deemed to be re-appointed for each succeeding financial year on the expiry of the time for appointing auditors for that year, unless—
  (a) a resolution has been passed under section 250 by virtue of which the company is exempt from the obligation to appoint auditors, or
  (b) a resolution has been passed under section 393 to the effect that their appointment should be brought to an end.

(3) If the election ceases to be in force, the auditors then holding office shall continue to hold office—
  (a) where section 385 then applies, until the conclusion of the next general meeting of the company at which accounts are laid;
  (b) where section 385A then applies, until the end of the time for appointing auditors for the next financial year under that section.

(4) No account shall be taken of any loss of the opportunity of further deemed re-appointment under this section in ascertaining the amount of any compensation or damages payable to an auditor on his ceasing to hold office for any reason.

Appointment by Secretary of State in default of appointment by company

387.—(1) If in any case no auditors are appointed, re-appointed or deemed to be re-appointed before the end of the time for appointing auditors, the Secretary of State may appoint a person to fill the vacancy.

(2) In such a case the company shall within one week of the end of the time for appointing auditors give notice to the Secretary of State of his power having become exercisable.

If a company fails to give the notice required by this subsection, the company and every officer of it who is in default is guilty of an offence and liable to a fine and, for continued contravention, to a daily default fine.

Filling of casual vacancies

388.—(1) The directors, or the company in general meeting, may fill a casual vacancy in the office of auditor.

(2) While such a vacancy continues, any surviving or continuing auditor or auditors may continue to act.

(3) Special notice is required for a resolution at a general meeting of a company—
  (a) filling a casual vacancy in the office of auditor, or
  (b) re-appointing as auditor a retiring auditor who was appointed by the directors to fill a casual vacancy.

(4) On receipt of notice of such an intended resolution the company shall forthwith send a copy of it—
  (a) to the person proposed to be appointed, and
  (b) if the casual vacancy was caused by the resignation of an auditor, to the auditor who resigned.

Dormant company exempt from obligation to appoint auditors

388A.—(1) A company which by virtue of section 250 (dormant companies: exemption from provisions as to audit of accounts) is exempt from the provisions of Part VII relating to the audit of accounts is also exempt from the obligation to appoint auditors.

(2) The following provisions apply if the exemption ceases.

(3) Where section 385 applies (appointment at general meeting at which accounts are laid), the directors may appoint auditors at any time before the next meeting of the company at which accounts are to be laid; and auditors so appointed shall hold office until the conclusion of that meeting.

(4) Where section 385A applies (appointment by private company not obliged to lay accounts), the directors may appoint auditors at any time before—
   (a) the end of the period of 28 days beginning with the day on which copies of the company's annual accounts are next sent to members under section 238, or
   (b) if notice is given under section 253(2) requiring the laying of the accounts before the company in general meeting, the beginning of that meeting;
and auditors so appointed shall hold office until the end of that period or, as the case may be, the conclusion of that meeting.

(5) If the directors fail to exercise their powers under subsection (3) or (4), the powers may be exercised by the company in general meeting.".

(2) In Schedule 24 to the Companies Act 1985 (punishment of offences), at the appropriate place insert—

"387(2)	Company failing to give Secretary of State notice of non-appointment of auditors.	Summary.	One-fifth of the statutory maximum.	One-fiftieth of the statutory maximum.".

(3) In section 46(2) of the Banking Act 1987 (duty of auditor of authorised institution to give notice to Bank of England of certain matters) for "appointed under section 384" substitute "appointed under Chapter V of Part XI"; and in section 46(4) (adaptation of references in relation to Northern Ireland) for "sections 384," substitute "Chapter V of Part XI and sections".

DEFINITIONS
"accounts laid before the company in general meeting": s.11.
"annual accounts": s.22; Sched. 10, para. 15.
"company auditor": ss.24(2), 119.
"directors": s.741 C.A. 1985.
"dormant company": s.14.
"financial year": s.3; Sched. 10, para. 15.
"general meetings": ss.366–375, C.A. 1985.
"members": s.22 C.A. 1985.
"officer who is in default": s.730(5) C.A. 1985.
"private company": s.1(3) C.A. 1985.
"public company": s.1(3) C.A. 1985.
"special notice": s.379 C.A. 1985.

GENERAL NOTE
S.119 deals with the appointment of auditors and inserts new ss.384, 385, 385A, 386, 387, 388 and 388A into the 1985 Act.

New s.384
This section deals with the duty of a company (except where it is dormant under s.250, inserted by s.14 of the new Act) to appoint auditors. Subs. (2) indicates that, except where a private company elects to dispense with the laying of accounts (see new s.385A), auditors will be appointed at a general meeting where accounts are laid (see new s.385).

New s.385
This section indicates that, except for private companies which elect to dispense with the laying of accounts (see new C.A. 1985, s.252, introduced by s.16 of C.A. 1989) the company

must appoint an auditor at each general meeting where accounts are laid until the next such meeting. However, the first auditors may be appointed by directors before the first general meeting at which accounts are laid, or—failing action by them—by the company in general meeting.

New s.385A
This section deals with the situation where a private company has elected, in accordance with s.252, (inserted by s.16 of this Act) to dispense with the laying of accounts before the company in general meeting. In such circumstances auditors must, under subs. (2), be appointed by the company at a general meeting held within four weeks of accounts for the previous year being sent to members, etc., under s.238 (inserted by s.10 of this Act); or, where such a meeting was held, the conclusion of a general meeting at which accounts for the previous year were laid. Such auditors hold office until the next date at which an appointment falls due. In the case of the first auditors of a private company taking advantage of an election under the new s.252, the directors (rather than the company in general meeting) can exercise the power of appointment outlined in subs. (2), failing which the company in general meeting will appoint.

New s.386
This section enables private companies to elect to dispense with the obligation to appoint auditors annually, in which case the existing auditors will, so long as the election continues, be deemed to have been reappointed unless the company either is a dormant company under s.250 (inserted by s.14 of this Act) or a resolution is passed ending the appointment.

New s.387
This section requires that where no auditors are appointed, the company shall, within a week of the time for making such an appointment elapsing, give notice to the Secretary of State so that he can fill the vacancy. Failure to give such notice renders the defaulting company and officers liable to be fined, the amounts of which are detailed in Sched.24 of the 1985 Act, as inserted by s.119(2) of this Act.

New s.388(1)
This section empowers the directors or the company in general meeting to fill a casual vacancy. In the latter case special notice is required, as it is when an auditor appointed to fill a casual vacancy by the directors is subject to reappointment by the company in general meeting. Copies of such notice have to be sent to the auditor concerned and to his predecessor if he resigned.

New s.388A(1)
This section indicates that a company which is dormant under the provisions of s.250 of the 1985 Act, as inserted by s.14 of this Act, is exempt from the obligations to appoint auditors. subss. (2)–(5) indicate the various ways auditors may be appointed if the "dormant" status ceases.
For derivations, see the annotations to s.118.

Rights of auditors

120.—(1) The following sections are inserted in Chapter V of Part XI of the Companies Act 1985 (auditors)—

"*Rights of auditors*

Rights to information
389A.—(1) The auditors of a company have a right of access at all times to the company's books, accounts and vouchers, and are entitled to require from the company's officers such information and explanations as they think necessary for the performance of their duties as auditors.

(2) An officer of a company commits an offence if he knowingly or recklessly makes to the company's auditors a statement (whether written or oral) which—
  (a) conveys or purports to convey any information or explanations

which the auditors require, or are entitled to require, as auditors of the company, and

(b) is misleading, false or deceptive in a material particular.

A person guilty of an offence under this subsection is liable to imprisonment or a fine, or both.

(3) A subsidiary undertaking which is a body corporate incorporated in Great Britain, and the auditors of such an undertaking, shall give to the auditors of any parent company of the undertaking such information and explanations as they may reasonably require for the purposes of their duties as auditors of that company.

If a subsidiary undertaking fails to comply with this subsection, the undertaking and every officer of it who is in default is guilty of an offence and liable to a fine; and if an auditor fails without reasonable excuse to comply with this subsection he is guilty of an offence and liable to a fine.

(4) A parent company having a subsidiary undertaking which is not a body corporate incorporated in Great Britain shall, if required by its auditors to do so, take all such steps as are reasonably open to it to obtain from the subsidiary undertaking such information and explanations as they may reasonably require for the purposes of their duties as auditors of that company.

If a parent company fails to comply with this subsection, the company and every officer of it who is in default is guilty of an offence and liable to a fine.

(5) Section 734 (criminal proceedings against unincorporated bodies) applies to an offence under subsection (3).

Right to attend company meetings, &c.

390.—(1) A company's auditors are entitled—
  (a) to receive all notices of, and other communications relating to, any general meeting which a member of the company is entitled to receive;
  (b) to attend any general meeting of the company; and
  (c) to be heard at any general meeting which they attend on any part of the business of the meeting which concerns them as auditors.

(2) In relation to a written resolution proposed to be agreed to by a private company in accordance with section 381A, the company's auditors are entitled—
  (a) to receive all such communications relating to the resolution as, by virtue of any provision of Schedule 15A, are required to be supplied to a member of the company,
  (b) to give notice in accordance with section 381B of their opinion that the resolution concerns them as auditors and should be considered by the company in general meeting or, as the case may be, by a meeting of the relevant class of members of the company,
  (c) to attend any such meeting, and
  (d) to be heard at any such meeting which they attend on any part of the business of the meeting which concerns them as auditors.

(3) The right to attend or be heard at a meeting is exercisable in the case of a body corporate or partnership by an individual authorised by it in writing to act as its representative at the meeting.".

(2) In section 734 of the Companies Act 1985 (criminal proceedings against unincorporated bodies), in subsection (1) (offences in relation to which the provisions apply), after "under" insert "section 389A(3) or".

(3) In Schedule 24 to the Companies Act 1985 (punishment of offences) at the appropriate place insert—

"389A(2)	Officer of company making false, misleading or deceptive statement to auditors.	1. On indictment. 2. Summary.	2 years or a fine; or both. 6 months or the statutory maximum; or both.
389A(3)	Subsidiary undertaking or its auditor failing to give information to auditors of parent company.	Summary.	One-fifth of the statutory maximum.
389A(4)	Parent company failing to obtain from subsidiary undertaking information for purposes of audit.	Summary.	One-fifth of the statutory maximum.".

(4) In Schedule 4 to the Iron and Steel Act 1982 (constitution and proceedings of publicly-owned companies that are private companies), in paragraph 3(6) (entitlement of auditors to attend and be heard at general meetings, &c.) for "387(1)" substitute "390(1)".

DEFINITIONS
"books, etc., of a company": s.744 C.A. 1985.
"body corporate": s.740, C.A. 1985.
"company auditor": ss.24(2), 119.
"general meetings": ss.366–375, C.A. 1985.
"member": s.22 C.A. 1985.
"officer": s.744 C.A. 1985.
"parent company": s.21; Sched. 9.
"private company": s.1(3) C.A. 1985.
"subsidiary undertaking": Sched. 9; s.144, SSAP.14, para. 7.

GENERAL NOTE
S.120(1) inserts new ss.389A and 390 into the 1985 Act, which deal with the rights of auditors to obtain information and to attend and be heard at meetings.

New s.389A
This section affirms the auditors' right of access at all times to a company's books, accounts and vouchers and to be given such explanations as are necessary to carry out their duties. Subs. (2) covers the position where officers of a company make false, misleading or deceptive statements, either deliberately or through reckless behaviour. Subs. (3) requires British subsidiaries and their auditors to give the parent company's auditors relevant information and explanations, in default of which they will be liable to a fine and (under subs. (5) and s.734) possible criminal proceedings. Subs. (4) requires parent companies to obtain relevant information and explanations from overseas subsidiaries for the benefit of their auditors.

New s.390
Subs. (1) establishes that a company's auditors are entitled to receive all communications relating to a general meeting and to attend and be heard on auditing matters at such meetings. Subs. (2) deals with the situation where, for a private company, under s.381A (inserted by s.113 of the new Act) a resolution in writing can be agreed without a meeting by those entitled to attend and vote at such a meeting. In such circumstances the auditors are entitled to receive all communications relating to such resolutions and shall give notice to the company within seven days if, following new s.381B (inserted by s.113) in their opinion the matter should be considered by the company in general meeting. They then have the right to attend such a meeting and be heard on matters which concern them as auditors.

S.120(3) inserts into Sched. 24 to the 1985 Act details of the penalties which can be imposed for failing to comply with the provisions of ss.389A and 390.
For derivations, see the annotations to s.118.

Remuneration of auditors

121. The following sections are inserted in Chapter V of Part XI of the Companies Act 1985 (auditors)—

"Remuneration of auditors

Remuneration of auditors

390A.—(1) The remuneration of auditors appointed by the company in general meeting shall be fixed by the company in general meeting or in such manner as the company in general meeting may determine.

(2) The remuneration of auditors appointed by the directors or the Secretary of State shall be fixed by the directors or the Secretary of State, as the case may be.

(3) There shall be stated in a note to the company's annual accounts the amount of the remuneration of the company's auditors in their capacity as such.

(4) For the purposes of this section "remuneration" includes sums paid in respect of expenses.

(5) This section applies in relation to benefits in kind as to payments in cash, and in relation to any such benefit references to its amount are to its estimated money value.

The nature of any such benefit shall also be disclosed.

Remuneration of auditors or their associates for non-audit work

390B.—(1) The Secretary of State may make provision by regulations for securing the disclosure of the amount of any remuneration received or receivable by a company's auditors or their associates in respect of services other than those of auditors in their capacity as such.

(2) The regulations may—
  (a) provide that "remuneration" includes sums paid in respect of expenses,
  (b) apply in relation to benefits in kind as to payments in cash, and in relation to any such benefit require disclosure of its nature and its estimated money value,
  (c) define "associate" in relation to an auditor,
  (d) require the disclosure of remuneration in respect of services rendered to associated undertakings of the company, and
  (e) define "associated undertaking" for that purpose.

(3) The regulations may require the auditors to disclose the relevant information in their report or require the relevant information to be disclosed in a note to the company's accounts and require the auditors to supply the directors of the company with such information as is necessary to enable that disclosure to be made.

(4) The regulations may make different provision for different cases.

(5) Regulations under this section shall be made by statutory instrument which shall be subject to annulment in pursuance of a resolution of either House of Parliament.".

DEFINITIONS
  "company auditor": ss.24(2), 119.
  "general meetings": ss.366–375, C.A. 1985.
  "notes to the accounts": s.22

GENERAL NOTE
  S.121 inserts new ss.390A and 390B into the 1985 Act.

New s.390A
This empowers the company in general meeting to fix the auditors' remuneration; or, where a vacancy is filled by the Secretary of State under the provisions of new s.387, the

Secretary of State. Remuneration (which includes benefits in kind and expenses) is to be disclosed in a note to the accounts.

New s.390B

This section is innovatory and empowers the Secretary of State to introduce regulations by statutory instrument relating to a group, including its associated companies, and the remuneration received by auditors or their related parties for non-audit services. Remuneration, once again, is defined to include benefits in kind and expenses, and the regulations may require the auditors either to disclose such details in their report on the accounts or to supply relevant information to the company's directors, who will then disclose it in a note to the financial statements.

For derivations, see the annotations to s.118.

Removal, resignation, &c. of auditors

122.—(1) The following sections are inserted in Chapter V of Part XI of the Companies Act 1985 (auditors)—

"Removal, resignation, &c. of auditors

Removal of auditors

391.—(1) A company may by ordinary resolution at any time remove an auditor from office, notwithstanding anything in any agreement between it and him.

(2) Where a resolution removing an auditor is passed at a general meeting of a company, the company shall within 14 days give notice of that fact in the prescribed form to the registrar.

If a company fails to give the notice required by this subsection, the company and every officer of it who is in default is guilty of an offence and liable to a fine and, for continued contravention, to a daily default fine.

(3) Nothing in this section shall be taken as depriving a person removed under it of compensation or damages payable to him in respect of the termination of his appointment as auditor or of any appointment terminating with that as auditor.

(4) An auditor of a company who has been removed has, notwithstanding his removal, the rights conferred by section 390 in relation to any general meeting of the company—

(a) at which his term of office would otherwise have expired, or

(b) at which it is proposed to fill the vacancy caused by his removal.

In such a case the references in that section to matters concerning the auditors as auditors shall be construed as references to matters concerning him as a former auditor.

Rights of auditors who are removed or not re-appointed

391A.—(1) Special notice is required for a resolution at a general meeting of a company—

(a) removing an auditor before the expiration of his term of office, or

(b) appointing as auditor a person other than a retiring auditor.

(2) On receipt of notice of such an intended resolution the company shall forthwith send a copy of it to the person proposed to be removed or, as the case may be, to the person proposed to be appointed and to the retiring auditor.

(3) The auditor proposed to be removed or (as the case may be) the retiring auditor may make with respect to the intended resolution representations in writing to the company (not exceeding a reasonable length) and request their notification to members of the company.

(4) The company shall (unless the representations are received by it too late for it to do so)—

(a) in any notice of the resolution given to members of the company, state the fact of the representations having been made, and
(b) send a copy of the representations to every member of the company to whom notice of the meeting is or has been sent.

(5) If a copy of any such representations is not sent out as required because received too late or because of the company's default, the auditor may (without prejudice to his right to be heard orally) require that the representations be read out at the meeting.

(6) Copies of the representations need not be sent out and the representations need not be read at the meeting if, on the application either of the company or of any other person claiming to be aggrieved, the court is satisfied that the rights conferred by this section are being abused to secure needless publicity for defamatory matter; and the court may order the company's costs on the application to be paid in whole or in part by the auditor, notwithstanding that he is not a party to the application.

Resignation of auditors

392.—(1) An auditor of a company may resign his office by depositing a notice in writing to that effect at the company's registered office.

The notice is not effective unless it is accompanied by the statement required by section 394.

(2) An effective notice of resignation operates to bring the auditor's term of office to an end as of the date on which the notice is deposited or on such later date as may be specified in it.

(3) The company shall within 14 days of the deposit of a notice of resignation send a copy of the notice to the registrar of companies.

If default is made in complying with this subsection, the company and every officer of it who is in default is guilty of an offence and liable to a fine and, for continued contravention, a daily default fine.

Rights of resigning auditors

392A.—(1) This section applies where an auditor's notice of resignation is accompanied by a statement of circumstances which he considers should be brought to the attention of members or creditors of the company.

(2) He may deposit with the notice a signed requisition calling on the directors of the company forthwith duly to convene an extraordinary general meeting of the company for the purpose of receiving and considering such explanation of the circumstances connected with his resignation as he may wish to place before the meeting.

(3) He may request the company to circulate to its members—
(a) before the meeting convened on his requisition, or
(b) before any general meeting at which his term of office would otherwise have expired or at which it is proposed to fill the vacancy caused by his resignation,

a statement in writing (not exceeding a reasonable length) of the circumstances connected with his resignation.

(4) The company shall (unless the statement is received too late for it to comply)—
(a) in any notice of the meeting given to members of the company, state the fact of the statement having been made, and
(b) send a copy of the statement to every member of the company to whom notice of the meeting is or has been sent.

(5) If the directors do not within 21 days from the date of the deposit of a requisition under this section proceed duly to convene a meeting for a day not more than 28 days after the date on which the

notice convening the meeting is given, every director who failed to take all reasonable steps to secure that a meeting was convened as mentioned above is guilty of an offence and liable to a fine.

(6) If a copy of the statement mentioned above is not sent out as required because received too late or because of the company's default, the auditor may (without prejudice to his right to be heard orally) require that the statement be read out at the meeting.

(7) Copies of a statement need not be sent out and the statement need not be read out at the meeting if, on the application either of the company or of any other person who claims to be aggrieved, the court is satisfied that the rights conferred by this section are being abused to secure needless publicity for defamatory matter; and the court may order the company's costs on such an application to be paid in whole or in part by the auditor, notwithstanding that he is not a party to the application.

(8) An auditor who has resigned has, notwithstanding his resignation, the rights conferred by section 390 in relation to any such general meeting of the company as is mentioned in subsection (3)(a) or (b).

In such a case the references in that section to matters concerning the auditors as auditors shall be construed as references to matters concerning him as a former auditor.

Termination of appointment of auditors not appointed annually

393.—(1) When an election is in force under section 386 (election by private company to dispense with annual appointment), any member of the company may deposit notice in writing at the company's registered office proposing that the appointment of the company's auditors be brought to an end.

No member may deposit more than one such notice in any financial year of the company.

(2) If such a notice is deposited it is the duty of the directors—
  (a) to convene a general meeting of the company for a date not more than 28 days after the date on which the notice was given, and
  (b) to propose at the meeting a resolution in a form enabling the company to decide whether the appointment of the company's auditors should be brought to an end.

(3) If the decision of the company at the meeting is that the appointment of the auditors should be brought to an end, the auditors shall not be deemed to be re-appointed when next they would be and, if the notice was deposited within the period immediately following the distribution of accounts, any deemed re-appointment for the financial year following that to which those accounts relate which has already occurred shall cease to have effect.

The period immediately following the distribution of accounts means the period beginning with the day on which copies of the company's annual accounts are sent to members of the company under section 238 and ending 14 days after that day.

(4) If the directors do not within 14 days from the date of the deposit of the notice proceed duly to convene a meeting, the member who deposited the notice (or, if there was more than one, any of them) may himself convene the meeting; but any meeting so convened shall not be held after the expiration of three months from that date.

(5) A meeting convened under this section by a member shall be convened in the same manner, as nearly as possible, as that in which meetings are to be convened by directors.

(6) Any reasonable expenses incurred by a member by reason of the failure of the directors duly to convene a meeting shall be made

good to him by the company; and any such sums shall be recouped by the company from such of the directors as were in default out of any sums payable, or to become payable, by the company by way of fees or other remuneration in respect of their services.

(7) This section has effect notwithstanding anything in any agreement between the company and its auditors; and no compensation or damages shall be payable by reason of the auditors' appointment being terminated under this section.".

(2) In Schedule 24 to the Companies Act 1985 (punishment of offences), at the appropriate place insert—

"391(2)	Failing to give notice to registrar of removal of auditor.	Summary.	One-fifth of the statutory maximum.	One-fiftieth of the statutory maximum.
392(3)	Company failing to forward notice of auditor's resignation to registrar.	1. On indictment. 2. Summary.	A fine. The statutory maximum.	 One-tenth of the statutory maximum.
392A(5)	Directors failing to convene meeting requisitioned by resigning auditor.	1. On indictment. 2. Summary.	A fine. The statutory maximum.".	

DEFINITIONS
"company auditor": ss.24(2), 119.
"directors": s.741, C.A. 1985.
"extraordinary general meeting": s.368, C.A. 1985.
"general meetings": ss.366–375, C.A. 1985.
"member": s.22 C.A. 1985.
"ordinary resolution": ss.376–7, C.A. 1985.
"private company": s.1(3), C.A. 1985.
"registered office": s.287, C.A. 1985.
"special notice": s.379, C.A. 1985.

GENERAL NOTE
This section deals with the removal and resignation of auditors, and subs. (1) inserts new ss.391, 391A, 392, 392A and 393 into the 1985 Act. Subs. (2) inserts into Sched. 24 of the 1985 Act the penalties for breaching new s.391(2) (failing to give notice to the Registrar of removal of an auditor), s.392(3) (failure by the company to forward notice of an auditor's resignation to the Registrar), and s.392A(5) (failure by the directors to convene a meeting requisitioned by a resigning auditor).

New s.391
This section deals with the removal of auditors. Under its provisions a company may, by ordinary resolution, remove an auditor before his period of office has expired and notwithstanding any agreement with him. Where he is so removed, the company must give notice in prescribed form within two weeks, failing which both it and defaulting officers are liable to a fine and, for continued contravention, a daily default fine, the penalties being specified in s.122(2). An auditor so removed retains his rights to compensation or damages in respect of the termination of his appointment; and he is also entitled under s.390 (inserted by s.120 of the new Act) to receive all communications relating to general meetings when his term of office would normally expire or at which it is proposed to appoint his successor, and to attend and be heard at such meetings.

New s.391A
Under this section, special notice is required for a resolution removing an auditor or appointing his successor, and such notice must be forwarded to the parties concerned. The auditor who is being removed or who is resigning may make representations of reasonable length to the company, which, if requested, must circulate them with the resolution, failing which the auditor may require them to be read out at the meeting. However, application

may be made to the Court by the company or other aggrieved party, and if such representations are deemed to be needlessly defamatory they need not be circulated or be read out at the meeting. In such circumstances, the Court may require the auditor to pay some or all of the costs involved.

New s.392
This section specifies that an auditor may resign by depositing notice in writing at a company's registered office, but it must be accompanied by a statement indicating whether or not there are any special circumstances leading to such action (see new s.394 inserted by s.123 of this Act). The auditor's period of office ends when such notice is lodged, unless it specifies another date. The company must deliver a copy of the notice to the Registrar within a fortnight of it being lodged at its registered office, failing which it and its defaulting officers are liable to a fine and for continued contravention, a daily default fine, such penalties being specified in s.122(2).

New s.392A
Under this section, when an auditor's resignation letter is accompanied by a statement of circumstances leading to such action (see s.394 inserted by s.123 of this Act), he may deposit a signed requisition calling on the directors to convene an extraordinary general meeting to receive such a statement and other explanations he may wish to give. He may request the company to circulate a written explanation of reasonable length concerning the circumstances before such a meeting is convened, or before a meeting at which his term of office would normally have expired. The company must indicate in the notice of the meeting that such a statement has been made and circulate it to members of the company. The directors must convene a meeting within three weeks of the requisition being lodged, and it must be held within four weeks of the date of the notice of the meeting being given. Failure to do so renders every director who did not take reasonable steps to secure compliance liable to a fine, penalties being specified in s.122(2). If the statement is not circulated, the auditor may require it to be read out at the meeting. However, application may be made to the Court by the company or other aggrieved party, and if such representations are deemed to be needlessly defamatory they need not be circulated or be read out at the meeting. In such circumstances, the Court may require the auditor to pay some or all of the costs involved.

New s.393
This section introduces provisions relating to the appointment of auditors not appointed annually. Under subs. (1), where a company by s.386 (inserted by s.119 of the new Act) has elected to dispense with the annual appointment of an auditor, any member can deposit up to one notice in writing in each financial year at its registered office proposing that the appointment shall be terminated. The directors must then hold a general meeting within four weeks at which a resolution shall be put concerning the termination of the auditor's appointment. If the decision is to end the appointment, the auditor shall be deemed not to be reappointed when next he would be. Moreover, if notice was lodged within a fortnight of the accounts being circulated, any deemed reappointment that has taken place will be invalid. Where the directors fail to take steps to convene a general meeting within a fortnight of a member depositing notice, he may himself convene such a meeting, being reimbursed by the company for his expenses, which in turn may then recoup them from the defaulting directors. However, no compensation or damages are payable directly as a result of termination of appointment under this section, although an agreement between the company and the auditor may still provide for compensation for loss of office.

For derivations, see the annotations to s.118.

Statement by person ceasing to hold office as auditor

123.—(1) The following section is inserted in Chapter V of Part XI of the Companies Act 1985 (auditors)—

"**Statement by person ceasing to hold office as auditor**

394.—(1) Where an auditor ceases for any reason to hold office, he shall deposit at the company's registered office a statement of any circumstances connected with his ceasing to hold office which he considers should be brought to the attention of the members or creditors of the company or, if he considers that there are no such circumstances, a statement that there are none.

(2) In the case of resignation, the statement shall be deposited along with the notice of resignation; in the case of failure to seek reappointment, the statement shall be deposited not less than 14 days before the end of the time allowed for next appointing auditors; in any other case, the statement shall be deposited not later than the end of the period of 14 days beginning with the date on which he ceases to hold office.

(3) If the statement is of circumstances which the auditor considers should be brought to the attention of the members or creditors of the company, the company shall within 14 days of the deposit of the statement either—

(a) send a copy of it to every person who under section 238 is entitled to be sent copies of the accounts, or

(b) apply to the court.

(4) The company shall if it applies to the court notify the auditor of the application.

(5) Unless the auditor receives notice of such an application before the end of the period of 21 days beginning with the day on which he deposited the statement, he shall within a further seven days send a copy of the statement to the registrar.

(6) If the court is satisfied that the auditor is using the statement to secure needless publicity for defamatory matter—

(a) it shall direct that copies of the statement need not be sent out, and

(b) it may further order the company's costs on the application to be paid in whole or in part by the auditor, notwithstanding that he is not a party to the application;

and the company shall within 14 days of the court's decision send to the persons mentioned in subsection (3)(a) a statement setting out the effect of the order.

(7) If the court is not so satisfied, the company shall within 14 days of the court's decision—

(a) send copies of the statement to the persons mentioned in subsection (3)(a), and

(b) notify the auditor of the court's decision;

and the auditor shall within seven days of receiving such notice send a copy of the statement to the registrar.

Offences of failing to comply with s.394

394A.—(1) If a person ceasing to hold office as auditor fails to comply with section 394 he is guilty of an offence and liable to a fine.

(2) In proceedings for an offence under subsection (1) it is a defence for the person charged to show that he took all reasonable steps and exercised all due diligence to avoid the commission of the offence.

(3) Sections 733 (liability of individuals for corporate default) and 734 (criminal proceedings against unincorporated bodies) apply to an offence under subsection (1).

(4) If a company makes default in complying with section 394, the company and every officer of it who is in default is guilty of an offence and liable to a fine and, for continued contravention, to a daily default fine.".

(2) In Schedule 24 to the Companies Act 1985 (punishment of offences), at the appropriate place insert—

"394A(1) Person ceasing to hold office as auditor failing to deposit statement as to circumstances.	1. On indictment. 2. Summary.	A fine. The statutory maximum.	
394A(4) Company failing to comply with requirements as to statement of person ceasing to hold office as auditor.	1. On indictment. 2. Summary.	A fine. The statutory maximum.	One-tenth of the statutory maximum.".

(3) In section 733 of the Companies Act 1985 (liability of individuals for corporate default), in subsection (1) (offences in relation to which provisions apply) after "216(3)" insert ", 394A(1)".

(4) In section 734 of the Companies Act 1985 (criminal proceedings against unincorporated bodies), in subsection (1) (offences in relation to which the provisions apply), after "under" insert "section 394A(1) or".

(5) In Schedule 22 to the Companies Act 1985 (unregistered companies), in the entry for sections 384 to 393, for "393" substitute "394A".

DEFINITIONS
"company auditor": ss.24(2), 119.
"members": s.22 C.A. 1985.
"registered office": s.287 C.A. 1985.

GENERAL NOTE
S.123 inserts new ss.394 and 394A into the 1985 Act.

New s.394
This section deals with statements made by a person who for any reason has ceased to hold office as auditor. It requires that he should deposit at the company's registered office within the periods specified in subs. (2) a statement detailing any circumstances connected with his departure which he considers should be brought to the members' or creditors' attention. Where the auditor considers there are no such circumstances, the statement should indicate that fact. However, where there are such circumstances, the company must either send copies of the statement to those persons entitled to receive copies of the accounts under s.238 of the principal Act (inserted by s.10 of the new legislation) or alternatively apply to the Court, in which case the auditor must be informed. For his part, the auditor must send a copy of his statement to the Registrar within four weeks of depositing it with the company, unless he receives notice within three weeks that the company has applied to the Court. If the Court is satisfied that the auditor is needlessly using his statement for defamatory purposes, it will direct that copies of it should not be circulated and may order the auditor to pay some or all of the costs involved. Moreover, the company will have to circulate another statement indicating the effect of the Court's order. If, however, the Court is not satisfied that the auditor's statement is vexatious, the company must circulate it within 14 days and notify the auditor, who will then send a copy to the Registrar within a week of being so informed.

New s.394A
This section identifies the offences of failing to comply with the provisions of new s.394, dealing with statements of an auditor ceasing to hold office.

Subss. (1)–(3) deal with the position of the auditor, stating that he, or a partnership acting as auditors, are guilty of an offence if they breach the provisions of new s.394, although it is a defence to show all reasonable steps were taken to comply. For its part, the company and every defaulting officer is liable to a fine; and, for continued contravention, a daily default fine.

The penalties for breaking s.394 (*i.e.* for committing the offences identified in new s.394A) are outlined in s.123(2), which inserts them into Sched. 24 of the 1985 Act.

For derivations, see the annotations to s.118.

Auditors of trade unions and employers' associations

124. In section 11 of the Trade Union and Labour Relations Act 1974 (duties of trade unions and employers' associations as to auditors, &c.), after subsection (8) insert—

"(9) Where a trade union or employers' association to which this section applies is a company within the meaning of the Companies Act 1985—
- (a) subsection (3) above, and the provisions of paragraphs 6 to 15 of Schedule 2 to this Act, do not apply, and
- (b) the rights and powers conferred, and duties imposed, by paragraphs 16 to 21 of that Schedule belong to the auditors of the company appointed under Chapter V of Part XI of that Act.".

GENERAL NOTE

This section inserts a new subsection to s.11 of the Trade Union and Labour Relations Act 1974. The effect is to achieve what was previously provided for in the former s.394 of the 1985 Companies Act, now superseded by a new section inserted by s.123 of the new Act.

S.124 provides that the auditors of the relatively few bodies which are both companies and trade unions or employers' associations must be appointed under the provisions of the Companies Acts but have the rights conferred and are subject to the duties imposed by paras. 16 to 21 of Sched. 2 to the Trade Union and Labour Relations Act 1974 (auditors' rights of access to books and information, right to be heard at meetings and reports) as well as those given and imposed by the Companies Acts.

Derivation: former s.394, C.A. 1985.

Company records and related matters

Delivery of documents to the registrar

125.—(1) For section 706 of the Companies Act 1985 (size, durability, &c. of documents delivered to the registrar) substitute—

"Delivery to the registrar of documents in legible form

706.—(1) This section applies to the delivery to the registrar under any provision of the Companies Acts of documents in legible form.

(2) The document must—
- (a) state in a prominent position the registered number of the company to which it relates,
- (b) satisfy any requirements prescribed by regulations for the purposes of this section, and
- (c) conform to such requirements as the registrar may specify for the purpose of enabling him to copy the document.

(3) If a document is delivered to the registrar which does not comply with the requirements of this section, he may serve on the person by whom the document was delivered (or, if there are two or more such persons, on any of them) a notice indicating the respect in which the document does not comply.

(4) Where the registrar serves such a notice, then, unless a replacement document—
- (a) is delivered to him within 14 days after the service of the notice, and
- (b) complies with the requirements of this section (or section 707) or is not rejected by him for failure to comply with those requirements,

the original document shall be deemed not to have been delivered to him.

But for the purposes of any enactment imposing a penalty for failure to deliver, so far as it imposes a penalty for continued contravention, no account shall be taken of the period between the delivery of the original document and the end of the period of 14 days after service of the registrar's notice.

(5) Regulations made for the purposes of this section may make different provision with respect to different descriptions of document.".

(2) For section 707 of the Companies Act 1985 (power of registrar to accept information on microfilm, &c.) substitute—

"**Delivery to the registrar of documents otherwise than in legible form**

707.—(1) This section applies to the delivery to the registrar under any provision of the Companies Acts of documents otherwise than in legible form.

(2) Any requirement to deliver a document to the registrar, or to deliver a document in the prescribed form, is satisfied by the communication to the registrar of the requisite information in any non-legible form prescribed for the purposes of this section by regulations or approved by the registrar.

(3) Where the document is required to be signed or sealed, it shall instead be authenticated in such manner as may be prescribed by regulations or approved by the registrar.

(4) The document must—
  (a) contain in a prominent position the registered number of the company to which it relates,
  (b) satisfy any requirements prescribed by regulations for the purposes of this section, and
  (c) be furnished in such manner, and conform to such requirements, as the registrar may specify for the purpose of enabling him to read and copy the document.

(5) If a document is delivered to the registrar which does not comply with the requirements of this section, he may serve on the person by whom the document was delivered (or, if there are two or more such persons, on any of them) a notice indicating the respect in which the document does not comply.

(6) Where the registrar serves such a notice, then, unless a replacement document—
  (a) is delivered to him within 14 days after the service of the notice, and
  (b) complies with the requirements of this section (or section 706) or is not rejected by him for failure to comply with those requirements,

the original document shall be deemed not to have been delivered to him.

But for the purposes of any enactment imposing a penalty for failure to deliver, so far as it imposes a penalty for continued contravention, no account shall be taken of the period between the delivery of the original document and the end of the period of 14 days after service of the registrar's notice.

(7) The Secretary of State may by regulations make further provision with respect to the application of this section in relation to instantaneous forms of communication.

(8) Regulations made for the purposes of this section may make different provision with respect to different descriptions of document and different forms of communication, and as respects delivery to the registrar for England and Wales and delivery to the registrar for Scotland.".

GENERAL NOTE

Ss.125–127 relate to the registration, filing and inspection of company data by the registrar. This section substitutes new ss.706 and 707 into the Companies Act 1985, which relate to the delivery of documents to the registrar. The prior sections tended to equate a document with a piece of paper. (Under C.A. 1989, new s.715A—see C.A. 1989, s.127—a *document* is defined to include information recorded in any form). The new distinction is between documents in a legible form (new s.706) and others (new s.707). For the definition of *legible form* see C.A. 1989, new s.715A (C.A. 1989, s.127).

New s.706

Documents in a legible form must be presented to the registrar with the company's registered number, comply with regulations made by the registrar and satisfy his requirements as to enable them to be copied. Under a new power, where the registrar receives a document which cannot be so processed or does not otherwise conform to his requirements he may, by notice, indicate the relevant defect. If a correct document is then supplied within fourteen days of the service of the notice there is to be no penalty for late delivery as a result of that delivery although the first document is deemed not to have been delivered.

New s.707

This applies to the delivery of electronic information. It gives the registrar powers to regulate the form and authentication of the information. It is also wide enough (in subs. (7)) to cover technological advances. The registrar's powers in relation to the submission of inaccurately processed information are similar to those in relation to legible documents in new s.706.

Keeping and inspection of company records

126.—(1) In Part XXIV of the Companies Act 1985 (the registrar of companies, his functions and offices), after the sections inserted by section 125 above, insert—

"**The keeping of company records by the registrar**

707A.—(1) The information contained in a document delivered to the registrar under the Companies Acts may be recorded and kept by him in any form he thinks fit, provided it is possible to inspect the information and to produce a copy of it in legible form.

This is sufficient compliance with any duty of his to keep, file or register the document.

(2) The originals of documents delivered to the registrar in legible form shall be kept by him for ten years, after which they may be destroyed.

(3) Where a company has been dissolved, the registrar may, at any time after the expiration of two years from the date of the dissolution, direct that any records in his custody relating to the company may be removed to the Public Record Office; and records in respect of which such a direction is given shall be disposed of in accordance with the enactments relating to that Office and the rules made under them.

This subsection does not extend to Scotland.

(4) In subsection (3) "company" includes a company provisionally or completely registered under the Joint Stock Companies Act 1844.".

(2) For sections 709 and 710 of the Companies Act 1985 (inspection of documents kept by the registrar) substitute—

"**Inspection, &c. of records kept by the registrar**

709.—(1) Any person may inspect any records kept by the registrar for the purposes of the Companies Acts and may require—
  (a) a copy, in such form as the registrar considers appropriate, of any information contained in those records, or
  (b) a certified copy of, or extract from, any such record.

(2) The right of inspection extends to the originals of documents delivered to the registrar in legible form only where the record kept

by the registrar of the contents of the document is illegible or unavailable.

(3) A copy of or extract from a record kept at any of the offices for the registration of companies in England and Wales or Scotland, certified in writing by the registrar (whose official position it is unnecessary to prove) to be an accurate record of the contents of any document delivered to him under the Companies Acts, is in all legal proceedings admissible in evidence as of equal validity with the original document and as evidence of any fact stated therein of which direct oral evidence would be admissible.

In England and Wales this is subject to compliance with any applicable rules of court under section 5 of the Civil Evidence Act 1968 or section 69(2) of the Police and Criminal Evidence Act 1984 (which relate to evidence from computer records).

(4) Copies of or extracts from records furnished by the registrar may, instead of being certified by him in writing to be an accurate record, be sealed with his official seal.

(5) No process for compelling the production of a record kept by the registrar shall issue from any court except with the leave of the court; and any such process shall bear on it a statement that it is issued with the leave of the court.

Certificate of incorporation

710. Any person may require a certificate of the incorporation of a company, signed by the registrar or authenticated by his official seal.

Provision and authentication by registrar of documents in non-legible form

710A.—(1) Any requirement of the Companies Acts as to the supply by the registrar of a document may, if the registrar thinks fit, be satisfied by the communication by the registrar of the requisite information in any non-legible form prescribed for the purposes of this section by regulations or approved by him.

(2) Where the document is required to be signed by him or sealed with his official seal, it shall instead be authenticated in such manner as may be prescribed by regulations or approved by the registrar.".

GENERAL NOTE

This section introduces a new s.707A into the Companies Act 1985, substitutes ss.709 and 710 of that Act and introduces new s.710A.

New s.707A

This section relates to three matters. First, it enables the registrar to keep information under his statutory duties in any form, provided inspection and copies of the material are possible. Secondly, it allows him to destroy the originals of any legible documents after ten years, and third, in England and Wales only, allows any records in his custody relating to a dissolved company to be transferred to the Public Record Office after two years. Note the definition of company in subs. (4) which relates to the third of those matters only. The second and third matters were formerly in ss.712 and 715 of the C.A. 1985 which have been repealed by s.127(3) of this Act.

New s.709

This section makes no major changes to the present rules on the inspection of records kept by the registrar as set out in the former ss.709 and 710 of the C.A. 1985. They are modernised, however, to take into account the fact that the information may be given or held in electronic form.

In subs. (3) the references as to evidence of any fact, etc., and to the Civil Evidence Act 1968 and Police and Criminal Evidence Act 1984 are new.

New s.710

This section re-enacts the former s.709(1)(b) of the C.A. 1985 in relation to the certificate of incorporation of a company.

New s.710A
This allows the registrar to provide any document requested in a electronic form, provided it complies with his regulations.

Supplementary provisions as to company records and related matters

127.—(1) In Part XXIV of the Companies Act 1985 (the registrar of companies, his functions and offices), after section 715 insert—

"Interpretation
715A.—(1) In this Part—
"document" includes information recorded in any form; and
"legible", in the context of documents in legible or non-legible form, means capable of being read with the naked eye.
(2) References in this Part to delivering a document include sending, forwarding, producing or (in the case of a notice) giving it.".

(2) In section 708(1) of the Companies Act 1985 (fees)—
  (a) in paragraph (a) for the words from "any notice or other document" to the end substitute "any document which under those Acts is required to be delivered to him", and
  (b) in paragraph (b) omit "or other material".

(3) Omit sections 712 and 715 of the Companies Act 1985 (removal and destruction of old records).

(4) In section 713(1) (enforcement of duty to make returns, &c.), for the words from "file with" to "or other document" substitute "deliver a document to the registrar of companies".

(5) In section 735A(2) of the Companies Act 1985 (provisions applying to Insolvency Act 1986 and Company Directors Disqualification Act 1986 as to the Companies Acts)—
  (a) after "707(1)," insert "707A(1),",
  (b) after "708(1)(a) and (4)," insert "709(1) and (3),", and
  (c) for "710(5)" substitute "710A".

(6) After section 735A of the Companies Act 1985 insert—

"Relationship of this Act to Parts IV and V of the Financial Services Act 1986
735B. In sections 704(5), 706(1), 707(1), 707A(1), 708(1)(a) and (4), 709(1) and (3), 710A and 713(1) references to the Companies Acts include Parts IV and V of the Financial Services Act 1986.".

(7) In Schedule 22 to the Companies Act 1985 (unregistered companies), in the entry for Part XXIV for "sections 706, 708 to 710, 712 and 713" substitute "sections 706 to 710A, 713 and 715A".

GENERAL NOTE
This section is supplementary and consequential to the changes in the registration and inspection of company documents contained in ss.125 and 126.

In particular it introduces important new definitions of *document*, *legible* and *delivery* by inserting new s.715A into the C.A. 1985. The repeal of ss.712 and 715 of C.A. 1985 is consequential on s.126 above.

Miscellaneous

Form of articles for partnership company

128. In Chapter I of Part I of the Companies Act 1985 (company formation), after section 8 (Tables A, C, D and E) insert—

"Table G
8A.—(1) The Secretary of State may by regulations prescribe a Table G containing articles of association appropriate for a partnership company, that is, a company limited by shares whose shares are

intended to be held to a substantial extent by or on behalf of its employees.

(2) A company limited by shares may for its articles adopt the whole or any part of that Table.

(3) If in consequence of regulations under this section Table G is altered, the alteration does not affect a company registered before the alteration takes effect, or repeal as respects that company any portion of the Table.

(4) Regulations under this section shall be made by statutory instrument which shall be subject to annulment in pursuance of a resolution of either House of Parliament.".

GENERAL NOTE

This section, introducing a new s.8A into the C.A. 1985, allows the Secretary of State to bring forward a new model set of articles for a "partnership company," to be known as Table G. The definition of a partnership company for this purpose is one whose shares are intended to be held to a substantial extent by or on behalf of its employees. It is therefore aimed at employee-controlled companies although numerical control is not required by this enabling section. The reason for this new power is the high cost for employees in framing appropriate articles for such companies.

Table G will be optional. The regulations introducing it will be subject to the negative resolution procedure, as are other model form of articles, etc.

Membership of holding company

129.—(1) In Chapter I of Part I of the Companies Act 1985 (company formation), for section 23 (membership of holding company) substitute—

"**Membership of holding company**

23.—(1) Except as mentioned in this section, a body corporate cannot be a member of a company which is its holding company and any allotment or transfer of shares in a company to its subsidiary is void.

(2) The prohibition does not apply where the subsidiary is concerned only as personal representative or trustee unless, in the latter case, the holding company or a subsidiary of it is beneficially interested under the trust.

For the purpose of ascertaining whether the holding company or a subsidiary is so interested, there shall be disregarded—

(a) any interest held only by way of security for the purposes of a transaction entered into by the holding company or subsidiary in the ordinary course of a business which includes the lending of money;

(b) any such interest as is mentioned in Part I of Schedule 2.

(3) The prohibition does not apply where the subsidiary is concerned only as a market maker.

For this purpose a person is a market maker if—

(a) he holds himself out at all normal times in compliance with the rules of a recognised investment exchange other than an overseas investment exchange (within the meaning of the Financial Services Act 1986) as willing to buy and sell securities at prices specified by him, and

(b) he is recognised as so doing by that investment exchange.

(4) Where a body corporate became a holder of shares in a company—

(a) before 1st July 1948, or

(b) on or after that date and before the commencement of section 129 of the Companies Act 1989, in circumstances in which this section as it then had effect did not apply, but at any time after the commencement of that section falls within the prohibition in subsection (1) above in respect of those shares, it may continue to be a member of that company; but for so long as that prohibition would apply, apart from this subsection, it has no right to vote in respect of those shares at meetings of the company or of any class of its members.

(5) Where a body corporate becomes a holder of shares in a company after the commencement of that section in circumstances in which the prohibition in subsection (1) does not apply, but subsequently falls within that prohibition in respect of those shares, it may continue to be a member of that company; but for so long as that prohibition would apply, apart from this subsection, it has no right to vote in respect of those shares at meetings of the company or of any class of its members.

(6) Where a body corporate is permitted to continue as a member of a company by virtue of subsection (4) or (5), an allotment to it of fully paid shares in the company may be validly made by way of capitalisation of reserves of the company; but for so long as the prohibition in subsection (1) would apply, apart from subsection (4) or (5), it has no right to vote in respect of those shares at meetings of the company or of any class of its members.

(7) The provisions of this section apply to a nominee acting on behalf of a subsidiary as to the subsidiary itself.

(8) In relation to a company other than a company limited by shares, the references in this section to shares shall be construed as references to the interest of its members as such, whatever the form of that interest.".

(2) In Schedule 2 to the Companies Act 1985 (interpretation of references to "beneficial interest"), in paragraphs 1(1), 3(1) and 4(2) for "as respects section 23(4)" substitute "as this paragraph applies for the purposes of section 23(2)".

GENERAL NOTE

This section substitutes a redrafted and expanded s.23 of the C.A. 1985. That section was, and the new section still is, designed to prevent a subsidiary company holding shares in its holding company, which would otherwise amount to a *de facto* reduction of capital. The new section contains two further exceptions to that prohibition.

New s.23

The basic prohibition in subs. (1), the trustee exemptions in subs. (2), the pre-1948 exemption in subs. (4), the nominee provision in subs. (7) and provisions relating to guarantee companies in subs. (8) are all substantially the same as in the original section.

Subs. (3)—Market-maker exception: This is a new exception to the prohibition. A subsidiary which is a market-maker under the Financial Services Act 1986 may, for that purpose only, hold shares in its holding company. Market-makers are subject to the controls imposed by the 1986 Act.

Subss. (5) and (6)—Pre-existing shareholding exemption: In 1962 the Jenkins Committee (Cmnd. 1749) in para. 156(c) recommended that where a company becomes a subsidiary company of a company in which it already holds shares it should be allowed to retain those shares provided it could not vote with them. Subs. (5) now implements this recommendation after 27 years. That Committee also recommended that in such a case the holding company should be allowed to allot shares to the subsidiary if they are by way of scrip issue subject again to a voting embargo. Subs. (6) implements that proposal and extends it to the pre-1948 exception in subs. (4).

Company contracts and execution of documents by companies

130.—(1) In Chapter III of Part I of the Companies Act 1985 (a company's capacity; the formalities of carrying on business), for section 36 (form of company contracts) substitute—

"**Company contracts: England and Wales**

36. Under the law of England and Wales a contract may be made—
   (a) by a company, by writing under its common seal, or
   (b) on behalf of a company, by any person acting under its authority, express or implied;

and any formalities required by law in the case of a contract made by an individual also apply, unless a contrary intention appears, to a contract made by or on behalf of a company.".

(2) After that section insert—

"**Execution of documents: England and Wales**

36A.—(1) Under the law of England and Wales the following provisions have effect with respect to the execution of documents by a company.

(2) A document is executed by a company by the affixing of its common seal.

(3) A company need not have a common seal, however, and the following subsections apply whether it does or not.

(4) A document signed by a director and the secretary of a company, or by two directors of a company, and expressed (in whatever form of words) to be executed by the company has the same effect as if executed under the common seal of the company.

(5) A document executed by a company which makes it clear on its face that it is intended by the person or persons making it to be a deed has effect, upon delivery, as a deed; and it shall be presumed, unless a contrary intention is proved, to be delivered upon its being so executed.

(6) In favour of a purchaser a document shall be deemed to have been duly executed by a company if it purports to be signed by a director and the secretary of the company, or by two directors of the company, and, where it makes it clear on its face that it is intended by the person or persons making it to be a deed, to have been delivered upon its being executed.

A "purchaser" means a purchaser in good faith for valuable consideration and includes a lessee, mortgagee or other person who for valuable consideration acquires an interest in property.".

(3) After the section inserted by subsection (2) insert—

"**Execution of documents: Scotland**

36B.—(1) Under the law of Scotland the following provisions have effect with respect to the execution of documents by a company.

(2) A document—
   (a) is signed by a company if it is signed on its behalf by a director, or by the secretary, of the company or by a person authorised to sign the document on its behalf, and
   (b) is subscribed by a company if it is subscribed on its behalf by being signed in accordance with the provisions of paragraph (a) at the end of the last page.

(3) A document shall be presumed, unless the contrary is shown, to have been subscribed by a company in accordance with subsection (2) if—
   (a) it bears to have been subscribed on behalf of the company by a director, or by the secretary, of the company or by a person bearing to have been authorised to subscribe the documents on its behalf; and
   (b) it bears—

(i) to have been signed by a person as a witness of the subscription of the director, secretary or other person subscribing on behalf of the company; or

(ii) (if the subscription is not so witnessed) to have been sealed with the common seal of the company.

(4) A presumption under subsection (3) as to subscription of a document does not include a presumption—
  (a) that a person bearing to subscribe the document as a director or the secretary of the company was such director or secretary; or
  (b) that a person subscribing the document on behalf of the company bearing to have been authorised to do so was authorised to do so.

(5) Notwithstanding subsection (3)(b)(ii), a company need not have a common seal.

(6) Any reference in any enactment (including an enactment contained in a subordinate instrument) to a probative document shall, in relation to a document executed by a company after the commencement of section 130 of the Companies Act 1989, be construed as a reference to a document which is presumed under subsection (3) above to be subscribed by the company.

(7) Subsections (1) to (4) above do not apply where an enactment (including an enactment contained in a subordinate instrument) provides otherwise.".

(4) After the section inserted by subsection (3) insert—

"**Pre-incorporation contracts, deeds and obligations**

36C.—(1) A contract which purports to be made by or on behalf of a company at a time when the company has not been formed has effect, subject to any agreement to the contrary, as one made with the person purporting to act for the company or as agent for it, and he is personally liable on the contract accordingly.

(2) Subsection (1) applies—
  (a) to the making of a deed under the law of England and Wales, and
  (b) to the undertaking of an obligation under the law of Scotland, as it applies to the making of a contract.".

(5) In Schedule 22 of the Companies Act 1985 (provisions applying to unregistered companies), at the appropriate place insert—

"Section 36	Company contracts.	Subject to section 718(3).
Section 36A and 36B	Execution of documents.	Subject to section 718(3).
Section 36C	Pre-incorporation contracts, deeds and obligations.	Subject to section 718(3).".

(6) The Secretary of State may make provision by regulations applying sections 36 to 36C of the Companies Act 1985 (company contracts; execution of documents; pre-incorporation contracts, deeds and obligations) to companies incorporated outside Great Britain, subject to such exceptions, adaptations or modifications as may be specified in the regulations.

Regulations under this subsection shall be made by statutory instrument which shall be subject to annulment in pursuance of a resolution of either House of Parliament.

(7) Schedule 17 contains further minor and consequential amendments relating to company contracts, the execution of documents by companies and related matters.

GENERAL NOTE
This section, redrafted only in the final stages of the Bill in the House of Commons, introduces a substituted s.36 and new ss.36A and 36B into the Companies Act 1985 which abolish the need for a company to have or to use its common seal. It also introduces a new s.36C which replaces the repealed s.36(4) of the C.A. 1985 on the legal consequences of pre-incorporation contracts. Companies incorporated outside Great Britain and unregistered companies will be dealt with by statutory instrument. Sched. 17, introduced by this section, makes minor and consequential amendments to the C.A. 1985.

Substituted s.36
This section states the current legal position in relation to company contracts in England and Wales. A company may contract either by writing under its common seal (see new s.36A below) or through an agent acting within his authority. The general rules as to contractual formalities continue to apply unless a contrary intention is shown. The former s.36(1) did not provide for contrary intention nor did it refer to the agency concept.

New s.36A
This section applies only to England and Wales (subs. (1)). Whilst a company may continue to execute a document by affixing its common seal (subs. (2)) it need not have such a seal (subs. (3)) and whether or not a company does have one, it may execute a document in such a way that it will have the same effect as one made under that seal (*e.g.* for formalities purposes or to create a contract—see substituted s.36). Any document signed by a director and the company secretary or by two directors and expressed to be executed by the company will be regarded as if the seal had been affixed. Further, if they intend it to be a deed and that is made clear on the face of the document, it will be a deed upon delivery. Such delivery will also be execution unless a contrary intention is proved (subss. (4) and (5)). This resolves a previous ambiguity. For similar changes for individuals see s.1 of the Law of Property Miscellaneous Amendments Act 1989.

To protect third parties acting in good faith for valuable consideration, a document which purports to be signed by a director and the secretary or by two directors will be as valid as if it was signed by an actual director and secretary, provided the other conditions are fulfilled. The intention is that such third parties will not be required to check the company's registered documents to establish the bona fides of the parties. The wording is based on a similar protection given to conveyancers in s.74 of the Law of Property Act 1925. Actual notice of an irregularity will defeat this presumption—*quaere* the effect of "Nelsonian" notice, *i.e.* deliberate ignorance?

New s.36B
This section applies only to Scotland (subs. (1)) following reforms proposed by the Scottish Law Commission. It provides for the methods by which a company may sign or subscribe a document. A company may sign a document through the medium of a director, the secretary or an authorised agent, signing on its behalf (subs. (2)(a)). Such a signature, at the end of the last page of the document, will be a valid subscription by the company (subs. (2)(b)).

A subscription will be presumed if the document bears to have been so signed and either such signature bears to have been witnessed or it has been sealed with the company's common seal, although such a presumption does not extend to the fact that the signatory was a director, secretary or authorised agent as appropriate. There is no requirement for a company to have a common seal, however.

These provisions apply to any enactment relating to probative documents but do not (except for the abolition of the requirement to have a common seal) apply to any enactment which provides to the contrary.

New s.36C
This section replaces the repealed C.A. 1985, s.36(4). It substantially re-enacts that provision, however, in fixing the liability of the "agent" for contracts entered into prior to the company's incorporation but extends it to deeds in England and Wales and to the undertaking of obligations in Scotland (see ss.36A, 36B above).

Unregistered and overseas companies
New ss.36–36C will apply to unregistered companies only so far as specified by regulations to be made by the Secretary of State (subs. (5)). With regard to companies incorporated outside Great Britain these sections will be applied as adopted, modified or excluded by

further regulations (subs. (6)). In both cases the regulations will be by statutory instrument, subject to the negative resolution procedure (C.A. 1985, s.718(6); subs. (6)).

Members' rights to damages, &c.

131.—(1) In Part IV of the Companies Act 1985 (allotment of shares and debentures), before section 112 and after the heading "*Other matters arising out of allotment &c.*", insert—

"**Right to damages, &c. not affected**
111A. A person is not debarred from obtaining damages or other compensation from a company by reason only of his holding or having held shares in the company or any right to apply or subscribe for shares or to be included in the company's register in respect of shares.".

(2) In section 116 of the Companies Act 1985 (extended operation of certain provisions applying to public companies) for "and 110 to 115" substitute ", 110, 111 and 112 to 115".

GENERAL NOTE
This section introduces a new s.111A of the Companies Act 1985 which abolishes the effect of the decision in *Houldsworth* v. *City of Glasgow Bank* (1880) 7 R (H.L.). 53 that a shareholder cannot claim damages against his company for a misrepresentation inducing him to acquire his shares unless he rescinds the contract (in that case the right to rescind was lost by the company's liquidation). The precise extent of that decision was unclear (*e.g.* was rescission possible once the shareholder's name appeared on the register of members?) and it is no longer applied in any event to listing particulars or a prospectus governed by Pts. IV and V of the Financial Services Act 1986. This new section will resolve any anomalies in this area. The section only removes a bar from any action; it does not create any new cause of action. There is a consequential amendment to C.A. 1985, s.116 so that the effects of that section will not apply to the new s.111A.

Financial assistance for purposes of employees' share scheme

132. In Chapter VI of Part V of the Companies Act 1985 (financial assistance by company for purchase of its own shares), in section 153 (transactions not prohibited), for subsection (4)(b) (provision of money in accordance with employees' share scheme) substitute—

"(b) the provision by a company, in good faith in the interests of the company, of financial assistance for the purposes of an employees' share scheme,".

GENERAL NOTE
This section amends s.153(4)(b) of the Companies Act 1985. Originally, this allowed a company, by way of exception to the prohibition on a company giving financial assistance for the acquisition of its own shares or those of its holding company, to provide money for the acquisition of such shares (if fully paid) in accordance with an employees' share scheme (as defined in C.A. 1985, s.743). This wording proved to be unduly narrow and was only appropriate for approved profit sharing schemes under s.186 of the Income and Corporation Taxes Act, 1988. The development of tax favoured schemes since 1981, culminating in the employee share ownership trusts in the Finance Act 1989, required a more flexible exception, *e.g.* under such schemes the trustees may borrow money, etc.

The new exception therefore allows a company to give financial assistance as distinct from money and to give that for the purpose of an employees' share scheme (not just for the acquisition of shares). Financial assistance as defined in C.A. 1985, s.152, is very wide and includes both repaying borrowings and giving guarantees. On the other hand, this new exception is now subject to the 'good faith' criteria which are also present in the larger purpose exceptions of C.A. 1985, ss.153(1) and (2). For judicial disagreement on the meaning of that phrase in that context see *Brady* v. *Brady* [1988] 2 W.L.R. 1308 and *Plaut* v. *Steiner* (1989) 5 BCC 352.

Issue of redeemable shares

133.—(1) In Part V of the Companies Act 1985 (share capital, its increase, maintenance and reduction), Chapter III (redeemable shares, purchase by a company of its own shares) is amended as follows.

(2) After section 159 (power to issue redeemable shares) insert—

"**Terms and manner of redemption**

159A.—(1) Redeemable shares may not be issued unless the following conditions are satisfied as regards the terms and manner of redemption.

(2) The date on or by which, or dates between which, the shares are to be or may be redeemed must be specified in the company's articles or, if the articles so provide, fixed by the directors, and in the latter case the date or dates must be fixed before the shares are issued.

(3) Any other circumstances in which the shares are to be or may be redeemed must be specified in the company's articles.

(4) The amount payable on redemption must be specified in, or determined in accordance with, the company's articles, and in the latter case the articles must not provide for the amount to be determined by reference to any person's discretion or opinion.

(5) Any other terms and conditions of redemption shall be specified in the company's articles.

(6) Nothing in this section shall be construed as requiring a company to provide in its articles for any matter for which provision is made by this Act.".

(3) In section 160 (financing, &c. of redemption)—
  (a) omit subsection (3) (which is superseded by the new section 159A), and
  (b) in subsection (4) (cancellation of shares on redemption) for "redeemed under this section" substitute "redeemed under this Chapter".

(4) In section 162 (power of company to purchase own shares), for subsection (2) (application of provisions relating to redeemable shares) substitute—

"(2) Sections 159, 160 and 161 apply to the purchase by a company under this section of its own shares as they apply to the redemption of redeemable shares.".

GENERAL NOTE

This section introduces a new s.159A into the Companies Act 1985 as a replacement for C.A. 1985, s.160(3) which is repealed. The new section details the terms and manner in which redeemable shares issued under s.159 may be redeemed. The existing requirements in s.159(3), *i.e.* that such shares must be fully paid before redemption and that the terms of redemption must provide for payment on redemption are not affected, nor are the rules relating to the financing of the redemption contained in the remainder of Chapter VII of Pt. V of the C.A. 1985.

The repealed s.160(3) simply provided that subject to the criteria set out above, the shares could be redeemed on such terms and in such manner as provided by the company's articles. New s.159A requires much more detailed provisions to be included in the articles in an attempt to clarify the powers of the directors in relation to the price and conditions of redemption.

There are consequential amendments to C.A. 1985, s.160(4), and to C.A. 1985, s.162(2). The latter ensures that the new s.159A does not apply to companies purchasing their own shares under that section.

New s.159A

This section applies mandatory rules regulating the terms and manner of the redemption of any redeemable shares. They relate first to the time of redemption. The date, or dates, within which the shares are to be or may be redeemed, must either be specified in the articles or delegated to the directors by the articles. In the latter case the date(s) of redemption must be fixed prior to the issue of the shares. Any other redemption triggers must also be specified in the articles.

The second area relates to the amount payable on redemption. The articles must either specify the amount payable or provide a formula for calculating that amount. The latter cannot involve any person's discretion or opinion. A formula is thus expressly allowed for.

Finally, all other terms and conditions of redemption must be included in the articles except for those already required by the Act itself, *e.g.* C.A. 1985, s.159(3).

This new section was introduced in the final stages of the parliamentary timetable and the Government stated that it would not bring the section into force until the position had been fully discussed.

Disclosure of interests in shares

134.—(1) Part VI of the Companies Act 1985 (disclosure of interests in shares) is amended as follows.

(2) In section 199(2) (notifiable interests), for the words from "the percentage" to the end substitute "3 per cent. of the nominal value of that share capital".

The order bringing the above amendment into force may make such provision as appears to the Secretary of State appropriate as to the obligations of a person whose interest in a company's shares becomes notifiable by virtue of the amendment coming into force.

(3) In sections 202(1) and (4) and 206(8) (which require notification of certain matters within a specified period) for "5 days" substitute "2 days".

(4) In section 202 (particulars to be contained in notification), for subsection (3) substitute—

"(3) A notification (other than one stating that a person no longer has a notifiable interest) shall include the following particulars, so far as known to the person making the notification at the date when it is made—
  (a) the identity of each registered holder of shares to which the notification relates and the number of such shares held by each of them, and
  (b) the number of such shares in which the interest of the person giving the notification is such an interest as is mentioned in section 208(5).".

(5) After section 210 insert—

"**Power to make further provision by regulations**

210A.—(1) The Secretary of State may by regulations amend—
  (a) the definition of "relevant share capital" (section 198(2)),
  (b) the percentage giving rise to a "notifiable interest" (section 199(2)),
  (c) the periods within which an obligation of disclosure must be fulfilled or a notice must be given (sections 202(1) and (4) and 206(8)),
  (d) the provisions as to what is taken to be an interest in shares (section 208) and what interests are to be disregarded (section 209), and
  (e) the provisions as to company investigations (section 212);
and the regulations may amend, replace or repeal the provisions referred to above and make such other consequential amendments or repeals of provisions of this Part as appear to the Secretary of State to be appropriate.

(2) The regulations may in any case make different provision for different descriptions of company; and regulations under subsection (1)(b), (c) or (d) may make different provision for different descriptions of person, interest or share capital.

(3) The regulations may contain such transitional and other supplementary and incidental provisions as appear to the Secretary of State to be appropriate, and may in particular make provision as to the obligations of a person whose interest in a company's shares becomes or ceases to be notifiable by virtue of the regulations.

(4) Regulations under this section shall be made by statutory instrument.

(5) No regulations shall be made under this section unless a draft of the regulations has been laid before and approved by a resolution of each House of Parliament.".

(6) Any regulations made under section 209(1)(j) which are in force immediately before the repeal of that paragraph by this Act shall have effect as if made under section 210A(1)(d) as inserted by subsection (5) above.

GENERAL NOTE
This section makes three specific amendments to Pt.VI of the Companies Act 1985 on the disclosure of interests in the shares of public companies, and by introducing new s.210A into the C.A. 1985 considerably extends the Secretary of State's powers to amend the primary legislation by statutory instrument.

Subs. (2)
Notifiable interests: The notification threshold is reduced from five per cent. to three per cent. by the amendment made in subs. (1) to s.199(2) of the C.A. 1985. (Former C.A. 1985, s.201(1) is repealed). Originally the threshold was ten per cent. This figure may be changed by statutory instrument: new s.210A.

Subs. (3)
Time limits for notification: The time limits for notification of various events in relation to shareholdings in public companies in ss.202(1) and (4) and 206(8) are reduced from five days to two. These may be changed by statutory instrument: new s.210A.

Subs. (4)
Disclosure in relation to options: S.202(3) of the C.A. 1985 is substituted by this subsection. The substance of the original s.202(3) is re-enacted by new s.202(3)(a); *i.e.* disclosure of the identity of the owner and the size of his holding. This also required disclosure of any shares held by way of an option (s.208(5) of the C.A. 1985 defines that as a notifiable interest) but not of the exercise of that option or the acquisition of the shares. The nature of the interest but not the size would have altered.

Under new s.202(3)(b) a shareholder will have to specify the number of shares held by way of option. Since any change to s.202 particulars must be notified under s.202(4), the exercise of such an option will have to be notified.

New s.210A
Subs. (5)
Powers of amendment: This new section subsumes ss.201 and 209(1)(j) of the C.A. 1985 in a much wider regulatory power for the Secretary of State. By way of statutory instrument subject to the affirmative resolution procedure he may amend, replace or repeal, etc., any of the following: (a) the definition of relevant share capital in C.A. 1985, s.198(2), (new power); (b) the notifiable percentage in C.A. 1985, s.199(2), (formerly in C.A. 1985, s.201); (c) time limits for notification in C.A. 1985, ss.202(1), (4) and 206(8) (new); (d) interests in shares and disregarded in ss.208 and 209 (the former is new, the latter was in C.A. 1985, s.109(1)(j) and thus subject to no parliamentary procedure at all); (e) company's own investigations into its shareholders in C.A. 1985, s.212, (new).

Existing regulations under C.A. 1985, s.209(1)(j) are preserved by subs.(6).

Orders imposing restrictions on shares

135.—(1) The Secretary of State may by regulations made by statutory instrument make such amendments of the provisions of the Companies Act 1985 relating to orders imposing restrictions on shares as appear to him necessary or expedient—

(a) for enabling orders to be made in a form protecting the rights of third parties;
(b) with respect to the circumstances in which restrictions may be relaxed or removed;
(c) with respect to the making of interim orders by a court.

(2) The provisions referred to in subsection (1) are section 210(5), section 216(1) and (2), section 445 and Part XV of the Companies Act 1985.

(3) The regulations may make different provision for different cases and may contain such transitional and other supplementary and incidental provisions as appear to the Secretary of State to be appropriate.

(4) Regulations under this section shall not be made unless a draft of the regulations has been laid before Parliament and approved by resolution of each House of Parliament.

GENERAL NOTE

This section allows the Secretary of State to amend by regulations those sections of the Companies Act 1985 which relate to orders imposing restrictions on shares. The provisions which may be so altered are as set out in subs. (2); *i.e.*

C.A. 1985, s.210(5)—an order imposed by the Secretary of State for an offence under the compulsory notification of interests in shares provisions of the Act;

C.A. 1985, s.216(1) and (2)—a court order made following a failure to comply with a s.212 notice served by the company concerned on a shareholder to disclose the true beneficial interest in that company's shares;

C.A. 1985, s.445—an order imposed by the Secretary of State in consequence of an investigation into the ownership, etc., of a company;

C.A. 1985 Pt. XV—the consequences of, and qualifications to, (ss.454–457) an order made under the above sections.

The amendments which may be made apply to three areas: to the protection of third parties; the relaxation or removal of such restrictions; or to interim orders. The need for such amendments was perceived following such cases as *Lonrho v. Bond (No.2)* (1989) 5 BCC 776, where the court held that it had no jurisdiction to make an order qualifying the restrictions as currently contained in Pt. XV of the Companies Act 1985 by excluding innocent third parties who had taken the shares as a security and were in no way responsible for the breach giving rise to the order. Such an order had to apply to all parties or to none.

The regulations will be made by the affirmative resolution procedure.

A company's registered office

136. For section 287 of the Companies Act 1985 (registered office) substitute—

"A company's registered office

287.—(1) A company shall at all times have a registered office to which all communications and notices may be addressed.

(2) On incorporation the situation of the company's registered office is that specified in the statement sent to the registrar under section 10.

(3) The company may change the situation of its registered office from time to time by giving notice in the prescribed form to the registrar.

(4) The change takes effect upon the notice being registered by the registrar, but until the end of the period of 14 days beginning with the date on which it is registered a person may validly serve any document on the company at its previous registered office.

(5) For the purposes of any duty of a company—
(a) to keep at its registered office, or make available for public inspection there, any register, index or other document, or
(b) to mention the address of its registered office in any document,

a company which has given notice to the registrar of a change in the situation of its registered office may act on the change as from such date, not more than 14 days after the notice is given, as it may determine.

(6) Where a company unavoidably ceases to perform at its registered office any such duty as is mentioned in subsection (5)(a) in circumstances in which it was not practicable to give prior notice to the registrar of a change in the situation of its registered office, but—
  (a) resumes performance of that duty at other premises as soon as practicable, and
  (b) gives notice accordingly to the registrar of a change in the situation of its registered office within 14 days of doing so,
it shall not be treated as having failed to comply with that duty.

(7) In proceedings for an offence of failing to comply with any such duty as is mentioned in subsection (5), it is for the person charged to show that by reason of the matters referred to in that subsection or subsection (6) no offence was committed.".

GENERAL NOTE

This section substitutes a new s.287 in the Companies Act 1985. It re-enacts in new s.287(1) the basic requirement that a company must have a registered office, although with the repeal of old s.287(3) there is no specific penalty for failure to do so. However, the penalties for failing to keep various registers, etc., remain.

The remainder of the new section is concerned with the change of address of the registered office. The first address is that specified in the statement sent on incorporation under C.A. 1985, s.10. Previously, notification of any change in that address had to be given to the registrar within 14 days of the change, but there was some doubt as to when such a change took effect—whether it was on notification or on registration. Under new s.287(3) and (4) such a change, which must be notified to the registrar, takes effect on that notice being registered by the registrar. However, since the new address will actually appear on the company's file a few days after registration, a third party may now validly serve a document at the old address for up to 14 days after the date of registration.

The company will also be unaware of the precise date of registration unless it makes a specific search to that effect. New s.287(5) allows the company to transfer its registers, etc., and to use the new address at any time within 14 days of giving the notice to the registrar. Any technical offences so committed are thus nullified.

Finally, under s.287(6) and (7), if a company is unavoidably unable to keep its registers, etc., at its registered office in circumstances in which it was impracticable to give the registrar due notice of the change, the company will not thereby commit any offence if (1) it resumes performance of such duties at a new address as soon as practicable, and (2) it gives notice of that new address within 14 days of doing so. The burden of proof is on the company.

Effecting of insurance for officers and auditors of company

137.—(1) In section 310 of the Companies Act 1985 (provisions exempting officers and auditors from liability), for subsection (3) (permitted provisions) substitute—

"(3) This section does not prevent a company—
  (a) from purchasing and maintaining for any such officer or auditor insurance against any such liability, or
  (b) from indemnifying any such officer or auditor against any liability incurred by him—
    (i) in defending any proceedings (whether civil or criminal) in which judgment is given in his favour or he is acquitted, or
    (ii) in connection with any application under section 144(3) or (4) (acquisition of shares by innocent nominee) or section 727 (general power to grant relief in case of honest and reasonable conduct) in which relief is granted to him by the court.".

(2) In Part I of Schedule 7 to the Companies Act 1985 (general matters to be dealt with in directors' report), after paragraph 5 insert—

"*Insurance effected for officers or auditors*

5A. Where in the financial year the company has purchased or maintained any such insurance as is mentioned in section 310(3)(a) (insurance of officers or auditors against liabilities in relation to the company), that fact shall be stated in the report."

GENERAL NOTE
This section substitutes a new subs. (3) into s.310 of the Companies Act 1985 and a new para. 5A into Sched. 7 to that Act (the Directors' Report).

New s.310(3) of the C.A. re-enacts the former provisions in new para. (b) and so preserves the exception to the general prohibition in that section against a company indemnifying its officers or auditors for any breach of duty, etc., in relation to the costs of a successful defence to any such action or where the court grants him relief. New para. (a) now includes a further exemption from the prohibition in relation to indemnity insurance policies taken out by companies in favour of their officers or auditors to cover such breaches. This will not affect policies existing prior to the date when this section comes into effect which are arguably void as a result of C.A. 1985, s.310(2).

Under new para. 5A of Sched. 7 to the C.A. 1985, any such policy must be disclosed in the Directors' Report. This will be so even if the officer is himself partly contributing to the policy.

Increase of limits on certain exemptions

138. Part X of the Companies Act 1985 (enforcement of fair dealing by directors) is amended as follows—
(a) in section 332(1)(b) (short-term quasi-loans) for "£1,000" substitute "£5,000,";
(b) in section 334 (loans of small amounts) for "£2,500" substitute "£5,000";
(c) in section 338(4) and (6) (loans or quasi-loans by money-lending company) for "£50,000" substitute "£100,000".

GENERAL NOTE
Pt. X of the Companies Act 1985, which relates to the prohibition and disclosure requirements imposed upon dealings between a company and its directors, contains many anomalies and difficulties. This section merely updates the monetary figures in three sections:
(a) the limit on short term quasi-loans in s.332(1)(b) is raised from £1,000 to £5,000;
(b) the limit on small loans in s.334 is raised from £2,500 to £5,000 (these two limits now correspond to that for minor transactions in C.A. 1985, s.335); and
(c) the limits for loans and quasi-loans by money lending companies in s.338 are raised from £50,000 to £100,000.

Annual returns

139.—(1) In Part XI of the Companies Act 1985 (company administration and procedure), for Chapter III (annual return) substitute—

"CHAPTER III

ANNUAL RETURN

Duty to deliver annual returns

363.—(1) Every company shall deliver to the registrar successive annual returns each of which is made up to a date not later than the date which is from time to time the company's "return date", that is—

(a) the anniversary of the company's incorporation, or
(b) if the company's last return delivered in accordance with this Chapter was made up to a different date, the anniversary of that date.

(2) Each return shall—
   (a) be in the prescribed form,
   (b) contain the information required by or under the following provisions of this Chapter, and
   (c) be signed by a director or the secretary of the company;

and it shall be delivered to the registrar within 28 days after the date to which it is made up.

(3) If a company fails to deliver an annual return in accordance with this Chapter before the end of the period of 28 days after a return date, the company is guilty of an offence and liable to a fine and, in the case of continued contravention, to a daily default fine.

The contravention continues until such time as an annual return made up to that return date and complying with the requirements of subsection (2) (except as to date of delivery) is delivered by the company to the registrar.

(4) Where a company is guilty of an offence under subsection (3), every director or secretary of the company is similarly liable unless he shows that he took all reasonable steps to avoid the commission or continuation of the offence.

(5) The references in this section to a return being delivered "in accordance with this Chapter" are—
   (a) in relation to a return made after the commencement of section 139 of the Companies Act 1989, to a return with respect to which all the requirements of subsection (2) are complied with;
   (b) in relation to a return made before that commencement, to a return with respect to which the formal and substantive requirements of this Chapter as it then had effect were complied with, whether or not the return was delivered in time.

Contents of annual return: general

364.—(1) Every annual return shall state the date to which it is made up and shall contain the following information—
   (a) the address of the company's registered office;
   (b) the type of company it is and its principal business activities;
   (c) the name and address of the company secretary;
   (d) the name and address of every director of the company;
   (e) in the case of each individual director—
      (i) his nationality, date of birth and business occupation, and
      (ii) such particulars of other directorships and former names as are required to be contained in the company's register of directors;
   (f) in the case of any corporate director, such particulars of other directorships as would be required to be contained in that register in the case of an individual;
   (g) if the register of members is not kept at the company's registered office, the address of the place where it is kept;
   (h) if any register of debenture holders (or a duplicate of any such register or a part of it) is not kept at the company's registered office, the address of the place where it is kept;
   (i) if the company has elected—
      (i) to dispense under section 252 with the laying of accounts and reports before the company in general meeting, or

(ii) to dispense under section 366A with the holding of annual general meetings,

a statement to that effect.

(2) The information as to the company's type shall be given by reference to the classification scheme prescribed for the purposes of this section.

(3) The information as to the company's principal business activities may be given by reference to one or more categories of any prescribed system of classifying business activities.

(4) A person's "name" and "address" mean, respectively—
   (a) in the case of an individual, his Christian name (or other forename) and surname and his usual residential address;
   (b) in the case of a corporation or Scottish firm, its corporate or firm name and its registered or principal office.

(5) In the case of a peer, or an individual usually known by a title, the title may be stated instead of his Christian name (or other forename) and surname or in addition to either or both of them.

(6) Where all the partners in a firm are joint secretaries, the name and principal office of the firm may be stated instead of the names and addresses of the partners.

Contents of annual return: particulars of share capital and shareholders

364A.—(1) The annual return of a company having a share capital shall contain the following information with respect to its share capital and members.

(2) The return shall state the total number of issued shares of the company at the date to which the return is made up and the aggregate nominal value of those shares.

(3) The return shall state with respect to each class of shares in the company—
   (a) the nature of the class, and
   (b) the total number and aggregate nominal value of issued shares of that class at the date to which the return is made up.

(4) The return shall contain a list of the names and addresses of every person who—
   (a) is a member of the company on the date to which the return is made up, or
   (b) has ceased to be a member of the company since the date to which the last return was made up (or, in the case of the first return, since the incorporation of the company);

and if the names are not arranged in alphabetical order the return shall have annexed to it an index sufficient to enable the name of any person in the list to be easily found.

(5) The return shall also state—
   (a) the number of shares of each class held by each member of the company at the date to which the return is made up, and
   (b) the number of shares of each class transferred since the date to which the last return was made up (or, in the case of the first return, since the incorporation of the company) by each member or person who has ceased to be a member, and the dates of registration of the transfers.

(6) The return may, if either of the two immediately preceding returns has given the full particulars required by subsections (4) and (5), give only such particulars as relate to persons ceasing to be or becoming members since the date of the last return and to shares transferred since that date.

(7) Subsections (4) and (5) do not require the inclusion of particulars entered in an overseas branch register if copies of those entries have not been received at the company's registered office by the date to which the return is made up.

Those particulars shall be included in the company's next annual return after they are received.

(8) Where the company has converted any of its shares into stock, the return shall give the corresponding information in relation to that stock, stating the amount of stock instead of the number or nominal value of shares.

Supplementary provisions: regulations and interpretation

365.—(1) The Secretary of State may by regulations make further provision as to the information to be given in a company's annual return which may amend or repeal the provisions of sections 364 and 364A.

(2) Regulations under this section shall be made by statutory instrument which shall be subject to annulment in pursuance of a resolution of either House of Parliament.

(3) For the purposes of this Chapter, except section 363(2)(c) (signature of annual return), a shadow director shall be deemed to be a director.".

(2) Where a company was, immediately before the commencement of this section, in default with respect to the delivery of one or more annual returns, this section does not affect its obligation to make such a return (in accordance with Chapter III of Part XI of the Companies Act 1985 as it then had effect) or any liability arising from failure to do so.

(3) In Schedule 24 to the Companies Act 1985 (punishment of offences) in the entry relating to section 363(7), in the first column for "363(7)" substitute "363(3)".

(4) In Schedule 1 to the Company Directors Disqualification Act 1986 (matters relevant to determining unfitness of directors), in paragraph 4 (failure of company to comply with certain provisions), for sub-paragraphs (f) and (g) substitute—

"(f) section 363 (duty of company to make annual returns);".

(5) In section 565(6) of the Income and Corporation Taxes Act 1988 (conditions for exemption from provisions relating to sub-contractors in construction industry: compliance with requirements of Companies Act 1985), in paragraph (d) for "sections 363, 364 and 365" substitute "sections 363 to 365".

GENERAL NOTE

This section substitutes a new Chapter III of Pt. XI of the Companies Act 1985 which sets out the requirements for the company's annual return. Old ss.363–365 of and Sched. 15 to the Companies Act 1985 are replaced by new ss.363, 364, 364A and 365, introduced by this section. The basic structure of the new regime is that s.363 sets out the obligation and procedures relating to the submission of an annual return, s.364 details its contents for all companies, s.364A requires further details from companies having a share capital and s.365 allows the Secretary of State to amend the contents sections. There are other consequential definitions and savings.

New s.363

Companies are obliged to deliver to the registrar a successive annual return made up to a date not later than each company's return date. That date is initially one year from incorporation and from then on it is one year from the date when the last return was made up. Because the only restriction is that a company may not leave a gap of more than 12 months between its returns, any company may, by bringing its return date forward, achieve flexibility in the date selected. Thus, groups may now harmonise the return dates of all member companies and link that to their accounting obligations.

The new concept of a return date is intended to facilitate the introduction of a shuttle system for annual returns. Companies House will, under this proposed system, send out to each company in advance of the return date an annual return form already completed with the information provided by the company in the previous return. The company will only have to amend it and have it signed by a director or the secretary.

The form of the annual return will be prescribed, the contents are set out in C.A. 1985, new ss.364 and 364A (see below) and it must be signed by a director (not a shadow director—see new s.365(3)) or the secretary. Delivery must be made within 28 days of the return being made up. The company and its officers are guilty of an offence for failure to comply with these obligations, including a daily default fine, although an officer may use the reasonable diligence defence. If a return is made up before this section comes into force, but is delivered afterwards, it must comply with the provisions relating to annual returns in force at the time it was made up.

New s.364

This section details the required contents of an annual return for all companies. It is supplemented by new s.364A for companies with a share capital. The following headings apply:
 (a) the registered office address;
 (b) the type of company it is (see new s.364(1A))—a new obligation;
 (c) the company's principal business activities (see new s.364(2))—a new obligation;
 (d) the name and address of the company secretary (see new s.364(3), (4) and (5));
 (e) the name and address of all directors, including shadow directors—new s.365(3)—(see new s.364(3) and (4));
 (f) further details of all directors, including shadow directors;
 (g) details of corporate directors;
 (h) location of the register of members if not at the registered office;
 (i) location of the register of debenture holders if not at the registered office; and
 (j) notification of any election to dispense with the laying of accounts or the holding of an annual general meeting (see ss.108 and 109 of this Act above).
Heads (b), (c) and (j) are new obligations.

New s.364A

This section largely re-enacts the obligations formerly in paras. 3 and 5 of Sched. 15 to the C.A. 1985 for companies with a share capital. Details are required of shares allotted or subscribed for as at the date when the return is made up, of each class of share, of current shareholders and those who have ceased to be shareholders since the last return was made up, including details as to classes of shares so held or formerly held. Once a list of such shareholders has been provided, subsequent returns need only specify changes. There are special provisions for overseas shareholders (see C.A. 1985, Sched. 14) and for shares converted into stock.

New s.365

The details of new s.364 and 364A may be amended by statutory instrument, subject to the negative resolution procedure.

Other savings and amendments: Any liability arising under the old provisions relating to annual returns is preserved by subs. (2) of this section. There are consequential amendments to Sched. 24 to the C.A. 1985, to the criteria for disqualification of directors under Sched. 1 to the Company Directors Disqualification Act 1986, and to s.565(6) of the Taxes Act 1988 (obligations to be complied with by sub-contractors in the construction industry for tax privileges) in subss. (3)–(5) of this section.

Floating charges (Scotland)

140.—(1) In section 463 of the Companies Act 1985 (effect of floating charge on winding up), in subsection (1) for the words "On the commencement of the winding up of a company," there shall be substituted the words "Where a company goes into liquidation within the meaning of section 247(2) of the Insolvency Act 1986,".

(2) Section 464 of the Companies Act 1985 (ranking of floating charges) is amended as follows.

(3) In subsection (1)(b) at the beginning there shall be inserted the words "with the consent of the holder of any subsisting floating charge or fixed security which would be adversely affected,".

(4) After subsection (1) there shall be inserted the following subsection—

"(1A) Where an instrument creating a floating charge contains any such provision as is mentioned in subsection (1)(a), that provision shall be effective to confer priority on the floating charge over any fixed security or floating charge created after the date of the instrument.".

(5) For subsection (3) there shall be substituted—

"(3) The order of ranking of the floating charge with any other subsisting or future floating charges or fixed securities over all or any part of the company's property is determined in accordance with the provisions of subsections (4) and (5) except where it is determined in accordance with any provision such as is mentioned in paragraph (a) or (b) of subsection (1).".

(6) In subsection (5) at the end there shall be added the following paragraph—

"; and

(e) (in the case of a floating charge to secure a contingent liability other than a liability arising under any further advances made from time to time) the maximum sum to which that contingent liability is capable of amounting whether or not it is contractually limited.".

(7) In subsection (6) after the words "subject to" there shall be inserted the words "Part XII and to".

(8) In section 466 of the Companies Act 1985 (alteration of floating charges), subsections (4) and (5) and in subsection (6) the words "falling under subsection (4) of this section" shall cease to have effect.

GENERAL NOTE

This section amends ss.463, 464 and 466 of the C.A. 1985, which apply to floating charges in Scotland only.

The amendment to s.463 which relates to the effect of a floating charge on a winding up, imports the definition in s.247(2) of the Insolvency Act 1986 as to when a company goes into liquidation. It is therefore a belated tidying-up amendment.

The amendments to s.464 are more substantial. First, the right of the holder of a floating charge to create a ranking order by his charge with other subsisting or future charges is now limited by the need to obtain the consent of the holder of any subsisting fixed or floating charge which would be adversely affected. Secondly, the right of the chargee to restrict the creation of subsequent fixed or floating charges taking priority over his floating charge is now expressly effective to give his charge priority over any later charge (new subs. (1A)). Thirdly, although the order of ranking in the absence of any ranking clause in the floating charge remains the same (s.464(4)), the provision for this is more accurately worded (substituted s.464(3)). Finally, the complex process whereby under s.464(5) the holder of a lower ranked floating charge may restrict the preference of a higher ranking charge is amended so that the restricted charge is entitled to preference for a contingent liability.

C.A. 1985, s.466 is amended by the repeal of subss. (4) and (5), which required the registration of any instrument altering a floating charge.

Application to declare dissolution of company void

141.—(1) Section 651 of the Companies Act 1985 (power of court to declare dissolution of company void) is amended as follows.

(2) In subsection (1) omit the words "at any time within 2 years of the date of the dissolution."

(3) After subsection (3) add—

"(4) Subject to the following provisions, an application under this section may not be made after the end of the period of two years from the date of the dissolution of the company.

(5) An application for the purpose of bringing proceedings against the company—

(a) for damages in respect of personal injuries (including any sum

claimed by virtue of section 1(2)(c) of the Law Reform (Miscellaneous Provisions) Act 1934 (funeral expenses)), or
  (b) for damages under the Fatal Accidents Act 1976 or the Damages (Scotland) Act 1976,
may be made at any time; but no order shall be made on such an application if it appears to the court that the proceedings would fail by virtue of any enactment as to the time within which proceedings must be brought.

(6) Nothing in subsection (5) affects the power of the court on making an order under this section to direct that the period between the dissolution of the company and the making of the order shall not count for the purposes of any such enactment.

(7) In subsection (5)(a) "personal injuries" includes any disease and any impairment of a person's physical or mental condition.".

(4) An application may be made under section 651(5) of the Companies Act 1985 as inserted by subsection (3) above (proceedings for damages for personal injury, &c.) in relation to a company dissolved before the commencement of this section notwithstanding that the time within which the dissolution might formerly have been declared void under that section had expired before commencement.

But no such application shall be made in relation to a company dissolved more than twenty years before the commencement of this section.

(5) Except as provided by subsection (4), the amendments made by this section do not apply in relation to a company which was dissolved more than two years before the commencement of this section.

GENERAL NOTE

This section amends s.651 of the Companies Act 1985, which allows the court to reverse the dissolution of a company to allow an action to be brought as if it had not been dissolved. Under the former wording of that section, a court could only make such a declaration on an application made within two years of the date of dissolution. This gave rise to problems, *e.g.* whereby an employee who contracted a disease in the course of his employment which did not become apparent until much later could not pursue a claim against the employer company or its insurance company if the former had been dissolved for more than two years by the date of the claim.

Under the amended s.651, the maximum period of two years is retained, except for claims for damages for personal injuries (and funeral expenses) as defined in new s.651(7), or for damages under the Fatal Accidents Act 1976 or the Damages (Scotland) Act 1976. In such cases, the period for applications can be extended up to the time allowed by ss.11 and 14 of the Limitation Act 1980. The Court may also declare that the period between dissolution and its reversal will not count for limitation purposes.

The effect of these changes to C.A. 1985, s.651 is qualified by subss. (4) and (5) of this section. In general they do not apply to companies dissolved more than two years prior to this section coming into force, but for applications under new s.651(5) (personal injuries, etc.) they will apply to any company dissolved within twenty years prior to that date. Thus, those changes are retrospective in their effect.

Abolition of doctrine of deemed notice

142.—(1) In Part XXIV of the Companies Act 1985 (the registrar of companies, his functions and offices), after section 711 insert—

"**Exclusion of deemed notice**

711A.—(1) A person shall not be taken to have notice of any matter merely because of its being disclosed in any document kept by the registrar of companies (and thus available for inspection) or made available by the company for inspection.

(2) This does not affect the question whether a person is affected by notice of any matter by reason of a failure to make such inquiries as ought reasonably to be made.

(3) In this section 'document' includes any material which contains information.

(4) Nothing in this section affects the operation of—
  (a) section 416 of this Act (under which a person taking a charge over a company's property is deemed to have notice of matters disclosed on the companies charges register), or
  (b) section 198 of the Law of Property Act 1925 as it applies by virtue of section 3(7) of the Land Charges Act 1972 (under which the registration of certain land charges under Part XII, or Chapter III of Part XXIII, of this Act is deemed to constitute actual notice for all purposes connected with the land affected).".

(2) In Schedule 22 to the Companies Act 1985 (unregistered companies), in the entry for Part XXIV at the appropriate place insert—

"Section 711A   Abolition of doctrine of deemed notice.   Subject to section 718(3).".

GENERAL NOTE

This section introduces new s.711A into the Companies Act 1985. This new section, following the recommendation of the Prentice and Diamond Reports, abolishes the doctrine of constructive notice which operated in relation to all documents kept by the registrar of companies on a company's file. The abolition of the *ultra vires* rule by C.A. 1985, new s.35 (C.A. 1989, s.108, see above) suggested this, as did the abolition of constitutional restrictions on company agents (C.A. 1985, new s.35A as inserted by C.A. 1989, s.108, see above).

The new section applies, however, to all information kept by the registrar for inspection, whether on a physical document or in electronic form, except for the constructive notice given by C.A. 1985, new s.416, to a person taking a charge over a company's property as to matters then on the register of charges.

The new section expressly saves other forms of notice, *e.g.* failure to make reasonable enquiries, and it also preserves registration of certain land charges as being actual notice for land law purposes under s.3(7) of the Land Charges Act 1972.

Subs. (2)

This provides that the new s.711A will only apply to unregistered companies in so far as the Secretary of State decides by regulations.

Rights of inspection and related matters

143.—(1) In Part XXV of the Companies Act 1985 (miscellaneous and supplementary provisions), after section 723 insert—

"Obligations of company as to inspection of registers, &c.

723A.—(1) The Secretary of State may make provision by regulations as to the obligations of a company which is required by any provision of this Act—
  (a) to make available for inspection any register, index or document, or
  (b) to provide copies of any such register, index or document, or part of it;
and a company which fails to comply with the regulations shall be deemed to have refused inspection or, as the case may be, to have failed to provide a copy.

(2) The regulations may make provision as to the time, duration and manner of inspection, including the circumstances in which and extent to which the copying of information is permitted in the course of inspection.

(3) The regulations may define what may be required of the company as regards the nature, extent and manner of extracting or

presenting any information for the purposes of inspection or the provision of copies.

(4) Where there is power to charge a fee, the regulations may make provision as to the amount of the fee and the basis of its calculation.

(5) Regulations under this section may make different provision for different classes of case.

(6) Nothing in any provision of this Act or in the regulations shall be construed as preventing a company from affording more extensive facilities than are required by the regulations or, where a fee may be charged, from charging a lesser fee than that prescribed or no fee at all.

(7) Regulations under this section shall be made by statutory instrument which shall be subject to annulment in pursuance of a resolution of either House of Parliament.".

(2) In section 169(5) of the Companies Act 1985 (contract for purchase by company of its own shares), omit the words from ", during business hours" to "for inspection)".

(3) In section 175(6) of the Companies Act 1985 (statutory declaration and auditors' report relating to payment out of capital), in paragraph (b) omit the words from "during business hours" to "period".

(4) In section 191 of the Companies Act 1985 (register of debenture holders)—
  (a) in subsection (1), omit the words from "(but" to "for inspection)" and for the words from "a fee of 5 pence" to the end substitute "such fee as may be prescribed";
  (b) in subsection (2) for the words from "10 pence" to the end substitute "such fee as may be prescribed"; and
  (c) in subsection (3), after "on payment" insert "of such fee as may be prescribed" and omit paragraphs (a) and (b).

(5) In section 219 of the Companies Act 1985 (register of interests in shares, &c.)—
  (a) in subsection (1), omit the words from "during" to "for inspection)"; and
  (b) in subsection (2) for the words from "10 pence" to "required to be copied" substitute "such fee as may be prescribed".

(6) In section 288 of the Companies Act 1985 (register of directors and secretaries), in subsection (3), omit the words from "during" to "for inspection)" and for the words from "5 pence" to the end substitute "such fee as may be prescribed".

(7) In section 318 of the Companies Act 1985 (directors' service contracts), in subsection (7) omit the words from ", during business hours" to "for inspection)".

(8) In section 356 of the Companies Act 1985 (register and index of members' names)—
  (a) in subsection (1), omit "during business hours" and for "the appropriate charge" substitute "such fee as may be prescribed";
  (b) omit subsection (2);
  (c) in subsection (3) for "the appropriate charge" substitute "such fee as may be prescribed"; and
  (d) omit subsection (4).

(9) In section 383 of the Companies Act 1985 (minutes of proceedings of general meetings)—
  (a) in subsection (1), omit "during business hours";
  (b) omit subsection (2); and
  (c) in subsection (3), after "entitled" insert "on payment of such fee as may be prescribed" and omit the words from "at a charge" to the end.

(10) In Part IV of Schedule 13 to the Companies Act 1985 (register of directors' interests)—
(a) in paragraph 25, omit the words from "during" to "for inspection)" and for the words from "5 pence" to the end substitute "such fee as may be prescribed"; and
(b) in paragraph 26(1), for the words from "10 pence" to the end substitute "such fee as may be prescribed."

(11) In Schedule 22 to the Companies Act 1985 (provisions applying to unregistered companies), in the entry relating to Part XXV at the appropriate place insert—

| "Section 723A | Rights of inspection and related matters. | To apply only so far as this provision has effect in relation to provisions applying by virtue of the foregoing provisions of this Schedule."." |

GENERAL NOTE

This section first introduces new s.723A into the Companies Act 1985. This gives the Secretary of State power to make regulations defining the nature of a company's obligations where that Act requires that an index, register or document must be made available for inspection and copying. At present there are several of these obligations with differing obligations as to time limits, access and fees chargeable. No such regulations will be made until late 1990 at the earliest. The regulations which will be subject to the negative procedure will prescribe the minimum obligations for companies and the maximum fees which may be charged.

The section then provides amendments to various sections of the Companies Act 1985 which will be consequential on the regulations under new s.723A coming into force. The amendments relate to the obligations and fees to be covered by the new regulations. It can therefore be anticipated that these subsections will not come into force until those regulations are in force. There is an addition to Sched. 22 to the 1985 Act limiting the new s.723A with respect to unregistered companies to their obligations under the 1985 Act.

"Subsidiary", "holding company" and "wholly-owned subsidiary"

144.—(1) In Part XXVI of the Companies Act 1985 (general interpretation provisions), for section 736 substitute—

" **"Subsidiary", holding company" and "wholly-owned subsidiary"**
736.—(1) A company is a "subsidiary" of another company, its "holding company", if that other company—
(a) holds a majority of the voting rights in it, or
(b) is a member of it and has the right to appoint or remove a majority of its board of directors, or
(c) is a member of it and controls alone, pursuant to an agreement with other shareholders or members, a majority of the voting rights in it,

or if it is a subsidiary of a company which is itself a subsidiary of that other company.

(2) A company is a "wholly-owned subsidiary" of another company if it has no members except that other and that other's wholly-owned subsidiaries or persons acting on behalf of that other or its wholly-owned subsidiaries.

(3) In this section "company" includes any body corporate.

Provisions supplementing s.736
736A.—(1) The provisions of this section explain expressions used in section 736 and otherwise supplement that section.

(2) In section 736(1)(a) and (c) the references to the voting rights in a company are to the rights conferred on shareholders in respect of their shares or, in the case of a company not having a share capital, on members, to vote at general meetings of the company on all, or substantially all, matters.

(3) In section 736(1)(b) the reference to the right to appoint or remove a majority of the board of directors is to the right to appoint or remove directors holding a majority of the voting rights at meetings of the board on all, or substantially all, matters; and for the purposes of that provision—
  (a) a company shall be treated as having the right to appoint to a directorship if—
    (i) a person's appointment to it follows necessarily from his appointment as director of the company, or
    (ii) the directorship is held by the company itself; and
  (b) a right to appoint or remove which is exercisable only with the consent or concurrence of another person shall be left out of account unless no other person has a right to appoint or, as the case may be, remove in relation to that directorship.

(4) Rights which are exercisable only in certain circumstances shall be taken into account only—
  (a) when the circumstances have arisen, and for so long as they continue to obtain, or
  (b) when the circumstances are within the control of the person having the rights;
and rights which are normally exercisable but are temporarily incapable of exercise shall continue to be taken into account.

(5) Rights held by a person in a fiduciary capacity shall be treated as not held by him.

(6) Rights held by a person as nominee for another shall be treated as held by the other; and rights shall be regarded as held as nominee for another if they are exercisable only on his instructions or with his consent or concurrence.

(7) Rights attached to shares held by way of security shall be treated as held by the person providing the security—
  (a) where apart from the right to exercise them for the purpose of preserving the value of the security, or of realising it, the rights are exercisable only in accordance with his instructions;
  (b) where the shares are held in connection with the granting of loans as part of normal business activities and apart from the right to exercise them for the purpose of preserving the value of the security, or of realising it, the rights are exercisable only in his interests.

(8) Rights shall be treated as held by a company if they are held by any of its subsidiaries; and nothing in subsection (6) or (7) shall be construed as requiring rights held by a company to be treated as held by any of its subsidiaries.

(9) For the purposes of subsection (7) rights shall be treated as being exercisable in accordance with the instructions or in the interests of a company if they are exercisable in accordance with the instructions of or, as the case may be, in the interests of—
  (a) any subsidiary or holding company of that company, or
  (b) any subsidiary of a holding company of that company.

(10) The voting rights in a company shall be reduced by any rights held by the company itself.

(11) References in any provision of subsections (5) to (10) to rights held by a person include rights falling to be treated as held by him by

virtue of any other provision of those subsections but not rights which by virtue of any such provision are to be treated as not held by him.

(12) In this section "company" includes any body corporate.".

(2) Any reference in any enactment (including any enactment contained in subordinate legislation within the meaning of the Interpretation Act 1978) to a "subsidiary" or "holding company" within the meaning of section 736 of the Companies Act 1985 shall, subject to any express amendment or saving made by or under this Act, be read as referring to a subsidiary or holding company as defined in section 736 as substituted by subsection (1) above.

This applies whether the reference is specific or general, or express or implied.

(3) In Part XXVI of the Companies Act 1985 (general interpretation provisions), after section 736A insert—

"Power to amend ss.736 and 736A

736B.—(1) The Secretary of State may by regulations amend sections 736 and 736A so as to alter the meaning of the expressions "holding company", "subsidiary" or "wholly-owned subsidiary".

(2) The regulations may make different provision for different cases or classes of case and may contain such incidental and supplementary provisions as the Secretary of State thinks fit.

(3) Regulations under this section shall be made by statutory instrument which shall be subject to annulment in pursuance of a resolution of either House of Parliament.

(4) Any amendment made by regulations under this section does not apply for the purposes of enactments outside the Companies Acts unless the regulations so provide.

(5) So much of section 23(3) of the Interpretation Act 1978 as applies section 17(2)(a) of that Act (effect of repeal and re-enactment) to deeds, instruments and documents other than enactments shall not apply in relation to any repeal and re-enactment effected by regulations made under this section.".

(4) Schedule 18 contains amendments and savings consequential on the amendments made by this section; and the Secretary of State may by regulations make such further amendments or savings as appear to him to be necessary or expedient.

(5) Regulations under this section shall be made by statutory instrument which shall be subject to annulment in pursuance of a resolution of either House of Parliament.

(6) So much of section 23(3) of the Interpretation Act 1978 as applies section 17(2)(a) of that Act (presumption as to meaning of references to enactments repealed and re-enacted) to deeds or other instruments or documents does not apply in relation to the repeal and re-enactment by this section of section 736 of the Companies Act 1985.

GENERAL NOTE

This section substitutes a new s.736 and introduces new ss.736A and 736B into the Companies Act 1985 to provide new definitions of holding companies, subsidiary companies and wholly-owned subsidiaries for that and other Acts. There are also transitional procedures for existing documents and legislation. Sched. 18 to the Companies Act 1989 makes consequential savings and amendments as a result of these new definitions.

The basic structure of this section is that subs. (1) introduces new s.736, which provides the new definitions, and new s.736A, which expands and supplements those definitions. Subs. (2) applies the new definitions to existing legislation which refer, even impliedly, to the former C.A. 1985, s.736 unless Sched. 18 applies. Subs. (3) introduces new s.736B which allows the Secretary of State to alter the definitions by statutory instrument. Subs. (4) introduces Sched. 18 and allows that to be expanded by the Secretary of State by statutory instrument introduced by the negative resolution procedure (subs. (5)). Finally, subs. (6) relates to existing documents, etc., which were drafted on the basis of the former definitions.

New ss.736 and 736A

These sections provide new definitions of a holding, subsidiary and wholly-owned subsidiary company. In parts they overlap with the definition of parent and subsidiary undertakings in s.21 of this Act (see above) for group accounts purposes, but they are more tightly drawn.

The *holding-subsidiary* company relationship may be established by one of three connections:

(a) where company A holds a majority of the voting rights in company B;
(b) where A is a member of B and has the right to appoint or dismiss a majority of the directors of B;
(c) where A is a member of B and controls alone under an agreement with other shareholders or members of B a majority of the voting rights in B.

A subsidiary of a subsidiary is also a subsidiary of the holding company: s.736(1).

These three connecting factors may be referred to as "voting control," "director control" and "contract control" respectively.

A wholly-owned subsidiary is one whose shares are all owned by another company, its wholly-owned subsidiaries and nominees of either: s.736(2).

This basic framework is expanded by s.736A.

In establishing voting control or contract control, only rights attached to shares are to count. If there are no shares, rights to vote at general meetings on all or substantially all matters are used.

In establishing director control, a majority of the board means not a numerical majority but control by appointment or dismissal of a majority of the directors' voting rights on all or substantially all matters.

Rights to appoint or remove a director which require the consent of another person do not count unless no-one else has the right to appoint or remove that director. One company (A) is deemed to have the right to appoint or dismiss a director of another company (B) if either his appointments follows necessarily from his appointment as a director of A or the directorship of B is held by A itself.

S.736A further defines what amount to rights for the purpose of voting rights or rights of appointment or dismissal as appropriate. These are:

(a) rights which apply only in certain circumstances will only be relevant if they are *de facto* exercisable at the relevant time. General rights will, however, be relevant, even if they are temporarily incapable of being exercised (*e.g.* on a probate dispute);
(b) purely fiduciary rights do not count;
(c) nominee rights (*i.e.* those exercisable only on instructions or with consent) are to be attributed to the beneficial owner;
(d) a chargee's rights over shares will be attributed to the chargee and not the borrower if, apart from normal creditor protection provisions, they are exercisable only on the chargee's or its subsidiary's instructions or, if the loan was part of the chargee's normal business activities, they are exercisable only in its or its subsidiary's interests;
(e) a subsidiary's rights are to be regarded as those of its holding company, but principles (c) and (d) above are not to be regarded as applying in this context;
(f) voting rights held by a company in itself are to be ignored; and
(g) principles (b) to (f) are cumulative where necessary.

New s.736B

This section allows the Secretary of State to amend new ss.736 and 736A by statutory instrument under the negative resolution procedure.

Existing documents

C.A. 1989, s.144(6), makes it clear that documents in existence when the new definitions come into effect which refer to a holding, subsidiary or wholly-owned subsidiary company, will continue to be interpreted under the former definition section and not the new.

Minor amendments

145. The Companies Act 1985 has effect with the further amendments specified in Schedule 19.

GENERAL NOTE

This section introduces Sched. 19 which contains further amendments to the Companies Act 1985. See the note to that Schedule.

Part VI

Mergers and Related Matters

Restriction on references which prior notice given

146. After section 75 of the Fair Trading Act 1973 there is inserted—

"Restriction on power to make merger reference where prior notice has been given

General rule where notice given by acquirer and no reference made within period for considering notice

75A.—(1) Notice may be given to the Director by a person authorised by regulations to do so of proposed arrangements which might result in the creation of a merger situation qualifying for investigation.

(2) The notice must be in the prescribed form and state that the existence of the proposal has been made public.

(3) If the period for considering the notice expires without any reference being made to the Commission with respect to the notified arrangements, no reference may be made under this Part of this Act to the Commission with respect to those arrangements or to the creation or possible creation of any merger situation qualifying for investigation which is created in consequence of carrying those arrangements into effect.

(4) Subsection (3) of this section is subject to sections 75B(5) and 75C of this Act.

(5) A notice under subsection (1) of this section is referred to in sections 75B to 75F of this Act as a "merger notice".

The role of the Director

75B.—(1) The Director shall, when the period for considering any merger notice begins, take such action as he considers appropriate to bring the existence of the proposal, the fact that the merger notice has been given and the date on which the period for considering the notice may expire to the attention of those who in his opinion would be affected if the arrangements were carried into effect.

(2) The period for considering a merger notice is the period of twenty days, determined in accordance with subsection (9) of this section, beginning with the first day after—
  (a) the notice has been received by the Director, and
  (b) any fee payable to the Director in respect of the notice has been paid.

(3) The Director may, and shall if required to do so by the Secretary of State, by notice to the person who gave the merger notice—
  (a) extend the period mentioned in subsection (2) of this section by a further ten days, and
  (b) extend that period as extended under paragraph (a) of this subsection by a further fifteen days.

(4) The Director may by notice to the person who gave the merger notice request him to provide the Director within such period as may be specified in the notice with such information as may be so specified.

(5) If the Director gives to the person who gave the merger notice (in this subsection referred to as "the relevant person") a notice stating that the Secretary of State is seeking undertakings under

section 75G of this Act, section 75A(3) of this Act does not prevent a reference being made to the Commission unless—
  (a) after the Director has given that notice, the relevant person has given a notice to the Director stating that he does not intend to give such undertakings, and
  (b) the period of ten days beginning with the first day after the notice under paragraph (a) of this subsection was received by the Director has expired.

(6) A notice by the Director under subsection (3), (4) or (5) of this section must either be given to the person who gave the merger notice before the period for considering the merger notice expires or be sent in a properly addressed and pre-paid letter posted to him at such time that, in the ordinary course of post, it would be delivered to him before that period expires.

(7) The Director may, at any time before the period for considering any merger notice expires, reject the notice if—
  (a) he suspects that any information given in respect of the notified arrangements, whether in the merger notice or otherwise, by the person who gave the notice or any connected person is in any material respect false or misleading,
  (b) he suspects that it is not proposed to carry the notified arrangements into effect, or
  (c) any prescribed information is not given in the merger notice or any information requested by notice under subsection (4) of this section is not provided within the period specified in the notice.

(8) If—
  (a) under subsection (3)(b) of this section the period for considering a merger notice has been extended by a further fifteen days, but
  (b) the Director has not made any recommendation to the Secretary of State under section 76(b) of this Act as to whether or not it would in the Director's opinion be expedient for the Secretary of State to make a reference to the Commission with respect to the notified arrangements,
then, during the last five of those fifteen days, the power of the Secretary of State to make a reference to the Commission with respect to the notified arrangements is not affected by the absence of any such recommendation.

(9) In determining any period for the purposes of subsections (2), (3) and (5) of this section no account shall be taken of—
  (a) Saturday, Sunday, Good Friday and Christmas Day, and
  (b) any day which is a bank holiday in England and Wales.

Cases where power to refer unaffected

75C.—(1) Section 75A(3) of this Act does not prevent any reference being made to the Commission if—
  (a) before the end of the period for considering the merger notice, it is rejected by the Director under section 75B(7) of this Act,
  (b) before the end of that period, any of the enterprises to which the notified arrangements relate cease to be distinct from each other,
  (c) any information (whether prescribed information or not) that—
    (i) is, or ought to be, known to the person who gave the merger notice or any connected person, and
    (ii) is material to the notified arrangements;

is not disclosed to the Secretary of State or the Director by such time before the end of that period as may be specified in regulations,
(d) at any time after the merger notice is given but before the enterprises to which the notified arrangements relate cease to be distinct from each other, any of those enterprises ceases to be distinct from any enterprise other than an enterprise to which those arrangements relate,
(e) the six months beginning with the end of the period for considering the merger notice expires without the enterprises to which the notified arrangements relate ceasing to be distinct from each other,
(f) the merger notice is withdrawn, or
(g) any information given in respect of the notified arrangements, whether in the merger notice or otherwise, by the person who gave the notice or any connected person is in any material respect false or misleading.
(2) Where—
(a) two or more transactions which have occurred or, if any arrangements are carried into effect, will occur may be treated for the purposes of a merger reference as having occurred simultaneously on a particular date, and
(b) subsection (3) of section 75A of this Act does not prevent such a reference with respect to the last of those transactions,
that subsection does not prevent such a reference with respect to any of those transactions which actually occurred less than six months before—
(i) that date, or
(ii) the actual occurrence of another of those transactions with respect to which such a reference may be made (whether or not by virtue of this subsection).
(3) In determining for the purposes of subsection (2) of this section the time at which any transaction actually occurred, no account shall be taken of any option or other conditional right until the option is exercised or the condition is satisfied.

Regulations
75D.—(1) The Secretary of State may make regulations for the purposes of sections 75A to 75C of this Act.
(2) The regulations may, in particular—
(a) provide for section 75B(2) or (3) or section 75C(1)(e) of this Act to apply as if any reference to a period of days or months were a reference to a period specified in the regulations for the purposes of the provision in question,
(b) provide for the manner in which any merger notice is authorised or required to be given, rejected or withdrawn, and the time at which any merger notice is to be treated as received or rejected,
(c) provide for the manner in which any information requested by the Director or any other material information is authorised or required to be provided or disclosed, and the time at which such information is to be treated as provided or disclosed,
(d) provide for the manner in which any notice under section 75B of this Act is authorised or required to be given,
(e) provide for the time at which any notice under section 75B(5)(a) of this Act is to be treated as received,

(f) provide for the address which is to be treated for the purposes of section 75B(6) of this Act and of the regulations as a person's proper address,
(g) provide for the time at which any fee is to be treated as paid, and
(h) provide that a person is, or is not, to be treated, in such circumstances as may be specified in the regulations, as acting on behalf of a person authorised by regulations to give a merger notice or a person who has given such a notice.

(3) The regulations may make different provision for different cases.

(4) Regulations under this section shall be made by statutory instrument.

Interpretation of sections 75A to 75D

75E. In this section and sections 75A to 75D of this Act—
"connected person", in relation to the person who gave a merger notice, means—
  (a) any person who, for the purposes of section 77 of this Act, is associated with him, or
  (b) any subsidiary of the person who gave the merger notice or of any person so associated with him,
"merger notice" is to be interpreted in accordance with section 75A(5) of this Act,
"notified arrangements" means the arrangements mentioned in the merger notice or arrangements not differing from them in any material respect,
"prescribed" means prescribed by the Director by notice having effect for the time being and published in the London, Edinburgh and Belfast Gazettes,
"regulations" means regulations under section 75D of this Act, and
"subsidiary" has the meaning given by section 75(4K) of this Act, and references to the enterprises to which the notified arrangements relate are references to those enterprises that would have ceased to be distinct from one another if the arrangements mentioned in the merger notice in question had been carried into effect at the time when the notice was given.

Power to amend sections 75B to 75D

75F.—(1) The Secretary of State may, for the purpose of determining the effect of giving a merger notice and the steps which may be or are to be taken by any person in connection with such a notice, by regulations made by statutory instrument amend sections 75B to 75D of this Act.

(2) The regulations may make different provision for different cases and may contain such incidental and supplementary provisions as the Secretary of State thinks fit.

(3) No regulations shall be made under this section unless a draft of the regulations has been laid before and approved by resolution of each House of Parliament.".

GENERAL NOTE

Pt. VI amends the provisions of the Fair Trading Act 1973 dealing with mergers and certain provisions in the related fields of monopolies and uncompetitive practices. There is no fundamental change of policy on mergers in these provisions. The emphasis remains on competition and the belief that decisions on mergers, in the main, should be left to shareholders. The provisions of Pt. VI aim to ensure that they have adequate information on which to base their decisions on what is best for the company and reflect the belief that only when a merger threatens the interests of customers by reducing competition should the law intervene. The two main provisions in Pt. VI are intended to counter threats to competition but without otherwise impeding the operation of the market. These provisions shift the emphasis away from the Monopolies and Mergers Commission (M.M.C.) to the Office of Fair Trading (O.F.T.) and should accelerate the process of desirable mergers and avoid the cost of a full inquiry. In addition they give the power to charge fees for the cost of policing mergers.

This section establishes a new procedure for voluntary pre-notification of proposed mergers by the addition of new ss.75A–F after s.75 of the Fair Trading Act 1973. They set out a formal system with a prescribed timetable and powers exercisable by the Director General of Fair Trading and the Secretary of State. A bidder who chooses to avail himself of this new opportunity to pre-notify will have to provide certain information to the O.F.T. and the proposed merger will be made public so that interested third parties can become aware of it. Having exercised this option, however, the bidder will know that unless he is told the contrary within 20 days from the time the Director receives the pre-notice and any fees payable in respect of it, the merger can go ahead without any possibility of it being subsequently referred to the M.M.C., provided the merger is carried out within six months and certain other conditions are met.

The vast majority of simple merger proposals which raise no competition or other public interest problems should be facilitated by this procedure. The more difficult cases now are provided for in that the Director General is given power to seek further information and, if necessary, to extend the period initially by ten days but subsequently by a further 15 days, for deciding whether to make a reference to the M.M.C. In such instances the Secretary of State retains the power, during the last five of the permissible 25 day extension period, to make a reference irrespective of whether or not the Director General recommends it.

The maximum limit on extensions means that negotiations of divestment undertakings under s.147 could run beyond the maximum 45 days allowed for considering a pre-notification merger. Note, however, that the power to make a reference is retained in such instances while undertakings are still being sought, and if a bidder formally declines to give undertakings, the clock starts again and a reference must then be made within ten days or the power to refer will be lost.

Note the time periods concerned throughout this section are to be measured in working days, leaving aside weekends and statutory holidays.

The Secretary of State is empowered to make regulations to govern the manner and form of these new pre-notifications procedures and in addition he is enabled even to amend the primary legislation, subject to approval by resolution of each House of Parliament.

This provision will come into force by statutory instrument on a date yet to be announced by the Secretary of State.

Undertakings as alternative to merger reference

147. In Part V of the Fair Trading Act 1973 after the sections inserted by section 146 of this Act there is inserted—

"*Undertakings as alternative to merger reference*

Acceptance of undertakings

75G.—(1) Where—
  (a) the Secretary of State has power to make a merger reference to the Commission under section 64 or 75 of this Act,
  (b) the Director has made a recommendation to the Secretary of State under section 76 of this Act that such a reference should be made, and
  (c) the Director has (in making that recommendation or subsequently) given advice to the Secretary of State specifying particular effects adverse to the public interest which in his opinion the creation of the merger situation qualifying for investigation may have or might be expected to have,

the Secretary of State may, instead of making a merger reference to the Commission, accept from such of the parties concerned as he considers appropriate undertakings complying with subsections (2) and (3) of this section to take specified action which the Secretary of State considers appropriate to remedy or prevent the effects adverse to the public interest specified in the advice.

(2) The undertakings must provide for one or more of the following—
   (a) the division of a business by the sale of any part of the undertaking or assets or otherwise (for which purpose all the activities carried on by way of business by any one person or by any two or more interconnected bodies corporate may be treated as a single business),
   (b) the division of a group of interconnected bodies corporate, and
   (c) the separation, by the sale of any part of the undertaking or assets concerned or other means, of enterprises which are under common control otherwise than by reason of their being enterprises of interconnected bodies corporate.

(3) The undertakings may also contain provision—
   (a) preventing or restricting the doing of things which might prevent or impede the division or separation,
   (b) as to the carrying on of any activities or the safeguarding of any assets until the division or separation is effected,
   (c) for any matters necessary to effect or take account of the division or separation, and
   (d) for enabling the Secretary of State to ascertain whether the undertakings are being fulfilled.

(4) If the Secretary of State has accepted one or more undertakings under this section, no reference may be made to the Commission with respect to the creation or possible creation of the merger situation qualifying for investigation by reference to which the undertakings were accepted, except in a case falling within subsection (5) of this section.

(5) Subsection (4) of this section does not prevent a reference being made to the Commission if material facts about the arrangements or transactions, or proposed arrangements or transactions, in consequence of which the enterprises concerned ceased or may cease to be distinct enterprises were not—
   (a) notified to the Secretary of State or the Director, or
   (b) made public,
before the undertakings were accepted.

(6) In subsection (5) of this section "made public" has the same meaning as in section 64 of this Act.

Publication of undertakings

75H.—(1) The Secretary of State shall arrange for—
   (a) any undertaking accepted by him under section 75G of this Act,
   (b) the advice given by the Director for the purposes of subsection (1)(c) of that section in any case where such an undertaking has been accepted, and
   (c) any variation or release of such an undertaking,
to be published in such manner as he may consider appropriate.

(2) In giving advice for the purposes of section 75G(1)(c) of this Act the Director shall have regard to the need for excluding, so far as practicable, any matter to which subsection (4) of this section applies.

(3) The Secretary of State shall exclude from any such advice as published under this section—
   (a) any matter to which subsection (4) of this section applies and

in relation to which he is satisfied that its publication in the advice would not be in the public interest, and

(b) any other matter in relation to which he is satisfied that its publication in the advice would be against the public interest.

(4) This subsection applies to—

(a) any matter which relates to the private affairs of an individual, where publication of that matter would or might, in the opinion of the Director or the Secretary of State, as the case may be, seriously and prejudicially affect the interests of that individual, and

(b) any matter which relates specifically to the affairs of a particular body of persons, whether corporate or unincorporate, where publication of that matter would or might, in the opinion of the Director or the Secretary of State, as the case may be, seriously and prejudicially affect the interests of that body, unless in his opinion the inclusion of that matter relating specifically to that body is necessary for the purposes of the advice.

(5) For the purposes of the law relating to defamation, absolute privilege shall attach to any advice given by the Director for the purposes of section 75G(1)(c) of this Act.

Review of undertakings

75J. Where an undertaking has been accepted by the Secretary of State under section 75G of this Act, it shall be the duty of the Director—

(a) to keep under review the carrying out of that undertaking, and from time to time consider whether, by reason of any change of circumstances, the undertaking is no longer appropriate and either—

(i) one or more of the parties to it can be released from it, or

(ii) it needs to be varied or to be superseded by a new undertaking, and

(b) if it appears to him that the undertaking has not been or is not being fulfilled, that any person can be so released or that the undertaking needs to be varied or superseded, to give such advice to the Secretary of State as he may think proper in the circumstances.

Order of Secretary of State where undertaking not fulfilled

75K.—(1) The provisions of this section shall have effect where it appears to the Secretary of State that an undertaking accepted by him under section 75G of this Act has not been, is not being or will not be fulfilled.

(2) The Secretary of State may by order made by statutory instrument exercise such one or more of the powers specified in paragraphs 9A and 12 to 12C and Part II of Schedule 8 to this Act as he may consider it requisite to exercise for the purpose of remedying or preventing the adverse effects specified in the advice given by the Director for the purposes of section 75G(1)(c) of this Act; and those powers may be so exercised to such extent and in such manner as the Secretary of State considers requisite for that purpose.

(3) In determining whether, or to what extent or in what manner, to exercise any of those powers, the Secretary of State shall take into account any advice given by the Director under section 75J(b) of this Act.

(4) The provision contained in an order under this section may be different from that contained in the undertaking.

(5) On the making of an order under this section, the undertaking and any other undertaking accepted under section 75G of this Act by reference to the same merger situation qualifying for investigation are released by virtue of this section.".

GENERAL NOTE

This section adds further new provisions, ss.75G–K, to those already inserted after s.75 of the Fair Trading Act 1973 by the previous section. These additional provisions allow for certain undertakings to be given instead of the proposed merger being referred to the Commission. In the past, even where proposed mergers gave rise to competition problems, the practice had developed of resolving the problem by selling off part of the merged business. Disposals were prominently included in the proposed merger arrangements to facilitate the proposal and avoid a reference to the Commission, but the power to order a disposal, under the previous law, only arose after an adverse report from the Commission. Consequently, should a promise to make a disposal be broken, the only remedy previously was then to make a reference to the Commission.

This new section ushers in procedures which allow the Secretary of State to accept binding promises or undertakings to divest parts of the merged business as a way of dealing with the possible adverse effects of the merger identified by the Director General of Fair Trading, instead of making a reference to the M.M.C. Once the Secretary of State has accepted one or more undertakings, no reference to the Commission can be made unless material facts were withheld or not made public prior to the acceptance of the undertakings.

Should any such undertakings not be carried out or complied with then the Secretary of State may now enforce them without having to make a reference to the Commission. He is empowered to enforce them either directly by taking appropriate court action or by making a suitable order by statutory instrument, enabling him to exercise any of the powers specified in Pt. II of Sched. 8 to the Fair Trading Act 1973. It is the duty of the Director of Fair Trading to keep under review all such undertakings and to advise the Secretary of State as to appropriate variations or releases.

This section came into force on November 17, 1989.

Enforcement of undertakings

148. After section 93 of the Fair Trading Act 1973 there is inserted—

"Enforcement of undertakings

93A.—(1) This section applies where a person (in this section referred to as "the responsible person") has given an undertaking which—

(a) has been accepted by the Secretary of State under section 75G of this Act,

(b) has been accepted by the appropriate Minister or Ministers under section 88 of this Act after the commencement of this section, or

(c) has been accepted by the Director under section 4 or 9 of the Competition Act 1980 after that time.

(2) Any person may bring civil proceedings in respect of any failure, or apprehended failure, of the responsible person to fulfil the undertaking, as if the obligations imposed by the undertaking on the responsible person had been imposed by an order to which section 90 of this Act applies.".

GENERAL NOTE

This section inserts a new provision after s.93 of the Fair Trading Act 1973, which entitles any interested person to bring civil court enforcement action against anyone who has failed to fulfil an undertaking given by virtue of s.147, rather than leaving that to the public authorities, although, in the main, enforcement action will be taken by either the Secretary of State or the Director General of Fair Trading.

Temporary restrictions on share dealings

149.—(1) In section 75 of the Fair Trading Act 1973 (reference in anticipation of merger), after subsection (4) there is inserted—

"(4A) Where a merger reference is made under this section, it shall be unlawful, except with the consent of the Secretary of State under subsection (4C) of this section—
  (a) for any person carrying on any enterprise to which the reference relates or having control of any such enterprise or for any subsidiary of his, or
  (b) for any person associated with him or for any subsidiary of such a person,

directly or indirectly to acquire, at any time during the period mentioned in subsection (4B) of this section, an interest in shares in a company if any enterprise to which the reference relates is carried on by or under the control of that company.

(4B) The period referred to in subsection (4A) of this section is the period beginning with the announcement by the Secretary of State of the making of the merger reference concerned and ending—
  (a) where the reference is laid aside at any time, at that time,
  (b) where the time (including any further period) allowed to the Commission for making a report on the reference expires without their having made such a report, on the expiration of that time,
  (c) where a report of the Commission on the reference not including such conclusions as are referred to in section 73(1)(b) of this Act is laid before Parliament, at the end of the day on which the report is so laid,
  (d) where a report of the Commission on the reference including such conclusions is laid before Parliament, at the end of the period of forty days beginning with the day on which the report is so laid,

and where such a report is laid before each House on different days, it is to be treated for the purposes of this subsection as laid on the earlier day.

(4C) The consent of the Secretary of State—
  (a) may be either general or special,
  (b) may be revoked by the Secretary of State, and
  (c) shall be published in such way as, in the opinion of the Secretary of State, to give any person entitled to the benefit of it an adequate opportunity of getting to know of it, unless in the Secretary of State's opinion publication is not necessary for that purpose.

(4D) Section 93 of this Act applies to any contravention or apprehended contravention of subsection (4A) of this section as it applies to a contravention or apprehended contravention of an order to which section 90 of this Act applies.

(4E) Subsections (4F) to (4K) of this section apply for the interpretation of subsection (4A).

(4F) The circumstances in which a person acquires an interest in shares include those where—
  (a) he enters into a contract to acquire the shares (whether or not for cash),
  (b) not being the registered holder, he acquires a right to exercise, or to control the exercise of, any right conferred by the holding of the shares, or
  (c) he acquires a right to call for delivery of the shares to himself

or to his order or to acquire an interest in the shares or assumes an obligation to acquire such an interest,

but does not include those where he acquires an interest in pursuance of an obligation assumed before the announcement by the Secretary of State of the making of the merger reference concerned.

(4G) The circumstances in which a person acquires a right mentioned in subsection (4F) of this section—
(a) include those where he acquires a right or assumes an obligation the exercise or fulfilment of which would give him that right, but
(b) does not include those where he is appointed as proxy to vote at a specified meeting of a company or of any class of its members or at any adjournment of the meeting or he is appointed by a corporation to act as its representative at any meeting of the company or of any class of its members,

and references to rights and obligations in this subsection and subsection (4F) of this section include conditional rights and conditional obligations.

(4H) Any reference to a person carrying on or having control of any enterprise includes a group of persons carrying on or having control of an enterprise and any member of such a group.

(4J) Sections 65(2) to (4) and 77(1) and (4) to (6) of this Act apply to determine whether any person or group of persons has control of any enterprise and whether persons are associated as they apply for the purposes of section 65 of this Act to determine whether enterprises are brought under common control.

(4K) "Subsidiary" has the meaning given by section 736 of the Companies Act 1985, but that section and section 736A of that Act also apply to determine whether a company is a subsidiary of an individual or of a group of persons as they apply to determine whether it is a subsidiary of a company and references to a subsidiary in subsections (8) and (9) of section 736A as so applied are to be read accordingly.

(4L) In this section—
"company" includes any body corporate, and
"share" means share in the capital of a company, and includes stock.

(4M) Nothing in subsection (4A) of this section makes anything done by a person outside the United Kingdom unlawful unless he is—
(a) a British citizen, a British Dependent Territories citizen, a British Overseas citizen or a British National (Overseas),
(b) a body corporate incorporated under the law of the United Kingdom or of a part of the United Kingdom, or
(c) a person carrying on business in the United Kingdom, either alone or in partnership with one or more other persons.".

(2) This section does not apply in relation to any merger reference made before the passing of this Act.

GENERAL NOTE

Subs. (1)

This inserts new subs. (4A)–(M) after subs. (4) of s.75 of the Fair Trading Act 1973. These provisions prohibit parties to a potential merger situation from acquiring, directly or indirectly, during the period following a reference of the proposed merger to the M.M.C., any interest in the shares of any other party to the merger, without the consent of the Secretary of State.

The new provisions specify the following: the persons who are prohibited from acquiring (subs. (4A)); the period during which the prohibition operates (subs. (4B)); the nature of the Secretary of State's consent (subs. (4C)); the effect of contravening temporary prohibition orders on share dealing (subs. (4D)); the meaning of: "acquiring an interest in shares" (subss. (4F–G)), "carrying or having control" (subs. (4H–J)) and "subsidiary" (subs. (4K)).

Subs. (2)
This makes it clear that these new provisions do not apply retrospectively to any merger referred to the M.M.C. prior to November 17, 1989, on which date these provisions came into force.

Obtaining control by stages

150.—(1) After section 66 of the Fair Trading Act 1973 there is inserted—

"**Obtaining control by stages**
66A.—(1) Where an enterprise is brought under the control of a person or group of persons in the course of two or more transactions (referred to in this section as a "series of transactions") falling within subsection (2) of this section, those transactions may, if the Secretary of State or, as the case may be, the Commission thinks fit, be treated for the purposes of a merger reference as having occurred simultaneously on the date on which the latest of them occurred.

(2) The transactions falling within this subsection are—
  (a) any transaction which—
    (i) enables that person or group of persons directly or indirectly to control or materially to influence the policy of any person carrying on the enterprise,
    (ii) enables that person or group of persons to do so to a greater degree, or
    (iii) is a step (whether direct or indirect) towards enabling that person or group of persons to do so, and
  (b) any transaction whereby that person or group of persons acquires a controlling interest in the enterprise or, where the enterprise is carried on by a body corporate, in that body corporate.

(3) Where a series of transactions includes a transaction falling within subsection (2)(b) of this section, any transaction occurring after the occurrence of that transaction is to be disregarded for the purposes of subsection (1) of this section.

(4) Where the period within which a series of transactions occurs exceeds two years, the transactions that may be treated as mentioned in subsection (1) of this section are any of those transactions that occur within a period of two years.

(5) Sections 65(2) to (4) and 77(1) and (4) to (6) of this Act apply for the purposes of this section to determine whether an enterprise is brought under the control of a person or group of persons and whether a transaction falls within subsection (2) of this section as they apply for the purposes of section 65 of this Act to determine whether enterprises are brought under common control.

(6) In determining for the purposes of this section the time at which any transaction occurs, no account shall be taken of any option or other conditional right until the option is exercised or the condition is satisfied.".

(2) This section does not apply in relation to any merger reference made before the passing of this Act.

GENERAL NOTE
This section inserts a new s.66A after s.66 of the Fair Trading Act 1973 to regulate situations where control of an enterprise is being obtained by stages. In effect, it provides that successive events over a period of up to two years, such as a series of share acquisitions

by a person or group of persons, may be treated for purposes of a merger reference to the M.M.C. as if they had all occurred when the last of them occurred.

The section goes on to define the transactions falling within it and those sections of the Fair Trading Act 1973 which determine whether an enterprise is brought under the control of another.

Subs. (2) states that this new provision is only operative for merger references made after November 17, 1989.

False or misleading information

151. At the end of Part VIII of the Fair Trading Act 1973 there is inserted—

> **"False or misleading information**
>
> 93B.—(1) If a person furnishes any information—
>
> (a) to the Secretary of State, the Director or the Commission in connection with any of their functions under Parts IV, V, VI or this Part of this Act or under the Competition Act 1980, or
>
> (b) to the Commission in connection with the functions of the Commission under the Telecommunications Act 1984 or the Airports Act 1986,
>
> and either he knows the information to be false or misleading in a material particular, or he furnishes the information recklessly and it is false or misleading in a material particular, he is guilty of an offence.
>
> (2) A person who—
>
> (a) furnishes any information to another which he knows to be false or misleading in a material particular, or
>
> (b) recklessly furnishes any information to another which is false or misleading in a material particular,
>
> knowing that the information is to be used for the purpose of furnishing information as mentioned in subsection (1)(a) or (b) of this section, is guilty of an offence.
>
> (3) A person guilty of an offence under subsection (1) or (2) of this section is liable—
>
> (a) on summary conviction, to a fine not exceeding the statutory maximum, and
>
> (b) on conviction on indictment, to imprisonment for a term not exceeding two years or to a fine or to both.
>
> (4) Section 129(1) of this Act does not apply to an offence under this section.".

GENERAL NOTE

This section inserts a new s.93B at the end of Pt. VIII of the Fair Trading Act 1973, making it an offence to provide any false or misleading information whatsoever to the Secretary of State, the Director General of Fair Trading or the M.M.C. in connection with their statutory functions. However, difficulties may arise in that merely breaking a promise or undertaking (whether or not made or given under s.147) is not necessarily an indication that the information given was false at the time. The section makes it an offence to knowingly or recklessly provide wrong information directly, or indirectly through an innocent agent. To obtain a conviction, the prosecution must prove *mens rea* (a guilty state of mind) either by proof that the accused intended (*i.e.* had as his object or goal) the giving of false information or that he was reckless. The latter state of mind can be proved in one of two ways. First, either by showing that the accused consciously took the risk that the information he provided might be false (*R. v. Cunningham* [1957] 2 Q.B.D. 396) or alternatively by showing that the accused gave the information without giving any thought as to whether or not it might be true or false or misleading in a situation where the risk that it might be false or misleading would have been obvious to any reasonable person (*R. v. Caldwell* [1982] A.C. 341). If the prosecution prove that the accused provided false or misleading information to any of the persons mentioned in subs. (1) of s.93B, together with proof of any one of the guilty states of mind mentioned above, then they will secure a conviction which in the magistrates' courts carries a maximum fine of £2,000 and in the Crown Court to a maximum of two years' imprisonment and/or an unlimited fine.

This provision will come into force on a date to be specified by statutory instrument.

Fees

152.—(1) The Secretary of State may by regulations made by statutory instrument require the payment to him or to the Director of such fees as may be prescribed by the regulations in connection with the exercise by the Secretary of State, the Director and the Commission of their functions under Part V of the Fair Trading Act 1973.

(2) The regulations may provide for fees to be payable—
  (a) in respect of—
    (i) an application for the consent of the Secretary of State under section 58(1) of the Fair Trading Act 1973 to the transfer of a newspaper or of newspaper assets, and
    (ii) a notice under section 75A(1) of that Act, and
  (b) on the occurrence of any event specified in the regulations.

(3) The events that may be specified in the regulations by virtue of subsection (2)(b) above include—
  (a) the making by the Secretary of State of a merger reference to the Commission under section 64 or 75 of the Fair Trading Act 1973,
  (b) the announcement by the Secretary of State of his decision not to make a merger reference in any case where, at the time the announcement is made, he would under one of those sections have power to make such a reference.

(4) The regulations may also contain provision—
  (a) for ascertaining the persons by whom fees are payable,
  (b) specifying whether any fee is payable to the Secretary of State or to the Director,
  (c) for the amount of any fee to be calculated by reference to matters which may include—
    (i) in a case involving functions of the Secretary of State under sections 57 to 61 of the Fair Trading Act 1973, the number of newspapers concerned, the number of separate editions (determined in accordance with the regulations) of each newspaper and the average circulation per day of publication (within the meaning of Part V of that Act) of each newspaper, and
    (ii) in any other case, the value (determined in accordance with the regulations) of any assets concerned,
  (d) as to the time when any fee is to be paid, and
  (e) for the repayment by the Secretary of State or the Director of the whole or part of any fee in specified circumstances.

(5) The regulations may make different provision for different cases.

(6) Subsections (2) to (5) above do not prejudice the generality of subsection (1) above.

(7) In determining the amount of any fees to be prescribed by the regulations, the Secretary of State may take into account all costs incurred by him and by the Director in respect of the exercise by him, by the Commission and by the Director of their respective functions—
  (a) under Part V of the Fair Trading Act 1973, and
  (b) under Parts I, VII and VIII of that Act in relation to merger references or other matters arising under Part V.

(8) A statutory instrument containing regulations under this section shall be subject to annulment in pursuance of a resolution of either House of Parliament.

(9) Fees paid to the Secretary of State or the Director under this section shall be paid into the Consolidated Fund.

(10) In this section—
"the Commission",
"the Director", and
"merger reference",
have the same meaning as in the Fair Trading Act 1973, and "newspaper" has the same meaning as in Part V of that Act.

(11) References in this section to Part V of the Fair Trading Act 1973 and to merger references under section 64 or 75 of that Act or under that Part include sections 29 and 30 of the Water Act 1989 and any reference under section 29 of that Act.

GENERAL NOTE

This section permits the Secretary of State to make regulations by statutory instrument requiring the payment of fees to him or the Director General of Fair Trading in connection with the exercise by either of them or the M.M.C. of their statutory functions in relation to mergers and proposed mergers. While the Government admitted that Pt. VI will result in a small increase in staffing and costs of the O.F.T., it maintains that those costs will be covered by the fees that it is proposed to charge.

Other amendments about mergers and related matters

153. Schedule 20 to this Act has effect.

GENERAL NOTE

This section brings into effect Sched. 20 to this Act, which makes various amendments to the Fair Trading Act 1973, the Competition Act 1980, the Telecommunications Act 1984 and the Financial Services Act 1986, in order to rectify deficiencies and improve procedures.

PART VII

FINANCIAL MARKETS AND INSOLVENCY

Introduction

Introduction

154. This Part has effect for the purposes of safeguarding the operation of certain financial markets by provisions with respect to—
(a) the insolvency, winding up or default of a person party to transactions in the market (sections 155 to 172),
(b) the effectiveness or enforcement of certain charges given to secure obligations in connection with such transactions (sections 173 to 176), and
(c) rights and remedies in relation to certain property provided as cover for margin in relation to such transactions or subject to such a charge (sections 177 to 181).

DEFINITIONS
"cover for margin": ss.177, 190(3).
"default": s.188.
"insolvency": s.190(b).
"winding-up": Insolvency Act 1986, Pt. IV.

GENERAL NOTE

S.154 states the general purpose of Pt. VII of this Act, which is to safeguard the operations of certain defined and nominated financial markets. The Act does not define financial market as such, but goes on to provide for recognised exchanges and clearing houses (s.155), as well as for other exchanges and clearing houses (s.170), money market institutions (s.171) and Bank of England settlement arrangements (s.172), to the extent provided for in regulations that might be issued by the Secretary of State.

Pursuant to this broad aim, s.154 lays down in its three paragraphs three different measures. First (s.154(a)), Pt. VII of this Act (in ss.155–172) is designed to safeguard the integrity of contract settlement procedures where one of the contracting parties defaults, becomes insolvent or is wound up. This is achieved by sanctioning a mini-liquidation of the type rejected by the House of Lords in *British Eagle International Air Lines Ltd.* v. *Compagnie Nationale Air France* [1975] 1 W.L.R. 758. The effect of this is to permit a deep inroad to be made into the principle of *pari passu* distribution enshrined in ss.107 and 328(3) of the Insolvency Act 1986. To the extent that existing settlement procedures in the various financial markets are at odds with insolvency law, Pt. VII of this Act requires insolvency law to abide by these procedures. Secondly (s.154(b)), Pt. VII of this Act (in ss.173–176) preserves and even advances the priority of a chargee in respect of market charges given to secure contract debts and liabilities. Thirdly (s.154(c)), Pt. VII (in ss.177–181) safeguards rights over property provided as margin, which will typically, for example, be the case with futures and options contracts.

Taken together, all three measures are framed to prevent a domino effect produced by the collapse of one market player. The other market players are assured thereby that their net exposures in the market truly are net and are not gross.

The structure of Pt. VII, which has not yet been brought into force, is particularly fluid given the Secretary of State's very broad regulation-making powers to add to, vary or detract from its various provisions. These powers were justified, in the Bill's progress through Parliament, on the grounds that financial markets are fast-moving, complex and constantly evolving, and that coverage is given in general terms to a wide variety of financial markets, instead of particular coverage to individual markets. There is no guarantee, therefore, that the Act as brought into force with the various supporting regulations will resemble closely the Act as passed. A further point to make is that this part of the Act was amended particularly heavily in the course of its passage. The Bill originally introduced was at one time substantially amended in light of the comments of insolvency practitioners, who had not been consulted when the Bill was first drafted and laid before Parliament. The various debates and discussions, together with the probing amendments pressed by the Opposition, tease out the meaning of the different sections, which are by no means self-evident in their scope and meaning.

Recognised investment exchanges and clearing houses

Market contracts

155.—(1) This Part applies to the following descriptions of contract connected with a recognised investment exchange or recognised clearing house.

The contracts are referred to in this Part as "market contracts".

(2) In relation to a recognised investment exchange, this Part applies to—

(a) contracts entered into by a member or designated non-member of the exchange which are made on or otherwise subject to the rules of the exchange; and

(b) contracts subject to the rules of the exchange entered into by the exchange for the purposes of or in connection with the provision of clearing services.

A "designated non-member" means a person in respect of whom action may be taken under the default rules of the exchange but who is not a member of the exchange.

(3) In relation to a recognised clearing house, this Part applies to contracts subject to the rules of the clearing house entered into by the clearing house for the purposes of or in connection with the provision of clearing services for a recognised investment exchange.

(4) The Secretary of State may by regulations make further provision as to the contracts to be treated as "market contracts", for the purposes of this Part, in relation to a recognised investment exchange or recognised clearing house.

(5) The regulations may add to, amend or repeal the provisions of subsections (2) and (3) above.

DEFINITIONS
"recognised clearing house": s.190(1).
"recognised investment exchange": s.190(1).

GENERAL NOTE
This section lists the principal contracts that are subject to the mini-liquidation process hereafter established. The contracts in question are known as "market contracts" and include contracts entered into on investment exchanges recognised under the Financial Services Act 1986 for the purpose of self-regulation. They include also those clearing house contracts entered into by a clearing house providing services for a recognised investment exchange. The clearing house in question also has to be recognised under the Financial Services Act 1986. Subs. (2) makes it clear that the section includes contracts concluded between brokers on the exchange, subject to its clearing rules, as well as contracts that are subject to novation, where the broker sells to the exchange which sells on to another broker. In the latter case, the exchange interposes itself between brokers wishing to do business with each other. Recognition as an investment exchange is given under s.37 (now fully in force) of the Financial Services Act 1986, under which the Secretary of State, according recognition, may do so where it appears that the requirements of Sched. 4 to the 1986 Act have been met. One of those requirements (para. 2(4)) is that the investment exchange must itself ensure the performance of exchange transactions or entrust the same to a recognised clearing house. Further requirements for recognition under the 1986 Act are to be found in s.156 and Sched. 21, Pt. I to the present Act. Sched. 21, para. 4, for example, prescribes the approach that a recognised investment exchange must adopt towards designated non-members doing business on the exchange.

Subs. (3)
This establishes that clearing houses fall within the section to the extent that they provide services for recognised investment exchanges. The clearing house must be recognised under s.39 (now fully in force) of the Financial Services Act 1986, which incorporates in part the requirements for a recognised investment exchange. Additional recognition requirements are to be found in s.156 and Sched. 21, Pt. II to the present Act.

Subss. (4) and (5)
These, together, constitute one of a number of examples of a very broad regulation-making power given to the Secretary of State in the interest of permitting a quick, and no doubt discreet, response to rapidly-changing conditions in the financial markets.

Additional requirements for recognition: default rules, &c.

156.—(1) The Financial Services Act 1986 shall have effect as if the requirements set out in Schedule 21 to this Act (the "additional requirements") were among those specified in that Act for recognition of an investment exchange or clearing house.

(2) In particular, that Act shall have effect—
  (a) as if the requirements set out in Part I of that Schedule were among those specified in Schedule 4 to that Act (requirements for recognition of UK investment exchange),
  (b) as if the requirements set out in Part II of that Schedule were among those specified in section 39(4) of that Act (requirements for recognition of UK clearing house), and
  (c) as if the requirement set out in Part III of that Schedule was among those specified in section 40(2) of that Act (requirements for recognition of overseas investment exchange or clearing house).

(3) The additional requirements do not affect the status of an investment exchange or clearing house recognised before the commencement of this section, but if the Secretary of State is of the opinion that any of those requirements is not met in the case of such a body, he shall within one month of commencement give notice to the body stating his opinion.

(4) Where the Secretary of State gives such a notice, he shall not—
  (a) take action to revoke the recognition of such a body on the ground that any of the additional requirements is not met, unless he considers it essential to do so in the interests of investors, or

(b) apply on any such ground for a compliance order under section 12 of the Financial Services Act 1986,

until after the end of the period of six months beginning with the date on which the notice was given.

(5) The Secretary of State may extend, or further extend, that period if he considers there is good reason to do so.

DEFINITIONS
"overseas": s.190(1).
"U.K.": s.190(1).

GENERAL NOTE
The object of this section is to add to the requirements of recognition under the Financial Services Act 1986 demanded of investment exchanges and clearing houses. This is done by incorporating into the 1986 Act requirements, the new requirements to be found in Pt. I (investment exchanges) and Pt. II (clearing houses) of Sched. 21 to the present Act. In addition, Sched. 21, Pt. III adds to the requirements for recognition of an overseas investment exchange or clearing house laid down by s.40(2) of the F.S.A. 1986. The addition concerns adequate default procedures as part of the procedures established by the local law in question or by the body itself. S.170 of the present Act accords to the Secretary of State a broad regulation-making power for applying Pt. VII of the present Act to the activities of overseas investment exchanges and clearing houses, thus extending the scope of Pt. VII beyond recognised investment exchanges and recognised clearing houses.

Subss. (1) and (2)
These establish that recognition under the 1986 Act will, in future (when Pt. VII of the present Act comes into force), have to be based also on the new requirements contained in the present Act.

Subs. (3)
This subsection shows that a recognition previously granted is not automatically revoked when the new requirements become operative. Nevertheless, the Secretary of State has a limited power (under subs. (4)) to revoke recognition if within one month of the commencement of the new requirements he first gives notice to the body concerned that in his opinion the new requirements are not being met.

Subs. (4)
This requires the Secretary of State to give the body concerned six months' notice (or such further period as permitted by subs. (5)) before either revoking the recognition previously granted under the F.S.A. 1986 or seeking a compliance order under s.12 of that Act. The order in question may be sought of the High Court or Court of Session, which has a broad discretion to prescribe any step or steps the body must take to satisfy the requirements for recognition.

Change in default rules

157.—(1) A recognised UK investment exchange or recognised UK clearing house shall give the Secretary of State at least 14 days' notice of any proposal to amend, revoke or add to its default rules; and the Secretary of State may within 14 days from receipt of the notice direct the exchange or clearing house not to proceed with the proposal, in whole or in part.

(2) A direction under this section may be varied or revoked.

(3) Any amendment or revocation of, or addition to, the default rules of an exchange or clearing house in breach of a direction under this section is ineffective.

GENERAL NOTE
This is a short section that makes it clear that continuing recognition as an investment exchange or clearing house depends upon changes in the default rules not being objected to by the Secretary of State. Presumably the section applies also to bodies already recognised

under the F.S.A. 1986 before the commencement of Pt. VII of the present Act, whether or not a notice was given by the Secretary of State under s.156(3) of the present Act.

Modifications of the law of insolvency

158.—(1) The general law of insolvency has effect in relation to market contracts, and action taken under the rules of a recognised investment exchange or recognised clearing house with respect to such contracts, subject to the provisions of sections 159 to 165.

(2) So far as those provisions relate to insolvency proceedings in respect of a person other than a defaulter, they apply in relation to—
  (a) proceedings in respect of a member or designated non-member of a recognised investment exchange or a member of a recognised clearing house, and
  (b) proceedings in respect of a party to a market contract begun after a recognised investment exchange or recognised clearing house has taken action under its default rules in relation to a person party to the contract as principal,

but not in relation to any other insolvency proceedings, notwithstanding that rights or liabilities arising from market contracts fall to be dealt with in the proceedings.

(3) The reference in subsection (2)(b) to the beginning of insolvency proceedings is to—
  (a) the presentation of a bankruptcy petition or a petition for sequestration of a person's estate, or
  (b) the presentation of a petition for an administration order or a winding-up petition or the passing of a resolution for voluntary winding up, or
  (c) the appointment of an administrative receiver.

(4) The Secretary of State may make further provision by regulations modifying the law of insolvency in relation to the matters mentioned in subsection (1).

(5) The regulations may add to, amend or repeal the provisions mentioned in subsection (1), and any other provision of this Part as it applies for the purposes of those provisions, or provide that those provisions have effect subject to such additions, exceptions or adaptations as are specified in the regulations.

DEFINITIONS
  "party": s.187.
  "sequestration": s.190(7)(a).

GENERAL NOTE
This section establishes that ss.159–165 apply in derogation of the general law of insolvency, which otherwise takes effect with regard to market contracts and action taken with respect to them by recognised investment exchanges or clearing houses. The exceptions in ss.159–165 are so large that the statement in subs. (1) of the general scope of involvency law seems rather hollow.

Subs. (2)
This subsection deals with the rather difficult question of whose insolvency proceedings are caught by ss.159–165. Definitely included are insolvency proceedings respecting "defaulters" (see s.188(2)) and other members or designated non-members of recognised investment exchanges and clearing houses (s.158(2)(a)). It would seem, however, that insolvency proceedings in respect of investors are not included, except in so far as the other contracting party, who must for this purpose be acting as principal and not as agent, has already had action taken against him under the default rules of a recognised investment exchange or clearing house before the insolvency proceedings in question are begun (s.159(2)(b)).

Subs. (3)
This subsection defines the meaning of the beginning of insolvency proceedings. This includes the presentation of a bankruptcy petition in the case of individuals (a sequestration

petition in Scotland); and petitioning for a winding-up or for an administration order, passing a voluntary winding-up resolution or appointing an administrative receiver, in the case of a company. Note that the Insolvency Act 1986 accords with subs. (3), in respect of the time when insolvency proceedings are deemed to have begun, in the case of windings-up (see ss.86 and 129 of the Insolvency Act 1986). But note that s.278 of the Insolvency Act 1986 states the bankruptcy of an individual to have commenced on the day the order is made, not when the petition is presented.

Subss. (4) and (5)
These contain the usual sweeping regulation-making powers granted to the Secretary of State.

Proceedings of exchange or clearing house take precedence over insolvency procedures

159.—(1) None of the following shall be regarded as to any extent invalid at law on the ground of inconsistency with the law relating to the distribution of the assets of a person on bankruptcy, winding up or sequestration, or in the administration of an insolvent estate—
  (a) a market contract,
  (b) the default rules of a recognised investment exchange or recognised clearing house,
  (c) the rules of a recognised investment exchange or recognised clearing house as to the settlement of market contracts not dealt with under its default rules.

(2) The powers of a relevant office-holder in his capacity as such, and the powers of the court under the Insolvency Act 1986 or the Bankruptcy (Scotland) Act 1985 shall not be exercised in such a way as to prevent or interfere with—
  (a) the settlement in accordance with the rules of a recognised investment exchange or recognised clearing house of a market contract not dealt with under its default rules, or
  (b) any action taken under the default rules of such an exchange or clearing house.

This does not prevent a relevant office-holder from afterwards seeking to recover any amount under section 163(4) or 164(4) or prevent the court from afterwards making any such order or decree as is mentioned in section 165(1) or (2) (but subject to subsections (3) and (4) of that section).

(3) Nothing in the following provisions of this Part shall be construed as affecting the generality of the above provisions.

(4) A debt or other liability arising out of a market contract which is the subject of default proceedings may not be proved in a winding up or bankruptcy, or in Scotland claimed in a winding up or sequestration, until the completion of the default proceedings.

A debt or other liability which by virtue of this subsection may not be proved or claimed shall not be taken into account for the purposes of any set-off until the completion of the default proceedings.

(5) For the purposes of subsection (4) the default proceedings shall be taken to be completed in relation to a person when a report is made under section 162 stating the sum (if any) certified to be due to or from him.

DEFINITIONS
  "office-holder": s.189(1).
  "settlement": s.190(2).

GENERAL NOTE
  This section provides detail on the extent to which the provisions of Pt. VII derogate from the general law of insolvency. Recognised investment exchanges and clearing houses are at

liberty to define their own internal settlement procedures without these being subject to overthrow because of a failure to comply with general insolvency law. Furthermore, office-holders are not allowed to interfere with the settlement process or with action taken under the default rules. Outside insolvency proceedings are in effect suspended to the extent that market settlement and default procedures have not yet been completed.

Subs. (1)
This subsection refers to the default rules of a recognised investment exchange or clearing house. Sched. 21 to this Act establishes that default rules must establish a netting out or set off of the various unsettled market contracts entered into between principals, one of whom is a defaulter. Subs. (1) also refers to the settlement of market contracts where there has been no default. In consequence, a settlement process could not be challenged on the ground, for example, that it prefers one class of creditors, market creditors, to other creditors (Insolvency Act 1986, s.239).

Subs. (2)
This subsection prevents office-holders, for example, company liquidators, from exercising their powers (see Sched. 4 to the Insolvency Act 1986) so as to interfere with the settlement process. See Sched. 5 to the 1986 Act for the powers of a trustee-in-bankruptcy. Once the settlement process is completed, however, the relevant officer may seek to have it dismantled in part under ss.163(4), 164(4) and 165.

Subs. (4)
This subsection deals with the particular cases of set off and proof of debts. While the settlement process is still pending, a debt may not be proved or a set off claimed. Proof of debts in a bankruptcy, for example, is dealt with by s.322 of the Insolvency Act 1986, which defines bankruptcy debt in terms wide enough to catch a liability (s.382 of the Insolvency Act 1986). Subs. (4) of the present Act, however, explicitly mentions liability as well as debt. As for set off, a creditor under a market contract could not set off that entitlement against the debtor if the debtor were bringing an action arising out of a transaction outside the settlement process. It is unlikely that the claim and cross-claim would be sufficiently connected for the purpose of equitable set-off, but common law set off is satisfied with unconnected but liquidated claim and cross-claim, and so could fall within this subsection. Similarly, the scope of insolvency set off (see s.323 of the Insolvency Act 1986 and r.4.90 of the Insolvency Rules) is not at all confined to cases where there is a close connection between the claim and the cross-claim. If the settlement process is delayed, the set off right in question could be extinguished rather than merely delayed.

Duty to give assistance for purposes of default proceedings

160.—(1) It is the duty of—
(a) any person who has or had control of any assets of a defaulter, and
(b) any person who has or had control of any documents of or relating to a defaulter,
to give a recognised investment exchange or recognised clearing house such assistance as it may reasonably require for the purposes of its default proceedings.

This applies notwithstanding any duty of that person under the enactments relating to insolvency.

(2) A person shall not under this section be required to provide any information or produce any document which he would be entitled to refuse to provide or produce on grounds of legal professional privilege in proceedings in the High Court or on grounds of confidentiality as between client and professional legal adviser in proceedings in the Court of Session.

(3) Where original documents are supplied in pursuance of this section, the exchange or clearing house shall return them forthwith after the completion of the relevant default proceedings, and shall in the meantime allow reasonable access to them to the person by whom they were supplied and to any person who would be entitled to have access to them if they were still in the control of the person by whom they were supplied.

(4) The expenses of a relevant office-holder in giving assistance under this section are recoverable as part of the expenses incurred by him in the

discharge of his duties; and he shall not be required under this section to take any action which involves expenses which cannot be so recovered, unless the exchange or clearing house undertakes to meet them.

There shall be treated as expenses of his such reasonable sums as he may determine in respect of time spent in giving the assistance.

(5) The Secretary of State may by regulations make further provision as to the duties of persons to give assistance to a recognised investment exchange or recognised clearing house for the purposes of its default proceedings, and the duties of the exchange or clearing house with respect to information supplied to it.

The regulations may add to, amend or repeal the provisions of subsections (1) to (4) above.

(6) In this section "document" includes information recorded in any form.

GENERAL NOTE
The object of this section is to lend assistance to recognised investment exchanges and clearing houses in implementing their settlement processes. This assistance should be compared, for example, with the assistance that office-holders are entitled to demand under s.235 of the Insolvency Act 1986. A person able to provide assistance of the type mentioned in subs. (1) may resist if he is able to claim a professional privilege (subs. (2)). But it seems that a lien over documents of the type possessed by a solicitor, for example, must temporarily be released for the purpose of the settlement process.

Subs. (1)
This subsection emphasises again that market settlement processes take precedence over ordinary insolvency procedure. It would seem, to take one example, that a liquidator's duties with regard to an official receiver (see s.143(2) of the Insolvency Act 1986) would have to be suspended to a degree if they could not be fulfilled while the market settlement process was still pending.

Subs. (3)
This subsection would require a return of documents (defined in subs. (6)), the effect of which would presumably be for a possessory lien to reattach to the documents.

Subs. (4)
This subsection establishes that the expenses of an office-holder in giving assistance are to be charged to the insolvent's estate rather than absorbed as costs of the market settlement process. It might be that such expenses are minimal (telephone calls, for example), and it should be realised that the market settlement process may well be of assistance to an office-holder in the sense that it produces a report after default proceedings have been taken (see s.162).

Subs. (5)
This subsection contains another example of the Secretary of State's broad regulation-making powers.

Supplementary provisions as to default proceedings

161.—(1) If the court is satisfied on an application by a relevant office-holder that a party to a market contract with a defaulter intends to dissipate or apply his assets so as to prevent the office-holder recovering such sums as may become due upon the completion of the default proceedings, the court may grant such interlocutory relief (in Scotland, such interim order) as it thinks fit.

(2) A liquidator or trustee of a defaulter or, in Scotland, a permanent trustee on the sequestrated estate of the defaulter shall not—
    (a) declare or pay any dividend to the creditors, or
    (b) return any capital to contributories,

unless he has retained what he reasonably considers to be an adequate reserve in respect of any claims arising as a result of the default proceedings of the exchange or clearing house concerned.

(3) The court may on an application by a relevant office-holder make such order as it thinks fit altering or dispensing from compliance with such of the duties of his office as are affected by the fact that default proceedings are pending or could be taken, or have been or could have been taken.

(4) Nothing in section 10(1)(c), 11(3), 126, 128, 130, 185 or 285 of the Insolvency Act 1986 (which restrict the taking of certain legal proceedings and other steps), and nothing in any rule of law in Scotland to the like effect as the said section 285, in the Bankruptcy (Scotland) Act 1985 or in the Debtors (Scotland) Act 1987 as to the effect of sequestration, shall affect any action taken by an exchange or clearing house for the purpose of its default proceedings.

GENERAL NOTE
This section contains a number of different provisions designed to resolve conflicts between the market settlement process and other processes. Subs. (1) provides what is in effect a *Mareva*-type of procedure where the delay inherent in the default procedure might otherwise permit a debtor of the defaulter to dissipate his assets.

Subs. (2)
This subsection establishes that, in the event that the market settlement procedure establishes a net debit on the part of the defaulter, a liquidator or trustee settling the balance of the estate should retain a reserve to meet that contingency. S.324 of the Insolvency Act 1986, for example, already contains in subs. (4) a number of cases where the distribution of a dividend is subject to contingent matters.

Subs. (3)
This subsection appears to provide an office-holder with the opportunity to obtain a judicial sanction for conduct or inactivity, relative to default proceedings, that might otherwise render him liable for a breach of duty. See, for example, s.304 of the Insolvency Act 1986, which deals with the liability of a trustee-in-bankruptcy.

Subs. (4)
This subsection deals with a variety of proceedings and attachments against companies and individuals that the relevant office-holder (such as a trustee-in-bankruptcy, liquidator or administrator), but for the integrity of the market settlement process, might otherwise have been able to have had stayed or stopped.

Duty to report on completion of default proceedings

162.—(1) A recognised investment exchange or recognised clearing house shall, on the completion of proceedings under its default rules, report to the Secretary of State on its proceedings stating in respect of each creditor or debtor the sum certified by them to be payable from or to the defaulter or, as the case may be, the fact that no sum is payable.

(2) The exchange or clearing house may make a single report or may make reports from time to time as proceedings are completed with respect to the transactions affecting particular persons.

(3) The exchange or clearing house shall supply a copy of every report under this section to the defaulter and to any relevant office-holder acting in relation to him or his estate.

(4) When a report under this section is received by the Secretary of State, he shall publish notice of that fact in such manner as he thinks appropriate for bringing it to the attention of creditors and debtors of the defaulter.

(5) An exchange or clearing house shall make available for inspection by a creditor or debtor of the defaulter so much of any report by it under

this section as relates to the sum (if any) certified to be due to or from him or to the method by which that sum was determined.

(6) Any such person may require the exchange or clearing house, on payment of such reasonable fee as the exchange or clearing house may determine, to provide him with a copy of any part of a report which he is entitled to inspect.

GENERAL NOTE
This section deals with the report that the recognised investment exchange or clearing house must issue at the end of the default process, or from time to time in the course of the process where interim reports are produced. Note that under subss. (5) and (6) the report is not regarded as a matter for public consumption. Investor confidentiality is to be maintained. Apart from the defaulter himself and the relevant office-holder (see subs. (3)), other interested individuals (creditors and debtors of the defaulter) are entitled only to such information as relates to them personally.

Net sum payable on completion of default proceedings

163.—(1) The following provisions apply with respect to the net sum certified by a recognised investment exchange or recognised clearing house, upon proceedings under its default rules being duly completed in accordance with this Part, to be payable by or to a defaulter.

(2) If, in England and Wales, a bankruptcy or winding-up order has been made, or a resolution for voluntary winding up has been passed, the debt—
  (a) is provable in the bankruptcy or winding up or, as the case may be, is payable to the relevant office-holder, and
  (b) shall be taken into account, where appropriate, under section 323 of the Insolvency Act 1986 (mutual dealings and set-off) or the corresponding provision applicable in the case of winding up,
in the same way as a debt due before the commencement of the bankruptcy, the date on which the body corporate goes into liquidation (within the meaning of section 247 of the Insolvency Act 1986) or, in the case of a partnership, the date of the winding-up order.

(3) If, in Scotland, an award of sequestration or a winding-up order has been made, or a resolution for voluntary winding up has been passed, the debt—
  (a) may be claimed in the sequestration or winding up or, as the case may be, is payable to the relevant office-holder, and
  (b) shall be taken into account for the purposes of any rule of law relating to set-off applicable in sequestration or winding up,
in the same way as a debt due before the date of sequestration (within the meaning of section 73(1) of the Bankruptcy (Scotland) Act 1985) or the commencement of the winding up (within the meaning of section 129 of the Insolvency Act 1986).

(4) However, where (or to the extent that) a sum is taken into account by virtue of subsection (2)(b) or (3)(b) which arises from a contract entered into at a time when the creditor had notice—
  (a) that a bankruptcy petition or, in Scotland, a petition for sequestration was pending, or
  (b) that a meeting of creditors had been summoned under section 98 of the Insolvency Act 1986 or that a winding-up petition was pending,
the value of any profit to him arising from the sum being so taken into account (or being so taken into account to that extent) is recoverable from him by the relevant office-holder unless the court directs otherwise.

(5) Subsection (4) does not apply in relation to a sum arising from a contract effected under the default rules of a recognised investment exchange or recognised clearing house.

(6) Any sum recoverable by virtue of subsection (4) ranks for priority, in the event of the insolvency of the person from whom it is due, immediately before preferential or, in Scotland, preferred debts.

DEFINITION
"notice": s.190(5).

GENERAL NOTE
This section deals with the net credit or debit that remains after the market settlement process has been completed (subs. (1)). In the event of a net debit, this may be proved in the winding up or bankruptcy of the defaulter in the normal way. A net credit accruing to the defaulter may be met by a set off in the usual way in the event of the defaulter pressing his claim. These two results are provided for by subs. (2) (England and Wales) and subs. (3) (Scotland). While notice of an impending insolvency on the part of a creditor is not to be allowed to impair the integrity of the market settlement process, the trustee-in-bankruptcy or liquidator, as the case may be, is permitted to claw back this illegitimate advantage from the creditor in question at a later date (subs. (4)). But this claw back provision does not apply if the default rules entail as part of their implementation the entry into another contract; such a contract might well be entered into at a time when the creditor in question has notice of the impending insolvency. Subs. (6) permits the trustee or liquidator, who claws back, a status higher than that of a preference creditor. If security is the appropriate analogy, the trustee or liquidator has the equivalent of a fixed rather than a floating interest (cf. ss.40 and 175 of Insolvency Act 1986). Taken as a whole, the effect of s.163 is apparently to make it unimportant how precisely the relevant market organisation works out its market settlement process.

Subs. (1)
This subsection refers to the possibility of a net credit after the default process has been completed. This is perfectly possible if the rules of the recognised investment exchange or clearing house allow contracts to be closed out at the market rate prevailing on default, with the contractual breach of the defaulter being disregarded.

Subs. (2)
This subsection would appear to involve a rewriting of s.323 of the Insolvency Act 1986 (and r.4.90 of the Insolvency Rules) since that provision would exclude debts that fall due after notice of a pending bankruptcy petition. The market settlement process may well involve the creation of a composite debt that in fact falls due after this time, but is deemed by subs. (2) to fall due before the commencement of the bankruptcy. Note that subs. (2) does not deem the debt to fall due before notice of the pending bankruptcy petition and that s.323 of the Insolvency Act 1986 distinguishes between notice of the petition and notice of the commencement of the bankruptcy itself (defined in s.278 of the Insolvency Act 1986 as the date when the order is made). Since debts that fall due between notice of the pending bankruptcy and bankruptcy order may be excluded under s.323 of the Insolvency Act 1986, the scope of the section may not have been modified sufficiently by subs. (2).

Subss. (4) and (5)
These subsections do not solve the above difficulty posed by the revision of the set off section (s.323 of the Insolvency Act 1986). They deal with contracts entered into after the notice date that eventually give rise to a debt. They do not deal with contracts made before that date, under which a debt falls due between notice of the impending bankruptcy and the making of the bankruptcy order.

Disclaimer of property, rescission of contracts, &c.

164.—(1) Sections 178, 186, 315 and 345 of the Insolvency Act 1986 (power to disclaim onerous property and court's power to order rescission of contracts, &c. do not apply in relation to—
   (a) a market contract, or
   (b) a contract effected by the exchange or clearing house for the purpose of realising property provided as margin in relation to market contracts.

In the application of this subsection in Scotland, the reference to sections 178, 315 and 345 shall be construed as a reference to any rule of law having the like effect as those sections.

(2) In Scotland, a permanent trustee on the sequestrated estate of a defaulter or a liquidator is bound by any market contract to which that defaulter is a party and by any contract as is mentioned in subsection (1)(b) above notwithstanding section 42 of the Bankruptcy (Scotland) Act 1985 or any rule of law to the like effect applying in liquidations.

(3) Sections 127 and 284 of the Insolvency Act 1986 (avoidance of property dispositions effected after commencement of winding up or presentation of bankruptcy petition), and section 32(8) of the Bankruptcy (Scotland) Act 1985 (effect of dealing with debtor relating to estate vested in permanent trustee), do not apply to—
    (a) a market contract, or any disposition of property in pursuance of such a contract,
    (b) the provision of margin in relation to market contracts,
    (c) a contract effected by the exchange or clearing house for the purpose of realising property provided as margin in relation to a market contract, or any disposition of property in pursuance of such a contract, or
    (d) any disposition of property in accordance with the rules of the exchange or clearing house as to the application of property provided as margin.
(4) However, where—
    (a) a market contract is entered into by a person who has notice that a petition has been presented for the winding up or bankruptcy or sequestration of the estate of the other party to the contract, or
    (b) margin in relation to a market contract is accepted by a person who has notice that such a petition has been presented in relation to the person by whom or on whose behalf the margin is provided,
the value of any profit to him arising from the contract or, as the case may be, the amount or value of the margin is recoverable from him by the relevant office-holder unless the court directs otherwise.

(5) Subsection (4)(a) does not apply where the person entering into the contract is a recognised investment exchange or recognised clearing house acting in accordance with its rules, or where the contract is effected under the default rules of such an exchange or clearing house; but subsection (4)(b) applies in relation to the provision of margin in relation to such a contract.

(6) Any sum recoverable by virtue of subsection (4) ranks for priority, in the event of the insolvency of the person from whom it is due, immediately before preferential or, in Scotland, preferred debts.

DEFINITION
"margin": s.190(3).

GENERAL NOTE
This section is designed to preserve the integrity of the market settlement process. It achieves this aim by preventing a trustee-in-bankruptcy or liquidator from challenging or striking down individual transactions that are part of the composite whole of the insolvent's trading position. For example, a liquidator is not allowed to "cherry pick" and disclaim unprofitable contracts, as he might do under s.178 of the Insolvency Act 1986 (subs. (1)); nor can the other contracting party seek the court's assistance to have a market contract rescinded, as he might do under s.186 of the Insolvency Act 1986 (subs. (1)). Likewise, the realisation by the recognised investment exchange or clearing house of property provided as "margin" (ss.177 and 190(3)) is not affected by the above provisions of the Insolvency Act. The same result is reached also in the case of Scotland (subss. (1) and (2)). Subs. (3) goes on to save transactions dealing, as part of the settlement process, with market contracts, dispositions of property thereunder and the disposition of property provided as margin from

those provisions that (subject to a saving judicial discretion) strike down transactions concluded after the presentation of a winding up petition (s.127 of the Insolvency Act 1986) or after the presentation of the bankruptcy petition. As in the previous section, there is a claw back provision where a market contract is entered into, or margin accepted, after notice of a bankruptcy or winding up petition (subs. (4)). Again, there is an exception to this claw back where the margin is taken or market contract entered into as part of the market settlement process (subs. (5)), and again the claw back entitlement of the liquidator or trustee-in-bankruptcy ranks higher than preferential debts (subs. (6)).

Adjustment of prior transactions

165.—(1) No order shall be made in relation to a transaction to which this section applies under—
  (a) section 238 or 339 of the Insolvency Act 1986 (transactions at an under-value),
  (b) section 239 or 340 of that Act (preferences), or
  (c) section 423 of that Act (transactions defrauding creditors).
(2) As respects Scotland, no decree shall be granted in relation to any such transaction—
  (a) under section 34 or 36 of the Bankruptcy (Scotland) Act 1985 or section 242 or 243 of the Insolvency Act 1986 (gratuitous alienations and unfair preferences), or
  (b) at common law on grounds of gratuitous alienations or fraudulent preferences.
(3) This section applies to—
  (a) a market contract to which a recognised investment exchange or recognised clearing house is a party or which is entered into under its default rules, and
  (b) a disposition of property in pursuance of such a market contract.
(4) Where margin is provided in relation to a market contract and (by virtue of subsection (3)(a) or otherwise) no such order or decree as is mentioned in subsection (1) or (2) has been, or could be, made in relation to that contract, this section applies to—
  (a) the provision of the margin,
  (b) any contract effected by the exchange or clearing house in question for the purpose of realising the property provided as margin, and
  (c) any disposition of property in accordance with the rules of the exchange or clearing house as to the application of property provided as margin.

GENERAL NOTE

This section represents the final major piece in a raft of provisions designed to protect the integrity of the market settlement process.

Market contracts and dispositions of property made under the default rules of a recognised investment exchange or clearing house (subs. (3)), together with the provision and disposition of property provided as margin (subs. (4)), are not open to attack in the usual way under insolvency legislation, whether as transactions at an undervalue, unlawful preferences or transactions in fraud of creditors (subs. (1)). The working presumption appears to be that competitive markets operate efficiently so as not to give rise to such abuses. Consequently, it can only disrupt the orderly operation of the market settlement process if it is open to challenge in this way. Such challenges might be difficult to handle where, for example, the market price of an asset is subject to wild fluctuations of price on a particular day. A similar provision is made for Scotland (subs. (2)).

Powers of Secretary of State to give directions

166.—(1) The powers conferred by this section are exercisable in relation to a recognised UK investment exchange or recognised UK clearing house.
(2) Where in any case an exchange or clearing house has not taken action under its default rules—

(a) if it appears to the Secretary of State that it could take action, he may direct it to do so, and
(b) if it appears to the Secretary of State that it is proposing to take or may take action, he may direct it not to do so.

(3) Before giving such a direction the Secretary of State shall consult the exchange or clearing house in question; and he shall not give a direction unless he is satisfied, in the light of that consultation—
(a) in the case of a direction to take action, that failure to take action would involve undue risk to investors or other participants in the market, or
(b) in the case of a direction not to take action, that the taking of action would be premature or otherwise undesirable in the interests of investors or other participants in the market.

(4) A direction shall specify the grounds on which it is given.

(5) A direction not to take action may be expressed to have effect until the giving of a further direction (which may be a direction to take action or simply revoking the earlier direction).

(6) No direction shall be given not to take action if, in relation to the person in question—
(a) a bankruptcy order or an award of sequestration of his estate has been made, or an interim receiver or interim trustee has been appointed, or
(b) a winding up order has been made, a resolution for voluntary winding up has been passed or an administrator, administrative receiver or provisional liquidator has been appointed;
and any previous direction not to take action shall cease to have effect on the making or passing of any such order, award or appointment.

(7) Where an exchange or clearing house has taken or been directed to take action under its default rules, the Secretary of State may direct it to do or not to do such things (being things which it has power to do under its default rules) as are specified in the direction.

The Secretary of State shall not give such a direction unless he is satisfied that it will not impede or frustrate the proper and efficient conduct of the default proceedings.

(8) A direction under this section is enforceable, on the application of the Secretary of State, by injunction or, in Scotland, by an order under section 45 of the Court of Session Act 1988; and where an exchange or clearing house has not complied with a direction, the court may make such order as it thinks fit for restoring the position to what it would have been if the direction had been complied with.

GENERAL NOTE

This section gives the Secretary of State a wide-ranging power to intervene in the default process, but not in the conventional insolvency process (subs. (6)). The recognised investment exchange or clearing house may be goaded into action or lulled into inaction (subs. (2)), in accordance with the Secretary of State's desire to strike the fine balance between the avoidance of undue risk to investors and the creation of unrest in the market (subs. (3)). The direction of the Secretary of State must be taken after appropriate consultation with the exchange or clearing house (subs. (3)) and must specify the grounds on which it is given (subs. (4)). A direction not to act may be temporary (subs. (5)). It may also give particular guidance as to the operation of the default rules (subs. (7)), though it may not as such modify those rules (subs. (7)). It is enforceable in judicial proceedings (subs. (8)).

Application to determine whether default proceedings to be taken

167.—(1) Where there has been made or passed in relation to a member or designated non-member of a recognised investment exchange or a member of a recognised clearing house—

(a) a bankruptcy order or an award of sequestration of his estate, or an order appointing an interim receiver of his property, or

(b) an administration or winding up order, a resolution for voluntary winding up or an order appointing a provisional liquidator,

and the exchange or clearing house has not taken action under its default rules in consequence of the order, award or resolution or the matters giving rise to it, a relevant office-holder appointed by, or in consequence of or in connection with, the order, award or resolution may apply to the Secretary of State.

(2) The application shall specify the exchange or clearing house concerned and the grounds on which it is made.

(3) On receipt of the application the Secretary of State shall notify the exchange or clearing house, and unless within three business days after the day on which the notice is received the exchange or clearing house—

(a) takes action under its default rules, or

(b) notifies the Secretary of State that it proposes to do so forthwith,

then, subject as follows, the provisions of sections 158 to 165 above do not apply in relation to market contracts to which the member or designated non-member in question is a party or to anything done by the exchange or clearing house for the purposes of, or in connection with, the settlement of any such contract.

For this purpose a "business day" means any day which is not a Saturday or Sunday, Christmas Day, Good Friday or a bank holiday in any part of the United Kingdom under the Banking and Financial Dealings Act 1971.

(4) The provisions of sections 158 to 165 are not disapplied if before the end of the period mentioned in subsection (3) the Secretary of State gives the exchange or clearing house a direction under section 166(2)(a) (direction to take action under default rules).

No such direction may be given after the end of that period.

(5) If the exchange or clearing house notifies the Secretary of State that it proposes to take action under its default rules forthwith, it shall do so; and that duty is enforceable, on the application of the Secretary of State, by injunction or, in Scotland, by an order under section 45 of the Court of Session Act 1988.

GENERAL NOTE

This section is designed to goad the recognised investment exchange or clearing house into action in those cases where it is slow to initiate default proceedings. A failure to take action within the allotted time of three business days (subs. (3)) will mean the disapplication of ss.159–165, which safeguard the integrity of the market settlement process (or mini-liquidation). The action in question may consist of the giving of an undertaking to act by the exchange or clearing house to the Secretary of State (subs. (5)) or the issuance by the latter of a direction to act (subs. (4)). It is enforceable in judicial proceedings (subs. (5) and s.166(8)).

Delegation of functions to designated agency

168.—(1) Section 114 of the Financial Services Act 1986 (power to transfer functions to designated agency) applies to the functions of the Secretary of State under this Part in relation to a UK investment exchange or clearing house, with the exception of his functions with respect to the making of orders and regulations.

(2) If immediately before the commencement of this section—

(a) a designated agency is exercising all functions in relation to such bodies which are capable of being transferred under that section, and

(b) no draft order is lying before Parliament resuming any of those functions, the order bringing this section into force shall have effect as a delegation order made under that section transferring to that agency all the functions which may be transferred by virtue of this section.

(3) The Secretary of State may—
  (a) in the circumstances mentioned in subsection (3), (4) or (5) of section 115 of the Financial Services Act 1986, or
  (b) if it appears to him that a designated agency is unable or unwilling to discharge all or any of the functions under this Part which have been transferred to it,

make an order under that section resuming all functions under this Part which have been transferred to the agency.

This does not affect his power to make an order under subsection (1) or (2) of that section with respect to such functions.

GENERAL NOTE

This section provides for the delegation by the Secretary of State of certain powers, such as the power to give directions under s.166, to designated agencies under s.114 of the Financial Services Act 1986. The body explicitly referred to in s.114 is the Securities and Investments Board Limited.

Supplementary provisions

169.—(1) Section 61 of the Financial Services Act 1986 (injunctions and restitution orders) applies in relation to a contravention of any provision of the rules of a recognised investment exchange or recognised clearing house relating to the matters mentioned in Schedule 21 to this Act as it applies in relation to a contravention of any provision of such rules relating to the carrying on of investment business.

(2) The following provisions of the Financial Services Act 1986—
  section 12 (compliance orders), as it applies by virtue of section 37(8) or 39(8),
  section 37(7)(b) (revocation of recognition of UK investment exchange), and
  section 39(7)(b) (revocation of recognition of UK clearing house),
apply in relation to a failure by a recognised investment exchange or recognised clearing house to comply with an obligation under this Part as to a failure to comply with an obligation under that Act.

(3) Where the recognition of an investment exchange or clearing house is revoked under the Financial Services Act 1986, the Secretary of State may, before or after the revocation order, give such directions as he thinks fit with respect to the continued application of the provisions of this Part, with such exceptions, additions and adaptations as may be specified in the direction, in relation to cases where a relevant event of any description specified in the directions occurred before the revocation order takes effect.

(4) The references in sections 119 and 121 of the Financial Services Act 1986 (competition) to what is necessary for the protection of investors shall be construed as including references to what is necessary for the purposes of this Part.

(5) Section 204 of the Financial Services Act 1986 (service of notices) applies in relation to a notice, direction or other document required or authorised by or under this Part to be given to or served on any person other than the Secretary of State.

GENERAL NOTE

The broad purpose of this section is to extend the reach of various provisions in the Financial Services Act 1986, so as to apply them to the conduct of the market settlement process by the recognised investment exchange or clearing house and to the matters introduced in the new default rules set out in Sched. 21 of the present Act. The provisions in question in the 1986 Act include various forms of order and the revocation of recognition, as well as the service of notices.

Subs. (3)
The revocation of recognition accorded to an investment exchange or clearing house is without prejudice to the conduct of a current market settlement process, which is allowed to run its course to the extent that this is so permitted by the Secretary of State.

Other exchanges and clearing houses

Certain overseas exchanges and clearing houses

170.—(1) The Secretary of State may by regulations provide that this Part applies in relation to contracts connected with an overseas investment exchange or clearing house which is approved by him in accordance with such procedures as may be specified in the regulations, as satisfying such requirements as may be so specified, as it applies in relation to contracts connected with a recognised investment exchange or clearing house.

(2) The Secretary of State shall not approve an overseas investment exchange or clearing house unless he is satisfied—
  (a) that the rules and practices of the body, together with the law of the country in which the body's head office is situated, provide adequate procedures for dealing with the default of persons party to contracts connected with the body, and
  (b) that it is otherwise appropriate to approve the body.

(3) The reference in subsection (2)(a) to default is to a person being unable to meet his obligations.

(4) The regulations may apply in relation to the approval of a body under this section such of the provisions of the Financial Services Act 1986 as the Secretary of State considers appropriate.

(5) The Secretary of State may make regulations which, in relation to a body which is so approved—
  (a) apply such of the provisions of the Financial Services Act 1986 as the Secretary of State considers appropriate, and
  (b) provide that the provisions of this Part apply with such exceptions, additions and adaptations as appear to the Secretary of State to be necessary or expedient;
and different provision may be made with respect to different bodies or descriptions of body.

(6) Where the regulations apply any provisions of the Financial Services Act 1986, they may provide that those provisions apply with such exceptions, additions and adaptations as appear to the Secretary of State to be necessary or expedient.

DEFINITION
"overseas": s.190(1).

GENERAL NOTE
This section gives a very broad discretion to the Secretary of State in the recognition of overseas investment exchanges and clearing houses for the purpose of Pt. VII of this Act. This discretion extends to modifying the impact of provisions in the Financial Services Act 1986 (subss. (4)–(6)). The Secretary of State's recognition is dependent on the matters listed in subss. (2)–(3), which appear to be the same as those also listed in Sched. 21, Pt. III of this Act, though this Part is not explicitly referred to in the present section. See however s.156(2)(c).

Certain money market institutions

171.—(1) The Secretary of State may by regulations provide that this Part applies to contracts of any specified description in relation to which settlement arrangements are provided by a person for the time being included in a list maintained by the Bank of England for the purposes of this section, as it applies to contracts connected with a recognised investment exchange or recognised clearing house.

(2) The Secretary of State shall not make any such regulations unless he is satisfied, having regard to the extent to which the contracts in question—
   (a) involve, or are likely to involve, investments falling within paragraph 2 of Schedule 5 to the Financial Services Act 1986 (money market investments), or
   (b) are otherwise of a kind dealt in by persons supervised by the Bank of England,

that it is appropriate that the arrangements should be subject to the supervision of the Bank of England.

(3) The approval of the Treasury is required for—
   (a) the conditions imposed by the Bank of England for admission to the list maintained by it for the purposes of this section, and
   (b) the arrangements for a person's admission to and removal from the list;

and any regulations made under this section shall cease to have effect if the approval of the Treasury is withdrawn, but without prejudice to their having effect again if approval is given for fresh conditions or arrangements.

(4) The Bank of England shall publish the list as for the time being in force and provide a certified copy of it at the request of any person wishing to refer to it in legal proceedings.

A certified copy shall be evidence (in Scotland, sufficient evidence) of the contents of the list; and a copy purporting to be certified by or on behalf of the Bank shall be deemed to have been duly certified unless the contrary is shown.

(5) Regulations under this section may, in relation to a person included in the list—
   (a) apply, with such exceptions, additions and adaptations as appear to the Secretary of State to be necessary or expedient, such of the provisions of the Financial Services Act 1986 as he considers appropriate, and
   (b) provide that the provisions of this Part apply with such exceptions, additions and adaptations as appear to the Secretary of State to be necessary or expedient.

(6) Before making any regulations under this section, the Secretary of State shall consult the Treasury and the Bank of England.

(7) In section 84(1) of the Banking Act 1987 (disclosure of information obtained under that Act), in the Table showing the authorities to which, and functions for the purposes of which, disclosure may be made, at the end add—

"A person included in the list maintained by the Bank for the purposes of section 171 of the Companies Act 1989.	Functions under settlement arrangements to which regulations under that section relate.".

GENERAL NOTE

The Secretary of State is granted a regulation-making power to apply Pt. VII of the Act to settlement processes run by individuals who feature on a Bank of England list, maintained with the approval of the Treasury. The reference to investments dealt with in Sched. 5, para. 2 to the Financial Services Act 1986 is to debentures, warrants, instruments and the like issued by a building society or by an authorised bank as well as contracts with such bodies for the supply of, or entered into in connection with, currency and bullion.

Settlement arrangements provided by the Bank of England

172.—(1) The Secretary of State may by regulations provide that this Part applies to contracts of any specified description in relation to which settlement arrangements are provided by the Bank of England, as it applies to contracts connected with a recognised investment exchange or recognised clearing house.

(2) Regulations under this section may provide that the provisions of this Part apply with such exceptions, additions and adaptations as appear to the Secretary of State to be necessary or expedient.

(3) Before making any regulations under this section, the Secretary of State shall consult the Treasury and the Bank of England.

GENERAL NOTE

This section deals with settlement arrangements provided by the Bank of England itself, such as the developing Central Money Markets Office.

Market charges

Market charges

173.—(1) In this Part "market charge" means a charge, whether fixed or floating, granted—
  (a) in favour of a recognised investment exchange, for the purpose of securing debts or liabilities arising in connection with the settlement of market contracts,
  (b) in favour of a recognised clearing house, for the purpose of securing debts or liabilities arising in connection with their ensuring the performance of market contracts, or
  (c) in favour of a person who agrees to make payments as a result of the transfer of specified securities made through the medium of a computer-based system established by the Bank of England and The Stock Exchange, for the purpose of securing debts or liabilities of the transferee arising in connection therewith.

(2) Where a charge is granted partly for purposes specified in subsection (1)(a), (b) or (c) and partly for other purposes, it is a "market charge" so far as it has effect for the specified purposes.

(3) In subsection (1)(c)—
  "specified securities" means securities for the time being specified in the list in Schedule 1 to the Stock Transfer Act 1982, and includes any right to such securities; and
  "transfer", in relation to any such securities or right, means a transfer of the beneficial interest.

(4) The Secretary of State may by regulations make further provision as to the charges granted in favour of any such person as is mentioned in subsection (1)(a), (b) or (c) which are to be treated as "market charges" for the purposes of this Part; and the regulations may add to, amend or repeal the provisions of subsections (1) to (3) above.

(5) The regulations may provide that a charge shall or shall not be treated as a market charge if or to the extent that it secures obligations of a specified description, is a charge over property of a specified description or contains provisions of a specified description.

(6) Before making regulations under this section in relation to charges granted in favour of a person within subsection (1)(c), the Secretary of State shall consult the Treasury and the Bank of England.

DEFINITIONS
"charge": s.190(1).
"ensuring the performance, etc.": s.190(4).
"the Stock Exchange": s.190(1).

GENERAL NOTE

This is the first of a number of sections dealing with market charges. It defines what a market charge is, leaving it to the following sections to state how the market charge is to be treated in relation to the general law of insolvency. A reading of the House of Lords debates reveals a fair degree of unfamiliarity with the concept, which was referred to as being of recent vintage. As true as that might be of the use to which market charges are put, it is not true of the concept of charge itself. A charge is the appropriation of property, recognised in equity, as security for the payment of a debt or performance of some other obligation. It is not a mortgage as such, though certain charges operate by way of mortgage and, in various ways, charge and mortgage are hard to keep separate in practice. There is no such thing as a common law charge; a charge is an equitable security and therefore subject to the equitable rules on priorities between competing interests. Note, however, how a charge is defined in this Act as "any form of security, including a mortgage and, in Scotland, a heritable security". Note also that there is no definition in the Act of security, which as a general expression embraces both possessory and non-possessory security devices. Since, however, the idea of margin itself expresses a possessory interest in property taken to guarantee the due performance and settlement of market contracts, a sensible interpretation of "security" could be any non-possessory device whose purpose is to secure the due performance of a market contract obligation. Finally, note that no attempt is made to define the property that may be subjected to a market charge.

Subs. (1)

This subsection raises the novel possibility that a market charge granted in favour of a recognised investment exchange may be used to secure the performance of obligations owed under market contracts to persons whose identity is not yet known at the date when the charge is granted. More particularly, in para. (c), it points to security granted to someone, other than a recognised investment exchange or clearing house, making payments as a result of the transfer of securities. The case that prompted this provision is the settlement process effected under the Bank of England's Central Gilts Office system. Transactions in gilts take place on the Stock Exchange (see s.190(1)), which is of course a recognised investment exchange, but the transactions in question are cleared, not on the Stock Exchange's settlement system, but through the Central Gilts Office. The charge that supports the clearing arrangements is given, neither to the Stock Exchange nor to the Central Gilts Office, but in favour of the particular member's settlement bank. This bank undertakes to make payments on the member's behalf in the settlement process.

Subs. (2)

This subsection shows, particularly in the case of a settlement bank under subs. (1)(c), that a charge may be given to secure market debts or liabilities as well as personal obligations of the member (by way of overdraft, for example) to his settlement bank. The charge is therefore severable to the extent that it also fulfils a market rôle.

Subs. (3)

This refers to Sched. 1 to the Stock Transfer Act 1982, which sets out a wide range of securities issued by government, central and local, and by nationalised industries, as well as by various international organisations, such as the European Investment Bank and the World Bank, and foreign bodies, such as the hydroelectric authority of Quebec.

Subss. (4) and (5)

These subsections confer on the Secretary of State regulation-making powers as to the scope of market charges. It seems to be contemplated, in the case of the Central Gilts Office settlement process, for example, that regulations would limit the reach of the market charge to the member's liability to his settlement bank in respect of transfers of specific securities (mainly gilts) into the member's account.

Modifications of the law of insolvency

174.—(1) The general law of insolvency has effect in relation to market charges and action taken in enforcing them subject to the provisions of section 175.

(2) The Secretary of State may by regulations make further provision modifying the law of insolvency in relation to the matters mentioned in subsection (1).

(3) The regulations may add to, amend or repeal the provisions mentioned in subsection (1), and any other provision of this Part as it applies for the purposes of those provisions, or provide that those

provisions have effect with such exceptions, additions or adaptations as are specified in the regulations.

(4) The regulations may make different provision for cases defined by reference to the nature of the charge, the nature of the property subject to it, the circumstances, nature or extent of the obligations secured by it or any other relevant factor.

(5) Before making regulations under this section in relation to charges granted in favour of a person within section 173(1)(c), the Secretary of State shall consult the Treasury and the Bank of England.

GENERAL NOTE

This provision mirrors s.158, which states that the general law of insolvency applies in relation to market contracts, subject to a number of wide-ranging exceptions in the ensuing sections. Likewise, s.174 gives forewarning of the way that the market charge will be permitted to have effect without interference from the general law of insolvency. The inroads into insolvency law are laid down in s.175 and may be added to by regulations issued under subs. (2) of the present section. Subss. (3) and (4) show that the regulation-making power is so widely defined as to make prediction of the final shape of the regulations an impossible matter.

Administration orders, &c.

175.—(1) The following provisions of the Insolvency Act 1986 (which relate to administration orders and administrators) do not apply in relation to a market charge—
  (a) sections 10(1)(b) and 11(3)(c) (restriction on enforcement of security while petition for administration order pending or order in force), and
  (b) section 15(1) and (2) (power of administrator to deal with charged property);
and section 11(2) of that Act (receiver to vacate office when so required by administrator) does not apply to a receiver appointed under a market charge.

(2) However, where a market charge falls to be enforced after an administration order has been made or a petition for an administration order has been presented, and there exists another charge over some or all of the same property ranking in priority to or *pari passu* with the market charge, the court may order that there shall be taken after enforcement of the market charge such steps as the court may direct for the purpose of ensuring that the chargee under the other charge is not prejudiced by the enforcement of the market charge.

(3) The following provisions of the Insolvency Act 1986 (which relate to the powers of receivers) do not apply in relation to a market charge—
  (a) section 43 (power of administrative receiver to dispose of charged property), and
  (b) section 61 (power of receiver in Scotland to dispose of an interest in property).

(4) Sections 127 and 284 of the Insolvency Act 1986 (avoidance of property dispositions effected after commencement of winding up or presentation of bankruptcy petition), and section 32(8) of the Bankruptcy (Scotland) Act 1985 (effect of dealing with debtor relating to estate vested in permanent trustee), do not apply to a disposition of property as a result of which the property becomes subject to a market charge or any transaction pursuant to which that disposition is made.

(5) However, if a person (other than the chargee under the market charge) who is party to a disposition mentioned in subsection (4) has notice at the time of the disposition that a petition has been presented for the winding up or bankruptcy or sequestration of the estate of the party

making the disposition, the value of any profit to him arising from the disposition is recoverable from him by the relevant office-holder unless the court directs otherwise.

(6) Any sum recoverable by virtue of subsection (5) ranks for priority, in the event of the insolvency of the person from whom it is due, immediately before preferential or, in Scotland, preferred debts.

(7) In a case falling within both subsection (4) above (as a disposition of property as a result of which the property becomes subject to a market charge) and section 164(3) (as the provision of margin in relation to a market contract), section 164(4) applies with respect to the recovery of the amount or value of the margin and subsection (5) above does not apply.

DEFINITIONS
"party":s.187.
"permanent trustee": s.190(1), (7)(b).

GENERAL NOTE
This section states to what extent the market charge is to be allowed to override the general law of insolvency. The administration process in Pt. II of the Insolvency Act 1986 is prevented from interfering with the market charges; administrative receivers are not permitted to dispose of charged property and the provisions that presumptively invalidate dispositions of property after the bankruptcy or winding-up petition are excluded. There are, however, a number of provisions dealing with notice and claw back of the type observed before in ss.163–164.

Subs. (1)
This subsection provides that a receiver under a market charge cannot be required to vacate office, in the way that a receiver of only part of a company's property may be required to step down by a company administrator appointed under Pt. II of the Insolvency Act 1986. Similarly, an administrator may not dispose of property subject to a market charge or prevent the disposal by someone else of property subject to a market charge, as would otherwise be the case. The laudable goal of mounting a rescue operation on ailing companies with the aid of the administrator is postponed to the orderly settlement of market contracts and the realisation of charged property for that purpose.

Subs. (2)
This subsection contemplates that property subject to a market charge may be subject to a prior-ranking or equal-ranking charge for non-market purposes. Generally, Pt. VII of this Act does not seek to overturn established security and alter the settled order of priority, except in the limited way contemplated by s.178. Except for the administration order, a prior-ranking or equal-ranking chargee could take care of his interests in the normal way, since no interference is created by Pt. VII of this Act. But the partial efficacy of the administration order, in preventing enforcement of his charge by the non-market chargee while not inhibiting the market chargee, prompts this subsection, which is designed to deal with a non-market chargee in that position. The court's discretion appears to be very broad. If the charged property is not sufficient to satisfy both charges, perhaps the court might charge on the unencumbered portion of the debtor's assets. Where such assets do not exist, it may well be that the market settlement process will be allowed to interfere with established rules of priority, unless the court decides that the latter should override the former.

Subs. (4)
This should be compared with s.164(3).

Subs. (5)
This subsection would appear to allow a claw back from an individual, such as a broker, who receives a commission when acting in the capacity of agent. (See the definition of "party" in s.187.) This provision is subject to sub. (7). Subs. (6) should be compared with ss.163(6) and 164(6).

Power to make provision about certain other charges

176.—(1) The Secretary of State may by regulations provide that the general law of insolvency has effect in relation to charges of such descriptions as may be specified in the regulations, and action taken in enforcing them, subject to such provisions as may be specified in the regulations.

(2) The regulations may specify any description of charge granted in favour of—
  (a) a body approved under section 170 (certain overseas exchanges and clearing houses),
  (b) a person included in the list maintained by the Bank of England for the purposes of section 171 (certain money market institutions),
  (c) the Bank of England,
  (d) an authorised person within the meaning of the Financial Services Act 1986, or
  (e) an international securities self-regulating organisation within the meaning of that Act,

for the purpose of securing debts or liabilities arising in connection with or as a result of the settlement of contracts or the transfer of assets, rights or interests on a financial market.

(3) The regulations may specify any description of charge granted for that purpose in favour of any other person in connection with exchange facilities or clearing services provided by a recognised investment exchange or recognised clearing house or by any such body, person, authority or organisation as is mentioned in subsection (2).

(4) Where a charge is granted partly for the purpose specified in subsection (2) and partly for other purposes, the power conferred by this section is exercisable in relation to the charge so far as it has effect for that purpose.

(5) The regulations may—
  (a) make the same or similar provision in relation to the charges to which they apply as is made by or under sections 174 and 175 in relation to market charges, or
  (b) apply any of those provisions with such exceptions, additions or adaptations as are specified in the regulations.

(6) Before making regulations under this section relating to a description of charges defined by reference to their being granted—
  (a) in favour of a person included in the list maintained by the Bank of England for the purposes of section 171, or in connection with exchange facilities or clearing services provided by a person included in that list, or
  (b) in favour of the Bank of England, or in connection with settlement arrangements provided by the Bank,

the Secretary of State shall consult the Treasury and the Bank of England.

(7) Regulations under this section may provide that they apply or do not apply to a charge if or to the extent that it secures obligations of a specified description, is a charge over property of a specified description or contains provisions of a specified description.

GENERAL NOTE

This section establishes a general regulation-making power permitting the Secretary of State to add to the list of institutions recognised for the purpose of the market charges provision in s.173(1). Guidance as to the institutions that may be designated in this way is provided by subs. (2). This list includes, for example, self-regulating organisations (see s.8 of the Financial Services Act 1986), authorised insurers and authorised friendly societies. The regulations produced are expected to be modelled on the general provisions relating to market charges (compare, for example, s.173(2) and s.176(4), s.173(5) and s.176(7)), and see subs. (5).

Market property

Application of margin not affected by certain other interests

177.—(1) The following provisions have effect with respect to the application by a recognised investment exchange or recognised clearing house of property (other than land) held by the exchange or clearing house as margin in relation to a market contract.

(2) So far as necessary to enable the property to be applied in accordance with the rules of the exchange or clearing house, it may be so applied notwithstanding any prior equitable interest or right, or any right or remedy arising from a breach of fiduciary duty, unless the exchange or clearing house had notice of the interest, right or breach of duty at the time the property was provided as margin.

(3) No right or remedy arising subsequently to the property being provided as margin may be enforced so as to prevent or interfere with the application of the property by the exchange or clearing house in accordance with its rules.

(4) Where an exchange or clearing house has power by virtue of the above provisions to apply property notwithstanding an interest, right or remedy, a person to whom the exchange or clearing house disposes of the property in accordance with its rules takes free from that interest, right or remedy.

GENERAL NOTE

This section deals with the issue of priority as between the interest of a recognised investment exchange or clearing house in property held as margin and the interest of a prior party with an equitable interest in that same property. The property is held by the recognised investment exchange or clearing house as security for the due performance or settlement of market contracts. If the interest of the above body in that property is analysed as being in the nature of a pledgee's interest, then s.177(2) can be seen as applying the long established equitable rule that a bona fide purchaser of the legal estate for value without notice overrides prior equitable interests. In so far as the margin property is held by the body in question in respect of contracts to which it is not party, then it can be seen as holding the property as agent on behalf of the other party or parties to the relevant market contract or contracts.

Subs. (2)

This subsection emphasises that, in so far as the provision of margin property creates a legal interest to secure the due performance or settlement of market contracts, it is fully in accordance with existing principles of title transfer.

Subs. (3)

This subsection shows that the interest created when property is provided and held as margin cannot be overridden by later transactions or dealings in the same property. There are, in other words, no relevant *nemo dat* exceptions and, indeed, it is hard to imagine any that would otherwise be available while the property continues to be held as margin by the recognised investment exchange or clearing house.

Subs. (4)

This subsection shows that, in accordance with normal title transfer principles, any person to whom the margin property is subsequently transferred under the rules of the exchange or clearing house (such as the other party to the relevant market contract or contracts) takes free of prior interests. It is hard to imagine that the person receiving the property would be a volunteer, and hard to imagine too that such a person would have notice of any prior overridden interest, which ought in any event to be irrelevant on normal title transfer principles.

Priority of floating market charge over subsequent charges

178.—(1) The Secretary of State may by regulations provide that a market charge which is a floating charge has priority over a charge subsequently created or arising, including a fixed charge.

(2) The regulations may make different provision for cases defined, as regards the market charge or the subsequent charge, by reference to the description of charge, its terms, the circumstances in which it is created or arises, the nature of the charge, the person in favour of whom it is granted or arises or any other relevant factor.

GENERAL NOTE
This section, by disregarding the distinction between fixed and floating charges, aims to protect the priority position of a market chargee with regard to subsequent chargees. Since both parties' interests in such a case are equitable, s.178 can be seen as not contradicting the proposition that a bona fide purchaser of the legal estate for value without notice ought to override the interest of a market chargee.

Subs. (1)
This subsection alters existing law in that it would prevent a later fixed charge from overriding an earlier floating charge that has not yet crystallised. It all depends, however, on the Secretary of State making regulations to that effect.

Subs. (2)
This would permit, if the regulations were drafted in such a form, distinctions to be made according, for example, to the relative range of the two charges. It is only where the equities are equal, after all, that the first in time prevails.

Priority of market charge over unpaid vendor's lien

179. Where property subject to an unpaid vendor's lien becomes subject to a market charge, the charge has priority over the lien unless the chargee had actual notice of the lien at the time the property became subject to the charge.

GENERAL NOTE
This is another priority provision; its meaning is rather obscure. Literally read, it is capable of covering goods still in the possession of an unpaid seller exercising a lien, the general property in which has passed to the buyer-chargor. If s.179 is read in this way, a later equitable interest under the market charge overrides a prior legal interest. That can hardly have been the intention of Parliament. It seems unlikely too that the provision was designed to override the prior equitable interest of an unpaid seller of land which is now in the possession of the purchaser. Again, s.179 is literally capable of applying in such a case. It seems that this provision was prompted by the experience of the Central Gilts Office and the possibility that an unpaid vendor's lien over stock might in certain cases bind a subsequent purchaser of the stock, thus undermining the market charge given by that subsequent purchaser to his settlement bank.

Proceedings against market property by unsecured creditors

180.—(1) Where property (other than land) is held by a recognised investment exchange or recognised clearing house as margin in relation to market contracts or is subject to a market charge, no execution or other legal process for the enforcement of a judgment or order may be commenced or continued, and no distress may be levied, against the property by a person not seeking to enforce any interest in or security over the property, except with the consent of—
  (a) in the case of property provided as cover for margin, the investment exchange or clearing house in question, or
  (b) in the case of property subject to a market charge, the person in whose favour the charge was granted.

(2) Where consent is given the proceedings may be commenced or continued notwithstanding any provision of the Insolvency Act 1986 or the Bankruptcy (Scotland) Act 1985.

(3) Where by virtue of this section a person would not be entitled to enforce a judgment or order against any property, any injunction or other

remedy granted with a view to facilitating the enforcement of any such judgment or order shall not extend to that property.

(4) In the application of this section to Scotland, the reference to execution being commenced or continued includes a reference to diligence being carried out or continued, and the reference to distress being levied shall be omitted.

GENERAL NOTE

This section is designed to put margin property and charged property beyond the reach of unsecured creditors. Thus, for example, a judgment creditor may not levy execution against such property without the consent of the investment exchange or clearing house in question. Subs. (3) would, for example, read down a *Mareva* injunction that might otherwise extend to the margin property.

Power to apply provisions to other cases

181.—(1) The power of the Secretary of State to make provision by regulations under—

(a) section 170, 171 or 172 (power to extend provisions relating to market contracts), or

(b) section 176 (power to extend provisions relating to market charges), includes power to apply sections 177 to 180 to any description of property provided as cover for margin in relation to contracts in relation to which the power is exercised or, as the case may be, property subject to charges in relation to which the power is exercised.

(2) The regulations may provide that those sections apply with such exceptions, additions and adaptations as may be specified in the regulations.

GENERAL NOTE

This section carries over the Secretary of State's regulation-making power, in relation to market contracts and market charges, under the sections mentioned, to connected cases of margin property.

Supplementary provisions

Powers of court in relation to certain proceedings begun before commencement

182.—(1) The powers conferred by this section are exercisable by the court where insolvency proceedings in respect of—

(a) a member of a recognised investment exchange or a recognised clearing house, or

(b) a person by whom a market charge has been granted,

are begun on or after 22nd December 1988 and before the commencement of this section.

That person is referred to in this section as "the relevant person".

(2) For the purposes of this section "insolvency proceedings" means proceedings under Part II, IV, V or IX of the Insolvency Act 1986 (administration, winding up and bankruptcy) or under the Bankruptcy (Scotland) Act 1985; and references in this section to the beginning of such proceedings are to—

(a) the presentation of a petition on which an administration order, winding-up order, bankruptcy order or award of sequestration is made, or

(b) the passing of a resolution for voluntary winding up.

(3) This section applies in relation to—

(a) in England and Wales, the administration of the insolvent estate of a deceased person, and

(b) in Scotland, the administration by a judicial factor appointed under section 11A of the Judicial Factors (Scotland) Act 1889 of the insolvent estate of a deceased person,

as it applies in relation to insolvency proceedings.

In such a case references to the beginning of the proceedings shall be construed as references to the death of the relevant person.

(4) The court may on an application made, within three months after the commencement of this section, by—
 (a) a recognised investment exchange or recognised clearing house, or
 (b) a person in whose favour a market charge has been granted,

make such order as it thinks fit for achieving, except so far as assets of the relevant person have been distributed before the making of the application, the same result as if the provisions of Schedule 22 had come into force on 22nd December 1988.

(5) The provisions of that Schedule ("the relevant provisions") reproduce the effect of certain provisions of this Part as they appeared in the Bill for this Act as introduced into the House of Lords and published on that date.

(6) The court may in particular—
 (a) require the relevant person or a relevant office-holder—
  (i) to return property provided as cover for margin or which was subject to a market charge, or to pay to the applicant or any other person the proceeds of realisation of such property, or
  (ii) to pay to the applicant or any other person such amount as the court estimates would have been payable to that person if the relevant provisions had come into force on 22nd December 1988 and market contracts had been settled in accordance with the rules of the recognised investment exchange or recognised clearing house, or a proportion of that amount if the property of the relevant person or relevant office-holder is not sufficient to meet the amount in full;
 (b) provide that contracts, rules and dispositions shall be treated as not having been void;
 (c) modify the functions of a relevant office-holder, or the duties of the applicant or any other person, in relation to the insolvency proceedings, or indemnify any such person in respect of acts or omissions which would have been proper if the relevant provisions had been in force;
 (d) provide that conduct which constituted an offence be treated as not having done so;
 (e) dismiss proceedings which could not have been brought if the relevant provisions had come into force on 22nd December 1988, and reverse the effect of any order of a court which could not, or would not, have been made if those provisions had come into force on that date.

(7) An order under this section shall not be made against a relevant office-holder if the effect would be that his remuneration, costs and expenses could not be met.

GENERAL NOTE

This section creates a body of retrospective law, applicable when this part of the Companies Act is proclaimed in force and dated back to December 22, 1988, the day after the Companies Bill was first introduced in the House of Lords. It is designed to undo the effect of administration orders, windings up and bankruptcies to the extent that property still remains with the administrator, liquidator and trustee (subject to subs. (7)) and is capable of being clawed back. The applicant (see subs. (4)) seeking to claw back this property has three months to do so from the commencement of the present section. Subject to the case where property has already been distributed, the court may make an order as if the provisions of Sched. 22 to this Act had been in force as from December 22, 1988. Sched.

22 embodies certain provisions of Pt. VII as they appeared in the Bill that was first introduced in the House of Lords (and so can be seen as a primitive form of the present Pt. VII). Their principal features are helpfully summarised in subs. (6) of the present section. Note that this section in effect extends the notion of insolvency proceedings (administration orders, windings up and bankruptcies) to include the administration of insolvent estates (subs. (3)).

Insolvency proceedings in other jurisdictions

183.—(1) The references to insolvency law in section 426 of the Insolvency Act 1986 (co-operation with courts exercising insolvency jurisdiction in other jurisdictions) include, in relation to a part of the United Kingdom, the provisions made by or under this Part and, in relation to a relevant country or territory within the meaning of that section, so much of the law of that country or territory as corresponds to any provisions made by or under this Part.

(2) A court shall not, in pursuance of that section or any other enactment or rule of law, recognise or give effect to—
  (a) any order of a court exercising jurisdiction in relation to insolvency law in a country or territory outside the United Kingdom, or
  (b) any act of a person appointed in such a country or territory to discharge any functions under insolvency law,
in so far as the making of the order or the doing of the act would be prohibited in the case of a court in the United Kingdom or a relevant office-holder by provisions made by or under this Part.

(3) Subsection (2) does not affect the recognition or enforcement of a judgment required to be recognised or enforced under or by virtue of the Civil Jurisdiction and Judgments Act 1982.

GENERAL NOTE

This section has two principal purposes. First of all, it extends s.426 of the Insolvency Act 1986 to Pt. VII of the present Act. S.426 is designed, so far as possible, to eliminate the boundaries between different legal systems within the U.K. so as to permit the implementation of a national insolvency procedure. This is obviously subject to some limitations (see s.426(2)). For example, a Scottish court would not have to comply with the order of an English court regarding property located in Scotland. The second purpose of s.183, which is subject to the recognition and enforcement of European Community judgments (subs. (3)), is to restrain a court from co-operating with a foreign court or office-holder in a way that would undermine the rules and goals of Pt. VII.

S.426 of the Insolvency Act enacts a general duty of co-operation or assistance (s.426(4)) which the Secretary of State is empowered by statutory instrument to extend to a country outside the U.K. (s.426(11)).

Indemnity for certain acts, &c.

184.—(1) Where a relevant office-holder takes any action in relation to property of a defaulter which is liable to be dealt with in accordance with the default rules of a recognised investment exchange or recognised clearing house, and believes and has reasonable grounds for believing that he is entitled to take that action, he is not liable to any person in respect of any loss or damage resulting from his action except in so far as the loss or damage is caused by the office-holder's own negligence.

(2) Any failure by a recognised investment exchange or recognised clearing house to comply with its own rules in respect of any matter shall not prevent that matter being treated for the purposes of this Part as done in accordance with those rules so long as the failure does not substantially affect the rights of any person entitled to require compliance with the rules.

(3) No recognised investment exchange or recognised clearing house, nor any officer or servant or member of the governing body of a recognised investment exchange or recognised clearing house, shall be liable in damages for anything done or omitted in the discharge or purported

discharge of any functions to which this subsection applies unless the act or omission is shown to have been in bad faith.

(4) The functions to which subsection (3) applies are the functions of the exchange or clearing house so far as relating to, or to matters arising out of—
(a) its default rules, or
(b) any obligations to which it is subject by virtue of this Part.

(5) No person exercising any functions by virtue of arrangements made pursuant to paragraph 5 or 12 of Schedule 21 (delegation of functions in connection with default procedures), nor any officer or servant of such a person, shall be liable in damages for anything done or omitted in the discharge or purported discharge of those functions unless the act or omission is shown to have been in bad faith.

GENERAL NOTE

This section enacts a number of immunities, personal and institutional, in relation to the conduct of an office-holder (see s.189(1)) interfering with property subject to a market charge (theoretically margin property too), and in relation to the activities of recognised investment exchanges and clearing houses, as well as their agents and employees, in implementing their own rules or in complying with the provisions of Pt. VII of this Act.

Subs. (1)

This subsection would protect an office-holder, such as an administrator, from liability in conversion for unlawfully interfering with chattels subject to a market charge, or from liability for unlawfully interfering with contractual relations, provided that he was not negligent in acting as he did. It is submitted that the failure of an office-holder to acquaint himself with the provisions of Pt. VII might well in a proper case be negligence.

Subs. (2)

This subsection would appear, for example, to provide that minor breaches of its own rules by an investment exchange in the conduct of its market settlement process ought not to upset the result of that process and its interaction with general insolvency law.

Subs. (3)

This subsection demonstrates that a high level of misconduct must be reached before a damages action can be maintained. The standard should be compared with that in subs. (2). The same immunity is extended to delegates of investment exchanges and clearing houses when these persons implement those organisations' default procedures (subs. (5)).

Power to make further provision by regulations

185.—(1) The Secretary of State may by regulations make such further provision as appears to him necessary or expedient for the purposes of this Part.

(2) Provision may, in particular, be made—
  (a) for integrating the provisions of this Part with the general law of insolvency, and
  (b) for adapting the provisions of this Part in their application to overseas investment exchanges and clearing houses.

(3) Regulations under this section may add to, amend or repeal any of the provisions of this Part or provide that those provisions have effect subject to such additions, exceptions or adaptations as are specified in the regulations.

GENERAL NOTE

This section, perhaps more than any other, demonstrates the very broad scope of the Secretary of State's regulation-making powers and suggests the possibility that Pt. VII might bear little relation to the system eventually brought into force. In the course of its passage through Parliament, the original Pt. VII was very heavily amended and, in this area of law in particular, the regulation-making power seems to be the legislative process carried on by other means. It is hard to imagine that the subject-matter of Pt. VII will ever have to be dealt with in the legislative process again, to the evident discomfiture of Government and Opposition alike.

Supplementary provisions as to regulations

186.—(1) Regulations under this Part may make different provision for different cases and may contain such incidental, transitional and other supplementary provisions as appear to the Secretary of State to be necessary or expedient.

(2) Regulations under this Part shall be made by statutory instrument which shall be subject to annulment in pursuance of a resolution of either House of Parliament.

GENERAL NOTE
It is not easy to see what powers are accorded to the Secretary of State under subs. (1) that he does not already possess under s.185.

Construction of references to parties to market contracts

187.—(1) Where a person enters into market contracts in more than one capacity, the provisions of this Part apply (subject as follows) as if the contracts entered into in each different capacity were entered into by different persons.

(2) References in this Part to a market contract to which a person is a party include (subject as follows, and unless the context otherwise requires) contracts to which he is party as agent.

(3) The Secretary of State may by regulations—
  (a) modify or exclude the operation of subsections (1) and (2), and
  (b) make provision as to the circumstances in which a person is to be regarded for the purposes of those provisions as acting in different capacities.

GENERAL NOTE
The market settlement process countenanced by Pt. VII involves going behind the identity of a contracting party in some cases, especially when he is acting as an agent. It should make no difference whether that party is acting for a named, unnamed or undisclosed principal.

Meaning of "default rules" and related expressions

188.—(1) In this Part "default rules" means rules of a recognised investment exchange or recognised clearing house which provide for the taking of action in the event of a person appearing to be unable, or likely to become unable, to meet his obligations in respect of one or more market contracts connected with the exchange or clearing house.

(2) References in this Part to a "defaulter" are to a person in respect of whom action has been taken by a recognised investment exchange or recognised clearing house under its default rules, whether by declaring him to be a defaulter or otherwise; and references in this Part to "default" shall be construed accordingly.

(3) In this Part "default proceedings" means proceedings taken by a recognised investment exchange or recognised clearing house under its default rules.

(4) If an exchange or clearing house takes action under its default rules in respect of a person, all subsequent proceedings under its rules for the purposes of or in connection with the settlement of market contracts to which the defaulter is a party shall be treated as done under its default rules.

GENERAL NOTE
See, for example, Sched. 21 to this Act.

Meaning of "relevant office holder"

189.—(1) The following are relevant office-holders for the purposes of this Part—
(a) the official receiver,
(b) any person acting in relation to a company as its liquidator, provisional liquidator, administrator or administrative receiver,
(c) any person acting in relation to an individual (or, in Scotland, any debtor within the meaning of the Bankruptcy (Scotland) Act 1985) as his trustee in bankruptcy or interim receiver of his property or as permanent or interim trustee in the sequestration of his estate,
(d) any person acting as administrator of an insolvent estate of a deceased person.

(2) In subsection (1)(b) "company" means any company, society, association, partnership or other body which may be wound up under the Insolvency Act 1986.

DEFINITIONS
"administrative receiver": Insolvency Act 1986, s.251.
"administrator": Insolvency Act 1986, Pt. II.
"company": Insolvency Act 1986, ss.70, 220.
"liquidator, provisional liquidator": Insolvency Act 1986, ss.143, 411(3).
"official receiver": Insolvency Act 1986, ss.399, 400.

Minor definitions

190.—(1) In this Part—
"administrative receiver" has the meaning given by section 251 of the Insolvency Act 1986;
"charge" means any form of security, including a mortgage and, in Scotland, a heritable security;
"clearing house" has the same meaning as in the Financial Services Act 1986;
"interim trustee" and "permanent trustee" have the same meaning as in the Bankruptcy (Scotland) Act 1985;
"investment" and "investment exchange" have the same meaning as in the Financial Services Act 1986;
"overseas", in relation to an investment exchange or clearing house, means having its head office outside the United Kingdom;
"recognised" means recognised under the Financial Services Act 1986;
"set-off", in relation to Scotland, includes compensation;
"The Stock Exchange" means The International Stock Exchange of the United Kingdom and the Republic of Ireland Limited;
"UK", in relation to an investment exchange or clearing house, means having its head office in the United Kingdom.

(2) References in this Part to settlement in relation to a market contract are to the discharge of the rights and liabilities of the parties to the contract, whether by performance, compromise or otherwise.

(3) In this Part the expressions "margin" and "cover for margin" have the same meaning.

(4) References in this Part to ensuring the performance of a transaction have the same meaning as in the Financial Services Act 1986.

(5) For the purposes of this Part a person shall be taken to have notice of a matter if he deliberately failed to make enquiries as to that matter in circumstances in which a reasonable and honest person would have done so.

This does not apply for the purposes of a provision requiring "actual notice".

(6) References in this Part to the law of insolvency include references to every provision made by or under the Insolvency Act 1986 or the Bankruptcy (Scotland) Act 1985; and in relation to a building society references to insolvency law or to any provision of the Insolvency Act 1986 are to that law or provision as modified by the Building Societies Act 1986.

(7) In relation to Scotland, references in this Part—
  (a) to sequestration include references to the administration by a judicial factor of the insolvent estate of a deceased person, and
  (b) to an interim or permanent trustee include references to a judicial factor on the insolvent estate of a deceased person,

unless the context otherwise requires.

DEFINITIONS
"clearing house": Financial Services Act 1986, s.207(1).
"investment": Financial Services Act 1986, s.1(1).
"investment exchange": Financial Services Act 1986, s.1(2).
"recognised": Financial Services Act 1986, s.18.

Index of defined expressions

191. The following Table shows provisions defining or otherwise explaining expressions used in this Part (other than provisions defining or explaining an expression used only in the same section or paragraph)—

administrative receiver	section 190(1)
charge	section 190(1)
clearing house	section 190(1)
cover for margin	section 190(3)
default rules (and related expressions)	section 188
designated non-member	section 155(2)
ensuring the performance of a transaction	section 190(4)
insolvency law (and similar expressions)	section 190(6)
interim trustee	section 190(1) and (7)(b)
investment	section 190(1)
investment exchange	section 190(1)
margin	section 190(3)
market charge	section 173
market contract	section 155
notice	section 190(5)
overseas (in relation to an investment exchange or clearing house)	section 190(1)
party (in relation to a market contract)	section 187
permanent trustee	section 190(1) and (7)(b)
recognised	section 190(1)
relevant office-holder	section 189
sequestration	section 190(7)(a)
set off (in relation to Scotland)	section 190(1)
settlement and related expressions (in relation to a market contract)	section 190(2)
The Stock Exchange	section 190(1)
trustee, interim or permanent (in relation to Scotland)	section 190(7)(b)
UK (in relation to an investment exchange or clearing house)	section 190(1).

Part VIII

Amendments of the Financial Services Act 1986

Statements of principle

192. In Chapter V of Part I of the Financial Services Act 1986 (conduct of investment business), after section 47 insert—

"**Statements of principle**

47A.—(1) The Secretary of State may issue statements of principle with respect to the conduct and financial standing expected of persons authorised to carry on investment business.

(2) The conduct expected may include compliance with a code or standard issued by another person, as for the time being in force, and may allow for the exercise of discretion by any person pursuant to any such code or standard.

(3) Failure to comply with a statement of principle under this section is a ground for the taking of disciplinary action or the exercise of powers of intervention, but it does not of itself give rise to any right of action by investors or other persons affected or affect the validity of any transaction.

(4) The disciplinary action which may be taken by virtue of subsection (3) is—
  (a) the withdrawal or suspension of authorisation under section 28 or the termination or suspension of authorisation under section 33,
  (b) the giving of a disqualification direction under section 59,
  (c) the making of a public statement under section 60, or
  (d) the application by the Secretary of State for an injunction, interdict or other order under section 61(1);

and the reference in that subsection to powers of intervention is to the powers conferred by Chapter VI of this Part.

(5) Where a statement of principle relates to compliance with a code or standard issued by another person, the statement of principle may provide—
  (a) that failure to comply with the code or standard shall be a ground for the taking of disciplinary action, or the exercise of powers of intervention, only in such cases and to such extent as may be specified; and
  (b) that no such action shall be taken, or any such power exercised, except at the request of the person by whom the code or standard in question was issued.

(6) The Secretary of State shall exercise his powers in such manner as appears to him appropriate to secure compliance with statements of principle under this section.

Modification or waiver of statements of principle in particular cases

47B.—(1) The relevant regulatory authority may on the application of any person—
  (a) modify a statement of principle issued under section 47A so as to adapt it to his circumstances or to any particular kind of business carried on by him, or
  (b) dispense him from compliance with any such statement of principle, generally or in relation to any particular kind of business carried on by him.

(2) The powers conferred by this section shall not be exercised unless it appears to the relevant regulatory authority—
  (a) that compliance with the statement of principle in question

would be unduly burdensome for the applicant having regard to the benefit which compliance would confer on investors, and
  (b) that the exercise of those powers will not result in any undue risk to investors.

(3) The powers conferred by this section may be exercised unconditionally or subject to conditions; and section 47A(3) applies in the case of failure to comply with a condition as in the case of failure to comply with a statement of principle.

(4) The relevant regulatory authority for the purposes of this section is—
  (a) in the case of a member of a recognised self-regulating organisation or professional body, in relation to investment business in the carrying on of which he is subject to the rules of the organisation or body, that organisation or body;
  (b) in any other case, or in relation to other investment business, the Secretary of State.

(5) The references in paragraph 4(1) of Schedule 2 and paragraph 4(2) of Schedule 3 (requirements for recognition of self-regulating organisations and professional bodies) to monitoring and enforcement of compliance with statements of principle include monitoring and enforcement of compliance with conditions imposed by the organisation or body under this section.".

GENERAL NOTE

The Financial Services Act 1986 aimed to protect investors by licensing and regulating the conduct of persons engaged in investment business or the securities industry. The Secretary of State delegated most of the day to day implementation of his regulatory function to the Securities and Investments Board (S.I.B.) which compiled a large rulebook applicable to persons directly authorised to conduct investment business by it and which served as a model for the rulebooks of the self regulatory organisations (SROs) and recognised professional bodies (RPBs) which had to be equivalent to that of the S.I.B. Membership of one or other of the SROs or RPBs provides the member with authorisation to conduct the type of investment business coming within the regulatory scope of that organisation or body.

The Government subsequently took the view that the various rulebooks had become too complex, cumbersome and costly to implement and that desired flexibility had gone out of the system. Pt. VIII, *inter alia*, aims to provide renewed flexibility. The new amendments are designed to enable the S.I.B. and the SROs to rewrite their existing rulebooks in the form of a new three-tier system comprising: statements of principle, codes of conduct and more detailed rules made to suit the particular needs of each SRO.

Note the provisions of Pt. VIII of this Act are merely enabling provisions and provide absolutely no clue as to the proposed content of principles or codes of conduct. The S.I.B. will promulgate general principles, breaches of which will give rise to disciplinary proceedings only and may require SROs to adopt these same principles for similar purposes. Secondly, the S.I.B. will be able to require all SROs to adopt so many of the S.I.B.'s rules as are designated for this purpose by the board. These so-called "core rules" or second tier will have the same status as any other rules. Any breach of them may give rise to civil liability under s.62.

The third tier will be provided by both the S.I.B. and the SROs in that they will be able to supplement the rules with guidance as to the application of those rules in particular cases. A breach of that guidance would not in itself constitute breach of a rule, but could be used as evidence of such a breach.

This section inserts two new sections after s.47 in the Financial Services Act 1986. The new s.47A empowers the S.I.B. to issue a statement of principles which will be the guiding light to firms engaged in investment business. The conduct expected may include compliance with a code or standard issued by it or by one of the SROs (namely: T.S.A., F.I.M.B.R.A., L.A.U.T.R.O., I.M.R.O. or A.F.B.D.) or by one of the RPBs (*e.g.* The Law Society).

The breach of such a statement will give rise to disciplinary consequences or the exercise of the S.I.B.'s powers of intervention. It will not give rise to a right of civil action for investors under s.62 of the Financial Services Act 1986, nor will it affect the validity of any transaction.

The section specifies the disciplinary action that may be taken by the S.I.B. or by any of the SROs or RPBs.

The new s.47B would permit any person who is subject to regulation to apply to the regulator concerned to modify or dispense with any of its statements of principle in so far as they apply to him. The regulator may do so if the likely benefit to investors is outweighed by the burden of compliance or because there is no undue risk to investors. Any modification or dispensation may be subject to conditions, and failure to comply with them gives rise to the same sort of disciplinary actions as in the case of failure to comply with a principle. The Secretary of State has made it clear, however, that the Government has no intention of implementing s.47B because of the way in which the S.I.B. proposes to exercise the power given in s.47A, but it may be that the S.I.B. in the future will choose to use its principle-making power more widely, at which point the waiving of certain principles might become appropriate in some cases.

Restriction of right to bring action for contravention of rules, regulations, &c.

193.—(1) In Chapter V of Part I of the Financial Services Act 1986 (conduct of investment business), after section 62 (actions for damages) insert—

"**Restriction of right of action**

62A.—(1) No action in respect of a contravention to which section 62 above applies shall lie at the suit of a person other than a private investor, except in such circumstances as may be specified by regulations made by the Secretary of State.

(2) The meaning of the expression "private investor" for the purposes of subsection (1) shall be defined by regulations made by the Secretary of State.

(3) Regulations under subsection (1) may make different provision with respect to different cases.

(4) The Secretary of State shall, before making any regulations affecting the right to bring an action in respect of a contravention of any rules or regulations made by a person other than himself, consult that person.".

(2) In section 114(5) of the Financial Services Act 1986 (transfer of functions to designated agency: excluded functions), after paragraph (d) insert—

"(dd) section 62A;".

(3) In Schedule 11 to the Financial Services Act 1986 (friendly societies), after paragraph 22 insert—

"22A.—(1) No action in respect of a contravention to which paragraph 22(4) above applies shall lie at the suit of a person other than a private investor, except in such circumstances as may be specified by regulations made by the Registrar.

(2) The meaning of the expression "private investor" for the purposes of sub-paragraph (1) shall be defined by regulations made by the Registrar.

(3) Regulations under sub-paragraph (1) may make different provision with respect to different cases.

(4) The Registrar shall, before making any regulations affecting the right to bring an action in respect of a contravention of any rules or regulations made by a person other than himself, consult that person.".

(4) In paragraph 28(5) of Schedule 11 to the Financial Services Act1986 (transfer of Registrar's functions to transferee body), after "paragraphs 2 to 25" insert "(except paragraph 22A)".

GENERAL NOTE

This section inserts a new s.62A after s.62 of the Financial Services Act 1986 which allows civil actions for damages if an investor suffers loss as a result of a breach of the rules made under that Act.

S.62A prevents certain categories of investors from suing under s.62. The aim is to limit the right of action to private investors and deny it to professionals. Professionals will not be able to sue each other for breach of rules. There is, however, power to extend the ambit of the section to include "non-private" investors by regulations made by the Secretary of State. Likewise the term "private investor" will be defined in due course in regulations made by him. Note, this power is not delegable to the S.I.B.

The section makes corresponding provision by amending Sched. 11 to that Act for friendly societies.

Application of designated rules and regulations to members of self-regulating organisations

194. In Chapter V of Part I of the Financial Services Act 1986 (conduct of investment business), after section 63 insert—

"**Application of designated rules and regulations to members of self-regulating organisations**

63A.—(1) The Secretary of State may in rules and regulations under—
 (a) section 48 (conduct of business rules),
 (b) section 49 (financial resources rules),
 (c) section 55 (clients' money regulations), or
 (d) section 56 (regulations as to unsolicited calls),
designate provisions which apply, to such extent as may be specified, to a member of a recognised self-regulating organisation in respect of investment business in the carrying on of which he is subject to the rules of the organisation.

(2) It may be provided that the designated rules or regulations have effect, generally or to such extent as may be specified, subject to the rules of the organisation.

(3) A member of a recognised self-regulating organisation who contravenes a rule or regulation applying to him by virtue of this section shall be treated as having contravened the rules of the organisation.

(4) It may be provided that, to such extent as may be specified, the designated rules or regulations may not be modified or waived (under section 63B below or section 50) in relation to a member of a recognised self-regulating organisation.

Where such provision is made any modification or waiver previously granted shall cease to have effect, subject to any transitional provision or saving contained in the rules or regulations.

(5) Except as mentioned in subsection (1), the rules and regulations referred to in that subsection do not apply to a member of a recognised self-regulating organisation in respect of investment business in the carrying on of which he is subject to the rules of the organisation.

Modification or waiver of designated rules and regulations

63B.—(1) A recognised self-regulating organisation may on the application of a member of the organisation—
 (a) modify a rule or regulation designated under section 63A so as to adapt it to his circumstances or to any particular kind of business carried on by him, or
 (b) dispense him from compliance with any such rule or regulation, generally or in relation to any particular kind of business carried on by him.

(2) The powers conferred by this section shall not be exercised unless it appears to the organisation—
 (a) that compliance with the rule or regulation in question would be unduly burdensome for the applicant having regard to the benefit which compliance would confer on investors, and

(b) that the exercise of those powers will not result in any undue risk to investors.

(3) The powers conferred by this section may be exercised unconditionally or subject to conditions; and section 63A(3) applies in the case of a contravention of a condition as in the case of contravention of a designated rule or regulation.

(4) The reference in paragraph 4(1) of Schedule 2 (requirements for recognition of self-regulating organisations) to monitoring and enforcement of compliance with rules and regulations includes monitoring and enforcement of compliance with conditions imposed by the organisation under this section.".

GENERAL NOTE
This section inserts two new sections after s.63 of the Financial Services Act 1986. The new s.63A provides that the Secretary of State may directly impose rules (the so-called "core rules" or "middle tier"), on members of the SROs in relation to investment business and in relation to which such members are also subject to the rules of the SRO to which they belong. In the way that s.192 permits principles to be waived in certain circumstances, so this section similarly provides for the waiver of these rules (s.63B). The effect of these provisions is to provide the S.I.B. with the power of direct rule of persons engaged in investment business by way of rules, codes of practice, principles and other regulations.

See the general note to s.192.

Codes of practice

195. In Chapter V of Part I of the Financial Services Act 1986 (conduct of investment business), after the sections inserted by section 194 above, insert—

"**Codes of practice**

63C.—(1) The Secretary of State may issue codes of practice with respect to any matters dealt with by statements of principle issued under section 47A or by rules or regulations made under any provision of this Chapter.

(2) In determining whether a person has failed to comply with a statement of principle—
 (a) a failure by him to comply with any relevant provision of a code of practice may be relied on as tending to establish failure to comply with the statement of principle, and
 (b) compliance by him with the relevant provisions of a code of practice may be relied on as tending to negative any such failure.

(3) A contravention of a code of practice with respect to a matter dealt with by rules or regulations shall not of itself give rise to any liability or invalidate any transaction; but in determining whether a person's conduct amounts to contravention of a rule or regulation—
 (a) contravention by him of any relevant provision of a code of practice may be relied on as tending to establish liability, and
 (b) compliance by him with the relevant provisions of a code of practice may be relied on as tending to negative liability.

(4) Where by virtue of section 63A (application of designated rules and regulations to members of self-regulating organisations) rules or regulations—
 (a) do not apply, to any extent, to a member of a recognised self-regulating organisation, or
 (b) apply, to any extent, subject to the rules of the organisation,
a code of practice with respect to a matter dealt with by the rules or regulations may contain provision limiting its application to a corresponding extent.".

GENERAL NOTE
This section inserts another new section after s.63 of the Financial Services Act 1986, which entitles the Secretary of State to issue codes of practice relating to any matters dealt with by statements of principle or rules or regulations made under Pt. VIII. These codes constitute the so-called "third tier" of the new regulatory system, and although breach of a code does not in itself amount to the breach of a rule, it may be used as evidence of such a breach.
See the General Note to s.192.

Relations with other regulatory authorities

196. In Part I of the Financial Services Act 1986 (regulation of investment business), after section 128 insert—

"CHAPTER XV

RELATIONS WITH OTHER REGULATORY AUTHORITIES

Relevance of other controls
128A. In determining—
 (a) in relation to a self-regulating organisation, whether the requirements of Schedule 2 are met, or
 (b) in relation to a professional body, whether the requirements of Schedule 3 are met,
the Secretary of State shall take into account the effect of any other controls to which members of the organisation or body are subject.

Relevance of information given and action taken by other regulatory authorities
128B.—(1) The following provisions apply in the case of—
 (a) a person whose principal place of business is in a country or territory outside the United Kingdom or
 (b) a person whose principal business is other than investment business;
and in relation to such a person "the relevant regulatory authority" means the appropriate regulatory authority in that country or territory or, as the case may be, in relation to his principal business.
(2) The Secretary of State may regard himself as satisfied with respect to any matter relevant for the purposes of this Part if—
 (a) the relevant regulatory authority informs him that it is satisfied with respect to that matter, and
 (b) he is satisfied as to the nature and scope of the supervision exercised by that authority.
(3) In making any decision with respect to the exercise of his powers under this Part in relation to any such person, the Secretary of State may take into account whether the relevant regulatory authority has exercised, or proposes to exercise, its powers in relation to that person.
(4) The Secretary of State may enter into such arrangements with other regulatory authorities as he thinks fit for the purposes of this section.
(5) Where any functions under this Part have been transferred to a designated agency, nothing in this section shall be construed as affecting the responsibility of the Secretary of State for the discharge of Community obligations or other international obligations of the United Kingdom.

Enforcement in support of overseas regulatory authority
128C.—(1) The Secretary of State may exercise his disciplinary

powers or powers of intervention at the request of, or for the purpose of assisting, an overseas regulatory authority.

(2) The disciplinary powers of the Secretary of State means his powers—
  (a) to withdraw or suspend authorisation under section 28 or to terminate or suspend authorisation under section 33,
  (b) to give a disqualification direction under section 59,
  (c) to make a public statement under section 60, or
  (d) to apply for an injunction, interdict or other order under section 61(1);

and the reference to his powers of intervention is to the powers conferred by Chapter VI of this Part.

(3) An "overseas regulatory authority" means an authority in a country or territory outside the United Kingdom which exercises—
  (a) any function corresponding to—
    (i) a function of the Secretary of State under this Act, the Insurance Companies Act 1982 or the Companies Act 1985,
    (ii) a function under this Act of a designated agency, transferee body or competent authority, or
    (iii) a function of the Bank of England under the Banking Act 1987, or
  (b) any functions in connection with the investigation of, or the enforcement of rules (whether or not having the force of law) relating to, conduct of the kind prohibited by the Company Securities (Insider Dealing) Act 1985, or
  (c) any function prescribed for the purposes of this subsection, being a function which in the opinion of the Secretary of State relates to companies or financial services.

(4) In deciding whether to exercise those powers the Secretary of State may take into account, in particular—
  (a) whether corresponding assistance would be given in that country or territory to an authority exercising regulatory functions in the United Kingdom;
  (b) whether the case concerns the breach of a law, or other requirement, which has no close parallel in the United Kingdom or involves the assertion of a jurisdiction not recognised by the United Kingdom;
  (c) the seriousness of the case and its importance to persons in the United Kingdom;
  (d) whether it is otherwise appropriate in the public interest to give the assistance sought.

(5) The Secretary of State may decline to exercise those powers unless the overseas regulatory authority undertakes to make such contribution towards the cost of their exercise as the Secretary of State considers appropriate.

(6) The reference in subsection (3)(c) to financial services includes, in particular, investment business, insurance and banking.".

GENERAL NOTE

This section inserts three new sections after s.128 of the Financial Services Act 1986. They provide that the Secretary of State may exercise his disciplinary powers or powers of intervention at the request of, or for the purpose of assisting, an overseas regulatory authority.

Note that no breach of U.K. law or rules is necessary before this power may come into operation.

This section also defines an "overseas regulatory authority" and specifies the matters the Secretary of State may take into account in deciding whether to exercise disciplinary or intervention powers. These matters both correspond closely to the provisions in s.82 relating to the exercise of investigative power to assist overseas regulators. In relation to s.196, the type of assistance available would be the withdrawal or suspension of authorisation, a disqualification direction under s.59, a public statement under s.60 of the Financial Services Act 1986, or an application for an injunction.

An overseas regulator must be one whose functions correspond generally to the D.T.I. responsibilities in relation to companies, banking, financial services and insurance, or which generally relates to companies or financial services. The overseas regulator may have to pay for the service provided.

Construction of references to incurring civil liability

197.—(1) In section 150(6) of the Financial Services Act 1986 (exclusion of liability in respect of false or misleading listing particulars), at the end insert—

"The reference above to a person incurring liability includes a reference to any other person being entitled as against that person to be granted any civil remedy or to rescind or repudiate any agreement.".

(2) In section 154(5) of the Financial Services Act 1986 (exclusion of civil liability in respect of advertisements or other information in connection with listing application), at the end insert—

"The reference above to a person incurring civil liability includes a reference to any other person being entitled as against that person to be granted any civil remedy or to rescind or repudiate any agreement.".

GENERAL NOTE

This section, together with ss.198, 199 and 202, deals with certain changes in Pts. IV and V of the Financial Services Act 1986 relating to listing particulars and prospectuses.

This section amends ss.150 and 154 of that Act. Those sections are concerned to provide *inter alia* that those persons responsible for listing particulars and advertising in respect of listing particulars are liable to pay compensation to anyone suffering loss as a result of omission of information which should have been included or for the failure to disclose significant changes which occur between publication of the listing particulars and the commencement of dealings. In addition, both sections provide exemptions from liability.

S.150(6) exempts a person responsible for false or misleading listing particulars if he was not required to disclose the omitted information in question or was entitled to omit it by virtue of s.148. S.154(5) exempts a person who issues, or who is responsible for the content of, listing particulars which have been authorised or approved in certain circumstances. The new subsections simply extend the scope of both these exemptions identically, so that nobody may be granted any civil remedy or be entitled to rescind or repudiate any agreement against someone who is excluded from liability for the content of listing particulars or associated advertisements. Those responsible for the published information who are exempt from liability are exempt from civil actions or rescission or repudiation of any consequent agreement.

Offers of unlisted securities

198.—(1) In Part V of the Financial Services Act 1986 (offers of unlisted securities), after section 160 insert—

"Exemptions

160A.—(1) The Secretary of State may by order exempt from sections 159 and 160 when issued in such circumstances as may be specified in the order—
 (a) advertisements appearing to him to have a private character, whether by reason of a connection between the person issuing them and those to whom they are addressed or otherwise;
 (b) advertisements appearing to him to deal with investments only incidentally;
 (c) advertisements issued to persons appearing to him to be sufficiently expert to understand any risks involved;
 (d) such other classes of advertisements as he thinks fit.

(2) The Secretary of State may by order exempt from sections 159 and 160 an advertisement issued in whatever circumstances which relates to securities appearing to him to be of a kind that can be expected normally to be bought or dealt in only by persons sufficiently expert to understand any risks involved.

(3) An order under subsection (1) or (2) may require a person who by virtue of the order is authorised to issue an advertisement to comply with such requirements as are specified in the order.

(4) An order made by virtue of subsection (1)(a), (b) or (c) or subsection (2) shall be subject to annulment in pursuance of a resolution of either House of Parliament; and no order shall be made by virtue of subsection (1)(d) unless a draft of it has been laid before and approved by a resolution of each House of Parliament.".

(2) The following amendments of the Financial Services Act 1986 are consequential on that above.

(3) In section 159, in subsection (1) omit the words from the beginning to "section 161 below," and after subsection (2) insert—

"(3) Subsection (1) above has effect subject to section 160A (exemptions) and section 161 (exceptions).".

(4) In section 160, in subsection (1) omit the words from the beginning to "section 161 below," and for subsections (6) to (9) substitute—

"(6) Subsection (1) above has effect subject to section 160A (exemptions) and section 161 (exceptions).".

(5) In section 171, in subsection (1)(b) and subsection (3) for "section 160(6) or (7)" substitute "section 160A".

GENERAL NOTE

This section amends Pt. V of the Financial Services Act 1986 concerning the offer to the public of unlisted securities. It inserts a new section after s.160 of that Act which enables the Secretary of State to exercise regulation-making powers in the same terms as the powers in s.160 (other offers of securities) and s.159 (offers of securities on admission to approved exchange), and makes the necessary changes to ss.159, 160 and 171 consequential on that new provision.

Offers of securities by private companies and old public companies

199. In Part V of the Financial Services Act 1986 (offers of unlisted securities), in section 170 (advertisements by private companies and old public companies), for subsections (2) to (4) substitute—

"(2) The Secretary of State may by order exempt from subsection (1) when issued in such circumstances as may be specified in the order—

(a) advertisements appearing to him to have a private character, whether by reason of a connection between the person issuing them and those to whom they are addressed or otherwise;

(b) advertisements appearing to him to deal with investments only incidentally;

(c) advertisements issued to persons appearing to him to be sufficiently expert to understand any risks involved;

(d) such other classes of advertisements as he thinks fit.

(3) The Secretary of State may by order exempt from subsection (1) an advertisement issued in whatever circumstances which relates to securities appearing to him to be of a kind that can be expected normally to be bought or dealt in only by persons sufficiently expert to understand any risks involved.

(4) An order under subsection (2) or (3) may require a person who by virtue of the order is authorised to issue an advertisement to comply with such requirements as are specified in the order.

(4A) An order made by virtue of subsection (2)(a), (b) or (c) or subsection (3) shall be subject to annulment in pursuance of a resolution of either House of Parliament; and no order shall be made by virtue of subsection (2)(d) unless a draft of it has been laid before and approved by a resolution of each House of Parliament.".

GENERAL NOTE

This section amends s.170 of the Financial Services Act 1986 (advertisement by private companies and old public companies) in Pt. V of that Act which regulates the offer of unlisted securities.

S.170 precludes such companies from issuing or causing to be issued in the U.K. any advertisement offering securities to be issued by that company. The new section substitutes three subsections which now permit the Secretary of State by order to make exemptions from that prohibition on the same grounds as provided in s.198 of this Act and in s.160 of the Act which it amended and which permits regulations to allow public limited companies making offerings of their securities to dispense with the requirement of publishing a prospectus.

Jurisdiction of High Court and Court of Session

200.—(1) In the Financial Services Act 1986, for section 188 (jurisdiction as respects actions concerning designated agency, &c.), substitute—

"**Jurisdiction of High Court and Court of Session**

188.—(1) Proceedings arising out of any act or omission (or proposed act or omission) of—
(a) a recognised self-regulating organisation,
(b) a designated agency,
(c) a transferee body, or
(d) the competent authority,
in the discharge or purported discharge of any of its functions under this Act may be brought in the High Court or the Court of Session.

(2) The jurisdiction conferred by subsection (1) is in addition to any other jurisdiction exercisable by those courts.".

(2) In Schedule 5 to the Civil Jurisdiction and Judgments Act 1982 (proceedings excluded from general provisions as to allocation of jurisdiction within the United Kingdom), for paragraph 10 substitute—

"*Financial Services Act 1986*

10. Proceedings such as are mentioned in section 188 of the Financial Services Act 1986.".

GENERAL NOTE

This section replaces the previous s.188 of the Financial Services Act 1986. It clarifies that proceedings can be taken against an SRO in any part of the U.K. regardless of whether it has a presence there. The previous s.188 had established that to be the case only in relation to the S.I.B. or the International Stock Exchange in its capacity as the competent authority under Pt. IV of that Act. Unlike those bodies, the SRO's powers depend on *contractual* relationships with their members, not statute, but because they perform functions analogous to those of a public authority they are now to be treated as such for jurisdictional purposes.

Directions to secure compliance with international obligations

201. In the Financial Services Act 1986, for section 192 (international obligations) substitute—

"**International obligations**

192.—(1) If it appears to the Secretary of State—
(a) that any action proposed to be taken by an authority or body to which this section applies would be incompatible

with Community obligations or any other international obligations of the United Kingdom, or

(b) that any action which that authority or body has power to take is required for the purpose of implementing any such obligation,

he may direct the authority or body not to take or, as the case may be, to take the action in question.

(2) The authorities and bodies to which this section applies are the following—

(a) a recognised self-regulating organisation,
(b) a recognised investment exchange (other than an overseas investment exchange),
(c) a recognised clearing house (other than an overseas clearing house),
(d) a designated agency,
(e) a transferee body,
(f) a competent authority.

(3) This section also applies to an approved exchange within the meaning of Part V of this Act in respect of any action which it proposes to take or has power to take in respect of rules applying to a prospectus by virtue of a direction under section 162(3) above.

(4) A direction under this section may include such supplementary or incidental requirements as the Secretary of State thinks necessary or expedient.

(5) Where the function of making or revoking a recognition order in respect of an authority or body to which this section applies is exercisable by a designated agency, any direction in respect of that authority or body shall be a direction requiring the agency to give the authority or body such a direction as is specified in the direction given by the Secretary of State.

(6) A direction under this section is enforceable, on the application of the person who gave it, by injunction or, in Scotland, by an order under section 45 of the Court of Session Act 1988.".

GENERAL NOTE

This section substitutes a new provision for s.192 of the Financial Services Act 1986 empowering the Secretary of State to give directions to secure compliance with international obligations. The new subs. (1) is largely the same in that it still provides that any SRO, designated agency (S.I.B.), transferee body or competent authority can be directed to cease to breach, or directed to comply with the Community or international obligations of the U.K. In addition, the section is now extended to include within that power RIEs and RCHs (*i.e.* recognised investment exchanges and clearing houses).

Offers of short-dated debentures

202. In section 195 of the Financial Services Act 1986 (circumstances in which certain offers of debentures not treated as offers to the public), for "repaid within less than one year of the date of issue" substitute "repaid within five years of the date of issue".

GENERAL NOTE

This section extends s.195 of the Financial Services Act 1986 to allow short-dated debentures, primarily sterling commercial paper to have a maturity date up to five years (compared to the previous limit of one year) without being treated as an offer to the public requiring a prospectus. This is a further step in the deregularisation of the sterling capital market which only concerns professional investors.

Standard protection for investors

203.—(1) In Schedule 2 to the Financial Services Act 1986 (requirements for recognition of self-regulating organisations), in paragraph 3 (safeguards for investors) for sub-paragraphs (1) and (2) substitute—

"(1) The organisation must have rules governing the carrying on of investment business by its members which, together with the statements of principle, rules, regulations and codes of practice to which its members are subject under Chapter V of Part I of this Act, are such as to afford an adequate level of protection for investors.

(2) In determining in any case whether an adequate level of protection is afforded for investors of any description, regard shall be had to the nature of the investment business carried on by members of the organisation, the kinds of investors involved and the effectiveness of the organisation's arrangements for enforcing compliance.".

(2) In Schedule 3 to the Financial Services Act 1986 (requirements for recognition of professional bodies), for paragraph 3 (safeguards for investors) substitute—

"3.—(1) The body must have rules regulating the carrying on of investment business by persons certified by it which, together with the statements of principle, rules, regulations and codes of practice to which those persons are subject under Chapter V of Part I of this Act, afford an adequate level of protection for investors.

(2) In determining in any case whether an adequate level of protection is afforded for investors of any description, regard shall be had to the nature of the investment business carried on by persons certified by the body, the kinds of investors involved and the effectiveness of the body's arrangements for enforcing compliance.".

(3) The order bringing this section into force may provide that, for a transitional period, a self-regulating organisation or professional body may elect whether to comply with the new requirement having effect by virtue of subsection (1) or (2) above or with the requirement which it replaces.

The Secretary of State may by order specify when the transitional period is to end.

GENERAL NOTE

This section amends Scheds. 2 and 3 of the Financial Services Act 1986 in what appears to be a relatively minor fashion but which is, in fact, of major significance. Under that Act the rulebooks of the SROs had to be "equivalent". The term "equivalence" was narrowly interpreted as requiring a close textual comparison of different sets of rules rather than a comparison of their effects. The S.I.B.'s emphasis on line-by-line equivalence meant in effect corresponding or the same rules and any deviation in the rulebook of one SRO was approved only with difficulty.

This section, by substituting in effect the term "adequate" for "equivalent", is a move away from the narrow view, so permitting SROs to draw up detailed rules that are appropriate for their particular membership and which deviate from the model rulebook provided by the S.I.B.

Note, again, this is only an enabling provision and tells the reader nothing about the content of such rules or how they will interact with principles (s.192) and codes (s.195). What s.203 requires is that for an SRO to be recognised, it must have rules governing the carrying on of investment business which together with the statements of principle, rules, regulations and codes of practice to which its members are subject "are such as to afford an adequate level of protection for investors". To determine whether that is satisfied, regard is to be had to the nature of the investment business of the members, the kinds of investors concerned and the effectiveness of the SRO's arrangements for compliance.

Similar provisions are made for recognised professional bodies (RPBs). SROs and RPBs will have a transitional period before the new test becomes mandatory.

Costs of compliance

204.—(1) In Schedule 2 to the Financial Services Act 1986 (requirements for recognition of self-regulating organisations), after paragraph 3 insert—

"Taking account of costs of compliance

3A. The organisation must have satisfactory arrangements for taking account, in framing its rules, of the cost to those to whom the rules would apply of complying with those rules and any other controls to which they are subject.";

and in Schedule 3 to that Act (requirements for recognition of professional body), after paragraph 3 insert—

"Taking account of costs of compliance

3A. The body must have satisfactory arrangements for taking account, in framing its rules, of the cost to those to whom the rules would apply of complying with those rules and any other controls to which they are subject.".

(2) The additional requirements having effect by virtue of subsection (1) do not affect the status of a self-regulating organisation or professional body recognised before the commencement of that subsection; but if the Secretary of State is of the opinion that any of those requirements is not met in the case of such an organisation or body, he shall within one month of commencement give notice to the organisation or body stating his opinion.

(3) Where the Secretary of State gives such a notice, he shall not—
   (a) take action to revoke the recognition of such an organisation or body on the ground that any of the additional requirements is not met, unless he considers it essential to do so in the interests of investors, or
   (b) apply on any such ground for a compliance order under section 12 of the Financial Services Act 1986,

until after the end of the period of six months beginning with the date on which the notice was given.

(4) In Schedule 7 to the Financial Services Act 1986 (qualifications of designated agency), after paragraph 2 insert—

"Taking account of costs of compliance

2A.—(1) The agency must have satisfactory arrangements for taking account, in framing any provisions which it proposes to make in the exercise of its legislative functions, of the cost to those to whom the provisions would apply of complying with those provisions and any other controls to which they are subject.

(2) In this paragraph "legislative functions" means the functions of issuing or making statements of principle, rules, regulations or codes of practice.".

(5) The additional requirement having effect by virtue of subsection (4) above does not affect the status of a designated agency to which functions have been transferred before the commencement of that subsection; but if the Secretary of State is of the opinion the requirement is not met in the case of such an agency, he shall within one month of commencement give notice to the agency stating his opinion.

(6) Where the Secretary of State gives such a notice, he shall not take action under section 115(2) of the Financial Services Act 1986 to resume

any functions exercisable by such an agency on the ground that the additional requirement is not met until after the end of the period of six months beginning with the date on which the notice was given.

(7) References in this section to a recognised self-regulating organisation include a recognised self-regulating organisation for friendly societies and references to a designated agency include a transferee body (within the meaning of that Act).

In relation to such an organisation or body—
> (a) references to the Secretary of State shall be construed as references to the Registrar (within the meaning of Schedule 11 to the Financial Services Act 1986), and
> (b) the reference to section 12 of that Act shall be construed as a reference to paragraph 6 of that Schedule.

GENERAL NOTE

This section inserts a new paragraph into Scheds. 2 and 3 of the Financial Services Act 1986 concerning the costs of compliance. These changes mean that one of the criteria by which "adequacy" will be judged is cost. An SRO or RPB is required to have satisfactory arrangements for taking account, in framing its rules, of the costs to its members of implementation or compliance. This is intended to ensure one of the original objects of the Act, which was to provide investor protection in an efficient, flexible and economic way. The Secretary of State is empowered to notify any SRO or RPB that he is not satisfied with their performance in this regard, but except in essential instances he cannot revoke recognition or seek a compliance order against such a body for a further period of six months.

Requirements for recognition of investment exchange

205.—(1) In Schedule 4 to the Financial Services Act 1986 (requirements for recognition of investment exchange), after paragraph 5 insert—

"Supplementary

> 6.—(1) The provisions of this Schedule relate to an exchange only so far as it provides facilities for the carrying on of investment business; and nothing in this Schedule shall be construed as requiring an exchange to limit dealings on the exchange to dealings in investments.
>
> (2) The references in this Schedule, and elsewhere in this Act, to ensuring the performance of transactions on an exchange are to providing satisfactory procedures (including default procedures) for the settlement of transactions on the exchange.".

(2) The above amendment shall be deemed always to have had effect.

(3) In section 207(1) of the Financial Services Act 1986 (interpretation), at the appropriate place insert—

> " "ensure" and "ensuring", in relation to the performance of transactions on an investment exchange, have the meaning given in paragraph 6 of Schedule 4 to this Act;".

GENERAL NOTE

This section makes it clear that the requirements for recognition of an investment exchange (RIE) set out in Sched. 4 to the Financial Services Act 1986 do not prevent an RIE from providing facilities for dealings in things other than investments as defined by Sched. 1 to that Act (*e.g.* physical commodities). Sched. 4 would not apply to these non-investments.

The section also clarifies that ensuring performance on an exchange means providing a satisfactory method for settling transactions including procedures in the event of default by one or other of the parties to a transaction on the exchange.

Consequential amendments and delegation of functions on commencement

206.—(1) The Financial Services Act 1986 has effect with the amendments specified in Schedule 23 which are consequential on the amendments made by sections 192, 194 and 195.

(2) If immediately before the commencement of any provision of this Part which amends Part I of the Financial Services Act 1986—
  (a) a designated agency is exercising by virtue of a delegation order under section 114 of that Act any functions of the Secretary of State under that Part, and
  (b) no draft order is lying before Parliament resuming any of those functions,

the order bringing that provision into force may make, in relation to any functions conferred on the Secretary of State by the amendment, any such provision as may be made by an order under that section.

(3) If immediately before the commencement of any provision of Schedule 23 which amends Part III of the Financial Services Act 1986—
  (a) a transferee body (within the meaning of that Act) is exercising by virtue of a transfer order under paragraph 28 of Schedule 11 to that Act any functions of the Registrar under that Part, and
  (b) no draft order is lying before Parliament resuming any of those functions,

the order bringing that provision into force may make, in relation to any functions conferred on the Registrar by the amendment, any such provision as may be made by an order under that paragraph.

(4) References in the Financial Services Act 1986 to a delegation order made under section 114 of that Act or to a transfer order made under paragraph 28 of Schedule 11 to that Act include an order made containing any such provision as is authorised by subsection (2) or (3).

GENERAL NOTE

This section will bring Sched. 23 into effect on a date to be announced by the Secretary of State by statutory instrument. That Schedule makes amendments to the Financial Services Act 1986 which are necessary to accommodate the amendments made by ss.192, 194 and 195 of this Act and makes those changes effective in situations where the Secretary of State's functions under the Act have been previously delegated to a designated agency.

PART IX

TRANSFER OF SECURITIES

Transfer of securities

207.—(1) The Secretary of State may make provision by regulations for enabling title to securities to be evidenced and transferred without a written instrument.

In this section—
  (a) "securities" means shares, stock, debentures, debenture stock, loan stock, bonds, units of a collective investment scheme within the meaning of the Financial Services Act 1986 and other securities of any description;
  (b) references to title to securities include any legal or equitable interest in securities; and
  (c) references to a transfer of title include a transfer by way of security.

(2) The regulations may make provision—
  (a) for procedures for recording and transferring title to securities, and

(b) for the regulation of those procedures and the persons responsible for or involved in their operation.

(3) The regulations shall contain such safeguards as appear to the Secretary of State appropriate for the protection of investors and for ensuring that competition is not restricted, distorted or prevented.

(4) The regulations may for the purpose of enabling or facilitating the operation of the new procedures make provision with respect to the rights and obligations of persons in relation to securities dealt with under the procedures.

But the regulations shall be framed so as to secure that the rights and obligations in relation to securities dealt with under the new procedures correspond, so far as practicable, with those which would arise apart from any regulations under this section.

(5) The regulations may include such supplementary, incidental and transitional provisions as appear to the Secretary of State to be necessary or expedient.

In particular, provision may be made for the purpose of giving effect to—
(a) the transmission of title to securities by operation of law;
(b) any restriction on the transfer of title to securities arising by virtue of the provisions of any enactment or instrument, court order or agreement;
(c) any power conferred by any such provision on a person to deal with securities on behalf of the person entitled.

(6) The regulations may make provision with respect to the persons responsible for the operation of the new procedures—
(a) as to the consequences of their insolvency or incapacity, or
(b) as to the transfer from them to other persons of their functions in relation to the new procedures.

(7) The regulations may for the purposes mentioned above—
(a) modify or exclude any provision of any enactment or instrument, or any rule of law;
(b) apply, with such modifications as may be appropriate, the provisions of any enactment or instrument (including provisions creating criminal offences);
(c) require the payment of fees, or enable persons to require the payment of fees, of such amounts as may be specified in the regulations or determined in accordance with them;
(d) empower the Secretary of State to delegate to any person willing and able to discharge them any functions of his under the regulations.

(8) The regulations may make different provision for different cases.

(9) Regulations under this section shall be made by statutory instrument; and no such regulations shall be made unless a draft of the instrument has been laid before and approved by resolution of each House of Parliament.

GENERAL NOTE
For background information see the Introductory Note to Part IX above.

Subss. (1) and (9)
These subsections confer power on the Secretary of State to introduce the paperless system for recording title and transfer of securities. The regulations are subject to the affirmative resolution mechanism for Parliamentary control. Some idea of the possible content of these regulations is furnished by the following subsections.

Subs. (2)
This confers discretion on the Secretary of State to make provision in the regulations for certain specified matters.

Subs. (3)
By way of contrast with subs. (2), these items *must* be covered in the forthcoming regulations but, notwithstanding this obligation, there is still considerable discretion vested in the Secretary of State.

Subs. (4)
There is an important rider to note in that the new system should not be constructed in such a way so as to create rights and obligations that are substantially out of line with those arising under the existing regime for recording title and transfer of shares.

Subss. (5)–(8)
These subsections give hints as to what the regulations might contain, though it is clear from ss.(5) and (8) that the Secretary of State has a Pandora's box at his disposal, including the now common Henry VIII clause in subs. (7).

Subs. (9)
The use of the affirmative resolution procedure is becoming rare in Company Law reform and its utilisation in this context is perhaps an indication of the sensitivity felt by the Government in introducing such a major change of Company Law philosophy by delegated legislation.

PART X

MISCELLANEOUS AND GENERAL PROVISIONS

Miscellaneous

Summary proceedings in Scotland for offences in connection with disqualification of directors

208. In section 21 of the Company Directors Disqualification Act 1986 (application of provisions of the Insolvency Act 1986), after subsection (3) add—

> "(4) For the purposes of summary proceedings in Scotland, section 431 of that Act applies to summary proceedings for an offence under section 11 or 13 of this Act as it applies to summary proceedings for an offence under Parts I to VII of that Act.".

GENERAL NOTE

This adds another subsection to s.21 of the Company Directors Disqualification Act 1986 so as to deal with the question of summary proceedings in Scotland for certain offences in connection with the disqualification of directors—*i.e.* an undischarged bankrupt acting as a director without the leave of the court or acting whilst disqualified. The effect of this amendment is to harmonise the law in England and Scotland—see the discussion in Standing Committee D, H.C., col. 686, June 26, 1989.

Prosecutions in connection with insider dealing

209. In section 8 of the Company Securities (Insider Dealing) Act 1985 (punishment of contraventions), in subsection (2) (institution of proceedings in England and Wales), for "by the Secretary of State or by, or with the consent of, the Director of Public Prosecutions" substitute "by, or with the consent of, the Secretary of State or the Director of Public Prosecutions".

GENERAL NOTE

This rewords s.8(2) of the Companies Securities (Insider Dealing) Act 1985 so as to clarify who has the power to institute, or give permission for, a prosecution for insider dealing. The effect of the change is to widen the prosecution options by allowing the Secretary of State to consent to prosecutions brought by third parties, such as the International Stock

Exchange—see the explanation given in Standing Committee D, H.C., col. 687, June 26, 1989.

Restriction of duty to supply statement of premium income

210.—(1) Schedule 3 to the Policyholders Protection Act 1975 (provisions with respect to levies on authorised insurance companies) is amended as follows.

(2) For paragraph 4 (statements of premium income to be sent to Secretary of State) substitute—

"4.—(1) The Secretary of State may by notice in writing require an authorised insurance company to send him a statement of—
  (a) any income of the company for the year preceding that in which the notice is received by the company which is income liable to the general business levy, and
  (b) any income of the company for that year which is income liable to the long term business levy.

(2) An authorised insurance company which receives a notice under this paragraph shall send the statement required by the notice to the Secretary of State within three months of receiving the notice.

(3) Where an authorised insurance company is required under this paragraph to send a statement to the Secretary of State in respect of income of both descriptions mentioned in sub-paragraph (1)(a) and (b) above it shall send a separate statement in respect of income of each description.".

(3) In paragraph 5(3) (application of provisions of the Insurance Companies Act 1982 to failure to meet obligation imposed by paragraph (4) for "the obligation imposed on an insurance company by paragraph 4" substitute "an obligation imposed on an insurance company under paragraph 4".

(4) In paragraph 6 (declaration and enforcement of levies) omit sub-paragraph (4) (provision about notices).

(5) After paragraph 7 insert—

"*Notices under paragraphs 4 and 6*

8. A notice under paragraph 4 or 6 above may be sent by post, and a letter containing such a notice shall be deemed to be properly addressed if it is addressed to the insurance company to which it is sent at its last known place of business in the United Kingdom.".

GENERAL NOTE

Subss. (1)–(5)

These provisions make a number of technical amendments to Sched. 3 of the Policyholders Protection Act 1975, which deals specifically with the supply by insurance companies of statements of premium income to the Secretary of State. The 1975 Act sets in place a scheme to protect policyholders of insurance companies that fail to meet their obligations by establishing a central rescue fund financed by levies from insurance companies to the Secretary of State. The main effect of these amendments, which surfaced in the original Bill, is to confer greater discretion on the Secretary of State when requiring statements of premium income from insurance companies and to relieve such companies from a general obligation to supply details unless requested to do so.

Building societies: miscellaneous amendments

211.—(1) In section 104 of the Building Societies Act 1986 (power to assimilate law relating to building societies and law relating to companies), in subsection (2) (relevant provisions of that Act), omit the word "and" before paragraph (d) and after that paragraph add—
  "; and

(e) section 110 (provisions exempting officers and auditors from liability).".

(2) In Schedule 15 to the Building Societies Act 1986 (application of companies winding-up legislation)—
  (a) in paragraph 1(a) (provisions of Insolvency Act 1986 applied) for "and XII" substitute ", XII and XIII";
  (b) in paragraph 3(2)(b) (adaptations: references to be omitted), omit ", a shadow director".

(3) In the Company Directors Disqualification Act 1986, after section 22 insert—

"**Application of Act to building societies**

22A.—(1) This Act applies to building societies as it applies to companies.

(2) References in this Act to a company, or to a director or an officer of a company include, respectively, references to a building society within the meaning of the Building Societies Act 1986 or to a director or officer, within the meaning of that Act, of a building society.

(3) In relation to a building society the definition of "shadow director" in section 22(5) applies with the substitution of "building society" for "company."

(4) In the application of Schedule 1 to the directors of a building society, references to provisions of the Insolvency Act or the Companies Act include references to the corresponding provisions of the Building Societies Act 1986.".

GENERAL NOTE

Subss. (1) and (2)
These subsections effect a number of amendments to the Building Societies Act 1986.

Subs. (3)
The broad effect of this change is to render directors of building societies subject to the general rules providing for the disqualification of company directors. This reform is consistent with the trend towards assimilating the rules governing building societies with those applicable to limited liability companies in general.

General

Repeals

212. The enactments mentioned in Schedule 24 are repealed to the extent specified there.

GENERAL NOTE
This is a general repealing provision that must be read in the light of Sched. 24. The number of additions introduced by new legislation far outweighs the repeals, with the result that the subject is becoming increasingly unwieldy. Of the repeals, note that there is no future rôle for the following provisions: ss.389, 435, 440, 712 and 715.

Provisions extending to Northern Ireland

213.—(1) The provisions of this Act extend to Northern Ireland so far as they amend, or provide for the amendment of, an enactment which so extends.

(2) So far as any provision of this Act amends the Companies Act 1985 or the Insolvency Act 1986, its application to companies registered or incorporated in Northern Ireland is subject to section 745(1) of the Companies Act 1985 or section 441(2) of the Insolvency Act 1986, as the case may be.

(3) In Part III (investigations and powers to obtain information), sections 82 to 91, (powers exercisable to assist overseas regulatory authorities) extend to Northern Ireland.

(4) Part VI (mergers and related matters) extends to Northern Ireland.

(5) In Part VII (financial markets and insolvency) the following provisions extend to Northern Ireland—
- (a) sections 154 and 155 (introductory provisions and definition of "market contract"),
- (b) section 156 and Schedule 21 (additional requirements for recognition of investment exchange or clearing house),
- (c) sections 157, 160, 162, and 166 to 169 (provisions relating to recognised investment exchanges and clearing houses),
- (d) sections 170 to 172 (power to extend provisions to other financial markets),
- (e) section 184 (indemnity for certain acts), and
- (f) sections 185 to 191 (supplementary provisions).

(6) Part VIII (amendments of Financial Services Act 1986) extends to Northern Ireland.

(7) Part IX (transfer of securities) extends to Northern Ireland.

Subject to any Order made after the passing of this Act by virtue of section 3(1)(a) of the Northern Ireland Constitution Act 1973, the transfer of securities shall not be a transferred matter for the purposes of that Act but shall for the purposes of section 3(2) be treated as specified in Schedule 3 to that Act.

(8) In Part X (miscellaneous and general provisions), this section and sections 214 to 216 (general provisions) extend to Northern Ireland.

(9) Except as mentioned above, the provisions of this Act do not extend to Northern Ireland.

GENERAL NOTE

This section (and the following section) outline how this Act will be rendered applicable (or not, as the case may be) to Northern Ireland. Direct incorporation or Orders in Council may be used to achieve this end—see s.214. Eventually, by whatever constitutional route is chosen, the bulk of the substantive reforms contained in the Companies Act 1989 will be enacted in that Province.

Making of corresponding provision for Northern Ireland

214.—(1) An Order in Council under paragraph 1(1)(b) of Schedule 1 to the Northern Ireland Act 1974 (legislation for Northern Ireland in the interim period) which contains a statement that it is only made for purposes corresponding to the purposes of provisions of this Act to which this section applies—
- (a) shall not be subject to paragraph 1(4) and (5) of that Schedule (affirmative resolution of both Houses of Parliament), but
- (b) shall be subject to annulment in pursuance of a resolution of either House of Parliament.

(2) The provisions of this Act to which this section applies are—
- (a) Parts I to V, and
- (b) Part VII, except sections 156, 157, 169 and Schedule 21.

GENERAL NOTE

These provisions deal with Northern Ireland—see the comment on the previous section.

Commencement and transitional provisions

215.—(1) The following provisions of this Act come into force on Royal Assent—
- (a) in Part V (amendments of company law), section 141 (application to declare dissolution of company void);

(b) in Part VI (mergers)—
   (i) sections 147 to 150, and
   (ii) paragraphs 2 to 12, 14 to 16, 18 to 20, 22 to 25 of Schedule 20, and section 153 so far as relating to those paragraphs;
(c) in Part VIII (amendments of the Financial Services Act 1986), section 202 (offers of short-dated debentures);
(d) in Part X (miscellaneous and general provisions), the repeals made by Schedule 24 in sections 71, 74, 88 and 89 of, and Schedule 9 to, the Fair Trading Act 1973, and section 212 so far as relating to those repeals.

(2) The other provisions of this Act come into force on such day as the Secretary of State may appoint by order made by statutory instrument; and different days may be appointed for different provisions and different purposes.

(3) An order bringing into force any provision may contain such transitional provisions and savings as appear to the Secretary of State to be necessary or expedient.

(4) The Secretary of State may also by order under this section amend any enactment which refers to the commencement of a provision brought into force by the order so as to substitute a reference to the actual date on which it comes into force.

GENERAL NOTE
This is the scheme relating to commencement dates and transitional matters.

Subs. (1)
Matters herein identified come into force on Royal Assent—*i.e.* November 16, 1989.

Subss. (2) and (3)
This is now the standard procedure for implementing companies legislation.

Subs. (4)
This confers latitude on the Secretary of State with regard to commencement dates.

Short title

216. This Act may be cited as the Companies Act 1989.

SCHEDULES

SCHEDULE 1

FORM AND CONTENT OF COMPANY ACCOUNTS

1. Schedule 4 to the Companies Act 1985 (form and content of company accounts) is amended as follows.

Group undertakings

2.—(1) For "group companies", wherever occurring, substitute "group undertakings".
(2) That expression occurs—
   (a) in Balance Sheet Format 1, in Items B.III.1 and 2, C.II.2, C.III.1, E.6 and H.6;
   (b) in Balance Sheet Format 2—
      (i) under the heading "ASSETS", in Items B.III.1 and 2, C.II.2 and C.III.1;
      (ii) under the heading "LIABILITIES", in Item C.6;
   (c) in the Profit and Loss Accounts Formats—
      (i) in Format 1, Item 7;
      (ii) in Format 2, Item 9;
      (iii) in Format 3, Item B.3;
      (iv) in Format 4, Item B.5;

(d) in Notes (15) and (16) to the profit and loss account formats; and
(e) in the second sentence of paragraph 53(2) (exclusion from requirement to state separately certain loans).

Participating interests

3.—(1) For "shares in related companies", wherever occurring, substitute "participating interests".
(2) That expression occurs—
(a) in Balance Sheet Format 1, Item B.III.3;
(b) in Balance Sheet Format 2, under the heading "ASSETS", in Item B.III.3;
(c) in the Profit and Loss Accounts Formats—
(i) in Format 1, Item 8;
(ii) in Format 2, Item 10;
(iii) in Format 3, Item B.4;
(iv) in Format 4, Item B.6.

4.—(1) For "related companies", wherever occurring in any other context, substitute "undertakings in which the company has a participating interest".
(2) Those contexts are—
(a) in Balance Sheet Format 1, in Items B.III.4, C.II.3, E.7 and H.7;
(b) in Balance Sheet Format 2—
(i) under the heading "ASSETS", in Items B.III.4 and C.II.3;
(ii) under the heading "LIABILITIES", in Item C.7.

Consistency of accounting policies

5. For paragraph 11 (consistency of accounting policy from one year to the next) substitute—
"11. Accounting policies shall be applied consistently within the same accounts and from one financial year to the next.".

Revaluation reserve

6. In paragraph 34 (revaluation reserve), for sub-paragraph (3) (circumstances in which reduction of reserve required or permitted) substitute—
"(3) An amount may be transferred from the revaluation reserve—
(a) to the profit and loss account, if the amount was previously charged to that account or represents realised profit, or
(b) on capitalisation;
and the revaluation reserve shall be reduced to the extent that the amounts transferred to it are no longer necessary for the purposes of the valuation method used.
(3A) In sub-paragraph (3)(b) "capitalisation", in relation to an amount standing to the credit of the revaluation reserve, means applying it in wholly or partly paying up unissued shares in the company to be allotted to members of the company as fully or partly paid shares.
(3B) The revaluation reserve shall not be reduced except as mentioned in this paragraph.".

Compliance with accounting standards

7. After paragraph 36 (disclosure of accounting policies) insert—
"36A. It shall be stated whether the accounts have been prepared in accordance with applicable accounting standards and particulars of any material departure from those standards and the reasons for it shall be given.".

Provision for taxation

8. For paragraph 47 (provision for taxation) substitute—
"47. The amount of any provision for deferred taxation shall be stated separately from the amount of any provision for other taxation.".

Loans in connection with assistance for purchase of company's own shares

9. In paragraph 51(2) (disclosure of outstanding loans in connection with certain cases of financial assistance for purchase of company's own shares), after "153(4)(b)" insert ", (bb)".

Obligation to show corresponding amounts for previous financial year

10. In paragraph 58(3) (exceptions from obligation to show corresponding amount for previous financial year), for paragraphs (a) to (c) substitute—
"(a) paragraph 13 of Schedule 4A (details of accounting treatment of acquisitions),
(b) paragraphs 2, 8(3), 16, 21(1)(d), 22(4) and (5), 24(3) and (4) and 27(3) and (4) of Schedule 5 (shareholdings in other undertakings),
(c) Parts II and III of Schedule 6 (loans and other dealings in favour of directors and others), and
(d) paragraphs 42 and 46 above (fixed assets and reserves and provisions).".

Special provisions where company is parent company or subsidiary undertaking

11.—(1) For the heading to Part IV (special provisions where the company is a holding or subsidiary company) substitute—

"PART IV

SPECIAL PROVISIONS WHERE COMPANY IS A PARENT COMPANY OR SUBSIDIARY UNDERTAKING".

(2) In that Part for paragraph 59 substitute—

"*Dealings with or interests in group undertakings*

59. Where a company is a parent company or a subsidiary undertaking and any item required by Part I of this Schedule to be shown in the company's balance sheet in relation to group undertakings includes—
(a) amounts attributable to dealings with or interests in any parent undertaking or fellow subsidiary undertaking, or
(b) amounts attributable to dealings with or interests in any subsidiary undertaking of the company,
the aggregate amounts within paragraphs (a) and (b) respectively shall be shown as separate items, either by way of subdivision of the relevant item in the balance sheet or in a note to the company's accounts.".

(3) After that paragraph insert—

"*Guarantees and other financial commitments in favour of group undertakings*

59A. Commitments within any of sub-paragraphs (1) to (5) of paragraph 50 (guarantees and other financial commitments) which are undertaken on behalf of or for the benefit of—
(a) any parent undertaking or fellow subsidiary undertaking, or
(b) any subsidiary undertaking of the company,
shall be stated separately from the other commitments within that sub-paragraph, and commitments within paragraph (a) shall also be stated separately from those within paragraph (b).".

DEFINITIONS
"accounting policies": Sched. 4, para. 36, C.A. 1985.
"accounting standards": s.19, Sched. 1, para. 7.
"annual accounts": s.22, Sched. 10, para. 15.
"capitalisation (on transfers from revaluation reserves)": Sched. 1, para. 6.
"deferred tax": Sched. 4, para. 54, C.A. 1985; SSAP. 15.
"fellow subsidiary": s.22.
"financial year": s.3, Sched. 10, para. 15.
"group": s.22, SSAP. 14, para. 9.
"group undertaking": s.22, Sched. 9.

"guarantees": Sched. 4, para. 50, C.A. 1985; SSAP. 18.
"parent undertaking": s.21, Sched. 9; SSAP. 14.
"participating interest": s.22, Sched. 3; SSAP. 1.
"provision": Sched. 4, paras. 46, 85–89, C.A. 1985.
"realised profits": s.22; Sched. 10, para. 15.
"subsidiary undertaking": s.144, Sched. 9; SSAP. 14, para. 7.
"undertaking": s.22.

GENERAL NOTE
This Schedule amends Sched. 4 to the 1985 Act, which deals with the Form and Content of Company Accounts.
The main adjustments are as follows:
Paras. 1–4: The phrases "group undertakings" and "participating interests" are respectively substituted for "group companies" and "related companies" throughout the text of Sched. 4.
Para. 5: Para. 11 of Sched. 4, dealing with the consistency of accounting policies, is reworded so that it encompasses consistency within accounts as well as from one year to another.
Para. 6: Para. 34 of Sched. 4, relating to revaluation reserves is modified in respect of the circumstances in which such a reserve may be reduced.
Para. 7: A new para., 36A, is inserted. It relates to the disclosure of accounting policies and requires that the notes to the accounts shall include a statement indicating whether accounting standards have been observed; and, if not, particulars of any material departure, the reasons for it, and its financial effects. This implements a recommendation of the Dearing Committee to the Consultative Committee of Accountancy Bodies in its report, "The Making of Accounting Standards", September 1988 (section 10.3).
Para. 8: Para. 47 is reworded to ensure that the balance on the deferred tax account is specifically stated by a company in the notes to its accounts.
Para. 9: A minor amendment is made to the text of para. 51(2).
Para. 10: Para. 58(3), relieving companies of the obligation to show corresponding previous year's figures for certain items, has been altered to recognise changes in Chapter I of Pt. VII to the 1985 Act introduced in ss.1–24 of the new Act and the implementation of Sched. 4A (see Sched. 2 to the new Act).
Para. 11: The wording of para. 59, covering dealings with or interests in group undertakings, has been amended slightly, and a new para., 59A, has been inserted requiring guarantees and financial commitments to other group undertakings to be shown separately from other guarantees and financial commitments in accordance with the provisions of para. 50.

Section 5(2)

SCHEDULE 2

[SCHEDULE 4A TO THE COMPANIES ACT 1985]

FORM AND CONTENT OF GROUP ACCOUNTS

General rules

1.—(1) Group accounts shall comply so far as practicable with the provisions of Schedule 4 as if the undertakings included in the consolidation ("the group") were a single company.
(2) In particular, for the purposes of paragraph 59 of that Schedule (dealings with or interests in group undertakings) as it applies to group accounts—
(a) any subsidiary undertakings of the parent company not included in the consolidation shall be treated as subsidiary undertakings of the group, and
(b) if the parent company is itself a subsidiary undertaking, the group shall be treated as a subsidiary undertaking of any parent undertaking of that company, and the reference to fellow-subsidiary undertakings shall be construed accordingly.
(3) Where the parent company is treated as an investment company for the purposes of Part V of that Schedule (special provisions for investment companies) the group shall be similarly treated.
2.—(1) The consolidated balance sheet and profit and loss account shall incorporate in full the information contained in the individual accounts of the undertakings included in the consolidation, subject to the adjustments authorised or required by the following provisions

of this Schedule and to such other adjustments (if any) as may be appropriate in accordance with generally accepted accounting principles or practice.

(2) If the financial year of a subsidiary undertaking included in the consolidation differs from that of the parent company, the group accounts shall be made up—
  (a) from the accounts of the subsidiary undertaking for its financial year last ending before the end of the parent company's financial year, provided that year ended no more than three months before that of the parent company, or
  (b) from interim accounts prepared by the subsidiary undertaking as at the end of the parent company's financial year.

3.—(1) Where assets and liabilities to be included in the group accounts have been valued or otherwise determined by undertakings according to accounting rules differing from those used for the group accounts, the values or amounts shall be adjusted so as to accord with the rules used for the group accounts.

(2) If it appears to the directors of the parent company that there are special reasons for departing from sub-paragraph (1) they may do so, but particulars of any such departure, the reasons for it and its effect shall be given in a note to the accounts.

(3) The adjustments referred to in this paragraph need not be made if they are not material for the purpose of giving a true and fair view.

4. Any differences of accounting rules as between a parent company's individual accounts for a financial year and its group accounts shall be disclosed in a note to the latter accounts and the reasons for the difference given.

5. Amounts which in the particular context of any provision of this Schedule are not material may be disregarded for the purposes of that provision.

Elimination of group transactions

6.—(1) Debts and claims between undertakings included in the consolidation, and income and expenditure relating to transactions between such undertakings, shall be eliminated in preparing the group accounts.

(2) Where profits and losses resulting from transactions between undertakings included in the consolidation are included in the book value of assets, they shall be eliminated in preparing the group accounts.

(3) The elimination required by sub-paragraph (2) may be effected in proportion to the group's interest in the shares of the undertakings.

(4) Sub-paragraphs (1) and (2) need not be complied with if the amounts concerned are not material for the purpose of giving a true and fair view.

Acquisition and merger accounting

7.—(1) The following provisions apply where an undertaking becomes a subsidiary undertaking of the parent company.

(2) That event is referred to in those provisions as an "acquisition", and references to the "undertaking acquired" shall be construed accordingly.

8. An acquisition shall be accounted for by the acquisition method of accounting unless the conditions for accounting for it as a merger are met and the merger method of accounting is adopted.

9.—(1) The acquisition method of accounting is as follows.

(2) The identifiable assets and liabilities of the undertaking acquired shall be included in the consolidated balance sheet at their fair values as at the date of acquisition.

In this paragraph the "identifiable" assets or liabilities of the undertaking acquired means the assets or liabilities which are capable of being disposed of or discharged separately, without disposing of a business of the undertaking.

(3) The income and expenditure of the undertaking acquired shall be brought into the group accounts only as from the date of the acquisition.

(4) There shall be set off against the acquisition cost of the interest in the shares of the undertaking held by the parent company and its subsidiary undertakings the interest of the parent company and its subsidiary undertakings in the adjusted capital and reserves of the undertaking acquired.

For this purpose—
  "the acquisition cost" means the amount of any cash consideration and the fair value of any other consideration, together with such amount (if any) in respect of fees and other expenses of the acquisition as the company may determine, and

"the adjusted capital and reserves" of the undertaking acquired means its capital and reserves at the date of the acquisition after adjusting the identifiable assets and liabilities of the undertaking to fair values as at that date.

(5) The resulting amount if positive shall be treated as goodwill, and if negative as a negative consolidation difference.

10.—(1) The conditions for accounting for an acquisition as a merger are—
  (a) that at least 90 per cent. of the nominal value of the relevant shares in the undertaking acquired is held by or on behalf of the parent company and its subsidiary undertakings,
  (b) that the proportion referred to in paragraph (a) was attained pursuant to an arrangement providing for the issue of equity shares by the parent company or one or more of its subsidiary undertakings,
  (c) that the fair value of any consideration other than the issue of equity shares given pursuant to the arrangement by the parent company and its subsidiary undertakings did not exceed 10 per cent. of the nominal value of the equity shares issued, and
  (d) that adoption of the merger method of accounting accords with generally accepted accounting principles or practice.

(2) The reference in sub-paragraph (1)(a) to the "relevant shares" in an undertaking acquired is to those carrying unrestricted rights to participate both in distributions and in the assets of the undertaking upon liquidation.

11.—(1) The merger method of accounting is as follows.

(2) The assets and liabilities of the undertaking acquired shall be brought into the group accounts at the figures at which they stand in the undertaking's accounts, subject to any adjustment authorised or required by this Schedule.

(3) The income and expenditure of the undertaking acquired shall be included in the group accounts for the entire financial year, including the period before the acquisition.

(4) The group accounts shall show corresponding amounts relating to the previous financial year as if the undertaking acquired had been included in the consolidation throughout that year.

(5) There shall be set off against the aggregate of—
  (a) the appropriate amount in respect of qualifying shares issued by the parent company or its subsidiary undertakings in consideration for the acquisition of shares in the undertaking acquired, and
  (b) the fair value of any other consideration for the acquisition of shares in the undertaking acquired, determined as at the date when those shares were acquired,
the nominal value of the issued share capital of the undertaking acquired held by the parent company and its subsidiary undertakings.

(6) The resulting amount shall be shown as an adjustment to the consolidated reserves.

(7) In sub-paragraph (5)(a) "qualifying shares" means—
  (a) shares in relation to which section 131 (merger relief) applies, in respect of which the appropriate amount is the nominal value; or
  (b) shares in relation to which section 132 (relief in respect of group reconstructions) applies, in respect of which the appropriate amount is the nominal value together with any minimum premium value within the meaning of that section.

12.—(1) Where a group is acquired, paragraphs 9 to 11 apply with the following adaptations.

(2) References to shares of the undertaking acquired shall be construed as references to shares of the parent undertaking of the group.

(3) Other references to the undertaking acquired shall be construed as references to the group; and references to the assets and liabilities, income and expenditure and capital and reserves of the undertaking acquired shall be construed as references to the assets and liabilities, income and expenditure and capital and reserves of the group after making the set-offs and other adjustments required by this Schedule in the case of group accounts.

13.—(1) The following information with respect to acquisitions taking place in the financial year shall be given in a note to the accounts.

(2) There shall be stated—
  (a) the name of the undertaking acquired or, where a group was acquired, the name of the parent undertaking of that group, and
  (b) whether the acquisition has been accounted for by the acquisition or the merger method of accounting;
and in relation to an acquisition which significantly affects the figures shown in the group accounts, the following further information shall be given.

(3) The composition and fair value of the consideration for the acquisition given by the parent company and its subsidiary undertakings shall be stated.

(4) The profit or loss of the undertaking or group acquired shall be stated—
   (a) for the period from the beginning of the financial year of the undertaking or, as the case may be, of the parent undertaking of the group, up to the date of the acquisition, and
   (b) for the previous financial year of that undertaking or parent undertaking;

and there shall also be stated the date on which the financial year referred to in paragraph (a) began.

(5) Where the acquisition method of accounting has been adopted, the book values immediately prior to the acquisition, and the fair values at the date of acquisition, of each class of assets and liabilities of the undertaking or group acquired shall be stated in tabular form, including a statement of the amount of any goodwill or negative consolidation difference arising on the acquisition, together with an explanation of any significant adjustments made.

(6) Where the merger method of accounting has been adopted, an explanation shall be given of any significant adjustments made in relation to the amounts of the assets and liabilities of the undertaking or group acquired, together with a statement of any resulting adjustment to the consolidated reserves (including the re-statement of opening consolidated reserves).

(7) In ascertaining for the purposes of sub-paragraph (4), (5) or (6) the profit or loss of a group, the book values and fair values of assets and liabilities of a group or the amount of the assets and liabilities of a group, the set-offs and other adjustments required by this Schedule in the case of group accounts shall be made.

14.—(1) There shall also be stated in a note to the accounts the cumulative amount of goodwill resulting from acquisitions in that and earlier financial years which has been written off.

(2) That figure shall be shown net of any goodwill attributable to subsidiary undertakings or businesses disposed of prior to the balance sheet date.

15. Where during the financial year there has been a disposal of an undertaking or group which significantly affects the figures shown in the group accounts, there shall be stated in a note to the accounts—
   (a) the name of that undertaking or, as the case may be, of the parent undertaking of that group, and
   (b) the extent to which the profit or loss shown in the group accounts is attributable to profit or loss of that undertaking or group.

16. The information required by paragraph 13, 14 or 15 above need not be disclosed with respect to an undertaking which—
   (a) is established under the law of a country outside the United Kingdom, or
   (b) carries on business outside the United Kingdom,

if in the opinion of the directors of the parent company the disclosure would be seriously prejudicial to the business of that undertaking or to the business of the parent company or any of its subsidiary undertakings and the Secretary of State agrees that the information should not be disclosed.

Minority interests

17.—(1) The formats set out in Schedule 4 have effect in relation to group accounts with the following additions.

(2) In the Balance Sheet Formats a further item headed "Minority interests" shall be added—
   (a) in Format 1, either after item J or at the end (after item K), and
   (b) in Format 2, under the general heading "LIABILITIES", between items A and B;

and under that item shall be shown the amount of capital and reserves attributable to shares in subsidiary undertakings included in the consolidation held by or on behalf of persons other than the parent company and its subsidiary undertakings.

(3) In the Profit and Loss Account Formats a further item headed "Minority interests" shall be added—
   (a) in Format 1, between items 14 and 15,
   (b) in Format 2, between items 16 and 17,
   (c) in Format 3, between items 7 and 8 in both sections A and B, and
   (d) in Format 4, between items 9 and 10 in both sections A and B;

and under that item shall be shown the amount of any profit or loss on ordinary activities attributable to shares in subsidiary undertakings included in the consolidation held by or on behalf of persons other than the parent company and its subsidiary undertakings.

(4) In the Profit and Loss Account Formats a further item headed "Minority interests" shall be added—
   (a) in Format 1, between items 18 and 19,
   (b) in Format 2, between items 20 and 21,
   (c) in Format 3, between items 9 and 10 in section A and between items 8 and 9 in section B, and
   (d) in Format 4, between items 11 and 12 in section A and between items 10 and 11 in section B;
and under that item shall be shown the amount of any profit or loss on extraordinary activities attributable to shares in subsidiary undertakings included in the consolidation held by or on behalf of persons other than the parent company and its subsidiary undertakings.

(5) For the purposes of paragraph 3(3) and (4) of Schedule 4 (power to adapt or combine items)—
   (a) the additional item required by sub-paragraph (2) above shall be treated as one to which a letter is assigned, and
   (b) the additional items required by sub-paragraphs (3) and (4) above shall be treated as ones to which an Arabic number is assigned.

Interests in subsidiary undertakings excluded from consolidation

18. The interest of the group in subsidiary undertakings excluded from consolidation under section 229(4) (undertakings with activities different from those of undertakings included in the consolidation), and the amount of profit or loss attributable to such an interest, shall be shown in the consolidated balance sheet or, as the case may be, in the consolidated profit and loss account by the equity method of accounting (including dealing with any goodwill arising in accordance with paragraphs 17 to 19 and 21 of Schedule 4).

Joint ventures

19.—(1) Where an undertaking included in the consolidation manages another undertaking jointly with one or more undertakings not included in the consolidation, that other undertaking ("the joint venture") may, if it is not—
   (a) a body corporate, or
   (b) a subsidiary undertaking of the parent company,
be dealt with in the group accounts by the method of proportional consolidation.

(2) The provisions of this Part relating to the preparation of consolidated accounts apply, with any necessary modifications, to proportional consolidation under this paragraph.

Associated undertakings

20.—(1) An "associated undertaking" means an undertaking in which an undertaking included in the consolidation has a participating interest and over whose operating and financial policy it exercises a significant influence, and which is not—
   (a) a subsidiary undertaking of the parent company, or
   (b) a joint venture dealt with in accordance with paragraph 19.

(2) Where an undertaking holds 20 per cent. or more of the voting rights in another undertaking, it shall be presumed to exercise such an influence over it unless the contrary is shown.

(3) The voting rights in an undertaking means the rights conferred on shareholders in respect of their shares or, in the case of an undertaking not having a share capital, on members, to vote at general meetings of the undertaking on all, or substantially all, matters.

(4) The provisions of paragraphs 5 to 11 of Schedule 10A (rights to be taken into account and attribution of rights) apply in determining for the purposes of this paragraph whether an undertaking holds 20 per cent. or more of the voting rights in another undertaking.

21.—(1) The formats set out in Schedule 4 have effect in relation to group accounts with the following modifications.

(2) In the Balance Sheet Formats the items headed "Participating interests", that is—
   (a) in Format 1, item B.III.3, and
   (b) in Format 2, item B.III.3 under the heading "ASSETS",
shall be replaced by two items, "Interests in associated undertakings" and "Other participating interests".

(3) In the Profit and Loss Account Formats, the items headed "Income from participating interests", that is—
(a) in Format 1, item 8,
(b) in Format 2, item 10,
(c) in Format 3, item B.4, and
(d) in Format 4, item B.6,
shall be replaced by two items, "Income from interests in associated undertakings" and "Income from other participating interests".

22.—(1) The interest of an undertaking in an associated undertaking, and the amount of profit or loss attributable to such an interest, shall be shown by the equity method of accounting (including dealing with any goodwill arising in accordance with paragraphs 17 to 19 and 21 of Schedule 4).

(2) Where the associated undertaking is itself a parent undertaking, the net assets and profits or losses to be taken into account are those of the parent and its subsidiary undertakings (after making any consolidation adjustments).

(3) The equity method of accounting need not be applied if the amounts in question are not material for the purpose of giving a true and fair view.

DEFINITIONS
"accounting principles": Sched. 4, paras. 9–15, C.A. 1985.
"acquisition accounting": Sched. 2; SSAPs. 14 and 23.
"associated undertaking": Sched. 2; SSAP. 1.
"balance sheet date": s.22.
"body corporate": s.740, C.A. 1985.
"consolidated balance sheet": s.5; SSAP. 14, para. 10.
"consolidated profit and loss account": s.5; SSAP. 14, para. 10.
"equity method of accounting": Sched. 2; SSAP. 1; SSAP. 14, para. 14.
"fair value": SSAP. 22, para. 25.
"fellow subsidiary": s.22.
"financial year": s.3, Sched. 10, para. 15.
"goodwill": Sched. 2; SSAPs. 14, 22.
"group": s.22; SSAP. 14, para. 9.
"group accounts": s.5; SSAP. 14.
"group undertaking": s.22, Sched. 9.
"individual accounts": ss.4, 22.
"interim accounts": ss.270(4)(a), 272, C.A. 1985.
"investment company": s.266, Sched. 4, paras. 71–73, C.A. 1985.
"joint ventures": Sched. 2, Sched. 3.
"merger accounting": Sched. 2; SSAP. 23.
"minority interests": Sched. 2; SSAP. 14, paras. 34–35.
"nominal value of shares": ss.2(5), 117(3), C.A. 1985.
"parent undertaking": s.21, Sched. 9; SSAP. 14.
"participating interest": s.22, Sched. 3; SSAP. 1.
"shares": s.22.
"subsidiary undertaking": s.144, Sched. 9; SSAP. 14, para. 7.
"true and fair view (in group accounts)": s.5.
"voting rights": s.370, C.A. 1985; Sched. 9.

GENERAL NOTE
This Schedule inserts a new Sched. 4A into the 1985 Act which deals with the Form and Content of Group Accounts. A summary of the contents, together with cross references, is given below.

		EC Seventh Directive, Art.	Sched. 4 to the 1985 Act, para.
Para.			
1(1)	Sched. 4 provisions to apply as far as possible.		
1(2)	Unconsolidated subsidiaries to be treated as part of the group for the purpose of para. 59 of Sched. 4.		
1(3)	Investment groups		71–73
2(1)	Basis of consolidation	25–28, 30	

		EC Seventh Directive, Art.	Sched. 4 to the 1985 Act, para.
Para.			
2(2)	Alignment of financial years within the group	27	
3(1)	Standardisation of valuation rules within a group	29	
3(2), (3)	Departures from para. 3(1) and disclosure of such departures	29(3)	
4	Disclosure where different accounting rules adopted within a group	29(2)	
5	Provisions of Sched. 4A need not apply if amounts involved are immaterial	13(1)	
6	Elimination of intra-group transactions in group accounts	26	
7	Conditions for acquisition and merger accounting	20	
8	Acquisition method to be applied unless conditions exist for merger accounting	19, 20	
9	Explanation of acquisition accounting	19	
10	Conditions for merger accounting	20	
11	Explanation of the merger method of accounting	20	
12	Modifications to the application of paras. 9–11 where a group is acquired		
13	Disclosures relating to acquisitions and mergers in the years of combination	28	75
14	Disclosure of cumulative amounts of purchased goodwill written off	19, 30	66
15	Disclosure of disposals of undertakings in a year		
16	Exemptions from the provisions of paras. 13–15 for overseas undertakings		
17	Disclosure of minority interests in the accounts format	17, 21, 23	
18	Disclosure of interests in unconsolidated subsidiaries	14, 15	69
19	Proportional consolidation of joint ventures	32	
20	Associated undertakings	33	
21	Disclosure of participating interests and income from participating interests in the accounts formats	17	
22	Application of the equity method of accounting for associated undertakings	33	

Section 6(2)

SCHEDULE 3

[SCHEDULE 5 TO THE COMPANIES ACT 1985]

DISCLOSURE OF INFORMATION: RELATED UNDERTAKINGS

PART I

COMPANIES NOT REQUIRED TO PREPARE GROUP ACCOUNTS

Subsidiary undertakings

1.—(1) The following information shall be given where at the end of the financial year the company has subsidiary undertakings.

(2) The name of each subsidiary undertaking shall be stated.

(3) There shall be stated with respect to each subsidiary undertaking—

(a) if it is incorporated outside Great Britain, the country in which it is incorporated;
(b) if it is incorporated in Great Britain, whether it is registered in England and Wales or in Scotland;
(c) if it is unincorporated, the address of its principal place of business.

(4) The reason why the company is not required to prepare group accounts shall be stated.

(5) If the reason is that all the subsidiary undertakings of the company fall within the exclusions provided for in section 229, it shall be stated with respect to each subsidiary undertaking which of those exclusions applies.

Holdings in subsidiary undertakings

2.—(1) There shall be stated in relation to shares of each class held by the company in a subsidiary undertaking—
(a) the identity of the class, and
(b) the proportion of the nominal value of the shares of that class represented by those shares.

(2) The shares held by or on behalf of the company itself shall be distinguished from those attributed to the company which are held by or on behalf of a subsidiary undertaking.

Financial information about subsidiary undertakings

3.—(1) There shall be disclosed with respect to each subsidiary undertaking—
(a) the aggregate amount of its capital and reserves as at the end of its relevant financial year, and
(b) its profit or loss for that year.

(2) That information need not be given if the company is exempt by virtue of section 228 from the requirement to prepare group accounts (parent company included in accounts of larger group).

(3) That information need not be given if—
(a) the subsidiary undertaking is not required by any provision of this Act to deliver a copy of its balance sheet for its relevant financial year and does not otherwise publish that balance sheet in Great Britain or elsewhere, and
(b) the company's holding is less than 50 per cent. of the nominal value of the shares in the undertaking.

(4) Information otherwise required by this paragraph need not be given if it is not material.

(5) For the purposes of this paragraph the "relevant financial year" of a subsidiary undertaking is—
(a) if its financial year ends with that of the company, that year, and
(b) if not, its financial year ending last before the end of the company's financial year.

Financial years of subsidiary undertakings

4. Where the financial year of one or more subsidiary undertakings did not end with that of the company, there shall be stated in relation to each such undertaking—
(a) the reasons why the company's directors consider that its financial year should not end with that of the company, and
(b) the date on which its last financial year ended (last before the end of the company's financial year).

Instead of the dates required by paragraph (b) being given for each subsidiary undertaking the earliest and latest of those dates may be given.

Further information about subsidiary undertakings

5.—(1) There shall be disclosed—
(a) any qualifications contained in the auditors' reports on the accounts of subsidiary undertakings for financial years ending with or during the financial year of the company, and
(b) any note or saving contained in such accounts to call attention to a matter which, apart from the note or saving, would properly have been referred to in such a qualification,

in so far as the matter which is the subject of the qualification or note is not covered by the company's own accounts and is material from the point of view of its members.

(2) The aggregate amount of the total investment of the company in the shares of subsidiary undertakings shall be stated by way of the equity method of valuation, unless—
  (a) the company is exempt from the requirement to prepare group accounts by virtue of section 228 (parent company included in accounts of larger group), and
  (b) the directors state their opinion that the aggregate value of the assets of the company consisting of shares in, or amounts owing (whether on account of a loan or otherwise) from, the company's subsidiary undertakings is not less than the aggregate of the amounts at which those assets are stated or included in the company's balance sheet.
(3) In so far as information required by this paragraph is not obtainable, a statement to that effect shall be given instead.

Shares and debentures of company held by subsidiary undertakings

6.—(1) The number, description and amount of the shares in and debentures of the company held by or on behalf of its subsidiary undertakings shall be disclosed.
(2) Sub-paragraph (1) does not apply in relation to shares or debentures in the case of which the subsidiary undertaking is concerned as personal representative or, subject as follows, as trustee.
(3) The exception for shares or debentures in relation to which the subsidiary undertaking is concerned as trustee does not apply if the company, or any subsidiary undertaking of the company, is beneficially interested under the trust, otherwise than by way of security only for the purposes of a transaction entered into by it in the ordinary course of a business which includes the lending of money.
(4) Schedule 2 to this Act has effect for the interpretation of the reference in sub-paragraph (3) to a beneficial interest under a trust.

Significant holdings in undertakings other than subsidiary undertakings

7.—(1) The information required by paragraphs 8 and 9 shall be given where at the end of the financial year the company has a significant holding in an undertaking which is not a subsidiary undertaking of the company.
(2) A holding is significant for this purpose if—
  (a) it amounts to 10 per cent. or more of the nominal value of any class of shares in the undertaking, or
  (b) the amount of the holding (as stated or included in the company's accounts) exceeds one-tenth of the amount (as so stated) of the company's assets.

8.—(1) The name of the undertaking shall be stated.
(2) There shall be stated—
  (a) if the undertaking is incorporated outside Great Britain, the country in which it is incorporated;
  (b) if it is incorporated in Great Britain, whether it is registered in England and Wales or in Scotland;
  (c) if it is unincorporated, the address of its principal place of business.
(3) There shall also be stated—
  (a) the identity of each class of shares in the undertaking held by the company, and
  (b) the proportion of the nominal value of the shares of that class represented by those shares.

9.—(1) Where the company has a significant holding in an undertaking amounting to 20 per cent. or more of the nominal value of the shares in the undertaking, there shall also be stated—
  (a) the aggregate amount of the capital and reserves of the undertaking as at the end of its relevant financial year, and
  (b) its profit or loss for that year.
(2) That information need not be given if—
  (a) the company is exempt by virtue of section 228 from the requirement to prepare group accounts (parent company included in accounts of larger group), and
  (b) the investment of the company in all undertakings in which it has such a holding as is mentioned in sub-paragraph (1) is shown, in aggregate, in the notes to the accounts by way of the equity method of valuation.
(3) That information need not be given in respect of an undertaking if—
  (a) the undertaking is not required by any provision of this Act to deliver a copy of its balance sheet for its relevant financial year and does not otherwise publish that balance sheet in Great Britain or elsewhere, and

(b) the company's holding is less than 50 per cent. of the nominal value of the shares in the undertaking.

(4) Information otherwise required by this paragraph need not be given if it is not material.

(5) For the purposes of this paragraph the "relevant financial year" of an undertaking is—

(a) if its financial year ends with that of the company, that year, and
(b) if not, its financial year ending last before the end of the company's financial year.

Arrangements attracting merger relief

10.—(1) This paragraph applies to arrangements attracting merger relief, that is, where a company allots shares in consideration for the issue, transfer or cancellation of shares in another body corporate ("the other company") in circumstances such that section 130 of this Act (share premium account) does not, by virtue of section 131(2) (merger relief), apply to the premiums on the shares.

(2) If the company makes such an arrangement during the financial year, the following information shall be given—

(a) the name of the other company,
(b) the number, nominal value and class of shares allotted,
(c) the number, nominal value and class of shares in the other company, issued, transferred or cancelled, and
(d) particulars of the accounting treatment adopted in the company's accounts in respect of the issue, transfer or cancellation.

(3) Where the company made such an arrangement during the financial year, or during either of the two preceding financial years, and there is included in the company's profit and loss account—

(a) any profit or loss realised during the financial year by the company on the disposal of—
    (i) any shares in the other company, or
    (ii) any assets which were fixed assets of the other company or any of its subsidiary undertakings at the time of the arrangement, or
(b) any part of any profit or loss realised during the financial year by the company on the disposal of any shares (other than shares in the other company) which was attributable to the fact that there were at the time of the disposal amongst the assets of the company which issued the shares, or any of its subsidiary undertakings, such shares or assets as are described in paragraph (a) above,

then, the net amount of that profit or loss or, as the case may be, the part so attributable shall be shown, together with an explanation of the transactions to which the information relates.

(4) For the purposes of this paragraph the time of the arrangement shall be taken to be—

(a) where as a result of the arrangement the other company becomes a subsidiary undertaking of the company, the date on which it does so or, if the arrangement in question becomes binding only on the fulfilment of a condition, the date on which that condition is fulfilled;
(b) if the other company is already a subsidiary undertaking of the company, the date on which the shares are allotted or, if they are allotted on different days, the first day.

Parent undertaking drawing up accounts for larger group

11.—(1) Where the company is a subsidiary undertaking, the following information shall be given with respect to the parent undertaking of—

(a) the largest group of undertakings for which group accounts are drawn up and of which the company is a member, and
(b) the smallest such group of undertakings.

(2) The name of the parent undertaking shall be stated.

(3) There shall be stated—

(a) if the undertaking is incorporated outside Great Britain, the country in which it is incorporated;
(b) if it is incorporated in Great Britain, whether it is registered in England and Wales or in Scotland;
(c) if it is unincorporated, the address of its principal place of business.

(4) If copies of the group accounts referred to in sub-paragraph (1) are available to the public, there shall also be stated the addresses from which copies of the accounts can be obtained.

Identification of ultimate parent company

12.—(1) Where the company is a subsidiary undertaking, the following information shall be given with respect to the company (if any) regarded by the directors as being the company's ultimate parent company.

(2) The name of that company shall be stated.

(3) If known to the directors, there shall be stated—
   (a) if that company is incorporated outside Great Britain, the country in which it is incorporated;
   (b) if it is incorporated in Great Britain, whether it is registered in England and Wales or in Scotland.

(4) In this paragraph "company" includes any body corporate.

Constructions of references to shares held by company

13.—(1) References in this Part of this Schedule to shares held by a company shall be construed as follows.

(2) For the purposes of paragraphs 2 to 5 (information about subsidiary undertakings)—
   (a) there shall be attributed to the company any shares held by a subsidiary undertaking, or by a person acting on behalf of the company or a subsidiary undertaking; but
   (b) there shall be treated as not held by the company any shares held on behalf of a person other than the company or a subsidiary undertaking.

(3) For the purposes of paragraphs 7 to 9 (information about undertakings other than subsidiary undertakings)—
   (a) there shall be attributed to the company shares held on its behalf by any person; but
   (b) there shall be treated as not held by a company shares held on behalf of a person other than the company.

(4) For the purposes of any of those provisions, shares held by way of security shall be treated as held by the person providing the security—
   (a) where apart from the right to exercise them for the purpose of preserving the value of the security, or of realising it, the rights attached to the shares are exercisable only in accordance with his instructions, and
   (b) where the shares are held in connection with the granting of loans as part of normal business activities and apart from the right to exercise them for the purpose of preserving the value of the security, or of realising it, the rights attached to the shares are exercisable only in his interests.

PART II

COMPANIES REQUIRED TO PREPARE GROUP ACCOUNTS

Introductory

14. In this Part of this Schedule "the group" means the group consisting of the parent company and its subsidiary undertakings.

Subsidiary undertakings

15.—(1) The following information shall be given with respect to the undertakings which are subsidiary undertakings of the parent company at the end of the financial year.

(2) The name of each undertaking shall be stated.

(3) There shall be stated—
   (a) if the undertaking is incorporated outside Great Britain, the country in which it is incorporated;
   (b) if it is incorporated in Great Britain, whether it is registered in England and Wales or in Scotland;
   (c) if it is unincorporated, the address of its principal place of business.

(4) It shall also be stated whether the subsidiary undertaking is included in the consolidation and, if it is not, the reasons for excluding it from consolidation shall be given.

(5) It shall be stated with respect to each subsidiary undertaking by virtue of which of the conditions specified in section 258(2) or (4) it is a subsidiary undertaking of its immediate parent undertaking.

That information need not be given if the relevant condition is that specified in subsection (2)(a) of that section (holding of a majority of the voting rights) and the immediate parent undertaking holds the same proportion of the shares in the undertaking as it holds voting rights.

Holdings in subsidiary undertakings

16.—(1) The following information shall be given with respect to the shares of a subsidiary undertaking held—
 (a) by the parent company, and
 (b) by the group;
and the information under paragraphs (a) and (b) shall (if different) be shown separately.
 (2) There shall be stated—
  (a) the identity of each class of shares held, and
  (b) the proportion of the nominal value of the shares of that class represented by those shares.

Financial information about subsidiary undertakings not included in the consolidation

17.—(1) There shall be shown with respect to each subsidiary undertaking not included in the consolidation—
 (a) the aggregate amount of its capital and reserves as at the end of its relevant financial year, and
 (b) its profit or loss for that year.
 (2) That information need not be given if the group's investment in the undertaking is included in the accounts by way of the equity method of valuation or if—
  (a) the undertaking is not required by any provision of this Act to deliver a copy of its balance sheet for its relevant financial year and does not otherwise publish that balance sheet in Great Britain or elsewhere, and
  (b) the holding of the group is less than 50 per cent. of the nominal value of the shares in the undertaking.
 (3) Information otherwise required by this paragraph need not be given if it is not material.
 (4) For the purposes of this paragraph the "relevant financial year" of a subsidiary undertaking is—
  (a) if its financial year ends with that of the company, that year, and
  (b) if not, its financial year ending last before the end of the company's financial year.

Further information about subsidiary undertakings excluded from consolidation

18.—(1) The following information shall be given with respect to subsidiary undertakings excluded from consolidation.
 (2) There shall be disclosed—
  (a) any qualifications contained in the auditors' reports on the accounts of the undertaking for financial years ending with or during the financial year of the company, and
  (b) any note or saving contained in such accounts to call attention to a matter which, apart from the note or saving, would properly have been referred to in such a qualification,
in so far as the matter which is the subject of the qualification or note is not covered by the consolidated accounts and is material from the point of view of the members of the parent company.
 (3) In so far as information required by this paragraph is not obtainable, a statement to that effect shall be given instead.

Financial years of subsidiary undertakings

19. Where the financial year of one or more subsidiary undertakings did not end with that of the company, there shall be stated in relation to each such undertaking—
 (a) the reasons why the company's directors consider that its financial year should not end with that of the company, and

(b) the date on which its last financial year ended (last before the end of the company's financial year).

Instead of the dates required by paragraph (b) being given for each subsidiary undertaking the earliest and latest of those dates may be given.

Shares and debentures of company held by subsidiary undertakings

20.—(1) The number, description and amount of the shares in and debentures of the company held by or on behalf of its subsidiary undertakings shall be disclosed.

(2) Sub-paragraph (1) does not apply in relation to shares or debentures in the case of which the subsidiary undertaking is concerned as personal representative or, subject as follows, as trustee.

(3) The exception for shares or debentures in relation to which the subsidiary undertaking is concerned as trustee does not apply if the company or any of its subsidiary undertakings is beneficially interested under the trust, otherwise than by way of security only for the purposes of a transaction entered into by it in the ordinary course of a business which includes the lending of money.

(4) Schedule 2 to this Act has effect for the interpretation of the reference in sub-paragraph (3) to a beneficial interest under a trust.

Joint ventures

21.—(1) The following information shall be given where an undertaking is dealt with in the consolidated accounts by the method of proportional consolidation in accordance with paragraph 19 of Schedule 4A (joint ventures)—
   (a) the name of the undertaking;
   (b) the address of the principal place of business of the undertaking;
   (c) the factors on which joint management of the undertaking is based; and
   (d) the proportion of the capital of the undertaking held by undertakings included in the consolidation.

(2) Where the financial year of the undertaking did not end with that of the company, there shall be stated the date on which a financial year of the undertaking last ended before that date.

Associated undertakings

22.—(1) The following information shall be given where an undertaking included in the consolidation has an interest in an associated undertaking.

(2) The name of the associated undertaking shall be stated.

(3) There shall be stated—
   (a) if the undertaking is incorporated outside Great Britain, the country in which it is incorporated;
   (b) if it is incorporated in Great Britain, whether it is registered in England and Wales or in Scotland;
   (c) if it is unincorporated, the address of its principal place of business.

(4) The following information shall be given with respect to the shares of the undertaking held—
   (a) by the parent company, and
   (b) by the group;
and the information under paragraphs (a) and (b) shall be shown separately.

(5) There shall be stated—
   (a) the identity of each class of shares held, and
   (b) the proportion of the nominal value of the shares of that class represented by those shares.

(6) In this paragraph "associated undertaking" has the meaning given by paragraph 20 of Schedule 4A; and the information required by this paragraph shall be given notwithstanding that paragraph 22(3) of that Schedule (materiality) applies in relation to the accounts themselves.

Other significant holdings of parent company or group

23.—(1) The information required by paragraphs 24 and 25 shall be given where at the end of the financial year the parent company has a significant holding in an undertaking

40/Sch. 3   *Companies Act 1989*

which is not one of its subsidiary undertakings and does not fall within paragraph 21 (joint ventures) or paragraph 22 (associated undertakings).

(2) A holding is significant for this purpose if—
  (a) it amounts to 10 per cent. or more of the nominal value of any class of shares in the undertaking, or
  (b) the amount of the holding (as stated or included in the company's individual accounts) exceeds one-tenth of the amount of its assets (as so stated).

24.—(1) The name of the undertaking shall be stated.
(2) There shall be stated—
  (a) if the undertaking is incorporated outside Great Britain, the country in which it is incorporated;
  (b) if it is incorporated in Great Britain, whether it is registered in England and Wales or in Scotland;
  (c) if it is unincorporated, the address of its principal place of business.
(3) The following information shall be given with respect to the shares of the undertaking held by the parent company.
(4) There shall be stated—
  (a) the identity of each class of shares held, and
  (b) the proportion of the nominal value of the shares of that class represented by those shares.

25.—(1) Where the company has a significant holding in an undertaking amounting to 20 per cent. or more of the nominal value of the shares in the undertaking, there shall also be stated—
  (a) the aggregate amount of the capital and reserves of the undertaking as at the end of its relevant financial year, and
  (b) its profit or loss for that year.
(2) That information need not be given in respect of an undertaking if—
  (a) the undertaking is not required by any provision of this Act to deliver a copy of its balance sheet for its relevant financial year and does not otherwise publish that balance sheet in Great Britain or elsewhere, and
  (b) the company's holding is less than 50 per cent. of the nominal value of the shares in the undertaking.
(3) Information otherwise required by this paragraph need not be given if it is not material.
(4) For the purposes of this paragraph the "relevant financial year" of an undertaking is—
  (a) if its financial year ends with that of the company, that year, and
  (b) if not, its financial year ending last before the end of the company's financial year.

26.—(1) The information required by paragraphs 27 and 28 shall be given where at the end of the financial year the group has a significant holding in an undertaking which is not a subsidiary undertaking of the parent company and does not fall within paragraph 21 (joint ventures) or paragraph 22 (associated undertakings).
(2) A holding is significant for this purpose if—
  (a) it amounts to 10 per cent. or more of the nominal value of any class of shares in the undertaking, or
  (b) the amount of the holding (as stated or included in the group accounts) exceeds one-tenth of the amount of the group's assets (as so stated).

27.—(1) The name of the undertaking shall be stated.
(2) There shall be stated—
  (a) if the undertaking is incorporated outside Great Britain, the country in which it is incorporated;
  (b) if it is incorporated in Great Britain, whether it is registered in England and Wales or in Scotland;
  (c) if it is unincorporated, the address of its principal place of business.
(3) The following information shall be given with respect to the shares of the undertaking held by the group.
(4) There shall be stated—
  (a) the identity of each class of shares held, and
  (b) the proportion of the nominal value of the shares of that class represented by those shares.

28.—(1) Where the holding of the group amounts to 20 per cent. or more of the nominal value of the shares in the undertaking, there shall also be stated—
   (a) the aggregate amount of the capital and reserves of the undertaking as at the end of its relevant financial year, and
   (b) its profit or loss for that year.
(2) That information need not be given if—
   (a) the undertaking is not required by any provision of this Act to deliver a copy of its balance sheet for its relevant financial year and does not otherwise publish that balance sheet in Great Britain or elsewhere, and
   (b) the holding of the group is less than 50 per cent. of the nominal value of the shares in the undertaking.
(3) Information otherwise required by this paragraph need not be given if it is not material.
(4) For the purposes of this paragraph the "relevant financial year" of an outside undertaking is—
   (a) if its financial year ends with that of the parent company, that year, and
   (b) if not, its financial year ending last before the end of the parent company's financial year.

Arrangements attracting merger relief

29.—(1) This paragraph applies to arrangements attracting merger relief, that is, where a company allots shares in consideration for the issue, transfer or cancellation of shares in another body corporate ("the other company") in circumstances such that section 130 of this Act (share premium account) does not, by virtue of section 131(2) (merger relief), apply to the premiums on the shares.
(2) If the parent company made such an arrangement during the financial year, the following information shall be given—
   (a) the name of the other company,
   (b) the number, nominal value and class of shares allotted,
   (c) the number, nominal value and class of shares in the other company issued, transferred or cancelled, and
   (d) particulars of the accounting treatment adopted in the parent company's individual and group accounts in respect of the issue, transfer or cancellation, and
   (e) particulars of the extent to which and manner in which the profit or loss for the financial year shown in the group accounts is affected by any profit or loss of the other company, or any of its subsidiary undertakings, which arose before the time of the arrangement.
(3) Where the parent company made such an arrangement during the financial year, or during either of the two preceding financial years, and there is included in the consolidated profit and loss account—
   (a) any profit or loss realised during the financial year on the disposal of—
      (i) any shares in the other company, or
      (ii) any assets which were fixed assets of the other company or any of its subsidiary undertakings at the time of the arrangement, or
   (b) any part of any profit or loss realised during the financial year on the disposal of any shares (other than shares in the other company) which was attributable to the fact that there were at the time of the disposal amongst the assets of the company which issued the shares, or any of its subsidiary undertakings, such shares or assets as are described in paragraph (a) above,
then, the net amount of that profit or loss or, as the case may be, the part so attributable shall be shown, together with an explanation of the transactions to which the information relates.
(4) For the purposes of this paragraph the time of the arrangement shall be taken to be—
   (a) where as a result of the arrangement the other company becomes a subsidiary undertaking of the company in question, the date on which it does so or, if the arrangement in question becomes binding only on the fulfilment of a condition, the date on which that condition is fulfilled;
   (b) if the other company is already a subsidiary undertaking of that company, the date on which the shares are allotted or, if they are allotted on different days, the first day.

Parent undertaking drawing up accounts for larger group

30.—(1) Where the parent company is itself a subsidiary undertaking, the following information shall be given with respect to that parent undertaking of the company which heads—
   (a) the largest group of undertakings for which group accounts are drawn up and of which that company is a member, and
   (b) the smallest such group of undertakings.
(2) The name of the parent undertaking shall be stated.
(3) There shall be stated—
   (a) if the undertaking is incorporated outside Great Britain, the country in which it is incorporated;
   (b) if it is incorporated in Great Britain, whether it is registered in England and Wales or in Scotland;
   (c) if it is unincorporated, the address of its principal place of business.
(4) If copies of the group accounts referred to in sub-paragraph (1) are available to the public, there shall also be stated the addresses from which copies of the accounts can be obtained.

Identification of ultimate parent company

31.—(1) Where the parent company is itself a subsidiary undertaking, the following information shall be given with respect to the company (if any) regarded by the directors as being that company's ultimate parent company.
(2) The name of that company shall be stated.
(3) If known to the directors, there shall be stated—
   (a) if that company is incorporated outside Great Britain, the country in which it is incorporated;
   (b) if it is incorporated in Great Britain, whether it is registered in England and Wales or in Scotland.
(4) In this paragraph "company" includes any body corporate.

Construction of references to shares held by parent company or group

32.—(1) References in this Part of this Schedule to shares held by the parent company or the group shall be construed as follows.
(2) For the purposes of paragraphs 16, 22(4) and (5) and 23 to 25 (information about holdings in subsidiary and other undertakings)—
   (a) there shall be attributed to the parent company shares held on its behalf by any person; but
   (b) there shall be treated as not held by the parent company shares held on behalf of a person other than the company.
(3) References to shares held by the group are to any shares held by or on behalf of the parent company or any of its subsidiary undertakings; but there shall be treated as not held by the group any shares held on behalf of a person other than the parent company or any of its subsidiary undertakings.
(4) Shares held by way of security shall be treated as held by the person providing the security—
   (a) where apart from the right to exercise them for the purpose of preserving the value of the security, or of realising it, the rights attached to the shares are exercisable only in accordance with his instructions, and
   (b) where the shares are held in connection with the granting of loans as part of normal business activities and apart from the right to exercise them for the purpose of preserving the value of the security, or of realising it, the rights attached to the shares are exercisable only in his interests.

DEFINITIONS
"(annual) accounts": Sched. 10, para. 15.
"allotment of shares": s.738 C.A. 1985.
"associated undertakings": Sched. 2; SSAP. 1.
"body corporate": s.740 C.A. 1985.
"consolidated accounts": s.5; SSAP. 14.
"debentures": s.774 C.A. 1985.
"directors": s.741 C.A. 1985.

"equity method of accounting": Sched. 2; SSAP. 1; SSAP. 14, para. 14.
"financial year": s.3, Sched. 10, para. 15.
"group": Sched. 3; SSAP. 14, para. 9.
"individual accounts": ss.4, 22, Scheds. 1–7.
"joint venture": Scheds. 2, 3.
"merger relief": s.131 C.A. 1985.
"nominal value of shares": ss.2(5), 117(3) C.A. 1985.
"parent company and parent undertaking": s.21, Sched. 9.
"profit and loss account": Scheds. 1–7.
"publication of a balance sheet": s.10.
"qualification in an auditors' report": s.22.
"realised profits and losses": Sched. 10, para. 15.
"share premium": ss.130–134 C.A. 1985.
"subsidiary undertakings": ss.21, 144; SSAP. 14, para. 7.
"undertakings": s.22.

GENERAL NOTE
This Schedule inserts a new Sched. 5 into the 1985 Act, which deals with Disclosure of Information: Related Undertakings. This incorporates provisions of the European Community's Seventh Directive on Consolidated Accounts, 83/349 (see Palmer, vol. IV, K–066).
A summary of the contents, together with cross references, is given below.

Pt. I—Companies not Required to Prepare Group Accounts.

Para.		EC's Seventh Directive	Former Sched. 4	Former Sched. 5
1	Disclosure of names and locations of each subsidiary and the reasons why the company is not required to prepare group accounts.	14(3), 34		
2	Disclosure of share holdings in subsidiaries.	34	65, 68–69	1–6, 16–17
3	Disclosure of financial information relating to subsidiaries where consolidated accounts are not prepared.	34		
4	Disclosure of reasons for differences in financial years within the group.		70	
5(1)	Disclosure of audit qualifications to, or significant items given in notes to, a subsidiary's accounts.		69(2)	
5(2)	Aggregate amount of investment stated by equity method where a subsidiary's accounts are not consolidated.	15, 34		
6	Disclosure of shares and debentures of the parent held by subsidiaries.		60	
7–9	Disclosures of financial information of an undertaking where the participating interest exceeds 10 per cent. and 20 per cent. of its nominal share capital or 10 per cent. of the holding company's assets.			7–19
10	Disclosures relating to merger relief.		75	
11	Disclosure of the names of ultimate parent undertakings.			20–21
12	Identification of the ultimate parent company.			
13	Meaning of references to shares held by a company.			13, 19

Section 6(4)

SCHEDULE 4

DISCLOSURE OF INFORMATION: EMOLUMENTS AND OTHER BENEFITS OF DIRECTORS AND OTHERS

1. Schedule 6 to the Companies Act 1985 is amended as follows.
2. For the heading substitute—

"DISCLOSURE OF INFORMATION: EMOLUMENTS AND OTHER BENEFITS OF DIRECTORS AND OTHERS".

3. Insert the following provisions (which reproduce, with amendments, the former Part V of Schedule 5 to that Act) as Part I—

"PART I

CHAIRMAN'S AND DIRECTORS' EMOLUMENTS, PENSIONS AND COMPENSATION FOR LOSS OF OFFICE

Aggregate amount of directors' emoluments

1.—(1) The aggregate amount of directors' emoluments shall be shown.
(2) This means the emoluments paid to or receivable by any person in respect of—
    (a) his services as a director of the company, or
    (b) his services while director of the company—
        (i) as director of any of its subsidiary undertakings, or
        (ii) otherwise in connection with the management of the affairs of the company or any of its subsidiary undertakings.
(3) There shall also be shown, separately, the aggregate amount within sub-paragraph (2)(a) and (b)(i) and the aggregate amount within sub-paragraph (2)(b)(ii).
(4) For the purposes of this paragraph the "emoluments" of a person include—
    (a) fees and percentages,
    (b) sums paid by way of expenses allowance (so far as those sums are chargeable to United Kingdom income tax),
    (c) contributions paid in respect of him under any pension scheme, and
    (d) the estimated money value of any other benefits received by him otherwise than in cash,
and emoluments in respect of a person's accepting office as director shall be treated as emoluments in respect of his services as director.

Details of chairman's and directors' emoluments

2. Where the company is a parent company or a subsidiary undertaking, or where the amount shown in compliance with paragraph 1(1) is £60,000 or more, the information required by paragraphs 3 to 6 shall be given with respect to the emoluments of the chairman and directors, and emoluments waived.

3.—(1) The emoluments of the chairman shall be shown.
(2) The "chairman" means the person elected by the directors to be chairman of their meetings, and includes a person who, though not so elected, holds an office (however designated) which in accordance with the company's constitution carries with it functions substantially similar to those discharged by a person so elected.
(3) Where there has been more than one chairman during the year, the emoluments of each shall be stated so far as attributable to the period during which he was chairman.
(4) The emoluments of a person need not be shown if his duties as chairman were wholly or mainly discharged outside the United Kingdom.

4.—(1) The following information shall be given with respect to the emoluments of directors.
(2) There shall be shown the number of directors whose emoluments fell within each of the following bands—
    not more than £5,000,
    more than £5,000 but not more than £10,000,
    more than £10,000 but not more than £15,000,
    and so on.

(3) If the emoluments of any of the directors exceeded that of the chairman, there shall be shown the greatest amount of emoluments of any director.

(4) Where more than one person has been chairman during the year, the reference in sub-paragraph (3) to the emoluments of the chairman is to the aggregate of the emoluments of each person who has been chairman, so far as attributable to the period during which he was chairman.

(5) The information required by sub-paragraph (2) need not be given in respect of a director who discharged his duties as such wholly or mainly outside the United Kingdom; and any such director shall be left out of account for the purposes of sub-paragraph (3).

5. In paragraphs 3 and 4 "emoluments" has the same meaning as in paragraph 1, except that it does not include contributions paid in respect of a person under a pension scheme.

Emoluments waived

6.—(1) There shall be shown—
    (a) the number of directors who have waived rights to receive emoluments which, but for the waiver, would have fallen to be included in the amount shown under paragraph 1(1), and
    (b) the aggregate amount of those emoluments.

(2) For the purposes of this paragraph it shall be assumed that a sum not receivable in respect of a period would have been paid at the time at which it was due, and if such a sum was payable only on demand, it shall be deemed to have been due at the time of the waiver.

Pensions of directors and past directors

7.—(1) There shall be shown the aggregate amount of directors' or past directors' pensions.

(2) This amount does not include any pension paid or receivable under a pension scheme if the scheme is such that the contributions under it are substantially adequate for the maintenance of the scheme; but, subject to this, it includes any pension paid or receivable in respect of any such services of a director or past director as are mentioned in paragraph 1(2), whether to or by him or, on his nomination or by virtue of dependence on or other connection with him, to or by any other person.

(3) The amount shown shall distinguish between pensions in respect of services as director, whether of the company or any of its subsidiary undertakings, and other pensions.

(4) References to pensions include benefits otherwise than in cash and in relation to so much of a pension as consists of such a benefit references to its amount are to the estimated money value of the benefit.

The nature of any such benefit shall also be disclosed.

Compensation to directors for loss of office

8.—(1) There shall be shown the aggregate amount of any compensation to directors or past directors in respect of loss of office.

(2) This amount includes compensation received or receivable by a director or past director for—
    (a) loss of office as director of the company, or
    (b) loss, while director of the company or on or in connection with his ceasing to be a director of it, of—
        (i) any other office in connection with the management of the company's affairs, or
        (ii) any office as director or otherwise in connection with the management of the affairs of any subsidiary undertaking of the company;
and shall distinguish between compensation in respect of the office of director, whether of the company or any of its subsidiary undertakings, and compensation in respect of other offices.

(3) References to compensation include benefits otherwise than in cash; and in relation to such compensation references to its amount are to the estimated money value of the benefit.

The nature of any such compensation shall be disclosed.

(4) References to compensation for loss of office include compensation in consideration for, or in connection with, a person's retirement from office.

Sums paid to third parties in respect of directors' services

9.—(1) There shall be shown the aggregate amount of any consideration paid to or receivable by third parties for making available the services of any person—
(a) as a director of the company, or
(b) while director of the company—
  (i) as director of any of its subsidiary undertakings, or
  (ii) otherwise in connection with the management of the affairs of the company or any of its subsidiary undertakings.

(2) The reference to consideration includes benefits otherwise than in cash; and in relation to such consideration the reference to its amount is to the estimated money value of the benefit.

The nature of any such consideration shall be disclosed.

(3) The reference to third parties is to persons other than—
(a) the director himself or a person connected with him or body corporate controlled by him, and
(b) the company or any of its subsidiary undertakings.

Supplementary

10.—(1) The following applies with respect to the amounts to be shown under paragraphs 1, 7, 8 and 9.

(2) The amount in each case includes all relevant sums paid by or receivable from—
(a) the company; and
(b) the company's subsidiary undertakings; and
(c) any other person,
except sums to be accounted for to the company or any of its subsidiary undertakings or, by virtue of sections 314 and 315 of this Act (duty of directors to make disclosure on company takeover; consequence of non-compliance), to past or present members of the company or any of its subsidiaries or any class of those members.

(3) The amount to be shown under paragraph 8 shall distinguish between the sums respectively paid by or receivable from the company, the company's subsidiary undertakings and persons other than the company and its subsidiary undertakings.

(4) References to amounts paid to or receivable by a person include amounts paid to or receivable by a person connected with him or a body corporate controlled by him (but not so as to require an amount to be counted twice).

11.—(1) The amounts to be shown for any financial year under paragraphs 1, 7, 8 and 9 are the sums receivable in respect of that year (whenever paid) or, in the case of sums not receivable in respect of a period, the sums paid during that year.

(2) But where—
(a) any sums are not shown in a note to the accounts for the relevant financial year on the ground that the person receiving them is liable to account for them as mentioned in paragraph 10(2), but the liability is thereafter wholly or partly released or is not enforced within a period of 2 years; or
(b) any sums paid by way of expenses allowance are charged to United Kingdom income tax after the end of the relevant financial year,
those sums shall, to the extent to which the liability is released or not enforced or they are charged as mentioned above (as the case may be), be shown in a note to the first accounts in which it is practicable to show them and shall be distinguished from the amounts to be shown apart from this provision.

12. Where it is necessary to do so for the purpose of making any distinction required by the preceding paragraphs in an amount to be shown in compliance with this Part of this Schedule, the directors may apportion any payments between the matters in respect of which these have been paid or are receivable in such manner as they think appropriate.

Interpretation

13.—(1) The following applies for the interpretation of this Part of this Schedule.
(2) A reference to a subsidiary undertaking of the company—

(a) in relation to a person who is or was, while a director of the company, a director also, by virtue of the company's nomination (direct or indirect) of any other undertaking, includes (subject to the following sub-paragraph) that undertaking, whether or not it is or was in fact a subsidiary undertaking of the company, and

(b) for the purposes of paragraphs 1 to 7 (including any provision of this Part of this Schedule referring to paragraph 1) is to an undertaking which is a subsidiary undertaking at the time the services were rendered, and for the purposes of paragraph 8 to a subsidiary undertaking immediately before the loss of office as director.

(3) The following definitions apply—

(a) "pension" includes any superannuation allowance, superannuation gratuity or similar payment,

(b) "pension scheme" means a scheme for the provision of pensions in respect of services as director or otherwise which is maintained in whole or in part by means of contributions, and

(c) "contribution", in relation to a pension scheme, means any payment (including an insurance premium) paid for the purposes of the scheme by or in respect of persons rendering services in respect of which pensions will or may become payable under the scheme except that it does not include any payment in respect of two or more persons if the amount paid in respect of each of them is not ascertainable.

(4) References in this Part of this Schedule to a person being "connected" with a director, and to a director "controlling" a body corporate, shall be construed in accordance with section 346.

Supplementary

14. This Part of this Schedule requires information to be given only so far as it is contained in the company's books and papers or the company has the right to obtain it from the persons concerned.".

4.—(1) For the heading to the present Part I substitute—

"PART II

LOANS, QUASI-LOANS AND OTHER DEALINGS IN FAVOUR OF DIRECTORS"

(2) Paragraphs 1 to 3 and 5 to 14 of that Part shall be renumbered 15 to 27, and internal cross-references in that Part shall be renumbered accordingly.

(3) Paragraph 4 is omitted.

(4) In paragraph 1 (renumbered 15) for "Group accounts" substitute "The group accounts of a holding company, or if it is not required to prepare group accounts its individual accounts,".

(5) For the heading before paragraph 11 (renumbered 24) substitute—

"Excluded transactions"

5. In paragraph 14 (renumbered 27), make the existing provision sub-paragraph (1) and after it insert—

"(2) In this Part of this Schedule "director" includes a shadow director.".

6.—(1) For the heading to the present Part II substitute—

"PART III

OTHER TRANSACTIONS, ARRANGEMENTS AND AGREEMENTS"

(2) Paragraphs 15 to 17 of that Part shall be renumbered 28 to 30, and internal cross-references in that Part shall be renumbered accordingly.

(3) In paragraph 16 (renumbered 29), for "made as mentioned in section 233(1)" substitute "made by the company or a subsidiary of it for persons who at any time during the financial year were officers of the company (but not directors or shadow directors)".

40/Sch. 5   *Companies Act* 1989

7. Omit the present Part III (disclosure required in case of banking companies), the substance of which is reproduced in Part IV of Schedule 7 to this Act.

DEFINITIONS
"chairman": Sched. 4, para. 3(2).
"compensation for loss of office": Sched. 4, para. 8(2).
"contribution": Sched. 4, para. 13(3).
"directors": s.741 C.A. 1985.
"emoluments": Sched. 4, para. 1(4).
"financial year": s.3, Sched. 10, para. 15.
"pensions": Sched. 4, para. 13(3).
"pension scheme": Sched. 4, para. 13(3).
"subsidiary undertakings": ss.21, 144, Sched. 9; SSAP. 14, para. 7.
"third parties": Sched. 4, para. 9(3).

GENERAL NOTE
This Schedule recasts Sched. 6 to the 1985 Act in the following way:
Pt. V of the former Sched. 5 (dealing with Chairman's and Directors' Emoluments, Pensions and Compensation for Loss of Office), becomes Pt. I of the new Sched. 6 (paras. 1–14).
Pt. I of the former Sched. 6 (dealing with Loans, Quasi-loans and Other Dealings in Favour of Directors), disclosed under the terms of the original s.232 of the 1985 Act, becomes Pt. II of the new Sched. 6.
Pt. II of the former Sched. 6 (dealing with Other Transactions, Arrangements and Arguments), disclosed under the terms of the original s.233 of the 1985 Act, becomes Pt. III of the new Sched. 6.
The old ss.232–233 of the 1985 Act have not been replaced by corresponding sections in the revised text of the Act under the new legislation. Likewise, old s.234 has not been replaced, and what was previously Pt. III of the former Sched. 6 (dealing with Recognised Banks: Disclosure of Dealings with and for Directors) becomes Pt. IV of Sched. 7 to the new Act (which deals with Special Provisions for Banking and Insurance Companies and Groups).
The old Pt. VI of the former Sched. 5 to the 1985 Act (dealing with Particulars Relating to Numbers of Higher Paid Employees) disappears from the legislation.

Section 8(2)   SCHEDULE 5

MATTERS TO BE INCLUDED IN DIRECTORS' REPORT

1. Schedule 7 to the Companies Act 1985 (matters to be included in directors' report) is amended as follows.

Subsidiary undertakings

2.—(1) In paragraph 1(1) (significant changes in fixed assets) for "subsidiaries" substitute "subsidiary undertakings".
(2) In paragraph 6 (general information), for "subsidiaries" in each place where it occurs (three times) substitute "subsidiary undertakings".

Directors' interests

3. For paragraph 2 (directors' interests) substitute—
"2.—(1) The information required by paragraphs 2A and 2B shall be given in the directors' report, or by way of notes to the company's annual accounts, with respect to each person who at the end of the financial year was a director of the company.
(2) In those paragraphs—
    (a) "the register" means the register of directors' interests kept by the company under section 325; and
    (b) references to a body corporate being in the same group as the company are to its being a subsidiary or holding company, or another subsidiary of a holding company, of the company.

2A.—(1) It shall be stated with respect to each director whether, according to the register, he was at the end of the financial year interested in shares in or debentures of the company or any other body corporate in the same group.

(2) If he was so interested, there shall be stated the number of shares in and amount of debentures of each body (specifying it) in which, according to the register, he was then interested.

(3) If a director was interested at the end of the financial year in shares in or debentures of the company or any other body corporate in the same group—
   (a) it shall also be stated whether, according to the register, he was at the beginning of the financial year (or, if he was not then a director, when he became one) interested in shares in or debentures of the company or any other body corporate in the same group, and
   (b) if he was so interested, there shall be stated the number of shares in and amount of debentures of each body (specifying it) in which, according to the register, he was then interested.

(4) In this paragraph references to an interest in shares or debentures have the same meaning as in section 324; and references to the interest of a director include any interest falling to be treated as his for the purposes of that section.

(5) The reference above to the time when a person became a director is, in the case of a person who became a director on more than one occasion, to the time when he first became a director.

2B.—(1) It shall be stated with respect to each director whether, according to the register, any right to subscribe for shares in or debentures of the company or another body corporate in the same group was during the financial year granted to, or exercised by, the director or a member of his immediate family.

(2) If any such right was granted to, or exercised by, any such person during the financial year, there shall be stated the number of shares in and amount of debentures of each body (specifying it) in respect of which, according to the register, the right was granted or exercised.

(3) A director's "immediate family" means his or her spouse and infant children; and for this purpose "children" includes step-children, and "infant", in relation to Scotland, means pupil or minor.

(4) The reference above to a member of the director's immediate family does not include a person who is himself or herself a director of the company.".

DEFINITIONS
"body corporate": s.740 C.A. 1985.
"debentures": s.744 C.A. 1985.
"directors": s.741 C.A. 1985.
"director's immediate family": Sched. 5, para. 2B(3)(4).
"directors' report": s.8, Sched. 5.
"financial year": s.3; Sched. 10, para. 15.
"shares": s.22.
"subsidiary undertakings": ss.21, 144, Sched. 9; SSAP. 14, para. 7.

GENERAL NOTE
This Schedule amends Sched. 7 to the 1985 Act, which concerns Matters Dealt With in Directors' Report. The main change relates to para. 2, which concerns directors' interests. This is replaced by new paras. 2, 2A and 2B, which extend disclosures to cover not merely interests in shares and debentures but also rights to subscribe for shares or debentures, not only by a director himself but also by his immediate family (defined in para. 2B(3)(4)).

Section 13(2)

SCHEDULE 6

[SCHEDULE 8 TO THE COMPANIES ACT 1985]

EXEMPTIONS FOR SMALL AND MEDIUM-SIZED COMPANIES

PART I

SMALL COMPANIES

Balance sheet

1.—(1) The company may deliver a copy of an abbreviated version of the full balance sheet, showing only those items to which a letter or Roman number is assigned in the balance sheet format adopted under Part I of Schedule 4, but in other respects corresponding to the full balance sheet.

(2) If a copy of an abbreviated balance sheet is delivered, there shall be disclosed in it or in a note to the company's accounts delivered—
  (a) the aggregate of the amounts required by note (5) of the notes on the balance sheet formats set out in Part I of Schedule 4 to be shown separately for each item included under debtors (amounts falling due after one year), and
  (b) the aggregate of the amounts required by note (13) of those notes to be shown separately for each item included under creditors in Format 2 (amounts falling due within one year or after more than one year).

(3) The provisions of section 233 as to the signing of the copy of the balance sheet delivered to the registrar apply to a copy of an abbreviated balance sheet delivered in accordance with this paragraph.

Profit and loss account

2. A copy of the company's profit and loss account need not be delivered.

Disclosure of information in notes to accounts

3.—(1) Of the information required by Part III of Schedule 4 (information to be given in notes to accounts if not given in the accounts themselves) only the information required by the following provisions need be given—
  paragraph 36 (accounting policies),
  paragraph 38 (share capital),
  paragraph 39 (particulars of allotments),
  paragraph 42 (fixed assets), so far as it relates to those items to which a letter or Roman number is assigned in the balance sheet format adopted,
  paragraph 48(1) and (4) (particulars of debts),
  paragraph 58(1) (basis of conversion of foreign currency amounts into sterling),
  paragraph 58(2) (corresponding amounts for previous financial year), so far as it relates to amounts stated in a note to the company's accounts by virtue of a requirement of Schedule 4 or under any other provision of this Act.

(2) Of the information required by Schedule 5 to be given in notes to the accounts, the information required by the following provisions need not be given—
  paragraph 4 (financial years of subsidiary undertakings),
  paragraph 5 (additional information about subsidiary undertakings),
  paragraph 6 (shares and debentures of company held by subsidiary undertakings),
  paragraph 10 (arrangements attracting merger relief).

(3) Of the information required by Schedule 6 to be given in notes to the accounts, the information required by Part I (directors' and chairman's emoluments, pensions and compensation for loss of office) need not be given.

Directors' report

4. A copy of the directors' report need not be delivered.

PART II

MEDIUM-SIZED COMPANIES

Profit and loss account

5. The company may deliver a profit and loss account in which the following items listed in the profit and loss account formats set out in Part 1 of Schedule 4 are combined as one item under the heading "gross profit or loss"—
  Items 1, 2, 3 and 6 in Format 1;
  Items 1 to 5 in Format 2;
  Items A.1, B.1 and B.2 in Format 3;
  Items A.1, A.2 and B.1 to B.4 in Format 4.

Disclosure of information in notes to accounts

6. The information required by paragraph 55 of Schedule 4 (particulars of turnover) need not be given.

PART III

SUPPLEMENTARY PROVISIONS

Statement that advantage taken of exemptions

7.—(1) Where the directors of a company take advantage of the exemptions conferred by Part I or Part II of this Schedule, the company's balance sheet shall contain—
  (a) a statement that advantage is taken of the exemptions conferred by Part I or, as the case may be, Part II of this Schedule, and
  (b) a statement of the grounds on which, in the directors' opinion, the company is entitled to those exemptions.

(2) The statements shall appear in the balance sheet immediately above the signature required by section 233.

Special auditors' report

8.—(1) If the directors of a company propose to take advantage of the exemptions conferred by Part I or II of this Schedule, it is the auditors' duty to provide them with a report stating whether in their opinion the company is entitled to those exemptions and whether the documents to be proposed to be delivered in accordance with this Schedule are properly prepared.

(2) The accounts delivered shall be accompanied by a special report of the auditors stating that in their opinion—
  (a) the company is entitled to the exemptions claimed in the directors' statement, and
  (b) the accounts to be delivered are properly prepared in accordance with this Schedule.

(3) In such a case a copy of the auditors' report under section 235 need not be delivered separately, but the full text of it shall be reproduced in the special report; and if the report under section 235 is qualified there shall be included in the special report any further material necessary to understand the qualification.

(4) Section 236 (signature of auditors' report) applies to a special report under this paragraph as it applies to a report under section 235.

Dormant companies

9. Paragraphs 7 and 8 above do not apply where the company is exempt by virtue of section 250 (dormant companies) from the obligation to appoint auditors.

Requirements in connection with publication of accounts

10.—(1) Where advantage is taken of the exemptions conferred by Part I or II of this Schedule, section 240 (requirements in connection with publication of accounts) has effect with the following adaptations.

(2) Accounts delivered in accordance with this Schedule and accounts in the form in which they would be required to be delivered apart from this Schedule are both "statutory accounts" for the purposes of that section.

(3) References in that section to the auditors' report under section 235 shall be read, in relation to accounts delivered in accordance with this Schedule, as references to the special report under paragraph 8 above.

DEFINITIONS
  "balance sheet formats": Sched. 4, para. 8, C.A. 1985.
  "director's report": s.8, Sched. 5.
  "profit and loss account": Scheds. 1–7.
  "qualified auditors' report": s.22.

40/Sch. 6   Companies Act 1989

GENERAL NOTE

This Schedule inserts a new and shortened Sched. 8 into the Companies Act 1985. This deals with the filing of modified accounts by small and medium-sized companies and refers to the new ss.246–249 of the 1985 Act as inserted by s.13. New s.246 deals with the exemptions available to small and medium-sized companies; and new s.247 with the qualifying criteria to be such types of company. New ss.248–249 correspondingly deal with the exemptions available to, and criteria for determining, small and medium-sized groups. The effect is that, whereas the former Sched. 8 dealt with the exemptions for individual companies in Pt. I, and those for group accounts in Pts. II and III, the new Sched. 8 deals with both simultaneously. The number of paragraphs is therefore reduced from 22 to ten, and Pts. I and II now deal respectively with small and medium-sized companies (including groups) while Pt. III covers supplementary provisions.

The substance of the provisions in the new Sched. 8 is very similar to that of its predecessor. The main changes are in para. 3(2), which offers certain exemptions from disclosing information dealt with in the revised Sched. 5 to the 1985 Act (see Sched. 3 to the new Act); and para. 3, which continues the exemptions from disclosing details of directors' emoluments, etc., which were formerly dealt with in Sched. 5, Pt. V, but which are now Pt. I of the revised Sched. 6 (as inserted by Sched. 4 to the new Act). (Pt. VI of the former Sched. 5, dealing with Particulars Relating to Numbers of Higher Paid Employees, is no longer in the Companies Acts).

Disclosure of Information: Emoluments and Other Benefits of Directors and Others:—

                                                                          Former Sched. 5 paras.

Pt. I—*Chairman's and Directors' Emoluments and Compensation for Loss of Office*

Para.

1	Disclosure of aggregate amount of directors' emoluments, and	22
2	—except where the company is a holding or subsidiary company and total emoluments do not exceed £60,000—	23
3	the chairman's emoluments,	24
4	the emoluments of the highest paid director (if other than the chairman) and the numbers of directors whose emoluments fell into bands of £5,000 intervals, *i.e.* £0–£5,000, £5001–£10,000; £10,001–£15,000; etc.,	25
5	Definition of emoluments as in para. 1,	26
6	Disclosure of the number of directors waiving their emoluments and the aggregate amount involved,	27
7	Disclosure of the aggregate amount of directors' and past directors' pensions,	28
8	Disclosure of the aggregate amount of compensation paid to directors and past directors,	29
9	Sums paid to third parties in respect of directors' services,	
10–12	Definitions in connection with paras. 1, 7, 8, 9,	30–32
13	Interpretation of paras. 1–12,	33
14	The information given under paras. 1–13 should be obtained from the company's books or from the persons concerned,	34

                                                      Former Sched. 5 paras.

Pt. II—*Loans, Quasi-Loans and Other Dealings in Favour of Directors*

Para.

15–17	1–3
18–27	5–14

Pt. III—*Other Transactions, Arrangements and Agreements*

Para.

28–30	15–17

Section 18(3) and (4) SCHEDULE 7

SPECIAL PROVISIONS FOR BANKING AND INSURANCE COMPANIES AND GROUPS

Preliminary

Schedule 9 to the Companies Act 1985 is amended in accordance with this Schedule, as follows—
(a) for the heading of the Schedule substitute "SPECIAL PROVISIONS FOR BANKING AND INSURANCE COMPANIES AND GROUPS";
(b) omit the introductory paragraph preceding Part I, together with its heading;
(c) make the present provisions of Parts I to V of the Schedule (as amended by Part I of this Schedule) Part I of the Schedule, and accordingly—
  (i) for the descriptive Part heading before paragraph 2 substitute "FORM AND CONTENT OF ACCOUNTS", and
  (ii) omit the Part headings before paragraphs 19, 27, 31 and 32;
(d) the provisions of Parts II, III and IV of this Schedule have effect as Parts II, III and IV of Schedule 9 to the Companies Act 1985.

PART I

FORM AND CONTENT OF ACCOUNTS

1. In paragraph 10(1)(c) of Schedule 9 to the Companies Act 1985 (disclosure of outstanding loans in connection with certain cases of financial assistance for purchase of company's own shares), after "153(4)(b)" insert ", (bb)".

2. In paragraph 13 of that Schedule (information supplementing balance sheet), omit sub-paragraph (3) (information as to acquisition of, or creation of lien or charge over, company's own shares).

3. In paragraph 17(5) of that Schedule (statement of turnover: companies exempt from requirement) for "neither a holding company nor a subsidiary of another body corporate" substitute "neither a parent company nor a subsidiary undertaking".

4. After paragraph 18 of that Schedule insert—

"Supplementary provisions

18A.—(1) Accounting policies shall be applied consistently within the same accounts and from one financial year to the next.

(2) If it appears to the directors of a company that there are special reasons for departing from the principle stated in sub-paragraph (1) in preparing the company's accounts in respect of any financial year, they may do so; but particulars of the departure, the reasons for it and its effect shall be given in a note to the accounts.

18B. It shall be stated whether the accounts have been prepared in accordance with applicable accounting standards, and particulars of any material departure from those standards and the reasons for it shall be given.

18C.—(1) In respect of every item shown in the balance sheet or profit and loss account, or stated in a note to the accounts, there shall be shown or stated the corresponding amount for the financial year immediately preceding that to which the accounts relate, subject to sub-paragraph (3).

(2) Where the corresponding amount is not comparable, it shall be adjusted and particulars of the adjustment and the reasons for it shall be given in a note to the accounts.

(3) Sub-paragraph (1) does not apply in relation to an amount shown—
  (a) as an amount the source or application of which is required by paragraph 8 above (reserves and provisions),
  (b) in pursuance of paragraph 13(10) above (acquisitions and disposals of fixed assets),
  (c) by virtue of paragraph 13 of Schedule 4A (details of accounting treatment of acquisitions),
  (d) by virtue of paragraph 2, 8(3), 16, 21(1)(d), 22(4) or (5), 24(3) or (4) or 27(3) or (4) of Schedule 5 (shareholdings in other undertakings), or
  (e) by virtue of Part II or III of Schedule 6 (loans and other dealings in favour of directors and others).".

40/Sch. 7 Companies Act 1989

5.—(1) Before paragraph 19 of that Schedule insert the heading "*Provisions where company is parent company or subsidiary undertaking*"; and that paragraph is amended as follows.

(2) In sub-paragraph (1) for the words from "is a holding company" onwards substitute "is a parent company".

(3) In sub-paragraph (2)—
    (a) for "subsidiaries" (four times) substitute "subsidiary undertakings", and
    (b) in paragraph (a), for "Part I" substitute "paragraphs 5, 6, 10, 13 and 14".

(4) Omit sub-paragraphs (3) to (7).

6. For paragraph 20 of that Schedule substitute—

"20.—(1) This paragraph applies where the company is a subsidiary undertaking.

(2) The balance sheet of the company shall show—
    (a) the aggregate amount of its indebtedness to undertakings of which it is a subsidiary undertaking or which are fellow subsidiary undertakings, and
    (b) the aggregate amount of the indebtedness of all such undertakings to it,
distinguishing in each case between indebtedness in respect of debentures and otherwise.

(3) The balance sheet shall also show the aggregate amount of assets consisting of shares in fellow subsidiary undertakings.".

7. Omit paragraphs 21 to 26 of that Schedule.

8.—(1) Before paragraph 27 of that Schedule insert the heading "*Exceptions for certain companies*"; and that paragraph is amended as follows.

(2) In sub-paragraph (2)—
    (a) for "Part I of this Schedule" substitute "paragraphs 2 to 18 of this Schedule", and
    (b) in paragraph (b) for the words from "paragraphs 15" to the end substitute "and paragraph 15".

(3) In sub-paragraph (4), omit "of the said Part I".

9. In paragraph 28 of that Schedule, in sub-paragraph (1) (twice) and in sub-paragraph (2) for "Part I" substitute "paragraphs 2 to 18".

10. After that paragraph insert—

"28A. Where a company is entitled to, and has availed itself of, any of the provisions of paragraph 27 or 28 of this Schedule, section 235(2) only requires the auditors to state whether in their opinion the accounts have been properly prepared in accordance with this Act.".

11. Omit paragraphs 29 to 31 of that Schedule.

12. Before paragraph 32 of that Schedule insert the heading "*Interpretation*"; and in sub-paragraphs (1) and (2) of that paragraph for "this Schedule" substitute "this Part of this Schedule".

13. In paragraph 36 of that Schedule for "this Schedule" substitute "this Part of this Schedule".

PART II

[PART II OF SCHEDULE 9 TO THE COMPANIES ACT 1985]

ACCOUNTS OF BANKING OR INSURANCE GROUP

Undertakings to be included in consolidation

1. The following descriptions of undertaking shall not be excluded from consolidation under section 229(4) (exclusion of undertakings whose activities are different from those of the undertakings consolidated)—
    (a) in the case of a banking group, an undertaking (other than a credit institution) whose activities are a direct extension of or ancillary to banking business;
    (b) in the case of an insurance group, an undertaking (other than one carrying on insurance business) whose activities are a direct extension of or ancillary to insurance business.

For the purposes of paragraph (a) "banking" means the carrying on of a deposit-taking business within the meaning of the Banking Act 1987.

General application of provisions applicable to individual accounts

2.—(1) In paragraph 1 of Schedule 4A (application to group accounts of provisions applicable to individual accounts), the reference in sub-paragraph (1) to the provisions of Schedule 4 shall be construed as a reference to the provisions of Part I of this Schedule; and accordingly—
  (a) the reference in sub-paragraph (2) to paragraph 59 of Schedule 4 shall be construed as a reference to paragraphs 19(2) and 20 of Part I of this Schedule; and
  (b) sub-paragraph (3) shall be omitted.

(2) The general application of the provisions of Part I of this Schedule in place of those of Schedule 4 is subject to the following provisions.

Treatment of goodwill

3.—(1) The rules in paragraph 21 of Schedule 4 relating to the treatment of goodwill, and the rules in paragraphs 17 to 19 of that Schedule (valuation of fixed assets) so far as they relate to goodwill, apply for the purpose of dealing with any goodwill arising on consolidation.

(2) Goodwill shall be shown as a separate item in the balance sheet under an appropriate heading; and this applies notwithstanding anything in paragraph 10(1)(b) or (2) of Part I of this Schedule (under which goodwill, patents and trade marks may be stated in the company's individual accounts as a single item).

Minority interests and associated undertakings

4. The information required by paragraphs 17 and 20 to 22 of Schedule 4A (minority interests and associated undertakings) to be shown under separate items in the formats set out in Part I of Schedule 4 shall be shown separately in the balance sheet and profit and loss account under appropriate headings.

Companies entitled to benefit of exemptions

5.—(1) Where a banking or insurance company is entitled to the exemptions conferred by paragraph 27 or 28 of Part I of this Schedule, a group headed by that company is similarly entitled.

(2) Paragraphs 27(4), 28(2) and 28A (accounts not to be taken to be other than true and fair; duty of auditors) apply accordingly where advantage is taken of those exemptions in relation to group accounts.

Information as to undertaking in which shares held as result of financial assistance operation

6.—(1) The following provisions apply where the parent company of a banking group has a subsidiary undertaking which—
  (a) is a credit institution of which shares are held as a result of a financial assistance operation with a view to its reorganisation or rescue, and
  (b) is excluded from consolidation under section 229(3)(c) (interest held with a view to resale).

(2) Information as to the nature and terms of the operation shall be given in a note to the group accounts and there shall be appended to the copy of the group accounts delivered to the registrar in accordance with section 242 a copy of the undertaking's latest individual accounts and, if it is a parent undertaking, its latest group accounts.

If the accounts appended are required by law to be audited, a copy of the auditors' report shall also be appended.

(3) If any document required to be appended is in a language other than English, the directors shall annex to the copy of that document delivered a translation of it into English, certified in the prescribed manner to be a correct translation.

(4) The above requirements are subject to the following qualifications—
  (a) an undertaking is not required to prepare for the purposes of this paragraph accounts which would not otherwise be prepared, and if no accounts satisfying the above requirements are prepared none need be appended;
  (b) the accounts of an undertaking need not be appended if they would not otherwise be required to be published, or made available for public inspection, anywhere in the world, but in that case the reason for not appending the accounts shall be stated in a note to the consolidated accounts.

40/Sch. 7 *Companies Act 1989*

(5) Where a copy of an undertaking's accounts is required to be appended to the copy of the group accounts delivered to the registrar, that fact shall be stated in a note to the group accounts.

(6) Subsections (2) to (4) of section 242 (penalties, &c. in case of default) apply in relation to the requirements of this paragraph as regards the delivery of documents to the registrar as they apply in relation to the requirements of subsection (1) of that section.

PART III

[PART III OF SCHEDULE 9 TO THE COMPANIES ACT 1985]

ADDITIONAL DISCLOSURE: RELATED UNDERTAKINGS

1. Where accounts are prepared in accordance with the special provisions of this Part relating to banking companies or groups, there shall be disregarded for the purposes of—
   (a) paragraphs 7(2)(a), 23(2)(a) and 26(2)(a) of Schedule 5 (information about significant holdings in undertakings other than subsidiary undertakings: definition of 10 per cent. holding), and
   (b) paragraphs 9(1), 25(1) and 28(1) of that Schedule (additional information in case of 20 per cent. holding),

any holding of shares not comprised in the equity share capital of the undertaking in question.

PART IV

[PART IV OF SCHEDULE 9 TO THE COMPANIES ACT 1985]

ADDITIONAL DISCLOSURE: EMOLUMENTS AND OTHER BENEFITS OF DIRECTORS AND OTHERS

1. The provisions of this Part of this Schedule have effect with respect to the application of Schedule 6 (additional disclosure: emoluments and other benefits of directors and others) to a banking company or the holding company of such a company.

Loans, quasi-loans and other dealings

2. Part II of Schedule 6 (loans, quasi-loans and other dealings) does not apply for the purposes of accounts prepared by a banking company, or a company which is the holding company of a banking company, in relation to a transaction or arrangement of a kind mentioned in section 330, or an agreement to enter into such a transaction or arrangement, to which that banking company is a party.

Other transactions, arrangements and agreements

3.—(1) Part III of Schedule 6 (other transactions, arrangements and agreements) applies for the purposes of accounts prepared by a banking company, or a company which is the holding company of a banking company, only in relation to a transaction, arrangement or agreement made by that banking company for—
   (a) a person who was a director of the company preparing the accounts, or who was connected with such a director, or
   (b) a person who was a chief executive or manager (within the meaning of the Banking Act 1987) of that company or its holding company.

(2) References in that Part to officers of the company shall be construed accordingly as including references to such persons.

(3) In this paragraph "director" includes a shadow director.

(4) For the purposes of that Part as it applies by virtue of this paragraph, a company which a person does not control shall not be treated as connected with him.

(5) Section 346 of this Act applies for the purposes of this paragraph as regards the interpretation of references to a person being connected with a director or controlling a company.

DEFINITIONS
 "accounting standards": Sched. 1, para. 7.
 "associated undertaking": Sched. 2.
 "banking company": Sched. 10, para. 16.

"banking group": s.18.
"credit institution": s.22.
"emoluments": Sched. 4, para. 3.
"goodwill": Sched. 2; SSAPs. 14, 22.
"insurance group": s.18.
"minority interests": Sched. 2.
"parent company": s.21, Sched. 9.
"quasi-loan": s.331(7), C.A. 1985.
"related undertakings": s.6, Sched. 3.
"subsidiary undertaking": ss.21, 144; Sched. 9; SSAP. 14, para. 7.

GENERAL NOTE

This Schedule recasts Sched. 9 to the 1985 Act, which deals with the Form and Content of Special Category Accounts. Now that the former ss.257–262, dealing with the Accounts of Banking, Shipping and Insurance Companies have been removed from the body of the 1985 Act, the title of Sched. 9 has had to be changed to "Special Provisions for Banking and Insurance Companies and Groups". Shipping companies no longer qualify for special treatment.

The main change to Sched. 9 is that paras. 21–26, dealing with the position where the company is a holding company or a subsidiary company, have been removed from the text. What remains now constitutes Pt. I of the revised Sched. 9, dealing with the Form and Content of Accounts, and has been the subject of minor amendments. A new Pt. II, dealing with the Accounts of Banking Groups, effectively replaces withdrawn paras. 21–22, 24–26; while new Pts. III and IV, respectively dealing with additional disclosures on related undertakings and emoluments and other benefits of directors, etc., replace the provisions of the withdrawn para. 23.

The modifications can thus be summarised as follows:

Sched. 7, Pt.	para.	
Pt. I:		*Pt. I—Form and Content of Accounts*
	1	Minor textual amendments.
	2	Omission of the former para. 13(3).
	3	Insertion of new paras. 18A, 18B and 18C, dealing with the specific disclosure that accounting policies have been consistently applied; and the disclosure of previous year's figures. Paras. 18A and 18B correspond to paras. 11 and 36A of the revised Sched. 4, as inserted by paras. 5 and 7 of Sched. 1 to the new Act (see annotations thereto). Para. 18C relates to paras. 13(18) and 18(5) of the old Sched. 9.
	5–7	Modifies the provisions where the company is a holding company or a subsidiary company, but removing paras. 21–26. These are replaced by Parts II and IV (see below).
	8–9	Minor textual amendments.
	10	Inserts para. 28A, which deals with the auditors' report, formerly covered by the old s.262.
	11	Omits paras. 29–31 of Sched. 9 to the 1985 Act.
	12–13	Minor textual amendments.
		Pt. II—Accounts of Banking or Insurance Group.
Pt. II	1	Undertakings to be included in consolidation.
	2	General application of provisions applicable to individual accounts.
	3	Treatment of goodwill.
	4	Minority interests and associated undertakings.
	5	Companies entitled to benefit of exemptions.
	6	Information as to undertaking in which shares held as a result of financial assistance operation.
		Pt. III—Additional Disclosure: Related Undertakings
Pt.III	1	Disclosure in notes.
		Pt. IV—Additional Disclosure: Emoluments and Other Benefits of Directors and Others
Pt. IV	1	Disclosure of emoluments under the new Sched. 6.
	2	Loans, quasi-loans and other dealings: Pt. II of the new Sched. 6 does not apply to banks.

3 Other transactions, arrangements and agreements: the extent of application of Pt. III of the new Sched. 6 to banks.

Section 18(5)

SCHEDULE 8

[SCHEDULE 10 TO THE COMPANIES ACT 1985]

DIRECTORS' REPORT WHERE ACCOUNTS PREPARED IN ACCORDANCE WITH SPECIAL PROVISIONS FOR BANKING OR INSURANCE COMPANIES OR GROUPS

Recent issues

1.—(1) This paragraph applies where a company prepares individual accounts in accordance with the special provisions of this Part relating to banking or insurance companies.

(2) If in the financial year to which the accounts relate the company has issued any shares or debentures, the directors' report shall state the reason for making the issue, the classes of shares or debentures issued and, as respects each class, the number of shares or amount of debentures issued and the consideration received by the company for the issue.

Turnover and profitability

2.—(1) This paragraph applies where a company prepares group accounts in accordance with the special provisions of this Part relating to banking or insurance groups.

(2) If in the course of the financial year to which the accounts relate the group carried on business of two or more classes (other than banking or discounting or a class prescribed for the purposes of paragraph 17(2) of Part I of Schedule 9) that in the opinion of the directors differ substantially from each other, there shall be contained in the directors' report a statement of—
  (a) the proportions in which the turnover for the financial year (so far as stated in the consolidated accounts) is divided amongst those classes (describing them), and
  (b) as regards business of each class, the extent or approximate extent (expressed in money terms) to which, in the opinion of the directors, the carrying on of business of that class contributed to or restricted the profit or loss of the group for that year (before taxation).

(3) In sub-paragraph (2) "the group" means the undertakings included in the consolidation.

(4) For the purposes of this paragraph classes of business which in the opinion of the directors do not differ substantially from each other shall be treated as one class.

Labour force and wages paid

3.—(1) This paragraph applies where a company prepares individual or group accounts in accordance with the special provisions of this Part relating to banking or insurance companies or groups.

(2) There shall be stated in the directors' report—
  (a) the average number of persons employed by the company or, if the company prepares group accounts, by the company and its subsidiary undertakings, and
  (b) the aggregate amount of the remuneration paid or payable to persons so employed.

(3) The average number of persons employed shall be determined by adding together the number of persons employed (whether throughout the week or not) in each week of the financial year and dividing that total by the number of weeks in the financial year.

(4) The aggregate amount of the remuneration paid or payable means the total amount of remuneration paid or payable in respect of the financial year; and for this purpose remuneration means gross remuneration and includes bonuses, whether payable under contract or not.

(5) The information required by this paragraph need not be given if the average number of persons employed is less than 100.

(6) No account shall be taken for the purposes of this paragraph of persons who worked wholly or mainly outside the United Kingdom.

(7) This paragraph does not apply to a company which is a wholly-owned subsidiary of a company incorporated in Great Britain.

DEFINITIONS
  "banking group": s.18.
  "debentures": s.744, C.A. 1985.
  "directors' report (for non-banking and non-insurance groups)": Sched. 5.

"financial year": s.3, Sched. 10, para. 15.
"individual company accounts": s.22, Scheds. 1–7.
"insurance group": s.18.
"shares": s.22.

GENERAL NOTE
This Schedule replaces the requirements of the old s.261(6) and the former Sched. 10, which dealt with the contents of the Directors' Report Where Accounts Are Prepared in Accordance with the Special Provisions for Banking or Insurance Companies or Groups. Although the text has been shortened, the content is substantially the same, dealing with matters not dealt with in the amended Sched. 7, which applies to non-banking and non-insurance companies. The points covered are:
(a) details of recent share issues;
(b) turnover and profit by lien of business; and
(c) the average number of employees and their remuneration.

Exemptions for Small and Medium-Sized Companies

Paras.	Pt. I—Small Companies	Corresponding material in the original 1985 Act	
		Paras. in Sched. 8	Sections
1(1)		2(1)(2), 13(1)(2)	
1(2)	Balance Sheet	6(16)	
1(3)		2(3)	
2	Profit and loss account	3, 14	
3(1)		5, 15	
3(2)	Disclosure in notes to the accounts		
3(3)		4, 17	
4	Directors' report	3, 14	
	Pt. II—Medium-sized Companies		
5	Profit and loss account	7, 18	
6	Disclosure in notes to the accounts	8, 19	
	Pt. III—Supplementary Provisions		
7	Statement that advantages taken of exemptions	9, 21	
8	Special auditors' report	10, 22	
9	Dormant companies		s.253(3)(b)
10	Requirements in connection with publication of accounts	11, 23	

Section 21(2)

SCHEDULE 9

[SCHEDULE 10A TO THE COMPANIES ACT 1985]

PARENT AND SUBSIDIARY UNDERTAKINGS: SUPPLEMENTARY PROVISIONS

Introduction

1. The provisions of this Schedule explain expressions used in section 258 (parent and subsidiary undertakings) and otherwise supplement that section.

Voting rights in an undertaking

2.—(1) In section 258(2)(a) and (d) the references to the voting rights in an undertaking are to the rights conferred on shareholders in respect of their shares or, in the case of an undertaking not having a share capital, on members, to vote at general meetings of the undertaking on all, or substantially all, matters.

(2) In relation to an undertaking which does not have general meetings at which matters are decided by the exercise of voting rights, the references to holding a majority of the voting rights in the undertaking shall be construed as references to having the right under the constitution of the undertaking to direct the overall policy of the undertaking or to alter the terms of its constitution.

Right to appoint or remove a majority of the directors

3.—(1) In section 258(2)(b) the reference to the right to appoint or remove a majority of the board of directors is to the right to appoint or remove directors holding a majority of the voting rights at meetings of the board on all, or substantially all, matters.
(2) An undertaking shall be treated as having the right to appoint to a directorship if—
   (a) a person's appointment to it follows necessarily from his appointment as director of the undertaking, or
   (b) the directorship is held by the undertaking itself.
(3) A right to appoint or remove which is exercisable only with the consent or concurrence of another person shall be left out of account unless no other person has a right to appoint or, as the case may be, remove in relation to that directorship.

Right to exercise dominant influence

4.—(1) For the purposes of section 258(2)(c) an undertaking shall not be regarded as having the right to exercise a dominant influence over another undertaking unless it has a right to give directions with respect to the operating and financial policies of that other undertaking which its directors are obliged to comply with whether or not they are for the benefit of that other undertaking.
(2) A "control contract" means a contract in writing conferring such a right which—
   (a) is of a kind authorised by the memorandum or articles of the undertaking in relation to which the right is exercisable, and
   (b) is permitted by the law under which that undertaking is established.
(3) This paragraph shall not be read as affecting the construction of the expression "actually exercises a dominant influence" in section 258(4)(a).

Rights exercisable only in certain circumstances or temporarily incapable of exercise

5.—(1) Rights which are exercisable only in certain circumstances shall be taken into account only—
   (a) when the circumstances have arisen, and for so long as they continue to obtain, or
   (b) when the circumstances are within the control of the person having the rights.
(2) Rights which are normally exercisable but are temporarily incapable of exercise shall continue to be taken into account.

Rights held by one person on behalf of another

6. Rights held by a person in a fiduciary capacity shall be treated as not held by him.
7.—(1) Rights held by a person as nominee for another shall be treated as held by the other.
(2) Rights shall be regarded as held as nominee for another if they are exercisable only on his instructions or with his consent or concurrence.

Rights attached to shares held by way of security

8. Rights attached to shares held by way of security shall be treated as held by the person providing the security—
   (a) where apart from the right to exercise them for the purpose of preserving the value of the security, or of realising it, the rights are exercisable only in accordance with his instructions, and
   (b) where the shares are held in connection with the granting of loans as part of normal business activities and apart from the right to exercise them for the purpose of preserving the value of the security, or of realising it, the rights are exercisable only in his interests.

Rights attributed to parent undertaking

9.—(1) Rights shall be treated as held by a parent undertaking if they are held by any of its subsidiary undertakings.
(2) Nothing in paragraph 7 or 8 shall be construed as requiring rights held by a parent undertaking to be treated as held by any of its subsidiary undertakings.

(3) For the purposes of paragraph 8 rights shall be treated as being exercisable in accordance with the instructions or in the interests of an undertaking if they are exercisable in accordance with the instructions of or, as the case may be, in the interests of any group undertaking.

Disregard of certain rights

10. The voting rights in an undertaking shall be reduced by any rights held by the undertaking itself.

Supplementary

11. References in any provision of paragraphs 6 to 10 to rights held by a person include rights falling to be treated as held by him by virtue of any other provision of those paragraphs but not rights which by virtue of any such provision are to be treated as not held by him.

DEFINITIONS
"dominant influence": s.21.
"parent undertaking": s.21, Sched. 9.
"subsidiary undertaking": s.21, Sched. 9.
"undertaking": s.22.
"voting rights": Sched. 9.

GENERAL NOTE
This Schedule inserts a new Sched. 10A, which deals with the meaning of expressions concerning parent and subsidiary undertakings. It therefore supplements the revised s.258 of the 1985 Act, inserted by s.21 of the new legislation.

Schedule 10A: Parent and Subsidiary Undertakings: Supplementary Provisions
Para.
1	Introduction
2	Meaning of voting rights in an undertaking.
3	Meaning of the right to appoint or remove a majority of the directors.
4	Meaning of the right to exercise dominant influence.
5	Rights exercisable only in certain circumstances or which are temporarily incapable of exercise.
6–7	Rights held by one person on behalf or another.
8	Rights attached to shares held by way of security.
9	Rights attached to parent undertaking.
10	Disregard of certain rights.
11	Supplementary.

Section 23

SCHEDULE 10

AMENDMENTS CONSEQUENTIAL ON PART I

PART I

AMENDMENTS OF THE COMPANIES ACT 1985

1. In section 46 (meaning of "unqualified" auditors' report in section 43(3)), for subsections (2) to (6) substitute—

"(2) If the balance sheet was prepared for a financial year of the company, the reference is to an auditors' report stating without material qualification the auditors' opinion that the balance sheet has been properly prepared in accordance with this Act.

(3) If the balance sheet was not prepared for a financial year of the company, the reference is to an auditors' report stating without material qualification the auditors' opinion that the balance sheet has been properly prepared in accordance with the provisions of this Act which would have applied if it had been so prepared.

For the purposes of an auditors' report under this subsection the provisions of this Act shall be deemed to apply with such modifications as are necessary by reason of the fact that the balance sheet is not prepared for a financial year of the company.

(4) A qualification shall be regarded as material unless the auditors state in their report that the matter giving rise to the qualification is not material for the purpose of determining (by reference to the company's balance sheet) whether at the balance sheet date the amount of the company's net assets was not less than the aggregate of its called up share capital and undistributable reserves.

In this subsection "net assets" and "undistributable reserves" have the meaning given by section 264(2) and (3).".

2. In section 209(5)(a)(i) for "an authorised institution" substitute "a banking company".

3. In sections 211(9) and 215(4) for "paragraph 3 or 10 of Schedule 5" substitute "section 231(3)".

4. In section 271(3), for "section 236" substitute "section 235".

5. In section 272(3)—
    (a) for "section 228" substitute "section 226", and
    (b) for "section 238" substitute "section 233".

6. In sections 272(5) and 273(7) for "section 241(3)(b)" substitute "the second sentence of section 242(1)".

7. In section 276(b) for "34(4)(b)" substitute "34(3)(a)".

8. For section 279 substitute—

"**Distributions by banking or insurance companies**

279. Where a company's accounts relevant for the purposes of this Part are prepared in accordance with the special provisions of Part VII relating to banking or insurance companies, sections 264 to 275 apply with the modifications shown in Schedule 11.".

9. In section 289(4) for "section 252(5)" substitute "section 250(3)".

10. In sections 338(4), 339(4), 343(1)(a) and 344(2) for "an authorised institution", wherever occurring, substitute "a banking company".

11. In section 343(2) and (4) for "paragraph 4 of Schedule 6, be required by section 232" substitute "paragraph 2 of Part IV of Schedule 9, be required".

12. In section 699(3) for "section 241(3)" substitute "section 242(1)".

13. In Part XXIII (oversea companies), for Chapter II (delivery of accounts) substitute—

"CHAPTER II

DELIVERY OF ACCOUNTS AND REPORTS

Preparation of accounts and reports by oversea companies

700.—(1) Every oversea company shall in respect of each financial year of the company prepare the like accounts and directors' report, and cause to be prepared such an auditors'report, as would be required if the company were formed and registered under this Act.

(2) The Secretary of State may by order—
  (a) modify the requirements referred to in subsection (1) for the purpose of their application to oversea companies;
  (b) exempt an oversea company from those requirements or from such of them as may be specified in the order.

(3) An order may make different provision for different cases or classes of case and may contain such incidental and supplementary provisions as the Secretary of State thinks fit.

(4) An order under this section shall be made by statutory instrument which shall be subject to annulment in pursuance of a resolution of either House of Parliament.

Oversea company's financial year and accounting reference periods

701.—(1) Sections 223 to 225 (financial year and accounting reference periods) apply to an oversea company, subject to the following modifications.

(2) For the references to the incorporation of the company substitute references to the company establishing a place of business in Great Britain.

(3) Omit section 225(4) (restriction on frequency with which current accounting reference period may be extended).

Delivery to registrar of accounts and reports of oversea company

702.—(1) An oversea company shall in respect of each financial year of the company deliver to the registrar copies of the accounts and reports prepared in accordance with section 700.

If any document comprised in those accounts or reports is in a language other than English, the directors shall annex to the copy delivered a translation of it into English, certified in the prescribed manner to be a correct translation.

(2) In relation to an oversea company the period allowed for delivering accounts and reports is 13 months after the end of the relevant accounting reference period.

This is subject to the following provisions of this section.

(3) If the relevant accounting reference period is the company's first and is a period of more than 12 months, the period allowed is 13 months from the first anniversary of the company's establishing a place of business in Great Britain.

(4) If the relevant accounting period is treated as shortened by virtue of a notice given by the company under section 225 (alteration of accounting reference date), the period allowed is that applicable in accordance with the above provisions or three months from the date of the notice under that section, whichever last expires.

(5) If for any special reason the Secretary of State thinks fit he may, on an application made before the expiry of the period otherwise allowed, by notice in writing to an oversea company extend that period by such further period as may be specified in the notice.

(6) In this section "the relevant accounting reference period" means the accounting reference period by reference to which the financial year for the accounts in question was determined.

Penalty for non-compliance

703.—(1) If the requirements of section 702(1) are not complied with before the end of the period allowed for delivering accounts and reports, or if the accounts and reports delivered do not comply with the requirements of this Act, the company and every person who immediately before the end of that period was a director of the company is guilty of an offence and liable to a fine and, for continued contravention, to a daily default fine.

(2) It is a defence for a person charged with such an offence to prove that he took all reasonable steps for securing that the requirements in question would be complied with.

(3) It is not a defence in relation to a failure to deliver copies to the registrar to prove that the documents in question were not in fact prepared as required by this Act.".

14. In section 711(1)(k) for "section 241 (annual accounts)" substitute "section 242(1) (accounts and reports)".

15. For section 742 (expressions used in connection with accounts) substitute—

"**Expressions used in connection with accounts**

742.—(1) In this Act, unless a contrary intention appears, the following expressions have the same meaning as in Part VII (accounts)—

"annual accounts",

"accounting reference date" and "accounting reference period",

"balance sheet" and "balance sheet date",

"current assets",

"financial year", in relation to a company,

"fixed assets",

"parent company" and "parent undertaking",

"profit and loss account", and

"subsidiary undertaking".

(2) References in this Act to "realised profits" and "realised losses", in relation to a company's accounts, shall be construed in accordance with section 262(3).".

16. In section 744 (interpretation), omit the definition of "authorised institution" and at the appropriate place insert—

" 'banking company' means a company which is authorised under the Banking Act 1987;".

17. In Schedule 1, in paragraph 2(2)(a) for "section 252(5)" substitute "section 250(3)".

18.—(1) Schedule 2 (interpretation of references to "beneficial interest") is amended as follows.

(2) After the heading at the beginning of the Schedule, and before the cross-heading preceding paragraph 1, insert the following heading—

40/Sch. 10 *Companies Act 1989*

"PART I

REFERENCES IN SECTIONS 23, 145, 146 AND 148".

(3) In paragraph 1—
  (a) in sub-paragraph (1) omit "paragraph 60(2) of Schedule 4, or paragraph 19(3) of Schedule 9"; and
  (b) omit sub-paragraph (5).
(4) In paragraph 3—
  (a) in sub-paragraph (1) omit ", paragraph 60(2) of Schedule 4 or paragraph 19(3) of Schedule 9"; and
  (b) omit sub-paragraph (3).
(5) In paragraph 4—
  (a) in sub-paragraph (1) omit "(whether as personal representative or otherwise)", and
  (b) in sub-paragraph (2) omit ", paragraph 60(2) of Schedule 4 and paragraph 19(3) of Schedule 9";
and at the end add—
  "(3) As respects sections 145, 146 and 148, sub-paragraph (1) above applies where a company is a personal representative as it applies where a company is a trustee.".
(6) In paragraph 5(1) for "this Schedule" substitute "this Part of this Schedule".
(7) After paragraph 5 insert the following—

"PART II

REFERENCES IN SCHEDULE 5

Residual interests under pension and employees' share schemes

6.—(1) Where shares in an undertaking are held on trust for the purposes of a pension scheme or an employees' share scheme, there shall be disregarded any residual interest which has not vested in possession, being an interest of the undertaking or any of its subsidiary undertakings.

(2) In this paragraph a "residual interest" means a right of the undertaking in question (the "residual beneficiary") to receive any of the trust property in the event of—
  (a) all the liabilities arising under the scheme having been satisfied or provided for, or
  (b) the residual beneficiary ceasing to participate in the scheme, or
  (c) the trust property at any time exceeding what is necessary for satisfying the liabilities arising or expected to arise under the scheme.

(3) In sub-paragraph (2) references to a right include a right dependent on the exercise of a discretion vested by the scheme in the trustee or any other person; and references to liabilities arising under a scheme include liabilities that have resulted or may result from the exercise of any such discretion.

(4) For the purposes of this paragraph a residual interest vests in possession—
  (a) in a case within sub-paragraph (2)(a), on the occurrence of the event there mentioned, whether or not the amount of the property receivable pursuant to the right mentioned in that sub-paragraph is then ascertained;
  (b) in a case within sub-paragraph (2)(b) or (c), when the residual beneficiary becomes entitled to require the trustee to transfer to that beneficiary any of the property receivable pursuant to that right.

Employer's charges and other rights of recovery

7.—(1) Where shares in an undertaking are held on trust, there shall be disregarded—
  (a) if the trust is for the purposes of a pension scheme, any such rights as are mentioned in sub-paragraph (2) below;
  (b) if the trust is for the purposes of an employees' share scheme, any such rights as are mentioned in paragraph (a) of that sub-paragraph,
being rights of the undertaking or any of its subsidiary undertakings.
(2) The rights referred to are—
  (a) any charge or lien on, or set-off against, any benefit or other right or interest

under the scheme for the purpose of enabling the employer or former employer of a member of the scheme to obtain the discharge of a monetary obligation due to him from the member, and

(b) any right to receive from the trustee of the scheme, or as trustee of the scheme to retain, an amount that can be recovered or retained under section 47 of the Social Security Pensions Act 1975 (deduction of premium from refund of pension contributions) or otherwise as reimbursement or partial reimbursement for any state scheme premium paid in connection with the scheme under Part III of that Act.

Trustee's right to expenses, remuneration, indemnity, &c.

8. Where an undertaking is a trustee, there shall be disregarded any rights which the undertaking has in its capacity as trustee including, in particular, any right to recover its expenses or be remunerated out of the trust property and any right to be indemnified out of that property for any liability incurred by reason of any act or omission of the undertaking in the performance of its duties as trustee.

Supplementary

9.—(1) The following applies for the interpretation of this Part of this Schedule.

(2) "Undertaking", and "shares" in relation to an undertaking, have the same meaning as in Part VII.

(3) This Part of this Schedule applies in relation to debentures as it applies in relation to shares.

(4) "Pension scheme" means any scheme for the provision of benefits consisting of or including relevant benefits for or in respect of employees or former employees; and "relevant benefits" means any pension, lump sum, gratuity or other like benefit given or to be given on retirement or on death or in anticipation of retirement or, in connection with past service, after retirement or death.

(5) In sub-paragraph (4) of this paragraph and in paragraph 7(2) "employee" and "employer" shall be read as if a director of an undertaking were employed by it.".

19.—(1) Part II of Schedule 3 (prospectuses: auditors' and accountants' reports to be set out) is amended as follows.

(2) In paragraph 16 (auditors' reports), in sub-paragraph (2) for "subsidiaries" substitute "subsidiary undertakings" and for sub-paragraph (3) substitute—

"(3) If the company has subsidiary undertakings, the report shall—

(a) deal separately with the company's profits or losses as provided by sub-paragraph (2), and in addition deal either—

(i) as a whole with the combined profits or losses of its subsidiary undertakings, so far as they concern members of the company, or

(ii) individually with the profits or losses of each of its subsidiary undertakings, so far as they concern members of the company,

or, instead of dealing separately with the company's profits or losses, deal as a whole with the profits or losses of the company and (so far as they concern members of the company) with the combined profits and losses of its subsidiary undertakings; and

(b) deal separately with the company's assets and liabilities as provided by sub-paragraph (2), and in addition deal either—

(i) as a whole with the combined assets and liabilities of its subsidiary undertakings, with or without the company's assets and liabilities, or

(ii) individually with the assets and liabilities of each of its subsidiary undertakings,

indicating, as respects the assets and liabilities of its subsidiary undertakings, the allowance to be made for persons other than members of the company.".

(3) For paragraph 18 (accountants' reports) substitute—

"18.—(1) The following provisions apply if—

(a) the proceeds of the issue are to be applied directly or indirectly in any manner resulting in the acquisition by the company of shares in any other undertaking, or any part of the proceeds is to be so applied, and

(b) by reason of that acquisition or anything to be done in consequence of or in connection with it, that undertaking will become a subsidiary undertaking of the company.

(2) There shall be set out in the prospectus a report made by accountants upon—

(a) the profits or losses of the other undertaking in respect of each of the five financial years immediately preceding the issue of the prospectus, and
(b) the assets and liabilities of the other undertaking at the last date to which its accounts were made up.

(3) The report shall—
(a) indicate how the profits or losses of the other undertaking would in respect of the shares to be acquired have concerned members of the company and what allowance would have fallen to be made, in relation to assets and liabilities so dealt with, for holders of other shares, if the company had at all material times held the shares to be acquired, and
(b) where the other undertaking is a parent undertaking, deal with the profits or losses and the assets and liabilities of the undertaking and its subsidiary undertakings in the manner provided by paragraph 16(3) above in relation to the company and its subsidiary undertakings.

(4) In this paragraph "undertaking" and "shares", in relation to an undertaking, have the same meaning as in Part VII.".

(4) In paragraph 22 (eligibility of accountants to make reports), for sub-paragraph (2) substitute—

"(2) Such a report shall not be made by an accountant who is an officer or servant, or a partner of or in the employment of an officer or servant, of—
(a) the company or any of its subsidiary undertakings,
(b) a parent undertaking of the company or any subsidiary undertaking of such an undertaking.".

20. In paragraph 12(b) of Schedule 4, for "section 238" substitute "section 233".

21.—(1) Schedule 11 is amended as follows.

(2) For the heading substitute "MODIFICATIONS OF PART VIII WHERE COMPANY'S ACCOUNTS PREPARED IN ACCORDANCE WITH SPECIAL PROVISIONS FOR BANKING OR INSURANCE COMPANIES".

(3) In paragraphs 1 and 2(a) for "Schedule 9" substitute "Part I of Schedule 9".

(4) In paragraph 4—
(a) in sub-paragraph (a) for "Schedule 9" substitute "Part I of Schedule 9", and
(b) omit sub-paragraphs (b) and (c).

(5) In paragraph 5—
(a) in sub-paragraph (a) for "Part III of Schedule 9" substitute "paragraph 27 or 28 of Schedule 9", and
(b) omit sub-paragraph (b).

(6) In paragraph 6—
(a) in sub-paragraph (a), for "section 228" substitute "section 226" and for "section 258 and Schedule 9" substitute "section 255 and Part I of Schedule 9", and
(b) in sub-paragraph (b), for "Part III of Schedule 9" substitute "paragraph 27 or 28 of Schedule 9".

(7) In paragraph 7(a) for "Schedule 9" substitute "Part I of Schedule 9".

22.—(1) In Schedule 15A (renumbered 15B) (provisions applicable to mergers and divisions of public companies), paragraph 6 (documents to be made available for inspection) is amended as follows.

(2) In sub-paragraph (1)(b) (directors' report on merger or division), after "directors' report" insert "referred to in paragraph 4 above".

(3) For sub-paragraph (1)(d) and (e) substitute—

"(d) the company's annual accounts, together with the relevant directors' report and auditors' report, for the last three financial years ending on or before the relevant date; and
(e) if the last of those financial years ended more than six months before the relevant date, an accounting statement in the form described in the following provisions.".

(4) In sub-paragraph (1), after the paragraphs add—

"In paragraphs (d) and (e) "the relevant date" means one month before the first meeting of the company summoned under section 425(1) or for the purposes of paragraph 1.".

(5) For sub-paragraphs (2) to (5) substitute—

"(2) The accounting statement shall consist of—
(a) a balance sheet dealing with the state of the affairs of the company as at a date not more than three months before the draft terms were adopted by the directors, and
(b) where the company would be required to prepare group accounts if that date

were the last day of a financial year, a consolidated balance sheet dealing with the state of affairs of the company and its subsidiary undertakings as at that date.

(3) The requirements of this Act as to balance sheets forming part of a company's annual accounts, and the matters to be included in notes thereto, apply to any balance sheet required for the accounting statement, with such modifications as are necessary by reason of its being prepared otherwise than as at the last day of a financial year.

(4) Any balance sheet required for the accounting statement shall be approved by the board of directors and signed on behalf of the board by a director of the company.

(5) In relation to a company within the meaning of Article 3 of the Companies (Northern Ireland) Order 1986, the references in this paragraph to the requirements of this Act shall be construed as reference to the corresponding requirements of that Order.".

23. In Schedule 22 (provisions applying to unregistered companies), in the entry relating to Part VII, in column 1, for "Schedule 10" substitute "Schedules 10 and 10A".

24.—(1) Schedule 24 (punishment of offences) is amended as follows.

(2) The existing entries for provisions in Part VII are amended as follows, and shall be re-ordered according to the new order of the sections in that Part:

Provisions of Part VII	Amendment
233(1)	In column 1, for "223(1)" substitute "221(5) or 222(4)".
223(2)	In column 1, for "223(2)" substitute "222(6)".
	In column 2, for "222(4)" substitute "222(5)".
231(3)	In column 1, for "231(3)" substitute "231(6)".
231(4)	In column 1, for "231(4)" substitute "232(4)".
	In column 2, for "Schedule 5, Part V" subsitute "Schedule 6, Part I".
235(7)	In column 1, for "235(7)" substitute "234(5)".
	In column 2, for "the section" substitute "Part VII".
238(2)	In column 1, for "238(2)" substitute "233(6)".
240(5)	In column 1, for "240(5)" substitute "238(5)".
	In column 2, for "company balance sheet" substitute "company's annual accounts".
243(1)	In column 1, for "243(1)" substitute "241(2) or 242(2)".
	In column 2, for "company accounts" substitute "company's annual accounts, directors' report and auditors' report".
245(1)	Omit the entry.
245(2)	Omit the entry.
246(2)	In column 1, for "246(2)" substitute "239(3)".
	In column 2, after "accounts" insert "and reports".
254(5)	In column 1, for "254(6)" substitute "240(6)".
	In column 2, for the present words substitute "Failure to comply with requirements in connection with publication of accounts".
255(5)	Omit the entry.
260(3)	Omit the entry.

(3) At the appropriate places insert the following new entries—

"233(5)	Approving defective accounts.	1. On indictment. 2. Summary.	A fine The statutory maximum.
234A(4)	Laying, circulating or delivering directors' report without required signature.	Summary.	One-fifth of the statutory maximum.
236(4)	Laying, circulating or delivering auditors' report without required signature.	Summary.	On-fifth of the statutory maximum.
251(6)	Failure to comply with requirements in relation to summary financial statements.	Summary.	One-fifth of the statutory maximum.".

(4) In the entry for section 703(1) (failure by oversea company to comply with requirements as to accounts and reports), in column 2 for the words from "s.700" to the end substitute "requirements as to accounts and reports".

Part II

Amendments of Other Enactments

Betting, Gaming and Lotteries Act 1963 (c.2)

25. In Schedule 2 to the Betting, Gaming and Lotteries Act 1963 (registered pool promoters), in paragraph 24(2) (duties with respect to delivery of accounts and audit) for the words from "and the following provisions" to "their report)" substitute "and sections 235(2) and 237(1) and (3) of the Companies Act 1985 (matters to be stated in auditors' report and responsibility of auditors in preparing their report)".

Harbours Act 1964 (c.40)

26.—(1) Section 42 of the Harbours Act 1964 (accounts and reports of statutory harbour undertakers) is amended as follows.

(2) For subsection (2) substitute—

"(2) Where a statutory harbour undertaker is a parent undertaking with subsidiary undertakings which carry on harbour activities or any associated activities, then, it shall be the duty of the company also to prepare group accounts relating to the harbour activities and associated activities carried on by it and its subsidiary undertakings."

(3) In subsection (6) (application of provisions of the Companies Act 1985)—
   (a) in paragraph (a) for "company accounts" substitute "individual company accounts";
   (b) in paragraph (c) omit the words "required to be attached to a company's balance sheet".

(4) In subsection (9), for the definition of "holding company" and "subsidiary" substitute—

" 'parent undertaking' and 'subsidiary undertaking' have the same meaning as in Part VII of the Companies Act 1985;".

Coal Industry Act 1971 (c.16)

27.—(1) Section 8 of the Coal Industry Act 1971 (further provisions as to accounts of British Coal Corporation) is amended as follows.

(2) In subsections (1) and (2) for "subsidiaries" (three times) substitute "subsidiary undertakings".

(3) After subsection (2) insert—

"(3) In this section 'subsidiary undertaking' has the same meaning as in Part VII of the Companies Act 1985.".

Aircraft and Shipbuilding Industries Act 1977 (c.3)

28.—(1) Section 17 of the Aircraft and Shipbuilding Industries Act 1977 (British Shipbuilders: accounts and audit) is amended as follows.

(2) In subsection (1)(c) (duty to prepare consolidated accounts) for "subsidiaries" substitute "subsidiary undertakings".

(3) In subsection (9) (copies of accounts to be sent to the Secretary of State) for "subsidiaries" substitute "subsidiary undertakings" and for "subsidiary" substitute "subsidiary undertaking".

(4) After subsection (9) add—

"(10) In this section "subsidiary undertaking" has the same meaning as in Part VII of the Companies Act 1985.".

Crown Agents Act 1979 (c.43)

29. In section 22 of the Crown Agents Act 1979 (accounts and audit), in subsection (2) (duty to prepare consolidated accounts) for "subsidiaries" (three times) substitute "subsidiary undertakings", and at the end of that subsection add—

"In this subsection "subsidiary undertaking" has the same meaning as in Part VII of the Companies Act 1985.".

British Telecommunications Act 1981 (c.38)

30. In section 75 of the British Telecommunications Act 1981 (accounts of the Post Office), in subsection (1)(c)(i) for "subsidiaries" substitute "subsidiary undertakings within the meaning of Part VII of the Companies Act 1985".

Transport Act 1981 (c.56)

31. In section 11(4) of the Transport Act 1981, for "section 235" substitute "section 234".

Iron and Steel Act 1982 (c.25)

32. In section 24(5) of the Iron and Steel Act 1982 (meaning of "directors' report") for the words from "which, under section 235" to the end substitute "which is required to be prepared under section 234 of the Companies Act 1985".

Oil and Pipelines Act 1985 (c.62)

33. In Schedule 3 to the Oil and Pipelines Act 1985 (Oil and Pipelines Agency: financial and other provisions), in paragraph 9(2) (duty to prepare consolidated accounts) for "subsidiaries" (three times) substitute "subsidiary undertakings", and at the end of that sub-paragraph add—
"In this sub-paragraph "subsidiary undertaking" has the same meaning as in Part VII of the Companies Act 1985.".

Patents, Designs and Marks Act 1986 (c.39)

34. In Schedule 2 to the Patents, Designs and Marks Act 1986 (service marks), in paragraph 1(2) (provisions in which reference to trade mark includes service mark) for sub-paragraph (ii) substitute—
"(ii) Part I of Schedule 4 and paragraphs 5(2)(d) and 10(1)(b) and (2) of Schedule 9 (form of company balance sheets); and".

Company Directors Disqualification Act 1986 (c.46)

35.—(1) The Company Directors Disqualification Act 1986 is amended as follows.
(2) In section 3(3)(b) (default orders)—
 (a) in sub-paragraph (i) for "section 244" substitute "section 242(4)", and
 (b) after that sub-paragraph insert—
 "(ia) section 245B of that Act (order requiring preparation of revised accounts),".
(3) In Schedule 1, for paragraph 5 substitute—
"5. The extent of the director's responsibility for any failure by the directors of the company to comply with—
 (a) section 226 or 227 of the Companies Act (duty to prepare annual accounts), or
 (b) section 233 of that Act (approval and signature of accounts).".

Financial Services Act 1986 (c.60)

36.—(1) The Financial Services Act 1986 is amended as follows.
(2) In section 117(4) and (5), for "section 227" substitute "section 226".
(3) In Schedule 1, for paragraph 30 substitute—
"30.—(1) For the purposes of this Schedule a group shall be treated as including any body corporate in which a member of the group holds a qualifying capital interest.
(2) A qualifying capital interest means an interest in relevant shares of the body corporate which the member holds on a long-term basis for the purpose of securing a contribution to its own activities by the exercise of control or influence arising from that interest.
(3) Relevant shares means shares comprised in the equity share capital of the body corporate of a class carrying rights to vote in all circumstances at general meetings of the body.
(4) A holding of 20 per cent. or more of the nominal value of the relevant shares of a body corporate shall be presumed to be a qualifying capital interest unless the contrary is shown.

40/Sch. 10 *Companies Act* 1989

(5) In this paragraph "equity share capital" has the same meaning as in the Companies Act 1985 and the Companies (Northern Ireland) Order 1986.".

Banking Act 1987 (c.22)

37.—(1) The Banking Act 1987 is amended as follows.
(2) In Section 46(2) (duties of auditor of authorised institution), in paragraph (c) for "section 236" substitute "section 235(2)" and for "section 237" substitute "section 235(3) or section 237"; and in section 46(4) (adaptation of references for Northern Ireland) for "236 and 237" substitute "235(2) and 235(3) and 237".
(3) After section 105 insert—

"Meaning of "related company"
105A.—(1) In this Act a "related company", in relation to an institution or the holding company of an institution, means a body corporate (other than a subsidiary) in which the institution or holding company holds a qualifying capital interest.

(2) A qualifying capital interest means an interest in relevant shares of the body corporate which the institution or holding company holds on a long-term basis for the purpose of securing a contribution to its own activities by the exercise of control or influence arising from that interest.

(3) Relevant shares means shares comprised in the equity share capital of the body corporate of a class carrying rights to vote in all circumstances at general meetings of the body.

(4) A holding of 20 per cent. or more of the nominal value of the relevant shares of a body corporate shall be presumed to be a qualifying capital interest unless the contrary is shown.

(5) In this paragraph "equity share capital" has the same meaning as in the Companies Act 1985 and the Companies (Northern Ireland) Order 1986.".
(4) In section 106(1) (interpretation), for the definition of "related company" substitute—
" "related company" has the meaning given by section 105A above;".

Income and Corporation Taxes Act 1988 (c.1)

38.—(1) The Income and Corporation Taxes Act 1988 is amended as follows.
(2) In section 180 (annual return of registered profit-related pay scheme), in subsection (3) for "section 242(3)" substitute "section 244(3)".
(3) In section 565(6) (conditions for exemption from provisions relating to sub-contractors in construction industry: compliance with requirements of Companies Act 1985), in paragraph (a) for "section 227 and 241" substitute "sections 226, 241 and 242".

Dartford–Thurrock Crossing Act 1988 (c.20)

39. In section 33 of the Dartford–Thurrock Crossing Act 1988 (duty to lay before Parliament copies of accounts of persons appointed to levy tolls), for subsection (2) substitute—

"(2) In relation to a company "accounts" in subsection (1) means the company's annual accounts for a financial year, together with the relevant directors' report and the auditors' report on those accounts.

Expressions used in this subsection have the same meaning as in Part VII of the Companies Act 1985.".

DEFINITIONS
"accounting reference date, accounting reference period": s.3.
"annual accounts": s.22; Sched. 10, para. 15.
"auditors' report": s.9.
"balance sheet date": s.22; Sched. 10, para. 15.
"banking company": Sched. 10, para. 16.
"banking group": s.18.
"company accounts": s.4(1).
"current assets": s.22.
"delivery of accounts to the Registrar": s.11.
"employee" and "employer": Sched. 10, para. 18(7).
"financial year": s.3; Sched. 10, para. 15.

"fixed assets": s.22.
"insurance group": s.18.
"net assets": s.264(2) C.A. 1985.
"pension scheme": Sched. 10, para. 18)7).
"profit and loss account (in relation to a company not trading for profit)": s.22.
"qualification an auditor's report": s.22.
"residual interest": Sched. 10, para. 18(7).
"shares": s.22.
"subsidiary undertaking": ss.22, 144; Sched. 9; SSAP. 14, para. 7.
"undertaking": s.24.

GENERAL NOTE
This Schedule deals with amendments consequential on Pt. I of the new Act. Pt. I of the Schedule deals with amendments to the Companies Act 1985, as Pt. II with amendments of other enactments.
The main enactments are as follows:

Pt. I. Amendments to the Companies Act 1985
Para. 1: S. 46 of the 1985 Act, which deals with the meaning of an unqualified auditor's report in s.43(3), is extensively modified, the provisions being explained in slightly more general terms, although the substance is not altered. Further reference should be made to the Auditing Standards and Guidelines of the Auditing Practices Committee, especially to the Standard on "The Audit Report".
Para. 8: A new s.279, dealing with distributions by banking and insurance companies, is inserted, although the substance is similar.
Para. 13: New ss.700–703, dealing with the Delivery of Accounts and Reports by oversea companies, is substituted for the corresponding sections in the 1985 Act. The text is simplified, but the substance is essentially the same.
Para. 15: A new s.742, dealing with expressions used in connection with accounts, is inserted into the 1985 Act. However, the substance is unchanged.
Para. 16: A new definition of a "banking company" is included in s.744 of the 1985 Act.
Para. 18(7): In Sched. 2 to the 1985 Act, which deals with the interpretation of references to "beneficial interest", new paras. 6–9 are inserted. These deal with references in Sched. 5 to the 1985 Act (as amended by Sched. 3 to this Act) relating to para. 6—residual interests under pension and employees' share schemes; para. 7—employer's charges and other rights of recovery; para. 8—trustee's right to expenses, remuneration, indemnity, etc.; para. 9—supplementary.
Para. 19: Sched. 3 to the 1985 Act, which deals with the Mandatory Contents of a Prospectus, is to be repealed (together with Pt. III of the 1985 Act, ss.56–79) under the provisions of Sched. 17 to the Financial Services Act 1986. However, this has yet to be implemented, and in the meantime para. 19 of Sched. 10 to the new Act makes minor amendments to the wording of paras. 16, 18 and 22 of Sched. 3 to the 1985 Act. The paragraphs in question are concerned with auditors' and accountants' reports and ensure that the words "subsidiary undertakings" are used.
Para. 22: Sched. 15A to the 1985 Act, which deals with provisions applicable to mergers and divisions of public companies, is renumbered 15B, and the wording of para. 6 (inspection of documents) is altered, although the substance is unchanged.
Para. 24(3): In Sched. 24 to the 1985 Act, which deals with the punishment of offences, four new offences and appropriate penalties are identified; (1) s.233(5)—approving defective accounts (see s.7 of the new Act); (2) s.234A(4)—laying, circulating or delivering directors' report without required signature (see s.8 of the new Act); (3) s.236(4)—laying, circulating or delivering auditors' report without required signature (see s.9 of the new Act); (4) s.251(6)—failure to comply with requirements in relation to summary financial statements (see s.15 of the new Act).

Part II—Amendments of Other Enactments
Para. 36(3): In Sched. 1 to the Financial Services Act 1986, a new para. 30 is submitted which specifies in more detail the meaning of a group for the purposes of the Schedule.
Para. 37(3): A new s.105A is substituted into the Banking Act 1987, dealing with the meaning of a "related company".

Section 30(5)

SCHEDULE 11

RECOGNITION OF SUPERVISORY BODY

PART I

GRANT AND REVOCATION OF RECOGNITION

Application for recognition of supervisory body

1.—(1) A supervisory body may apply to the Secretary of State for an order declaring it to be a recognised supervisory body for the purposes of this Part of this Act.
(2) Any such application—
   (a) shall be made in such manner as the Secretary of State may direct, and
   (b) shall be accompanied by such information as the Secretary of State may reasonably require for the purpose of determining the application.
(3) At any time after receiving an application and before determining it the Secretary of State may require the applicant to furnish additional information.
(4) The directions and requirements given or imposed under sub-paragraphs (2) and (3) may differ as between different applications.
(5) Any information to be furnished to the Secretary of State under this paragraph shall, if he so requires, be in such form or verified in such manner as he may specify.
(6) Every application shall be accompanied by a copy of the applicant's rules and of any guidance issued by the applicant which is intended to have continuing effect and is issued in writing or other legible form.

Grant and refusal of recognition

2.—(1) The Secretary of State may, on an application duly made in accordance with paragraph 1 and after being furnished with all such information as he may require under that paragraph, make or refuse to make an order (a "recognition order") declaring the applicant to be a recognised supervisory body for the purposes of this Part of this Act.
(2) The Secretary of State shall not make a recognition order unless it appears to him, from the information furnished by the body and having regard to any other information in his possession, that the requirements of Part II of this Schedule are satisfied as respects that body.
(3) The Secretary of State may refuse to make a recognition order in respect of a body if he considers that its recognition is unnecessary having regard to the existence of one or more other bodies which maintain and enforce rules as to the appointment and conduct of company auditors and which have been or are likely to be recognised.
(4) Where the Secretary of State refuses an application for a recognition order he shall give the applicant a written notice to that effect specifying which requirements in the opinion of the Secretary of State are not satisfied or stating that the application is refused on the ground mentioned in sub-paragraph (3).
(5) A recognition order shall state the date on which it takes effect.

Revocation of recognition

3.—(1) A recognition order may be revoked by a further order made by the Secretary of State if at any time it appears to him—
   (a) that any requirement of Part II of this Schedule is not satisfied in the case of the body to which the recognition order relates ("the recognised body"),
   (b) that the recognised body has failed to comply with any obligation to which it is subject by virtue of this Part of this Act, or
   (c) that the continued recognition of the body is undesirable having regard to the existence of one or more other bodies which have been or are to be recognised.
(2) An order revoking a recognition order shall state the date on which it takes effect and that date shall not be earlier than three months after the day on which the revocation order is made.
(3) Before revoking a recognition order the Secretary of State shall give written notice of his intention to do so to the recognised body, take such steps as he considers reasonably practicable for bringing the notice to the attention of members of the body and publish it in such manner as he thinks appropriate for bringing it to the attention of any other persons who are in his opinion likely to be affected.

(4) A notice under sub-paragraph (3) shall state the reasons for which the Secretary of State proposes to act and give particulars of the rights conferred by sub-paragraph (5).

(5) A body on which a notice is served under sub-paragraph (3), any member of the body and any other person who appears to the Secretary of State to be affected may within three months after the date of service or publication, or within such longer time as the Secretary of State may allow, make written representations to the Secretary of State and, if desired, oral representations to a person appointed for that purpose by the Secretary of State; and the Secretary of State shall have regard to any representations made in accordance with this sub-paragraph in determining whether to revoke the recognition order.

(6) If in any case the Secretary of State considers it essential to do so in the public interest he may revoke a recognition order without regard to the restriction imposed by sub-paragraph (2) and notwithstanding that no notice has been given or published under sub-paragraph (3) or that the time for making representations in pursuance of such a notice has not expired.

(7) An order revoking a recognition order may contain such transitional provisions as the Secretary of State thinks necessary or expedient.

(8) A recognition order may be revoked at the request or with the consent of the recognised body and any such revocation shall not be subject to the restrictions imposed by sub-paragraphs (1) and (2) or the requirements of sub-paragraphs (3) to (5).

(9) On making an order revoking a recognition order the Secretary of State shall give the body written notice of the making of the order, take such steps as he considers reasonably practicable for bringing the making of the order to the attention of members of the body and publish a notice of the making of the order in such manner as he thinks appropriate for bringing it to the attention of any other persons who are in his opinion likely to be affected.

Part II

Requirements for Recognition

Holding of appropriate qualification

4.—(1) The body must have rules to the effect that a person is not eligible for appointment as a company auditor unless—
   (a) in the case of an individual, he holds an appropriate qualification;
   (b) in the case of a firm—
      (i) the individuals responsible for company audit work on behalf of the firm hold an appropriate qualification, and
      (ii) the firm is controlled by qualified persons (see paragraph 5 below).

(2) This does not prevent the body from imposing more stringent requirements.

(3) A firm which has ceased to comply with the conditions mentioned in sub-paragraph (1)(b) may be permitted to remain eligible for appointment as a company auditor for a period of not more than three months.

5.—(1) The following provisions explain what is meant in paragraph 4(1)(b)(ii) by a firm being "controlled by qualified persons".

(2) For this purpose references to a person being qualified are, in relation to an individual, to his holding an appropriate qualification, and in relation to a firm, to its being eligible for appointment as a company auditor.

(3) A firm shall be treated as controlled by qualified persons if, and only if—
   (a) a majority of the members of the firm are qualified persons, and
   (b) where the firm's affairs are managed by a board of directors, committee or other management body, a majority of the members of that body are qualified persons or, if the body consists of two persons only, at least one of them is a qualified person.

(4) A majority of the members of a firm means—
   (a) where under the firm's constitution matters are decided upon by the exercise of voting rights, members holding a majority of the rights to vote on all, or substantially all, matters;
   (b) in any other case, members having such rights under the constitution of the firm as enable them to direct its overall policy or alter its constitution.

(5) A majority of the members of the management body of a firm means—
   (a) where matters are decided at meetings of the management body by the exercise of voting rights, members holding a majority of the rights to vote on all, or substantially all, matters at such meetings;

(b) in any other case, members having such rights under the constitution of the firm as enable them to direct its overall policy or alter its constitution.

(6) The provisions of paragraphs 5 to 11 of Schedule 10A to the Companies Act 1985 (rights to be taken into account and attribution of rights) apply for the purposes of this paragraph.

Auditors to be fit and proper persons

6.—(1) The body must have adequate rules and practices designed to ensure that the persons eligible under its rules for appointment as a company auditor are fit and proper persons to be so appointed.

(2) The matters which the body may take into account for this purpose in relation to a person must include—
   (a) any matter relating to any person who is or will be employed by or associated with him for the purposes of or in connection with company audit work; and
   (b) in the case of a body corporate, any matter relating to any director or controller of the body, to any other body corporate in the same group or to any director or controller of any such other body; and
   (c) in the case of a partnership, any matter relating to any of the partners, any director or controller of any of the partners, any body corporate in the same group as any of the partners and any director or controller of any such other body.

(3) In sub-paragraph (2)(b) and (c) "controller", in relation to a body corporate, means a person who either alone or with any associate or associates is entitled to exercise or control the exercise of 15 per cent. or more of the rights to vote on all, or substantially all, matters at general meetings of the body or another body corporate of which it is a subsidiary.

Professional integrity and independence

7.—(1) The body must have adequate rules and practices designed to ensure—
   (a) that company audit work is conducted properly and with integrity, and
   (b) that persons are not appointed company auditor in circumstances in which they have any interest likely to conflict with the proper conduct of the audit.

(2) The body must also have adequate rules and practices designed to ensure that no firm is eligible under its rules for appointment as a company auditor unless the firm has arrangements to prevent—
   (a) individuals who do not hold an appropriate qualification, and
   (b) persons who are not members of the firm,
from being able to exert any influence over the way in which an audit is conducted in circumstances in which that influence would be likely to affect the independence or integrity of the audit.

Technical standards

8. The body must have rules and practices as to the technical standards to be applied in company audit work and as to the manner in which those standards are to be applied in practice.

Procedures for maintaining competence

9. The body must have rules and practices designed to ensure that persons eligible under its rules for appointment as a company auditor continue to maintain an appropriate level of competence in the conduct of company audits.

Monitoring and enforcement

10.—(1) The body must have adequate arrangements and resources for the effective monitoring and enforcement of compliance with its rules.

(2) The arrangements for monitoring may make provision for that function to be performed on behalf of the body (and without affecting its responsibility) by any other body or person who is able and willing to perform it.

Membership, eligibility and discipline

11. The rules and practices of the body relating to—
    (a) the admission and expulsion of members,
    (b) the grant and withdrawal of eligibility for appointment as a company auditor, and
    (c) the discipline it exercises over its members,
must be fair and reasonable and include adequate provision for appeals.

Investigation of complaints

12.—(1) The body must have effective arrangements for the investigation of complaints—
    (a) against persons who are eligible under its rules to be appointed company auditor, or
    (b) against the body in respect of matters arising out of its functions as a supervisory body.

(2) The arrangements may make provision for the whole or part of that function to be performed by and to be the responsibility of a body or person independent of the body itself.

Meeting of claims arising out of audit work

13.—(1) The body must have adequate rules or arrangements designed to ensure that persons eligible under its rules for appointment as a company auditor take such steps as may reasonably be expected of them to secure that they are able to meet claims against them arising out of company audit work.

(2) This may be achieved by professional indemnity insurance or other appropriate arrangements.

Register of auditors and other information to be made available

14. The body must have rules requiring persons eligible under its rules for appointment as a company auditor to comply with any obligations imposed on them by regulations under section 35 or 36.

Taking account of costs of compliance

15. The body must have satisfactory arrangements for taking account, in framing its rules, of the cost to those to whom the rules would apply of complying with those rules and any other controls to which they are subject.

Promotion and maintenance of standards

16. The body must be able and willing to promote and maintain high standards of integrity in the conduct of company audit work and to co-operate, by the sharing of information and otherwise, with the Secretary of State and any other authority, body or person having responsibility in the United Kingdom for the qualification, supervision or regulation of auditors.

DEFINITIONS
"appropriate qualification": s.31.
"company auditor": s.24(2).
"company audit work": s.24(2).
"firm (*i.e.* partnership)": s.52(1).
"guidance of a supervisory body": s.30(4).
"recognition order": Sched. 11, para. 2.
"revocation order": Sched. 11, para. 3.
"rules of a supervisory body": s.30(3).
"supervisory body": s.30(1).
"technical standards": Sched. 11, para. 8.

GENERAL NOTE
This Schedule relates to the provisions of s.30, which refer to the recognition of "Supervisory Bodies". Professional bodies (such as the Institutes of Chartered Accountants)

can only secure recognition if they have adequate rules and arrangements to ensure that only eligible members will undertake company audits.

A summary outline of the Schedule, together with cross references to articles in the European Community's Eighth Council Directive on Company Law (84/253 of April 10, 1984), is given below. (For the text of the Eighth Directive, see *Palmer* K.120–K.151.)

Recognition of a Supervisory Body

	Articles in the EC's Eighth Directive
Pt. I Grant and Revocation of Recognition	
Para.	
1 Procedures for applying for recognition as a supervisory body.	
2 Procedures for granting or refusing such recognition.	
3 Grounds for and procedures for revoking recognition.	
Pt. II Requirements for Recognition	
4 The supervisory body's rules relating to eligibility as a company's auditor,	2
5 including those relating to an auditing partnership.	
6 The supervisory body's rules to ensure that auditors are fit and proper persons.	3
7 The supervisory body must have rules which ensure company audits are conducted with professional integrity and independence.	23
8 The supervisory body must have rules and practices which ensure proper technical standards are applied to company audit work.	
9 There must be procedures to ensure that those persons eligible to be appointed as company auditors maintain an appropriate level of competence.	
10 The supervisory body must monitor and ensure compliance with its rules.	
11 There must be adequate rules relating to the admission, expulsion and discipline of members, as well as procedures relating to eligibility of members to act as company auditors.	26
12 There must be effective arrangements for the investigation of complaints.	
13 There must be rules ensuring eligible members are properly insured against professional negligence liability.	
14 The body must keep a register of auditors under ss.35–36.	28
15 The body must have satisfactory procedures for taking into account the costs of complying with its rules when it frames them.	
16 Obligation to promote and maintain standards.	

Section 32(4)

SCHEDULE 12

RECOGNITION OF PROFESSIONAL QUALIFICATION

PART I

GRANT AND REVOCATION OF RECOGNITION

Application for recognition of professional qualification

1.—(1) A qualifying body may apply to the Secretary of State for an order declaring a qualification offered by it to be a recognised professional qualification for the purposes of this Part of this Act.

(2) Any such application—
(a) shall be made in such manner as the Secretary of State may direct, and
(b) shall be accompanied by such information as the Secretary of State may reasonably require for the purpose of determining the application.

(3) At any time after receiving an application and before determining it the Secretary of State may require the applicant to furnish additional information.

(4) The directions and requirements given or imposed under sub-paragraphs (2) and (3) may differ as between different applications.

(5) Any information to be furnished to the Secretary of State under this section shall, if he so requires, be in such form or verified in such manner as he may specify.

In the case of examination standards, the verification required may include independent moderation of the examinations over such period as the Secretary of State considers necessary.

(6) Every application shall be accompanied by a copy of the applicant's rules and of any guidance issued by it which is intended to have continuing effect and is issued in writing or other legible form.

Grant and refusal of recognition

2.—(1) The Secretary of State may, on an application duly made in accordance with paragraph 1 and after being furnished with all such information as he may require under that paragraph, make or refuse to make an order (a "recognition order") declaring the qualification in respect of which the application was made to be a recognised professional qualification for the purposes of this Part of this Act.

In this Part of this Act a "recognised qualifying body" means a qualifying body offering a recognised professional qualification.

(2) The Secretary of State shall not make a recognition order unless it appears to him, from the information furnished by the applicant and having regard to any other information in his possession, that the requirements of Part II of this Schedule are satisfied as respects the qualification.

(3) Where the Secretary of State refuses an application for a recognition order he shall give the applicant a written notice to that effect specifying which requirements, in his opinion, are not satisfied.

(4) A recognition order shall state the date on which it takes effect.

Revocation of recognition

3.—(1) A recognition order may be revoked by a further order made by the Secretary of State if at any time it appears to him—
 (a) that any requirement of Part II of this Schedule is not satisfied in relation to the qualification to which the recognition order relates, or
 (b) that the qualifying body has failed to comply with any obligation to which it is subject by virtue of this Part of this Act.

(2) An order revoking a recognition order shall state the date on which it takes effect and that date shall not be earlier than three months after the day on which the revocation order is made.

(3) Before revoking a recognition order the Secretary of State shall give written notice of his intention to do so to the qualifying body, take such steps as he considers reasonably practicable for bringing the notice to the attention of persons holding the qualification or in the course of studying for it and publish it in such manner as he thinks appropriate for bringing it to the attention of any other persons who are in his opinion likely to be affected.

(4) A notice under sub-paragraph (3) shall state the reasons for which the Secretary of State proposes to act and give particulars of the rights conferred by sub-paragraph (5).

(5) A body on which a notice is served under sub-paragraph (3), any person holding the qualification or in the course of studying for it and any other person who appears to the Secretary of State to be affected may within three months after the date of service or publication, or within such longer time as the Secretary of State may allow, make written representations to the Secretary of State and, if desired, oral representations to a person appointed for that purpose by the Secretary of State; and the Secretary of State shall have regard to any representations made in accordance with this subsection in determining whether to revoke the recognition order.

(6) If in any case the Secretary of State considers it essential to do so in the public interest he may revoke a recognition order without regard to the restriction imposed by sub-paragraph (2) and notwithstanding that no notice has been given or published under sub-paragraph (3) or that the time for making representations in pursuance of such a notice has not expired.

(7) An order revoking a recognition order may contain such transitional provisions as the Secretary of State thinks necessary or expedient.

(8) A recognition order may be revoked at the request or with the consent of the qualifying body and any such revocation shall not be subject to the restrictions imposed by sub-paragraphs (1) and (2) or the requirements of sub-paragraphs (3) to (5).

(9) On making an order revoking a recognition order the Secretary of State shall give the qualifying body written notice of the making of the order, take such steps as he considers reasonably practicable for bringing the making of the order to the attention of persons holding the qualification or in the course of studying for it and publish a notice of the making of the order in such manner as he thinks appropriate for bringing it to the attention of any other persons who are in his opinion likely to be affected.

Part II

Requirements for Recognition

Entry requirements

4.—(1) The qualification must only be open to persons who have attained university entrance level or have a sufficient period of professional experience.

(2) In relation to a person who has not been admitted to a university or other similar establishment in the United Kingdom, attaining university entrance level means—
   (a) being educated to such a standard as would entitle him to be considered for such admission on the basis of—
       (i) academic or professional qualifications obtained in the United Kingdom and recognised by the Secretary of State to be of an appropriate standard, or
       (ii) academic or professional qualifications obtained outside the United Kingdom which the Secretary of State considers to be of an equivalent standard; or
   (b) being assessed on the basis of written tests of a kind appearing to the Secretary of State to be adequate for the purpose, with or without oral examination, as of such a standard of ability as would entitle him to be considered for such admission.

(3) The assessment, tests and oral examination referred to in sub-paragraph (2)(b) may be conducted by the qualifying body or by some other body approved by the Secretary of State.

Course of theoretical instruction

5. The qualification must be restricted to persons who have completed a course of theoretical instruction in the subjects prescribed for the purposes of paragraph 7 or have a sufficient period of professional experience.

Sufficient period of professional experience

6.—(1) The references in paragraphs 4 and 5 to a sufficient period of professional experience are to not less than seven years' experience in a professional capacity in the fields of finance, law and accountancy.

(2) Periods of theoretical instruction in the fields of finance, law and accountancy may be deducted from the required period of professional experience, provided the instruction—
   (a) lasted at least one year, and
   (b) is attested by an examination recognised by the Secretary of State for the purposes of this paragraph;
but the period of professional experience may not be so reduced by more than four years.

(3) The period of professional experience together with the practical training required in the case of persons satisfying the requirement in paragraph 5 by virtue of having a sufficient period of professional experience must not be shorter than the course of theoretical instruction referred to in that paragraph and the practical training required in the case of persons satisfying the requirement of that paragraph by virtue of having completed such a course.".

Examination

7.—(1) The qualification must be restricted to persons who have passed an examination (at least part of which is in writing) testing—
   (a) theoretical knowledge of the subjects prescribed for the purposes of this paragraph by regulations made by the Secretary of State, and
   (b) ability to apply that knowledge in practice,

and requiring a standard of attainment at least equivalent to that required to obtain a degree from a university or similar establishment in the United Kingdom.

(2) The qualification may be awarded to a person without his theoretical knowledge of a subject being tested by examination if he has passed a university or other examination of equivalent standard in that subject or holds a university degree or equivalent qualification in it.

(3) The qualification may be awarded to a person without his ability to apply his theoretical knowledge of a subject in practice being tested by examination if he has received practical training in that subject which is attested by an examination or diploma recognised by the Secretary of State for the purposes of this paragraph.

(4) Regulations under this paragraph shall be made by statutory instrument which shall be subject to annulment in pursuance of a resolution of either House of Parliament.

Practical training

8.—(1) The qualification must be restricted to persons who have completed at least three years' practical training of which—
  (a) part was spent being trained in company audit work, and
  (b) a substantial part was spent being trained in company audit work or other audit work of a description approved by the Secretary of State as being similar to company audit work.

For this purpose "company audit work" includes the work of a person appointed as auditor under the Companies (Northern Ireland) Order 1986 or under the law of a country or territory outside the United Kingdom where it appears to the Secretary of State that the law and practice with respect to the audit of company accounts is similar to that in the United Kingdom.

(2) The training must be given by persons approved by the body offering the qualification as persons as to whom the body is satisfied, in the light of undertakings given by them and the supervision to which they are subject (whether by the body itself or some other body or organisation), that they will provide adequate training.

(3) At least two-thirds of the training must be given by a fully-qualified auditor, that is, a person—
  (a) eligible in accordance with this Part of this Act to be appointed as a company auditor, or
  (b) satisfying the corresponding requirements of the law of Northern Ireland or another member State of the European Economic Community.

The body offering the qualification

9.—(1) The body offering the qualification must have—
  (a) rules and arrangements adequate to ensure compliance with the requirements of paragraphs 4 to 8, and
  (b) adequate arrangements for the effective monitoring of its continued compliance with those requirements.

(2) The arrangements must include arrangements for monitoring the standard of its examinations and the adequacy of the practical training given by the persons approved by it for that purpose.

DEFINITIONS
"company auditor": s.24(2).
"company audit work": s.24(2).
"examinations": Sched. 12, para. 7.
"qualifying body": s.32(1).
"recognised professional qualification": s.32(4).
"recognised qualifying body": Sched. 12, para. 2(1).

GENERAL NOTE
This Schedule relates to the provisions of s.32, which refer to recognition of professional qualifications. Pt. I deals with the granting and revoking of recognition to a qualifying body of its professional qualifications; Pt. II deals with the requirements for recognition of such a professional qualification and effectively implements the articles of the European Community's Eighth Council Directive on Company Law (84/253 of April 10, 1984: see *Palmer* K.120–151).

Recognition of Professional Qualification

Pt. I–Grant and Revocation of Recognition

Articles in the EC's Eighth Directive

Para.
1 Application by a qualifying body for recognition of its professional qualification.
2 Procedures relating to the grant or refusal of recognition by the Secretary of State.
3 Revocation of recognition by the Secretary of State.

Pt. II—Requirements for Recognition

Para.		Articles
4	Professional qualification entry requirements.	4, 8–11
5	Requirement to have completed a course of theoretical instruction.	5
6	Sufficient period of professional experience before qualification, subject to a reduction if periods of specialist theoretical instruction have been undertaken.	9–10
7	Qualification is restricted to those who have passed an examination.	4, 5, 7
8	Qualification is restricted to those who have undergone at least three years' practical training.	8
9	The qualifying body must have adequate rules and arrangements to ensure its compliance with statutory regulations.	

Section 46(6)

SCHEDULE 13

SUPPLEMENTARY PROVISIONS WITH RESPECT TO DELEGATION ORDER

Introductory

1. The following provisions have effect in relation to a body established by a delegation order under section 46; and any power to make provision by order is to make provision by order under that section.

Status

2. The body shall not be regarded as acting on behalf of the Crown and its members, officers and employees shall not be regarded as Crown servants.

Name, members and chairman

3.—(1) The body shall be known by such name as may be specified in the delegation order.

(2) The body shall consist of such persons (not being less than eight) as the Secretary of State may appoint after such consultation as he thinks appropriate; and the chairman of the body shall be such person as the Secretary of State may appoint from amongst its members.

(3) The Secretary of State may make provision by order as to the terms on which the members of the body are to hold and vacate office and as to the terms on which a person appointed as chairman is to hold and vacate the office of chairman.

Financial provisions

4.—(1) The body shall pay to its chairman and members such remuneration, and such allowances in respect of expenses properly incurred by them in the performance of their duties, as the Secretary of State may determine.

(2) As regards any chairman or member in whose case the Secretary of State so determines, the body shall pay or make provision for the payment of—

(a) such pension, allowance or gratuity to or in respect of that person on his retirement or death, or

(b) such contributions or other payment towards the provision of such a pension, allowance or gratuity,

as the Secretary of State may determine.

(3) Where a person ceases to be a member of the body otherwise than on the expiry of his term of office and it appears to the Secretary of State that there are special circumstances which make it right for him to receive compensation, the body shall make a payment to him by way of compensation of such amount as the Secretary of State may determine.

Proceedings

5.—(1) The delegation order may contain such provision as the Secretary of State considers appropriate with respect to the proceedings of the body.

(2) The order may, in particular—

(a) authorise the body to discharge any functions by means of committees consisting wholly or partly of members of the body;

(b) provide that the validity of proceedings of the body, or of any such committee, is not affected by any vacancy among the members or any defect in the appointment of any member.

Fees

6.—(1) The body may retain fees payable to it.

(2) The fees shall be applied for meeting the expenses of the body in discharging its functions and for any purposes incidental to those functions.

(3) Those expenses include any expenses incurred by the body on such staff, accommodation, services and other facilities as appear to it to be necessary or expedient for the proper performance of its functions.

(4) In prescribing the amount of fees in the exercise of the functions transferred to it the body shall prescribe such fees as appear to it sufficient to defray those expenses, taking one year with another.

(5) Any exercise by the body of the power to prescribe fees requires the approval of the Secretary of State; and the Secretary of State may, after consultation with the body, by order vary or revoke any regulations made by it prescribing fees.

Legislative functions

7.—(1) Regulations made by the body in the exercise of the functions transferred to it shall be made by instrument in writing, but not by statutory instrument.

(2) The instrument shall specify the provision of this Part of this Act under which it is made.

(3) The Secretary of State may by order impose such requirements as he thinks necessary or expedient as to the circumstances and manner in which the body must consult on any regulations it proposes to make.

8.—(1) Immediately after an instrument is made it shall be printed and made available to the public with or without payment.

(2) A person shall not be taken to have contravened any regulation if he shows that at the time of the alleged contravention the instrument containing the regulation had not been made available as required by this paragraph.

9.—(1) The production of a printed copy of an instrument purporting to be made by the body on which is endorsed a certificate signed by an officer of the body authorised by it for the purpose and stating—

(a) that the instrument was made by the body,

(b) that the copy is a true copy of the instrument, and

(c) that on a specified date the instrument was made available to the public as required by paragraph 8, is prima facie evidence or, in Scotland, sufficient evidence of the facts stated in the certificate.

(2) A certificate purporting to be signed as mentioned in sub-paragraph (1) shall be deemed to have been duly signed unless the contrary is shown.

(3) Any person wishing in any legal proceedings to cite an instrument made by the body may require the body to cause a copy of it to be endorsed with such a certificate as is mentioned in this paragraph.

Report and accounts

10.—(1) The body shall at least once in each year for which the delegation order is in force make a report to the Secretary of State on the discharge of the functions transferred to it and on such other matters as the Secretary of State may by order require.

(2) The Secretary of State shall lay before Parliament copies of each report received by him under this paragraph.

(3) The Secretary of State may, with the consent of the Treasury, give directions to the body with respect to its accounts and the audit of its accounts and it is the duty of the body to comply with the directions.

(4) A person shall not be appointed auditor of the body unless he is eligible for appointment as a company auditor under section 25.

Other supplementary provisions

11.—(1) The transfer of a function to a body established by a delegation order does not affect anything previously done in the exercise of the function transferred; and the resumption of a function so transferred does not affect anything previously done in exercise of the function resumed.

(2) The Secretary of State may by order make such transitional and other supplementary provision as he thinks necessary or expedient in relation to the transfer or resumption of a function.

(3) The provision that may be made in connection with the transfer of a function includes, in particular, provision—
  (a) for modifying or excluding any provision of this Part of this Act in its application to the function transferred;
  (b) for applying to the body established by the delegation order, in connection with the function transferred, any provision applying to the Secretary of State which is contained in or made under any other enactment;
  (c) for the transfer of any property, rights or liabilities from the Secretary of State to that body;
  (d) for the carrying on and completion by that body of anything in process of being done by the Secretary of State when the order takes effect;
  (e) for the substitution of that body for the Secretary of State in any instrument, contract or legal proceedings.

(4) The provision that may be made in connection with the resumption of a function includes, in particular, provision—
  (a) for the transfer of any property, rights or liabilities from that body to the Secretary of State;
  (b) for the carrying on and completion by the Secretary of State of anything in process of being done by that body when the order takes effect;
  (c) for the substitution of the Secretary of State for that body in any instrument, contract or legal proceedings.

12. Where a delegation order is revoked, the Secretary of State may by order make provision—
  (a) for the payment of compensation to persons ceasing to be employed by the body established by the delegation order; and
  (b) as to the winding up and dissolution of the body.

DEFINITIONS
"delegation order": s.46.
"revocation of a delegation order": s.46(4), Sched. 13, para. 12.

GENERAL NOTE
This Schedule relates to the provisions of s.46, which refer to a delegated body that can exercise the Secretary of State's powers under Pt. II of the Act concerning Eligibility for Appointment as Company Auditor.

Section 47(1)

SCHEDULE 14

Supervisory and Qualifying Bodies: Restrictive Practices

Part I

Prevention of Restrictive Practices

Refusal of recognition on grounds related to competition

1.—(1) The Secretary of State shall before deciding whether to make a recognition order in respect of a supervisory body or professional qualification send to the Director General of Fair Trading (in this Schedule referred to as "the Director") a copy of the rules and of any guidance which the Secretary of State is required to consider in making that decision together with such other information as the Secretary of State considers will assist the Director.

(2) The Director shall consider whether the rules or guidance have, or are intended or likely to have, to any significant extent the effect of restricting, distorting or preventing competition, and shall report to the Secretary of State; and the Secretary of State shall have regard to his report in deciding whether to make a recognition order.

(3) The Secretary of State shall not make a recognition order if it appears to him that the rules and any guidance of which copies are furnished with the application have, or are intended or likely to have, to any significant extent the effect of restricting, distorting or preventing competition, unless it appears to him that the effect is reasonably justifiable having regard to the purposes of this Part of this Act.

Notification of changes to rules or guidance

2.—(1) Where a recognised supervisory or qualifying body amends, revokes or adds to its rules or guidance in a manner which may reasonably be regarded as likely—
  (a) to restrict, distort or prevent competition to any significant extent, or
  (b) otherwise to affect the question whether the recognition order granted to the body should continue in force,
it shall within seven days give the Secretary of State written notice of the amendment, revocation or addition.

(2) Notice need not be given under sub-paragraph (1) of the revocation of guidance not intended to have continuing effect or issued otherwise than in writing or other legible form, or of any amendment or addition to guidance which does not result in or consist of guidance which is intended to have continuing effect and is issued in writing or other legible form.

Continuing scrutiny by the Director General of Fair Trading

3.—(1) The Director shall keep under review the rules made or guidance issued by a recognised supervisory or qualifying body, and if he is of the opinion that any rules or guidance of such a body have, or are intended or likely to have, to any significant extent the effect of restricting, distorting or preventing competition, he shall report his opinion to the Secretary of State, stating what in his opinion the effect is or is likely to be.

(2) The Secretary of State shall send to the Director copies of any notice received by him under paragraph 2, together with such other information as he considers will assist the Director.

(3) The Director may report to the Secretary of State his opinion that any matter mentioned in such a notice does not have, and is not intended or likely to have, to any significant extent the effect of restricting, distorting or preventing competition.

(4) The Director may from time to time consider whether—
  (a) any practices of a recognised supervisory or qualifying body in its capacity as such, or
  (b) any relevant practices required or contemplated by the rules or guidance of such a body or otherwise attributable to its conduct in its capacity as such,
have, or are intended or likely to have, to any significant extent the effect of restricting, distorting or preventing competition and, if so, what that effect is or is likely to be; and if he is of that opinion he shall make a report to the Secretary of State stating his opinion and what the effect is or is likely to be.

(5) The practices relevant for the purposes of sub-paragraph (4)(b) in the case of a recognised supervisory body are practices engaged in for the purposes of, or in connection with, appointment as a company auditor or the conduct of company audit work by persons who—
  (a) are eligible under its rules for appointment as a company auditor, or
  (b) hold an appropriate qualification and are directors or other officers of bodies corporate which are so eligible or partners in, or employees of, partnerships which are so eligible.

(6) The practices relevant for the purposes of sub-paragraph (4)(b) in the case of a recognised qualifying body are—
  (a) practices engaged in by persons in the course of seeking to obtain a recognised professional qualification from that body, and
  (b) practices engaged in by persons approved by the body for the purposes of giving practical training to persons seeking such a qualification and which relate to such training.

Investigatory powers of the Director

4.—(1) The following powers are exercisable by the Director for the purpose of investigating any matter in connection with his functions under paragraph 1 or 3.

(2) The Director may by a notice in writing require any person to produce, at a time and place specified in the notice, to the Director or to any person appointed by him for the purpose, any documents which are specified or described in the notice and which are documents in his custody or under his control and relating to any matter relevant to the investigation.

(3) The Director may by a notice in writing require any person to furnish to the Director such information as may be specified or described in the notice, and specify the time within which and the manner and form in which any such information is to be furnished.

(4) A person shall not under this paragraph be required to produce any document or disclose any information which he would be entitled to refuse to produce or disclose on grounds of legal professional privilege in proceedings in the High Court or on the grounds of confidentiality as between client and professional legal adviser in proceedings in the Court of Session.

(5) Subsections (6) to (8) of section 85 of the Fair Trading Act 1973 (enforcement provisions) apply in relation to a notice under this paragraph as they apply in relation to a notice under subsection (1) of that section but as if, in subsection (7) of that section, for the words from "any one" to "the Commission" there were substituted "the Director".

Publication of Director's reports

5.—(1) The Director may, if he thinks fit, publish any report made by him under paragraph 1 or 3.

(2) He shall exclude from a published report, so far as practicable, any matter which relates to the affairs of a particular person (other than the supervisory or qualifying body concerned) the publication of which would or might in his opinion seriously and prejudicially affect the interests of that person.

Powers exercisable by the Secretary of State in consequence of report

6.—(1) The powers conferred by this section are exercisable by the Secretary of State if, having received and considered a report from the Director under paragraph 3(1) or (4), it appears to him that—
  (a) any rules made or guidance issued by a recognised supervisory or qualifying body, or
  (b) any such practices as are mentioned in paragraph 3(4),
have, or are intended or likely to have, to any significant extent the effect of restricting, distorting or preventing competition and that that effect is greater than is reasonably justifiable having regard to the purposes of this Part of this Act.

(2) The powers are—
  (a) to revoke the recognition order granted to the body concerned,
  (b) to direct it to take specified steps for the purpose of securing that the rules, guidance or practices in question do not have the effect mentioned in sub-paragraph (1), and
  (c) to make alterations in the rules of the body for that purpose.

(3) The provisions of paragraph 3(2) to (5), (7) and (9) of Schedule 11 or, as the case may be, Schedule 12 have effect in relation to the revocation of a recognition order under sub-paragraph (2)(a) above as they have effect in relation to the revocation of such an order under that Schedule.

(4) Before the Secretary of State exercises the power conferred by sub-paragraph (2)(b) or (c) above he shall—

(a) give written notice of his intention to do so to the body concerned and take such steps (whether by publication or otherwise) as he thinks appropriate for bringing the notice to the attention of any other person who in his opinion is likely to be affected by the exercise of the power, and

(b) have regard to any representation made within such time as he considers reasonable by the body or any such other person.

(5) A notice under sub-paragraph (4) shall give particulars of the manner in which the Secretary of State proposes to exercise the power in question and state the reasons for which he proposes to act; and the statement of reasons may include matters contained in any report received by him under paragraph 4.

Supplementary provisions

7.—(1) A direction under paragraph 6 is, on the application of the Secretary of State, enforceable by injunction or, in Scotland, by an order under section 45 of the Court of Session Act 1988.

(2) The fact that any rules made by a recognised supervisory or qualifying body have been altered by the Secretary of State, or pursuant to a direction of the Secretary of State, under paragraph 6 does not preclude their subsequent alteration or revocation by that body.

(3) In determining for the purposes of this Part of this Schedule whether any guidance has, or is likely to have, any particular effect the Secretary of State and the Director may assume that the persons to whom it is addressed will act in conformity with it.

PART II

CONSEQUENTIAL EXEMPTIONS FROM COMPETITION LAW

Fair Trading Act 1973 (c. 41)

8.—(1) For the purpose of determining whether a monopoly situation within the meaning of the Fair Trading Act 1973 exists by reason of the circumstances mentioned in section 7(1)(c) of that Act (supply of services by or for group of two or more persons), no account shall be taken of—

(a) the rules of or guidance issued by a recognised supervisory or qualifying body, or

(b) conduct constituting such a practice as is mentioned in paragraph 3(4) above.

(2) Where a recognition order is revoked there shall be disregarded for the purpose mentioned in sub-paragraph (1) any such conduct as is mentioned in that sub-paragraph which occurred while the order was in force.

(3) Where on a monopoly reference under section 50 or 51 of the Fair Trading Act 1973 falling within section 49 of that Act (monopoly reference not limited to the facts) the Monopolies and Mergers Commission find that a monopoly situation within the meaning of that Act exists and—

(a) that the person (or, if more than one, any of the persons) in whose favour it exists is—

(i) a recognised supervisory or qualifying body, or

(ii) a person of a description mentioned in paragraph 3(5) or (6) above, or

(b) that any such person's conduct in doing anything to which the rules of such a body relate is subject to guidance issued by the body,

the Commission in making their report on that reference shall exclude from their consideration the question whether the rules or guidance of the body concerned, or the acts or omissions of that body in its capacity as such, operate or may be expected to operate against the public interest.

Restrictive Trade Practices Act 1976 (c. 34)

9.—(1) The Restrictive Trade Practices Act 1976 does not apply to an agreement for the constitution of a recognised supervisory or qualifying body in so far as it relates to rules of or guidance issued by the body, and incidental matters connected therewith, including any term deemed to be contained in it by virtue of section 8(2) or 16(3) of that Act.

(2) Nor does that Act apply to an agreement the parties to which consist of or include—
   (a) a recognised supervisory or qualifying body, or
   (b) any such person as is mentioned in paragraph 3(5) or (6) above,

by reason that it includes any terms the inclusion of which is required or contemplated by the rules or guidance of that body.

(3) Where an agreement ceases by virtue of this paragraph to be subject to registration—
   (a) the Director shall remove from the register maintained by him under the Act of 1976 any particulars which are entered or filed in that register in respect of the agreement, and
   (b) any proceedings in respect of the agreement which are pending before the Restrictive Practices Court shall be discontinued.

(4) Where a recognition order is revoked, sub-paragraphs (1) and (2) above shall continue to apply for a period of six months beginning with the day on which the revocation takes effect, as if the order were still in force.

(5) Where an agreement which has been exempt from registration by virtue of this paragraph ceases to be exempt in consequence of the revocation of a recognition order, the time within which particulars of the agreement are to be furnished in accordance with section 24 of and Schedule 2 to the Act of 1976 shall be the period of one month beginning with the day on which the agreement ceased to be exempt from registration.

(6) Where in the case of an agreement registered under the 1976 Act a term ceases to fall within sub-paragraph (2) above in consequence of the revocation of a recognition order and particulars of that term have not previously been furnished to the Director under section 24 of that Act, those particulars shall be furnished to him within the period of one month beginning with the day on which the term ceased to fall within that sub-paragraph.

Competition Act 1980 (c. 21)

10.—(1) No course of conduct constituting any such practice as is mentioned in paragraph 3(4) above shall constitute an anti-competitive practice for the purposes of the Competition Act 1980.

(2) Where a recognition order is revoked there shall not be treated as an anti-competitive practice for the purposes of that Act any such course of conduct as is mentioned in sub-paragraph (1) which occurred while the order was in force.

DEFINITIONS
"Director (*i.e.* Director General of Fair Trading)": Sched. 14, para. 1.
"guidance of a qualifying body": s.32(3).
"guidance of a supervisory body": s.30(4).
"qualifying body": s.32(1).
"recognised qualifying body": Sched. 12, para. 2(1).
"recognised professional qualification": s.32(4), Sched. 12.
"recognised supervisory body": s.30(5), Sched. 11.
"rules of a qualifying body": s.32(2).
"rules of a supervisory body": s.30(3).

GENERAL NOTE
This Schedule relates to the provisions of s.47, which refer to restrictive practices and competition law in connection with the activities of supervisory and qualifying bodies. The Secretary of State is placed under a duty not to recognise a body unless he is satisfied that its rules and guidance do not restrict, distort or prevent competition to a greater extent than is reasonably justifiable having regard to the purpose of Pt. II of the Act, concerning Eligibility for Appointment as a Company Auditor. He may only exercise his powers after he has considered any report from the Director General of Fair Trading, who is also charged with keeping the rules and guidance in question under review.

Para. 2, dealing with the notification to the Secretary of State by supervisory or qualifying bodies of relevant changes to their rules or to the guidance they give, was inserted into the Schedule during the progress of the bill through Parliament.

A summary outline of the Schedule is given below.

Supervisory and qualifying bodies: Restrictive practices

Pt. I—Prevention of restrictive practices

Para.
1. Refusal of recognition by the Secretary of State after consultation with the Director General of Fair Trading on grounds related to the restriction, distribution or prevention of competition.
2. Notification by supervisory or qualifying bodies to the Secretary of State of relevant changes in their rules.
3. Continuing scrutiny by the Director General of Fair Trading of the rules of a guidance given by supervisory or qualifying bodies.
4. Investigating powers of the Director General of Fair Trading in relation to supervisory and qualifying bodies.
5. Publication of reports by the Director General of Fair Trading.
6. Powers exercisable by the Secretary of State in consequence of a report by the Director General of Fair Trading.
7. Supplementary provisions relating to the Secretary of State's directions, including the use of injunctions.

Pt. II—Consequential exemptions from Competition Law

8. Fair Trading Act 1973, ss.7, 49–51.
9. Restrictive Trade Practices Act 1976.
10. Competition Act 1980.

SCHEDULE 15

CHARGES ON PROPERTY OF OVERSEA COMPANIES

The following provisions are inserted in Part XXIII of the Companies Act 1985—

"CHAPTER III

REGISTRATION OF CHARGES

Introductory provisions
703A.—(1) The provisions of this Chapter have effect for securing the registration in Great Britain of charges on the property of a registered oversea company.

(2) Section 395(2) and (3) (meaning of "charge" and "property") have effect for the purposes of this Chapter.

(3) A "registered oversea company", in relation to England and Wales or Scotland, means an oversea company which has duly delivered documents to the registrar for that part of Great Britain under section 691 and has not subsequently given notice to him under section 696(4) that it has ceased to have an established place of business in that part.

(4) References in this Chapter to the registrar shall be construed in accordance with section 703E below and references to registration, in relation to a charge, are to registration in the register kept by him under this Chapter.

Charges requiring registration
703B.—(1) The charges requiring registration under this Chapter are those which if created by a company registered in Great Britain would require registration under Part XII of this Act.

(2) Whether a charge is one requiring registration under this Chapter shall be determined—
  (a) in the case of a charge over property of a company at the date it delivers documents for registration under section 691, as at that date,
  (b) in the case of a charge created by a registered oversea company, as at the date the charge is created, and
  (c) in the case of a charge over property acquired by a registered oversea company, as at the date of the acquisition.

(3) In the following provisions of this Chapter references to a charge are, unless the context otherwise requires, to a charge requiring registration under this Chapter.

Where a charge not otherwise requiring registration relates to property by virtue of which it requires to be registered and to other property, the references are to the charge so far as it relates to property of the former description.

The register

703C.—(1) The registrar shall keep for each registered oversea company a register, in such form as he thinks fit, of charges on property of the company.

(2) The register shall consist of a file containing with respect to each such charge the particulars and other information delivered to the registrar under or by virtue of the following provisions of this Chapter.

(3) Section 397(3) to (5) (registrar's certificate as to date of delivery of particulars) applies in relation to the delivery of any particulars or other information under this Chapter.

Company's duty to deliver particulars of charges for registration

703D.—(1) If when an oversea company delivers documents for registration under section 691 any of its property is situated in Great Britain and subject to a charge, it is the company's duty at the same time to deliver the prescribed particulars of the charge, in the prescribed form, to the registrar for registration.

(2) Where a registered oversea company—
    (a) creates a charge on property situated in Great Britain, or
    (b) acquires property which is situated in Great Britain and subject to a charge,

it is the company's duty to deliver the prescribed particulars of the charge, in the prescribed form, to the registrar for registration within 21 days after the date of the charge's creation or, as the case may be, the date of the acquisition.

This subsection does not apply if the property subject to the charge is at the end of that period no longer situated in Great Britain.

(3) Where the preceding subsections do not apply and property of a registered oversea company is for a continuous period of four months situated in Great Britain and subject to a charge, it is the company's duty before the end of that period to deliver the prescribed particulars of the charge, in the prescribed form, to the registrar for registration.

(4) Particulars of a charge required to be delivered under subsections (1), (2) or (3) may be delivered for registration by any person interested in the charge.

(5) If a company fails to comply with subsection (1), (2) or (3), then, unless particulars of the charge have been delivered for registration by another person, the company and every officer of it who is in default is liable to a fine.

(6) Section 398(2), (4) and (5) (recovery of fees paid in connection with registration, filing of particulars in register and sending of copy of particulars filed and note as to date) apply in relation to particulars delivered under this Chapter.

Registrar to whom particulars, &c. to be delivered

703E.—(1) The particulars required to be delivered by section 703D(1) (charges over property of oversea company becoming registered in a part of Great Britain) shall be delivered to the registrar to whom the documents are delivered under section 691.

(2) The particulars required to be delivered by section 703D(2) or (3) (charges over property of registered oversea company) shall be delivered—
    (a) if the company is registered in one part of Great Britain and not in the other, to the registrar for the part in which it is registered, and
    (b) if the company is registered in both parts of Great Britain but the property subject to the charge is situated in one part of Great Britain only, to the registrar for that part;

and in any other case the particulars shall be delivered to the registrars for both parts of Great Britain.

(3) Other documents required or authorised by virtue of this Chapter to be delivered to the registrar shall be delivered to the registrar or registrars to whom particulars of the charge to which they relate have been, or ought to have been, delivered.

(4) If a company gives notice under section 696(4) that it has ceased to have an established place of business in either part of Great Britain, charges over property of the company shall cease to be subject to the provisions of this Chapter, as regards registration in that part of Great Britain, as from the date on which notice is so given.

This is without prejudice to rights arising by reason of events occurring before that date.

Effect of failure to deliver particulars, late delivery and effect of errors and omissions

703F.—(1) The following provisions of Part XII—
   (a) section 399 (effect of failure to deliver particulars),
   (b) section 400 (late delivery of particulars), and
   (c) section 402 (effect of errors and omissions in particulars delivered),
apply, with the following modifications, in relation to a charge created by a registered oversea company of which particulars are required to be delivered under this Chapter.

(2) Those provisions do not apply to a charge of which particulars are required to be delivered under section 703D(1) (charges existing when company delivers documents under section 691).

(3) In relation to a charge of which particulars are required to be delivered under section 703D(3) (charges registrable by virtue of property being within Great Britain for requisite period), the references to the period of 21 days after the charge's creation shall be construed as references to the period of four months referred to in that subsection.

Delivery of further particulars or memorandum

703G. Sections 401 and 403 (delivery of further particulars and memorandum of charge ceasing to affect company's property) apply in relation to a charge of which particulars have been delivered under this Chapter.

Further provisions with respect to voidness of charges

703H.—(1) The following provisions of Part XII apply in relation to the voidness of a charge by virtue of this Chapter—
   (a) section 404 (exclusion of voidness as against unregistered charges),
   (b) section 405 (restrictions on cases in which charge is void),
   (c) section 406 (effect of exercise of power of sale), and
   (d) section 407 (effect of voidness on obligation secured).

(2) In relation to a charge of which particulars are required to be delivered under section 703D(3) (charges registrable by virtue of property being within Great Britain for requisite period), the reference in section 404 to the period of 21 days after the charge's creation shall be construed as a reference to the period of four months referred to in that subsection.

Additional information to be registered

703I.—(1) Section 408 (particulars of taking up of issue of debentures) applies in relation to a charge of which particulars have been delivered under this Chapter.

(2) Section 409 (notice of appointment of receiver or manager) applies in relation to the appointment of a receiver or manager of property of a registered oversea company.

(3) Regulations under section 410 (notice of crystallisation of floating charge, &c.) may apply in relation to a charge of which particulars have been delivered under this Chapter; but subject to such exceptions, adaptations and modifications as may be specified in the regulations.

Copies of instruments and register to be kept by company

703J.—(1) Sections 411 and 412 (copies of instruments and register to be kept by company) apply in relation to a registered oversea company and any charge over property of the company situated in Great Britain.

(2) They apply to any charge, whether or not particulars are required to be delivered to the registrar.

(3) In relation to such a company the references to the company's registered office shall be construed as references to its principal place of business in Great Britain.

Power to make further provision by regulations

703K.—(1) The Secretary of State may by regulations make further provision as to the application of the provisions of this Chapter, or the provisions of Part XII applied by this Chapter, in relation to charges of any description specified in the regulations.

(2) The regulations may apply any provisions of regulations made under section 413 (power to make further provision with respect to application of Part XII) or make any provision which may be made under that section with respect to the application of provisions of Part XII.

Provisions as to situation of property

703L.—(1) The following provisions apply for determining for the purposes of this Chapter whether a vehicle which is the property of an oversea company is situated in Great Britain—

40/Sch. 16   *Companies Act* 1989

      (a) a ship, aircraft or hovercraft shall be regarded as situated in Great Britain if, and only if, it is registered in Great Britain;

      (b) any other description of vehicle shall be regarded as situated in Great Britain on a day if, and only if, at any time on that day the management of the vehicle is directed from a place of business of the company in Great Britain;

and for the purposes of this Chapter a vehicle shall not be regarded as situated in one part of Great Britain only.

(2) For the purposes of this Chapter as it applies to a charge on future property, the subject-matter of the charge shall be treated as situated in Great Britain unless it relates exclusively to property of a kind which cannot, after being acquired or coming into existence, be situated in Great Britain; and references to property situated in a part of Great Britain shall be similarly construed.

Other supplementary provisions

703M. The following provisions of Part XII apply for the purposes of this Chapter—

      (a) section 414 (construction of references to date of creation of charge),
      (b) section 415 (prescribed particulars and related expressions),
      (c) section 416 (notice of matters disclosed on the register),
      (d) section 417 (power of court to dispense with signature),
      (e) section 418 (regulations) and
      (f) section 419 (minor definitions).

Index of defined expressions

703N. The following Table shows the provisions of this Chapter and Part XII defining or otherwise explaining expressions used in this Chapter (other than expressions used only in the same section)—

charge	sections 703A(2), 730B(3) and 395(2)
charge requiring registration	sections 703B(1) and 396
creation of charge	sections 703M(f) and 419(2)
date of acquisition (of property by a company)	sections 703M(f) and 419(3)
date of creation of charge	sections 703M(a) and 414
property	sections 703A(2) and 395(2)
registered oversea company	section 703A(3)
registrar and registration in relation to a charge	sections 703A(4) and 703E
situated in Great Britain	
in relation to vehicles	section 703L(1)
in relation to future property	section 703L(2)".

GENERAL NOTE
See the annotation to s.105.

Section 107   SCHEDULE 16

AMENDMENTS CONSEQUENTIAL ON PART IV

Land Charges Act 1972 (c. 61)

1.—(1) Section 3 of the Land Charges Act 1972 (registration of land charges) is amended as follows.

(2) In subsection (7) (registration in companies charges register to have same effect as registration under that Act), for "any of the enactments mentioned in subsection (8) below" substitute "Part XII, or Chapter III of Part XXIII, of the Companies Act 1985 (or corresponding earlier enactments)".

(3) In subsection (8) for "The enactments" substitute "The corresponding earlier enactments" and at the end insert "as originally enacted".

Companies Act 1985 (c. 6)

2.—(1) Schedule 24 to the Companies Act 1985 (punishment of offences) is amended as follows.

(2) For the entries relating to sections 399(3) to 423(3) (offences under Part XII: registration of charges) substitute—

"398(3)	Company failing to deliver particulars of charge to registrar.	1. On indictment. 2. Summary.	A fine. The statutory maximum.
408(3)	Company failing to deliver particulars of taking up of issue of debentures.	Summary.	One-fifth of the statutory maximum.
409(4)	Failure to give notice to registrar of appointment of receiver or manager, or of his ceasing to act.	Summary.	One-fifth of the statutory maximum.
410(4)	Failure to comply with requirements of regulations under s.410.	Summary.	One-fifth of the statutory maximum.
411(4)	Failure to keep copies of charging instruments or register at registered office.	1. On indictment. 2. Summary.	A fine. The statutory maximum.
412(4)	Refusing inspection of charging instrument or register or failing to supply copies.	Summary.	One-fifth of the statutory maximum.".

(3) After the entry relating to section 703(1) insert—

"703D(5)	Oversea company failing to deliver particulars of charge to registrar.	1. On indictment. 2. Summary.	A fine. The statutory maximum.".

Insolvency Act 1986 (c. 45)

3.—(1) The Insolvency Act 1986 is amended as follows.

(2) In section 9(3) (restrictions on making administration order where administrative receiver has been appointed), in paragraph (b) (exceptions) insert—

"(i) be void against the administrator to any extent by virtue of the provisions of Part XII of the Companies Act 1985 (registration of company charges),";

and renumber the existing sub-paragraphs as (ii) to (iv).

(3) In sections 45(5), 53(2), 54(3) and 62(5) (offences of failing to deliver documents relating to appointment or cessation of appointment of receiver) omit the words "and, for continued contravention, to a daily default fine".

Company Directors Disqualification Act 1986 (c. 46)

4. In Schedule 1 to the Company Directors Disqualification Act 1986 (matters relevant to determining unfitness of directors), in paragraph 4 (failure of company to comply with certain provisions), for sub-paragraph (h) substitute—

"(h) sections 398 and 703D (duty of company to deliver particulars of charges on its property).".

GENERAL NOTE
See the annotation to s.107.

Section 130(7)　　　　　　　　SCHEDULE 17

COMPANY CONTRACTS, SEALS, &C.: FURTHER PROVISIONS

Execution of deeds abroad

1.—(1) Section 38 of the Companies Act 1985 (execution of deeds abroad) is amended as follows.

(2) In subsection (1) (appointment of attorney to execute deeds), after "A company may" insert "under the law of England and Wales".

(3) For subsection (2) (effect of deed executed by attorney) substitute—

"(2) A deed executed by such an attorney on behalf of the company has the same effect as if it were executed under the company's common seal.".

Official seal for use abroad

2.—(1) Section 39 of the Companies Act 1985 (power to have official seal for use abroad) is amended as follows.

(2) In subsection (1), after "A company" insert "which has a common seal" and for "the common seal of the company" substitute "its common seal".

(3) For subsection (2) (effect of sealing with official seal) substitute—

"(2) The official seal when duly affixed to a document has the same effect as the company's common seal.".

(4) In subsection (3) (instrument authorising person to affix official seal), after "by writing under its common seal" insert "or, in the case of a company registered in Scotland, subscribed in accordance with section 36B,".

Official seal for share certificates, &c.

3.—(1) Section 40 of the Companies Act 1985 (official seal for share certificates, &c.) is amended as follows.

(2) After "A company" insert "which has a common seal" and for "the company's common seal" substitute "its common seal".

(3) At the end add—

"The official seal when duly affixed to a document has the same effect as the company's common seal.".

Authentication of documents

4. In section 41 of the Companies Act 1985 (authentication of documents), for the words from "may be signed" to the end substitute "is sufficiently authenticated for the purposes of the law of England and Wales by the signature of a director, secretary or other authorised officer of the company.".

Share certificate as evidence of title

5. For section 186 of the Companies Act 1985 (certificate to be evidence of title) substitute—

"Certificate to be evidence of title

186.—(1) A certificate under the common seal of the company (or in the case of a company registered in Scotland, subscribed in accordance with section 36B) specifying any shares held by a member is—

(a) in England and Wales, prima facie evidence, and
(b) in Scotland, sufficient evidence unless the contrary is shown,

of his title to the shares.".

Share warrants to bearer

6. For section 188 of the Companies Act 1985 (issue and effect of share warrant to bearer) substitute—

"Issue and effect of share warrant to bearer

188.—(1) A company limited by shares may, if so authorised by its articles, issue with respect to any fully paid shares a warrant (a "share warrant") stating that the bearer of the warrant is entitled to the shares specified in it.

(2) A share warrant issued under the company's common seal (or, in the case of a company registered in Scotland, subscribed in accordance with section 36B) entitles the bearer to the shares specified in it; and the shares may be transferred by delivery of the warrant.

(3) A company which issues a share warrant may, if so authorised by its articles, provide (by coupons or otherwise) for the payment of the future dividends on the shares included in the warrant.".

Identification of company on common seal

7. In section 350 of the Companies Act 1985 (identification of company on company seal), for subsection (1) substitute—

"(1) A company which has a common seal shall have its name engraved in legible characters on the seal; and if it fails to comply with this subsection it is liable to a fine.".

Floating charges under Scots law

8. In section 462 of the Companies Act 1985 (power of company to create floating charge), for subsections (2) and (3) substitute—
"(2) In the case of a company which the Court of Session has jurisdiction to wind up, a floating charge may be created only by a written instrument which is presumed under section 36B to be subscribed by the company.".

9. In section 466(2) of the Companies Act 1985 (execution of instrument altering floating charge)—
   (a) at the beginning of the subsection insert "Without prejudice to any enactment or rule of law regarding the execution of documents,";
   (b) omit paragraph (a);
   (c) at the end of paragraph (b) insert "; or," and
   (d) omit paragraph (d) and the word "or" preceding it.

10. In section 53(3) of the Insolvency Act 1986 (execution of instrument appointing receiver), in paragraph (a) for "in accordance with the provisions of section 36 of the Companies Act as if it were a contract" substitute "in accordance with section 36B of the Companies Act 1985".

GENERAL NOTE

This Schedule, introduced by s.123(7), makes minor and consequential amendments to the Companies Act 1985 following the new provisions relating to the execution of documents in England and Wales (C.A. 1985, new s.36A) and in Scotland (C.A. 1985, new s.36B) and the abolition of the requirement for a company to have a common seal.

The amendments relate in the main either to the fact that a common seal is no longer compulsory or to the new separate regime for Scotland. Other amendments are simply a rewriting of the existing provisions. They apply to C.A. 1985, s.38 (execution of deeds abroad); C.A. 1985, s.39 (use of the seal abroad); C.A. 1985, s.40 (the official seal for share certificates); C.A. 1985, s.41 (authentication of documents); C.A. 1985, s.186 (share certificate as evidence of title); C.A. 1985, s.188 (share warrants); C.A. 1985, s.350(1) (penalty for incorrect type of seal) and C.A. 1985, ss. 462(2) and 466(2) and Insolvency Act 1985, s.53(3) (floating charges in Scotland).

Section 144(4)   SCHEDULE 18

"SUBSIDIARY" AND RELATED EXPRESSIONS: CONSEQUENTIAL AMENDMENTS AND SAVINGS

Coal Industry Nationalisation Act 1946 (c. 59)

1. In Schedule 2A to the Coal Industry Nationalisation Act 1946 (eligibility for superannuation benefits), in the definition of "subsidiary" in paragraph 5 of the Table, for "section 154 of the Companies Act 1948" substitute "section 736 of the Companies Act 1985".

Electricity Act 1947 (c. 54)

2. In section 67 of the Electricity Act 1947 (interpretation)—
   (a) in the definition of "holding company" for "the definition contained in the Companies Act 1947" substitute "section 736 of the Companies Act 1985", and
   (b) in the definition of "subsidiary company" for "the Companies Act 1947" substitute "section 736 of the Companies Act 1985".

Landlord and Tenant Act 1954 (c. 56)

3. In section 42 of the Landlord and Tenant Act 1954 (groups of companies), in subsection (1) for "the same meaning as is assigned to it for the purposes of the Companies Act 1985 by section 736 of that Act" substitute "the meaning given by section 736 of the Companies Act 1985".

Transport Act 1962 (c. 46)

4. In the Transport Act 1946, in the definition of "subsidiary" in section 92(1) (interpretation) omit the words "(taking references in that section to a company as being references to a body corporate)".

Harbours Act 1964 (c. 40)

5. In section 57(1) of the Harbours Act 1964 (interpretation), in the definition of "marine work" for "section 154 of the Companies Act 1948" substitute "section 736 of the Companies Act 1985".

General Rate Act 1967 (c. 9)

6. In section 32A of the General Rate Act 1967 (rateable premises of Transport Boards), in the definition of "subsidiary" in subsection (6) omit the words "(taking references in that section to a company as being references to a body corporate)".

Transport Act 1968 (c. 73)

7. For the purposes of Part V of the Transport Act 1968 (licensing of road haulage operators) as it applies in relation to licences granted before the commencement of section 144(1), the expression "subsidiary" has the meaning given by section 736 of the Companies Act 1985 as originally enacted.

Post Office Act 1969 (c. 48)

8. In section 86 of the Post Office Act 1969 (interpretation), in subsection (2) for "736(5)(b)" substitute "736".

Industry Act 1972 (c. 63)

9. In section 10 of the Industry Act 1972 (construction credits), in subsection (9) for "for the purposes of the Companies Act 1985 by section 736 of that Act" substitute "by section 736 of the Companies Act 1985".

Coal Industry Act 1973 (c. 8)

10. In section 12(1) of the Coal Industry Act 1973 (interpretation) for the definition of "subsidiary" and "wholly-owned subsidiary" substitute—
    " 'subsidiary' and 'wholly-owned subsidiary' have the meanings given by section 736 of the Companies Act 1985;".

Industry Act 1975 (c. 68)

11. In section 37(1) of the Industry Act 1975 (interpretation), in the definition of "wholly-owned subsidiary" for "section 736(5)(b)" substitute "section 736".

Scottish Development Agency Act 1975 (c. 69)

12. In section 25(1) of the Scottish Development Agency Act 1975 (interpretation), in the definition of "wholly-owned subsidiary" for "section 736(5)(b)" substitute "section 736".

Welsh Development Agency Act 1975 (c. 70)

13. In section 27(1) of the Welsh Development Agency Act 1975 (interpretation), in the definition of "wholly-owned subsidiary" for "section 736(5)(b)" substitute "section 736".

Restrictive Trade Practices Act 1976 (c. 41)

14.—(1) This paragraph applies to agreements (within the meaning of the Restrictive Trade Practices Act 1976) made before the commencement of section 144(1); and "registrable" means subject to registration under that Act.

(2) An agreement which was not registrable before the commencement of section 144(1) shall not be treated as registrable afterwards by reason only of that provision having come into force; and an agreement which was registrable before the commencement of that provision shall not cease to be registrable by reason of that provision coming into force.

Industrial Common Ownership Act 1976 (c. 78)

15. In section 2(5) of the Industrial Common Ownership Act 1976 (common ownership and co-operative enterprises) for "for the purposes of the Companies Act 1985" substitute "as defined by section 736 of the Companies Act 1985 or for the purposes of".

Aircraft and Shipbuilding Industries Act 1977 (c. 3)

16. In section 56(1) of the Aircraft and Shipbuilding Industries Act 1977 (interpretation), in the definition of "subsidiary" for "the same meaning as in" substitute "the meaning given by section 736 of".

Nuclear Industry (Finance) Act 1977 (c. 7)

17. In section 3 of the Nuclear Industry (Finance) Act 1977 (expenditure on acquisition of shares in National Nuclear Corporation Ltd and subsidiaries), after "within the meaning of" insert "section 736 of".

Coal Industry Act 1977 (c. 39)

18. In section 14(1) of the Coal Industry Act 1977 (interpretation), in the definition of "wholly-owned subsidiary" for "section 736(5)(b)" substitute "section 736".

Shipbuilding (Redundancy Payments) Act 1978 (c. 11)

19. In section 1(4) of the Shipbuilding (Redundancy Payments) Act 1978 (schemes for payments to redundant workers), for the definitions of "subsidiary" and "wholly-owned subsidiary" substitute—
" 'subsidiary' and 'wholly-owned subsidiary' have the meanings given by section 736 of the Companies Act 1985;".

Capital Gains Tax Act 1979 (c. 14)

20. In section 149 of the Capital Gains Tax Act 1979 (employee trusts), in subsection (7) for "the same meaning as in" substitute "the meaning given by section 736 of".

Crown Agents Act 1979 (c. 43)

21. In section 31(1) of the Crown Agents Act 1979 (interpretation), in the definition of "wholly-owned subsidiary" for "section 736(5)(b)" substitute "section 736(2)".

Competition Act 1980 (c. 21)

22. In sections 11(3)(f) and 12 of the Competition Act 1980 (references relating to public bodies, &c.), after "within the meaning of" insert "section 736 of".

British Aerospace Act 1980 (c. 26)

23. In section 14(1) of the British Aerospace Act 1980 (interpretation)—
 (a) in the definition of "subsidiary" for "the same meaning as in", and
 (b) in the definition of "wholly-owned subsidiary" for "the same meaning as it has for the purposes of section 150 of the Companies Act 1948",
substitute "the meaning given by section 736 of the Companies Act 1985".

Local Government, Planning and Land Act 1980 (c. 65)

24. In sections 100(1), 141(7) and 170(1)(d) and (2) of the Local Government, Planning and Land Act 1980 (which refer to wholly-owned subsidiaries) for "within the meaning of section 736(5)(b)" substitute "as defined by section 736".

British Telecommunications Act 1981 (c. 38)

25. In section 85 of the British Telecommunications Act 1981 (interpretation), for subsection (2) substitute—
   "(2) Any reference in this Act to a subsidiary or wholly-owned subsidiary shall be construed in accordance with section 736 of the Companies Act 1985.".

Transport Act 1981 (c. 56)

26. In section 4(2) of the Transport Act 1981 (interpretation of provisions relating to activities of British Railways Board), for "section 154 of the Companies Act 1985" substitute "section 736 of the Companies Act 1985".

Value Added Tax Act 1983 (c. 55)

27. In section 29 of the Value Added Tax Act 1983 (groups of companies), in subsection (8) after "within the meaning of" insert "section 736 of".

Telecommunications Act 1984 (c. 12)

28. In section 73(1) of the Telecommunications Act 1984 (interpretation of Part V), for "the same meaning as in" substitute "the meaning given by section 736 of".

London Regional Transport Act 1984 (c. 32)

29. In section 68 of the London Regional Transport Act 1984 (interpretation), for the definition of "subsidiary" substitute—
   " "subsidiary" (subject to section 62 of this Act) has the meaning given by section 736 of the Companies Act 1985;".

Inheritance Tax Act 1984 (c. 51)

30.—(1) The Inheritance Tax Act 1984 is amended as follows.
(2) In section 13 (dispositions by close companies for benefit of employees), in the definition of "subsidiary" in subsection (5) for "the same meaning as in" substitute "the meaning given by section 736 of".
(3) In section 103 (introductory provisions relating to relief for business property), in subsection (2) for "the same meanings as in" substitute "the meanings given by section 736 of".
(4) In section 234 (interest on instalments) in subsection (3) for "within the meaning of" substitute "as defined in section 736 of".

Ordnance Factories and Military Services Act 1984 (c. 59)

31. In section 14 of the Ordnance Factories and Military Services Act 1984 (interpretation), for the definitions of "subsidiary" and "wholly-owned subsidiary" substitute—
   " "subsidiary" and "wholly-owned subsidiary" have the meanings given by section 736 of the Companies Act 1985.".

Companies Act 1985 (c. 6)

32.—(1) The following provisions have effect with respect to the operation of section 23 of the Companies Act 1985 (prohibition on subsidiary being a member of its holding company).
(2) In relation to times, circumstances and purposes before the commencement of section 144(1) of this Act, the references in section 23 to a subsidiary or holding company shall be construed in accordance with section 736 of the Companies Act 1985 as originally enacted.

(3) Where a body corporate becomes or ceases to be a subsidiary of a holding company by reason of section 144(1) coming into force, the prohibition in section 23 of the Companies Act 1985 shall apply (in the absence of exempting circumstances), or cease to apply, accordingly.

33.—(1) Section 153 of the Companies Act 1985 (transactions excepted from prohibition on company giving financial assistance for acquisition of its own shares) is amended as follows.

(2) In subsection (4)(bb) (employees' share schemes) for "a company connected with it" substitute "a company in the same group".

(3) For subsection (5) substitute—

"(5) For the purposes of subsection (4)(bb) a company is in the same group as another company if it is a holding company or subsidiary of that company, or a subsidiary of a holding company of that company.".

34. Section 293 of the Companies Act 1985 (age limit for directors) does not apply in relation to a director of a company if—

(a) he had attained the age of 70 before the commencement of section 144(1) of this Act, and

(b) the company became a subsidiary of a public company by reason only of the commencement of that subsection.

35. Nothing in section 144(1) affects the operation of Part XIIIA of the Companies Act 1985 (takeover offers) in relation to a takeover offer made before the commencement of that subsection.

36. For the purposes of section 719 of the Companies Act 1985 (power to provide for employees on transfer or cessation of business), a company which immediately before the commencement of section 144(1) was a subsidiary of another company shall not be treated as ceasing to be such a subsidiary by reason of that subsection coming into force.

37. For the purposes of section 743 of the Companies Act 1985 (meaning of "employees' share scheme"), a company which immediately before the commencement of section 144(1) was a subsidiary of another company shall not be treated as ceasing to be such a subsidiary by reason of that subsection coming into force.

38. In Schedule 25 to the Companies Act 1985 "subsidiary" has the meaning given by section 736 of that Act as originally enacted.

Transport Act 1985 (c. 67)

39. In section 137(1) of the Transport Act 1985 (interpretation), in the definition of "subsidiary" for the words from "as defined" to the end substitute "within the meaning of section 736 of the Companies Act 1985 as originally enacted (and not as substituted by section 144(1) of the Companies Act 1989);".

Housing Act 1985 (c. 68)

40. In section 622 of the Housing Act 1985 (minor definitions: general), in the definition of "subsidiary" for "the same meaning as in" substitute "the meaning given by section 736 of".

Housing Associations Act 1985 (c. 69)

41. In section 101 of the Housing Associations Act 1985 (minor definitions: Part II), in the definition of "subsidiary" for "the same meaning as in" substitute "the meaning given by section 736 of".

Atomic Energy Authority Act 1986 (c. 3)

42. In section 9 of the Atomic Energy Authority Act 1986 (interpretation), in the definition of "subsidiary" and "wholly-owned subsidiary" for "have the same meaning as in" substitute "have the meaning given by section 736 of".

Airports Act 1986 (c. 31)

43. In section 82 of the Airports Act 1986 (general interpretation), in the definition of "subsidiary" for "has the same meaning as in" substitute "has the meaning given by section 736 of".

40/Sch. 19　　　　　　*Companies Act* 1989

Gas Act 1986 (c. 44)

44. In the Gas Act 1986—
    (a) in section 48(1) (interpretation of Part I), in the definitions of "holding company" and "subsidiary", and
    (b) in section 61(1) (interpretation of Part II), in the definition of "subsidiary",
for "has the same meaning as in" substitute "has the meaning given by section 736 of".

Building Societies Act 1986 (c. 53)

45. In section 119 of the Building Societies Act 1986 (interpretation), in the definition of "subsidiary" for "has the same meaning as in" substitute "has the meaning given by section 736 of".

Income and Corporation Taxes Act 1988 (c. 1)

46. In section 141 of the Income and Corporation Taxes Act 1988 (benefits in kind: non-cash vouchers), in the definition of "subsidiary" in subsection (7) for "section 736(5)(b)" substitute "section 736".

British Steel Act 1988 (c. 35)

47. In section 15(1) of the British Steel Act 1988 (interpretation), in the definition of "subsidiary" for "has the same meaning as in" substitute "has the meaning given by section 736 of".

GENERAL NOTE

This Schedule makes amendments and savings in relation to various statutes consequent on the new definitions of a holding company, subsidiary company and wholly-owned subsidiary in s.134 of this Act. In particular it amends and makes transitional provisions for ss.23, 134, 153, 193, 428–430F, 719 and 743 of the Companies Act 1985 (paras. 32–38).

Section 145　　　　　　SCHEDULE 19

MINOR AMENDMENTS OF THE COMPANIES ACT 1985

Correction of cross-reference

1. In section 131(1) of the Companies Act 1985 (merger relief) for "section 132(4)" substitute "section 132(8)".
This amendment shall be deemed always to have had effect.

Particulars to be given of directors and secretaries

2.—(1) Section 289 of the Companies Act 1985 (particulars of directors required to be entered in register) is amended as follows.
(2) In subsection (1)(a) (particulars of individual directors)—
   (a) in sub-paragraph (i) for "Christian name and surname" and in sub-paragraph (ii) for "Christian name or surname" substitute "name", and
   (b) for sub-paragraph (vii) substitute—
      "(vii) the date of his birth;".
(3) In subsection (1)(b) (particulars of other directors) after "corporation" insert "or Scottish firm" and after "corporate" insert "or firm".
(4) For subsection (2) substitute—
   "(2) In subsection (1)(a)—
      (a) "name" means a person's Christian name (or other forename) and surname, except that in the case of a peer, or an individual usually known by a title, the title may be stated instead of his Christian name (or other forename) and surname, or in addition to either or both of them; and
      (b) the reference to a former name does not include—

(i) in the case of a peer, or an individual normally known by a British title, the name by which he was known previous to the adoption of or succession to the title, or

(ii) in the case of any person, a former name which was changed or disused before he attained the age of 18 years or which has been changed or disused for 20 years or more, or

(iii) in the case of a married woman, the name by which she was known previous to the marriage.".

3.—(1) Section 290 of the Companies Act 1985 (particulars of secretaries to be entered in register) is amended as follows.

(2) In subsection (1)(a) (particulars of individuals) for "Christian name and surname" and "Christian name or surname" substitute "name".

(3) For subsection (3) substitute—

"(3) Section 289(2)(a) and (b) apply for the purposes of the obligation under subsection (1)(a) of this section to state the name or former name of an individual.".

4.—(1) Section 305 of the Companies Act 1985 (directors' names on company correspondence, &c.) is amended as follows.

(2) In subsection (1) for the words from "the Christian name" onwards substitute "the name of every director of the company".

(3) For subsection (4) substitute—

"(4) For the purposes of the obligation under subsection (1) to state the name of every director of the company, a person's "name" means—

(a) in the case of an individual, his Christian name (or other forename) and surname; and

(b) in the case of a corporation or Scottish firm, its corporate or firm name.

(5) The initial or a recognised abbreviation of a person's Christian name or other forename may be stated instead of the full Christian name or other forename.

(6) In the case of a peer, or an individual usually known by a title, the title may be stated instead of his Christian name (or other forename) and surname or in addition to either or both of them.

(7) In this section "director" includes a shadow director and the reference in subsection (3) to an "officer" shall be construed accordingly.".

5.—(1) Section 686 of the Companies Act 1985 (documents to be delivered to registrar on registration of company not formed under companies legislation) is amended as follows.

(2) In subsection (1) (particulars to be delivered to registrar), for paragraph (b) (particulars of directors and managers) substitute—

"(b) a list showing with respect to each director or manager of the company—

(i) in the case of an individual, his name, address, occupation and date of birth,

(ii) in the case of a corporation or Scottish firm, its corporate or firm name and registered or principal office.".

(3) After that subsection insert—

"(1A) For the purposes of subsection (1)(b)(i) a person's'name' means his Christian name (or other forename) and surname, except that in the case of a peer, or an individual usually known by a title, the title may be stated instead of his Christian name (or other forename) and surname or in addition to either or both of them.".

6. In section 691 of the Companies Act 1985 (documents to be delivered to registrar on registration of oversea company), for subsection (2) (particulars of directors and secretary) substitute—

"(2) The list referred to in subsection (1)(b)(i) shall contain the following particulars with respect to each director—

(a) in the case of an individual—

(i) his name,

(ii) any former name,

(iii) his usual residential address,

(iv) his nationality,

(v) his business occupation (if any),

(vi) if he has no business occupation but holds other directorships, particulars of them, and

(vii) his date of birth;

(b) in the case of a corporation or Scottish firm, its corporate or firm name and registered or principal office.

(3) The list referred to in subsection (1)(b)(i) shall contain the following particulars with respect to the secretary (or, where there are joint secretaries, with respect to each of them)—

(a) in the case of an individual, his name, any former name and his usual residential address;

(b) in the case of a corporation or Scottish firm, its corporate or firm name and registered or principal office.

Where all the partners in a firm are joint secretaries of the company, the name and principal office of the firm may be stated instead of the particulars required by paragraph (a).

(4) In subsections (2)(a) and (3)(a) above—

(a) "name," means a person's Christian name (or other forename) and surname, except that in the case of a peer, or an individual usually known by a title, the title may be stated instead of his Christian name (or other forename) and surname, or in addition to either or both of them; and

(b) the reference to a former name does not include—

(i) in the case of a peer, or an individual normally known by a British title, the name by which he was known previous to the adoption of or succession to the title, or

(ii) in the case of any person, a former name which was changed or disused before he attained the age of 18 years or which has been changed or disused for 20 years or more, or

(iii) in the case of a married woman, the name by which she was known previous to the marriage.".

7.—(1) Schedule 1 to the Companies Act 1985 (particulars of directors and secretaries to be sent to registrar) is amended as follows.

(2) In paragraph 1(a) (particulars of individual directors)—

(a) for "Christian name and surname" and "Christian name or surname" substitute "name"; and

(b) for the words from "and, in the case" to the end substitute "and his date of birth".

(3) In paragraph 1(b) (particulars of other directors) after "corporation" insert "or Scottish firm" and after "corporate" insert "or firm".

(4) In paragraph 3(1)(a) (particulars of individual secretaries) for "Christian name and surname" (twice) substitute "name".

(5) For paragraph 4 substitute—

"4. In paragraphs l(a) and 3(1)(a) above—

(a) "name" means a person's Christian name (or other forename) and surname, except that in the case of a peer, or an individual usually known by a title, the title may be stated instead of his Christian name (or other forename) and surname or in addition to either or both of them; and

(b) the reference to a former name does not include—

(i) in the case of a peer, or an individual normally known by a British title, the name by which he was known previous to the adoption of or succession to the title, or

(ii) in the case of any person, a former name which was changed or disused before he attained the age of 18 years or which has been changed or disused for 20 years or more, or

(iii) in the case of a married woman, the name by which she was known previous to the marriage.".

Transactions with directors not requiring authorisation

8. In section 321 of the Companies Act 1985 (exceptions from provisions requiring authorisation for substantial property transactions with directors, &c.), after subsection (3) insert—

"(4) Section 320(1) does not apply to a transaction on a recognised investment exchange which is effected by a director, or a person connected with him, through the agency of a person who in relation to the transaction acts as an independent broker.

For this purpose an "independent broker" means—

(a) in relation to a transaction on behalf of a director, a person who independently of the director selects the person with whom the transaction is to be effected, and

(b) in relation to a transaction on behalf of a person connected with a director, a person who independently of that person or the director selects the person with whom the transaction is to be effected;

and "recognised", in relation to an investment exchange, means recognised under the Financial Services Act 1986.".

Time limit for holding extraordinary general meeting convened on members' requisition

9. In section 368 of the Companies Act 1985 (extraordinary general meeting on members' requisition), after subsection (7) add—
"(8) The directors are deemed not to have duly convened a meeting if they convene a meeting for a date more than 28 days after the date of the notice convening the meeting.".

Removal of restriction on transfer of shares

10.—(1) In section 456(3) of the Companies Act 1985 (removal of restrictions by order of court), in paragraph (b) (order where shares to be sold)—
 (a) for "sold" substitute "transferred for valuable consideration", and
 (b) for "sale" substitute "transfer".
(2) In section 454(2) and (3) (which refer to section 456(3)(b)) for "sell" and "sale" substitute "transfer".

Protection of company's members against unfair prejudice

11. In Part XVII of the Companies Act 1985 (protection of company's members against unfair prejudice)—
 (a) in section 459(1) (application by company member), and
 (b) in section 460(1)(b) (application by Secretary of State),
for "unfairly prejudicial to the interests of some part of the members" substitute "unfairly prejudicial to the interests of its members generally or of some part of its members".

Requirements for registration by joint stock companies

12. In section 684(1) of the Companies Act 1985 (requirements for registration by joint stock companies: documents to be delivered to registrar), in paragraph (b) (list of members on specified day) for "(not more than 6 clear days before the day of registration)" substitute "(not more than 28 clear days before the day of registration)".

Delivery of documents by oversea companies

13. In Chapter I of Part XXIII of the Companies Act 1985 (oversea companies: registration, &c.), for section 696 (office where documents to be filed) substitute—

 "Registrar to whom documents to be delivered
 696.—(1) References to the registrar in relation to an oversea company (except references in Chapter III of this Part (registration of charges): see section 703E), shall be construed in accordance with the following provisions.

 (2) The documents which an oversea company is required to deliver to the registrar shall be delivered—
  (a) to the registrar for England and Wales if the company has established a place of business in England and Wales, and
  (b) to the registrar for Scotland if the company has established a place of business in Scotland;
 and if the company has an established place of business in both parts of Great Britain, the documents shall be delivered to both registrars.

 (3) If a company ceases to have a place of business in either part of Great Britain, it shall forthwith give notice of that fact to the registrar for that part; and from the date on which notice is so given it is no longer obliged to deliver documents to that registrar.".

Companies' registered numbers

14. For section 705 of the Companies Act 1985 (companies' registered numbers) substitute—

 "Companies registered numbers

705.—(1) The registrar shall allocate to every company a number, which shall be known as the company's registered number.

(2) Companies' registered numbers shall be in such form, consisting of one or more sequences of figures or letters, as the registrar may from time to time determine.

(3) The registrar may upon adopting a new form of registered number make such changes of existing registered numbers as appear to him necessary.

(4) A change of a company's registered number has effect from the date on which the company is notified by the registrar of the change; but for a period of three years beginning with the date on which that notification is sent by the registrar the requirement of section 351(1)(a) as to the use of the company's registered number on business letters and order forms is satisfied by the use of either the old number or the new.

(5) In this section "company" includes—
  (a) any oversea company which has complied with section 691 (delivery of statutes to registrar, &c.), other than a company which appears to the registrar not to have a place of business in Great Britain; and
  (b) any body to which any provision of this Act applies by virtue of section 718 (unregistered companies).".

Exemptions from limit of 20 on members of partnership

15.—(1) Section 716 of the Companies Act 1985 (prohibition of formation of company, association or partnership with more than 20 members unless registered as company, &c.) is amended as follows.

(2) In subsection (2) (exemptions), after paragraph (c) insert—
  "(d) for any purpose prescribed by regulations (which may include a purpose mentioned above), of a partnership of a description so prescribed.";
and omit the words inserted by paragraph 22 of Schedule 16 to the Financial Services Act 1986.

(3) For subsections (3) and (4) substitute—
  "(3) In subsection (2)(a) "solicitor"—
  (a) in relation to England and Wales, means solicitor of the Supreme Court, and
  (b) in relation to Scotland, means a person enrolled or deemed enrolled as a solicitor in pursuance of the Solicitors (Scotland) Act 1980.
  (4) In subsection (2)(c) "recognised stock exchange" means—
  (a) The International Stock Exchange of the United Kingdom and the Republic of Ireland Limited, and
  (b) any other stock exchange for the time being recognised for the purposes of this section by the Secretary of State by order made by statutory instrument.".

16.—(1) Section 717 of the Companies Act 1985 (limited partnerships: limit on number of members) is amended as follows.

(2) In subsection (1) (exemptions from limit of 20 members under section 4(2) of Limited Partnerships Act 1907), after paragraph (c) insert—
  "(d) to a partnership carrying on business of any description prescribed by regulations (which may include a business of any description mentioned above), of a partnership of a description so prescribed.";
and omit the words inserted by paragraph 22 of Schedule 16 to the Financial Services Act 1986.

(3) For subsections (2) and (3) substitute—
  "(2) In subsection (1)(a) "solicitor"—
  (a) in relation to England and Wales, means solicitor of the Supreme Court, and
  (b) in relation to Scotland, means a person enrolled or deemed enrolled as a solicitor in pursuance of the Solicitors (Scotland) Act 1980.
  (3) In subsection (1)(c) "recognised stock exchange" means—
  (a) The International Stock Exchange of the United Kingdom and the Republic of Ireland Limited, and
  (b) any other stock exchange for the time being recognised for the purposes of this section by the Secretary of State by order made by statutory instrument.".

Meaning of "officer who is in default"

17. In section 730 of the Companies Act 1985 (punishment of offences), in subsection (5) (meaning of "officer who is in default"), after "company" (twice) insert "or other body".

Offences committed by partnerships and other unincorporated bodies

18. In section 734 of the Companies Act 1985 (criminal proceedings against unincorporated bodies), at the end add—

"(5) Where such an offence committed by a partnership is proved to have been committed with the consent or connivance of, or to be attributable to any neglect on the part of, a partner, he as well as the partnership is guilty of the offence and liable to be proceeded against and punished accordingly.

(6) Where such an offence committed by an unincorporated body (other than a partnership) is proved to have been committed with the consent or connivance of, or to be attributable to any neglect on the part of, any officer of the body or any member of its governing body, he as well as the body is guilty of the offence and liable to be proceeded against and punished accordingly.".

Meaning of "office copy" in Scotland

19. In Part XXVI of the Companies Act 1985 (interpretation), after section 743 insert—

"Meaning of "office copy" in Scotland

743A. References in this Act to an office copy of a court order shall be construed, as respects Scotland, as references to a certified copy interlocutor.".

Index of defined expressions

20. In Part XXVI of the Companies Act 1985 (interpretation), after section 744 insert—

"Index of defined expressions

744A. The following Table shows provisions defining or otherwise explaining expressions for the purposes of this Act generally—

accounting reference date, accounting reference period	sections 244 and 742(1)
acquisition (in relation to a non-cash asset)	section 739(2)
agent	section 744
allotment (and related expressions)	section 738
annual accounts	sections 261(2), 262(1) and 742(1)
annual general meeting	section 366
annual return	section 363
articles	section 744
authorised minimum	section 118
balance sheet and balance sheet date	sections 261(2), 262(1) and 742(1)
bank holiday	section 744
banking company	section 744
body corporate	section 740
books and papers, books or papers	section 744
called-up share capital	section 737(1)
capital redemption reserve	section 170(1)
the Companies Acts	section 744
companies charges register	section 397
company	section 735(1)
the Consequential Provisions Act	section 744
corporation	section 740
the court (in relation to a company)	section 744
current assets	sections 262(1) and 742(1)
debenture	section 744
director	section 741(1)
document	section 744
elective resolution	section 379A
employees' share scheme	section 743
equity share capital	section 744
existing company	section 735(1)
extraordinary general meeting	section 368
extraordinary resolution	section 378(1)

40/Sch. 19 *Companies Act* 1989

financial year (of a company)	sections 223 and 742(1)
fixed assets	sections 262(1) and 742(1)
floating charge (in Scotland)	section 462
the former Companies Acts	section 735(1)
the Gazette	section 744
hire-purchase agreement	section 744
holding company	section 736
the Insider Dealing Act	section 744
the Insolvency Act	section 735A(1)
insurance company	section 744
the Joint Stock Companies Acts	section 735(3)
limited company	section 1(2)
member (of a company)	section 22
memorandum (in relation to a company)	section 744
non-cash asset	section 739(1)
number (in relation to shares)	section 744
ofice copy (in relation to a court order in Scotland)	section 743A
officer (in relation to a body corporate)	section 744
official seal (in relation to the registrar of companies)	section 744
oversea company	section 744
overseas branch register	section 362
paid up (and related expressions)	section 738
parent company and parent undertaking	sections 258 and 742(1)
place of business	section 744
prescribed	section 744
private company	section 1(3)
profit and loss account	sections 261(1), 262(1) and 742(1)
prospectus	section 744
public company	section 1(3)
realised profits or losses	sections 262(3) and 742(2)
register number (of a company)	section 705(1)
registered office (of a company)	section 287
registrar and registrar of companies	section 744
resolution for reducing share capital	section 135(3)
shadow director	section 741(2) and (3)
share	section 744
share premium account	section 130(1)
share warrant	section 188
special notice (in relation to a resolution)	section 379
special resolution	section 378(2)
subsidiary	section 736
subsidiary undertaking	sections 258 and 742(1)
transfer (in relation to a non-cash asset)	section 739(2)
uncalled share capital	section 737(2)
undistributable reserves	section 264(3)
unlimited company	section 1(2)
unregistered company	section 718
wholly-owned subsidiary	section 736(2)".

Fraudulent trading by unregistered companies

21. In Schedule 22 to the Companies Act 1985 (provisions applying to unregistered companies), at the appropriate place insert—
   "Part XVI   Fraudulent trading   —".
                     by a company.

GENERAL NOTE

This Schedule contains amendments to the Companies Act 1985.

Merger relief—correction of cross reference (para. 1): Para. 1 amends the reference to C.A. 1985, s.132(4), in s.131(1) of that Act, to a reference to s.132(8). This rectifies a simple error in the original text and ensures that the two forms of merger relief in ss.131 and 132 are mutually exclusive as they were always intended to be. This amendment is retrospective.

Statement of names of directors and secretaries (paras. 2–7): Para. 2 amends C.A. 1985, s.289 (particulars of directors to be kept in a register). The main change is that all references to Christian names and surnames will be read as references to the director's name. This is now defined as his or her Christian or forename and surname. It also now requires that a director's date of birth be included for all companies. The other change is to include a Scottish firm name if such is a director of a company.

Similar amendments (except for date of birth) are made to C.A. 1985, s.290 (particulars of secretary of register) by para. 3, and to C.A. 1985, Sched. 1 (statement of directors and secretary to be sent to the registrar on formation under C.A. 1985, s.10 by para. 7.

Para. 4 amends C.A. 1985, s.305 (disclosure of directors' names on company correspondence), similarly including the date of birth. Initials or a "recognised abbreviation" of a Christian or forename may be used.

Para. 5 amends C.A. 1985, s.686 (details to be supplied on registration of companies not formed by registration) to require the date of birth of directors to be included, and to allow for corporate or Scottish partnership directors. The provisions for names are harmonised with the above changes.

Para. 6 applies similar changes as to the names of directors and the secretary required of an overseas company under Pt. XXIII of the 1985 Act.

Transactions with directors not requiring authorisation (para. 8): Para. 8 adds a new subs. (4) to C.A. 1985, s.320. That section requires directors to seek shareholder approval before acquiring non-cash assets from their company above certain limits. The new subsection will apply to the case, *e.g.* of a director of a holding company in a financial services group which includes a market maker who buys shares from that market maker through a broker without being aware of it. This new exception to the general rule will only apply to transactions on a recognised investment exchange (under the Financial Services Act 1986) through an independent broker, *i.e.* one who selects the market maker independently of the director.

Time limit for holding extraordinary general meeting convened on members' requisition (para. 9): Para. 9 makes a long awaited amendment to C.A. 1985, s.368, under which a percentage of the members may require the directors to convene an emergency general meeting and by s.368(4) such a meeting must be called within 21 days of the request being deposited. But there was no time limit as to when the meeting need actually be held. The Jenkins Committee in 1962 recommended a change and the courts confirmed this defect in *Re Windward Enterprises Ltd.* [1983] B.C.L.C. 293, so that the purpose of the section could be defeated. In *McGuiness* v. *Bremner* [1988] BCLC 673, the Court of Session confirmed this but allowed a s.459 petition as a remedy. Under the amendment the directors will be compelled to fix the actual date of the meeting within 28 days of its being summoned, a maximum 49-day period in all.

Removal of restriction on transfer of shares (para. 10): Para. 10 makes technical amendments to C.A. 1985, s.456 (court removing restrictions imposed on the transfer of shares) by replacing the concept of a sale of shares to one of transfer for valuable considerations (*e.g.* an exchange).

Protection of company's members against unfair prejudice (para. 11): Para. 11 amends C.A. 1985, s.459 (petition for unfairly prejudicial conduct) following the decision in *Re A Company,* ex p. *Glossop* [1988] BCLC 570, that conduct which was unfair to all the members would not found a petition since the conduct had to be unfair to a part of the members. Although this decision was doubted in *Re Sam Weller & Sons Ltd.* (1989) 5 BCC 810, this amendment will rectify any anomaly.

Requirements for registration by joint stock companies (para. 12): Para. 12 amends C.A. 1985, s.684(1)(b), by requiring a joint stock company to deliver a list of members made up to no more than 28 days before to the registrar, and not six days before as previously.

Delivery of documents by overseas companies (para. 13): Para. 13 substitutes a new s.696 to the C.A. 1985, which specifies which is the appropriate registrar in relation to the notification requirements imposed upon overseas companies (except for the register of charges). The registrar concerned is the one in England and Wales or Scotland, or both, in which the company has established a place of business. It is also obliged to notify the appropriate registrar on cesser of such business since it thereby ceases to have the notification requirements.

Companies' registered numbers (para. 14): This paragraph substitutes a new s.705 into the C.A. 1985. This section relates to the allocation of a registered number to each company. Under the new section this number is to consist of any sequence of figures or letters as the registrar may decide. This will enable additional "check digits" to be introduced which should facilitate speed and accuracy on retrieval. The registrar may decide to change existing company numbers to the new format, the change taking effect on notification of that number to the company. However, the old or new number may be used on business letters and order forms (to comply with C.A. 1985, s.351(1)(c)) for three years from the date when notification was sent to the company.

Exemptions from limit of 20 members (paras. 15, 16). Para. 15 amends C.A. 1985, s.716, which prohibits any partnership with more than 20 members and then contains several exceptions. The only change of substance is that the former reference to the Stock Exchange now reads as a reference to the International Stock Exchange of the United Kingdom and the Republic of Ireland Ltd. Other changes are not substantive and relate mainly to the order.

Para. 16 makes similar changes to C.A. 1985, s.717, which applies to limited partnerships.

Meaning of "officer who is in default" (para. 17): Para. 17 amends C.A. 1985, s.730, to include in the definition of an officer who is in default for the C.A. 1985 purposes an officer of the company *or other body* involved.

Offences committed by partnerships and other unincorporated bodies (para. 18): Para. 18 adds new subss. (5) and (6) to C.A. 1985, s.734. That section applies to offences committed under C.A. 1985, ss.447 to 451 (refusal to produce documents, mutilation of documents, etc., as requested by D.T.I. inspection) by unincorporated bodies. Under new subs. (5) a partner commits a separate offence if the crime is committed by the firm with his consent, connivance or neglect. Under new subs. (6) similar provision is made with respect to any such officer or member of the governing body of any other unincorporated association.

Meaning of "office copy" in Scotland (para. 19): Para. 19 introduces new s.734A into the C.A. 1985 and defines an office copy of a court order for Scotland.

Index of defined expressions (para. 20): Para. 20 introduces new s.744A into the C.A. 1985, which sets out an index of defined expressions to the C.A. 1985 as amended by C.A. 1989.

Fraudulent trading by unregistered companies (para. 21): Para. 21 introduces an amendment into Sched. 22 to the C.A. 1985 so that s.458 of that Act (fraudulent trading) will apply to unregistered companies (*i.e.* statutory and chartered companies).

Section 153

SCHEDULE 20

AMENDMENTS ABOUT MERGERS AND RELATED MATTERS

Fair Trading Act 1973 (c. 41)

1. In section 46 of the Fair Trading Act 1973, subsection (3) is omitted.

2.—(1) In section 60 of that Act—
   (a) in subsection (1) for "the period of three months beginning with the date of the" there is substituted "such period (not being longer than three months beginning with the date of the reference) as may be specified in the",
   (b) in subsection (2) for "original period of three months" there is substituted "period specified in the newspaper merger reference", and
   (c) in subsection (3) for "subsection (1)" there is substituted "the newspaper merger reference".

(2) This paragraph does not apply in relation to any newspaper merger reference made before the passing of this Act.

3. In section 63(1) of that Act, for "to 75 of this Act shall have effect in relation to merger references other than" there is substituted "to 75K of this Act shall not have effect in relation to".

4. In section 66 of that Act—
   (a) in subsections (1) and (3), after "the Secretary of State" there is inserted "or the Commission", and
   (b) in subsection (4), after "this section" there is inserted "and to section 66A of this Act".

5.—(1) In section 67 of that Act, in subsection (2)(a), for the words from "any enterprise" to the end there is substituted—
   "(i) any enterprise which remains under the same ownership and control, or
   (ii) if none of the enterprises remains under the same ownership and control, the enterprise having the assets with the highest value, and".

(2) In subsection (4) of that section—
   (a) after "section 66" there is inserted "or subsection (1) of section 66A", and

(b) for "that subsection" there is substituted "either of those subsections".

6. In section 68(4) of that Act, after "the Secretary of State" there is inserted "or, as the case may be, the Commission".

7. In section 71 of that Act—
   (a) in subsection (1) the words "made under section 69(4) of this Act", and
   (b) subsection (2), are omitted.

8. In section 74(1) of that Act—
   (a) the words "and does not impose on the Commission a limitation under section 69(4) of this Act" are omitted, and
   (b) in paragraph (d), for "paragraph 12" there is substituted "paragraphs 12 and 12A".

9. In section 75(4) of that Act—
   (a) after "sections 66" there is inserted "66A," and
   (b) for paragraphs (a) and (b) there is substituted—
      "(a) section 66 shall apply, where an event by which any enterprises cease as between themselves to be distinct enterprises will occur if the arrangements are carried into effect, as if the event had occurred immediately before the date of the reference;
      (aa) section 66A shall apply, where a transaction falling within subsection (2) of that section will occur if the arrangements are carried into effect, as if the transaction had occurred immediately before the date of the reference;
      (b) in section 67(4) the references to subsection (1) of section 66 and subsection (1) of section 66A shall be construed as references to those subsections as modified in accordance with paragraph (a) or (aa) of this subsection;".

10. Paragraphs 4 to 9 (and the repeals in Schedule 24 corresponding to paragraphs 7 and 8(a)) do not apply in relation to any merger reference made before the passing of this Act.

11. At the end of section 76 of that Act there is added—
   "(2) In exercising his duty under this section the Director shall take into consideration any representations made to him by persons appearing to him to have a substantial interest in any such arrangements or transactions or by bodies appearing to him to represent substantial numbers of persons who have such an interest.".

12.—(1) In section 83 of that Act, after subsection (3) there is inserted—
   "(3A) Without prejudice to subsection (3) above, if the Minister or Ministers to whom any such report is made consider that it would not be in the public interest to disclose—
      (a) any matter contained in the report relating to the private affairs of an individual whose interests would, in the opinion of the Minister or Ministers, be seriously and prejudicially affected by the publication of that matter, or
      (b) any matter contained in the report relating specifically to the affairs of a particular person whose interests would, in the opinion of the Minister or Ministers, be seriously and prejudicially affected by the publication of that matter,
   the Minister or Ministers shall exclude that matter from the copies of the report as laid before Parliament and from the report as published under this section.".

(2) This paragraph does not apply in relation to any report made before the passing of this Act.

13.—(1) In section 85 of that Act, for subsection (7) there is substituted—
   "(7) If any person (referred to in subsection (7A) of this section as 'the defaulter') refuses or otherwise fails to comply with any notice under subsection (1) of this section, any one of those who, in relation to the investigation in question, are performing the functions of the Commission may certify that fact in writing to the court and the court may enquire into the case.
   (7A) If, after hearing any witness who may be produced against or on behalf of the defaulter and any statement which may be offered in defence, the court is satisfied that the defaulter did without reasonable excuse refuse or otherwise fail to comply with the notice, the court may punish the defaulter (and, in the case of a body corporate, any director or officer) in like manner as if the defaulter had been guilty of contempt of court.".

(2) Subsections (5) and (6)(b) of that section are omitted.

14.—(1) In section 88 of that Act, in subsection (1) for the words from "if requested" to "the relevant parties" there is substituted "to comply with any request of the appropriate

Minister or Ministers to consult with any persons mentioned in the request (referred to below in this section as 'the relevant parties')".

(2) After subsection (2) of that section there is inserted—

"(2A) Where—
(a) an undertaking is given under this section after the commencement of this subsection, or
(b) an undertaking given under this section is varied or released after that time,

the Minister to whom the undertaking is or was given shall cause the undertaking or, as the case may be, the variation or release to be published in such manner as the Minister may consider appropriate.".

(3) In subsection (4) of that section—
(a) in paragraph (a) for "it" there is substituted "the undertaking is no longer appropriate and either the relevant parties (or any of them) can be released from the undertaking or the undertaking", and
(b) in paragraph (b) for "that it" there is substituted "that any person can be so released or that an undertaking",

and in subsection (5), after "varied" (in both places) there is inserted "or revoked".

(4) In subsection (6) of that section the words from " 'the relevant parties' " to the "and" immediately following paragraph (c) are omitted.

(5) Sub-paragraphs (1) and (4) (and the repeal in Schedule 24 corresponding to sub-paragraph (4)) do not apply in relation to any report made before the passing of this Act.

15.—(1) In section 89 of that Act, in subsection (1), for paragraphs (a) and (b) there is substituted—

"(a) in the circumstances specified in subsection (1) of any of the following sections—
   (i) sections 56, 73 and 75K of this Act, and
   (ii) section 10 of the Competition Act 1980,
the Secretary of State makes, has made, or has under consideration the making of, an order under the section in question exercising any of the powers specified in Schedule 8 to this Act, or
(b) in the circumstances specified in subsection (1) of section 12 of the Competition Act 1980 the Secretary of State makes, has made, or has under consideration the making of, an order under subsection (5) of that section exercising any of those powers.".

(2) In subsection (2) of that section, "Part II of" is omitted.

(3) In subsection (3) of that section, after paragraph (b) there is inserted—

"(bb) require any person to furnish any such information to the Director as may be specified or described in the order;".

(4) The amendments made by sub-paragraphs (1) to (3) have effect in relation to the making of any order under section 89 of the Fair Trading Act 1973 after the passing of this Act, whether the principal order (within the meaning of that section) was made before or after that time.

16.—(1) Section 90 of that Act is amended as follows.

(2) In subsection (1) after "section 74" there is inserted ", section 75K".

(3) For subsection (5) there is substituted—

"(5) Nothing in any order to which this section applies shall have effect so as to—
(a) cancel or modify conditions in licences granted—
   (i) under a patent granted under the Patents Act 1949 or the Patents Act 1977 or a European patent (UK) (within the meaning of the Patents Act 1977), or
   (ii) in respect of a design registered under the Registered Designs Act 1949,
by the proprietor of the patent or design, or
(b) require an entry to be made in the register of patents or the register of designs to the effect that licences under such a patent or such a design are to be available as of right.".

17. In section 132(1) of that Act, after "85(6)" there is inserted "section 93B".

18.—(1) In Schedule 3 to that Act, in paragraph 16(2) for "75" there is substituted "73".

(2) This paragraph does not apply in relation to any report made before the passing of this Act.

19.—(1) Schedule 8 to that Act is amended as follows.

(2) After paragraph 9 there is inserted—

"9A.—(1) An order may require a person supplying goods or services to publish—
(a) any such accounting information in relation to the supply of the goods or services, and
(b) any such information in relation to—

(i) the quantities of goods or services supplied, or
(ii) the geographical areas in which they are supplied,
as may be specified or described in the order.

(2) In this paragraph "accounting information", in relation to a supply of goods or services, means information as to—
(a) the costs of the supply, including fixed costs and overheads,
(b) the manner in which fixed costs and overheads are calculated and apportioned for accounting purposes of the supplier, and
(c) the income attributable to the supply.".

(3) After paragraph 12 there is inserted—

"12A. An order may require any person to furnish any such information to the Director as may be specified or described in the order.

12B. An order may require any activities to be carried on separately from any other activities.

12C. An order may prohibit or restrict the exercise of any right to vote exercisable by virtue of the holding of any shares, stock or securities.".

20.—(1) In Schedule 9 to that Act, in paragraph 4 the words from "either" to the end are omitted.

(2) This paragraph has effect in relation to the laying of any draft order under paragraph 4 of Schedule 9 to the Fair Trading Act 1973 after the passing of this Act, whether the notice under that Schedule was published before or after that time.

Competition Act 1980 (c. 21)

21. In section 3(8) of the Competition Act 1980—
(a) for "(5)" there is substituted "(6)", and
(b) at the end there is inserted "but as if, in subsection (7) of that section, for the words from 'any one' to 'the Commission' there were substituted 'the Director' ".

22. In section 4(4) of that Act for paragraph (a) there is substituted—
"(a) to arrange for—
(i) any undertaking accepted by him under this section, and
(ii) any variation or release of such an undertaking after the passing of the Companies Act 1989,
to be published in such manner as appears to him to be appropriate,".

23. In section 9(4) of that Act—
(a) in paragraph (a), after "undertaking" there is inserted "and of any variation of it after the passing of the Companies Act 1989", and
(b) in paragraph (b), after "undertaking" there is inserted "and any variation or release of it after that time".

24. In section 29(1)(a) of that Act after "section" there is inserted "75G or".

Telecommunications Act 1984 (c. 12)

25.—(1) In section 13(9) of the Telecommunications Act 1984, after "Commission)" there is inserted "together with section 24 of the Competition Act 1980 (modification of provisions about performance of Commission's functions)".

(2) The Monopolies and Mergers Commission (Performance of Functions) Order 1989 shall have effect as if sub-paragraph (1) above had come into force immediately before the making of the Order.

Financial Services Act 1986 (c. 60)

26. In section 123(3) of the Financial Services Act 1986—
(a) for "(5)" there is substituted "(6)", and
(b) at the end there is inserted "but as if, in subsection (7) of that section, for the words from 'any one' to 'the Commission' there were substituted 'the Director' ".

GENERAL NOTE
See the General Note to s.153.
This Schedule makes the necessary amendments to the Fair Trading Act 1973, the Competition Act 1980, the Telecommunications Act 1984 and the Financial Services Act 1986 consequent on the provisons in Part IV of this Act.

Section 156(1)

SCHEDULE 21

ADDITIONAL REQUIREMENTS FOR RECOGNITION

PART I

U.K. INVESTMENT EXCHANGES

Default rules

1.—(1) The exchange must have default rules which, in the event of a member of the exchange appearing to be unable to meet his obligations in respect of one or more market contracts, enable action to be taken in respect of unsettled market contracts to which he is party.

(2) The rules may authorise the taking of the same or similar action in relation to a member who appears to be likely to become unable to meet his obligations in respect of one or more market contracts.

(3) The rules must enable action to be taken in respect of all unsettled market contracts, other than those entered into by a recognised clearing house for the purposes of or in connection with the provision of clearing services for the exchange.

(4) As regards contracts entered into by the exchange for the purposes of or in connection with the provision of its own clearing services, the rules must contain provision corresponding to that required by paragraphs 9 to 11 below in the case of a UK clearing house.

(5) As regards other contracts the rules must contain provision complying with paragraphs 2 and 3 below.

Content of rules

2.—(1) The rules must provide for all rights and liabilities between those party as principal to unsettled market contracts to which the defaulter is party as principal to be discharged and for there to be paid by one party to the other such sum of money (if any) as may be determined in accordance with the rules.

(2) The rules must further provide—
  (a) for the sums so payable in respect of different contracts between the same parties to be aggregated or set off so as to produce a net sum, and
  (b) for the certification by or on behalf of the exchange of the net sum payable or, as the case may be, of the fact that no sum is payable.

(3) The rules may make special provision with respect to, or exclude from the provisions required by sub-paragraphs (1) and (2), contracts of any description prescribed for the purposes of this sub-paragraph by regulations made by the Secretary of State.

Notification to other parties affected

3. The exchange must have adequate arrangements for securing that—
  (a) parties to unsettled market contracts with a defaulter acting as principal are notified as soon as reasonably practicable of the default and of any decision taken under the rules in relation to contracts to which they are a party; and
  (b) parties to unsettled market contracts with a defaulter acting as agent and the defaulter's principals are notified as soon as reasonably practicable of the default and of the identity of the other party to the contract.

Application of default rules to designated non-members

4.—(1) The rules may make the same or similar provision in relation to designated non-members as in relation to members of the exchange.

(2) If such provision is made, the exchange must have adequate procedures—
  (a) for designating the persons, or descriptions of person, in respect of whom action may be taken,
  (b) for keeping under review the question which persons or descriptions of person should be or remain so designated, and
  (c) for withdrawing such designation.

(3) The procedures shall be designed to secure that a person is not or does not remain designated if failure by him to meet his obligations in respect of one or more market

contracts would be unlikely adversely to affect the operation of the market, and that a description of persons is not or does not remain designated if failure by a person of that description to meet his obligations in respect of one or more market contracts would be unlikely adversely to affect the operation of the market.

(4) The exchange must have adequate arrangements—
   (a) for bringing a designation or withdrawal of designation to the attention of the person or description of persons concerned, and
   (b) where a description of persons is designated, or the designation of a description of persons is withdrawn, for ascertaining which persons fall within that description.

Delegation of functions in connection with default procedures

5. The rules may make provision for the whole or part of the functions mentioned in paragraphs 1 to 4 to be performed by another body or person on behalf of the exchange.

Co-operation with other authorities

6. The exchange must be able and willing to co-operate, by the sharing of information and otherwise, with the Secretary of State, any relevant office-holder and any other authority or body having responsibility for any matter arising out of, or connected with, the default of a member of the exchange or any designated non-member.

Margin

7. Where the exchange provides its own clearing arrangements and margined transactions are effected, paragraph 14 below applies as it applies in relation to a clearing house.

PART II

U.K. CLEARING HOUSES

Default rules

8.—(1) The clearing house must have default rules which, in the event of a member of the clearing house appearing to be unable to meet his obligations in respect of one or more market contracts, enable action to be taken to close out his position in relation to all unsettled market contracts to which he is a party.

(2) The rules may authorise the taking of the same or similar action where a member appears to be likely to become unable to meet his obligations in respect of one or more market contracts.

Content of rules

9.—(1) The rules must provide for all rights and liabilities of the defaulter under or in respect of unsettled market contracts to be discharged and for there to be paid by or to the defaulter such sum of money (if any) as may be determined in accordance with the rules.

(2) The rules must further provide—
   (a) for the sums so payable by or to the defaulter in respect of different contracts to be aggregated or set off so as to produce a net sum;
   (b) for that sum—
      (i) if payable by the defaulter to the clearing house, to be set off against any property provided by or on behalf of the defaulter as cover for margin (or the proceeds of realisation of such property) so as to produce a further net sum, and
      (ii) if payable by the clearing house to the defaulter to be aggregated with any property provided by or on behalf of the defaulter as cover for margin (or the proceeds of realisation of such property); and
   (c) for the certification by or on behalf of the clearing house of the sum finally payable or, as the case may be, of the fact that no sum is payable.

10.—(1) The reference in paragraph 9 to the rights and liabilities of a defaulter under or in respect of an unsettled market contract includes (without prejudice to the generality of

that provision) rights and liabilities arising in consequence of action taken under provisions of the rules authorising—
   (a) the effecting by the clearing house of corresponding contracts in relation to unsettled market contracts to which the defaulter is a party;
   (b) the transfer of the defaulter's position under an unsettled market contract to another member of the clearing house;
   (c) the exercise by the clearing house of any option granted by an unsettled market contract.

(2) A "corresponding contract" means a contract on the same terms (except as to price or premium) as the market contract, but under which the person who is the buyer under the market contract agrees to sell and the person who is the seller under the market contract agrees to buy.

This sub-paragraph applies with any necessary modifications in relation to a market contract which is not an agreement to sell.

(3) The reference in paragraph 9 to the rights and liabilities of a defaulter under or in respect of an unsettled market contract does not include, where he acts as agent, rights or liabilities of his arising out of the relationship of principal and agent.

Notification to other parties affected

11. The clearing house must have adequate arrangements for securing that parties to unsettled market contracts with a defaulter are notified as soon as reasonably practicable of the default and of any decision taken under the rules in relation to contracts to which they are a party.

Delegation of functions in connection with default procedures

12. The rules may make provision for the whole or part of the functions mentioned in paragraphs 8 to 11 to be performed by another body or person on behalf of the clearing house.

Co-operation with other authorities

13. The clearing house must be able and willing to co-operate, by the sharing of information and otherwise, with the Secretary of State, any relevant office-holder and any other authority or body having responsibility for any matter arising out of, or connected with, the default of a member of the clearing house.

Margin

14.—(1) The rules of the clearing house must provide that, in the event of a default, margin provided by the defaulter for his own account is not to be applied to meet a shortfall on a client account.

(2) This is without prejudice to the requirements of any relevant regulations under section 55 of the Financial Services Act 1986 (clients' money).

PART III

OVERSEAS INVESTMENT EXCHANGES AND CLEARING HOUSES

15.—(1) The rules and practices of the body, together with the law of the country in which the body's head office is situated, must be such as to provide adequate procedures for dealing with the default of persons party to market contracts connected with the body.

(2) The reference in sub-paragraph (1) to default is to a person being unable to meet his obligations.

GENERAL NOTE
See the General Note to s.156 and the further express references to default and similar expressions (especially s.188) in ss.157–64, 166–67, 170, 174 and 188.

Section 182(4)

SCHEDULE 22

FINANCIAL MARKETS AND INSOLVENCY: PROVISIONS APPLYING TO PRE-COMMENCEMENT CASES

Introductory

1. The provisions of this Schedule have effect for the purpose of safeguarding the operation of certain financial markets—
    (a) in the event of the insolvency, winding up or default of a person party to transactions in the market (paragraphs 2 to 8), and
    (b) as regards the effectiveness or enforcement of certain charges given to secure obligations in connection with such transactions (paragraphs 9 to 12).

Recognised investment exchanges and clearing houses

2.—(1) This Schedule applies to the following descriptions of contract connected with a recognised investment exchange or recognised clearing house.
The contracts are referred to in this Schedule as "market contracts".
(2) In relation to a recognised investment exchange, this Schedule applies to—
    (a) contracts entered into by a member or designated non-member of the exchange which are—
        (i) made on or otherwise subject to the rules of the exchange,
        (ii) on terms expressed to be as traded on the exchange, or
        (iii) on the same terms as those on which an equivalent contract would be made on the exchange; and
    (b) contracts subject to the rules of the exchange entered into by the exchange for the purposes of or in connection with the provision of clearing services.
A "designated non-member" means a person in respect of whom action may be taken under the default rules of the exchange but who is not a member of the exchange.
(3) In relation to a recognised clearing house, this Schedule applies to contracts subject to the rules of the clearing house entered into by the clearing house for the purposes of or in connection with the provision of clearing services for a recognised investment exchange.
This includes contracts effected under or in consequence of action taken by the clearing house under its default rules.

3. The general law of insolvency has effect in relation to market contracts, and action taken under the rules of a recognised investment exchange or recognised clearing house with respect to such contracts, subject to the following provisions of this Schedule.

4.—(1) None of the following shall be regarded as to any extent invalid at law on the ground of inconsistency with the law relating to the distribution of the assets of a person on bankruptcy, winding up or sequestration, or in the administration of an insolvent estate—
    (a) a market contract,
    (b) the rules of a recognised investment exchange or recognised clearing house as to the settlement of market contracts,
    (c) the default rules of a recognised investment exchange or recognised clearing house.
(2) The powers of a relevant office-holder in his capacity as such, and the powers of the court under the Insolvency Act 1986 or the Bankruptcy (Scotland) Act 1985, shall not be exercised in such a way as to prevent or interfere with—
    (a) the settlement of a market contract in accordance with the rules of a recognised investment exchange or recognised clearing house,
    (b) any action taken under the default rules of such an exchange or clearing house.
(3) Nothing in the following provisions of this Schedule shall be construed as affecting the generality of sub-paragraph (2).
(4) A debt or other liability arising out of a market contract which is the subject of default proceedings may not be proved in a winding up or bankruptcy, or in Scotland claimed in a winding up or sequestration, until the completion of the default proceedings.
A debt or other liability which by virtue of this sub-paragraph may not be proved or claimed shall not be taken into account for the purposes of any set-off until the completion of the default proceedings.

5.—(1) A liquidator or trustee of a defaulter shall not—
    (a) declare or pay any dividend to the creditors, or
    (b) return any capital to contributories,
unless he has retained what he reasonably considers to be an adequate reserve in respect of any claims arising as a result of the default proceedings of the exchange or clearing house concerned.

(2) Nothing in section 11(3), 130 or 285 of the Insolvency Act 1986 (which restrict the taking of certain legal proceedings and other steps), and nothing in the Bankruptcy (Scotland) Act 1985, shall affect any action taken by an exchange or clearing house for the purpose of its default proceedings.

6.—(1) The following provisions apply with respect to the net sum certified by a recognised investment exchange or recognised clearing house, upon the completion of proceedings under its default rules, to be payable by or to a defaulter.

(2) If, in England and Wales, a bankruptcy or winding up order has been made, or a resolution for voluntary winding up has been passed, the debt—
  (a) is provable in the bankruptcy or winding up or, as the case may be, is payable to the relevant office-holder, and
  (b) shall be taken into account, where appropriate, under section 323 of the Insolvency Act 1986 (mutual dealings and set-off) or the corresponding provision applicable in the case of a winding up,
in the same way as a debt due before the commencement of the bankruptcy or winding up.

(3) If, in Scotland, an award of sequestration or a winding-up order has been made, or a resolution for voluntary winding up has been passed, the debt—
  (a) may be claimed in the sequestration or winding up or, as the case may be, is payable to the relevant office-holder, and
  (b) shall be taken into account for the purposes of any rule of law relating to compensation or set-off applicable in sequestration or winding up,
in the same way as a debt due before the date of sequestration (within the meaning of section 73(1) of the Bankruptcy (Scotland) Act 1985) or the commencement of the winding up.

7.—(1) Sections 178, 186, 315 and 345 of the Insolvency Act 1986 (power to disclaim onerous property and court's power to order rescission of contracts, &c.) do not apply in relation to—
  (a) a market contract, or
  (b) a contract effected by the exchange or clearing house for the purpose of realising property provided as margin in relation to market contracts.
In the application of this sub-paragraph in Scotland, the reference to sections 178 and 315 shall be construed as a reference to any rule of law having the like effect as those sections.

(2) Sections 127 and 284 of the Insolvency Act 1986 (avoidance of property dispositions effected after commencement of winding up or presentation of bankruptcy petition) do not apply to—
  (a) a market contract, or any disposition of property in pursuance of such a contract,
  (b) the provision of margin in relation to market contracts,
  (c) a contract effected by the exchange or clearing house for the purpose of realising property provided as margin in relation to a market contract, or any disposition of property in pursuance of such a contract, or
  (d) any disposition of property in accordance with the rules of the exchange or clearing house as to the application of property provided as margin.

(3) However, if a person enters into a market contract knowing that a petition has been presented for the winding up or bankruptcy of the other party to the contract, the value of any profit or benefit to him arising from the contract is recoverable from him by the relevant office-holder unless the court directs otherwise.

(4) Any sum recoverable by virtue of sub-paragraph (3) has the same priority, in the event of the insolvency of the person from whom it is due, as if it were secured by a fixed charge.

8.—(1) No order shall be made in relation to a market contract under—
  (a) section 238 or 339 of the Insolvency Act 1986 (transactions at an under-value),
  (b) section 239 or 340 of that Act (preferences), or
  (c) section 423 of that Act (transactions defrauding creditors),
unless the court is satisfied that the person in favour of whom the contract was made knew at the time he entered into it that it was at an under-value (within the meaning of the relevant provision) or, as the case may be, that a preference was being given.

(2) As respects Scotland, no decree shall be granted in relation to a market contract—
  (a) under section 34 or 36 of the Bankruptcy (Scotland) Act 1985 or section 242 or 243 of the Insolvency Act 1986 (gratuitous alienations and unfair preferences), or
  (b) at common law,
unless the court is satisfied that the person with whom the contract was made knew at the time he entered into it that it was challengeable under any of the provisions mentioned in paragraph (a) or at common law.

(3) Sub-paragraphs (1) and (2) apply in relation to—

(a) a disposition of property in pursuance of a market contract,
(b) the provision of margin in relation to market contracts,
(c) a contract effected by a recognised investment exchange or recognised clearing house for the purpose of realising property provided as margin, or
(d) a disposition of property in accordance with the rules of the exchange or clearing house as to the application of property provided as margin,

as they apply in relation to the making of a market contract.

Market charges

9.—(1) The charges to which paragraphs 10 to 12 apply are charges, whether fixed or floating, granted—
(a) in favour of a recognised investment exchange, for the purpose of securing debts or liabilities arising in connection with the settlement of market contracts,
(b) in favour of a recognised clearing house, for the purpose of securing debts or liabilities arising in connection with their ensuring the performance of market contracts, or
(c) in favour of a person who agrees to make payments as a result of the transfer of specified securities made through the medium of a computer-based system established by the Bank of England and The Stock Exchange, for the purpose of securing debts or liabilities of the transferee arising in connection with the payments.

Those charges are referred to in this Schedule as "market charges".

(2) Where a charge is granted partly for purposes specified in sub-paragraph (1)(a), (b) or (c) and partly for other purposes, paragraphs 10 to 12 apply to it so far as it has effect for the specified purposes; and the expression "market charge" shall be construed accordingly.

(3) In this paragraph and paragraphs 10 to 12—

"charge" means any form of security, including a mortgage and, in Scotland, a heritable security; and

"specified securities" means securities for the time being specified in the list in Schedule 1 to the Stock Transfer Act 1982, and includes any right to such securities.

10. The general law of insolvency has effect in relation to market charges and action taken in enforcing them subject to the following provisions of this Schedule.

11.—(1) Sections 10(1)(b) and 11(3)(c) of the Insolvency Act 1986 (no enforcement of security while petition for administration order pending or order in force) do not apply to a market charge.

(2) Section 11(2) of that Act (receiver to vacate office when so required by administrator) does not apply to a receiver appointed under a market charge.

(3) Section 15(1) and (2) of that Act (administrator's power to deal with charged property) do not apply to a market charge.

(4) Sections 127 and 284 of that Act (avoidance of property dispositions effected after commencement of winding up or presentation of bankruptcy petition) do not apply to—
(a) a disposition of property as a result of which the property becomes subject to a market charge, or any transaction pursuant to which that disposition is made, or
(b) any disposition of property made in enforcing a market charge.

(5) However, if a person (other than the chargee under the market charge) who is a party to a disposition mentioned in sub-paragraph (4)(a) knows at the time of the disposition that a petition has been presented for the winding up or bankruptcy of the party making the disposition, the value of any profit or benefit to him arising from the disposition is recoverable from him by the relevant office-holder unless the court directs otherwise.

(6) Any sum recoverable by virtue of sub-paragraph (5) has the same priority, in the event of the insolvency of the person from whom it is due, as if it were secured by a fixed charge.

12.—(1) No legal proceedings, execution or other legal process may be commenced or continued, and no distress may be levied against property which is, or becomes, subject to a market charge except with the consent of the person in whose favour the charge was granted or the leave of the court.

(2) The court may give leave subject to such terms as it thinks fit.

(3) Sub-paragraph (1) does not apply to proceedings to enforce any security over, or any equitable interest in, the property.

(4) Sections 10(1)(c), 11(3)(d), 130(3) and 285(3) of the Insolvency Act 1986 (which restrict the taking of certain legal proceedings and other steps) have effect accordingly.

(5) In the application of this paragraph to Scotland, the reference to execution being commenced or continued includes a reference to diligence being carried out or continued, and the reference to distress being levied shall be omitted.

40/Sch. 23 *Companies Act 1989*

Supplementary provisions

13.—(1) In this Schedule "default rules" means—
(a) in relation to a recognised investment exchange, rules which provide in the event of a member or designated non-member of the exchange appearing to be unable, or likely to become unable, to meet his obligations in respect of one or more market contracts, for the settlement forthwith of all unsettled market contracts to which he is a party as principal, other than those whose performance is ensured by a recognised clearing house;
(b) in relation to a recognised clearing house, rules which provide in the event of a member of the clearing house appearing to be unable, or likely to become unable, to meet his obligations in respect of any market contract, for the closing out of his position in relation to all market contracts to which he is a party.

(2) References in this Schedule to a "defaulter" are to a person in respect of whom action has been taken by a recognised investment exchange or recognised clearing house under its default rules, whether by declaring him to be a defaulter or otherwise; and references in this Schedule to "default" shall be construed accordingly.

(3) In this Schedule "default proceedings" means proceedings taken by a recognised investment exchange or recognised clearing house under its default rules.

14.—(1) The following are relevant office-holders for the purposes of this Schedule—
(a) the official receiver,
(b) any person acting in relation to a company as its liquidator, provisional liquidator, administrator or administrative receiver,
(c) any person acting in relation to an individual (or, in Scotland, a deceased debtor) as his trustee in bankruptcy or interim receiver of his property or as permanent or interim trustee in the sequestration of his estate,
(d) any person acting as administrator (or, in Scotland, as judicial factor) of an insolvent estate of a deceased person.

(2) Sub-paragraph (1)(c) applies in relation to a partnership, and any debtor within the meaning of the Bankruptcy (Scotland) Act 1985, as it applies in relation to an individual.

(3) In this paragraph—
"administrative receiver" has the meaning given by section 251 of the Insolvency Act 1986;
"company" means a company within the meaning of section 735(1) of the Companies Act 1985 or a company which may be wound up under Part V of the Insolvency Act 1986 (unregistered companies); and
"interim trustee" and "permanent trustee" have the same meaning as in the Bankruptcy (Scotland) Act 1985.

15.—(1) In this Schedule—
"clearing house" has the same meaning as in the Financial Services Act 1986;
"investment" and "investment exchange" have the same meaning as in the Financial Services Act 1986;
"recognised" means recognised under the Financial Services Act 1986;
"The Stock Exchange" means The International Stock Exchange of the United Kingdom and the Republic of Ireland Limited.

(2) References in this Schedule to ensuring the performance of a transaction have the same meaning as in the Financial Services Act 1986.

(3) References in this Schedule to a market contract to which a person is a party include, unless the contrary intention appears, contracts to which he is party as agent.

GENERAL NOTE
See the General Note to s.182.

Section 206(1) SCHEDULE 23

CONSEQUENTIAL AMENDMENTS OF THE FINANCIAL SERVICES ACT 1986

PART I

GENERAL AMENDMENTS

1.—(1) Section 13 of the Financial Services Act 1986 (power to direct alteration of rules of recognised self-regulating organisation) is amended as follows.

(2) Omit subsection (1).

(3) For subsection (2) substitute—

"(2) If at any time it appears to the Secretary of State that—

(a) a recognised self-regulating organisation is concerned with two or more kinds of investment business, and

(b) the requirement in paragraph 3(1) of Schedule 2 to this Act is not satisfied in respect of investment business of one or more but not all of those kinds,

he may, instead of revoking the recognition order or making an application under section 12 above, direct the organisation to alter, or himself alter, its rules so that they preclude a member from carrying on investment business of a kind in respect of which that requirement is not satisfied, unless he is an authorised person otherwise than by virtue of membership of the organisation or is an exempted person in respect of that business.".

(4) For subsection (3) substitute—

"(3) A direction under this section is enforceable on the application of the Secretary of State by injunction or, in Scotland, by an order under section 45 of the Court of Session Act 1988.".

(5) Omit subsections (4) to (6).

2.—(1) Section 48 of the Financial Services Act 1986 (conduct of business rules) is amended as follows.

(2) In subsection (1) omit the words "members of a recognised self-regulating organisation or" and "organisation or".

(3) After subsection (10) insert—

"(11) Section 63A below (application of designated rules) has effect as regards the application of rules under this section to members of recognised self-regulating organisations in respect of investment business in the carrying on of which they are subject to the rules of the organisation.".

3.—(1) Section 49 of the Financial Services Act 1986 (financial resources rules) is amended as follows.

(2) For subsection (1) substitute—

"(1) The Secretary of State may make rules requiring—

(a) a person authorised to carry on investment business by virtue of section 25 or 31 above, or

(b) a member of a recognised self-regulating organisation carrying on investment business in the carrying on of which he is subject to the rules of the organisation,

to have and maintain in respect of that business such financial resources as are required by the rules.".

(3) After subsection (2) insert—

"(3) Section 63A below (application of designated rules) has effect as regards the application of rules under this section to members of recognised self-regulating organisations in respect of investment business in the carrying on of which they are subject to the rules of the organisation.".

4. In section 50 of the Financial Services Act 1986 (power of Secretary of State to modify conduct of business and financial resources rules for particular cases), after subsection (3) insert—

"(4) The powers conferred by subsection (1) above shall not be exercised in a case where the powers conferred by section 63B below are exercisable (powers of recognised self-regulating organisation in relation to designated rules).".

5. In section 52 of the Financial Services Act 1986 (notification regulations), in subsection (3) (application to member of recognised self-regulating organisation or professional body), for "subject to any of the rules made under section 48 above" substitute "not subject to the rules of that organisation or body".

6.—(1) Section 55 of the Financial Services Act 1986 (clients' money) is amended as follows.

(2) In subsection (2)(b) and (e) omit the words "a member of a recognised self-regulating organisation or" and "organisation or".

(3) In subsection (3) omit the words "organisation or".

(4) After subsection (5) insert—

"(6) Section 63A below (application of designated regulations) has effect as regards the application of regulations under this section to members of recognised self-regulating organisations in respect of investment business in the carrying on of which they are subject to the rules of the organisation.".

7. In section 56 of the Financial Services Act 1986 (unsolicited calls), for subsection (7) substitute—

"(7) Section 63A below (application of designated regulations) has effect as regards the application of regulations under this section to members of recognised self-regulating organisations in respect of investment business in the carrying on of which they are subject to the rules of the organisation.

As it applies to such persons in respect of such business the reference in subsection (1) above to conduct permitted by regulations made by the Secretary of State shall be construed—

(a) where or to the extent that the regulations do not apply, as a reference to conduct permitted by the rules of the organisation; and

(b) where or to the extent that the regulations do apply but are expressed to have effect subject to the rules of the organisation, as a reference to conduct permitted by the regulations together with the rules of the organisation.

(7A) In the application of this section to anything done by a person certified by a recognised professional body in carrying on investment business in the carrying on of which he is subject to the rules of the body, the reference in subsection (1) above to conduct permitted by regulations made by the Secretary of State shall be construed as a reference to conduct permitted by the rules of the body.".

8. In section 86 of the Financial Services Act 1986 (collective investment schemes constituted in other member States), in subsection (7) (restriction on application of conduct of business rules), at the end add—

"This subsection also applies to statements of principle under section 47A and codes of practice under section 63A so far as they relate to matters falling within the rule-making power in section 48.".

9. In section 95 of the Financial Services Act 1986 (collective investment schemes: contraventions), after subsection (2) add—

"(3) The disciplinary action which may be taken by virtue of section 47A(3) (failure to comply with statement of principle) includes—

(a) the giving of a direction under section 91(2), and

(b) the application by the Secretary of State for an order under section 93;

and subsection (6) of section 47A (duty of the Secretary of State as to exercise of powers) has effect accordingly.".

10.—(1) Section 107 of the Financial Services Act 1986 (appointment of auditors) is amended as follows.

(2) For subsection (1) (power to make rules) substitute—

"(1) The Secretary of State may make rules requiring—

(a) a person authorised to carry on investment business by virtue of section 25 or 31 above, or

(b) a member of a recognised self-regulating organisation carrying on investment business in the carrying on of which he is subject to the rules of the organisation,

and who, apart from the rules, is not required by or under any enactment to appoint an auditor, to appoint as an auditor a person satisfying such conditions as to qualifications and otherwise as may be specified in or imposed under the rules.".

(3) After subsection (3) add—

"(4) In its application to members of recognised self-regulating organisations, this section has effect subject to section 107A below.".

11. After section 107 of the Financial Services Act 1986 insert—

"**Application of audit rules to members of self-regulating organisations**

107A.—(1) The Secretary of State may in rules under section 107 designate provisions which apply, to such extent as may be specified, to a member of a recognised self-regulating organisation in respect of investment business in the carrying on of which he is subject to the rules of the organisation.

(2) It may be provided that the designated rules have effect, generally or to such extent as may be specified, subject to the rules of the organisation.

(3) A member of a recognised self-regulating organisation who contravenes a rule applying to him by virtue of that section shall be treated as having contravened the rules of the organisation.

(4) Except as mentioned above, rules made under section 107 do not apply to members of recognised self-regulating organisations in respect of investment business in the carrying on of which they are subject to the rules of the organisation.

(5) A recognised self-regulating organisation may on the application of a member of the organisation—

(a) modify a rule designated under this section so as to adapt it to his circumstances or to any particular kind of business carried on by him, or

(b) dispense him from compliance with any such rule, generally or in relation to any particular kind of business carried on by him.

(6) The powers conferred by subsection (5) shall not be exercised unless it appears to the organisation—

(a) that compliance with the rule in question would be unduly burdensome for the applicant having regard to the benefit which compliance would confer on investors, and

(b) that the exercise of those powers will not result in any undue risk to investors.

(7) The powers conferred by subsection (5) may be exercised unconditionally or subject to conditions; and subsection (3) applies in the case of a contravention of a condition as in the case of contravention of a designated rule.

(8) The reference in paragraph 4(1) of Schedule 2 (requirements for recognition of self-regulating organisations) to monitoring and enforcement of compliance with rules includes monitoring and enforcement of compliance with conditions imposed by the organisation under subsection (7).".

12.—(1) Section 114 of the Financial Services Act 1986 (power to transfer functions to designated agency) is amended as follows.

(2) For subsection (9) substitute—

"(9) The Secretary of State shall not make a delegation order transferring any legislative functions unless—

(a) the agency has furnished him with a copy of the instruments it proposes to issue or make in the exercise of those functions, and

(b) he is satisfied that those instruments will afford investors an adequate level of protection and, in the case of such provisions as are mentioned in Schedule 8 to this Act, comply with the principles set out in that Schedule.

In this subsection "legislative functions" means the functions of issuing or making statements of principle, rules, regulations or codes of practice.".

(3) In subsection (12) for "rules or regulations made" substitute "statements of principle, rules, regulations or codes of practice issued or made".

13.—(1) Section 115 of the Financial Services Act 1986 (resumption of transferred functions) is amended as follows.

(2) For subsection (5) substitute—

"(5) Where the transferred functions consist of or include any legislative functions, an order may be made under subsection (2) above if at any time it appears to the Secretary of State that the instruments issued or made by the agency do not satisfy the requirements of section 114(9)(b) above.".

(3) In subsection (7)—

(a) in the opening words, for "subsection (2)(b) above" substitute "this section", and

(b) in paragraph (a) for "functions of making rules or regulations" substitute "functions of issuing or making statements of principle, rules, regulations or codes of practice".

14.—(1) Section 119 of the Financial Services Act 1986 (competition scrutiny: recognition orders) is amended as follows.

(2) In subsection (1) (considerations relevant to making of recognition order), for paragraphs (a) and (b) substitute—

"(a) in the case of a self-regulating organisation, the rules and any guidance of which copies are furnished with the application for the order, together with any statements of principle, rules, regulations or codes of practice to which members of the organisation would be subject by virtue of Chapter V of this Part,

(b) in the case of an investment exchange, the rules and any guidance of which copies are furnished with the application for the order, together with any arrangements of which particulars are furnished with the application,

(c) in the case of a clearing house, the rules and any guidance of which copies are furnished with the application for the order,".

(3) In subsection (2) (circumstances in which powers are exercisable in relation to recognised body), for paragraphs (a) to (c) substitute—

"(a) in the case of a self-regulating organisation—

(i) any rules made or guidance issued by the organisation,

(ii) any practices of the organisation, or

(iii) any practices of persons who are members of, or otherwise subject to the rules made by, the organisation,
together with any statements of principle, rules, regulations or codes of practice to which members of the organisation are subject by virtue of Chapter V of this Part,
   (b) in the case of a recognised investment exchange—
      (i) any rules made or guidance issued by the exchange,
      (ii) any practices of the exchange, or
      (iii) any practices of persons who are members of, or otherwise subject to the rules made by, the exchange,
   (c) in the case of a recognised clearing house—
      (i) any rules made or guidance issued by the clearing house,
      (ii) any practices of the clearing house, or
      (iii) any practices of persons who are members of, or otherwise subject to the rules made by, the clearing house,
or any clearing arrangements made by the clearing house,".
(4) In subsection (3) (powers exercisable in relation to recognised body)—
   (a) in paragraph (b) for "the rules" substitute "its rules, or the", and
   (b) in paragraph (c) for "the rules" substitute "its rules".
(5) In subsection (5) (construction of references to practices)—
   (a) for "paragraph (b)" substitute "paragraph (a)(ii), (b)(ii) and (c)(ii)", and
   (b) omit the words from "and the practices referred to in paragraph (c)" to the end.
(6) After that subsection insert—

"(6) The practices referred to in paragraph (a)(iii), (b)(iii) and (c)(iii) of subsection (2) above are—
   (a) in relation to a recognised self-regulating organisation, practices in relation to business in respect of which the persons in question are subject to—
      (i) the rules of the organisation, or
      (ii) statements of principle, rules, regulations or codes of practice to which its members are subject by virtue of Chapter V of this Part,
   and which are required or contemplated by the rules of the organisation or by those statements, rules, regulations or codes, or by guidance issued by the organisation,
   (b) in relation to a recognised investment exchange or clearing house, practices in relation to business in respect of which the persons in question are subject to the rules of the exchange or clearing house, and which are required or contemplated by its rules or guidance,
or which are otherwise attributable to the conduct of the organisation, exchange or clearing house as such.".

15.—(1) Section 121 of the Financial Services Act 1986 (competition scrutiny: designated agencies) is amended as follows.

(2) In subsection (1) for "rules, regulations" substitute "statements of principle, rules, regulations, codes of practice".

(3) In subsection (2)(a) and (c) for "rules or regulations made" substitute "statements of principle, rules, regulations or codes of practice issued or made".

(4) In subsection (3)(b) for "rules, regulations" substitute "statements of principle, rules, regulations, codes of practice".

(5) In subsection (4) for "rules or regulations" (twice) substitute "statements of principle, rules, regulations or codes of practice".

16.—(1) Section 122 of the Financial Services Act 1986 (reports by Director General of Fair Trading) is amended as follows.

(2) In subsection (1) for "and regulations" substitute ", statements of principle, regulations and codes of practice".

(3) In subsection (2) for "regulations," substitute "statements of principle, regulations, codes of practice,".

(4) In subsection (4)—
   (a) in paragraph (a) for "rules, guidance, arrangements and regulations" substitute "rules, statements of principle, regulations, codes of practice, guidance and arrangements", and
   (b) in the words following the paragraphs, for "rules, guidance, arrangements, regulations" substitute "rules, statements of principle, regulations, codes of practice, guidance, arrangements", and for "rules, guidance, arrangements or regulations" substitute "rules, statements of principle, regulations, codes of practice, guidance or arrangements".

17.—(1) Section 124 of the Financial Services Act 1986 (matters to be left out of account for certain purposes in connection with competition scrutiny) is amended as follows.

(2) In subsection (1) (matters to be left out of account in determining whether monopoly situation exists), in paragraph (c) for "rules or regulations made or guidance issued" substitute "statements of principle, rules, regulations, codes of practice or guidance issued or made".

(3) In subsection (3) (matters to be excluded from consideration where monopoly situation exists)—
  (a) in paragraph (a), for "rules or regulations made" substitute "statements of principle, rules, regulations or codes of practice issued or made",
  (b) in paragraph (b), for "rules or regulations" substitute "statements of principle, rules, regulations or codes of practice", and
  (c) in the closing words, for "rules, regulations" substitute "statements of principle, rules, regulations, codes of practice".

18. For section 205 of the Financial Services Act 1986 (regulations, rules and orders) substitute—

"General power to make regulations

205. The Secretary of State may make regulations prescribing anything which by this Act is authorised or required to be prescribed.

Supplementary provisions with respect to subordinate legislation

205A.—(1) The following provisions apply to any power of the Secretary of State under this Act—
  (a) to issue statements of principle,
  (b) to make rules or regulations,
  (c) to make orders (other than such orders as are excepted by subsection (4) below), or
  (d) to issue codes of practice.

(2) Any such power is exercisable by statutory instrument and includes power to make different provision for different cases.

(3) Except as otherwise provided, a statutory instrument containing statements of principle, rules or regulations shall be subject to annulment in pursuance of a resolution of either House of Parliament.

(4) The above provisions do not apply to a recognition order, an order declaring a collective investment scheme to be an authorised unit trust scheme or a recognised scheme or to an order revoking any such order.".

19. In section 206(1) of the Financial Services Act 1986 (publication of information and advice)—
  (a) in paragraph (a), for "rules and regulations made" substitute "statements of principle, rules, regulations and codes of practice issued or made", and
  (b) in paragraph (b) for "rules or regulations" substitute "statements of principle, rules, regulations or codes of practice".

20. In Schedule 2 to the Financial Services Act 1986 (requirements for recognition of self-regulating organisations), in paragraph 4(1) (monitoring and enforcement) for "rules or regulations" substitute "statements of principle, rules, regulations or codes of practice".

21. In Schedule 3 to the Financial Services Act 1986 (requirements for recognition of professional bodies), in paragraph 4(2) (monitoring and enforcement) for "rules or regulations" substitute "statements of principle, rules, regulations or codes of practice".

22. In Schedule 7 to the Financial Services Act 1986 (qualifications of designated agency), in paragraph 2(2) (arrangements for discharge of functions: matters to be decided upon by the governing body) for "rules or regulations must be made" substitute "statements of principle, rules, regulations and codes of practice must be issued or made".

23.—(1) Schedule 8 to the Financial Services Act 1986 (principles applicable to designated agency's rules and regulations) is amended as follows.

(2) In the heading for "RULES AND REGULATIONS" substitute "LEGISLATIVE PROVISIONS".

(3) For paragraph 1, and the cross-heading preceding it, substitute—

"Introduction

1.—(1) In this Schedule "legislative provisions" means the provisions of statements of principle, rules, regulations and codes of practice issued or made under Part I of this Act.

(2) References in this Schedule to "conduct of business provisions" are to rules made under section 48 of this Act and statements of principle and codes of practice so far as they relate to matters falling within that rule-making power.

(3) References in this Schedule to provisions made for the purposes of a specified section or Chapter are to rules or regulations made under that section or Chapter and statements of principle and codes of practice so far as they relate to matters falling within that power to make rules or regulations.

Standards

1A. The conduct of business provisions and the other legislative provisions must promote high standards of integrity and fair dealing in the conduct of investment business.".

(4) In paragraphs 2 to 7, 9, 11 and 12 for "conduct of business rules" substitute "conduct of business provisions".

(5) In paragraph 7 for "those rules and rules under" substitute "those provisions and provisions made for the purposes of".

(6) In paragraph 8 for "Rules made under" substitute "Provisions made for the purposes of".

(7) In paragraph 9 for "regulations made under" substitute "provisions made for the purposes of".

(8) In paragraph 10 for "Rules made under" substitute "Provisions made for the purposes of" and for "under those sections" substitute "for the purposes of those sections".

(9) In paragraph 12 for "rules and regulations made under" substitute "provisions made for the purposes of".

24.—(1) Schedule 9 to the Financial Services Act 1986 (designated agency: exercise of transferred functions) is amended as follows.

(2) In paragraph 4(1) (copies of instruments to be sent to Secretary of State), for "any rules or regulations made" substitute "any statements of principle, rules, regulations or codes of practice issued or made".

(3) For paragraphs 5 and 6 substitute—

"5. Paragraphs 6 to 9 below have effect instead of section 205A of this Act in relation to statements of principle, rules, regulations and codes of practice issued or made by a designated agency in the exercise of powers transferred to it by a delegation order.

6. Any such power is exercisable by instrument in writing and includes power to make different provision for different cases.".

(4) In paragraph 8 (instruments to be printed and made available to public)—
  (a) in sub-paragraph (1) for "is made" substitute "is issued or made," and
  (b) in sub-paragraph (2) for "rule or regulation" (twice) substitute "statement of principle, rule, regulation or code of practice".

(5) In paragraph 9 (proof of instruments), for "made by the agency" (twice) substitute "made or issued by the agency".

(6) For paragraph 12 (consultation) substitute—

"12.—(1) Where a designated agency proposes, in the exercise of powers transferred to it by a delegation order, to issue or make any statements of principle, rules, regulations or codes of practice, it shall publish the proposed instrument in such manner as appears to it best calculated to bring the proposals to the attention of the public, together with a statement that representations about the proposals (and, in particular, representations as to the cost of complying with the proposed provisions) can be made to the agency within a specified time.

(2) Before issuing or making the instrument the agency shall have regard to any representations duly made in accordance with that statement.

(3) The above requirements do not apply—
  (a) where the agency considers that the delay involved in complying with them would be prejudicial to the interests of investors;
  (b) to the issuing or making of an instrument in the same, or substantially the same, terms as a proposed instrument which was furnished by the agency to the Secretary of State for the purposes of section 114(9) of this Act.".

25.—(1) Schedule 10 to the Financial Services Act 1986 (application of investment business provisions to regulated insurance companies) is amended as follows.

(2) In paragraph 4 (modification of conduct of business rules), after sub-paragraph (2) insert—

"(2A) Sub-paragraphs (1) and (2) also apply to statements of principle under section 47A and codes of practice under section 63A so far as they relate to matters falling within the rule-making power in section 48.".

(3) In paragraph 7 (withdrawal of authorisation) after sub-paragraph (2) insert—

"(3) The disciplinary action which may be taken by virtue of section 47A(3) of this Act (failure to comply with statement of principle) includes—
  (a) the withdrawal of authorisation under section 11(2)(a) of the Insurance Companies Act 1982, and
  (b) the giving of a direction under section 13(2A) of that Act;
and subsection (6) of section 47A (duty of the Secretary of State as to exercise of powers) has effect accordingly.".

PART II

AMENDMENTS RELATING TO FRIENDLY SOCIETIES

26. Schedule 11 to the Financial Services Act 1986 (friendly societies) is amended as follows.

27. In paragraph 3(2) (competition scrutiny: recognition of self-regulating organisation for friendly societies), after "sent to him under this sub-paragraph" insert ", together with any statements of principle, rules, regulations or codes of practice to which members of the organisation would be subject by virtue of this Schedule,".

28.—(1) Paragraph 4 (requirements for recognition of self-regulating organisation for friendly societies) is amended as follows.
  (2) In sub-paragraph (4)—
    (a) in paragraph (a) for "22" substitute "22D", and
    (b) omit paragraph (b).
  (3) In sub-paragraph (5) for "22" substitute "22D".

29. Omit paragraph 7.

30.—(1) Paragraph 10 (competition scrutiny: circumstances in which powers are exercisable in relation to recognised self-regulating organisation for friendly societies) is amended as follows.
  (2) In sub-paragraph (1), after paragraph (c) insert "together with any statements of principle, rules, regulations or codes of practice to which members of the organisation are subject by virtue of this Schedule,".
  (3) In sub-paragraph (2)—
    (a) in paragraph (b), for "the rules" substitute "its rules, or the", and
    (c) in paragraph (c), for "the rules" substitute "its rules".
  (4) In sub-paragraph (3) (construction of references to practices), omit the words from "and the practices referred to in paragraph (c)" to the end; and after that sub-paragraph insert—

  "(3A) The practices referred to in paragraph (c) of sub-paragraph (1) above are practices in relation to business in respect of which the persons in question are subject to—
    (a) the rules of the organisation, or
    (b) statements of principle, rules, regulations or codes of practice to which its members are subject by virtue of this Schedule,
  and which are required or contemplated by the rules of the organisation or by those statements, rules, regulations or codes, or by guidance issued by the organisation, or which are otherwise attributable to the conduct of the organisation as such.".

31. In paragraph 13, for "Paragraphs 14 to 25" substitute "Paragraphs 13A to 25".

32. Before paragraph 14 and after the heading "*Conduct of investment business*", insert—

  "13A.—(1) The Registrar may issue statements of principle with respect to the conduct expected of regulated friendly societies.
  (2) The conduct expected may include compliance with a code or standard issued by another person, as for the time being in force, and may allow for the exercise of discretion by any person pursuant to any such code or standard.
  (3) Failure to comply with a statement of principle under this paragraph is a ground for the taking of disciplinary action or the exercise of powers of intervention, but it does not give rise to any right of action by investors or other persons affected or affect the validity of any transaction.
  (4) The disciplinary action which may be taken by virtue of sub-paragraph (3) is—
    (a) the making of a public statement under paragraph 21, or
    (b) the application by the Registrar for an injunction, interdict or other order under paragraph 22(1), or
    (c) any action under paragraph 26 or 27 of this Schedule;

and the reference in that sub-paragraph to powers of intervention is to the powers conferred by Chapter VI of Part I of this Act.

(5) Where a statement of principle relates to compliance with a code or standard issued by another person, the statement of principle may provide—
(a) that failure to comply with the code or standard shall be a ground for the taking of disciplinary action, or the exercise of powers of intervention, only in such cases and to such extent as may be specified; and
(b) that no such action shall be taken, or any such power exercised, except at the request of the person by whom the code or standard in question was issued.

(6) The Registrar shall exercise his powers in such manner as appears to him appropriate to secure compliance with statements of principle under this paragraph.

13B.—(1) The relevant regulatory authority may on the application of a regulated friendly society—
(a) modify a statement of principle issued under paragraph 13A so as to adapt it to the circumstances of the society or to any particular kind of business carried on by it, or
(b) dispense the society from compliance with any such statement of principle, generally or in relation to any particular kind of business carried on by it.

(2) The powers conferred by this paragraph shall not be exercised unless it appears to the relevant regulatory authority—
(a) that compliance with the statement of principle in question would be unduly burdensome for the applicant having regard to the benefit which compliance would confer on investors, and
(b) that the exercise of those powers will not result in any undue risk to investors.

(3) The powers conferred by this paragraph may be exercised unconditionally or subject to conditions; and paragraph 13A(3) applies in the case of failure to comply with a condition as in the case of failure to comply with a statement of principle.

(4) The relevant regulatory authority for the purposes of this paragraph is—
(a) in the case of a member society of a recognised self-regulating organisation for friendly societies, in relation to investment business in the carrying on of which it is subject to the rules of the organisation, that organisation;
(b) in any other case, or in relation to other investment business, the Registrar.

(5) The reference in paragraph 4(1) of Schedule 2 as applied by paragraph 4 above (requirements for recognition of self-regulating organisation for friendly societies) to monitoring and enforcement of compliance with statements of principle includes monitoring and enforcement of compliance with conditions imposed by the organisation under this paragraph.".

33.—(1) Paragraph 14 (conduct of business rules) is amended as follows.

(2) In sub-paragraph (1), omit the words "other than a member society".

(3) After sub-paragraph (2) insert—
"(2A) Paragraph 22B below has effect as regards the application of rules under this paragraph to member societies in respect of investment business in the carrying on of which they are subject to the rules of a recognised self-regulating organisation for friendly societies.".

(4) In sub-paragraph (3), omit the word "and" after paragraph (a); and after paragraph (b) insert—
"; and
(c) for the references in subsection (4) to section 63B and a recognised self-regulating organisation there shall be substituted references to paragraph 13B and a recognised self-regulating organisation for friendly societies.".

34.—(1) Paragraph 19 (clients' money regulations) is amended as follows.

(2) In sub-paragraph (2) for the words from "(but with the substitution" to the end substitute "(but with the substitution for the reference in paragraph (e) of subsection (2) to the Secretary of State of a reference to the Registrar)".

(3) After that sub-paragraph insert—
"(3) Paragraph 22B below has effect as regards the application of regulations under this paragraph to member societies in respect of investment business in the carrying on of which they are subject to the rules of a recognised self-regulating organisation for friendly societies.".

35. For paragraph 20 (unsolicited calls) substitute—
"20.—(1) Regulations under section 56(1) of this Act shall not permit anything to be done by a regulated friendly society but that section shall not apply to anything done by such a society in the course of or in consequence of an unsolicited call which, as respects the society, constitutes the carrying on of regulated business, if it is permitted

to be done by the society by regulations made by the Registrar with the consent of the Secretary of State.

(2) Paragraph 22B below has effect as regards the application of regulations under this paragraph to member societies in respect of investment business in the carrying on of which they are subject to the rules of a recognised self-regulating organisation for friendly societies.

(3) As it applies to such persons in respect of such business, the reference in sub-paragraph (1) above to conduct permitted by regulations made by the Registrar with the consent of the Secretary of State shall be construed—

(a) where or to the extent that the regulations do not apply, as a reference to conduct permitted by the rules of the organisation; and

(b) where or to the extent that the regulations do apply but are expressed to have effect subject to the rules of the organisation, as a reference to conduct permitted by the regulations together with the rules of the organisation.".

36. After paragraph 22 (and after the paragraph inserted by section 193(3)) insert—

"22B.—(1) The Registrar may in rules and regulations under—

(a) paragraph 14 (conduct of business rules),

(b) paragraph 19 (clients' money regulations), or

(c) paragraph 20 (regulations as to unsolicited calls),

designate provisions which apply, to such extent as may be specified, to a member society in respect of investment business in the carrying on of which it is subject to the rules of a recognised self-regulating organisation for friendly societies.

(2) It may be provided that the designated rules or regulations have effect, generally or to such extent as may be specified, subject to the rules of the organisation.

(3) A member society which contravenes a rule or regulation applying to it by virtue of this paragraph shall be treated as having contravened the rules of the relevant recognised self-regulating organisation for friendly societies.

(4) It may be provided that, to such extent as may be specified, the designated rules or regulations may not be modified or waived (under paragraph 22C below or section 50) in relation to a member society.

Where such provision is made any modification or waiver previously granted shall cease to have effect, subject to any transitional provision or saving contained in the rules or regulations.

(5) Except as mentioned in sub-paragraph (1), the rules and regulations referred to in that sub-paragraph do not apply to a member society in respect of investment business in the carrying on of which it is subject to the rules of a recognised self-regulating organisation for friendly societies.

22C.—(1) A recognised self-regulating organisation for friendly societies may on the application of a society which is a member of the organisation—

(a) modify a rule or regulation designated under paragraph 22B so as to adapt it to the circumstances of the society or to any particular kind of business carried on by it, or

(b) dispense the society from compliance with any such rule or regulation, generally or in relation to any particular kind of business carried on by it.

(2) The powers conferred by this paragraph shall not be exercised unless it appears to the organisation—

(a) that compliance with the rule or regulation in question would be unduly burdensome for the applicant having regard to the benefit which compliance would confer on investors, and

(b) that the exercise of those powers will not result in any undue risk to investors.

(3) The powers conferred by this paragraph may be exercised unconditionally or subject to conditions; and paragraph 22B(3) applies in the case of a contravention of a condition as in the case of contravention of a designated rule or regulation.

(4) The reference in paragraph 4(1) of Schedule 2 as applied by paragraph 4 above (requirements for recognition of self-regulating organisation for friendly societies) to monitoring and enforcement of compliance with rules and regulations includes monitoring and enforcement of compliance with conditions imposed by the organisation under this paragraph.

22D.—(1) The Registrar may issue codes of practice with respect to any matters dealt with by statements of principle issued under paragraph 13A or by rules or regulations made under any provision of this Schedule.

(2) In determining whether a society has failed to comply with a statement of principle—

(a) a failure by it to comply with any relevant provision of a code of practice may be relied on as tending to establish failure to comply with the statement of principle, and

(b) compliance by it with the relevant provisions of a code of practice may be relied on as tending to negative any such failure.

(3) A contravention of a code of practice with respect to a matter dealt with by rules or regulations shall not of itself give rise to any liability or invalidate any transaction; but in determining whether a society's conduct amounts to contravention of a rule or regulation—

(a) contravention by it of any relevant provision of a code of practice may be relied on as tending to establish liability, and

(b) compliance by it with the relevant provisions of a code of practice may be relied on as tending to negative liability.

(4) Where by virtue of paragraph 22B (application of designated rules and regulations to member societies) rules or regulations—

(a) do not apply, to any extent, to a member society of a recognised self-regulating organisation for friendly societies, or

(b) apply, to any extent, subject to the rules of the organisation,

a code of practice with respect to a matter dealt with by the rules or regulations may contain provision limiting its application to a corresponding extent.".

37. For paragraph 29 (transfer of functions of making rules or regulations) substitute—

"29.—(1) The Registrar shall not make a transfer order transferring any legislative functions to a transferee body unless—

(a) the body has furnished him and the Secretary of State with a copy of the instruments it proposes to issue or make in the exercise of those functions, and

(b) they are both satisfied that those instruments will—

(i) afford investors an adequate level of protection,

(ii) in the case of provisions corresponding to those mentioned in Schedule 8 to this Act, comply with the principles set out in that Schedule, and

(iii) take proper account of the supervision of friendly societies by the Registrar under the enactments relating to friendly societies.

(2) In this paragraph "legislative functions" means the functions of issuing or making statements of principle, rules, regulations or codes of practice.

38. In paragraph 30(2), for "rules or regulations made" substitute "statements of principle, rules, regulations or codes of practice issued or made".

39. In paragraph 31(6)(c), for "as if the reference to section 205(2) were a reference to paragraph 45(1) below" substitute "as if the reference to section 205A were a reference to paragraph 45(1) and (3) below".

40. For paragraph 34 substitute—

"34.—(1) A transferee body to which the Registrar has transferred any legislative functions may exercise those functions without the consent of the Secretary of State.

(2) In this paragraph "legislative functions" means the functions of issuing or making statements of principle, rules, regulations or codes of practice.".

41. In paragraph 36 (competition scrutiny: transferee bodies) in sub-paragraphs (1) and (3)(b) for "rules, regulations" substitute "statements of principle, rules, regulations, codes of practice".

42. In paragraph 38(1) (publication of information and advice)—

(a) in paragraph (a), for "rules and regulations made" substitute "statements of principle, rules, regulations and codes of practice issued or made," and

(b) in paragraph (b) for "rules or regulations" substitute "statements of principle, rules, regulations or codes of practice".

43. In paragraph 45—

(a) in sub-paragraph (1) for "make regulations, rules or orders" substitute "issue or make statements of principle, rules, regulations, orders or codes of practice", and

(b) in sub-paragraph (3) for "regulations, rules or orders" substitute "statements of principle, rules, regulations, orders or codes of practice.".

GENERAL NOTE

See the General Note to s.206.

This Schedule makes the necessary amendments to the Financial Services Act 1986 consequent on the provisions in ss.192, 194 and 195 of this Act giving the Secretary of State and S.I.B. power to issue statements of principle, core rules and codes of practice for the regulation of the financial services industry.

Section 212

SCHEDULE 24

REPEALS

Chapter	Short title	Extent of repeal
1964 c. 40.	Harbours Act 1964.	In section 42(6), the words "required to be attached to a company's balance sheet".
1973 c. 41.	Fair Trading Act 1973.	Section 46(3). In section 71, in subsection (1) the words "made under section 69(4) of this Act" and subsection (2). In section 74(1), the words from "and does not" to "section 69(4) of this Act". In section 85, subsection (5) and, in subsection (6), paragraph (b) and the word "or" preceding it. In section 88(6), the words from "the relevant parties" to the "and" immediately following paragraph (c). In section 89(2), the words "Part II of". In Schedule 9, in paragraph 4 the words from "either" to the end.
1985 c. 6.	Companies Act 1985.	Section 160(3). In section 169(5), the words from ", during business hours" to "for inspection)". In section 175(6)(b), the words from "during business hours" to "period". In section 191— (a) in subsection (1), the words from "(but" to "for inspection)"; (b) in subsection (3), paragraphs (a) and (b). Section 201. In section 202(1), the words "(except where section 201(3) applies)". Section 209(1)(j). In section 219(1), the words from "during" to "for inspection)". In section 288(3), the words from "during" to "for inspection)". In section 318(7), the words from "during" to "for inspection)". In section 356— (a) in subsection (1), the words "during business hours"; (b) subsections (2) and (4). In section 383— (a) in subsection (1), the words "during business hours"; (b) subsection (2); (c) in subsection (3), the words from "at a charge" to the end. Section 389. Section 435. Section 440. Section 443(4). In section 466— (a) in subsection (3), paragraph (b), and the word "and" preceding it; (b) subsection (7). Section 447(1).

Chapter	Short title	Extent of repeal
1985 c. 6—cont.	Companies Act 1985—cont.	In section 449(1)— (a) the words "or 448"; (b) paragraph (e). Section 452(1)(b). In section 460(1), the words "(inspection of company's books and papers)" and "under section 440". In section 464(5), at the end of paragraph (c), the word "and". In section 466— (a) in subsection (2), paragraph (a) and (d) and the word "or" preceding the latter; (b) subsections (4) and (5); (c) in subsection (6), the words "falling under subsection (4) of this section". In section 651(1), the words "at any time within 2 years of the date of the dissolution". In section 708(1)(b), the words "or other material". Sections 712 and 715. In section 716(2), the words following paragraph (c). In section 717(1), the words following paragraph (c). In section 733(3), the words from "then" to "216(3)". In section 735A(1), the words "440, 449(1)(a) and (d)". In section 744, the definitions of "annual return", "authorised institution", "authorised minimum", "expert", "floating charge", "joint stock company" and "undistributable reserves". In section 746, the words "Except as provided by section 243(6),". In Schedule 2— (a) in paragraph 1(1), the words "paragraph 60(2) of Schedule 4 or paragraph 19(3) of Schedule 9"; (b) paragraph 1(5); (c) in paragraph 2(1), the word "23,"; (d) paragraph 2(2); (e) in paragraph 3(1), the words "paragraph 60(2) of Schedule 4 or paragraph 19(3) of Schedule 9"; (f) paragraph 3(3); (g) in paragraph 4(1), the words "(whether as personal representative or otherwise)"; (h) in paragraph 4(2), the words "paragraph 60(2) of Schedule 4 or paragraph 19(3) of Schedule 9". In Schedule 4, paragraphs 50(6), 53(7), 60 to 70, 74, 75, 77 to 81, 87, 90 to 92 and 95.

Chapter	Short title	Extent of repeal
1985 c. 6—cont.	Companies Act 1985—cont.	In Schedule 9— (a) paragraphs 1, 13(3) and (18), 16, 18(5), 19(3) to (7) and 21 to 26; (b) in paragraph 27(4), the words "of the said Part I"; (c) in paragraph 28, in sub-paragraph (1) the words "to which Part II of the Insurance Companies Act 1982 applies" and in sub-paragraph (2) the words "of Part I of this Schedule"; (d) paragraphs 29 to 31. In Schedule 11— (a) paragraph 4(b) and (c); (b) paragraph 5(b). In Schedule 13, in paragraph 25, the words from "during" to "for inspection)". Schedule 15. In Schedule 22— (a) the entry relating to section 36(4); (b) in the entry relating to sections 363 to 365, the words "(with Schedule 15)"; (c) in the entry relating to sections 384 to 393, in column 2, the word "qualifications". In Schedule 24, the entries relating to sections 245(1), 245(2), 255(5), 260(3), 287(3), 365(3), 384(5), 386(2), 389(10), 390(7), 391(4), 392(2) and 393.
1985 c. 65.	Insolvency Act 1985.	In Schedule 6, paragraphs 7(3), 23 and 45.
1986 c. 45.	Insolvency Act 1986.	In sections 45(5), 53(2), 54(3) and 62(5), the words "and, for continued contravention, to a daily default fine". In Schedule 10, the entries in column 5 relating to sections 45(5), 53(2), 54(3) and 62(5). In Part I of Schedule 13, the entries relating to sections 222(4), 225 and 733(3).
1986 c. 46.	Company Directors Disqualification Act 1986.	In section 21(2), the words "and section 431 (summary proceedings)".
1986 c. 53.	Building Societies Act 1986.	In Schedule 15, in paragraph 3(2)(b), the words ", a shadow director". In Schedule 18, paragraphs 16 and 17.
1986 c. 60.	Financial Services Act 1986.	In section 13— (a) subsection (1); (b) subsections (4) to (6). In section 48(1), the words "members of a recognised self-regulating organisation or" and "organisation or". In section 55— (a) in subsection (2)(b) and (e), the words "a member of a recognised self-regulating organisation or" and "organisation or"; (b) in subsection (3), the words "organisation or". In section 94— (a) in subsection (3), the words "except section 435(1)(a) and (b) and (2)";

40/Sch. 24   *Companies Act* 1989

Chapter	Short title	Extent of repeal
1986 c. 60— *cont.*	Financial Services Act 1986—*cont.*	(b) in subsection (4), the words "or its affairs", "and the affairs mentioned in subsection (1) or (2) above" and "or director". Section 105(7). In section 119(5), the words from "and the practices referred to in paragraph (c)" to the end. In sections 159(1) and 160(1), the words from the beginning to "section 161 below". In section 179(3), the word "and" preceding paragraph (i). Section 180(6). Section 196(3). Section 198(1). In section 199(9), the words from "and, in relation" to the end. In Schedule 11— (a) paragraph 4(4)(b); (b) paragraph 7; (c) in paragraph 10(3), the words from "and the practices referred to in paragraph (c)" to the end; (d) in paragraph 14(1), the words "other than a member society"; (e) in paragraph 14(3), the word "and" after paragraph (a). In Schedule 16, paragraph 22.
1987 c. 22.	Banking Act 1987.	In the Table in section 84(1), the entry relating to persons appointed under section 94, 106 or 177 of the Financial Services Act 1986. Section 90(1). In Schedule 6— (a) paragraph 18(1) to (6); (b) in paragraph 18(7), the words "and (1A)"; (c) paragraph 18(8) and (9); (d) in paragraph 27(3), the words "and (6)"
1987 c. 41.	Criminal Justice (Scotland) Act 1987.	Section 55(a).
1988 c. 1.	Income and Corporation Taxes Act 1988.	Section 565(6)(b).
1988 c. 33.	Criminal Justice Act 1988.	Section 145(a).
1988 c. 48.	Copyright, Designs and Patents Act 1988.	In Schedule 7, paragraph 31.

GENERAL NOTE
See the annotation to s.212.

INDEX

References are to section and Schedule number

ACCOUNTANCY BODIES,
  amendment of enactments, s.51
  qualifying. *See* QUALIFYING BODIES.
  supervisory. *See* RECOGNISED SUPERVISORY
    BODY.
ACCOUNTING RECORDS,
  abroad, kept, s.2
  auditors, investigation by, s.9
  contents of, s.2
  duty to keep, s.2
  period of preservation, s.2
  registered office, kept at, s.2
ACCOUNTING REFERENCE DATE,
  alteration of, s.3
  meaning, s.3
ACCOUNTING REFERENCE PERIOD,
  determination of, s.3
  financial year, determining, s.3
  previous, s.3
  relevant, s.11
ACCOUNTING REQUIREMENTS,
  failure to comply with, s.12
  power to alter, s.20
  small and medium-sized companies, s.13, Sch. 6
ACCOUNTING STANDARDS,
  compliance with, Sch. 1
  grants for, s.19
  meaning, s.19
ACCOUNTS,
  amendment of enactments, Sch. 10
  annual, meaning, s.22
  approval and signing, s.7
  auditors' report, s.8
  banking companies, of, s.18, Sch. 7
  company in general meeting, laying before, s.11
    private company dispensing with, s.16
  defective, application in respect of, s.12
  failure to deliver, s.11
  flow of funds statement, s.4
  form and content of, Sch. 1
  group, s.5
  individual, s.4
  insurance companies, of, s.18
  non-statutory, s.10
  notes,
    disclosure required in, s.6, Schs. 3, 4
    information in, s.22
  period for laying and delivering, s.11
  persons entitled to receive, s.10
  publication, requirements, s.10
  realised profits and losses, s.22
  registrar, delivery to, s.11
    unlimited companies, exemption of, s.17
    revised, court directing, s.12
  Secretary of State, notice of, s.12
  small and medium-sized companies, of, s.13

ACCOUNTS—*cont.*
  subsidiary undertaking, of, s.11
  summary financial statement, s.15
  true and fair view, giving, s.4
  voluntary revision, of, s.12
ANNUAL RETURN,
  contents of, s.139
  duty to deliver, s.139
  regulations, s.139
ARTICLES,
  partnership company, for, s.129
AUDITORS,
  amendment of provisions, s.118
  appointment,
    duty of, s.119
    private companies, by, s.119
    Secretary of State, by s.119
    termination, s.122
  casual vacancies, s.119
  company,
    appointment,
      duty to, s.119
      eligibility for, s.25
      partnership, of, s.26
    firms eligible to act, information on, s.36
    ineligibility,
      effect of, s.28
      lack of independence, on grounds of, s.27
      second audit, requirement of, s.29
    meaning, s.24
    unquoted company, s.34
  dormant companies, not appointed by, ss.14, 119
  duties of, s.9
  duty to appoint, s.119
  employers' association, of, s.124
  false and misleading statements, s.41
  general meeting, attendance at, ss.119, 120
  information, receiving, s.120
  insurance for, s.137
  not appointed annually, termination of, appointment, s.12
  offences, s.122
  person ceasing to hold office, statement by, s.123
  private companies,
    appointment by, s.119
    written resolution, rights in relation, to s.113
  qualification,
    appropriate, s.31
    authorisation, under 1967 Act, s.34
    overseas, approval of, s.33
    recognised professional, s.32
  qualifying body. *See* QUALIFYING BODY.
  register of, s.35

INDEX

AUDITORS—cont.
　removal of, s.122
　removed or not re-appointed, rights of, s.122
　remuneration, s.121
　report,
　　company in general meeting, laid before, s.11
　　duty to prepare, s.9
　　failure to deliver, s.11
　　period for laying and delivering, s.11
　　persons entitled to receive, s.10
　　qualified, s.22
　　registrar, delivery to, s.11
　　signature, s.9
　　summary financial statement, s.15
　resignature, s.122
　rights of, s.120
　Secretary of State, delegation of functions of, s.46, Sch. 13
　supervisory body. *See* RECOGNISED SUPERVISORY BODY.
　trade unions, of, s.124
　unquoted company, of, s.34

BANK OF ENGLAND,
　market charges,
　　administration provisions not applying to, s.175
　　insolvency law, modification of, ss.174, 175
　　meaning, s.173
　　other charges, application of provisions to, s.176
　　regulations, s.173
　　settlement arrangements, provisions applying to, s.172
BANKING,
　duty of confidentiality, s.72
　information, protection of, s.69
BANKING COMPANIES,
　accounts, s.18, Sch. 7
　directors' report, s.18, Sch. 8
　disclosure requirements, s.18, Sch. 7
BANKING PARTNERSHIPS,
　meaning, s.18
　provisions applying to, s.18
BODY CORPORATE,
　holding company, membership of, s.129
　offences, by, ss.42, 90
　service of notices, s.49
BUILDING SOCIETIES
　amendment of provisions, s.211
　Commission, disclosure of information by, s.80
　directors, disqualification of, s.211

CHARGES,
　ceasing to affect company property, memorandum of, s.98
　companies, information to be kept by, s.101
　date of creation, references to, s.103
　floating,
　　notice of crystallisation, s.100
　　Scottish, ss.100, 140

CHARGES—cont.
　market. *See* MARKET CHARGES.
　meaning, ss.93, 190
　power of sale, effect of exercise, s.99
　prescribed particulars of, s.103
　property, on, s.93
　　date of acquisition, s.104
　　oversea company, of, s.105, Sch. 15
　registration of. *See* REGISTRATION OF CHARGES.
　regulations, power to make, ss.102, 104
　unregistered, exclusion of voidness against, s.99
　voidness of, s.99
CHARITABLE COMPANIES,
　invalidity of transactions, s.110
　objects clause, alterations of, s.110
　Scotland, in, s.112
　status appearing on correspondence, s.110
　winding-up, s.110
CLEARING HOUSE,
　meaning, s.190
　overseas, provisions applying to, s.170, Sch. 22
　recognised. *See* RECOGNISED CLEARING HOUSE.
COLLECTIVE INVESTMENT SCHEMES,
　investigations into, s.72
COMPANIES,
　annual return, s.139
　auditors. *See* AUDITORS.
　capacity,
　　memorandum not limiting, s.108
　　no duty to enquire as to, s.108
　certificate of incorporation, s.126
　charges, registration of. *See* REGISTRATION OF CHARGES.
　charitable. *See* CHARITABLE COMPANIES.
　common seal, s.130, Sch. 17
　contracts, s.130
　damages, members' rights to, s.131
　dissolution, power to declare void, s.141
　documents, execution of, s.130, Sch. 17
　holding, membership of, s.129
　investigations. *See* INVESTIGATIONS.
　meaning, s.53
　objects, statement of, s.110
　officers, insurance for, s.137
　partnership, s.128
　power of directors to bind, s.108
　pre-incorporation contracts, s.130
　private. *See* PRIVATE COMPANIES.
　property,
　　date of acquisition, s.104
　　overseas company, of, s.105, Sch. 15
　　registration of charges, on, s.93
　receiver or manager, notice of appointment, s.100
　records,
　　amendment of provisions, s.127
　　inspection of, s.126
　　registrar, kept by, s.126
　registered numbers, Sch. 19
　registered office, s.136
　registers, right of inspection, s.143
　voting rights, meaning, s.144

[2]

Index

COMPANIES ACT 1985,
amendment, generally, s.1, Schs. 10, 19
COMPETITION,
  supervisory and qualifying bodies, in respect of, s.47, Sch. 14

DEBENTURES,
  issue of, meaning, s.104
  particulars of taking up issue, registration of, s.100
  series of, meaning, s.104
  short-dated, offers of, s.202
DIRECTOR GENERAL OF FAIR TRADING,
  false or misleading information, furnishing to, s. 151
  prior notice of merger given to, s.146
  supervisory and qualifying bodies, examination of rules, Sch. 14
  undertakings, accepting, s.147
DIRECTORS,
  accounts, approval and signing, s.7
  authorisation, transactions not requiring, Sch. 19
  authority, no duty to enquire as to, s.108
  company, power to bind, s.108
  disqualification,
    after investigation of company, s.79
    building society, s.211
    summary proceedings for offences, s.208
  emoluments, disclosure required in notes to accounts, s.6, Sch. 4
  fair dealing, enforcement of, s.138
  majority, right to appoint or remove, s.144
  meaning, s.50
  particulars of, Sch. 19
  report,
    accounts, published with, s.10
    annual, meaning, s.22
    approval and signing, s.8
    banking companies, s.18, Sch. 8
    company in general meeting, laid before, s.11
    contents of, Sch. 5
    duty to prepare, s.8
    failure to deliver, s.11
    insurance companies, s.18, Sch. 8
    period for laying and delivering, s.11
    persons entitled to receive, s.10
    registrar, delivery to, s.11
    revision, court directing, s.12
    summary financial statement, s.15
    voluntary revision of, s.12
  voidable transactions, s.109
DOCUMENTS,
  authenication of, Sch. 17
  delivery, meaning, s.127
  destruction, mutilation, etc., of, s.66
  entry and search of premises for, s.64
  execution, of, s.130
  meaning, ss.56, 66, 77, 83, 127
  non-legible form, in,
    delivery to registrar, s.125
    provision and authentication of, s.126
  oversea companies, delivery by, Sch. 19

DOCUMENTS—*cont.*
  production of,
    inspectors, to, s.56
    power to require, ss.83, 85
    Secretary of State, power of to require, s.63
  registrar, delivery to, s.125
DORMANT COMPANIES,
  Auditors, not appointing, ss.9, 14, 119
  meaning, s.14

EMPLOYEES' SHARE SCHEMES,
  financial assistance for, s.132
  residual interests, Sch. 10
EMPLOYERS' ASSOCIATIONS,
  auditors, s.125
EUROPEAN COMMUNITY LAW,
  Seventh Company Law Directive, ss.1, 5

FINANCIAL MARKETS,
  insolvency, protection in case of, ss. 154, 158. *See also* RECOGNISED CLEARING HOUSE; RECOGNISED INVESTMENT EXCHANGE.
  market contracts, s.155
  money market institutions, provisions applying to, s.171
FINANCIAL STATEMENT,
  summary, company providing, s.15
FINANCIAL YEAR,
  alteration of, s.3
  determination of, s.3
FRIENDLY SOCIETIES,
  amendment of provisions, Sch. 23

GENERAL MEETING,
  auditors, attendance of, ss.119, 120
  laying of accounts and reports, before, s.11
    private company dispensing with, s.16
    shareholder requiring, s.16
  private company dispensing with, s.115
GROUP ACCOUNTS,
  banking and insurance companies, of, s.18, Sch. 7
  duty to prepare, s.5
  form and content of, Sch. 2
  individual profit and loss account, treatment of, s.5
  notes, disclosure in, s.6, Schs. 3, 4
  parent company included in larger group, exemption for, s.5
  publication, requirements, s.10
  small and medium-sized groups, s.13, Sch. 6
  special category, s.18
  subsidiary undertakings, including in, s.5
  true and fair view, ss.5, 22

HOLDING COMPANY,
  meaning, s.144
  membership of, s.129

Index

INDIVIDUAL ACCOUNTS,
  banking and insurance companies, of, s.18
  meaning, s.4
  true and fair view, ss.4, 22
  preparation of, s.4

INSIDER DEALING,
  entry and search of premises, s.76
  investigations into, s.74
  prosecutions, s.209

INSOLVENCY PROVISIONS,
  market charges, modification in respect of, ss.174, 175
  recognised clearing house or investment exchange, in relation to. *See* RECOGNISED CLEARING HOUSE; RECOGNISED INVESTMENT EXCHANGE.
  reference to, s.190

INSURANCE,
  officers and auditors of company, for, s.137

INSURANCE COMPANIES,
  accounts, s.18, Sch. 7
  directors' report, s.18, Sch. 8
  statement of premium income, s.210

INVESTIGATIONS,
  banking information, protection of, s.69
  civil proceedings on company's behalf, bringing, s.58
  collective investment schemes, into, s.72
  company ownership, of, s.62
  delegation of powers, s.84
  destruction, mutilation, etc., of documents, s.66
  director, disqualification of, s.79
  disclosure of information,
    bankers, by, ss.69, 72
    Banking Act, under, s.81
    Building Societies Commission, by, s.80
    inspector, by, s.68
    power to require, ss.83, 85
    restrictions on, ss.75, 86
      exceptions, s.87
      proceedings, ss.89–91
    Secretary of State, by, s.68
  entry and search of premises, ss.64, 76, 77
  expenses of, s.59
  false information, furnishing, s.67
  Financial Services Act, under,
    entry and search of premises, s.76
    restrictions on disclosure of information, s.75
  information, documents, etc., power to require, s.83
    failure to comply, s.85
  insider dealing, into, s.73
  Insolvency Act, under, s.78
  inspectors,
    disclosure of information by, s.68
    production of documents and evidence to, s.56
    report, duty to, s.57
  Insurance Companies Act, under, s.77
  investment business, affairs of persons carrying on, s.73
  oversea company, of, s.69
  overseas regulatory authority, assisting, s.82

INVESTIGATIONS—*cont.*
  proceedings for offences, s.89
  report,
    duty to, s.57
    evidence, as, s.61
    published, investigation not leading to, s.55
  security for information received, s.65
  unregistered companies, of, s.71

INVESTMENT BUSINESS,
  action for contravention of rules, restriction on, s.193
  amendment of provisions, s.206
  codes of practice, s.195
  costs of compliance, taking account of, s.204
  Financial Services Act, consequential amendments of, Sch. 23
  High Court and Court of Session jurisdiction, s.200
  international obligations, compliance with, s.201
  investigation of persons carrying on, s.73
  self-regulatory organisations, application of rules to members of, s.194
  short-dated debentures, offers of, s.202
  standard protection for investors, s.203
  statements of principle, s.192

INVESTMENT EXCHANGE,
  overseas, provisions applying to, s.170, Sch. 21
  recognised. *See* RECOGNISED INVESTMENT EXCHANGE.
  requirements for recognition, s.205, Sch. 22

LIQUIDATOR,
  investigation after report from, s.78
  recognised clearing house or investment exchange, insolvency proceedings involving. *See* RECOGNISED CLEARING HOUSE; RECOGNISED INVESTMENT EXCHANGE.

LISTED PUBLIC COMPANY,
  summary financial statements, s.15

LISTING PARTICULARS,
  civil liability in respect of, s.197

MARKET CHARGES,
  administration provisions, not applying to, s.175
  floating, priority of, s.178
  insolvency law, modification of, ss.174, 175
  meaning, s.173
  other charges, application of provisions to, s.176.
  regulations, s.173
  unpaid vendor's lien, priority over, s.179

MARKET CONTRACTS,
  meaning, s.155
  parties to, s.187
  regulations, s.155

Index

MARKET PROPERTY,
  extension of provisions, s.181
  floating market charge, priority of, s.178
  margin, application of, s.177
  unpaid vendor's lien, priority of charge over, s.179
  unsecured creditors, proceedings by, s.180

MEDIUM-SIZED COMPANIES,
  accounting requirements, s.13, Sch. 6
  qualification as, s.13

MEMORANDUM,
  company's capacity, not limiting, s.108
  objects, statement of, s.110

MERGERS,
  amendment of provisions, Sch.20
  false or misleading information, furnishing, s.151
  fees, regulations as to, s.152
  reference,
    prior notice, where, s.146
    share dealings, restrictions on, s.149
    undertakings as alternative to, s.147
      enforcement of, s.148
  stages, obtaining control by, s.150

NORTHERN IRELAND,
  assistance of overseas regulatory authority, powers in relation to, s.88
  corresponding provisions for, s.214
  provisions, extending to, s.213

NOTICE,
  deemed, abolition of doctrine, s. 142
  service of, s.49

OFFENCES,
  Accounting records, relating to, s.2
  auditors, relating to, ss.122, 123
  auditors' report, relating to, s.9
  body corporate, by ss.42, 90
  company auditor, ineligible person acting as, s.28
  destruction, mutilation, etc., of documents, s.66
  directors' report, relating to, s.8
  directors, disqualification of, summary proceedings, s.208
  disclosure of information, restrictions on, s.86
  disclosure requirements, relating to, s.6
  entry and search of premises, s.64
  false and misleading statements, making, s.41
  false information, furnishing, ss.67, 151
  jurisdiction,
    company accounts, in relation to, s.44
    investigations, in relation to, s.91
  misleading information, furnishing, s.151
  partnership, by, ss.42, 90, Sch. 19
  procedure,
    company accounts, in relation to, s.44
    investigations, in relation to, s.91
  prosecutions,
    company accounts, relating to, s.43
    disclosure of information requirements, as to, s.89
    insider dealing, for, s.209

OFFENCES—*cont.*
  report and accounts, failure to provide, ss.10, 11
  requirement to supply documents, etc., failure to comply with, s.85
  second audit, failure to provide, s.29
  time limit for prosecution, s.43
  unincorporated association, by, ss.42, 90, Sch. 19

OVERSEA COMPANY,
  accounts and reports, delivery of, Sch. 10
  charge on property of, s.105, Sch. 15
  contracts, s.130
  delivery of documents, Sch. 19
  execution of documents, s.130
  investigation of, s.69

OVERSEAS REGULATORY AUTHORITY,
  banking supervisor, being, s.82
  disclosure of information, restrictions on, s.86
  meaning, ss.75, 82, 196
  Northern Ireland, powers in relation to, s.88
  other regulatory authorities, relations with, s.196
  request for assistance by, s.82

PARENT UNDERTAKING,
  meaning, ss.21, 53
  supplementary provisions, Sch. 9

PARTNERSHIP,
  company auditor, appointment as, s.26
  information, recognised body holding, s.36
  number of members, exemption form restriction, Sch. 19
  offences by, ss.42, 90, Sch. 19.

PARTNERSHIP COMPANIES,
  articles, form of, s.128
  definition, s.128

PENSION SCHEMES,
  residual interests, Sch. 10

PREMISES,
  entry and search, ss.64, 76, 77

PRIVATE COMPANIES,
  auditors, appointment of, s.119
  elective resolutions,
    annual general meetings, as to, s.115
    duration of authority, as to, s.115
    further provision, regulations as to, s.117
    making, s.116
  general meeting,
    dispensing with, s.115
    laying of accounts and report before, dispensing with, s.16
  written resolutions,
    auditors, rights of, s.113
    exceptions, s.114
    making, s.113
    procedural requirements, adaptation of, s.114
    recording, s.113

QUALIFYING BODIES,
  compliance orders, s.39

INDEX

QUALIFYING BODIES—*cont.*
  damages, exemption from liability for, s.48
  examples of, s.32
  false and misleading statements, s.41
  fees, payment of, s.45
  guidance, s.32
  international obligations, directions to comply with, s.40
  meaning, s.32
  recognised professional qualification, s.32
    compliance order, s.39
  recognition, Sch. 12
  restrictive practices, Sch. 14
  rules, s.32
  Secretary of State,
    information, calling for, s.38
    matters notified to, s.37

RECOGNISED CLEARING HOUSE,
  default proceedings,
    assistance for purposes of, s.160
    completion, report on, s.162
    disclaimers, restriction on, s.164
    interlocutory relief, s.161
    meaning, s.188
    net sum payable on completion, s.163
    office-holder, alteration of duties, s.161
    prior transactions, adjustment of, s.165
    reserve, retention of, s.161
    whether to be taken, determining, s.167
  default rules,
    changes in, s.157
    indemnities, s.184
    meaning, s.188
    requirement of, Sched. 21
  delegation of function, s.168
  Financial Services Act provisions,
    application of, s.169
  insolvency proceedings,
    commencement of provision, begun before, s.182, Sch. 22
    modification of provisions, s.158
    other jurisdictions, in, s.183
    priority, s.159
  market charges,
    administration provisions not applying to, s.175
    floating, priority of, s.178
    insolvency law, modification of, ss.174, 175
    meaning, s.173
    other charges, application of provisions to, s.176
    regulations, s.173
    unpaid vendor's lien, priority over, s.179
  market contracts, ss.155, 187
  market property,
    extension of provisions, s.181
    floating market charge, priority of, s.178
    margin, application of, s.177
    unpaid vendor's lien, priority of charge over, s.179
    unsecured creditors, proceedings by, s.180

RECOGNISED CLEARING HOUSE—*cont.*
  regulations, power to make, ss.185, 186
  relevant office-holders, s.189
  requirements for recognition, s.156, Sch. 21
  Secretary of State, directions by, s.166

RECOGNISED INVESTMENT EXCHANGE,
  default proceedings,
    assistance for purposes of, s.160
    completion, report on, s.162
    disclaimers, restriction on, s.164
    interlocutory relief, s.161
    meaning, s.188
    net sum payable on completion, s.163
    office-holder, alteration of duties, s.161
    prior transactions, adjustment of, s.165
    reserve, retention of, s.161
    whether to be taken, determining, s.167
  default rules,
    changes in, s.157
    indemnities, s.184
    meaning, s.188
    requirement of, Sch. 21
  delegation of function, s.168
  designated non-member, s.155
  Financial Services Act provisions,
    application of, s.169
  insolvency proceedings,
    commencement of provision, begun before, s.182, Sch. 22
    modification of provisions, s.158
    other jurisdictions, in, s.183
    priority, s.159
  market charges,
    administration provisions not applying to, s.175
    floating, priority of, s.178
    insolvency law, modification of, ss.174, 175
    meaning, s.173
    other charges, application of provisions to, s.176
    regulations, s.173
    unpaid vendor's lien, priority over, s.179
  market contracts, ss.155, 187
  market property,
    extension of provisions, s.181
    floating market charge, priority of, s.178
    margin, application of, s.177
    unpaid vendor's lien, priority of charge over, s.179
    unsecured creditors, proceedings by, s.180
  regulations, power to make, ss.185, 186
  relevant office-holders, s.189
  requirements for recognition, ss.156, 205, Sch. 21
  Secretary of State, directions by, s.166

RECOGNISED PROFESSIONAL BODIES,
  costs of compliance, taking account of, s.204
  other regulatory authorities, relations with, s.196
  standard protection for investors, s.203
  statement of principle, s. 192

Index

RECOGNISED SUPERVISORY BODY,
  compliance orders, s.39
  damages, exemption form liability for, s.48
  examples of, s.30
  false and misleading statements, s.41
  fees, payment of, s.45
  firms eligible to act as auditor, information about, s.36
  guidance issued by, s.30
  international obligations, directions to comply with, s.40
  meaning, s.30
  members, references to, s.30
  recognition of, Sch. 11
  register of auditors, keeping, s.35
  restrictive practices, Sch. 14
  rules,
    references to, s.30
    requirements of, Sch. 11
  Secretary of State,
    information, calling for, s.38
    matters notified to, s.37
REGISTERED OFFICE,
  accounting records kept at, s.2
REGISTRAR,
  accounts and reports, delivery to, s.11
    unlimited companies, exemption of, s.17
  certificate of incorporation, providing, s.126
  company records, s.126
  deemed notice, abolition of doctrine, s.142
  documents,
    delivery of, s.125
    non-legible form, in, provision and authentication, s.126
  register of charges, keeping, s.95
REGISTRATION OF CHARGES,
  additional information, s.100
  amendment of provisions, ss.92, 107, Sch. 16
  certificate of, s.94
  charge ceasing to affect company property, memorandum of, s.98
  charges requiring, s.93
  company charges register,
    registrar keeping, s.94
    registration in, s.93
  delivery of particulars for,
    company, duty of, s.95
    failure, effect of, s.95
    further, s.96
    late, s.95
    omissions and errors, s.97
    signature, power to dispense with, s.103
  floating charge, crystallisation of, s.100
  generally, intro.
  issue of debentures, particulars of taking up, s.100
  notice of matters disclosed, s.103
  particulars, references to, s.103
  power of sale, effect of, s.99
    receiver or manager, notice of appointment, s.100
  regulations, power to make, ss.102, 104
  Slavenburg Register, intro.

REGISTRATION OF CHARGES—*cont.*
  unregistered company, of, s.106
  voidness, provisions on, s.99
RELATED UNDERTAKINGS,
  notes to accounts, disclosure in, s.6, Sch. 3
RESTRICTIVE PRACTICES,
  supervisory and qualifying bodies, in respect of, s.47, Sch. 14

SCOTLAND,
  charitable companies, s.112
  disqualification of directors, summary proceedings for offences, s.208
  execution of documents, s.130, Sch. 17
  floating charges, s.100, Sch. 17
    winding-up, effect of, Sch. 140
  office copy, meaning, Sch. 19
  registration of charges, s.93
SECRETARY OF STATE,
  accountancy bodies, amendment of enactments concerning, s.51
  accounting standards, power to alter, s.20
  annual accounts, notice in respect of, s.12
  auditors, appointment of, s.119
  civil proceedings on company's behalf, bringing, s.58
  codes of practice, issuing, s.195
  compliance order, application for, s.39
  consequential amendments, power to make, s.50
  defective accounts, application in respect of, s.12
  delegation of functions, s.46, Sch. 13
    designated agency, to, s.168
    restrictive practices, as to, s.47
  disclosure of information by, s.68
  documents, requiring production of, s.63
  evidence, requiring, s.83
    failure to comply, s.85
  false or misleading information, furnishing to, s.151
  information, calling for, s.38
  international obligations, directions to comply with, s.40
  investigation, stopping, s.57
  matters to be notified to, s.37
  merger undertakings, and, s.147
  offers securities, exemption of advertisements, ss.198, 199
  officer, exercise of powers by, s.84
  overseas regulatory authority, assisting, s.82
  persons authorised to apply to court by, s.12
  recognised clearing house or investment exchange, directions to, s.166
  regulations,
    annual return, as to, s.139
    Bank of England settlement arrangements, provisions to apply to, s.172
    charges, on, ss.102, 104
    disclosure of interests in shares, on, s.134
    elective resolutions, as to, s.117

[7]

INDEX

SECRETARY OF STATE—*cont.*
  regulations—*cont.*
    financial markets and insolvency, as to, ss.185, 186
    Financial Services Act, under, Sch. 23
    inspection of registers, etc., as to, s.143
    market charges, as to, ss.173, 178
    market contracts, as to, s.155
    market property, as to, s.181
    mergers, fees as to, s.152
    money market institutions, provisions to apply to, s.171
    paperless transfer of securities, as to, s.207
    prior notice of merger, as to, s.146
    shares, imposing restrictions on, s.135
    regulatory authorities, powers in relation to, s.196
  second audit, requiring, s.29
  statements of principle as to investment business, s.192
  winding-up petition, presenting, s.60
SECURITIES,
  meaning, ss.5, 207
  offers of,
    old public companies, by, s.199
    private companies, by, s.199
    unlisted, s.198
  paperless transfer of, s.207
SECURITIES AND INVESTMENT BOARD,
  international obligations, compliance with, s.201
  statements of principle, s.192
SELF-REGULATORY ORGANISATIONS,
  alteration of rules, Sch. 23
  audit rules, Sch. 23
  costs of compliance, taking account of, s.204
  designated rules and regulations, s.194
  international obligations, compliance with, s.201
  other regulatory authorities, relations with, s.196
  proceedings against, s.200
  standard protection for investors, s.203
  statements of principle, s.192
SHARES,
  certificate as evidence ot title, Sch. 17
  disclosure of interests in, s.134
  merger reference, restrictions on dealings in case of, s.149
  redeemable, issue of, s.133
  references to s.22
  restrictions, orders imposing, s.135
  warrants, issue of, Sch. 17
SMALL COMPANIES,
  accounting requirements, s.13, Sch. 6
  qualification as, s.13
STOCK EXCHANGE,
  market charges,
    administration provisions not applying to, s.175
    insolvency law, modification of, ss.174, 175
    meaning, s.173

STOCK EXCHANGE—*cont.*
  market charges—*cont.*
    other charges, application of provisions to, s.176
    regulations, s.173
    meaning, s.190
SUBSIDIARY,
  amendment of provisions with reference to, Sch. 18
  meaning, s.144
  wholly-owned, s.144
SUBSIDIARY UNDERTAKING,
  accounting records, s.2
  accounts, appending to parent company's, s.11
  consolidation, included in, s.5
  fellow, meaning, s.22
  financial year, s.3
  group accounts. *See* GROUP ACCOUNTS.
  meaning, ss.21, 53
  supplementary provisons, Sch. 9

TRADE UNIONS,
  auditors, s.125

ULTRA VIRES,
  abolition of doctrine, s.108
UNDERTAKING,
  associated, s.27, Sch. 2
  group, s.22
  meaning, s.22
  members of, s.21
  parent. *See* PARENT UNDERTAKING.
  participating interest in, s.22
  related, disclosure of information, Sch. 3
  subsidiary. *See* SUBSIDIARY UNDERTAKING.
UNINCORPORATED ASSOCIATIONS,
  offences by, ss.42, 90, Sch. 19
UNLIMITED COMPANIES,
  delivery of report and accounts, exemption from requirement, s.17
UNLISTED SECURITIES,
  offers of, s.198
UNREGISTERED COMPANIES,
  contracts, s.130
  execution of documents, s.130
  fraudulent trading by, Sch. 19
  investigation of, s.71
  registration of charges, s.106

WARRANT,
  entry and search of premises, for, ss.64, 76, 77
WINDING-UP,
  charitable company, of, s.110
  floating charges, effect on (Scotland), s.140
  public interest, on grounds of, s.60
WORDS AND PHRASES,
  accounting standards, s.19
  address, s.53
  administrative receiver, s.190
  annual accounts, s.22

Index

WORDS AND PHRASES—*cont.*
annual report, s.22
appropriate qualification, s.31
associate, s.52
associated undertaking, s.27, Sch. 2
balance sheet date, s.22
banking partnership, s.18
banking supervisor, s.82
capitalisation, s.22
charge, ss.93, 189
chargee, s.104
clearing house, s.190
company, s.53
company audit work, Sch. 12
company auditor, s.24
connected person, s.146
control contract, Sch. 9
corresponding contract, Sch. 21
credit institution, s.22
default proceedings, s.188
default rules, s.188
defaulter, s.188
designated non-member, s.155
director, s.53
documents, ss.56, 66, 77, 83, 127
dormant company, s.14
elective resolution, s.116
emoluments, Sch. 4
enactment, s.53
fellow subsidiary undertakings, s.22
firm, s.53
fixed assets, s.22
goods, s.93
group, ss.22, 53
group undertaking, s.22
holding company, ss.53, 144
included in the consolidation, s.22
index of, ss.54, 104, 191
individual accounts, s.4
interim trustee, s.190
investment, s.190
investment exchange, s.190
issue of debentures, s.104

WORDS AND PHRASES—*cont.*
listed, s.15
market charge, s.173
market contracts, s.155
merger notice, s.146
next annual return, s.6
notified arrangements, s.146
office copy, Sch. 19
overseas, s.190
overseas regulatory authority, ss.75, 82, 196
parent undertaking, ss.21, 53
participating interest in, s.22
permanent trustee, s.190
power of sale, s.99
previous accounting reference period, s.3
primary recipient, s.86
property in charge, s.93
public servant, ss.65, 75, 87
purchase price, s.22
purchaser, ss.99, 130
qualified auditors' report, s.22
qualifying body, s.32
realised losses, s.22
realised profits, s.22
recognised qualifying body, Sch. 12
recognition order, Sch. 12
regulatory functions, s.75, 82
related company, Sch. 10
relevant accounting reference period, s.11
remuneration, s.121
securities, ss.5, 207
series of debentures, s.104
specified securities, s.173
Stock Exchange, s.190
subsidiary, ss.53, 144
subsidiary undertaking, ss.21, 53
supervisory body, s.30
true and fair view, s.22
turnover, s.22
undertaking, s.22
unquoted conmpany, s.34
wholly-owned subsidiary, s.144